BEST OF THE BADMEN

by

Boyd Magers

Bob Nareau

Bobby Copeland

*with forewords by Morgan Woodward,
House Peters Jr.,
Michael Pate and Jan Merlin*

Published by
Empire Publishing, Inc.
PO Box 717
Madison, NC 27025-0717
Phone: 336-427-5850 • Fax: 336-427-7372
www.empirepublishinginc.com

Best of the Badmen copyright © 2005 by Boyd Magers, Bob Nareau, and Bobby Copeland

All rights reserved under International and Pan American copyright convention. No part of this book may be reproduced in any manner whatsoever without written permission from the author, except in the case of brief quotations embodied in reviews and articles.

Library of Congress Control Number: 2005931378
ISBN Number: 978-0-944019-43-6

Published and printed in the United States of America

First Printing: 2005
Second Printing: 2008

1 2 3 4 5 6 7 8 9

FRONT COVER PHOTOS (L-R top): Jack Elam, Lee Van Cleef and Roy Barcroft. (L-R bottom): Frank Ellis, Charles King and George Chesebro. BACK COVER (L-R): Emmett Lynn, Bill Elliott as Red Ryder, Dick Curtis, and George Chesebro in a scene from "Wagon Wheels Westward."

Publisher's note: Gathering photos of 300+ lesser-known actors from the early film days proved to be quite challenging. We apologize for the poor quality of some photos, but the best available shots were used in this compilation of Western movie bad guys.

TABLE OF CONTENTS

Acknowledgments 5
Dedications 7
Forewords 9
Introduction 17
The Badmen:

Ernie Adams	20	Harry Cording	85	Myron Healey	146
Ted Adams	21	Jim Corey	86	Edward Hearn	148
Chris Alcaide	23	Don Costello	87	Carol Henry	149
Dick Alexander	24	Richard Cramer	88	William "Bill" Henry	150
James Anderson	25	James Craven	89	Weldon Heyburn	152
John Anderson	26	Dick Curtis	89	Riley Hill	154
Morris Ankrum	27	Donald Curtis	91	Rex Holman	155
R. G. Armstrong	29	Steve Darrell	92	Reed Howes	156
Hooper Atchley	30	Jim Davis	93	Mauritz Hugo	157
Jimmy Aubrey	31	Ted de Corsia	95	Jack Ingram	158
Holly Bane / Mike Ragan	32	John Dehner	96	Arch Johnson	160
Roy Barcroft	34	Bruce Dern	97	I. Stanford Jolley	161
Trevor Bardette	37	Richard Devon	98	L. Q. Jones	162
Rayford Barnes	38	John Doucette	100	Victor Jory	164
Robert Barrat	39	Curley Dresden	101	Ian Keith	166
Gregg Barton	40	Douglass Dumbrille	102	DeForest Kelley	167
Hal Baylor	43	Bob Duncan	103	Cy Kendall	169
Alfonso Bedoya	44	Kenne Duncan	104	Bill Kennedy	170
Noah Beery, Sr.	44	Dan Duryea	106	Douglas Kennedy	171
Ray Bennett	46	Earl Dwire	108	George Keymas	172
Lyle Bettger	47	Jack Elam	109	Charles King	174
Robert (Bob) Bice	48	George Eldredge	111	Jack Kirk	177
William Bishop	49	John Eldredge	112	Fred Kohler Jr.	179
Monte Blue	50	Frank Ellis	113	Fred Kohler Sr.	179
Stanley Blystone	51	Douglas Evans	114	Bob Kortman	181
Ward Bond	53	Gene Evans	115	Frank Lackteen	182
Richard (Dick) Botiller	54	Frank Fenton	117	Ethan Laidlaw	183
Lane Bradford	55	Al Ferguson	117	Jack Lambert	185
Neville Brand	57	Frank Ferguson	119	Harry Lauter	186
Henry Brandon	58	Robert Fiske	119	George J. Lewis	188
Roy Brent	59	Paul Fix	120	Arthur Loft	190
Al Bridge	60	Robert Foulk	121	Tom London	191
Steve Brodie	61	Douglas Fowley	122	Walter Long	193
Budd Buster	63	Olin Francis	124	Theodore (Ted) Lorch	194
Ace Cain	64	Robert Frazer	125	Pierce Lyden	195
Yakima Canutt	65	Terry Frost	126	Frank McCarroll	198
Anthony Caruso	67	Bud Geary	128	Merrill McCormick	199
John Cason	68	Leo Gordon	129	Philo McCullough	200
Ed Cassidy	70	Fred Graham	132	Francis McDonald	200
Lane Chandler	71	Duane Grey	133	Ian MacDonald	202
Alden (Stephen) Chase	72	James Griffith	134	Kenneth MacDonald	203
George Chesebro	73	William Haade	136	J. P. McGowan	204
Steve Clark	75	Herman Hack	137	Joe McGuinn	205
John Cliff	75	Karl Hackett	138	Barton MacLane	206
Edmund Cobb	77	Kevin Hagen	139	George Macready	207
James Coburn	79	Don Haggerty	141	Rory Mallinson	208
Iron Eyes Cody	80	Frank Hagney	142	Ted Mapes	209
Tris (Tristram) Coffin	82	Kenneth Harlan	143	Lee Marvin	210
Ben Corbett	83	Don Harvey	144	LeRoy Mason	211

Carl Mathews	213	Leonard Penn	249	Lyle Talbot	284
Kermit Maynard	214	House Peters Jr.	250	Hal Taliaferro (Wally Wales)	285
Lew Meehan	215	Bill Phipps	252	Sherry Tansey	287
Don Megowan	216	Stanley Price	253	Forrest Taylor	288
Jan Merlin	217	Hugh Prosser	254	Ray Teal	290
John Merton	219	Denver Pyle	254	Tex Terry	291
Emile Meyer	221	Marshall Reed	256	Guy Usher	292
Charles Middleton	221	Tom Reese	258	Rick Vallin	293
Robert Middleton	223	Richard Reeves	260	Lee Van Cleef	294
John Milford	224	Addison Richards	260	Gregory Walcott	296
Walter Miller	225	Keith Richards	261	Francis Walker	297
Mort Mills	226	Paul Richards	262	Robert Walker	298
Steve Mitchell	227	Warner Richmond	263	Anthony Warde	299
Art Mix	228	Lee Roberts	265	Wally West	300
Gerald Mohr	230	Jack Rockwell	266	Charles "Slim" Whitaker	301
Tom Monroe	231	Gene Roth	267	Dan White	303
Monte Montague	232	Henry Rowland	269	Blackie Whiteford	304
Dennis Moore	233	Bing Russell	270	Peter Whitney	305
Lee Morgan	235	John (Jack) Rutherford	271	Frank Wilcox	306
Chuck Morrison	235	Walter Sande	272	Robert J. (Bob) Wilke	307
Zon Murray	236	Hugh Sanders	272	Roger Williams	309
Jay Novello	238	Allan Sears	274	Norman Willis	310
Wheeler Oakman	238	Fred Sears	274	Grant Withers	311
Artie Ortego	240	Carl Sepulveda	275	Harry Woods	312
Bud Osborne	241	Mickey Simpson	276	Bob Woodward	313
Jack O'Shea	242	Arthur Space	277	Morgan Woodward	314
Gregg Palmer	244	Charles Stevens	278	Harry Worth	315
Tex Palmer	245	Harold J. Stone	279	H. M. Wynant	316
Eddie Parker	246	Glenn Strange	280	Carleton Young	317
Michael Pate	247				

The Rest of the Gang:

Rodolfo (Rudy) Acosta	319	William Gould	326	Jack Palance	334
Richard Anderson	319	Chick Hannon	327	Dennis Patrick	334
Robert G. (Bob) Anderson	319	Joe Haworth	327	Gaylord "Steve" Pendleton	334
Stanley Andrews	320	Ron Hayes	327	John Pickard	334
Jacques Aubuchon	320	"Skip" (George) Homeier	327	Walter Reed	335
Tol Avery	320	Charles Horvath	328	Dick Rich	336
Robert Barron	321	Edward M. Howard	328	Frank Richards	336
Matthew Betz	321	John Ireland	328	Roy Roberts	337
Lynton Brent	321	Frank Jaquet	328	Jack Roper	337
David Brian	321	Noble Johnson	329	William Royle	337
William Bryant	322	Donald Kirke	329	William H. Ruhl	338
Bruce Cabot	322	John Larch	329	Lee Shumway	338
John Davis Chandler	322	George Lloyd	330	K. L. (Kenneth L.) Smith	338
Jeff Corey	323	Ken Lynch	330	William Smith	339
John Crawford	323	Cactus Mack	330	Ron Soble	339
Royal Dano	323	Peter Mamakos	331	Kelly Thorsden	339
Ray Danton	324	James (Jim) Mason	331	Michael Vallon	340
Albert Dekker	324	George Meeker	331	Niles Welch	340
Jim Diehl	324	John Miljan	332	Alan Wells	340
Charles "Art" Dillard	325	Ivan Miller	332	Norman (Rusty) Wescoatt	341
Earl Douglas	325	Boyd "Red" Morgan	332	Adam Williams	341
Victor French	325	Perry Murdock	333	Maston P. "Mack" Williams	341
Barney Furey	326	Bradley Page	333	Clifton Young	342

Bibliography   343
About the Authors   345

ACKNOWLEDGMENTS

No book of this type could be completed without assistance from a myriad of people. For the research, information, memories, scrutiny, and interviews all of the people listed provided, we offer a heartfelt "Thank you."

Les Adams, Chris Alcaide, Chuck Anderson, Ralph Absher, Malcolm Arthur, Tom Bahn, Bonita Barker, Dale Berry, John Bickler, Jim Bradbury, Conrad Brooks, Harry Carey Jr., Marilyn Carey, Joe Collura, Joe Copeland, Lance Copeland, Edith Correale, Dale Crawford, Don Durant, Michael Fitzgerald, Bobby Fluker, Jean Fowley, Leota Gandrau, Tom and Jim Goldrup, Gary Gray, John Hall, G. D. Hamann, Jim Hamby, John Hart, Luther Hathcock, Kelo Henderson, Whitey and Dotti Hughes, Greg Jackson, Dick Jones, Ken Jones, Marty Kelly, Pat King, Doris Lauter, Rhonda Lemons, Donna Magers, Leonard Maltin, Jack Mathis, Jan Merlin, Colin Momber, John Nelson, Francis Nevins, Nick Nicholls, Jack Oakman, Gregg Palmer, Michael Pate, Evelyn and Michael Patrick, House Peters Jr., Pamela Lee Powers, Buck Rainey, Tom Reese, Rex Rossi, Bill Russell, Blackie Seymour, Jan Shepard, Pat Shields, Jim Shoenberger, Richard Silverman, Dave Smith, Richard Smith III, Jim Sorenson, Neil Summers, Ed Tabor, Frankie Thomas, Clint Walker, Tom Walker, Morgan Woodward, the Academy of Motion Picture Arts and Sciences and the Vital Statistics Department for the State of California.

We are quite sure some of these people are unaware they played a part in making this book come together, but whether their contributions were large or small, assuredly they all contributed in some way.

All photos from the collection of Boyd Magers.

Some of the Best of the Badmen seem more than happy to rob, rustle, and shoot 'em up! Overjoyed they're finally getting a book about themselves and their cohorts in crime are (L-R) Carl Mathews, Tom Tyler, Dennis Moore, John Cason and Bud Osborne ("Marshal of Heldorado" '50 Lippert).

DEDICATIONS

Some may find it a bit of a dichotomy that a book about Hollywood's western "bad guys" should be dedicated to one of Hollywood's western "good guys". But, dichotomy be damned, I dedicate this book to Gary Gray, one of Hollywood's, and the world's nice people.

—Bob Nareau

Pierce Lyden had a long career as a movie and TV badman. While he does not rate near the top as a film villain like Roy Barcroft, Charlie King, or Harry Woods, he did menace practically every B cowboy star in the '40s. We became friends and exchanged letters, Christmas cards, and phone calls right up until a few weeks before his death. I was proud to call him my friend, and I am now pleased to dedicate our "Badmen" book to one of the best of the badmen, Pierce Lyden.

—Bobby Copeland

Dedicated to the memory of a posse of badmen now riding Heaven's range that I watched and admired as a kid, then had the very fortunate privilege to call close friends as an adult:

Chris Alcaide, Gregg Barton, Lyle Talbot, Walter Reed, John Cliff, Duane Grey, James Griffith, Harry Lauter, Pierce Lyden.

—Boyd Magers

Johnny Mack Brown (R) gets the drop on the Best of the Badmen—(L-R) Harry Woods, Roy Barcroft, and Charlie King in Universal's "West of Carson City" ('39).

FOREWORD
By MORGAN WOODWARD

I've been called "The Bad Guy," "The Heavy," "The Villain," even "The Depraved, Base-Minded Scoundrel", and I've loved it. In fact, one of the greatest compliments I ever received was from the legendary Jimmy Cagney. We met many years ago at a Hollywood affair. He recognized me and turned to his wife while exclaiming, "Look Honey, here's that sinister guy!"

Is this the way in which I am to be remembered? I hope so. For the moment though forget me; I want to pay tribute to the other evil, wicked, sinful and sinister scoundrels that you loved to hate.

So often we view the movies through star-studded eyes, focusing on the leading actors while much of the real work in getting the story across is laid on the shoulders of those rough-and-ready, hell-raising, jaw-busting characters who came to be called "The Heavies." These experienced and talented players encompassed every type of man imaginable, and played a vital role in bringing the story to life. Despised and hated as the villains they portrayed, this often times was at odds with who they really were—gentle, intelligent and loving men.

While working at their craft, many of them suffered injuries, some often fatal, because most did their own stunt work long before stunt doubles and special effects became commonplace. Some might say that, in a sense, these "Bad Guys" were often the true "Leading Men" because in the film the "Star" was so weak the audience seemed certain the "Damsel in Distress" would have happily chosen to ride off into the sunset with her kidnapper!

These men were the sergeant-majors of the movie industry because the plots so often spun around them. They were artists who plied their trade with quiet efficiency, but were rarely given the accolades they so richly deserved. They moved easily from movie set to movie set, secure in the knowledge they occupied a place in film history that only very few could attain. This is their story, one that is rich with history, humor and the heartbreak that mirrored the motion pictures they brought to life.

FOREWORD
By HOUSE PETERS JR.

You have just picked up a book that will give you a thorough review of yesterday's westerns by Boyd Magers (with much help from his wife Donna), Bob Nareau and Bobby Copeland. Their knowledge, effort and ability to give you a true story of the western era for television and motion pictures relating here to the character heavies is immense. They have a particular knack with years of experience to anything pertaining to westerns. I am proud to have been a part of that industry. I am sure these fellows' hours of research will bring you many hours of enjoyment.

My father, silent screen star House Peters Sr., did many outdoor films including westerns. His star was placed on Hollywood Blvd. many years ago.

For myself, I made many westerns from 1935 to 1967. I am well aware of the impact westerns made on the audience. Westerns provided me a variety of roles to play…heavies, leads, drunks, Indians, convicts, etc. I've just about done it all. Now hugging 90 years, I can still recall what a delightful experience it was. I often think of the time we were filming a "Cisco Kid" with Duncan Renaldo and Leo Carrillo. In Chatsworth, out at Iverson Ranch in Southern California, one foggy early morning as we stood around the heated fire-drums waiting for the sun to break through, imagine horses talking to each other. Heads down, ears back, one horse says to the others, "Here we go again fellows, chases with half of our riders never having been in our saddles"—suddenly, all ten or twelve horses lift their heads, sniff the air at the sound of a truck grinding its way up the grade with its main cargo to be used for shooting that day. One big elephant! Well, I won't go into detail but you can imagine how every boulder looked like an elephant to the horses as we spent the day shooting chases. There certainly were a few good riders that came out of their saddles as they rounded a huge boulder that resembled an elephant! As the day ended, I imitated the horses all the way into the barn as they munched their hay and told their stablemates about working with that elephant—"You should have been with us, fellows! It was quite a day!"

William Witney, the director of many Roy Rogers' films, recalled the impact a heavy can make on an audience. Republic received over 1,000 letters demanding I never be hired again at the studio after the script of "Under California Stars" called for me to hit Roy's dog and club Roy's horse Trigger with the butt end of a rifle; made all the more vivid as this picture was shot in color.

Repeating again, you have purchased a western book I'm sure you'll find most interesting and worthy of your library.

FOREWORD
By MICHAEL PATE

The great physical body of western films of the golden years of Hollywood, which began in the early years of the 20th century and extended into the first decade of this, the 21st century, was made up of flesh-and-blood men and women until it finally became a colossus of filmic achievement which straddled a whole world of movie-making and the vast multitude of cinema-going audiences in every country around the globe.

No doubt the stars of those western films of that golden century from Broncho Billy Anderson and Williams S. Hart on through Tom Mix, Ken Maynard, Hoot Gibson, Buck Jones, Tim McCoy, Roy Rogers and many others to John Wayne, Gary Cooper, James Stewart, Robert Mitchum, Glenn Ford, Charlton Heston, Clint Eastwood, and the others who came after them, could be said to make up the public face of that great body of movies. The stuntmen and stuntwomen, the horsebackers on their sturdy mounts, were surely the arms and legs of the colossus. But without question, the heavies were the spine of the body itself.

Although I'm sure the writers, producers and directors involved will claim to have been the brain of this incredible body of film-making, I'm equally sure the heavies were a very large part of the heart and soul of those ten decades of western movie-making—from the beginnings in 1903, then in the early epics, the A-listers, B-listers, oaters, serials, western TV series, the whole conglomerate of this magnificent American creation we have come to know as: The Western Films and Western Television Series of Hollywood.

Although I was born some 8,000 miles away across the South Pacific Ocean from the western plains and ranges of the golden years of westerns in Hollywood, those wonderful locations I came to know and love so well, I was fortunate to be introduced to the American West at an early age.

In the mid-'20s, when I was about six or seven, my beloved father, Barney, himself a well-known, highly respected horseman, a renowned horsebreaker of both thoroughbreds and brumbies to bridle and saddle or to harness, and a man confessedly addicted to westerns, would take me almost every Saturday afternoon to the matinees at a picture-house in our neighborhood to see a William S. Hart, Tom Mix, Ken Maynard, Tim McCoy, Hoot Gibson or Buck Jones movie.

There, in the seducing, exciting darkness of that flea-pit of a movie-house, I saw the most wonderful happenings flickering up there on that huge silver screen. I saw all the giants of the western screen of those times gallop by. I grew up wanting to *be* a cowboy!

A decade or so later when I first started in the business as a professional actor, I always played heroes—the young boy, the young juvenile, the young leading man. But when I got to Hollywood a decade or a half after that in 1950, after spending a few years playing all kinds of character parts in the movies of that era, I was handed heavies to play, and for the next two decades, I loved every moment of it.

Try to imagine what I felt like my first time up for a big role in a western being tossed into the pool of available actors for the part with this collection of heavies: Rodolfo (Rudy) Acosta, Claude Akins, Michael Ansara, R. G. Armstrong, Lyle Bettger, Charles Bickford, Richard Boone, Ernest Borgnine, Neville Brand, Henry Brandon, Charles Bronson, Timothy Carey, Anthony Caruso, John

Davis Chandler, Elisha Cook Jr., Jeff Corey, Ray Danton, Ted De Corsia, John Dehner, Albert Dekker, Richard Devon, Larry Dobkin, Paul Dubov, Jack Elam, Richard Emhardt, Thomas Gomez, Bruce Gordon, Leo Gordon, James Gregory, Skip Homeier, John Ireland, Richard Jaeckel, Victor Jory, Arthur Kennedy, George Kennedy, Jack Lambert, John Larch, Marc Lawrence, Mike Mazurki, Charles McGraw, George Macready, Lee Marvin, Emile Meyer, Robert Middleton, Alex Nicol, Simon Oakland, Warren Oates, Jack Palance, Nehemiah Persoff, Denver Pyle, Robert Ryan, Henry Silva, Frank Silvera, Warren Stevens, Lyle Talbot, William Talman, Akim Tamiroff, Ray Teal, Lee Van Cleef, Eli Wallach, Robert Webber, Robert Wilke, Adam Williams, Peter Whitney and many, many others.

I was very fortunate in my time in Hollywood to have met, known and/or worked with most of the guys listed above. And you are equally, if not more, fortunate because this book, meticulously researched as always, lovingly written by America's finest western lore writers, will acquaint you with or remind you once again of all these wonderful heavies of the movies and the films they appeared in.

Sit down, settle back, keep turning the pages. You are about to take a wonderful trip through a memory lane lined with and illuminated by an incredible myriad of personalities who frequented the Silver Screen and created such memorable cinema history over four exciting decades of movie-making from 1930 through the '60s.

FOREWORD
By JAN MERLIN

Before you knew us and saw us grown, we were little runts in chaps and wide-brimmed hats aiming a wooden six-gun straight at you. We had mischievous eyes and grins to match…just like you and your brothers, and no one suspected we'd become the badmen of the future…the heavies…dangerous characters earning boos and whistles of disdain in darkened theaters and not much lighter living rooms.

During the halcyon days of radio, film and television, we fearful men (every one of us six feet tall, no matter our actual height) were the vicious engines fueling the plot, we fought with blazing guns firing unlimited ammunition. Silent films established that desperadoes wore black hats as unmistakable badges they were the opponents of handsome fellows in white Stetsons; over the years, these toughs revealed gruff voices, were given menacing musical backgrounds, and became more colorful, vicious as ever, cruel eyes squinting above tight-lipped jaws while fleeing across plains and deserts from a vengeful posse. Though they were always cast as being on the wrong side of the law, some played heroes upon occasion.

But most of us inevitably ended up horizontal on the screen.

In this fondly executed volume, we are resurrected and shown to be quite different from our violent images. Boyd Magers' extensive study and personal friendship with a majority of us has given him a more accurate understanding of these scoundrels. I invite you to belly up to this book and peruse his and his cohorts' findings.

Jan Merlin was a badman even at a young age.

INTRODUCTION

In any western the audience's attention is primarily focused, quite naturally, on the screen exploits of our favorite western heroes. However, much of the success and popularity of western films—be they B, A or TV—is directly attributable to the performances turned in by an excellent stock company of actors who played the badmen, known in the movie business as The Heavies.

Growing up, one of the real pleasures we relished in watching a western was seeing how increasingly despicable Roy Barcroft, Harry Woods, Charlie King, Jack Elam, Chris Alcaide, Noah Beery, Ted Adams and scores of others could be from week to week.

No other group of pictures has ever produced such a colorful, varied and marvelous horde of villains as has the western. The bad guys, or heavies, are often much more interesting than the hero. Although their survival rate is extremely low, they are usually given the most satisfying lines to say. Even in bad westerns, if there is one unusual line of dialogue, odds are it will come from the heavy.

The heavy's suitability for his part is often more a matter of appearance than it is any great talent for acting. Truthfully, the screen appearance of many heavies is often so fleeting that acting is hardly required. The main requirement is a sleazy, crafty, mean, shifty-eyed, menacing, contemptible set of features. In general, the heavies have the most striking faces in westerns. However, this is not meant to belittle the excellent thespian qualities of many actors described in this book. Many of them *were* fine actors, more than adept at portraying any form of ruthless, loathsome scoundrel called for in the script.

In one of his columns several years ago in CLASSIC IMAGES, writing about his many years as a movie badman, Pierce Lyden explained quite well, "The most important group of supporting players in western pictures were the baddies—the heavies—who supported the action. They traditionally wore black hats as opposed to the good guys who dressed in white. This may have been true in the silent pictures because of bad lighting, poor filming or because black was depicted as the devil. White represented purity, honesty and goodness. Techniques, lighting and film changed, however, and so did the villain with the black hat. With the advent of talkies, he became more clever, sophisticated and able to fool the audience as to his identity—if the black hat was missing."

"This probably applied to the actor called the dress heavy, also known as the lead heavy. He was the mayor or banker of the town (the leading citizen) who was out to take over the town."

"All this was with the help of the second group which appeared in all western pictures, the real rotten guys in black hats, led by the second heavy or the top heavy. He was the most corrupt, ruthless and rotten of them all. As the henchman, he carried out the orders of the dress heavy. The orders given to him at various clandestine meetings were to burn buildings, ranches, to kill sheepmen, sodbusters and ranchers. He had to ride, fight, rob stagecoaches and carry the action in general. He was expected to be an all-around stuntman/badman and be able to read lines as an actor. His gang may have been scattered, put in jail or just forgotten, but the top heavy was always brought to justice in the end. He had to pay for his rotten life of crime. He was usually beaten up by the star once or twice during each picture."

The final group, which Pierce didn't allude to, were the "dog-heavy" henchmen, the brainless, unsightly lot who blindly followed the right-hand-man henchman of The Boss…the dress heavy. They often had little or no dialogue. They were there to ride hard, throw lead, rustle cattle, rob banks, bushwhack people and just generally look mean.

This book is dedicated to all the thrills, chills and excitement these polecats, varmints and skunks of all stripes provided us when we were kids. And still do today in videotape and DVD reruns.

But unless one maintained a full interest in western films as an adult, chances are the names of most of these men remain unknown. This book is aimed at acquainting you with…and refreshing your memory of…the best of the badmen.

In preparing BEST OF THE BADMEN, what we considered were A and B westerns basically from 1930 to the '60s, including actors who worked primarily in TV. You will, of course, find references to some silent films in various actor's bios. Only U.S. made westerns are included (with a rare exception here and there), so don't look for actors such as Aldo Sambrell and his dozens of Euro-westerns.

Actors closely identified with playing western heavies are those we chose to research and profile. The snakes who made a living being bad on screen. Therefore, there are reasons for several categories of actors you won't find in this book. Many former B-western stars, as they grew older, began to accept roles as heavies in A-films and TV—Don Barry, Tom Keene, Lash LaRue, Bob Livingston, Tom Tyler, Bob Steele, Rex Lease, Big Boy Williams, Jim Bannon, etc. With a couple of exceptions, we prefer to let these men remain stars of their own series.

There are also those men who, although they played some vicious heavies in their time, managed to later, one way or another, overshadow their badman roles. George Hayes, Forrest Tucker, Charles Bronson, Dave O'Brien, Eddie Dean, Robert Mitchum, Richard Boone, Lee J. Cobb, Stephen McNally, Claude Akins and others fall into this category.

We often saw stuntmen play lesser heavies when needed. Men like Tom Steele, Dale Van Sickel, John Day, Chuck Roberson, Fred Krone, Bobby Hoy, Ken Terrell, Bill Catching, etc. Certainly, they were indispensable to westerns, but these "action actors" are worthy of a book of their own.

Many actors with long careers were considered by the industry as character people. This is not to say they didn't play heavies from time to time, it is just to say they can't quite be classified as such because of all the fathers, brothers, military officers, bankers, deputies, ranchers, et al they also essayed. Into this broad and hazy category fall names like Earle Hodgins, George Wallace, William Tannen, Earl Askam, Hank Bell, Fred Burns, John Dennis, John Mitchum, Harry Dean Stanton, John Alderson, Robert F. Simon, Hal Price, among others.

Yet another important classification is the men with familiar faces referred to as background players. These guys could always be spotted populating western after western, men like the Bucko brothers, Roy and Buck, Art Dillard, Jack Montgomery, George Plues, Ray Jones, Tommy Coats, Frosty Royce, Victor Cox, Bill Hale, Silver Tip Baker, Pascale Perry, Blackjack Ward, Buck Morgan, etc.

Also eliminated from consideration were the ladies, of which Jean Willes, Christine McIntyre and Ruta Lee would head the list if we had included women. However, we prefer not to diminish the loveliness of our western ladies by mixing them in with a nasty bunch of ruffians.

Sometimes the reason for an exclusion was a combination of the stated reasons, after all, nearly every actor played a badman or outlaw at some point in his career, even Humphrey Bogart.

Sure there are some exceptions. Many of the badmen we included were close judgment calls. But one has to stop somewhere or this book would be too unwieldy and pricey.

Nearly two years went into the research and writing of BEST OF THE BADMEN. Bobby Copeland and Bob Nareau were both working on similar ideas when Boyd Magers joined the project as principal writer, pulling together and continuing the research both men had started. At great expense Bob Nareau bought and paid for hundreds of California death certificates which yielded scads of information on correct birth years, state of birth, family names, military information, cause and time of death.

Evelyn Patrick checked family records through <ancestry.com> and also came up with loads of information by accessing census records, newspaper articles, military records and more. Also useful was the California Death Index, the Social Security Death Index, the Social Security Database and various other states' death records.

Certainly, work done previously by other researchers and writers was considered, but we did not *rely* on these works as, during our research, we found numerous, often glaring, errors in some material. A source many have come to rely on is the IMDb (Internet Movie Database), but early on, we found it loaded with mistakes. So unless we knew conscientious researchers such as Les Adams, Tom Weaver, or others had "worked" on a particular IMDb entry, we found it best to do our own independent research.

In so doing our research, this book corrects many errors and fills in omitted gaps in previously published articles, books and internet postings.

Doing our research we constantly encountered specific problem areas.

1. Incorrect or made-up-from-whole-cloth studio biographies. This information may hold a kernel of truth, but is always suspect as to the truth, especially when it comes to dates.
2. Actors themselves who fabricated tales of their birth year, schooling and birthplace.
3. Census records are nice to have, but often the census taker at the time wrote down incorrect information because they "heard" it wrong, or the person giving the information was incorrect with their own family data, or just plain told an untruth. In doing basic math with census records, one finds many errors in ages of children listed, etc.
4. Death certificates are generally fairly accurate, but only to the point of who is providing the information to the state. We found certain relatives who gave out information at the time of a death to be just plain uninformed about their famous relative.

In general, we tried as best we could, with every source we could locate, to verify with as much accuracy as is possible (oftentimes looking back 70 years on some fairly obscure actors) all the facts and figures presented in BEST OF THE BADMEN. All things considered, we believe it to be the most accurate and comprehensive information ever published on over 300 western screen heavies.

Please note in the representative film listing for each heavy the films listed are only a sampling of their work as a badman. These film-lists are not meant to be all inclusive; if they were this book would be hundreds of pages longer than it is. These samplings are meant to direct you to some of that actor's better bad guy appearances. In these samplings, on TV series listed, if the show featured an ensemble cast ("Bonanza", "Wagon Train" etc.) the star of that episode may be the only one listed rather than the whole ensemble cast.

The ruthless behavior onscreen of the 315 heavies represented in this book often led to hatred for them off-screen in private life. This was the brand of a convincing badman. Stories are legion of "tough-guys" in bars attempting to pick a fight with a screen badman who was simply trying to enjoy a quiet drink. Or of kids who, when they saw one of these famous heavies in person, either were brave enough to run up and kick them in the shin while calling them a bad name, or more often, simply retreat to the other side of the street.

Only now do we realize what fine gentlemen and family men they were…and are. The three of us compiling this book have met, interviewed or had contact one way or another over the years with over a third of the men contained in this book. We can honestly—and happily—report, every one of them is in real life a gentleman (some of them are even real pussycats). Therefore, they can all be respectfully called—The Best of the Badmen.

ERNIE ADAMS

Weasely little Ernie Adams was one of the more talented B-western performers. Proof of this is found by viewing his various roles in large-budget films. But it is his badman parts in B-westerns for which he is best remembered. Not only did he become type-cast as a badman, he specialized in whimpering fink "stool pigeon" roles. Whenever a cowboy hero threatened to beat up Ernie, you always knew he would "spill the beans". A prime example of this can be seen in "Bar-Z Badmen" with Johnny Mack Brown.

Occasionally Ernie would step out of character and portray a nice guy, or perhaps even have a meaty role. Two examples are his portrayal of the Phantom's ally Rusty Denton in Columbia's "Phantom" serial ('43) which starred Tom Tyler, and as legendary baseball manager Miller Huggins in "The Pride of the Yankees" ('42) with Gary Cooper as baseball legend Lou Gehrig.

He was one of the stable of players at Nat Levine's Mascot serial factory, appearing in "Miracle Rider" ('35) with Tom Mix, "Hurricane Express" ('32) and "Shadow of the Eagle" ('32), both with John Wayne, "Galloping Ghost" ('31) with Red Grange, "Law of the Wild" ('34) with Bob Custer, and others. In all, Adams appeared in 32 serials (including one silent—"Melting Millions" for Pathe in '27), splitting his time almost equally between Mascot, Universal and Republic. Often his role was worked in for a specific reason, as when the script called for a "squealer". Other prominent serial roles for Ernie were in "Jungle Raiders" ('45 Columbia), "Hop Harrigan" ('46 Columbia) and "Son of Zorro" ('47 Republic). His last, in "Black Widow" (Republic), was completed in '47 just prior to his death.

Ernest S. Adams was born in San Francisco, California, June 18, 1885, the son of Leon D. Adams, a San Francisco native, and Laurence G. Girard of Paris, France.

Ernie was married to Berdonna Gilbert. The couple spent the early years of their entertainment careers as the vaudeville team of Adams and Gilbert. According to reports, at that time Ernie was quite a song and dance man.

Adams came to the film business in 1919 with a role (appropriately) as Shorty in "A Regular Girl". This film was made back East and Ernie didn't arrive in Hollywood until 1924. His first film "out west" was "Hutch of the U.S.A.", a Charles Hutchinson action film. His first western came a year later in support of Dick Hatton in "My Pal" for Arrow. Ernie actually made only about six

Jack Randall forces a confession from squealer Ernie Adams while Sherry Tansey, Glenn Strange and Forrest Taylor look on in Monogram's "Gun Packer" ('38).

westerns in the silent era where he was usually cast as a convict, ex-con, valet, pitchman of some sort—or low-rent gangster.

As sound came his western roles began to increase. He was a saloon singer/henchman in Gary Cooper's classic "The Virginian" in 1929. By 1936 he was in westerns almost exclusively until about 1939 when he began to obtain roles in A-films as well ("Young Tom Edison", "Sea Wolf", "Jack London", "Merry Monahans", "Murder My Sweet", "Blue Dahlia", "Buck Privates Come Home", etc.). Not that Ernie ever stopped making westerns—his last film was "Return of the Bad Men", released after his death.

Besides his outlaw and fink squealer roles, there were a couple of departures into sidekick parts. He's one of Tom Keene's fun-loving singing/roving buckaroos in "Beyond the Rockies" ('32 RKO), rode with Bob Steele in "Colorado Kid" ('37 Republic) and partnered up with Jack Randall in "Riders From Nowhere" ('40 Monogram).

From '30-'47, 17 years, Ernie worked in over 350 films!

Badman Pierce Lyden remembered Ernie as "always jumpin' around. He was like a kid that gets into everything. Asking to do something, suggesting things to the director. He was a volunteer and he loved the business. The people in charge loved him and kept him busy. He was great to have around."

Adams lived at 1830 N. Cherokee Ave. in Los Angeles with Berdonna and their daughter Robin until his death at 62 on November 26, 1947. He spent a week at West Olympic Sanitarium in L.A. before dying of pulmonary disease. His wife, 58 at the time, died February 12, 1961. Adams is at rest at Valhalla Cemetery in North Hollywood.

Suggested Sampling of Adams' Western Heavies:

- Fighting Legion ('30 Universal) Ken Maynard
- Shadow Ranch ('30 Columbia) Buck Jones
- Breed of the Border ('33 Monogram) Bob Steele
- Fighting With Kit Carson ('33 Mascot serial) Johnny Mack Brown
- Galloping Romeo ('33 Monogram) Bob Steele
- Ranger's Code ('33 Monogram) Bob Steele
- Law of the Wild ('34 Mascot serial) Bob Custer
- Prescott Kid ('34 Columbia) Tim McCoy
- Miracle Rider ('35 Mascot serial) Tom Mix
- Gun Ranger ('37 Republic) Bob Steele
- Bar-Z Badmen ('37 Republic) Johnny Mack Brown
- Law of the Ranger ('37 Columbia) Bob Allen
- Hopalong Rides Again ('37 Paramount) William Boyd
- Ridin' the Lone Trail ('37 Republic) Bob Steele
- Arizona Gunfighter ('37 Republic) Bob Steele
- Stars Over Arizona ('37 Monogram) Jack Randall
- West of Cheyenne ('38 Columbia) Charles Starrett
- Rollin' Plains ('38 Grand National) Tex Ritter
- Durango Valley Raiders ('38 Republic) Bob Steele
- Sundown on the Prairie ('39 Monogram) Tex Ritter
- Phantom Stage ('39 Universal) Bob Baker
- Overland With Kit Carson ('39 Columbia serial) Bill Elliott
- Man From Tumbleweeds ('40 Columbia) Bill Elliott
- Fargo Kid ('40 RKO) Tim Holt
- Bury Me Not On the Lone Prairie ('41 Universal) Johnny Mack Brown
- Robbers of the Range ('41 RKO) Tim Holt
- Stagecoach Buckaroo ('42 Universal) Johnny Mack Brown
- Riding the Wind ('42 RKO) Tim Holt
- Lone Prairie ('42 Columbia) Russell Hayden
- Hail to the Rangers ('43 Columbia) Charles Starrett
- Raiders of the Border ('44 Monogram) Johnny Mack Brown
- Arizona Whirlwind ('44 Monogram) Trail Blazers
- Son of Zorro ('47 Republic serial) George Turner

TED ADAMS

Richard Theodore "Ted" Adams was destined to become an actor as he was literally born in a theatre dressing room in New York City, March 17, 1890. His parents were vaudeville performers there at the time.

Adams gave up the stage at 18 to enter Cornell University but, after graduation, returned to the theatre where he spent three seasons in stock before going to New York City. For more than half his life he performed on the stage before coming to films in his mid 30s. There was a brief time out for service in the Navy during WWI.

Adams was a good friend of Leo Carrillo, both appearing in Porter Emerson Brown's play "The Bad Man" in 1920. Adams did an occasional revival of the play and also performed in the hit Broadway production of "Kongo" which starred Walter Huston in 1926.

His earliest documented role is as the family doctor in Al Hoxie's "Road Agent" for Rayart in 1926. Adams made his sound film debut in Bob Custer's "Under Texas Skies" in 1930.

With a strong voice and a solid screen presence Ted quickly established himself in westerns in which he worked almost exclusively for a quarter century in over 200 films. In his first few films he was cast as a good guy, and to truly appreciate his acting abilities one needs to watch "Rider of the Plains" ('31 Syndicate) in which Ted plays a reformed owlhoot, now a Parson, in love with the same girl hero Tom Tyler favors.

Adams found his badman niche by '32 and worked steadily for, mostly, the low budget independent outfits such as Puritan, PRC, Supreme, Victory, Metropolitan,

Colony and Grand National, only seldom venturing over to Republic, Columbia, Paramount and Universal.

Serials didn't escape Adams either. Making 12 cliffhangers, his best roles came in "Holt of the Secret Service" ('41 Columbia), "Daredevils of the West" ('43 Republic) and "King of the Rocketmen" ('49 Republic).

Circa 1942, now 52, Adams didn't totally give up badman roles, but he began to undertake more sheriff and rancher parts. Even at an advanced age, Adams spent time in the Navy during WWII (1944-'45).

He honed in on Monogram in the late '40s and was a staple in Johnny Mack Brown, Jimmy Wakely and Whip Wilson B's.

Parts becoming smaller, the B-westerns he enjoyed so much coming to an end, at 62, after a role in Bill Elliott's "Kansas Territory" ('52 Monogram) and some TV work on Russell Hayden's "Cowboy G-Men", Ted Adams hung up his spurs.

For a man who worked so much in westerns, very little is known about him. Obviously a quiet man, the best insight came from friend and fellow owlhoot Pierce Lyden. "He lived in a room on Western Ave. just off Hollywood Blvd. and I used to visit him there. Ted loved to cook. We almost burned down the hotel one time. He invited me over, and was going to show me how to make a pot of chili. Then we would invite some friends over. We had everything ready. Ted was burning up a pork chop in the bottom of an iron pot, which was the 'way to start chili'. He tells me to light the other burner, to sauté the onions, peppers, etc. and with a kitchen match, I light it, shake the match, and throw it into what I thought was an empty can. The match wasn't completely out—in the can was some old bacon grease and some paper towels. A few minutes later, it was blazing and so was the old varnish on the cabinet the can was sitting under. Fortunately, Ted knew where the fire extinguisher in the hall was, and we put out the fire. It took days to get rid of the smell of old varnish and grease, and clean up the mess."

During the '40s, Adams teamed up with another badman, Jack Ingram, to go on tours of small theaters around the country.

Adams lived quietly in retirement until his death from heart disease at 83. Widowed at the time of his death, September 24, 1973, he was at Braewood Convalescence Hospital in South Pasadena, his place of residence prior to his death. His cremated remains were placed at Chapel of the Pines Cemetery in Los Angeles.

Suggested Sampling of Adams' Western Heavies:

- Cyclone Kid ('31 Big 4) Buzz Barton
- Cavalier of the West ('31 Artclass) Harry Carey
- Ghost Valley ('32 RKO) Tom Keene
- Man of Action ('33 Columbia) Tim McCoy
- Law of the Wild ('34 Mascot serial) Bob Custer
- Gunfire ('35 Resolute) Rex Bell
- Lawless Border ('35 Spectrum) Bill Cody
- Law of .45s ('35 First Division) Big Boy Williams
- Border Caballero ('36 Puritan) Tim McCoy
- Desert Phantom ('36 Supreme) Johnny Mack Brown
- Song of the Gringo ('36 Grand National) Tex Ritter
- Lawless Land ('37 Republic) Johnny Mack Brown
- Rustler's Valley ('37 Paramount) William Boyd
- Smoke Tree Range ('37 Universal) Buck Jones
- Arizona Gunfighter ('37 Republic) Bob Steele
- Gunsmoke Trail ('38 Monogram) Jack Randall
- Desert Patrol ('38 Republic) Bob Steele
- Durango Valley Raiders ('38 Republic) Bob Steele
- Pals of the Saddle ('38 Republic) 3 Mesquiteers
- Lightning Carson Rides Again ('38 Victory) Tim McCoy
- Code of the Cactus ('39 Victory) Tim McCoy
- Smoky Trails ('39 Metropolitan) Bob Steele
- Fighting Renegades ('39 Victory) Tim McCoy
- Fighting Mad ('39 Monogram) James Newill
- El Diablo Rides ('39 Metropolitan) Bob Steele
- Pioneer Days ('40 Monogram) Jack Randall
- Phantom Rancher ('40 Colony) Ken Maynard
- Gaucho Serenade ('40 Republic) Gene Autry
- Straight Shooter ('40 Victory) Tim McCoy
- Riders of Pasco Basin ('40 Universal) Johnny Mack Brown

- Billy the Kid Outlawed ('40 PRC) Bob Steele
- Riders of Black Mountain ('40 PRC) Tim McCoy
- Law and Order ('40 Universal) Johnny Mack Brown
- Billy the Kid's Range War ('41 PRC) Bob Steele
- Lone Rider in Frontier Fury ('41 PRC) George Houston
- Fighting Bill Fargo ('41 Universal) Johnny Mack Brown
- Rolling Down the Great Divide ('42 PRC) Lee Powell/Art Davis/Bill Boyd
- King of the Stallions ('42 Monogram) Dave O'Brien
- Sundown Kid ('42 Republic) Don Barry
- Daredevils of the West ('43 Republic serial) Allan Lane
- Under Arizona Skies ('46 Monogram) Johnny Mack Brown
- Tumbleweed Trail ('46 PRC) Eddie Dean
- Red River Renegades ('46 Republic) Sunset Carson
- Shadows On the Range ('46 Monogram) Johnny Mack Brown
- Stagecoach To Denver ('46 Republic) Allan Lane
- Valley of Fear ('47 Monogram) Johnny Mack Brown
- Range Beyond the Blue ('47 PRC) Eddie Dean
- Prairie Express ('47 Monogram) Johnny Mack Brown
- Gun Runner ('49 Monogram) Jimmy Wakely
- Across the Rio Grande ('49 Monogram) Jimmy Wakely
- Stallion Canyon ('49 Astor) Ken Curtis
- I Killed Geronimo ('50 Eagle Lion) Jimmy Ellison
- Cisco Kid: Freight Line Feud ('51) Duncan Renaldo

CHRIS ALCAIDE

One of the meanest, nastiest badmen of the TV era—and one of the most prolific—was the always enjoyable Chris Alcaide, who received a Golden Boot Award for his 15 years of western dirty deeds in 2003.

Born October 23, 1922, in the tough steel mill town of Youngstown, Ohio, after a few odd jobs, Chris migrated west to California in 1942, becoming a bouncer at the Hollywood Palladium until he entered the Army in 1943. Discharged in '46, he was back at the Palladium until he enrolled with the Ben Bard Players which led to several plays and a film role in "Glass Menagerie" ('50).

Still working at the Palladium, but now house manager doing the band announcing, no other film roles came his way until he was cast as a heavy in a couple of George Montgomery's westerns ("Cripple Creek", "Texas Rangers") and several Durango Kid B's at Columbia in '51-'52. "When I finally saw Chuck Roberson in my outfit, I knew I'd arrived because now I was being doubled instead of doing my own fights and falls," Chris chuckles.

About this time a car wreck that crushed part of his chest curtailed his active westerns for awhile but Chris was able to do a small but showy role in Glenn Ford's "The Big Heat" ('53) which led to other gangster films and finally back into westerns by '54 where his snarling, mustached presence was sorely needed, especially with the onslaught of TV westerns then being made.

For movies Chris had some great lines in "Overland Pacific" and roles in "Black Dakotas" and "Massacre Canyon" among others—but TV became his forté as we found him on the small screen week after week through the late '60s.

In 1958 Chris almost turned his career around and became the hero in a series. In fact, he *was* Clay Culhane in the pilot for "Black Saddle" shown on "Zane Grey Theatre" as "Threat of Violence" but studio reps thought he'd played too many heavies too convincingly and recast the series with Peter Breck. A back-handed compliment if there ever was one! Also during that pilot, he injured his back which continued to bother him until he decided in the late '60s to leave the film business.

He and his wife, Peri (born in Turkey), who became a foreign correspondent, operated an antique photo business from '72-'85 at an L.A. storefront, catering quite heavily to people in the film industry. They later moved it to their residence in Palm Springs.

The acting bug bit again in '80 and Chris accepted a few roles with his last part being opposite Charles Bronson in "Assassin" ('86).

"I enjoyed the hell out of it! I loved it, very few guys I knew enjoyed it as much as I did," Chris smiled. And to the viewer, his enjoyment showed. Chris always put everything he had into his work as one of the television era's best badmen.

Chris died of cancer June 30, 2004, in Palm Springs.

Suggested Sampling of Alcaide's Western Heavies:

- Laramie Mountains ('52 Columbia) Charles Starrett
- Smoky Canyon ('52 Columbia) Charles Starrett
- Kid From Broken Gun ('52 Columbia) Charles Starrett
- Cripple Creek ('52 Columbia) George Montgomery
- Kit Carson: Renegade Wires ('53) Bill Williams
- Annie Oakley: Cinder Trail ('54) Gail Davis
- Overland Pacific ('54 United Artists) Jock Mahoney
- Massacre Canyon ('54 Columbia) Phil Carey
- Kit Carson: Counterfeit Country ('54) Bill Williams
- Tales of the Texas Rangers: Uranium Pete ('55) Willard Parker
- Gunslinger ('56 American Releasing) John Ireland
- Tales of the Texas Rangers: Trail Herd ('57) Willard Parker
- Maverick: Stampede ('57) James Garner
- Man Without a Gun: Teen Age Idol ('58) Rex Reason
- Have Gun Will Travel: High Graders ('58) Richard Boone
- Broken Arrow: Hired Killer ('58) John Lupton/Michael Ansara
- Trackdown: Deadly Decoy ('58) Robert Culp
- Day of the Badman ('58 Universal) Fred MacMurray
- Man Without a Gun: The Hero ('59) Rex Reason
- Black Saddle: Long Rider ('59) Peter Breck
- Rifleman: Obituary ('59) Chuck Connors
- Law of the Plainsman: Blood Trails ('59) Michael Ansara
- Shotgun Slade: Freight Line ('59) Scott Brady
- Wanted Dead Or Alive: Chain Gang ('59) Steve McQueen
- Laramie: Death Wind ('60) Robert Fuller/John Smith
- Bonanza: Escape to the Ponderosa ('60) Lorne Greene
- Rawhide: Incident of the Arana Sacar ('60) Eric Fleming
- Rifleman: Wyoming Story (Pt. 1-3) ('61) Chuck Connors
- Lawman: Cold Fear ('61) John Russell
- Have Gun Will Travel: Lazarus ('62) Richard Boone
- Cheyenne: Quick and the Deadly ('62) Clint Walker
- Dakotas: Thunder In Pleasant Valley ('63) Larry Ward/Jack Elam/Chad Everett
- Destry: Ride to Rio Verde ('64) John Gavin
- Man Called Shenandoah: The Locket ('65) Robert Horton
- Branded: This Stage of Fools ('66) Chuck Connors

DICK ALEXANDER

The large, 6' 3" imposing figure of Dick Alexander is probably best remembered as Buster Crabbe's ally, Prince Barin, in the first two Flash Gordon Universal serials ('36 and '38), but Alexander was one of the busiest and meanest of western movie badmen in the '30s and '40s.

Born in Dallas, Texas, November 18, 1902, Alexander graduated high school there, but the years circa 1920-1925 are unaccounted for til his first film, "Old Ironsides", in which he was an extra, coming in 1926. His first western came a year later with Pathé's "Fightin' Comeback" starring Buddy Roosevelt.

By the early '30s Alexander had found his calling and westerns became his forte. In a myriad of oaters from '30-'53 the brutish Alexander, often named Bull, made trouble for Ken Maynard, Tim McCoy, Tom Tyler, Jack Randall, Charles Starrett, Tex Ritter, 3 Mesquiteers, Dave O'Brien/James Newill, Rod Cameron, Jimmy Wakely and others.

Alexander enacted roles in many A-films throughout his 39 year career ("Sign of the Cross" '32, "Cleopatra" '34, "Babes In Toyland" '34, "Charlie Chan in Honolulu" '38, "Abbott and Costello In the Navy" '41, "Ali Baba and the Forty Thieves" '44, "A Southern Yankee" '48, "Father of the Bride" '50, "Dangerous When Wet" '53, "So Big" '53, "Great Race" '65, etc.) but he always returned to westerns, with his last being a role for producer Alex Gordon in "Requiem For a Gunfighter" in '65 and a bit in "Cheyenne Social Club" ('70).

Following a stoke after his retirement, he resided at the Motion Picture Home in Woodland Hills, Califor-

nia, where he died of pulmonary edema, heart disease and chronic lung obstruction on August 9, 1989.

Dick never served in the military and, at the time of his death, he was divorced. He's buried at Forest Lawn Memorial Park in Glendale.

Pierce Lyden told us at the time of Dick's death, "He was one of the oldtimers…from the old school. Very large, impressive man. Always very happy—everybody knew him."

Suggested Sampling of Alexander's Western Heavies:

- Sunset Trail ('32 Tiffany) Ken Maynard
- Law and Order ('32 Universal) Walter Huston
- Daring Danger ('32 Columbia) Tim McCoy
- Single Handed Saunders ('32 Monogram) Tom Tyler
- Law of the Wild ('34 Mascot serial) Bob Custer
- Cowboy Holiday ('34 Beacon) Big Boy Williams
- Coyote Trails ('35 Reliable) Tom Tyler
- Cowboy and the Bandit ('35 Superior) Rex Lease
- Riding Wild ('35 Columbia) Tim McCoy
- Mystery Range ('37 Victory) Tom Tyler
- Zorro Rides Again ('37 Republic serial) John Carroll
- Outlaws of the Prairie ('37 Columbia) Charles Starrett
- Where the West Begins ('38 Monogram) Jack Randall
- Six Shootin' Sheriff ('38 Grand National) Ken Maynard
- Where the Buffalo Roam ('38 Monogram) Tex Ritter
- Santa Fe Stampede ('38 Republic) 3 Mesquiteers
- Boss of Bullion City ('40 Universal) Johnny Mack Brown
- Man From Montana ('41 Universal) Johnny Mack Brown
- Return of the Rangers ('43 PRC) Dave O'Brien/James Newill
- Oklahoma Raiders ('44 Universal) Tex Ritter
- Spook Town ('44 PRC) Dave O'Brien/James Newill
- Raiders of the Border ('44 Monogram) Johnny Mack Brown
- Trigger Trail ('44 Universal) Rod Cameron
- Renegades of the Rio Grande ('45 Universal) Rod Cameron
- His Brother's Ghost ('45 PRC) Buster Crabbe
- Riders of the Dawn ('45 Monogram) Jimmy Wakely
- 'Neath Canadian Skies ('46 Screen Guild) Russell Hayden
- The Marauders ('47 United Artists) William Boyd
- False Paradise ('48 United Artists) William Boyd
- Lone Ranger: Pardon For Curley ('50) Clayton Moore
- Range Rider: Hidden Gold ('51) Jock Mahoney
- Range Rider: Romeo Goes West ('52) Jock Mahoney
- Wild Bill Hickok: Blacksmith Story ('52) Guy Madison
- Lone Ranger: Ghost of Coyote Canyon ('53) Clayton Moore

JAMES ANDERSON

Audie Murphy called him "Rat Face" in "Duel At Silver Creek". Apropos for one of the rottenest perpetrators of merciless deeds to come along in the '50s and '60s.

His sinister good looks made him a natural for westerns and he appeared in over 100 of them on TV, usually as a cruel gunman or hired killer, but sometimes as a spineless whiner.

Although he racked up over 45 screen credits, including impressive work in Arch Oboler's "Five" ('51) and as a redneck farmer in "To Kill A Mockingbird" ('62), it's his TV badmen for which Anderson is best known.

Kyle James Anderson was born in Wetumpka, Alabama, July 13, 1921, and entered films using his first two names in '39's "Story of Vernon and Irene Castle" with an unbilled role as a delivery boy.

A credits hiatus of a couple of years ('39-'41) suggests time in the military during WWII. He returned, still uncredited, in two war films, "Sergeant York" ('41) and "Dive Bomber" ('41). By '51 he'd found his ruthless niche as a screen and TV badman which he always played to the hilt.

According to Bill Phipps, interviewed by Tom Weaver for his ATTACK OF THE MONSTER MOVIE MAKERS book, "James Anderson was at the Actor's Lab when I was, and he was in Charles Laughton's acting group. Anderson was a very nice, very talented person, but a person out of control. He'd let his emotions carry him away. He would get almost irrational at times. He was a very heavy drinker and he died very early—it was brought on by dissipation."

At only 48, while on location in Billings, Montana, during the filming of Dustin Hoffman's "Little Big Man", Anderson died of a sudden heart attack on September 14, 1969.

His sister is noted actress Mary Anderson (born Bebe Anderson April 3, 1920, in Birmingham, Alabama). She was Maybelle Meriweather in "Gone With the Wind".

Suggested Sampling of Anderson's Western Heavies:

- Along the Great Divide ('51 Warner Bros.) Kirk Douglas
- Last Musketeer ('52 Republic) Rex Allen
- Gene Autry: Lawless Press ('52) Gene Autry
- Duel At Silver Creek ('52 Universal) Audie Murphy
- Great Jesse James Raid ('53 Lippert) Willard Parker
- Drums Across the River ('54 Universal) Audie Murphy
- Cisco Kid: Caution of Whitey Thompson ('54) Duncan Renaldo
- Rin Tin Tin: Star Witness ('55) Lee Aaker
- Gunsmoke: Magnus ('55) James Arness
- Fury at Gunsight Pass ('56 Columbia) Richard Long
- Circus Boy: White Eagle ('56) Mickey Braddock
- Casey Jones: Lost Train ('57) Alan Hale Jr.
- Maverick: Long Hunt ('57) James Garner
- Big Land ('57 Warner Bros.) Alan Ladd
- Restless Gun: Gold Star ('58) John Payne
- Mackenzie's Raiders: Hostage ('58) Richard Carlson
- Laramie: Star Trail ('59) Robert Fuller/John Smith
- Laramie: Ride the Wild Wind ('60) John Smith
- Bronco: Ordeal At Dead Tree ('61) Ty Hardin
- Dakotas: Sanctuary At Crystal Springs ('63) Larry Ward, Jack Elam
- Laramie: Violent Ones ('63) Robert Fuller
- Destry: Red Brady's Kid ('64) John Gavin
- Gunsmoke: Violators ('64) James Arness
- Gunsmoke: Vengeance (Pt. 1-2) ('67) James Arness

JOHN ANDERSON

Tall, lanky John Anderson was born on a farm October 20, 1922, near Clayton, Illinois, but grew up in the larger nearby city of Quincy.

Observing traveling medicine shows as a child on the farm, John became interested in acting, becoming involved in high school plays.

Following high school, John moved to St. Louis, Missouri, where he worked as a radio announcer. He soon was working as an actor on a Mississippi showboat, The Goldenrod, in what he termed "corny melodramas," for about six months in 1942.

After Coast Guard service during WWII, John returned to Quincy where he worked in radio, married, and took advantage of the G. I. Bill to study drama at the University of Iowa. During his last year he got a job in summer stock in Buffalo, New York. When the summer stock season closed, John joined the Cleveland Playhouse, one of only two resident companies in the country, the other being the Pasadena Playhouse. After one season, John decided to try his luck in New York in 1950 where he worked for six years in off Broadway shows, winter stock and live TV, finally landing a Broadway show, "Cat On a Hot Tin Roof" in '56. The show then toured the country, including five weeks in L.A.

Picking up an agent, he was cast in a lead guest star role on an episode of "Gunsmoke". John remembered, "It's like an actor's dream. The show was a big hit and the role I was playing was a very showy villain with heavy make-up, just a crazy man ("Buffalo Man"). It really opened doors, I just ran from one show to another. I did the craziest, nuttiest guys in the world and I had a ball doing it." Anderson returned to appear on 10 other "Gunsmoke" episodes.

In the '50s John segued from "Gunsmoke" to "Trackdown", "Have Gun Will Travel", "Tales of Wells Fargo", "Rifleman", "Bonanza", "Wanted Dead Or Alive", "Johnny Ringo", "Big Valley", "Laramie", "Maverick", "Virginian", to all of the other TV westerns of the period. In all, John worked on over 500 TV shows.

From '58-'61 John played the recurring role of brother Virgil Earp on Hugh O'Brian's "Life and Legend of Wyatt Earp".

By 1960, John began to obtain roles in major films such as Alfred Hitchcock's "Psycho" and Sam Peckinpah's "Ride the High Country".

He lost his wife of over 40 years, Patricia, in 1989.

He was still working in 1992 when he died of a heart attack at his home in Sherman Oaks, California, on August 7 at only 69.

Having received a Western Heritage Award at the Cowboy Hall of Fame in '67, John summed up his ca-

reer, "If I had it to do all over again, I would. I wouldn't change a thing."

His friend of 33 years, Marsha Hunt (herself a co-star in many late '30s Zane Grey westerns), told us, "We were so close…so comfortable together after I lost my husband and he lost his wife. He was a thorough professional…almost the ideal actor. He had a rich background in theatre. He'd done a great number of musicals—sang and danced…Broadway, off Broadway, a lot of regional professional theatre. He was the most working actor I've ever known. One never said 'Are you doing anything right now, John?' What you said was, 'What are you doing now, John?' He loved acting, he loved theatre, he loved the Screen Actors Guild; he worked on improvements of film actors' conditions. He really cared about the profession in a way not many performers do. He was a very bright, caring person. Johnny Crawford was almost like a son to him because he played in so many 'Rifleman' episodes. When Johnny was a little boy they really formed quite a bond of friendship. John was not a star…but he *was* in everything but fact."

Johnny Crawford, Mark McCain on "The Rifleman", said, "When I was shooting 'Rifleman' I enjoyed working with him, he seemed like a very serious actor and I always admired him. I thought he was so unique…very professional, prepared. He was an inspiration to work with. Then I didn't see him for many years, but a few years back I ran into him at a benefit. We struck up a conversation, had a great time and became pretty close. He started coming to performances of my music and was a real staunch supporter. He'd come to more performances than any friend I have. He was very conscientious and thoughtful about his work and his beliefs, very active in his support of people and things and political choices. He was a real artist."

Suggested Sampling of Anderson's Western Heavies:

- Gunsmoke: Buffalo Man ('55) James Arness
- Have Gun Will Travel: 24 Hours to North Fork ('58) Richard Boone
- Law of the Plainsman: Appointment in Santa Fe ('59) Michael Ansara
- Rawhide: The Retreat ('59) Eric Fleming
- Rifleman: Day of the Hunter ('60) Chuck Connors
- Rifleman: Shotgun Man ('60) Chuck Connors
- Lawman: Left Hand of the Law ('60) John Russell
- Cheyenne: Retaliation ('61) Clint Walker
- Tall Man: Night of the Hawk ('62) Barry Sullivan
- Ride the High Country ('62 MGM) Randolph Scott/Joel McCrea
- Big Valley: Guilt of Matt Bentell ('65) Lee Majors
- Virginian: Day of the Scorpion ('65) James Drury
- Gunsmoke: The Raid ('66) James Arness
- Welcome to Hard Times ('67 MGM) Henry Fonda
- Day of the Evil Gun ('68 MGM) Glenn Ford
- Lancer: Blood Rock ('68) Andrew Duggan
- Soldier Blue ('70 Avco Embassy) Peter Strauss

MORRIS ANKRUM

Morris Ankrum distinguished himself as an actor and established himself as a nasty heavy in a terrific string of six-in-a-row Hopalong Cassidy westerns in '36-'37 and seven more (again 6 in a row) in '40-'41.

Born Morris Nussbaum August 27, 1897, in Danville, Illinois, he prepared to be a lawyer (no wonder he could essay such evil portrayals) and graduated with a law degree from USC.

He first became interested in acting while an associate professor of economics at the University of California at Berkeley, founding The Little Theatre there. Ankrum made his professional acting bow with George Arliss on Broadway in "The Green Goddess", circa 1923. After appearing in New York from 1923-mid 1929 in a number of plays, he moved to Tacoma, Washington, where he headed a little theatre company. Ankrum became a teacher and director at the Pasadena Playhouse in 1930, encouraging many young actors, including Gloria Stuart, who credits him for helping her screen career evolve through a play in which he cast her. He remained there five years. During this period he also served as screentest director for Fox Films.

Ankrum also cast veteran B-western badman Pierce Lyden in his first production at the Playhouse—as Lord Chamberlain in Shakespeare's "Henry the Eighth".

Although his first film role was a bit as a musician in MGM's "Reunion in Vienna" ('33), Ankrum was primarily doing stage work (including Broadway with Orson Welles) until his true film debut as a psychotic gunman in "Hopalong Cassidy Returns" ('36).

Already 40 years old, this Hoppy and the next five sent Ankrum (known as Stephen Morris through '37) on a life-long acting journey of close to 300 films and TVers until 1963, only a year before his untimely death.

In order to return to Broadway, the actor took a two year hiatus after these six Hoppys. In New York he was producer-director for the Federal Theatre, producing "Prologue to Glory", "Pinocchio" and others.

When Morrie returned to the screen in '40 he made seven more Hoppys (five of them as heavies) over a two year period as well as essaying roles in Pop Sherman's bigger budgeted Zane Grey and Richard Dix westerns.

Also, when he returned to the screen after that two year hiatus, he assumed the more memorable Morris

Ankrum name which he used the rest of his lengthy 31 year screen career.

Pierce Lyden once described Morrie (as his friends called him) as "…studious but moody. He wasn't a cowboy…he was an *actor*…and a great guy." That moodiness came across on screen, he seldom looked "happy," but his strong, resonant, controlled, identifiable voice and serious manner served him well in westerns.

Francis "Mike" Nevins, in his FILMS OF HOPALONG CASSIDY book, described Ankrum's dual role as derelict, half-wit Loco and the cunning Fox in "Borderland" as "the most stunning enactment of a villain in any of the 66 pictures (in the Hopalong Cassidy) series."

Ankrum continued to appear in B-westerns opposite Tim Holt, Dick Foran and others while expanding his repertoire to A-films such as "I Wake Up Screaming", "Time To Kill", "Sea of Grass", "Adventure", "Thin Man Goes Home" and many others at MGM to whom he was under contract from mid '42 to '47.

By now, Ankrum could play tweedy country-club types, seedy villains, professional men, ranchers, and was ideal as low-key, patriotic father figures especially in sci-fi films of the '50s where he became a fixture as military officers, mayors, scientists, police captains and judges.

Freelancing from the late '40s, often sporting a gray mustache, Ankrum became a dependable character actor with a handsome, distinguished, weathered countenance. The western roles began to return—"Colorado Territory", "Short Grass", "Along the Great Divide", "Fort Osage", "Man Behind the Gun", "Cattle Queen of Montana", "Silver Lode", "Taza, Son of Cochise", "Two Guns and a Badge", "Vera Cruz", "Naked Gun", "Badman's Country", "Saga of Hemp Brown". He now played not only heavies but ranchers, fathers, sheriffs, mayors—even Indian chiefs.

His presence was felt on TV as well—"Rin Tin Tin", "Wyatt Earp", "Cheyenne", "Sugarfoot", "Tombstone Territory", "Have Gun Will Travel", "Rawhide", "Gunsmoke" and dozens more. His last work was on a "Destry" episode, "Infernal Triangle", which aired in May '64 only months before he died at 67 on September 2, 1964, at Huntington Memorial Hospital in Pasadena, California. Cause of death was a myocardial infarction due to coronary heart disease. He also suffered from trichinosis for two weeks before he died.

Morris was married twice. There was an early marriage to a Gillian Gilbert but at the time of his death he was married to Joan Wheeler, whom he'd met at the Pasadena Playhouse. Wheeler, an actress for about a year in '34, died at 88, December 20, 2001. Their son David was an actor for a while in the '70s.

Suggested Sampling of Ankrum's Western Heavies:

- Hopalong Cassidy Returns ('36 Paramount) William Boyd
- Trail Dust ('36 Paramount) William Boyd
- Borderland ('37 Paramount) William Boyd
- Hills of Old Wyoming ('37 Paramount) William Boyd
- North of the Rio Grande ('37 Paramount) William Boyd
- Showdown ('40 Paramount) William Boyd
- Cherokee Strip ('40 Paramount) Richard Dix
- Knights of the Range ('40 Paramount) Russell Hayden
- Three Men From Texas ('40 Paramount) William Boyd
- Doomed Caravan ('41 Paramount) William Boyd
- In Old Colorado ('41 Paramount) William Boyd
- Bandit Trail ('41 RKO) Tim Holt
- Road Agent ('41 Universal) Dick Foran
- Ride 'Em Cowboy ('42 Universal) Abbott and Costello
- Short Grass ('50 Allied Artists) Rod Cameron
- Fort Osage ('52 Monogram) Rod Cameron
- The Raiders ('52 Universal) Richard Conte
- Cowboy G-Men: Hang the Jury ('52) Russell Hayden
- Cowboy G-Men: Mysterious Decoy ('52) Russell Hayden
- Hopalong Cassidy: Black Sombrero ('54) William Boyd
- Cheyenne: The Travelers ('56) Clint Walker
- Sugarfoot: Strange Land ('57) Will Hutchins
- Tales of the Texas Rangers: Trail Herd ('57) Willard Parker
- Badman's Country ('58 WB) George Montgomery
- Adventures of Rin Tin Tin: The Foot Soldier ('58) Lee Aaker
- Bronco: Brand of Courage ('58) Ty Hardin
- Tales of Wells Fargo: That Washburn Girl ('61) Dale Robertson

R. G. ARMSTRONG

Director Sam Peckinpah once said, "R. G. Armstrong played righteous villainy better than anybody I've ever seen."

Armstrong played a crazy preacher who would drag blonde-headed girls around by the hair, then take them into the church where he was going to whip them in one episode of TV's "Jefferson Drum". In fact, Armstrong played crazed, demented, backwoods preachers better than anyone ever has. "I've always loved Walter Huston in 'Duel In the Sun' as a preacher," R. G. stated. "I've always wanted to play some preachers like that 'cause my mother wanted me to be a preacher so bad, it broke her heart when I didn't. That wasn't my cup of tea. I had repressed a lot of things in me from my father's action and behavior towards his children. I didn't want to be a man like that, I didn't want to be violent, so I repressed it. When they started giving me these villains, I started drawing on that and I saw I had all the fury of hell and violence there, that I was really psychotic inside, because I could go into an instant rage or hostility. It was not acting, it was real. And they just kept giving these parts to me."

Big, balding, boisterous, R. G. (Robert Golden) Armstrong was born April 17, 1917, in Wylam (Birmingham), Alabama. After growing up on a rural Alabama farm, he won a scholarship to college by playing high school football.

In college he took a writing course as he wanted to be a poet. He also wrote plays and acted in them. WWII intervened, but when he returned, he came back to the University of North Carolina on his G.I. bill and earned a Master's Degree in dramatic art.

R. G. taught a year after receiving his Master's, but he wanted to be an author in the league of William Faulkner.

Actress Eva Marie Saint introduced R. G. into the Actor's Studio in New York. Within three months he'd obtained a role on Broadway. Director Elia Kazan saw

him and cast him as Big Daddy in "Cat On a Hot Tin Roof" when Burl Ives took a two week vacation. An agent spotted Armstrong and recommended him to director Henry Hathaway for a heavy in "From Hell to Texas". That started his career in 1957.

R. G.'s hard-nosed, blustery, often brutal characterizations remained in constant demand during the '60s and '70s, including all the major TV westerns. R. G. continued to work on through the '90s including a showy role in "Dick Tracy" (as Pruneface) ('90).

Suggested Sampling of Armstrong's Western Heavies:

- From Hell To Texas ('58 20th Century Fox) Don Murray
- Jefferson Drum: Law and Order ('58) Jeff Richards
- Bronco: Turning Point ('58) Ty Hardin
- Sugarfoot: The Hunted ('59) Will Hutchins
- Lawman: Brand Release ('59) John Russell
- Rawhide: Incident of the Dog Days ('59) Eric Fleming
- Wanted Dead Or Alive: The Tyrant ('59) Steve McQueen
- Sugarfoot: Giant Killer ('59) Will Hutchins
- Lawman: Battle Scar ('59) John Russell
- Maverick: People's Friend ('60) Jack Kelly
- Laramie: License to Kill ('60) Robert Fuller
- Tall Man: Bitter Ashes ('60) Barry Sullivan
- Cheyenne: Alibi For a Scalped Man ('60) Clint Walker
- Cheyenne: Return of Mr. Grimm ('61) Clint Walker
- Gunsmoke: Indian Ford ('61) James Arness
- Laramie: Run of the Hunted ('61) John Smith
- Ride the High Country ('62 MGM) Randolph Scott/Joel McCrea
- Tales of Wells Fargo: Winter Storm ('62) Dale Robertson
- Laramie: Time of the Traitor ('62) Robert Fuller/John Smith
- Major Dundee ('65 Columbia) Charlton Heston
- Big Valley: My Son, My Son ('65) Linda Evans
- Gunsmoke: Which Doctor ('66) James Arness
- Guns of Will Sonnett: Turkey Shoot ('67) Walter Brennan
- Lancer: Foley ('68) Wayne Maunder
- Pat Garrett and Billy the Kid ('73 MGM) James Coburn

HOOPER ATCHLEY

Born on a mountain top in Tennessee…Ebenezer, Tennessee, a hamlet now part of Knoxville to be specific…on April 30, 1887, Hooper Atchley didn't make his way to Hollywood until 1929 when he was already in his early 40s, during the closing days of the silent film era.

At 5' 11" with brown hair and eyes, Atchley attended Knoxville High School and the University of Tennessee before deciding on a stage career. He eventually landed on Broadway in 1913 with Marie Dressler's "All Star Gambol". After service in WWI, he was back on Broadway for "White Cargo" ('23), "Across the Street" ('24), "Night Hawk" ('25), and Jarnegan" ('28), before eventually making his way to Hollywood at the dawn of talkies. The thin-mustached Atchley found his niche playing slick, slippery, conniving crooks with a weak backbone who always needed his dog-heavies to back him up.

Of Atchley's over 180 screen credits, some 35 are westerns in which he generally faced-off against Hoot Gibson, Ken Maynard, Tim McCoy or Gene Autry.

His first screen credit is "Love At First Sight", an early 1929 Chesterfield drawing room drama with Norman Foster.

Atchley always took work where he could find it, whether it was the lead heavy or an unbilled role as a hotel desk clerk, doctor or conductor. However, by the late '30s on through the '40s nearly all his roles, westerns or otherwise, tended to be uncredited bit parts, every now and then restored to his past villainy as in "Black Hills Express" ('43 Republic) with Don Barry.

Serials also gave Atchley employment and he was featured in nine cliffhangers at Mascot, Universal and Republic between 1933 and 1941, but in only one did he have something other than a minor role. In "The Three Musketeers" ('33 Mascot) he was El Kadur, one of the major suspects as being the mysterious El Shaitan.

At 56, with his uncredited parts dwindling down to one line bits, and despondent over fear he was losing his eyesight, Atchley committed suicide by shooting himself in the head at the family home (602 North Kilkea Dr. in Los Angeles) on the evening of November 16, 1943.

The full name and status of Atchley's father is clouded as information provided by Atchley's widow, Violet Yakar Atchley, upon his demise, only indicates the father's surname was Atchley, first name unknown, possibly indicating the father was of the absentee variety. His mother was Elizabeth Phillips, a Tennessee native. Following Atchley's death, the body was shipped back to Newport, Tennessee, where he lies at rest at the Church of the Open Door Cemetery.

Suggested Sampling of Atchley's Western Heavies:

- Sundown Tail ('31 RKO) Tom Keene
- Arizona Terror ('31 Tiffany) Ken Maynard
- Branded Men ('31 Tiffany) Ken Maynard
- Clearing the Range ('31 Allied) Hoot Gibson
- Near the Trail's End ('31 Tiffany) Bob Steele
- Spirit of the West ('32 Allied) Hoot Gibson
- Gold ('32 Majestic) Jack Hoxie
- Local Bad Man ('32 Allied) Hoot Gibson
- Fighting For Justice ('32 Columbia) Tim McCoy
- Prescott Kid ('34 Columbia) Tim McCoy
- Outlaw Deputy ('35 Puritan) Tim McCoy
- Roarin' Lead ('36 Republic) 3 Mesquiteers
- Sagebrush Troubadour ('35 Republic) Gene Autry
- Old Barn Dance ('38 Republic) Gene Autry

JIMMY AUBREY

Posse member, ranch hand, deputy, cook, townsman, sidekick, barfly and outlaw—comic Englishman Jimmy Aubrey played them all, in scores of westerns, all with his Cockney accent.

Aubrey was always a welcome sight in the independent poverty row westerns of the '30s and at PRC where he seemed to find a home in the '40s.

Often, in poverty row westerns, Aubrey played more than one role so the producer could save a few dollars. In Robert J. Horner's painfully crude "Border Menace" ('34 Aywon) Aubrey is comic relief Polecat Pete, so far over the top it's astounding! But watch closely, ol' Jimmy also plays a rustler. Additionally, he's the film's editor! Aubrey is once again overacting in a tour de force of three or four different roles in Reliable's "Mystery Ranch" ('34) with Tom Tyler, including an exaggerated "melodrama"-style opening.

Jimmy has probably his best role as Tweedle, the duded-up English butler to Oxford dandy John Meredith, in PRC's "Ghost of Hidden Valley" ('46) with Buster Crabbe.

Matter of fact, Aubrey was in so many PRC westerns in the '40s for producer Sig Neufeld, they sneaked an in-joke into "Law of the Saddle" ('43) with Bob Livingston. As Livingston and sidekick Fuzzy St. John talk, the previously unseen-in-the-picture Aubrey walks by as the duo comment on him looking familiar. Nothing more is made of it.

Over the course of his well over 200 westerns, Aubrey had the opportunity to play the hero's sidekick a few times. He's the Mountie pal to John Preston (as Morton of the Mounted) in the ultra low-budget "Courage of the North" ('35 Stage & Screen), he's Jack Randall's friend in "Kid From Santa Fe" ('40 Monogram), rides with Ted Wells in the double-dreadful "Phantom Cowboy" ('35 Aywon) and "Defying the Law" ('35 American), and is Bob Steele's saddlepal in "Wild Horse Valley" and "Pinto Canyon" (both '40 Metropolitan).

James (Jimmy) Aubrey was born in Liverpool, England, October 23, 1887. When Boyd Magers met him at the Motion Picture Country Home in Woodland Hills, California, in 1982, Jimmy was still quite spry at 94. He said he'd gotten his start in the English music halls. The 5' 6", 165 pound youth with brown hair and blue eyes, came to films in 1916 as Heine, star of a series of Heine and Louie comedies.

Previously coming to the U.S. in 1913, for vaudeville, he toured as the Terrible Turk in Fred Karno's "Night in the English Music Hall". Other members of the troupe included Charles Chaplin and Stan Laurel. In 1920 Aubrey was under contract to Vitagraph for two years and by 1923 he formed his own company to make two-reel comedies.

Aubrey told Magers he was on location in Kernville shooting a purported drama when the director needed actors for a big scene. He was asked if he could ride and said yes although he'd never been on a horse in his life. He held on for dear life, got through the scene and found himself a staple in westerns for the next nearly 20 years. (That film was most likely "A Gentleman Preferred", a 1928 First Division semi-western starring Gaston Glass.)

Aubrey is not in, but co-scripted with prolific Bennett Cohen, "Under Montana Skies" for Tiffany in 1930, an odd mixture of western action, comedy and music starring one-time silent matinee idol Kenneth Harlan.

Aubrey retired in 1953, with 37 years of screen credits, after playing a bartender in MGM's Esther Williams swim-fest, "Dangerous When Wet".

Aubrey left a rich film legacy when he died at 95 at the Woodland Hills Motion Picture Home September 2, 1983.

Suggested Sampling of Aubrey's Western Heavies:

- Lariats and Sixshooters ('31 Robert J. Horner) Jack Perrin
- Border Guns ('34 Aywon) Bill Cody
- Arizona Nights ('34 Reliable) Bud (Jack Perrin) and Ben (Ben Corbett)
- The Test ('35 Reliable) Rin Tin Tin Jr.
- Silent Valley ('35 Reliable) Tom Tyler
- Fast Bullets ('36 Reliable) Tom Tyler
- Men of the Plains ('36 Colony) Rex Bell
- Songs and Bullets ('38 Spectrum) Fred Scott
- Covered Wagon Trails ('40 Monogram) Jack Randall
- The Renegades ('43 PRC) Buster Crabbe
- Ghost of Hidden Valley ('46 PRC) Buster Crabbe

HOLLY BANE / MIKE RAGAN

Holly Bane, who changed his name to the more male sounding Mike Ragan midway in his badman career, was one of the best and busiest "second generation" B-western heavies of those that came along after WWII.

Co-badman Myron Healey remembers, "He was always good for a laugh if he was on the show…always into something. He was a hell of a personality. Everybody seemed to like him, including myself."

Hollis Alan Bane was born February 18, 1918, in Los Angeles, California. His father, John Bentley Bane, hailed from Illinois while his mom, Gladys Opal Turnmire, was from Indiana.

As a boy Holly lived in San Francisco as well as Los Angeles where he obtained his first job as an office boy at MGM circa 1932.

At the young age of 15 he left on his own for San Francisco once again to try his hand at the big band business. However, he soon returned to Los Angeles, taking an interest in the makeup department and becoming an apprentice in the craft. One of the first films he worked on was MGM's "The Good Earth" ('37) under the supervision of Jack Dawn. As a makeup artist at MGM and RKO he worked with such stars as Clark Gable, Greta Garbo, Hedy Lamarr and Spencer Tracy.

As an actor, he first appeared as a 1st Lieutenant in "Wake Island" ('42).

His makeup work and aspirations to be an actor were then interrupted when he spent four years with the Marines during WWII.

Returning to RKO circa 1945, he did makeup on various Robert Ryan and Robert Mitchum pictures before deciding to make acting a full time job with "Buffalo Bill Rides Again" ('47 Screen Guild).

Another friend, Pierce Lyden, said, "He was quite a heavy, as I was. A good type…good face. He was easy to get along with. One of the old gang, one of the few of us that did a lot of B-westerns—and worked at Republic." Holly apparently would have preferred to have done makeup as a career but as Pierce recalled, "It was a pretty closed union at that time, run by the Westmores. Pretty hard to get a foothold in the makeup union."

Still another frequent badman of the period, Gregg Barton, thought of Bane as "…a hard worker, good worker. He was kinda rough on the cob I thought, but was never lacking for doing his work. I knew him under both names—but mostly Holly."

Holly Bane interrupts Jimmy Wakely's dinner with Gail Davis, putting the strongarm on Jimmy for his boss William Ruhl in "Brand of Fear" ('49 Monogram).

Earl Bellamy directed Holly in "Gunpoint" (Bane's last film), "Blackjack Ketchum, Desperado" and several "Lone Ranger" episodes. Earl recalled, "He was *one* character! If I got on a show he would call me right away and say, 'I'm ready. I'm available.' He was so funny that way. 'Course I would hire him 'cause I liked him so darn much. If a company was down, he'd do something just for kicks to spark things up. When he would get shot—supposed to die in the scene, everybody would gather 'round to watch because Holly would take five minutes before he was dead. We'd get a kick out of it. Unbeknownst to him the crew would say, 'I'll betcha a dollar it'll take him three minutes…' or so on. They'd bet to see how long it would take Mike to die. The one last thing would be the twitch of the foot. (Laughs) I knew he'd gone into makeup. Fact is, I was doing some show and he came in that morning…we needed extra help…and I was very surprised but very pleased because he was doing really well and had a steady job for a change."

Bane connected at Republic, becoming an actor they frequently used in the latter days in "Rocky" Lane, Monte Hale and Roy Rogers pictures as well as seven serials beginning with "Jesse James Rides Again" ('47) and ending with his biggest role in "Panther Girl of the Kongo" in '55.

In 1961, Bane briefly returned to makeup when he did the makeup for the TV pilot of George Nader's syndicated "Shannon". When the show sold, Nader asked Bane to remain, but he preferred to stick with acting.

However, with work in westerns nearly dried up by 1966, he returned to makeup once again, later working on such popular series as "Welcome Back Kotter", "Fish", "Barney Miller" (where he was makeup department head for a time), "Family Feud" and "General Hospital".

Bane's hobbies were many—he was an inventor, painter, designer, avid swimmer and sportsman (at one time he played pro-baseball and boxed).

He was married for 30 years to character actress Dorothy Ford ("Three Godfathers", "Sands of Iwo Jima", a couple of Bowery Boys titles, among others) and they lived at 13906 Fiji Way in Marina Del Rey, California. He did a stint in makeup for the local ABC news affiliate in Los Angeles in the early '90s but retired in '92.

Bane, 77, died August 25, 1995, at Vencor Hospital in Los Angeles of cardiorespiratory arrest, complicated by emphysema. He'd been hospitalized for five months, with a tracheostomy performed on April 11, 1995. Bane's remains were cremated and scattered at sea by the Neptune Society off the coast of San Pedro, California.

Suggested Sampling of Bane's Western Heavies:

- Buffalo Bill Rides Again ('47 Screen Guild) Richard Arlen
- Overland Trails ('48 Monogram) Johnny Mack Brown
- Return of Wildfire ('48 Screen Guild) Richard Arlen
- Night Time In Nevada ('48 Republic) Roy Rogers
- Renegades of Sonora ('48 Republic) Allan "Rocky" Lane
- Far Frontier ('48 Republic) Roy Rogers
- Brand of Fear ('49 Monogram) Jimmy Wakely
- Riders of the Dusk ('49 Monogram) Whip Wilson
- Red Desert ('49 Lippert) Don Barry
- Fence Riders ('50 Monogram) Whip Wilson
- West of Wyoming ('50 Monogram) Johnny Mack Brown
- Storm Over Wyoming ('50 RKO) Tim Holt
- Lone Ranger: Bullets or Ballots ('50) Clayton Moore
- Gene Autry: Doublecross Valley ('50) Gene Autry
- Cisco Kid: Wedding Blackmail ('50) Duncan Renaldo
- Range Rider: Fatal Bullet ('51) Jock Mahoney
- Lone Ranger: Silent Voice ('51) Clayton Moore
- Cisco Kid: Haven For Heavies ('51) Duncan Renaldo
- Gene Autry: The Raiders ('51) Gene Autry
- Wild Bill Hickok: Tax Collecting Story ('51) Guy Madison
- Roy Rogers: Train Robbery ('52) Roy Rogers
- Sky King: Stagecoach Robbers ('52) Kirby Grant
- Cisco Kid: Puppeteer ('52) Duncan Renaldo
- Target ('52 RKO) Tim Holt
- Lone Ranger: Through the Wall ('52) John Hart
- Roy Rogers: Go For Your Gun ('52) Roy Rogers
- Wild Bill Hickok: Doctor Story ('53) Guy Madison
- Roy Rogers: Bad Company ('53) Roy Rogers
- Gunsmoke ('53 Universal-International) Audie Murphy
- Canadian Mounties Vs. Atomic Invaders ('53 Republic serial) Bill Henry
- Cisco Kid: Marriage By Mail ('54) Duncan Renaldo
- Roy Rogers: Land Swindle ('54) Roy Rogers
- Stories of the Century: Henry Plummer ('54) Jim Davis
- Annie Oakley: The Runaways ('54) Gail Davis
- Buffalo Bill Jr.: Empire Pass ('55) Dick Jones
- Annie Oakley: Thunder Hill ('55) Gail Davis
- Gene Autry: Million Dollar Fiddle ('55) Gene Autry
- Champion: Return of Red Cloud ('56) Jim Bannon
- Buffalo Bill Jr.: Secret of the Silverado ('56) Dick Jones
- Lone Ranger: White Hawk's Decision ('56) Clayton Moore
- Last of the Desperadoes ('56 Associated) James Craig
- Annie Oakley: Amateur Outlaw ('56) Gail Davis
- Lone Ranger: Ghost Canyon ('56) Clayton Moore
- Fury: Man Killer ('59) Peter Graves
- Laramie: Queen of Diamonds ('60) John Smith/Robert Fuller
- Bronco: Moment of Doubt ('62) Ty Hardin
- Gunpoint ('66 Universal) Audie Murphy

ROY BARCROFT

Pierce Lyden said Roy Barcroft turned his parts "into the deserved title, King of the Badmen."

Terry Frost called him "one of the nicest people I ever met in the business."

Monte Hale wrote that Roy "was the most likable, kindly, soft-spoken gentleman you ever crossed trails with. But when the cameras started rolling, he was the meanest, low-down, orneriest son-of-a-gun on the face of the earth. He always made the leading man look really good, no matter with whom he was working. He could always handle his part with the best of actors."

Rex Allen smiled, "When I think of Barcroft, I think of him coming to work on a motorcycle, roaring through the front gate. Off-screen, he was the nicest, big, old Saint Bernard you could ever want to be around. I had a very high respect for his acting ability and his photographic memory. He was a real pro."

Sunset Carson remembered, "One of the greatest you'd ever want to meet. He enjoyed a good laugh and was always telling jokes and pulling tricks on somebody. He enjoyed parties, hanging out with the guys and riding his motorcycle."

Eddie Dean recalled, "He was a musician, too. He enjoyed a jam session and played the clarinet and saxophone really well."

Tris Coffin said, "He was as beloved as anybody in the entire business."

Peggy Stewart calls him "a wonderful guy."

"You never met a nicer guy than Roy Barcroft," Harry Lauter commented. "And he was a fine actor. I'm sure he would have gone on to greater things if he hadn't gotten typed as a western heavy."

Fellow badman I. Stanford Jolley smiled, "Wonderful Roy Barcroft. We were the top heavies in 'Desperadoes of the West'. We made things tough for cowboy star Tom Keene, whom for some reason we never learned, used the name of Richard Powers in the film. Roy and I were friends socially as well as on the film set. We and our wives would often travel to Las Vegas together. Roy loved to play roulette. He had a 'system' and would sit at the tables for hours. He often liked to talk about a book he planned to write but never did. He wanted to entitle it, 'A 1,001 Ways to Lose at Gambling'."

Roy Rogers referred to Roy as "almost like family. He was a great actor. In his personal life he was just the opposite of the villain he portrayed. He was loving and kind as well as a comic at times. He looked mean, but he wasn't. Roy was one of the nicest guys I ever worked with."

In her book COWBOY PRINCESS, Roy Rogers' daughter Cheryl writes, "Roy Barcroft, the ultimate bad guy, was the biggest softy you ever saw with little kids. At the Hitching Post Theater on Saturday, it was funny how it usually took Dad a good 45 minutes to figure Barcroft for the bad guy—every kid in the audience knew

it was him from his very first scene. But on the set or at our house, he was a very sweet man. Dad often hunted with Barcroft and with Glenn Strange, who played both bad men and monsters."

Howard Harold Ravenscroft was born September 7, 1902, the youngest of seven children, to William Ravenscroft and Lillian Williams, both from Illinois. According to Social Security records in '37, Roy listed his birthplace as Omaha, Nebraska. However, close friends knew he was born in nearby Crab Orchard, Nebraska, and merely listed Omaha as his birthplace due to the city's greater name recognition. Weeping Water, Nebraska, is also often listed as his birthplace. The two small towns are near one another, so it's likely he was born in-between the two sites on his father's farm where he grew up.

After his father died when he was 13, Roy lied about his age and at the young age of 15 he managed to enlist in the U.S. Army at Lincoln, Nebraska, and was sent to France with the A.E.F. during WWI where he was wounded in action and returned home at 16 for discharge. He then spent about four years wandering, working at odd jobs—short order cook, dishwasher, oil well roughneck, gandy dancer (laborer on railroad tracks), truck driver, and a sailor-fireman on a tramp freighter in Constantinople. Sometime during this period, while working on a ranch in Oregon, he met his first wife by whom he had two children, a son and a daughter. They were divorced in '31.

Earlier, in 1923 he re-enlisted in the Army, serving until 1926 in Hawaii and at Fort Lewis, Washington.

During his time in the service he learned to play the clarinet and saxophone, playing professionally after leaving the Islands in '26. He played with various bands around Chicago until the market crash of '29 at which time he packed up his Model-A Roadster and he, his wife, and child headed for California, establishing a residence in Culver City near several movie studios.

There was a call for well-drilled ex-soldiers so, curious about the industry, he obtained an extra part in Greta Garbo's "Mata Hari" ('31).

For the next six years, during the Great Depression, Roy worked for two years in a tunnel for the Metropolitan Water District bringing water to L.A. and spent the rest of the time selling radios and automobiles.

In order to improve his sales, he took a course in public speaking where a friend suggested dramatics. He appeared in several little theatre productions where, one day, an agent offered to represent him.

Roy's first real film role was in the Republic serial "S.O.S. Coastguard" in July of '37. He was paid $66 per week.

Meanwhile, in 1932, Roy married again, to Vera Thompson. They had one son, Michael.

Roy's rough voice, tough look and demeanor were perfect for heavy roles in B-westerns and Barcroft spent the next 33 years in the film business.

As to his name, Barcroft once explained, "My real name was Ravenscroft, but it was too much for the marquee, or for anybody to pronounce correctly, or remember. So I thought I'd like to keep part of it. All this went through my mind. I thought, 'Well, let me see now...I could keep Croft and I'd like to be high on the alphabetical list.' So instead of being way down in the R's, if somebody was looking for an actor, they'd be going down the line, and they might come to one, and never finish the list. I thought I'd like to be up there fairly high, which is the B's, and I thought I'd choose a name no one else had in the business, but kind of similar to an actor who is well established...like George Bancroft. Then they would, maybe, say, 'See if you can find a guy's name something like Bancroft.' Then I thought, 'What's a better three-letter first name; make it short for the marquee, or whatever it was.' So I came up with Roy Barcroft; it *sounds* like a heavy."

His first western was as one of the heavies in Johnny Mack Brown's Universal serial "Flaming Frontiers" ('38).

Barcroft worked steadily at Paramount, RKO, Monogram, Universal and Republic for the next several years.

Reminiscing to writer Ken Jones for WESTERN FILM COLLECTOR in 1973 Barcroft said, "I will never forget my first 'chase'. I thought I could handle a horse. In this scene there were 15 horses involved and some of the best western players, men like Charlie King, Karl Hackett, Ethan Laidlaw, Kenne Duncan and Yakima Canutt. We started on top of the hill. The shot was fired which was the signal for the horses to go...and they did! I was in the middle of the pack and down the steep side we went, across an open grassy prairie, some cactus, ditches, prairie dog holes, over boulders and into the river. I won't try to say what went through my mind, but one thing was for certain; if I intended to remain in western pictures and all in one piece I was going to have to learn how to *really* ride. I sneaked away and practiced riding and falling by myself time and time again until I was accepted by the others. I can look back on some pretty miserable days when it was cold, windy and dusty and we 'chased' all day long and wore out three or four horses. That night it was Epsom salt baths and liniment. I think I liked the roles best where I could be the dirtiest, meanest, unkempt individual possible, such as the film 'Night Train to Memphis' with Roy Acuff in 1946. I also enjoyed films where the costumes were elaborate such as 'The Purple Monster Strikes' and my own favorite, 'Manhunt of Mystery Island,' both serials."

Having performed well and developed a following, Barcroft was signed to a term-contract at Republic on July 7, 1943. Over the next 10 years his salary rose from $125 a week to $300 a week. His contract ended July 11, 1953.

Before joining Republic exclusively, Barcroft had already worked in 17 serials at Universal, Columbia and Republic. Beginning in '43 he became Republic's prominent serial badman, appearing in 19 serials for them through 1954. For two he was a modern day pirate: "Haunted Harbor" ('44) "Manhunt of Mystery Island" ('45); two as outer space invaders: "Purple Monster Strikes" ('45), "Radar Men From the Moon" ('52); two as gangsters: "Daughter of Don Q" ('46), "Federal Agents Vs. Underworld Inc." ('49); one as a crooked police commissioner: "G Men Never Forget" ('48); two non-villain sheriffs: "Phantom Rider" ('46), "Man with the Steel Whip" ('54); six as western badmen: "Son of Zorro" ('47), "Jesse James Rides Again" ('47), "James Brothers of Missouri" ('49), Ghost of Zorro" ('49), "Desperadoes of the West" ('50), "Don Daredevil Rides Again" ('51) and a couple of bit or voiceover roles in "Masked Marvel" ('43), "Radar Patrol Vs. Spy King" ('50), "Government Agents Vs. Phantom Legion" ('51) and "Zombies of the Stratosphere" ('52). His personal favorite was as Capt. Mephisto in "Manhunt of Mystery Island".

Barcroft remembered for writer Ken Jones, "There was always a lot of horseplay with the movie crew during the filming of a feature. One didn't dare lie down on a hot rock for a nap for fear of a hot foot or having his spurs wired together or having a nice, warm snake released across your chest. The western actors were a great bunch of guys. I took it in stride the times when they loosened my saddle cinch just before running out of a saloon for a fast getaway…or even better yet riding up alongside of me in a wide open chase and taking off my horse's bridle and handing it to me."

When his contract ended at Republic in '53, Roy, continuing to play badmen, easily moved into television on "Annie Oakley", "Cowboy G-Men", "Kit Carson", "Fury" and "Lone Ranger".

In later years stuntman Whitey Hughes remembers how Roy Barcroft "built his own home out there in the San Fernando Valley with his own hands then complained about having to work real hard to keep from getting taxed out of it."

Gaining a little heft, Barcroft began to play sheriffs and lawmen on "Have Gun Will Travel", "Trackdown", "26 Men", "Tales of Wells Fargo", "Maverick", "Laredo" and others.

Still later, he became a terrific character actor on "Gunsmoke", "Johnny Ringo", "Texan", "Have Gun Will Travel", "Zane Grey Theatre", "Rifleman", "Shotgun Slade", "Rawhide", "Bonanza" and others. For Walt Disney in the late '50s Roy worked regularly on "Spin and Marty", "Elfego Baca" and "Texas John Slaughter". On theatre screens he played character roles in some 40 major westerns of the '50s and '60s—"Oklahoma" ('55), "Man Without a Star" ('55), "Domino Kid" ('57), "Escort West" ('58), "Six Black Horses" ('62), "Texas Across the River" ('66), "Way West" ('67), "The Reivers" ('69) and his final film, "Monte Walsh" ('70), released after his death on November 28, 1969, at the Motion Picture Hospital in Woodland Hills, California, of kidney cancer. His body was donated to UCLA for research.

The incredibly prolific (310 movies, over 110 TV shows) and talented 6' 2", 200 lb. Roy Barcroft always managed to bring something extra to his western badmen, making him stand out when the script often had little to offer. His screen fights with Allan "Rocky" Lane in 38 of Lane's 51 films are legendary realistic brawls. Without a doubt, Roy Barcroft tops the Best of the Badmen list at #1.

Suggested Sampling of Barcroft's Western Heavies:

- Flaming Frontiers ('38 Universal serial) Johnny Mack Brown
- Stranger From Arizona ('38 Columbia) Buck Jones
- Renegade Trail ('39 Paramount) William Boyd
- West of Carson City ('40 Universal) Johnny Mack Brown
- Stage to Chino ('40 RKO) George O'Brien
- White Eagle ('41 Columbia serial) Buck Jones
- Outlaws of Cherokee Trail ('41 Republic) 3 Mesquiteers
- Bandit Trail ('41 RKO) Tim Holt
- Masked Rider ('41 Universal) Johnny Mack Brown
- Lone Rider In Cheyenne ('42 PRC) George Houston
- Land of the Open Range ('42 RKO) Tim Holt
- West of the Law ('42 Monogram) Rough Riders
- Riders of the Rio Grande ('43 Republic) 3 Mesquiteers
- Stranger From Pecos ('43 Monogram) Johnny Mack Brown
- Bordertown Gunfighters ('43 Republic) Bill Elliott
- False Colors ('43 United Artists) William Boyd
- Hidden Valley Outlaws ('44 Republic) Bill Elliott
- Cheyenne Wildcat ('44 Republic) Bill Elliott
- Code of the Prairie ('44 Republic) Sunset Carson
- Sheriff of Sundown ('44 Republic) Allan Lane
- Lone Texas Ranger ('45 Republic) Bill Elliott
- Marshal of Laredo ('45 Republic) Bill Elliott
- Wagon Wheels Westward ('45 Republic) Bill Elliott
- Home On the Range ('46 Republic) Monte Hale
- Sun Valley Cyclone ('46 Republic) Bill Elliott
- Stagecoach to Denver ('46 Republic) Allan Lane
- Son of Zorro ('47 Republic serial) George Turner
- Oregon Trail Scouts ('47 Republic) Allan Lane
- Springtime In the Sierras ('47 Republic) Roy Rogers
- Jesse James Rides Again ('47 Republic serial) Clayton Moore
- Wild Frontier ('47 Republic) Allan "Rocky" Lane
- Oklahoma Badlands ('48 Republic) Allan "Rocky" Lane
- Bold Frontiersman ('48 Republic) Allan "Rocky" Lane
- Timber Trail ('48 Republic) Monte Hale
- Eyes of Texas ('48 Republic) Roy Rogers
- Renegades of Sonora ('48 Republic) Allan "Rocky" Lane
- Far Frontier '('48 Republic) Roy Rogers
- Outcasts of the Trail ('49 Republic) Monte Hale
- Ghost of Zorro ('49 Republic serial) Clayton Moore
- Frontier Investigator ('49 Republic) Allan "Rocky" Lane
- Powder River Rustlers ('49 Republic) Allan "Rocky" Lane
- Sheriff of Wichita ('49 Republic) Allan "Rocky" Lane
- South of Rio ('49 Republic) Monte Hale
- Code of the Silver Sage ('50 Republic) Allan "Rocky" Lane
- Vanishing Westerner ('50 Republic) Monte Hale
- Salt Lake Raiders ('50 Republic) Allan "Rocky" Lane
- Desperadoes of the West ('50 Republic serial) Richard (Tom Keene) Powers
- The Missourians ('50 Republic) Monte Hale
- In Old Amarillo ('51 Republic) Roy Rogers
- Fort Dodge Stampede ('51 Republic) Allan "Rocky" Lane
- Desert of Lost Men ('51 Republic) Allan "Rocky" Lane
- Wild Horse Ambush ('52 Republic) Rough Ridin' Kids
- Black Hills Ambush ('52 Republic) Allan "Rocky" Lane
- Thundering Caravans ('52 Republic) Allan "Rocky" Lane
- Old Oklahoma Plains ('52 Republic) Rex Allen
- South Pacific Trail ('52 Republic) Rex Allen
- Iron Mountain Trail ('53 Republic) Rex Allen
- Old Overland Trail ('53 Republic) Rex Allen
- Marshal of Cedar Rock ('53 Republic) Allan "Rocky" Lane
- El Paso Stampede ('53 Republic) Allan "Rocky" Lane
- Shadows of Tombstone ('53 Republic) Rex Allen
- Cowboy G-Men: Sidewinder ('53) Russell Hayden
- Kit Carson: Lost Treasure of the Panamints ('53) Bill Williams
- Champion: Diehards ('56) Jim Bannon
- Annie Oakley: Renegade's Return ('56) Gail Davis
- Domino Kid ('57 Columbia) Rory Calhoun
- Lone Ranger: The Avenger ('57) Clayton Moore
- 26 Men: Last Rebellion ('58) Kelo Henderson/Tris Coffin
- 26 Men: Has Been ('59) Kelo Henderson/Tris Coffin
- Gunsmoke: Say Uncle ('60) James Arness
- Have Gun Will Travel: Tax Gatherer ('61) Richard Boone
- Have Gun Will Travel: Long Weekend ('61) Richard Boone
- Laramie: Badge of the Outsider ('61) Robert Fuller/John Smith

TREVOR BARDETTE

"Trevor Bardette achieved his deception with a demeanor of sincerity," observed William C. Cline in his treatise on serials IN THE NICK OF TIME. Bardette usually portrayed a sad-faced, downtrodden individual, seldom called on to smile. In a role for which he will never be forgotten, that of the murderous Pegleg in Bill Elliott's classic Columbia serial, "Overland With Kit Carson" ('39), so effective was his desire to be helpful (when not in his Pegleg guise) it seemed nigh impossible he could be the mysterious renegade.

Then in Republic's "Jungle Girl" ('41) serial, his assumption of his murdered twin brother's identity brought no trace of suspicion from Nyoka. In Columbia's "Secret Code" ('42) as a spy leader he was a bit more forthright in his evil deeds.

Throughout his career, he seemed to play important roles in B-films (Roy Rogers, Rex Allen, Rocky Lane, etc.) and smaller character roles in important films ("Oklahoma Kid" '39, "Gone With the Wind" '39, "Abe Lincoln In Illinois" '40, "Uncertain Glory" '44, "Dragonwyck" '46, "Big Sleep" '46, "Sea of Grass" '47, "T-Men" '47, "Union Station" '50, "Thunder Road" '58, etc.). For TV he specialized in fathers and slightly off-kilter older miners, trappers, ranchers and the like.

Perhaps Bardette is best remembered by TV audiences as Old Man Ike Clanton during the Tombstone episodes of Hugh O'Brian's "Life and Legend of Wyatt Earp" (Sept. '59-May '61).

One-fourth Cherokee, Bardette was born November 19, 1902, in Nashville, Arkansas, of Scotch, Irish, French and Cherokee heritage. After graduating from Oregon University, his adventurous spirit found him in Mexico on a gold mining venture. That might have been his life's work if he hadn't run into a bit of gun-play with some Mexican peons and decided to pursue a less hazardous existence.

Bardette then attended Northwestern University, achieving a Master's degree, intending to be a mechanical engineer, but was sidetracked into drama through course work while in college.

After working in various stock companies throughout the Northwest, he began his acting career in earnest in New York in the musical "Flossie". Various other stage engagements kept him busy through 1936 when he went to Hollywood to pursue a screen career.

In his first film, Bardette befriended Hopalong

Dress-heavy Trevor Bardette (L) gives henchman Roy Barcroft strong orders in Monte Hale's "San Antone Ambush. ('49 Republic).

Cassidy as Mexican Secret Service Agent Col. Gonzales in "Borderland" ('37 Paramount), a role he repeated a year later in Hoppy's "In Old Mexico" ('38 Paramount).

From then until 1970, the broodingly handsome, usually mustachioed Bardette never stopped working in a wide variety of over 170 films and nearly 100 TV episodes. His last work was on a "Gunsmoke" episode in November '70.

Bardette was residing in Green Valley, Pima County, Arizona, when he died, reportedly, in Los Angeles, California, November 28, 1977. Exact circumstances are unknown, but speculation is he was living in Arizona and being treated in California.

Suggested Sampling of Bardette's Western Heavies:

- Overland With Kit Carson ('39 Columbia serial) Bill Elliott
- Young Buffalo Bill ('40 Republic) Roy Rogers
- Doomed Caravan ('41 Paramount) William Boyd
- Red River Valley ('41 Republic) Roy Rogers
- Wild Bill Hickok Rides ('42 Warner Bros.) Bruce Cabot
- Law of the Badlands ('45 Warner Bros.) Robert Shayne
- Marshal of Cripple Creek ('47 Republic) Allan Lane
- Marshal of Amarillo ('48 Republic) Allan "Rocky" Lane
- Sundown in Santa Fe ('48 Republic) Allan "Rocky" Lane
- Sheriff of Wichita ('49 Republic) Allan "Rocky" Lane
- Blazing Trail ('49 Columbia) Charles Starrett
- San Antone Ambush ('49 Republic) Monte Hale
- Hills of Oklahoma ('50 Republic) Rex Allen
- Fort Dodge Stampede ('51 Republic) Allan "Rocky" Lane
- Red River Shore ('53 Republic) Rex Allen
- Broken Arrow: The Captive ('56) John Lupton/Michael Ansara
- Wyatt Earp: (Recurring role as Clanton '59-'61) Hugh O'Brian
- Gunsmoke: Small Water ('60) James Arness
- Have Gun will Travel: The Road ('61) Richard Boone

RAYFORD BARNES

The man with the mean looking smirk, Rayford Barnes was one of the busiest badmen on episodic TV from '54-'69, besides working in some classic westerns of the period—"Hondo", "Wichita", "Shenandoah" and "The Wild Bunch".

Born October 23, 1920, near Whitesboro, Texas, the WWII Navy and Merchant Marine vet began his career in New York training with Stella Adler at the Neighborhood Playhouse, later moving to San Francisco to open his own theatre.

Rayford actually came from a showbiz "family". He was a nephew of comic actress Binnie Barnes who married producer Mike Frankovitch in 1940. Producer Peter Frankovitch and screenwriter Mike Frankovitch Jr. are his cousins.

His first film was a western, "Stranger Wore a Gun" in 1953 with Randolph Scott. John Wayne's "Hondo" was the same year and Rafe was on his way.

Husband and wife actors Jan Shepard and Dirk London have slightly varying views of Rayford. Jan recalls him as "serious" while Dirk found him "funny". Jan said, "He was sweet, friendly, very professional. Reminded me of a young Richard Widmark. Blonde, blue-eyed. Widmark was more pronounced; Ray was a little more nondescript." Dirk says, "He had a very infectious, contagious smile. He was Ike Clanton on our 'Wyatt Earp' show. (Dirk was Morgan Earp.) He was the type of guy who knew what he was doing, but had a lot of fun along with it."

Kelo Henderson, star of TV's "26 Men," knew Rayford. "The first time I met Rayford was on location in El Centro, California, for MGM's 'Gun Glory' in '57. The second time was when he came to Phoenix, Arizona, in '58 to appear in four episodes of my '26 Men' series. He was professional, a very versatile actor, having the rare talent of being able to portray a mousey, cowardly type with real conviction, then easily make the transition to a villainous heavy."

Barnes was still working up until his death, having just completed jobs on "ER" and "Walker Texas Ranger".

He married wife Debra in 1973. He may possibly have been married before.

Barnes died November 11, 2000, at St. John's Health Center in Santa Monica.

Suggested Sampling of Barnes' Western Heavies:

- Red River Shore ('53 Republic) Rex Allen
- The Desperado ('54 Allied Artists) Wayne Morris
- Roy Rogers: Outcasts of Paradise Valley ('55) Roy Rogers
- Wild Bill Hickok: Buckshot Comes Home ('55) Guy Madison
- Fury: Joey and the Stranger ('56) Bobby Diamond
- Stagecoach to Fury ('56 20th Century Fox) Forrest Tucker
- Colt .45: Small Man ('57) Wayde Preston
- Ride a Crooked Trail ('57 Universal) Audie Murphy
- Tombstone Territory: Shoot Out at Dark ('58) Pat Conway
- Have Gun Will Travel: Road to Wickenburg ('58) Richard Boone
- Rin Tin Tin: Deadman's Valley ('58) Lee Aaker
- Tales of the Texas Rangers: Desert Fury ('58) Willard Parker
- Have Gun Will Travel: Something To Live For ('58) Richard Boone
- Man Without A Gun: Quiet Stranger ('58) Rex Reason
- Lone Texan ('59 20th Century Fox) Willard Parker
- 26 Men: Death in the Dragoons ('59) Kelo Henderson
- Lawman: The Conclave ('59) John Russell
- Rin Tin Tin: Apache Stampede ('59) Lee Aaker
- Young Jesse James ('60 20th Century Fox) Willard Parker
- 13 Fighting Men ('60 20th Century Fox) Grant Williams
- Overland Trail: High Bridge ('60) Doug McClure
- Wyatt Earp: Series—as Ike Clanton ('60-'61) Hugh O'Brian
- Bat Masterson: Bull Whacker's Bounty ('61) Gene Barry
- Have Gun Will Travel: The Revenger ('61) Richard Boone
- Laramie: Fall Into Darkness ('62) John Smith
- Gunsmoke: Carter Caper ('63) James Arness
- Gunsmoke: No Hands ('64) James Arness
- Rawhide: Blood Harvest ('65) Eric Fleming
- Iron Horse: Through Ticket To Gunsight ('66) Dale Robertson
- Big Valley: Image of Yesterday ('67) Barbara Stanwyck
- High Chaparral: The Kinsman ('68) Leif Erickson
- Guns of Will Sonnett: Time Is the Rider ('69) Walter Brennan
- The Wild Bunch ('69 Warner Bros.) William Holden
- Cahill, United States Marshal ('73 Warner Bros.) John Wayne

ROBERT BARRAT

Big, powerful, banana-nosed character player Robert Barrat was a master at dialects (French, Polish, German) and was often seen as imposing, sometimes harsh, authority figures—sheriffs, mayors, attorneys, judges, counts and military men—including historical figures: Davy Crockett in "Man of Conquest" ('39 Republic); Chingachgook in "Last of the Mohicans" ('36 United Artists), President Abraham Lincoln in "Trailin' West" ('36 Warner Bros.); General Douglas MacArthur in both "They Were Expendable" ('45 MGM) and "American Guerrilla In the Philippines" ('50 20th Century Fox); Governor Lew Wallace in "Kid From Texas' ('50 Universal-International) and General Zachary Taylor in "Distant Drums" ('51 Warner Bros.).

Barrat was equally at home in comedies, murder mysteries, costume dramas and westerns, of which he appeared in nearly 40 from '35-'55. Whatever the genre, he was seldom seen without an ever present pipe in his mouth.

Robert H. (Harriot) Barrat was born July 10, 1889, in New York City, the son of Robert Barrat of England and Dora Mary Schneider of New York.

Barrat gained entrance into the thespian world through stock companies which led to a successful career on Broadway from 1918-1932, including the long-running "Kid Boots" (December 1923-February 1925).

Barrat appeared in three New York made silent films in 1915, 1920 and 1921, then came to Hollywood in the very early '30s as did many stage-trained, strong-voiced actors with the new medium of sound. He was under contract to Warner Bros. for four years ('33-'37) which is where he made his first western, "Moonlight On the Prairie" ('35) opposite Dick Foran.

The well-respected actor died at 80, January 7, 1970, at Midway Hospital in Los Angeles. The primary cause of death was heart disease, complicated by pneumonia and the failure of a post operative pacemaker.

Barrat had resided at 1737 N. Orange Grove Ave. in Los Angeles and was survived by his wife Mary Bean Barrat who acted a bit under the name Mary Dean. He is buried at Valhalla Cemetery in North Hollywood.

Suggested Sampling of Barrat's Western Heavies:

- Moonlight On the Prairie ('35 Warner Bros.) Dick Foran
- Trail of the Lonesome Pine ('36 Paramount) Fred MacMurray
- The Texans ('38 Paramount) Randolph Scott
- Union Pacific ('39 Paramount) Joel McCrea
- Colorado Sunset ('39 Republic) Gene Autry
- Return of the Cisco Kid ('39 20th Century Fox) Warner Baxter
- Cisco Kid and the Lady ('39 20th Century Fox) Cesar Romero
- Go West ('40 MGM) Marx Brothers
- Riders of the Purple Sage ('41 20th Century Fox) George Montgomery
- Wanderer of the Wasteland ('45 RKO) James Warren
- Tall Man Riding ('55 Warner Bros.) Randolph Scott

GREGG BARTON

"I've been knocked on my rear by every western star, including Annie Oakley. When the price is right, I'd let anyone knock me down." One of the busiest heavies of the late '40s on through the '50s, particularly on the TV screen, was stubbly bearded Gregg Barton—especially in Gene Autry's Columbia westerns and TV series.

Born Harold Wilsea Barker June 5, 1912, on Long Island City, New York, during the time the Infantile Paralysis epidemic swept through the city, Hal's father was George Wilsea Barker born in Kent, England, and his mother was Mae Malcolm, born in New York of Scottish heritage. Hal's father, an electrical engineer, died at 33 when Hal was only 3. As his father was a Mason, Hal and his older brother, age 4, were accepted into the Masonic Home and sent to their Home for Boys in Burlington, New Jersey, where Hal grew up. His younger brother did not go as he was only one year old. Interestingly, prior to that, when Hal was younger, the children's babysitter was a teenaged Ethel Merman.

Finishing high school, Hal attended the University of North Carolina at Chapel Hill on a football scholarship.

Hal went to work as a sales rep for a textile company but soon tired of this and headed west for greener pastures in California where he worked at odd jobs until he stumbled into the acting profession during a party at a friend's house circa 1939.

MGM tested him and put him through their school, although nothing transpired. Hal studied at Bliss-Hayden Theatre and did little theatre work. He acquired an agent and switched his name to Gregg Barton to avoid confusion with Lex Barker or Jess Barker.

He was just getting started with a bit in "A Yank At Eton" ('42 MGM) and a decent role in John Wayne's "Flying Tigers" ('42 Republic) when he enlisted in the Marine Corps the day after the attack on Pearl Harbor.

During WWII Gregg served as a tank commander with the 5th Tank Battalion, 5th Marine Division in the Pacific, taking part in the invasion of Iwo Jima. For his heroism in that battle he received the Silver Star. Reminded of this in later years, Gregg remarked, "They're all heroes, all of them." During his service period, '41-'46, he achieved the rank of Major.

Back in Hollywood, Gregg was hired to play the lead heavy in Eddie Dean's "West To Glory" ('47) which started him on his villainous career.

Besides roles in A-films such as "Joan Of Arc" ('48), "Tap Roots" ('48), "Jet Pilot" ('50) and others, Gregg menaced B-cowboys Charles Starrett, Rex Allen, Whip Wilson, Johnny Mack Brown, Bill Elliott, Wayne Morris and, of course, Gene Autry (11 features, 24 TVers), in the waning days of the B-western.

Gregg found work too in A-westerns—"The Outriders" ('50 MGM), "The Gunfighter" ('50 20th Century Fox), "Distant Drums" ('51 Warner Bros.), "Bend of the River" ('52 Universal), "Drums Across the River" ('54 Universal), "Man From Laramie" ('55 Columbia), "Raw Edge" ('56 Universal), "Joe Dakota" ('57 Universal), "Gunfight At Dodge City" ('59 United Artists), among others. Gregg's also in four of the latter-day serials, "Gunfighters of the Northwest" ('54 Columbia), "Riding With Buffalo Bill" ('54 Columbia), "Man With the Steel Whip" ('54 Republic) and "Blazing the Overland Trail" ('56 Columbia).

But it was on the '50s-'60s TV screen where Gregg amassed well over 150 credits. Besides those 24 Autrys, Gregg rode the outlaw trail on "Lone Ranger", "Wild Bill Hickok", "Roy Rogers", "Range Rider", "Annie Oakley", "Tales of the Texas Rangers", "My Friend Flicka", "Wyatt Earp", "Sgt. Preston", "Zane Grey Theatre", "26 Men", "Kit Carson", "Buffalo Bill Jr.", "Colt .45", "Cisco Kid", "Casey Jones", "Champion", "Death Valley Days",

"Deputy", "Hopalong Cassidy", "Laramie", "Maverick" and others.

Working on so many Autry productions, Gregg became close friends with Armand "Mandy" Schaefer of whom he said, "Mandy steered me very nicely, advised me what not to do and I'll be forever indebted to him for his clear-sightedness."

For over ten years, in between his TV and movie work, Gregg managed a 1,600 acre cattle ranch at Bonsail, California. Retiring from films (his last was an episode of "Death Valley Days" in '66), Gregg worked for Safeco Title Insurance for 22 years where he became top sales rep in Southern California.

Gregg was married in the late '40s, for about 14 years, to a lady named Helen Norris. After a long stretch as a bachelor, Gregg and Bonita Cooper were wed in 1983 until the time of his death at 88 on November 28, 2000, in the Fallbrook, California, convalescent center. His health had been failing since he had knee surgery earlier in the month. He is buried at Fort Rosecrans in San Diego, California.

Richard ("Sgt. Preston") Simmons recalled, "Gregg was a good man. Ironically, he played just the opposite characters in pictures. Perhaps his reason being most heavy parts had more to do, and for the most were better parts. He was truly a good actor. He was so well-liked by all that knew him. I clearly recall we were at a party one night. In the course of the evening a rather elderly lady came to me and said in no uncertain terms, 'Mr. Simmons, I've seen you in several shows along with my dear friend Gregg Barton. And I'm sick and tired of seeing you try to beat the tar out of him. He's a very nice young man and deserves much better. Please pick on someone else.' That says it all. The people who knew Gregg knew him for what he really was. A very nice, honest, good person. To this lady he was everything a gentleman should be. Gregg was such a fine actor he could portray quite the opposite very convincingly."

Dick Jones: "What a great guy he was, how much fun he was to work with. We had a lot of fun doing 'Range Rider' and 'Buffalo Bill Jr.' He was a good fight routine man. We had a lot of fun tearing the sets apart. He did *all* of his own fights. He was dependable. He didn't phony it up by looking back to where he was gonna go and staggering to it…getting down on one knee and then the next knee when he took a fall. He did it like a true athlete. He worked it out. When he was gonna go back over a table, he knew where the table was and he went over it just like you would actually do it. One time we were doing a fight routine in Judge Ben 'Fair and Square' Wiley's general store. They had all these beautiful props…barber chair, counter, back shelves full of goodies. So we routined a

Kenne Duncan and Gregg Barton are up to no-good in Gene Autry's "The Blazing Sun" ('50 Columbia.)

fight to go completely around the room, into the barber chair, over the chair, into the counter, over the counter, up on the shelves and pull the whole thing down. I reached over to grab him by the shirt, to do a body throw, but when I let go on the body throw I heard this blood curdling scream. I had reached through his shirt and grabbed hold of his chest hairs. He said, 'You scalped me!' All this talk was going, but with my back to the camera they didn't pick it up and kept on going. Besides all that, he was a good actor. His physique allowed him to play a stripped to the waist blacksmith or he could let his beard grow, put a dirty old slouch hat on and be the toughest villain there ever was. And he was handy on a horse. He looked good on a horse. I really liked him."

Walter Reed: "He was a hard working man who worked an awful lot. He was a very dear friend—and a friend to a lot of people. He was a wonderful husband to Bonita, he was very, very good to her. The first picture I ever did with him was 'Tripoli'. I loved him."

Rand Brooks: "Most all of our western friends were on the very, very gentlemanly, fun side, but Gregg was a notch above."

Stuntman Jack Williams: "Gregg and I were up in Canada on 'The Far Country' with Anthony Mann directing. Jimmy Stewart, Walter Brennan—a bunch up there. At the end of the picture they were trying to save a little money. They had used three railroad cars taking stuff to location, but now they tried to condense it into one. I had bought some maple syrup. There's nothing better than Canadian maple syrup. Now, Gregg was perhaps the nattiest dresser that ever lived in the picture business. He was immaculate. Gregg was wearing doeskin pants that cost $100 a pair when actors were making $35 a day. (Laughs) Cut to the studio—they're unloading all this stuff. Incidentally, when it was loaded in Canada, they were just throwing it in. It looked like everybody was on some of that Canadian whiskey…just tossing it in this boxcar. Got back—and Gregg's clothes looked like they'd been dipped in my syrup! (Laughs) Gregg was upset and so was I, 'cause it was my syrup! One of the greatest guys that was ever in the business."

Donna Martell: "He was one of the nicest gentlemen—and a gentle man—that I met in the business. Just so quiet, refined. A serious actor. He took his work seriously. He wasn't the kind who horsed around or made jokes, he was just a really nice guy. A sweet person."

John Hart: "The guy was a Marine officer. That's pretty hard to do. He was certainly a competent actor. I admired him as an actor and war veteran."

Myron Healey: "We worked together a lot. I was doing the lead heavy and he was doing the dog-heavy. He was a very nice guy that I admired greatly. Back in the days of Flying A and Monogram, he mentioned he and his wife were moving onto a ranch down in Fallbrook. They were gonna raise strawberries. I said, 'That happens to be my favorite food. We're working together a lot, next time you're scheduled to work with old Dad, bring me a basket of berries.' For years after that, every few months we'd get a job together and I'd look at him and say, 'Well…?' and he'd say, 'Oh God, No strawberries.' This went on for years and years and years. It got to a point where I'd really be disappointed if he ever brought me any strawberries. (Laughs) At the Golden Boot awards, I didn't have to ask him. When we went backstage, just before we came on, he looked at me and smiled, 'No berries.' (Laughs)"

Suggested Sampling of Barton's Western Heavies:

- West To Glory ('47 PRC) Eddie Dean
- Texas Dynamo ('50 Columbia) Charles Starrett
- Blazing Sun ('50 Columbia) Gene Autry
- Gene Autry: Doodle Bug ('50) Gene Autry
- Gene Autry and the Mounties ('51 Columbia) Gene Autry
- Valley of Fire ('51 Columbia) Gene Autry
- Silver City Bonanza ('51 Republic) Rex Allen
- Wild Bill Hickok: Ex Convict Story ('51)
- Gene Autry: Killer's Trail ('51) Gene Autry
- Dead Man's Trail ('52 Monogram) Johnny Mack Brown
- The Maverick ('52 Monogram) Bill Elliott
- Apache Country ('52 Columbia) Gene Autry
- Gene Autry: Ruthless Renegades ('52) Gene Autry
- Roy Rogers: Minister's Son ('52) Roy Rogers
- Range Rider: Silver Blade ('52) Jock Mahoney
- Range Rider: Indian War Party ('53) Jock Mahoney
- Range Rider: Marshal From Madero ('53) Jock Mahoney
- Kit Carson: Badman's Escape ('53) Bill Williams
- Winning of the West ('53 Columbia) Gene Autry
- Hopalong Cassidy: Arizona Troubleshooters ('53) William Boyd
- Cisco Kid: Fool's Gold ('54) Duncan Renaldo
- Cisco Kid: Trouble in Tonopah ('54) Duncan Renaldo
- Annie Oakley: A Gal For Grandma ('54) Gail Davis
- Gene Autry: Outlaw Warning ('54) Gene Autry
- Kit Carson: Eyes of the Outlaw ('54) Bill Williams
- Riding With Buffalo Bill ('54 Columbia serial) Marshall Reed
- Wild Bill Hickok: Sagebrush Manhunt ('55) Guy Madison
- Adventures of Champion: Deer Hunters ('55) Jim Bannon
- Annie Oakley: Flint and Steel ('56) Gail Davis
- Tales of the Texas Rangers: Horsemen of the Sierras ('56) Willard Parker
- Lone Ranger: Cross of Santo Domingo ('56) Clayton Moore
- Buffalo Bill Jr.: Jayhawkers ('56) Dick Jones
- Blazing the Overland Trail ('56 Columbia serial) Lee Roberts
- Lone Ranger: Mission for Tonto ('57) Clayton Moore
- 26 Men: Incident at Yuma ('57) Tris Coffin

HAL BAYLOR

Hal Baylor got into movies via the boxing ring. He was more than adept at portraying bullies, ruffians and malcontents and wound up making over 50 movies and some 150 TV episodes between 1948 and 1977.

Born Hal Brittan December 10, 1918, in San Antonio, Texas, his parents divorced when he was young so he never knew his father. He moved with his mother to Vallejo, California, where she established a beauty salon. His mother remarried to a Walter Fieberling and Hal took on his surname. His great-great grandfather was the original founder of Baylor University, which is from where Hal later drew his screen name.

Hal played football and boxed during his college years at Chico State University. Taking physical education courses, he transferred to Washington State on a football scholarship and studied business administration.

While at Chico State in '38 he and several other big football players were chosen to play Merry Men in "The Adventures of Robin Hood", but he never gave acting a second thought at that time.

Finishing college, he entered the amateur ranks of boxing, winning the Pacific Coast Championship in '39. Turning pro, Hal won 52 out of 57 fights.

In 1942 Hal entered the Marine Corps during WWII making landings on Saipan and Tinian. He was discharged in '46.

Trying to quit boxing at his parent's request, Hal enrolled in medical school in Oakland, California, after the war but found it not to his liking.

Moving back to Los Angeles to re-enter the ring, he ran into old friend Joe Kirkwood who was now starring in Monogram's Joe Palooka series. Joe asked Hal to do a fight scene with him in "Winner Take All" ('48) which then led to another fight picture, perhaps the best ever made, "The Set-Up" ('49 RKO) with Robert Ryan. A good role in John Wayne's "Sands of Iwo Jima" the same year convinced Hal to be an actor.

Being able to ride well, he was soon cast in every TV western aired for the next 20 years.

By 1983, disgruntled with a changing Hollywood, Hal retired to play golf, hunt and fish.

Hal died of heart failure at 79 January 5, 1998, in Van Nuys, California.

Fellow screen badman and good friend Duane Grey remembered, "They used Hal as a big lug to start a problem or have a fight. You always felt safe with Hal in a fight scene because of his prizefight background." Kelo Henderson, star of "26 Men" recalls, "I first met Hal in Arizona and worked with him in four episodes of '26 Men'. He knew his profession well, had good timing in his fight scenes, rode horseback well, and did a certain amount of his own stunts. Hal got along great with the cast and crew, and was well liked on the series for the good actor and fine gentleman he was."

Suggested Sampling of Baylor's Western Heavies:

- Lone Ranger: Mission Bells ('50) Clayton Moore
- Lone Ranger: Six Gun Sanctuary ('54) Clayton Moore
- River of No Return ('54 20th Century Fox) Robert Mitchum
- Outlaw Treasure ('55 American) Johnny Carpenter
- Gunsmoke: Hack Prine ('56) James Arness
- Cheyenne: Lone Gun ('56) Clint Walker
- Jefferson Drum: $50 For a Dead Man ('58) Jeff Richards
- Californians: Long Night ('58) Richard Coogan
- 26 Men: Hellion ('59) Kelo Henderson/Tris Coffin
- Lawman: The Gunman ('59) John Russell
- 26 Men: Death In the Dragoons ('59) Kelo Henderson/Tris Coffin
- Bronco: Borrowed Glory ('59) Ty Hardin
- Maverick: Sheriff of Duck 'n' Shoot ('59) James Garner
- Texan: Blue Norther ('59) Rory Calhoun
- Cheyenne: Outcast of Cripple Creek ('60) Clint Walker
- Bat Masterson: Debt of Honor ('60) Gene Barry
- Deputy: The Challenger ('61) Henry Fonda/Allen Case
- Rifleman: Short Rope For a Tall Man ('61) Chuck Connors
- Laramie: The Runaway ('62) John Smith/Robert Fuller
- Tales of Wells Fargo: Incident at Crossbow ('62) Dale Robertson
- Lawman: Man Behind the News ('62) John Russell
- Wagon Train: Alias Bill Hawks ('63) Terry Wilson
- Gunsmoke: Now That April's Here ('64) James Arness
- Bonanza: A Man to Admire ('64) Dan Blocker
- A Man Called Shenandoah: The Siege ('65) Robert Horton
- Rawhide: Hostage For Hanging ('65) Clint Eastwood
- Bonanza: Old Charlie ('66) Dan Blocker
- Laredo: Above the Law ('66) Neville Brand

ALFONSO BEDOYA

Mexican character actor Alfonso Bedoya cemented his claim as one of the westerns' most evil badmen with one memorable performance as the smiling cutthroat of "The Treasure of the Sierra Madre" who delivered the famous line about not needing any "stinking badges".

One of 20 children, he was born in the tiny village of Vicam, Sonora, Mexico, April 16, 1904. He reportedly had a nomadic upbringing, moving from place to place as a child until his parents shipped him off at 14 to a private school in Houston, Texas. Unconfirmed, but stated by Bedoya later in life, his father was B. Traven, a noted German born author. The private school was apparently not to his liking as he dropped out and roamed about working at an assortment of odd jobs until his family brought him back to Mexico City where he found work in the struggling Mexican film industry.

From 1937 til 1947 Bedoya appeared in over 100 Mexican films, including several westerns, until he gained a small role of a guard at the pass in the Duncan Renaldo produced "Bells of San Fernando" ('47 Screen Guild) with Donald Woods.

His career took a major leap in 1948 when director John Huston offered him the role of Mexican bandido Gold Tooth in "The Treasure of the Sierra Madre". In 1948 the L.A. DAILY NEWS described him as "friendly and likeable as they come. His eyes are smiling, his accent is soft and musical, and he's always happy."

For "Man in the Saddle", besides his known role, Bedoya is reputed to have doubled, in long shots, Ellen Drew when Drew was confined to bed with scurvy, an unfortunate holdover from her earlier "Fortunes of Captain Blood".

A report from noted director Peter Bogdanovitch says Bedoya produced Universal's "Border River" ('54) with Joel McCrea using the name "Albert J. Cohen," thereby confirming Bedoya's sense of humor.

Capitalizing on his success in "Treasure...", Bedoya appeared in nearly 20 more films for the next nine years until a drinking problem destroyed his health and he died at only 53 in Mexico City on December 15, 1957. His last role was opposite Gregory Peck in the large scale western, "The Big Country", released after his death in 1958.

Suggested Sampling of Bedoya's Western Heavies:

- The Treasure of the Sierra Madre ('48 Warner Bros.) Humphrey Bogart
- Streets of Laredo ('49 Paramount) William Holden
- Man In the Saddle ('51 Columbia) Randolph Scott
- California Conquest ('52 Columbia) Cornell Wilde
- Stranger Wore a Gun ('53 Columbia) Randolph Scott
- Ten Wanted Men ('55) Columbia) Randolph Scott

NOAH BEERY SR.

One of the great villains of the silent and sound screen, Noah Beery Sr., was in reality a kind, gentle, charitable man, but he could personify evil with his broadfaced grin and chortling laugh emanating from his rotund 6' 1" 230 pound frame—usually a smoking stogie poking out one side of his snarl. "The real make-up for a character must come from within," he once explained. "It is the result of studying the man until you can feel as he must feel—then your body, your whole features will become responsive to your own mental picture."

Born Noah Nicholas Beery February 17, 1882, in Smithville, Missouri, his father, Noah W. Beery, a native of Smithville (near Kansas City), was, reportedly, of Swiss descent and worked as a police officer. His mother, Mary Margaret Fitzgerald, was from Ridgley, Missouri. Noah was the elder brother of the more famous of the acting Beery brothers, Wallace Beery. Another brother, William Beery, was also an actor of much less stature who later entered the oil business quite successfully. Noah grew up on a farm in western Missouri. Reportedly, he went to grade school in Kansas City with outlaw Jesse James' son.

Still a boy, he sold lemon drops to actors at the Gillis theatre in Kansas City. Amused by his already booming, deep voice, various actors urged him to cultivate it and go on the stage, which he did at the youthful age of 16.

Apparently, Beery was possessed of a rich singing voice, and after some lessons, performed as a singer for a year in the Kansas City area and for a week at the fashionable Hammerstein's Resort in New York state as well as at Kansas City's Electric Park.

Finding he preferred melodrama, he worked under the noted William Brady, scoring a moderate success in a three year tour of a "Trail of the Lonesome Pine" production with brother Wallace.

By age 23, he was touring for a year (1905-1906) with Brady's "As Ye Sow", eventually playing for a month on Broadway.

In 1910 Beery married Marguerite Walker Lindsey, a stage actress. They had a son who died. The second child, Noah Lindsey Beery (later called simply Noah Beery Jr.) was born August 10, 1913, in New York. Seriously ill for months, doctors advised a milder climate so the Beerys moved to Florida where Noah Sr. made some early films and worked at any job he could find until the family finally reached California in 1917 where he found film work immediately, eventually appearing in over 110 silents. Of his silents, 22 were westerns, including many Zane Grey epics with either Jack Holt or Richard Dix. But he's also in the classic "Mark of Zorro" ('20) with Douglas Fairbanks Sr. and the 1923 version of "The Spoilers".

Probably his finest roles were as the sadistic sergeant major of "Beau Geste" ('26) and as the guard who beat and tortured little children of a reformatory in "The Godless Girl" ('29–last two scenes have dialog added).

Achieving success, the Beerys bought a ranch in the San Fernando Valley on which they grew tobacco. There were also grapevines, avocado, orange and lemon trees. His chief avocation was his famous Paradise Trout Club, located 100 miles from L.A., a popular year-round rendezvous for sports.

As talkies came in, Beery was in his late 40s, and even with his powerful voice and fabulous persona, his star began to slip—although he worked in nearly 90 films on through 1945.

Regarding Beery's contemptible skullduggery as Ace Hanlon in the Republic serial, "Adventures of Red Ryder", star Don Barry asked, "How can you describe a man who loved his profession and everyone in it? I shall always remember how he helped a brash, smart ass, young punk. I loved him."

His wife died in 1935 but 1940 saw his son Noah Jr. join with another respected Hollywood family when he married Maxine Jones, daughter of Buck Jones.

Leonard Maltin spoke with Noah Jr. in 1983 for an interview that eventually saw print in his MOVIE CRAZY publication in 2004. Jr. confirmed both his father and uncle, Wallace, began on the stage in New York. "They had done musicals. Then my dad and mother came out ahead of Wally, three years, something like that. Then when he sent word to Wal how good the pickings were out here in Hollywood, why he came, too. Pretty soon the whole outfit was here. (Dad) was not an intimidating man, except on screen where he was a classical deep, dark villain. But he was quite the opposite actually. (Working with him in pictures) was strange at first, but he could generally iron me out pretty good the night before (so) I wouldn't make too many blunders." As for any resentment being typecast as a heavy, Noah Jr. stated his father "loved it. He was always thinking of new ways to be mean. He liked it."

Beery had completed a role in his last film, a western, "Sing Me a Song of Texas" ('45 Columbia) with Tom Tyler, and in 1946 was residing in a New York City hotel while playing the role of Tammany Hall's Boss Tweed in a stage production of "Up In Central Park". He was taking a two-week vacation from the play to visit California where he, his brother Wallace, and Wallace's daughter, Carol Ann, were to appear together on a Lux Radio Theatre presentation. On April 1, 1946, while running their lines at Wallace's home on Colgate Avenue in L.A. during the afternoon of their scheduled evening performance, Noah suffered a fatal heart attack and died in his brother's arms. True to the show-biz adage, the show went on that evening—minus Noah. He was 64. He is buried at Forest Lawn, Hollywood Hills.

Noah's lecherous, sadistic, coarse and uncouth roles set a standard for heavies to come.

Suggested Sampling of Beery's Western Heavies:

- Mark of Zorro ('20 United Artists) Douglas Fairbanks Sr.
- Good Men and True ('22 FBO) Harry Carey
- The Spoilers ('23 Goldwyn) Milton Sills
- To the Last Man ('23 Paramount) Richard Dix
- Wild Horse Mesa ('25 Paramount) Jack Holt
- Thundering Herd ('25 Paramount) Jack Holt
- Vanishing American ('25 Paramount) Richard Dix
- Riders of the Purple Sage ('31 Fox) George O'Brien
- Big Stampede ('32 Warner Bros.) John Wayne
- Devil Horse ('32 Mascot serial) Harry Carey
- Thundering Herd ('33 Paramount) Randolph Scott
- Fighting With Kit Carson ('33 Mascot serial) Johnny Mack Brown
- Man of the Forest ('33 Paramount) Randolph Scott
- Zorro Rides Again ('37 Republic serial) John Carroll
- Panamint's Bad Man ('38 20th Century Fox) Smith Ballew
- Mexicali Rose ('39 Republic) Gene Autry
- Adventures of Red Ryder ('40 Republic serial) Don Barry
- Pioneers of the West ('40 Republic) 3 Mesquiteers
- Tulsa Kid ('40 Republic) Don Barry
- Devil's Trail ('42 Columbia) Bill Elliott/Tex Ritter
- Overland Mail ('42 Universal serial) Lon Chaney Jr.

RAY BENNETT

Equally at home as the dress heavy (crooked mayor or saloon owner) or the henchman (dog-heavy) Ray Bennett started right off with westerns in four of Tom Keene's historical Crescent films in 1937 ("Battle of Greed", "Drums of Destiny", "Old Louisiana", "Raw Timber").

Bennett's most productive period was '40-'46 with one of his most noticeable roles as a throat-slashing, crazed "ghost" with a straight razor stalking the secret passageways of Johnny Mack Brown's "Haunted Mine" ('46).

Raphael Fabian Bennett was born March 21, 1895, in Portland, Oregon. His father, George S. Bennett, was from Kentucky and his mother, Ella Costello, was a native of Tennessee.

In the beginning, he alternated between Rafael Bennett and Raphael Bennett, eventually settling on just plain Ray Bennett. His background was performing in Shakespearean plays.

Bennett worked almost exclusively in westerns and serials until about 1947-'48 when he began accepting character roles in bigger productions such as "Canon City" ('48), "Heaven Only Knows" ('47), "Ma and Pa Kettle" ('49), Samson and Delilah" ('49), "Winchester 73" ('50), "French Line" ('54), etc.

His 19 year film career came to an end with "Greater Love", an episode of "Gunsmoke" that aired December 1, 1956.

Bennett died December 18, 1957, at 62, of a heart attack at his home on South Kenmore Avenue in Los Angeles. Emphysema was a contributing factor. His remains were cremated.

As he was never married, he was survived only by a sister, Mary Bennett.

Suggested Sampling of Bennett's Western Heavies:

- Old Louisiana ('37 Crescent) Tom Keene
- Prairie Moon ('38 Republic) Gene Autry
- Old Barn Dance ('38 Republic) Gene Autry
- Man From Tumbleweeds ('40 Columbia) Bill Elliott
- Hidden Gold ('40 Paramount) William Boyd
- Knights of the Range ('40 Paramount) Russell Hayden
- Thundering Frontier ('40 Columbia) Charles Starrett
- Doomed Caravan ('41 Paramount) William Boyd
- Romance of the Rio Grande ('41 20th Century Fox) Cesar Romero
- Robbers of the Range ('41 RKO) Tim Holt
- Return of Daniel Boone ('41 Columbia) Bill Elliott
- Gauchos of El Dorado ('41 Republic) 3 Mesquiteers
- Lawless Plainsmen ('42 Columbia) Charles Starrett/Russell Hayden
- Death Rides the Plains ('43 PRC) Bob Livingston
- The Renegades ('43 PRC) Buster Crabbe
- Marshal of Gunsmoke ('44 Universal) Tex Ritter
- Raiders of the Border ('44 Monogram) Johnny Mack Brown
- Dead Or Alive ('44 PRC) Tex Ritter/Dave O'Brien

- Gun Smoke ('45 Monogram) Johnny Mack Brown
- Return of the Durango Kid ('45 Columbia) Charles Starrett
- Border Badmen ('45 PRC) Buster Crabbe
- Haunted Mine ('46 Monogram) Johnny Mack Brown
- Gun Town ('46 Universal) Kirby Grant
- Prairie Raiders ('47 Columbia) Charles Starrett
- Frontier Revenge ('49 Western Adventure) Lash LaRue
- Rimfire ('49 Lippert) James Millican
- Lone Ranger: The Tenderfeet ('49) Clayton Moore
- Dalton Gang ('49 Lippert) Don Barry
- Gene Autry: Ghost Town Raiders ('51) Gene Autry
- Waco ('52 Monogram) Bill Elliott
- Black Lash ('52 Western Adventure) Lash LaRue
- Man From the Black Hills ('52 Monogram) Johnny Mack Brown
- Cisco Kid: Spanish Dagger ('52) Duncan Renaldo
- Roy Rogers: Death Medicine ('52) Roy Rogers
- Champion: Bad Men of the Valley ('56) Jim Bannon

LYLE BETTGER

Handsome, blond-haired, steely-eyed western heavy Lyle Bettger was never the stubbly-bearded henchman sort, but always the immaculate, nattily dressed, respectable-in-appearance type who would double-cross you behind your back. Never more evident than in "Destry" opposite Audie Murphy.

Born February 13, 1915, in Philadelphia, Pennsylvania, Lyle was the son of St. Louis Cardinals third baseman Franklin Bettger who was born February 15, 1888, in Philadelphia and played ball under the name Franklin Lyle Betcher for 27 games in 1910.

In 1935, Lyle left Philly to attend the American Academy of Dramatic Arts in New York City from which he graduated in '37. After honing his craft in summer stock and on Broadway for over a decade, he made his film debut in 1950 in "No Man of Her Own" opposite Barbara Stanwyck.

Being under contract to Paramount for a while, producer A. C. Lyles remembered Bettger as "…one of the nicest guys we had at Paramount. So professional. He was, oddly enough, cast as a heavy while in real life he was just a dear, dear man. Extremely friendly with everyone. Very, very popular on the lot with cast members. People all over the world, the minute they saw him on screen, knew he was gonna be a mean man. His role in De Mille's 'The Greatest Show on Earth' was tailor-made for him." (Bettger, the elephant trainer, is spurned by showgirl Gloria Grahame whom he loves desperately but who mistreats him at every turn. Bettger eventually wrecks the circus train in a jealous rage.)

Other major roles in "Carnival Story" ('54) and "All I Desire" ('53) followed, but Bettger found his true calling as a slick villain in A-westerns and western TVers of the '50s and '60s.

He did pause long enough in '57-'59 to star first in "Court of Last Resort" (NBC) and then co-star with Harold J. Stone, another great screen heavy, in the short-lived syndicated "Grand Jury".

A. C. Lyles continued, "He had a place in Hawaii where he lived a lot of the time and when he retired, lived there all of the time." This did allow him to work on the "Hawaii Five-O" TV series and accept roles in films such as "The Hawaiians" ('70) and the TV movie "M Station: Hawaii" ('80), his last.

Bettger was married for 56 years to former actress Mary Rolfe who preceded him in death in '96. They had two sons, Frank and Lyle R. Bettger.

Bettger had lived on Maui, Hawaii, since '79, but died at 88 at his son Lyle's home in Atascadero, California, September 24, 2003.

Suggested Sampling of Bettger's Western Heavies:

- Denver and Rio Grande ('52 Paramount) Edmond O'Brien
- The Vanquished ('53 Paramount) John Payne
- The Great Sioux Uprising ('53 Universal) Jeff Chandler
- Drums Across the River ('54 Universal) Audie Murphy
- Destry ('54 Universal) Audie Murphy
- Lone Ranger ('56 Warner Bros.) Clayton Moore
- Showdown at Abilene ('56 Universal) Jock Mahoney
- Tales of Wells Fargo: John Wesley Hardin ('57) Dale Robertson
- Gunfight at the OK Corral ('57 Paramount) Burt Lancaster
- Zane Grey Theatre: Threat of Violence ('58) Chris Alcaide
- Texas John Slaughter: Killers From Kansas ('58) Tom Tryon
- Rifleman: The Wrong Man ('58) Chuck Connors
- Law of the Plainsman: Full Circle ('59) Michael Ansara
- Deputy: Deadly Breed ('60) Henry Fonda/Allen Case
- Laramie: Rimrock ('59) Robert Fuller
- Guns of the Timberland ('60 Warner Bros.) Alan Ladd
- Tall Man: Hard Justice ('60) Clu Gulager
- Tales of Wells Fargo: Mr. Mute ('61) Dale Robertson
- Laramie: Lawless Seven ('61) Robert Fuller
- Rifleman: Skull ('62) Chuck Connors
- Bonanza: The Guilty ('62) Lorne Greene
- Laramie: Beyond Justice ('62) John Smith
- Rawhide: Incident of the Dowry Dundee ('64) Clint Eastwood
- Gunsmoke: The Kite ('64) James Arness
- Town Tamer ('65 Paramount) Dana Andrews
- Johnny Reno ('66 Paramount) Dana Andrews

ROBERT (BOB) BICE

Robert Lee Bice was born in Dallas, Texas, March 4, 1913. His father, Oscar E. Bice, and his mother, Laura Isabell Barnes, were both natives of Texas.

After a brief fling at journalism, Bice made his way to Hollywood where his good looks got him into films as a sleazy tenderfoot in "Fighting Valley" ('43 PRC) with Dave O'Brien/James Newill. His acting is quite amateurish in this early picture, but a parade of smaller roles in major pictures ("Thirty Seconds Over Tokyo" '44, "Dragon Seed" '44, "Canon City" '48) and others greatly improved his screen skills.

An absence of film work in '45 and much of '46 indicates military service of some kind.

Bice turned to westerns with a vengeance in 1949 as those half-hour juvenile TVers came into prominence.

Perhaps Bice's most notable role was as Frank James (brother to Jesse—played by Keith Richards) in Republic's 1949 serial, "James Brothers of Missouri".

Now and then Bice also worked as a dialogue coach in films.

Bice's last role was on a "Death Valley Days" in October of '67. On January 8, 1968, at the age of 54, Bice committed suicide by overdosing on barbiturates in his apartment at 6753 Selma Avenue in Los Angeles. The informing party of his death was his wife, Lorraine L. Bice, who at the time of his death was living in Long Beach, leading to speculation they were separated and domestic discord may have led to Bice's drastic act.

He was laid to rest at Eternal Valley Memorial Park in Newhall, California.

In his 24 year screen career as a character actor Robert Bice played Germans, Indians, detectives, thugs, military men, reporters, natives, businessmen, and a fair share of badmen, especially in the half-hour westerns of "The Lone Ranger", "Cisco Kid", "Wild Bill Hickok", "Kit Carson", "Gene Autry", "Cowboy G-Men", "Annie Oakley", "Roy Rogers", "Tales of the Texas Rangers", "Rin Tin Tin", "Hopalong Cassidy" and others.

Suggested Sampling of Bice's Western Heavies:

- Fighting Valley ('43 PRC) Dave O'Brien/James Newill
- Susanna Pass ('49 Republic) Roy Rogers
- Bandit King of Texas ('49 Republic) Allan "Rocky" Lane
- Lone Ranger: Backtrail ('49) Clayton Moore
- Lone Ranger: Friend in Need ('51) Clayton Moore
- Cisco Kid: Ghost Story ('51) Duncan Renaldo
- Wild Bill Hickok: Hepsibah ('51) Guy Madison
- Night Stage to Galveston ('52 Columbia) Gene Autry

- Junction City ('52 Columbia) Charles Starrett
- Cripple Creek ('52 Columbia) George Montgomery
- Kit Carson: Gunsmoke Valley ('53) Bill Williams
- Cisco Kid: Runaway Kid ('53) Duncan Renaldo
- On Top of Old Smoky ('53 Columbia) Gene Autry
- Bandits of the West ('53 Republic) Allan "Rocky" Lane
- Hopalong Cassidy: Steel Rails West ('54) William Boyd
- Roy Rogers: Brothers O'Dell ('55) Roy Rogers
- Roy Rogers: Three Masked Men ('55) Roy Rogers
- Rin Tin Tin: Fort Adventure ('56) Lee Aaker
- Roy Rogers: High Stakes ('57) Roy Rogers
- Sgt. Preston: Lost River Roundup ('57) Richard Simmons

WILLIAM BISHOP

Although William Bishop came to films in 1943 and made eleven movies that year, his new found career was cut short by military service in WWII from 1944-'46. His career blossomed at Columbia in '48, although they couldn't decide whether to cast the handsome Bishop as a good guy or bad guy. Therefore, he alternated back and forth for the next 10 years before an untimely death at only 41.

Chris Alcaide, who worked a lot at Columbia, remembered Bishop as having…"a big jaw (Laughs)…I don't think Columbia used him properly or knew what to do with him. He was a cordial, gregarious guy. I liked him."

When playing a heavy, he was a villain of infinite control, smooth and charming, reasonable and plausible with a slightly crooked "too bright" smile.

William Paxton Bishop was born July 16, 1918, in Oak Park, Illinois. A nephew of Helen Hayes and Charles MacArthur, he launched his career after first receiving a law degree from the University of West Virginia. However, his first job after college was as assistant stage manager for Billy Rose's "Jumbo".

A successful stage career followed with roles on Broadway in "Victoria Regina", "Tobacco Road" and others. He was a leading man for a time at Steve Cochran's theatre in Olney, Maryland.

Bishop came to Hollywood under contract to MGM in 1941 but received no screen credits til '43, the year he became a workhorse, appearing in eleven movies starting with "Young Ideas" with Susan Peters.

His first western in 1948 was a starring role in Columbia's "Adventures in Silverado". He also starred that year at Columbia in "Black Eagle" and "Thunderhoof" as well as being featured in Randolph Scott's "Coroner Creek" ('48 Columbia) and "The Walking Hills" ('49 Columbia).

From there Bishop switched to badmen with a smile that belied his treachery.

From September '54 to June '56 he and Michael O'Shea teamed up to star on NBC TV's "It's a Great Life", a sit-com about two ex-GI's rooming together in California.

Then, it was back to the heroic roles at Columbia for "White Squaw" ('56) and "Phantom Stagecoach" ('57).

Unfortunately, Bishop died of cancer at 41 on October 3, 1959, in Malibu, California, before he had an opportunity to reach his full screen potential. He is, sadly, today, largely forgotten.

Suggested Sampling of Bishop's Western Heavies:

- Untamed Breed ('48 Columbia) Sonny Tufts
- Texas Rangers ('51 Columbia) George Montgomery
- Cripple Creek ('52 Columbia) George Montgomery
- Redhead From Wyoming ('53 Universal) Maureen O'Hara
- Gun Belt ('53 United Artists) George Montgomery
- Overland Pacific ('54 United Artists) Jock Mahoney
- Wyoming Renegades ('54 Columbia) Phil Carey
- Top Gun ('55 United Artists) Sterling Hayden
- Rifleman: Outlaw's Inheritance ('59) Chuck Connors

MONTE BLUE

Stalwart, durable Monte Blue, a romantic leading man in silent films, had a strong, cultivated voice that transferred well into talkies where he enjoyed a quality reputation as a noted character player for 30 years. All in all, a glorious 45 year screen career that encompassed many scoundrelous characterizations, especially in Zane Grey and Gene Autry westerns.

He was born Gerard Montgomery Blue on January 11, 1887, in Indianapolis, Indiana, as one of four sons born to William Jackson Blue (of French and Cherokee descent) and his wife Orphalena Louisa Springer who was Irish. Blue was one-sixteenth Cherokee. The Indian translation for Monte Blue is Blue Mountain.

Rupert Blue, former surgeon general of the Army, and Rear Admiral Victor Blue were kinsman of his father who served four years with Company C of the 33rd Indiana Volunteers and Company H of the 57th Indiana Volunteers during the Civil War. Blue's father later became a railroad engineer and was killed in a train accident in 1895 when Monte was only 7.

Blue's two older brothers were able to find work, but their poverty-stricken mother sent Monte and a younger brother to the Soldiers and Sailors Orphans Home in Knightstown, Indiana. It was here his birthdate was listed as January 11, 1887, as well as in the 1900 census in contradiction to an 1889 date Blue himself stated was accurate in a 1930 press interview.

Younger brother Maurice remained in the home for nine years till he was 14, then returned to Indiana to help support his mother. Monte stayed at the home for eleven years.

At age 12, Monte became interested in journalism, becoming a printer's devil on the weekly orphanage newspaper. At 14 he became the junior editor and at 16 he left the home and returned to Indiana to help his mother who was now a nurse.

At 17, against his mother's wishes, he became a fireman on the same railroad that had killed his father. Shortly thereafter, he too was involved in a train wreck from which he was rescued with both arms and legs and several ribs broken. He spent the next 18 months recovering in St. Vincent's Hospital in Indianapolis.

During his 18th year he went to Benton Harbor, Michigan, where he worked for a steel company. Drifting, he quit and moved to Pennsylvania where he learned coal mining. He was working in a coal mine near Wilkes Barre when he and six others were trapped in a cave-in for 36 hours.

Drifting west, he found a ranch job on the Bar S near Opal, Wyoming, where he learned to ride. After a year or so, he took a job with the Flying V Ranch in Montana. With two other cowboys, he returned east to join Ringling Brothers Circus as horsemen. In the Spring of 1910 he became a clown.

In late Fall of 1910 he headed west again, obtaining a job as a forest ranger in Montana. Still not satisfied, he headed for Washington where he became a lumberjack for a time.

1912 found him in Los Angeles working as a roustabout for a wrecking company until he was laid off.

Literally bumming a living for a while, he eventually scored a day laborer job at $1.50 a day at the D. W. Griffith studio. Soon feeling secure once again, he began to argue to other workers that the pay was too low…that they should be paid $2.50 a day. When he noticed Griffith himself observing his tirade, he returned to his job. A few days later, Griffith approached Blue to do the same sort of haranguing for a mob scene in "The Absentee". The non-actor performed the scene in the 1915 film so well, Griffith put him under contract at $10 a week, soon raised to $15, appearing in Griffith's "Birth of a Nation" ('15) and "Intolerance" ('16). With Griffith he was also a stuntman, script clerk and assistant director. As Blue could ride, he also began to double western stars for other directors.

As he gained a foothold in Hollywood, his star began to rise and he worked for many companies, especially Famous Players-Lasky. By 1923 he was under a long term contract to Warner Bros. Blue was not considered a handsome man, but his magnetic personality transferred well to the screen. The camera liked him. At last he'd found his life's work.

Blue was first married to Erma Gladys but they were divorced in 1923. He met his second wife, Tove

Janson of Seattle, while he was making "Peacock Alley" in 1922. Tove was a Harrison Fisher model who had provided the inspiration for many COSMOPOLITAN covers. The daughter of silent screen actress Bodil Rosing, her stage name was Tova Dancer but Monte called her "Jimmy".

After making several talkies for Warner Bros. in 1929 he "retired" from the screen while he, Tove and their two children (Barbara Ann and Richard) took a world cruise. However, when he returned during the Great Depression, bad investments had nearly wiped out his considerable savings.

Once again, as he had so many times before, he regrouped and became one of the screen's most dependable character players. Blue once commented, "I looked in the mirror and saw I was no Little Lord Fauntleroy. I decided to build my new career on rock instead of sand. So I started out at the bottom. I was in the awkward stage between stardom and character parts." Over the ensuing years, Blue essayed many heavies and, in later years, Indians ("Hawk of the Wilderness" serial as Yellow Weasel in '38, "Ranger of Cherokee Strip" in '49, "Iroquois Trail" in '50, "Rose of Cimarron" in '52 and on TV episodes of "Range Rider", "Rin Tin Tin", "Lone Ranger" and "Wagon Train" in the '50s) and Sheriffs ("Lone Ranger", "Sky King" and many A and B-westerns including his last feature, "Adventures of the Texas Kid: Border Ambush"). Blue continued to work until 1960, with his last role as an Indian on TV's "Rawhide: Incident at Tinker's Dam".

Actor House Peters Jr. told us Blue was "…a personable guy. He respected my Dad's work. Paul Robeson, Jim Thorpe and Blue came up to me on the set, shook hands and we sat down and talked about my Dad. All three admired the old man."

Blue's serial output was not extensive (six serials), but the roles were significant. He was the vicious bottom of the ocean ruler Unga Khan in Republic's "Undersea Kingdom" ('36), the Belgravian Baron Michael Karsten in "Secret Agent X-9" ('37 Universal), Colonel Cameron in "Great Adventures of Wild Bill Hickok" ('38 Columbia), the treacherous Yellow Weasel in "Hawk of the Wilderness" ('38 Republic), crooked Rance Davis in "Riders of Death Valley" ('41 Universal), and, finally, Sammy Baugh's murdered Texas Ranger father in "King of the Texas Rangers" ('41 Republic).

Blue's wife, Tove, died at 55 March 23, 1956. His son Richard died in 1962. There was also a daughter, Barbara. Blue remarried, Betty Jane Munson Mess, a former Indiana portrait artist, in 1959.

Just prior to his death Blue was working as an advance man for the Hamid-Morton Circus which was playing in Milwaukee, Wisconsin, where he died of a heart attack, complicated by influenza, on February 18, 1963. He is buried at Forest Lawn in Los Angeles.

Blue was a member of the Masons, the Elks, The Shrine, the Rodeo Cowboy's Association and Optimist International.

Suggested Sampling of Blue's Western Heavies:

- Hands Up ('17 Triangle) Wilfred Lucas
- M'Liss ('18 Artcraft) Thomas Meighan
- Last Round-Up ('34 Paramount) Randolph Scott
- Wagon Wheels ('34 Paramount) Randolph Scott
- Wanderer of the Wasteland ('35 Paramount) Dean Jagger
- Nevada ('35 Paramount) Buster Crabbe
- The Test ('35 Reliable) Rin Tin Tin
- Desert Gold ('36 Paramount) Tom Keene
- Ride, Ranger, Ride ('36 Republic) Gene Autry
- Rootin' Tootin' Rhythm ('37 Republic) Gene Autry
- Born to the West (aka Hell Town) ('37 Paramount) John Wayne/Johnny Mack Brown
- Mysterious Rider ('38 Paramount) Douglass Dumbrille
- Bad Man of Deadwood ('41 Republic) Roy Rogers
- Riders of Death Valley ('41 Universal serial) Dick Foran/Buck Jones
- Snake River Desperadoes ('51 Columbia) Charles Starrett
- Hangman's Knot ('52 Columbia) Randolph Scott
- Rin Tin Tin: Warrior's Promise ('57) Lee Aaker
- Rin Tin Tin: Luck of O'Hara ('59) Lee Aaker

STANLEY BLYSTONE

Large, burly, muscular Stanley Blystone with his booming, gravelly voice excelled in gruff, authoritarian or villainous roles, whether it be in B-westerns up against Hoot Gibson, Buck Jones, Tim McCoy, Don Barry, Rex Bell, Jack Randall, Ken Maynard and many others—or in comedies, be they two reelers or features, with the Three Stooges, Laurel and Hardy, Abbott and Costello, Marx Brothers, Harry Langdon, Vera Vague, El Brendel and others. In A-films, Blystone often played jailers, guards, deputies, sheriffs, detectives and police officers. As his career waned in the '50s, the parts of bank clerk/crew foreman/train conductor/seaman/passenger/posseman/card player grew smaller, but Blystone kept working for 32 years (with two years deducted for time spent overseas during WWI) until his death from a heart attack at 61 on July 16, 1956. He collapsed on the sidewalk enroute to play a small role on the "Wyatt Earp" TV series.

William Stanley Blystone was born in Rice Lake, Wisconsin, on August 1, 1894. His mother's maiden name was Oliver.

In all likelihood, it was his film director brother,

Stanley Blystone (center) and his boys, Charlie King (left) and Edward Howard (right) give comic Syd Saylor some trouble in his diner in Bob Steele's "Navajo Kid" ('45 PRC).

John G. Blystone (1892-1938) who was responsible for getting Stanley into the acting profession in the silent era. John started directing as early as 1915 including work with Tom Mix, the big hit "Tol'able David" and two of Laurel and Hardy's best comedies, "Swiss Miss" and "Blockheads". Blystone's first credited film is "Excitement" in 1924. Another brother, Jasper Blystone (1899-1965), became an assistant director. Blystone's wife was actress Alma Tell who died in 1937.

Stan may hold the record for the most "face in the crowd" scenes in films. It's estimated that in over fifty percent of his film appearances, over 400 movies, shorts and serials, he is uncredited.

As for those serials, he was in over 30 of them, with his earlier roles that of just henchmen in "Burn 'Em Up Barnes" ('34 Mascot), "Wolf Dog" ('33 Mascot) "Mandrake the Magician" ('39 Columbia), "Flying G-Men" ('39 Columbia) and others. Often his roles in serials bore a nautical slant ("Sea Raiders" '41 Universal, "Brick Bradford" '47 Columbia, "Sea Hound" '47 Columbia, "Adventures of Smilin' Jack" '43 Universal). Producer Sam Katzman used Blystone frequently in the late '40s and early '50s, giving him a good role in "Jack Armstrong" ('47 Columbia).

Suggested Sampling of Blystone's Western Heavies:

- The Circus Ace ('27 Fox) Tom Mix
- Parade of the West ('30 Universal) Ken Maynard
- Fighting Legion ('30 Universal) Ken Maynard
- Sundown Trail ('31 RKO) Tom Keene
- Honor of the Mounted ('32 Monogram) Tom Tyler
- Lucky Larrigan ('32 Monogram) Rex Bell
- Man of Action ('33 Columbia) Tim McCoy
- Fighting Parson ('33 Allied) Hoot Gibson
- Ivory Handled Gun ('35 Universal) Buck Jones
- Fighting Pioneers ('35 Resolute) Rex Bell
- Saddle Aces ('35 Resolute) Rex Bell
- Riding Avenger ('36 Diversion) Hoot Gibson
- Goofs and Saddles ('37 Columbia short) 3 Stooges
- Galloping Dynamite ('37 Ambassador) Kermit Maynard
- Headin' East ('37 Columbia) Buck Jones
- Stranger From Arizona ('38 Columbia) Buck Jones
- California Frontier ('38 Columbia) Buck Jones
- Drifting Westward ('39 Monogram) Jack Randall
- Three Texas Steers ('39 Republic) 3 Mesquiteers
- Crashing Thru ('39 Monogram) James Newill
- Tulsa Kid ('40 Republic) Don Barry
- Pony Post ('40 Universal) Johnny Mack Brown
- Sunset in Wyoming ('41 Republic) Gene Autry
- King of the Texas Rangers ('41 Republic serial) Sammy Baugh
- Jesse James Jr. ('42 Republic) Don Barry
- Navajo Kid ('45 PRC) Bob Steele
- Moon Over Montana ('46 Monogram) Jimmy Wakely
- Range Rider: Red Jack ('51) Jock Mahoney
- Roy Rogers: Blind Justice ('52) Roy Rogers
- Roy Rogers: Mingo Kid ('53) Roy Rogers

WARD BOND

Ward Bond's contribution to westerns is indisputable. Cast in a variety of roles, from villain to reverend, he could play them all with complete conviction. With a distinctive screen presence, it's unusual that he wasn't elevated to major roles earlier than he was.

Although he worked steadily from 1929 til his death, making as many as 28 pictures a year in the mid-'30s, Bond didn't achieve real stardom til the late '40s when his close association with John Wayne and John Ford cast him in terrific parts in a succession of films—"Tall In the Saddle" ('44), "They Were Expendable" ('45), "Dakota" ('45), "My Darling Clementine" ('46), "Fort Apache" ('48), "Three Godfathers" ('48), "Wagon Master" ('50), "Quiet Man" ('52), "Hondo" ('53), "Long Gray Line" ('55), "The Searchers" ('56). All these led to his crowning achievement, the role of Major Seth Adams, wagon boss on TV's "Wagon Train" in 1957.

But it all had its genesis as a heavy in the B-westerns of Buck Jones, Tim McCoy and George O'Brien.

Ward Edwin Bond was born April 9, 1903, in Benkelman, Nebraska, to John Bond and Mabel Huntley. He attended the University of Southern California where he obtained work as an extra through football teammate John Wayne. Director John Ford promoted Bond from extra to supporting player in "Salute" ('29). This cemented another long lasting friendship.

An arrogant man of little tact, yet fun-loving to the extreme, Bond was either loved or hated by those who knew him. An ardent but anti-intellectual patriot, among actors he was a vehement proponent of the blacklisting witch hunts of the '50s. He served as a most unforgiving president of the ultra-right-wing Motion Picture Alliance for the Preservation of American Ideals. An outspoken foe of communism, it was at his home on the coast that the American flag flew at half-mast during Premier Krushchev's visit to Hollywood in 1959. His rabid anti-Communist stance made him many enemies in liberal Hollywood.

A closely guarded secret is the fact Bond was an epileptic.

On a hunting trip, accidentally shot by John Wayne, Bond later left Wayne his shotgun.

Bond was posthumously inducted into the Hall of Great Western Performers at the National Cowboy and Western Heritage Museum in 2001.

Bond was twice married. From 1936-1944 he was wed to Doris Sellers. The marriage ended in divorce. From 1954 til Bond's death, he was married to Mary Louise May. The Bonds resided at 9510 Cherokee Lane in Beverly Hills.

On November 5, 1960, Bond and his wife were in Dallas, Texas, to attend a Dallas Cowboys/Los Angeles Rams pro football game when Bond died suddenly of a heart attack while sitting on the toilet in their hotel room, according to friend Harry Carey Jr.'s book COMPANY OF HEROES. He was 57. Bond's remains are at rest at Forest Lawn Cemetery in Glendale, California.

Bond was also in Dallas to meet with singer Johnny Horton ("Battle of New Orleans", "North to Alaska") to sign Horton to a contract to appear on "Wagon Train". Ironically, Horton died in an auto accident, hit by a drunk driver on the same day Bond died.

Buck Jones has the drop on Ward Bond in "Crimson Trail" ('35 Universal).

Suggested Sampling of Bond's Western Heavies:

- Hello Trouble ('32 Columbia) Buck Jones
- Sundown Rider ('33 Columbia) Buck Jones
- Unknown Valley ('33 Columbia) Buck Jones
- Fighting Code ('33 Columbia) Buck Jones
- Frontier Marshal ('34 20th Century Fox) George O'Brien
- Fighting Ranger ('34 Columbia) Buck Jones
- Crimson Trail ('35 Universal) Buck Jones
- Western Courage ('35 Columbia) Ken Maynard
- Fighting Shadows ('35 Columbia) Tim McCoy
- Avenging Waters ('36 Columbia) Ken Maynard
- Cattle Thief ('36 Columbia) Ken Maynard
- Conflict ('36 Universal) John Wayne
- Park Avenue Logger ('37 RKO) George O'Brien
- Gun Law ('38 RKO) George O'Brien
- Trouble In Sundown ('39 RKO) George O'Brien
- Buck Benny Rides Again ('40 Paramount) Jack Benny
- Tall In the Saddle ('44 RKO) John Wayne
- Dakota ('45 Republic) John Wayne

- Canyon Passage ('46 Universal) Dana Andrews
- Great Missouri Raid ('51 Paramount) Macdonald Carey
- Hellgate ('52 Lippert) Sterling Hayden
- The Moonlighter ('53 Warner Bros.) Fred MacMurray
- A Man Alone ('55 Republic) Ray Milland
- Halliday Brand ('57 United Artists) Joseph Cotten

RICHARD (DICK) BOTILLER

Richard (Dick) Botiller became quite adept at portraying scalawag looking Mexican bandits, vicious Indians and just plain reprehensible, odious henchmen in his 20 year western film career.

Botiller, born in Bakersfield, California, October 12, 1896, was uncredited as a rustler in his first film, "Lawless Valley" in 1932 with George O'Brien. Over the ensuing years, through 1952, he was uncredited more often than not. Nevertheless, he usually left a memorable nasty impression on not only Buck Jones, Tim McCoy, Charles Starrett, Gene Autry and others, but on the audience as well.

If an actor was one of the bad guys in B-westerns, chances are he could be seen in the serial that was part of the Saturday afternoon experience. Such is the case for Botiller beginning with "Return of Chandu" ('34 Principal) followed by "Radio Patrol" ('37 Universal), "Great Adventures of Wild Bill Hickok" ('38 Columbia), "Oregon Trail" ('39 Universal), "Overland With Kit Carson" ('39 Columbia)...11 in all.

Now and then Botiller would be hired by a major studio for a small role in an A-production, so look for Dick as a native in "Charge of the Light Brigade" ('36 Warner Bros.), as the escape boat pilot in "Devil's Island" ('40 Warner Bros.), an Indian in "Union Pacific" ('39 Paramount), a waiter in "Across the Pacific" ('42 Warner Bros.) or a sergeant in "For Whom the Bell Tolls" ('43 Paramount).

Botiller said adios to Hollywood in 1952 with the Durango Kid's "Smoky Canyon" and died a year later at only 56 on March 24, 1953, of unknown causes.

Suggested Sampling of Botiller's Western Heavies:

- Thunder Over Texas ('34 Beacon) Big Boy Williams
- Man Trailer ('34 Columbia) Buck Jones
- Arizona Bad Man ('35 Kent) Reb Russell
- Lightning Triggers ('35 Kent) Reb Russell
- Wild Mustang ('35 Ajax) Harry Carey
- Circle of Death ('35 Kent) Montie Montana
- West of Nevada ('36 Colony) Rex Bell
- Lightning Bill Carson ('36 Puritan) Tim McCoy
- Rio Grande Ranger ('36 Columbia) Bob Allen
- South of Arizona ('38 Columbia) Charles Starrett
- Mexicali Rose ('39 Republic) Gene Autry
- Overland With Kit Carson ('39 Columbia serial) Bill Elliott
- Wyoming Wildcat ('41 Republic) Don Barry
- Vigilantes Ride ('43 Columbia) Russell Hayden

LANE BRADFORD

Square-jawed Lane Bradford learned his dirty deeds from one of the best serial and B-western badmen—his father, John Merton.

Born Myrtland Viviene LaVarre Jr. August 29, 1922, in New York City, his father was Myrtland Viviene LaVarre Sr. who changed his screen name to John Merton (1901-1959). Bradford's mother was Esther Anita Swarts.

As John was a stage actor, the family came west in 1932. Lane started to do extra and stuntman work circa 1939. Lane worked extensively in B-westerns at PRC, Columbia and Republic with his career picking up considerably in the mid '40s.

"My brother, Lane (Bradford), had a lot of good qualities and I believe he was a far better, harder working and more thoughtful actor than my father (John Merton) was," Bob LaVarre told Tom and Jim Goldrup for their FEATURE PLAYERS Vol. 1. When Lane first came on the set of a new show, those who didn't know him were often "scared to death of him because he had that countenance, he had that mug on him, his broken nose and hawk-jaw, but he was just a teddy bear and loved everyone and wouldn't hurt anyone or anything."

LaVarre, Lane's younger brother and a sometime actor ("Sky King", "Hawaii 5-0") who became a cameraman on films ("Against A Crooked Sky") and TV ("Dukes of Hazzard" etc.), told the Goldrups Lane was "all over everywhere" during his younger days in California and soon found a love for Hawaii and Hawaiian music, learning to play the guitar and ukulele for his own amusement. Lane brought a love of Hawaii to the whole family.

After the family moved from the San Fernando Valley into the heart of Hollywood in 1939, 18 year old Lane started to work as an extra (at $7.50 a day) and stuntman with two of his earliest noticeable roles being in "Frontier Crusader" and "Riders of Black Mountain" (both '40) with Tim McCoy at PRC. This is the time he started using the name Lane Bradford, but LaVarre is unsure how the name was chosen.

Over the next few years Lane worked small roles in westerns with George Houston, Charles Starrett, Bill Elliott, 3 Mesquiteers and Buster Crabbe.

Some sort of military service in 1944-'45 but exactly what branch is unconfirmed. With his love of the sea, one would suspect the Navy or Coast Guard.

Lane's career started to come into focus post WWII and work picked up considerably from '46 on. He was seen in the westerns of Lash LaRue, Eddie Dean, Allan "Rocky" Lane, Johnny Mack Brown, Jim Bannon, Monte Hale, Roy Rogers, Rex Allen, Whip Wilson, Bill Elliott and others.

Lane was one of the busiest heavies on TV in the early days, appearing on "Annie Oakley", "Buffalo Bill Jr.", "Champion", "Cowboy G-Men", "Cisco Kid", "Fury", "Frontier Doctor", "Gene Autry", "Lone Ranger", "Hopalong Cassidy" right on through the heyday of TV westerns with "Cheyenne", "Bronco", "Black Saddle", "Bonanza", "Gunsmoke", "Have Gun Will Travel", "Laramie", "Lawman", "Tales of Wells Fargo", "Sugarfoot", "Wagon Train", "Maverick", "Rawhide"— virtually every TV western ever made. Well over 220 shows. And still he found time to continue working in the A-westerns of the period—"Drums Across the River", "Kansas Pacific", "Shootout at Medicine Bend", "Lone Ranger and the Lost City of Gold" etc.

Another veteran heavy, Pierce Lyden, recalls Lane as "One of the best. A great fight man, a cowboy. I think he'd do anything—if the price was right. We were on a 'Rin Tin Tin' at Traintown in Hollywood and were supposed to catch onto the train, climb on top, run along to the mail car and hold it up. I was 'rigging' some hand holds to climb down between the cars when Lane comes back and says, 'Forget it, they won't pay us!' and he was mad. I said, 'But I thought it was settled.' Lane says, 'But now they only want to pay us half of what we asked.' We didn't do it, but it took a half hour to change the shooting to us running through the cars instead of on top and a lot more money. But such is the thinking of Hollywood at times. In his last years, he accomplished what he always wanted to do—have a boat and be on the water. I heard he finally had a charter service out of Malibu and lived on his boat."

Lane's last film was as the prison warden in "Shoot Out" ('71) with Gregory Peck. Bradford also ventured into the burgeoning sci-fi field. He was Marex in Republic's '52 serial "Zombies of the Stratosphere". He was also in Republic's "Commando Cody" TV/film se-

Vicious Lane Bradford is about to put Al "Fuzzy" St. John's lights out in Lash LaRue's "Return of the Lash" ('47 PRC).

ries, several episodes of "Superman", "Rocky Jones, Space Ranger" and a "Lost In Space".

Lane's big love in life was boats. He first built an 18 ft. outrigger canoe and sailed it from his home in Malibu. Next he bought a 26 ft. ocean-going Folk Boat and later a P-28 which he took to Hawaii where he lived his last few years until he suffered a massive heart attack June 2, 1973, while on his boat at Ala Wai Yacht Harbor on the island of Oahu in Hawaii. Four days later, June 6, while a patient at Kaiser Foundation Hospital in Honolulu, Lane Bradford died. Cause of death was a massive cerebral hemorrhage.

Survivors included his wife, Mary Schrock, his mother, brother Bob, and four sisters. There is no evidence of any children.

Richard "Sgt. Preston" Simmons praised Bradford's professionalism: "When you had someone like Walter Reed, Lane Bradford, or Terry Frost on the show ("Sergeant Preston of the Yukon"), I never had to worry."

Suggested Sampling of Bradford's Western Heavies:

- Prairie Raiders ('47 Columbia) Charles Starrett
- Pioneer Justice ('47 PRC) Lash LaRue
- Ghost Town Renegades ('47 PRC) Lash LaRue
- Check Your Guns ('48 PRC) Eddie Dean
- Hawk of Powder River ('48 PRC) Eddie Dean
- Frontier Agent ('48 Monogram) Johnny Mack Brown
- Dead Man's Gold ('48 PRC) Lash LaRue
- Sundown in Santa Fe ('48 Republic) Allan "Rocky" Lane
- Far Frontier ('48 Republic) Roy Rogers
- Death Valley Gunfighter ('49 Republic) Allan "Rocky" Lane
- Prince of the Plains ('49 Republic) Monte Hale
- Law of the Golden West ('49 Republic) Monte Hale
- Roll, Thunder, Roll! ('49 Eagle Lion) Jim Bannon
- Fighting Redhead ('49 Eagle Lion) Jim Bannon
- Bandit King of Texas ('49 Republic) Allan "Rocky" Lane
- James Brothers of Missouri ('49 Republic serial) Keith Richards
- Lone Ranger: Legion of Old Timers ('49) Clayton Moore
- Lone Ranger: Desert Adventure ('50) Clayton Moore
- Old Frontier ('50 Republic) Monte Hale
- Frisco Tornado ('50 Republic) Allan "Rocky" Lane
- Missourians ('50 Republic) Monte Hale
- Don Daredevil Rides Again ('51 Republic serial) Ken Curtis
- Wells Fargo Gunmaster ('51 Republic) Allan "Rocky" Lane
- Stagecoach Driver ('51 Monogram) Whip Wilson
- Oklahoma Justice ('51 Monogram) Johnny Mack Brown
- Longhorn ('51 Monogram) Bill Elliott
- Stage to Blue River ('51 Monogram) Whip Wilson
- Fort Osage ('52 Monogram) Rod Cameron
- Target ('52 RKO) Tim Holt
- Kansas Territory ('52 Monogram) Bill Elliott
- Desert Passage ('52 RKO) Tim Holt
- Desperadoes Outpost ('52 Republic) Allan "Rocky" Lane
- Dead Man's Trail ('52 Monogram) Johnny Mack Brown
- Sky King: Carrier Pigeon ('52) Kirby Grant
- Cowboy G-Men: Ozark Gold ('52) Russell Hayden
- Hopalong Cassidy: The Trap ('52) William Boyd
- Roy Rogers: Mayor of Ghost Town ('52) Roy Rogers
- Savage Frontier ('53 Republic) Allan "Rocky" Lane
- Annie Oakley: Annie and the Silver Ace ('54) Gail Davis
- Forty-Niners ('54 Monogram) Bill Elliott
- Man With the Steel Whip ('54 Republic serial) Richard Simmons
- Lone Ranger: Stage to Tishomingo ('54) Clayton Moore
- Cisco Kid: Lowest Bidder ('54) Duncan Renaldo
- Buffalo Bill Jr.: Runaway Renegade ('55) Dick Jones
- Rin Tin Tin: Dead Man's Gold ('55) Lee Aaker
- Wyatt Earp: The Killer ('55) Hugh O'Brian
- Rin Tin Tin: Iron Horse ('55) Lee Aaker
- Tales of the Texas Rangers: Blazing Across the Pecos ('55) Willard Parker
- Judge Roy Bean: The Fugitive ('56) Edgar Buchanan
- Buffalo Bill Jr.: Gun Talk ('56) Dick Jones
- Annie Oakley: Outlaw Brand ('56) Gail Davis
- Annie Oakley: Annie and the Miser ('57) Gail Davis
- Lone Ranger: Mission For Tonto ('57) Clayton Moore
- Tales of Wells Fargo: Man In the Box ('57) Dale Robertson
- 26 Men: Destination Nowhere ('57) Kelo Henderson/Tris Coffin
- Sgt. Preston: Jailbreaker ('57) Richard Simmons
- Broken Arrow: Kingdom of Terror ('58) John Lupton
- Fury: Robber's Roost ('58) Bobby Diamond
- 26 Men: Chain Gang ('58) Kelo Henderson/Tris Coffin
- Toughest Gun In Tombstone ('58 United Artists) George Montgomery
- Restless Gun: Hiram Grover's Strike ('58) John Payne
- Frontier Doctor: San Francisco Story ('58) Rex Allen
- Texan: Eyes of Capt. Wylie ('59) Rory Calhoun
- 26 Men: Scorpion ('59) Kelo Henderson/Tris Coffin
- Fury: Man Killer ('59) Bobby Diamond
- Deputy: The Orphans ('59) Allen Case
- Gunsmoke: Moo Moo Raid ('60) James Arness
- Hotel de Paree: Vengeance For Sundance ('60) Earl Holliman
- Johnny Ringo: Cave-In ('60) Don Durant
- Tall Man: Counterfeit Law ('60) Barry Sullivan
- Tales of Wells Fargo: Mr. Mute ('61) Dale Robertson
- Gunsmoke: Caleb ('64) James Arness

NEVILLE BRAND

Neville Brand joined the U.S. Army in March 1941 meaning to make a career in the military. He emerged as the fourth most decorated GI of WWII, a statement Brand often denied, saying "I'm way up there, but Hollywood publicity took over." It was while he was in the Army that the craggy-faced, hard drinking, gravel-voiced Brand made his acting debut in Army training films. This experience apparently changed the direction of his life. A civilian again, he used his GI bill education assistance to study drama.

His rugged features and coarse, blaring attitude made him a natural unsophisticated heavy.

One of six children, Brand was born in Kewanee, Illinois, August 13, 1921. His father was Leo Brand, a steel worker and WWI Signal Corps vet. With his father and mother, Helen Milnes, he traveled up and down the Mississippi River to wherever a bridge was under construction.

Graduating from Kewanee High School, he falsified his birth date to read 1920 and joined the Illinois National Guard. In March '41 he enlisted in the Army and went through infantry training.

Brand was sent to Camp Carson at Colorado Springs, Colorado, where he was promoted to platoon sergeant and assigned to Company B, 331st Infantry, 83rd Infantry Division (the Thunderbolts).

Brand landed at Normandy in July 1944, then saw action in France, Luxembourg, Belgium and Germany, fighting in the Ardennes, through the Rhineland, Westphalia, Hanover and Saxony. On April 7, 1945, he was wounded near the Elbe River, spent time in a hospital in France, and, having enough, was discharged in October 1945.

While fighting in Europe he received the Silver Star, a Purple Heart, the American Defense Service Medal, and the European–African–Middle Eastern Campaign Medal with three Bronze Service Stars.

Following the war, Brand migrated to New York, settling in Greenwich Village amongst actors and writers. Hearing about the American Theatre Wing he enrolled as a student using his GI Bill entitlement.

After two years in New York, he moved to California and enrolled in the Geller Drama School.

After a couple of bit roles in 1949, he received plaudits for a strong performance in "D.O.A." ('50). Among other early films was the Oscar winning "Stalag 17".

In 1954 he scored in "Riot in Cell Block 11". "With this kisser," Brand chuckled, "I knew early in the game I wasn't going to make the world forget Clark Gable." He was perfect as Al Capone in "The George Raft Story" ('61), "The Scarface Mob" ('59) and several times on TV's "The Untouchables".

Brand explained to BAD AT THE BIJOU author William R. Horner, "I don't go in thinking he's a villain. The audience might, but the villain doesn't think he's a villain. Even a killer condones what he's done. I just create this human being under the circumstances that are given. I don't *think* he's a villain. Everybody just condones his own actions." As to being a "tough guy", "I'm a *rough* guy, let's put it that way. No, I am not a tough guy, but I can do all those things. Like in the war. I try not to be a tough guy, not in my personal life—but I can be, if the situation calls for it."

But, aside from his loathsome portrayals, perhaps Brand is best known for soft-hearted, loud-mouthed, none-too-bright, but tough as nails Texas Ranger Reese Bennett of TV's "Laredo" ('65-'67).

Brand was married three times and had two daughters with his second wife.

He died of emphysema April 16, 1992, in Sacramento, California.

Suggested Sampling of Brand's Western Heavies:

- Charge at Feather River ('53 Warner Bros.) Guy Madison
- Gun Fury ('53 Columbia) Rock Hudson
- Lone Gun ('54 United Artists) George Montgomery
- Return of Jack Slade ('55 Allied Artists) John Ericson
- Fury at Gunsight Pass ('56 Columbia) Richard Long
- Raw Edge ('56 Universal-International) Rory Calhoun
- Three Outlaws ('56 Associated) Bruce Bennett
- Gun Brothers ('56 United Artists) Buster Crabbe
- Lonely Man ('57 Paramount) Jack Palance
- Tin Star ('57 Paramount) Henry Fonda
- Badman's Country ('58 Warner Bros.) George Montgomery
- Texan: Law of the Gun ('58) Rory Calhoun
- Zane Grey Theatre: Trouble at Tres Cruces ('59) Brian Keith
- Rawhide: Incident of the Devil and His Due ('60) Eric Fleming
- Bonanza: The Last Viking ('60) Michael Landon/Lorne Greene
- Rawhide: Incident of the Red Wind ('63) Eric Fleming/Clint Eastwood
- Wagon Train: Jed Whitmore Story ('64) John McIntire
- Destry: Solid Gold Girl ('64) John Gavin
- Gunsmoke: Kioga ('65) James Arness
- Daniel Boone: Tanner ('67) Fess Parker
- Bonanza: Luck of Pepper Shannon ('70) Lorne Greene/Mitch Vogel
- Alias Smith and Jones: Shootout at Diablo Station ('71) Ben Murphy/Peter Duel

HENRY BRANDON

Handsome enough to play leads, Henry Brandon was typecast as a villain, whether it be Caucasian, oriental, Indian or Nazi. From age 21-22, for five decades, he made his mark as a memorable heavy in such films as "Babes In Toyland" (as Silas Barnaby), "Trail Of the Lonesome Pine" (as Wade Falin), and "The Searchers" (as Comanche Chief Scar).

Universal recognized his serial potential and cast him as the dastardly Cobra in "Jungle Jim" ('36), mastermind criminal Blackstone in "Secret Agent X-9" ('37) and treacherous Capt. Lasca in "Buck Rogers" ('39). In 1940, at Republic, he became the epitome of evil in the role for which he will always be associated, Dr. Fu Manchu in "Drums of Fu Manchu".

Born Heinrich Von Kleinbach in Berlin, Germany, June 8, 1912, his parents, Richard Kleinbach and Hidegard Brandenburg, migrated to the U.S. shortly after Henry's birth.

After 14 years of formal education, Brandon began to study acting at the famed Pasadena Playhouse when he was 17.

Brandon was playing an old man in a stage presentation of "The Drunkard" when producer Hal Roach spotted him and cast him in Laurel and Hardy's perennial Christmas classic, "Babes in Toyland" ('34) (later retitled "March of the Wooden Soldiers").

In 1936 the 6' 5" actor adopted the stage name Henry Brandon. His imposing features, muscular build and rich voice made him a much-in-demand bad guy in all types of films, including westerns. His chilling role as Comanche Chief Scar in "The Searchers" seemed to nearly typecast him as an Indian, a role he played at least 25 more times in film and on TV.

His career was interrupted from '42-'45 for active duty in WWII. He restarted his film career in 1947 with a small role in "Northwest Outpost".

Originally, Brandon hoped to play romantic leads but felt the competition was too great. As a result, he chose the villain route.

As television came along, Brandon split his time between films, TV and the legit stage. Brandon's many stage roles include Jason in "Medea" ('47-'48) opposite Judith Anderson (a role he also played in a TV production), and "Tower Beyond Tragedy" with Anderson. He appeared with her as Ross in Maurice Evans' "Macbeth" and L.A. and N.Y. productions of "The Lady's Not For Burning" ('57). He played Rochester in "Jane Eyre" at the opening of Hollywood's Huntington Hartford Theater, and was Alessandro for two seasons in California's "Ramona" pageant, as well as appearing frequently at the Pasadena Playhouse and other California legit houses.

Widely unknown, he was the animation model for Captain Hook in Disney's "Peter Pan" in '53. At a film

Looks like a disagreement over money between Henry Brandon and Joel McCrea in Universal's "Cattle Drive" ('51). Trailhand Bob Steele observes.

festival in the '80s, Brandon revealed his favorite role was as the mountain man in "When the North Wind Blows" ('74).

Brandon also did many commercial voiceovers and was scheduled to appear in his first music video two days before his death February 16, 1990, at Cedars Sinai Medical Center in Los Angeles. The cause was heart disease. His remains were cremated and returned to his home address on North Spaulding Ave. in L.A.

He was survived by a brother, name unknown, and sister, Marie Phillips of Glendale. Several sources indicate Brandon was a confirmed lifelong bachelor, but his California death certificate states he was divorced at the time of his death.

Director William Witney called him, "One of the fine actors that somehow got overlooked in Hollywood."

Suggested Sampling of Brandon's Western Heavies:

- Trail of the Lonesome Pine ('36 Paramount) Fred MacMurray
- Marshal of Mesa City ('39 RKO) George O'Brien
- Ranger and the Lady ('40 Republic) Roy Rogers
- Under Texas Skies ('40 Republic) 3 Mesquiteers
- Bad Man of Deadwood ('41 Republic) Roy Rogers
- Cattle Drive ('51 Universal) Joel McCrea
- Wagons West ('52 Monogram) Rod Cameron
- Pony Express ('53 Paramount) Charlton Heston
- War Arrow ('54 Universal) Jeff Chandler
- Stories of the Century: Nate Champion ('55) Jim Davis
- Broken Arrow: Passage Deferred ('55) John Lupton
- The Searchers ('56 Warner Bros.) John Wayne
- Jim Bowie: Epitaph For an Indian ('57) Scott Forbes
- Restless Gun: New Sheriff ('57) John Payne
- Lawman: Last Man ('59) John Russell
- Have Gun Will Travel: Treasure Trail ('59) Richard Boone
- Deputy: Big Four ('59) Allen Case
- Bronco: Legacy of Twisted Creek ('60) Ty Hardin
- Gunslinger: Death of Yellow Singer ('61) Tony Young
- Whispering Smith: Mortal Coil ('61) Audie Murphy
- Daniel Boone: The Deserter ('66) Fess Parker

ROY BRENT

Not a particularly talented actor, Roy Brent still managed to appear in at least 33 B-westerns and seven serials over an eleven year period 1935-1946. Perhaps his "shining hour" was "Raiders of Red Gap" ('43 PRC) as a flashy dressing, tough gunman who switches duds with Al "Fuzzy" St. John. Otherwise, he was "one of the gang" at PRC, Republic and Universal.

Born in Chicago, Illinois (not in Lafayette, Louisiana, as studio bios allege) on August 29, 1903, Brent was christened Manierre Alexander Williamson. His father worked concessions, traveling with various carnivals, leaving his son to grow up with his mother. Later, Roy too traveled a bit with carnivals but his passion was baseball.

When WWI came along, the boy enlisted at a young age in the U.S. Navy.

After the war, he hung around Chicago for a bit, was briefly married and divorced, then headed for California determined to play professional baseball. Indeed, he did play semi-pro ball in the '20s for the Utah-Idaho league.

A chance meeting at a party in 1921 with Christie Comedies' star Bobby Vernon landed Williamson a job as a movie extra and sometime stuntman. It was Vernon who re-christened him Roy Brent.

He knocked around Hollywood for years before he began to get small roles in 1933 (one of the ship's crew on "King Kong") and 1935 ("Best Man Wins" as a sailor, "Cappy Ricks Returns" as a workman, etc.). The late '30s and early '40s found him with uncredited bits in four serials—"Spider's Web" ('38 Columbia) "Daredevils of the Red Circle" ('39 Republic), "Adventures of Red Ryder" ('40 Republic) and "Spy Smasher" ('42 Republic).

By 1942-'43 he was at last receiving better parts in westerns with Don Barry ("Outlaws of Pine Ridge"), Bill Elliott ("Man From Thunder River") and Johnny Mack Brown ("Deep In the Heart of Texas", "Cheyenne Roundup") as well as Buster Crabbe and Bob Livingston B's at PRC.

Never achieving any outstanding roles, Brent nevertheless was steadily employed through 1946 at which time he decided, in his early '40s, to seek other employment. His last released film—for awhile—was "Outlaws of the Plains" ('46 PRC) with Buster Crabbe.

Brent tried a variety of jobs—selling stocks, selling encyclopedias, working with a giveaway "Green Sheet" newspaper, selling diapers door-to-door, selling carpeting, selling 'Invitation Dinners'—none of which brought him any modicum of income. He made a brief return to film as the sheriff on a couple of Roy Rogers TV episodes in '53 ("Knockout" and "Silver Fox Hunt").

Brent married Ruth Corbett, a commercial artist and illustrator at Universal-International, on February 23, 1957, but the union was a rocky one as Brent was unable to make much money and Ruth felt she was supporting the family. (She had a daughter, Jana, by a previous marriage.)

Even as late as 1962 Brent was seeking movie work in the annual trade casting directory.

Brent died of emphysema at 75 on February 10, 1979, in Sun City, California. Ruth died in December 1997 at 85.

PRC's Lone Rider, Bob Livingston, corrals one of the "Wolves of the Range" ('43), Roy Brent, while saddlepal Fuzzy St. John defangs him.

Suggested Sampling of Brent's Westerns:

- Wolves of the Range ('43 PRC) Bob Livingston
- Cattle Stampede ('43 PRC) Buster Crabbe
- Arizona Trail ('43 Universal) Tex Ritter
- Raiders of Red Gap ('43 PRC) Bob Livingston
- Cattle Stampede ('43 PRC) Buster Crabbe
- Blazing Guns ('43 Monogram) Trail Blazers
- The Drifter ('44 PRC) Buster Crabbe
- His Brother's Ghost ('45 PRC) Buster Crabbe
- Wild Beauty ('46 Universal) Don Porter

AL BRIDGE

Al Bridge was equally at home playing the boss heavy (dress heavy) or a grizzled henchman. He gave the impression in dozens of B-westerns the only fun he got out of life was obtained by cheating, lying, rustling and killing. He seemed to always have a cigarette in his hand. His voice sounded like a person who had been a heavy smoker.

Bridge spent 24 years in front of a camera, from '31-'54, menacing Tom Tyler, Bob Steele, Rex Bell, Hoot Gibson, Ken Maynard, Tom Keene, Buck Jones, Charles Starrett, 3 Mesquiteers, Gene Autry, Bill Elliott, Johnny Mack Brown and others before finally seeing the light towards the end of the trail and playing the Sheriff role in several Roy Rogers and Rex Allen films and on TV with Gene Autry and a few others.

Alan Marton Bridge was born in Pennsylvania on February 26, 1891. His parents, Charles Bridge and Louise Blackburn, were both Pennsylvania natives.

After serving with the armed forces in WWI, Bridge was a reporter for the KANSAS CITY JOURNAL and attended Georgia Brown Dramatic School in Kansas City. Bridge then managed and starred in his own musical-comedy stock company which also included his sister, actress Loie Bridge (Barnett) (1889-1974).

Arriving in Hollywood at the time of transition to sound, his first billed appearance was in Tom Tyler's "God's Country and the Man" in '31 for which he also was credited with additional dialogue.

Besides westerns, Bridge worked in 16 serials, his best roles coming in "Devil Horse" ('32 Mascot), "Fighting With Kit Carson" ('33 Mascot), "Mystery Mountain" ('34 Mascot), "Burn 'Em Up Barnes" ('34 Mascot), "Adventures of Rex and Rinty" ('35 Mascot), "Adventures of Frank Merriwell" ('36 Universal) and "Jungle Jim" ('36 Universal).

Bridge also appeared in many A-films and was a member of the famed Preston Sturges stock company of characters.

Once married to Hazel Belford, Bridge was divorced at the time of his death at age 66 on December 27, 1957, at his home on South Gramercy Park in Los Angeles. Primary cause of death stated to be heart disease with emphysema as a contributing factor. Remember—on screen he usually held a cigarette.

The veteran badman, whom Rex Allen once said was "a better rider than many professionals," is buried at Valhalla Memorial Park in North Hollywood where you'll note that his birth year is given at 1891 rather than 1890 (as reported on his death certificate) and his first name is spelled Alford (not Alan).

Suggested Sampling of Bridge's Westerns:

- God's County and the Man ('31 Syndicate) Tom Tyler
- Ridin' Fool ('31 Tiffany) Bob Steele
- South of Santa Fe ('32 Tiffany) Bob Steele
- Spirit of the West ('32 Allied) Hoot Gibson
- Devil Horse ('32 Mascot serial) Harry Carey
- Wyoming Whirlwind ('32 Kent) Lane Chandler
- When a Man Rides Alone ('33 Monarch) Tom Tyler
- Drum Taps ('33 World Wide) Ken Maynard
- Son of the Border ('33 RKO) Tom Keene
- Cheyenne Kid ('33 RKO) Tom Keene
- North of Arizona ('35 Reliable) Jack Perrin
- Outlaw Rule ('35 Kent) Reb Russell
- Silent Valley ('35 Reliable) Tom Tyler
- New Frontier ('35 Republic) John Wayne
- Lawless Nineties ('36 Republic) John Wayne
- Call of the Prairie ('36 Paramount) William Boyd
- Three Mesquiteers ('36 Republic) 3 Mesquiteers
- Dodge City Trail ('36 Columbia) Charles Starrett
- Two Gun Law ('37 Columbia) Charles Starrett
- Western Gold ('37 20th Century Fox) Smith Ballew
- Springtime in the Rockies ('37 Republic) Gene Autry
- Partners of the Plains ('38 Paramount) William Boyd
- Colorado Trail ('38 Columbia) Charles Starrett
- Man From Sundown ('38 Columbia) Charles Starrett
- Pioneers of the Frontier ('40 Columbia) Bill Elliott
- Blazing Six Shooters ('40 Columbia) Charles Starrett
- Kid's Last Ride ('41 Monogram) Range Busters
- Law of the Range ('41 Universal) Johnny Mack Brown
- Both Barrels Blazing ('45 Columbia) Charles Starrett
- Blazing the Western Trial ('45 Columbia) Charles Starrett
- Last Days of Boot Hill ('47 Columbia) Charles Starrett

STEVE BRODIE

One of the latecomers to westerns, Steve Brodie's first time in the saddle was as Bob Dalton in Randolph Scott's all-star-outlaw adventure, "Badman's Territory" in 1946.

An RKO contract player, he left a lasting impression in the early post-war Tim Holt B's. At the Knoxville western Film Fair in 1991 Steve smiled, "I loved making pictures with Tim Holt. I particularly liked playing a villain. When people booed you and hated you for the way you performed, it meant you had done your job well. Those western pictures were fun, and Tim Holt and Richard Martin were great guys to work with."

Steve was born John Stephens in El Dorado, Kansas, November 25, 1919. His father, Alexander Lewis Stephens, was from Ohio, and his mother, Lena Blanche Daugherty, was a native of Illinois.

As a teenager in the midst of the Great Depression, to his way of thinking, the best jobs were the flamboyant ones, so Steve raced cars, worked on oil rigs, boxed and made bootleg whiskey. He aspired to be a criminal lawyer, but when forced to drop out of school decided to try acting.

Auditioning in New York, he found nothing for over a year using the name John Stephens. Then he got the idea to come up with a memorable name, hence Steve Brodie—fashioned after the famous New York saloon owner who, in 1886, claimed he jumped off the Brooklyn Bridge into the East River. Pulling a "Brodie" soon became synonymous to publicity stunts.

When casting agents assumed he was related to the famous man, he didn't correct them and soon began receiving acting jobs. An MGM talent scout saw him and brought Steve to Hollywood as a $75 a week contract player. His first film was "Ladies Courageous" with Loretta Young in '44 (on loan-out to Universal).

Unfortunately, he was dropped by MGM after a year. He freelanced for a while and was then signed by RKO, along with good friend Robert Mitchum.

Steve was first married to actress Lois Andrews (with whom he later worked in Holt's "Rustlers" in '49).

"Arizona Ranger" Tim Holt and nasty Steve Brodie square off over Brodie's mistreatment of his wife Nan Leslie.

She was followed by a marriage to a lady named Barbara Savitt. They later divorced, and Steve married Virginia Carol Hefner. They lived on Sunnybrae Avenue in Canoga Park, California. Steve fathered two sons, one of whom, Kevin, became and actor/director.

Steve worked in films and on TV heavily til '68-'69, at which time he slowed down considerably. He made a bit of a comeback in '75 starring in "The Giant Spider Invasion" alongside former RKO stablemate Barbara Hale. But his appearances on TV after that were scant and the few films he did were ones he probably shouldn't have made.

Apart from westerns, he starred in a few B-pics at RKO such as "Desperate" ('47), but really made a mark in several classic A-films. He was part of the Texas Division platoon who took "A Walk in the Sun" on Salerno beachhead in 1945. He was Robert Mitchum's blackmailing private eye partner in the film noir "Out of the Past" ('47). He was Robert Ryan's drunken and sadistic ex-Army buddy helping to beat to death Sam Levine in Edward Dmytryk's controversial "Crossfire" ('47). He was Academy Award material as the bigoted corporal in Stanley Kramer's "Home of the Brave" ('49).

But still, it is the western films and TV shows for which we best remember Steve—the Tim Holt and Randolph Scott westerns…and his portrayal of vicious Sheriff Johnny Behan on TV's "Life and Legend of Wyatt Earp" from '59-'61.

RKO alumni Richard (Chito) Martin said, "He was a happy-go-lucky guy. I don't think he had too many problems in life. He always had a good time…but he studied and worked hard, he didn't take his job lightly. He got along with everybody, but he *was* outspoken. He enjoyed telling stories, laughing. I don't think he missed too much (in life) and that's good because we only go 'round once."

Walter Reed remembered, "I knew Steve socially also. I liked Steve. He was a real nice guy—funny guy—fun to be with. Also a very good actor, very competent. He was right there when he was needed. He lived hard, but he worked hard too. One day he just quit (films) and went into business. I don't think he pushed hard enough to really become big. He didn't realize how good he was."

Steve died January 9, 1992, at Humana Hospital in West Hills, California, of cardio respiratory arrest and myocardial infarction. Lactic acidosis and esophageal cancer were also contributing factors. His remains were cremated and taken to the family home.

"Everybody wants to be a leading man," said Brodie at the 1991 Knoxville Fest, "but early on I discovered it is much better to be a heavy because you work more. When a part was given to me, I went at it hard. If I had my life to live over again, I wouldn't change a thing. I've had a ball."

Suggested Sampling of Brodie's Westerns:

- Sunset Pass ('46 RKO) James Warren
- Code of the West ('47 RKO) James Warren
- Thunder Mountain ('47 RKO) Tim Holt
- Arizona Ranger ('48 RKO) Tim Holt
- Return of the Bad Men ('48 RKO) Randolph Scott
- Guns of Hate ('48 RKO) Tim Holt
- Brothers in the Saddle ('49 RKO) Tim Holt
- Rustlers ('49 RKO) Tim Holt
- Massacre River ('49 Allied Artists) Rory Calhoun/Guy Madison
- Winchester 73 ('50 Universal) James Stewart
- Charge At Feather River ('53 Warner Bros.) Guy Madison
- Lone Ranger: Tumblerock Law ('53) Clayton Moore
- Wild Bill Hickok: Young Witness ('53) Guy Madison
- Stories of the Century: Harry Tracy ('54) Jim Davis
- Gun Duel In Durango ('57 United Artists) George Montgomery
- Sugarfoot: Reluctant Hero ('57) Will Hutchins
- Trackdown: Matter of Justice ('58) Robert Culp
- Wanted Dead Or Alive: Call Your Shot ('59) Steve McQueen
- Rough Riders: A Matter of Instinct ('59) Jan Merlin
- Wanted Dead Or Alive: Montana Kid ('59) Steve McQueen
- Life and Legend of Wyatt Earp: Series—as Sheriff Johnny Behan ('59-'61)
- Pony Express: Vendetta ('60) Grant Sullivan
- Maverick: Devil's Necklace ('61) Jack Kelly
- Cheyenne: Winchester Quarantine ('61) Clint Walker
- Bronco: The Equalizer ('61) Ty Hardin
- Laramie: Confederate Express ('62) Robert Fuller
- Cheyenne: Man Alone ('62) Clint Walker
- Bonanza: Any Friend of Walter's ('63) Dan Blocker
- A Bullet For Billy the Kid ('63 Associated Dist.) Gaston Santos
- Bonanza: Walter and the Outlaws ('64) Dan Blocker

BUDD BUSTER

Wiry, feisty, little Budd Buster was a real B-western workhorse, a versatile character actor who could play any role from heavy to the girl's father convincingly. He was adept at sheriffs, fathers, bankers, townsmen…bit parts or major roles, he never turned in a bad performance.

Budd was even the sidekick in one Jack Randall at Monogram, "Covered Wagon Trails" ('40), played Tom Keene's friend Kentuck in several of Keene's Crescent historical dramas, and did comedy relief or pure sidekick work with Bob Steele in "Cavalry" ('36 Republic) (in which he played President Lincoln in silhouette), "Desert Patrol" ('38 Republic) and "Feud of the Range ('39 Metropolitan).

After playing plenty of badmen in the '30s and early '40s, as Budd got older you'd see him less frequently as an outlaw and cast more in sympathetic roles such as in "Trail of Terror" ('43 PRC), "Riders of the Santa Fe" ('44 Universal), "Gangs of Sonora" ('41 Republic), "Guns of the Law" ('44 PRC), "Song of the Sierras" ('46 Monogram) and "Rainbow Over the Rockies" ('47 Monogram).

Budd Leland Buster was born in Colorado Springs, Colorado, June 14, 1891. His mother's maiden name was Moore.

In addition to a vaudeville and road show stage career from age six, and prior to entering films first in 1909 at Ft. Lee, New Jersey, Buster was a makeup artist. His makeup tricks gave him wide latitude in portraying various characters and kept him in demand by national ad agencies who used him on national billboards for Studebaker, Eastside Beer and others. Budd also appeared on Broadway in 1908-1909 in "Mary Jane's Pa". He'd left films early on but returned in 1933 and worked nonstop in over 275 pictures until the early '50s.

Some listings mistakenly credit Budd with a lot of television and film roles played by character actor George Selk. However, Selk is a separate individual actor. The prolific Buster is listed as Budd L. Buster on the Social Security Database and on his grave marker.

Buster worked for practically every studio that made westerns and with most of the '30s and '40s cowboy stars but he especially found employment at PRC where he was almost a fixture.

Out of the 17 serials Buster appeared in, his prime roles were of grizzled old Vinegar Smith in Republic's "King of the Royal Mounted" ('40) and as Jungle Jack in Universal's "Jungle Queen" ('45).

Budd Buster, living in Los Angeles, died of a heart attack December 22, 1965, at 74.

Suggested Sampling of Buster's Western Heavies:

- Reckless Buckaroo ('35 Spectrum) Bill Cody
- Silent Valley ('35 Reliable) Tom Tyler
- Between Men ('35 Supreme) Johnny Mack Brown
- Lawless Border ('35 Spectrum) Bill Cody
- Desert Justice ('36 Atlantic) Jack Perrin
- Gun Ranger ('37 Republic) Bob Steele
- Colorado Kid ('37 Republic) Bob Steele
- Paroled To Die ('38 Republic) Bob Steele

- Man's Country ('38 Monogram) Jack Randall
- Stranger From Arizona ('38 Columbia) Buck Jones
- Adventures of the Masked Phantom ('39 Equity) Monte Rawlins
- Fighting Renegade ('39 Victory) Tim McCoy
- Pinto Canyon ('40 Metropolitan) Bob Steele
- Texas Marshal ('41 PRC) Tim McCoy
- West of Tombstone ('42 Columbia) Charles Starrett/Russell Hayden
- Billy the Kid Trapped ('42 PRC) Bob Steele
- Overland Stagecoach ('42 PRC) Bob Livingston
- Santa Fe Scouts ('43 Republic) 3 Mesquiteers
- Cowboy Commandos ('43 Monogram) Range Busters
- Outlaw Roundup ('44 PRC) Dave O'Brien/James Newill
- Pinto Bandit ('44 PRC) Dave O'Brien/James Newill
- Wild Horse Phantom ('44 PRC) Buster Crabbe
- Border Badmen ('45 PRC) Buster Crabbe
- Six Gun Man ('46 PRC) Bob Steele
- Wild Frontier ('47 Republic) Allan "Rocky" Lane

ACE CAIN

Ace Cain worked in less than 20 poverty row B-westerns of the early '30s, but his life was a fascinating one.

According to his nephew Everett Truman Cain, "Ace Cain was born Horace Truman Cain in Chickasaw Nation, Oklahoma, August 23, 1903. He died May 18, 1973, in Saugus, California, and was buried at Eternal Valley Memorial Park, Newhall, California."

"He married Beatress 'Skeeter' Willys in the early '30s, and they remained together his entire life. His boyhood days were spent in Wichita Falls, Texas, on the Cain family farm."

"Upon reaching manhood, Ace and his brother Jim joined the U.S. Army to see the world, mostly the Pacific Rim nations—China, Philippines, Hawaii, etc. Ace and Jim became expert gamblers during their service careers and banded substantial sums to be used for business purposes after discharge. Ace could throw the dice and unerringly come up with the desired numbers. Brother Jim played poker, memorizing the cards played and calculating the odds, and came up winner most of the time. After a few years saving up his gambling gains from the Army, Ace entered the bootlegging business in Hollywood during the Prohibition Era. He had a very outgoing and likeable personality, and ran a successful operation, often 'cooperating' with the police when they needed to make a raid. He would have his boys leave an old car with a few cases of cheap booze in it, so the cops could report that they had raided Ace Cain's. It was during this period, the middle '30s, that Ace met some of the B-western movie directors and actors. They convinced him he would make a great bad guy in their 7-day movie epics."

"He donned the black cowboy hat and dark clothes and did his best to make the movie audiences hate him. Being about six and a half feet tall and weighing in at 240, he made an excellent bad guy, doing his own fights, falls, and stunts. The minor B-western studios Ace worked for eventually were squeezed out of business by the big studios, so he quit the acting business after the Repeal and opened up Ace Cain's Café, a 'legal' watering hole on Western Avenue near Sunset Blvd. right across from 20th Century Fox. It was complete with live floor shows featuring scantily clad chorus girls, singing waiters, jugglers, acrobats, animal acts, and the works."

"Brother Jim operated a 'legal' package retail liquor store right next door. Ace Cain's was one of the top nighteries in Hollywood during WWII and he and his chorus beauties were featured in some of the early men's magazines. After the War, the nightclub business tapered off and Ace sold the property to the U.S. government, which placed a Post Office where the famous Ace Cain's Café had once stood."

"Ace opened up the Uncle Ace Liquor Store and Uncle Ace Motel down the street on Western Avenue near Santa Monica Blvd. He later sold these businesses and bought and operated the Rocky Springs Country Club on Sand Canyon Road in Saugus, California. His club achieved a dubious reputation during his remaining years, because of the 'very friendly' women—ex-models, ex-show girls, etc.—that frequented his establishment. Even after his passing in '73, he was featured in numerous write-ups in the local newspapers as one of the area's colorful historical characters."

Suggested Sampling of Cain's Western Heavies:

- Shotgun Pass ('31 Columbia) Tim McCoy
- Cyclone Ranger ('35 Spectrum) Bill Cody
- Danger Trails ('35 Beacon) Big Boy Williams
- Rio Rattler ('35 Reliable) Tom Tyler
- Six Gun Justice ('35 Spectrum) Bill Cody
- Texas Rambler ('35 Spectrum) Bill Cody
- Vanishing Riders ('35 Spectrum) Bill Cody
- Toll of the Desert ('36 Commodore) Fred Kohler Jr.
- Irish Gringo ('36 Keith) Pat Carlyle

YAKIMA CANUTT

Hollywood's most renowned stuntman and second unit director, Yakima Canutt, set the standard for achievement within that select group of action-actors performing some of the screen's most incredible feats of daring in early B-westerns. He also innovated many of the safety devices still used by stuntmen today. Meanwhile, Yak has to be considered one of the best of the '30s and '40s badmen for his roles opposite John Wayne, Reb Russell, Lane Chandler, Rex Lease, Johnny Mack Brown, 3 Mesquiteers, Jack Hoxie, Gene Autry, Tom Keene and others.

Yak's 60 years before and behind the camera encompassed that of stuntman par excellence, silent western star, western film heavy, second unit action director and director. Prior to that, he was a World Champion rodeo cowboy for seven years.

Born November 29, 1895, on a ranch in the Snake River Hills 16 miles from Colfax, Washington, Enos Edward Canutt grew up riding and roping. Yak entered his first rodeo at 16 and proved to be a natural bucking horse rider and bulldogger.

By 17 Canutt was riding in the Pendleton, Oregon, rodeo where he earned the nickname that he carried through life. He was hanging around with some bronc riders from the Yakima country of Washington when a newspaper photographer snapped a picture of Canutt upside down above a bronc captioning it "Yakima Canutt leaving the deck of a Pendleton bronc." The cowboys picked it up and started calling him "Yakima," soon shortened to "Yak". This is also from where the misconcep-

Sidekick Smiley Burnette approves as Bob Livingston convinces outlaw Yakima Canutt he is Republic's "Pride of the Plains" ('44).

tion grew that Canutt was of Indian descent, he is not, his heritage is strictly European.

Yak won All-Around Cowboy at Pendleton four times, 1917, 1919, 1920, 1923. He was also saddle bronc riding champ at Pendleton in 1917, 1919 and 1923 as well as in Calgary, Canada, in 1919. Yak took top points in steer wrestling in Pendleton in 1920 and '21.

In 1918 Yak joined the Navy, the 13th Naval District in Bremerton, Washington, and was with the Ordinance Class of Gunnery stateside. In the Fall of 1918 he was given a 30 day furlough to go to Pendleton where he competed. Soon after returning to military duty the Armistice was signed and, as he had enlisted for the duration, Yak was discharged in the Spring of 1919.

In 1916, at 21, Yak married the 28 year old rodeo cowgirl Kitty Wilks in Kalispell, Montana. The marriage ended in divorce in 1919.

With stunt riders in great demand, Yak entered the movies on a part-time basis in 1919. He performed stunts and was cast as the sheriff in the 15 chapter Jack Hoxie serial "Lightning Bryce" ('19 National).

By 1924, after roles and stunts in several other silents, Yak began to star in westerns for Arrow, FBO and Davis…"Branded a Bandit" ('24), "Ridin' Comet" ('25), "Scar Hanan" ('25), "Desert Greed" ('26), "Devil Horse" ('26), "Iron Rider" ('26), "Hellhounds of the Plains" ('26), "Riders of the Storm" ('29), among others.

A severe case of the flu while he was in the Navy in 1918 permanently damaged Yak's vocal chords making him sound, in his words, "Like a hillbilly in a well." Certainly his oddly-pitched, raspy voice was unsuited to leading man status, even in B-westerns, and he starred in only one talkie, the poverty row "Canyon Hawks" ('30 Big 4).

Within a year Yak saw the opportunity for extended excitement and thrills in motion pictures by being an all around professional stuntman. He quickly became known as Hollywood's premier stuntman in the '30s, meanwhile continuing to play heavies.

Yak and John Wayne created a new technique for filming screen fist fights more believably. Canutt created or refined most of the stunt techniques used in westerns and action films for years to come. Many of these took much of the risk out of stuntwork. He first astounded audiences in 1931's "Lightning Warrior" Mascot serial when he astonishingly fell between a galloping team of horses and laid prone as the stagecoach rolled over him. It was an amazing feat which he repeated, or variations of it, in "Branded a Coward" ('35), "Rootin' Tootin' Rhythm" ('37), "Zorro's Fighting Legion" serial ('39), "Stagecoach" ('39) and others. His famous flying leap over the neck of a stumbling horse was another of the legendary feats he perfected.

Applying his know-how and know-no-fear attitude, Canutt raised Mascot and Republic serials to new heights in "Lightning Warrior" ('31), "Devil Horse" ('32), "Darkest Africa" ('36), "Painted Stallion" ('37), "Dick Tracy Returns" ('38), "Jungle Girl" ('41) and so many others. He even gave Columbia a boost on "Mysterious Pilot" ('37), "Secret of Treasure Island" ('38), "Deadwood Dick" ('40) and "White Eagle" ('41). Regarding "Devil Horse", Yak once stated, "I was doubling Harry Carey. I was to grab Rex (the horse) around the neck and hold on to him. He couldn't shake me off, so he fell on me—knocking me unconscious and breaking several ribs. I spent quite sometime in the hospital over that. Rex was the meanest horse I ever saw."

Yak married again in 1931 to Minnie Andrea Rice. His son Edward Clay "Tap" Canutt was born in 1932, Harry Joe Canutt was born in 1937.

As the years and imaginative stunt work went on, Canutt was elevated to second unit director on major films such as "Stagecoach" ('39), "Dark Command" ('40), "Doolins of Oklahoma" ('49), "Ivanhoe" ('52), "Westward Ho the Wagons" ('56), "Spartacus" ('60), "El Cid" ('61), "Cat Ballou" ('65) and his crowning achievement, "Ben Hur" ('59) with the staging of the famed chariot race in which his own son Joe doubled for Charlton Heston.

Yak was awarded a special Oscar in 1966 for his contributions to the making of movies.

His friend Glenn Strange said, "In all the time I worked with Yak, I never saw a guy get hurt if they did what Yak told them to do. They tell me Yak got hurt one time over at MGM, a mule fell back on him—on 'Boom Town'. That was just a freak accident thing, but I'm talking about things he would rig up. For instance, he'd hook a four-up to a wagon, then come down a road and you'd see him bend 'em, he had a way of pulling the king pin which let the horses loose and he'd go with the horses and the wagon would just pick itself up and wrap itself around a tree. The guy somehow had a knack for rigging the thing where he got just the effect he wanted. He'd jump from the stagecoach boot to the first team, then the second team, then go underneath and crawl back up on the coach again. He's a perfectionist when it comes to figuring out a stunt and how to get the maximum out of it. Still, it's safe for everybody involved in it, if they do what he tells them to do."

It's been estimated Canutt's total film work as an actor, stuntman, stunt coordinator, second unit director and director would approach 1,000 entries. Without a doubt, Yakima Canutt was one of the most respected men in the film world. As Charlton Heston once said, "He's simply the best that ever was at what he does best."

Yak was residing at Valley Village in Los Angeles, California, when he died May 24, 1986. He was cremated and his ashes scattered over the Steptoe Butte near his birthplace in Washington. However, there is a marker for him at the Valhalla Cemetery in North Hollywood.

Suggested Sampling of Canutt's Western Heavies:

- Cheyenne Cyclone ('32 Kent) Lane Chandler
- Texas Tornado ('32 Kent) Lane Chandler
- Law and Lawless ('32 Majestic) Jack Hoxie
- Telegraph Trail ('33 Warner Bros.) John Wayne
- Riders of Destiny ('33 Lone Star) John Wayne
- Sagebrush Trail ('33 Lone Star) John Wayne
- Lucky Texan ('34 Lone Star) John Wayne
- Blue Steel ('34 Lone Star) John Wayne
- Randy Rides Alone ('34 Lone Star) John Wayne
- Carrying the Mail ('34 Imperial) Wally Wales
- Pals of the West ('34 Imperial) Wally Wales
- 'Neath the Arizona Skies ('34 Lone Star) John Wayne
- Outlaw Rule ('35 Kent) Reb Russell
- Pals of the Range ('35 Superior) Rex Lease
- Cyclone of the Saddle ('35 Superior) Rex Lease
- Paradise Canyon ('35 Lone Star) John Wayne
- Westward Ho ('35 Republic) John Wayne
- Lawless Range ('35 Republic) John Wayne
- Rough Riding Ranger ('35 Superior) Rex Lease
- Winds of the Wasteland ('36 Republic) John Wayne
- Wildcat Trooper ('36 Ambassador) Kermit Maynard
- Ghost Town Gold ('36 Republic) 3 Mesquiteers
- Riders of the Whistling Skull ('37 Republic) 3 Mesquiteers
- Hit the Saddle ('37 Republic) 3 Mesquiteers
- Gunsmoke Ranch ('37 Republic) 3 Mesquiteers
- Trouble In Texas ('37 Grand National) Tex Ritter
- Heart of the Rockies ('37 Republic) 3 Mesquiteers
- Pioneers of the West ('40 Republic) 3 Mesquiteers
- Prairie Pioneers ('41 Republic) 3 Mesquiteers
- Gauchos of El Dorado ('41 Republic) 3 Mesquiteers
- Pride of the Plains ('44 Republic) Bob Livingston

ANTHONY CARUSO

Solidly built and darkly handsome, Anthony Caruso of Sicilian descent, established a strong reputation playing, at first, hoodlums and mobsters in the '40s, gravitating to western badmen with Roy Rogers' last, "Pals of the Golden West" ('51 Republic). From there on he played dozens of renegade Indians, Mexican banditos and ruthless cutthroats in many A-westerns of the '50s and on dozens of TV episodes.

Caruso's parents were both born in Trabia, Sicily, immigrating to the U.S. Tony was born April 7, 1916, in Frankfort, Indiana, the oldest of six children.

The family moved to Long Beach, California, when Tony was about 10. While he was in Long Beach Poly High he hung around a Long Beach stock company, the Harvey and Ruby Hart Players. The moment he graduated in 1934 he joined the troupe, eventually spending two years with them. During that time he performed in 150 shows.

Following that, Tony studied and performed at the Pasadena Playhouse and then the Federal Theatre in L.A. for a couple of years. He also did several radio shows in this period. Off of this, he landed a showcase henchman role in Tyrone Power's "Johnny Apollo" ('40 20th Century Fox).

Shortly thereafter Caruso met his wife, Tonia Valente, while performing in a play in San Francisco. They were married in 1940. They later had two children.

Alan Ladd became one of Tony's best friends in the business and the star cast him in many of his pictures. Ladd wanted Tony for the part of gunfighter Wilson in "Shane" but Caruso was busy on another picture.

Besides his screen work, Tony spent 16 years serving on the board of directors of the Screen Actors Guild and was Harlequin (president) of the Masquers Club for many years.

Actress Lyn Thomas told us, "He was just a sweetheart. Very charming even though he played these horrible villains. He was so sweet and so gentle, and he was such a gentleman. If you were gettin' ready to get in line to have lunch on location, it was—'Oh, go first, my dear.' That type of thing. He was just a doll. It always amazed me, he appeared so large in the shows but he was not that big a man. You could not help but like Tony."

Caruso died April 4, 2003, at his Brentwood, California, home after a protracted illness.

Whether playing Italians, Sicilians, Mexicans, Indians, Greeks or any other ethnic heavy, Tony Caruso was always believable. "I've dispensed a lot of pain on screen," Caruso used to say. "I've acted in a lot of things for television that I thought were fairly good, but when it comes to theatrical films, I'm most proud of 'Asphalt Jungle'."

Suggested Sampling of Caruso's Western Heavies:

- Pals of the Golden West ('51 Republic) Roy Rogers
- Desert Pursuit ('52 Monogram) Wayne Morris
- Iron Mistress ('52 Warner Bros.) Alan Ladd
- Man Behind the Gun ('53 Warner Bros.) Randolph Scott
- Boy From Oklahoma ('54 Warner Bros) Will Rogers Jr.
- Stories of the Century: Tiburcio Vasquez ('54) Jim Davis
- Lone Ranger: Tell-Tale Bullet ('55) Clayton Moore
- Cattle Queen of Montana ('55 RKO) Ronald Reagan
- Walk the Proud Land ('56 Universal) Audie Murphy
- Big Land ('57 Warner Bros.) Alan Ladd
- Broken Arrow: The Challenge ('57) John Lupton/Michael Ansara
- Gunsmoke: Born to Hang ('57) James Arness
- Tombstone Territory: Mexican Bandido ('58) Pat Conway
- Zorro: Unmasking of Zorro ('58) Guy Williams
- The Badlanders ('58) MGM) Alan Ladd
- Sugarfoot: Extra Hand ('59) Will Hutchins
- Have Gun Will Travel: Long Hunt ('59) Richard Boone
- Bonanza: Paiute War ('59) Lorne Greene/Michael Landon/Pernell Roberts/Dan Blocker
- Deputy: Truly Yours ('60) Henry Fonda/Allen Case
- Gunsmoke: Shooting Stopover ('60) James Arness
- Gunslinger: Appointment in Cascabel ('61) Tony Young
- Have Gun Will Travel: The Revenger ('61) Richard Boone
- Gunsmoke: Cody's Code ('62) James Arness
- Gunsmoke: Quest For Asa Janin ('63) James Arness
- Rawhide: Prairie Fire ('65) Paul Brinnegar
- High Chaparral: The Covey ('68) Henry Darrow
- Gunsmoke: Ring of Darkness ('69) James Arness
- Gunsmoke: Sarah ('72) James Arness
- Gunsmoke: A Family of Killers ('74) James Arness
- Gunsmoke: Larkin ('75) James Arness

JOHN CASON

Tough Texan John Cason came to films at 23 in 1941 after a brief career in the boxing ring.

John Lacey Cason was born July 30, 1918, in Amarillo, Texas. His parents John J. Cason and Frances Johns were both Texas natives, moving to Dallas when John was 15.

At 6 ft. tall, 190 lbs., Cason won a light heavyweight Golden Gloves Tournament in Dallas then turned pro. He fought Tony Musto and won by a TKO. A group of spectators watching this semi-windup took a liking to him and bought his contract. "You could have knocked me over with a feather," John once said, "because when I was introduced to my new owners it was George Raft and Hugh Herbert."

Obviously, through these showbiz connections, Cason obtained an uncredited role as a prizefighter in Abbott and Costello's "Buck Privates" ('41). His first western was the same year, uncredited as a deputy in Don Barry's "Apache Kid".

Cason joined the Marine Corps in '42-'43, returning to film work in '44.

From there on, through 1961, Cason worked steadily in westerns. He practically became a fixture in Buster Crabbe's PRC series.

Besides acting, Cason worked heavily as a stunt double for Bill Williams on "Kit Carson" ('51-'55), Guy Madison on "Wild Bill Hickok" (although Madison had several doubles during the run of the series from '51-'58) and Jack Kelly on "Maverick" ('57-'62).

Perhaps the best description of Cason came from fellow badman Pierce Lyden, "I don't know if his name was John or Bob, but most of us who worked with him called him Bob. I never heard him say which he preferred. He was the kind that didn't care about a thing like that. Having had a somewhat 'speckled' career as a professional fighter, I guess it was only natural he was very good at motion picture fights. Bob never said exactly how many pro or semi-pro fights he had, but once when I asked him he said, 'I won a few and lost too many.' He had the bone in his nose removed, and his ears were a little thick, so he knew his way around the ring. I always liked Bob, he was great to work with. He was always good at everything we did. He was at his best in a part where he had a good fight scene. He told me once, 'It's hard sometimes to pull your punches.' I knew what he meant. There are times with some guys that you'd like to let one go. I never saw Bob lose his temper, but it was common knowledge 'you don't want to be around him when he does,' and I, for one, believed it. There were rumors that he 'mixed it up' once in a while at various watering holes in the Valley, but I never knew him to be in any great trouble."

Cason had worked in over 130 movies and hundreds of TVers when his life was foolishly cut short in a drunken driving auto accident. Jackie Lents Hoofman, the daughter of the man Cason was with on July 7, 1961, explains, "My dad Alton Lents aka Charlie Lents was with John in the auto accident. They were going on a coon hunt. John was driving his black El Camino and they went off the road near Buelton, California, close to Santa Barbara. John was killed instantly and my dad died two days later. Both were drinking when the accident happened. My dad and John were good friends and went on many hunts together. John went with my dad to Ninnekah, Oklahoma, to my grandmother's farm and they went on hunts there. John lived in Sylmar, California, where we also lived. John was a good cook and a fast driver, he came to our home many times. John called Glenn Ford from our house and called him Pappy, he took some friends and I to see Glenn when he was filming 'Pocket Full of Miracles'. John had a brother, Glen, who lived in Hanford, California."

The accident occurred approximately three miles

west of Buelton on county road 101 at about 8pm. Cason's massive injuries included a fractured skull, extensive brain damage, as well as fracturing his cervical vertebrae, pelvis and right arm. Actual death occurred at Cottage Hospital in Santa Barbara.

Cason was known to be a heavy drinker by those who worked with him, as director Oliver Drake related, "It was early in the morning and the crew and cast were preparing for action. The fight was to take place between Sunset Carson and Steve Keyes. Steve plays the heavy in the picture. Then Sunset's flashy Cadillac pulled into the parking area and stopped nearby. Bob Cason, one of the heavies in the picture, and also a fine stuntman, opened the driver's side door and stumbled drunkenly out to open the rear door. Ice and beer cans spewed out from the rear floor of the Cadillac onto the ground. Sunset got out of the passenger's side and walked around the car. He stared at the mess and then at Cason. 'What the hell have you done Bob?' he asked sharply. Guiltily, Bob grinned. 'I thought we'd need some cool drinks,' he mumbled and started to pick up the cans and put them back into the car."

Whatever his personal faults, John (Bob) Cason gave his all on the screen, rewarding us with many exciting fights, chases and menacing moments.

He is buried at Grangeville Cemetery in Amore, California.

Suggested Sampling of Cason's Western Heavies:

- Death Valley Outlaws ('41 Republic) Don Barry
- Spook Town ('44 PRC) Dave O'Brien/James Newill
- Wild Horse Phantom ('44 PRC) Buster Crabbe
- Lightning Raiders ('45 PRC) Buster Crabbe
- His Brother's Ghost ('45 PRC) Buster Crabbe
- Shadows of Death ('45 PRC) Buster Crabbe
- Gangster's Den ('45 PRC) Buster Crabbe
- Stagecoach Outlaws ('45 PRC) Buster Crabbe
- Flaming Bullets ('45 PRC) Tex Ritter/Dave O'Brien
- Ambush Trail ('46 PRC) Bob Steele
- Ghost of Hidden Valley ('46 PRC) Buster Crabbe
- Overland Riders ('46 PRC) Buster Crabbe
- Outlaws of the Plains ('46 PRC) Buster Crabbe
- Last Round-Up ('47 Columbia) Gene Autry
- Lone Hand Texan ('47 Columbia) Charles Starrett
- Six Gun Law ('48 Columbia) Charles Starrett
- Sunset Carson Rides Again ('48 Yucca) Sunset Carson
- Dead Man's Gold ('48 Western Adventure) Lash LaRue
- Mark of the Lash ('48 Western Adventure) Lash LaRue
- Big Sombrero ('49 Columbia) Gene Autry
- Rimfire ('49 Lippert) James Millican
- Red Desert ('49 Lippert) Don Barry
- Range Land ('49 Monogram) Whip Wilson
- Lone Ranger: War Horse ('49) Clayton Moore

John Cason (right) and Kermit Maynard (left) think they have the best of Buster Crabbe, but things will soon change because he's "Fighting Bill Carson" ('45 PRC).

- West of the Brazos ('50 Lippert) James Ellison/Russell Hayden
- Colorado Ranger ('50 Lippert) James Ellison/Russell Hayden
- Redwood Forest Trail ('50 Republic) Rex Allen
- Wyoming Mail ('50 Universal-International) Stephen McNally
- Rustlers On Horseback ('50 Republic) Allan "Rocky" Lane
- Gene Autry: Devil's Brand ('50) Gene Autry
- Lone Ranger: Desert Adventure ('50) Clayton Moore
- Range Rider: Ten Thousand Reward ('51) Jock Mahoney
- Kit Carson: Fury at Red Gulch ('51) Bill Williams
- Prairie Roundup ('51 Columbia) Charles Starrett
- Fort Savage Raiders ('51 Columbia) Charles Starrett
- Don Daredevil Rides Again ('51 Republic serial) Ken Curtis
- Cisco Kid: Jewelry Holdup ('52) Duncan Renaldo
- Wild Bill Hickok: Photographer Story ('52) Guy Madison
- Sky King: Deadly Cargo ('52) Kirby Grant
- Kit Carson: Roaring Challenge ('52) Bill Williams
- Hopalong Cassidy: Ghost Trails ('52) William Boyd
- Cowboy G-Men: Frontier Smugglers ('52) Russell Hayden
- Black Lash ('52 Western Adventure) Lash LaRue
- Black Hills Ambush ('52 Republic) Allan "Rocky" Lane
- Kid From Broken Gun ('52 Columbia) Charles Starrett
- Wagon Team ('52) Columbia) Gene Autry
- Cowboy G-Men: Empty Mailbags ('53) Russell Hayden
- Roy Rogers: Gun Trouble ('53) Roy Rogers
- Savage Frontier ('53 Republic) Allan "Rocky" Lane
- Gun Fury ('53 Columbia) Rock Hudson
- Red River Shore ('53 Republic) Rex Allen
- Annie Oakley: Valley of the Shadows ('54) Gail Davis
- Lone Ranger: Ex-Marshal ('54) Clayton Moore
- Roy Rogers: Last of the Larabee Kid ('54) Roy Rogers
- Rin Tin Tin: Education of Corporal Rusty ('54) Lee Aaker
- Wild Bill Hickok: Sundown Valley ('55) Guy Madison
- Lone Ranger: Tell-Tale Bullet ('55) Clayton Moore
- Tales of the Texas Rangers: Rough, Tough West ('55) Willard Parker
- Judge Roy Bean: Deliver the Body ('56) Edgar Buchanan
- Champion: Rails West ('56) Jim Bannon
- Roy Rogers: Empty Saddles ('56) Roy Rogers
- Wyatt Earp: Wyatt Meets Doc Holiday ('57) Hugh O'Brian
- Hard Man ('57 Columbia) Guy Madison
- Rough Riders: Counterfeiters ('58) Jan Merlin/Kent Taylor
- Snowfire ('58 Allied Artists) Don Megowan
- Deputy: The Border Between ('60) Allen Case
- Sugarfoot: Angel ('61) Will Hutchins

ED CASSIDY

The Sheriff. The Marshal. The Ranger Captain. While a huge amount of Ed Cassidy's over 250 screen roles were on the right side of the law wearing a badge of some sort—or as a rancher/father, doc, mayor, banker—he was not adverse to being one of the dirty, underhanded polecats. Most of his shifty roles came early in his screen career, once he became typecast as a star packer he couldn't seem to get away from the role.

Brown haired, brown eyed Edward Bottemley Cassidy was born March 21, 1893, in Chicago, Illinois. His father was Edward Cassidy and his mother was Maryann Mackeown, both from Ireland.

Following graduation from prestigious McGill University in Montreal, Canada, with a degree in optometry, his eyes were directed toward a career on the stage. Sometime prior to 1920, Cassidy was married; his wife's name was Pearl, noted as a vaudeville actress in the 1920 census. In 1920 Ed was working in vaudeville in Chicago, but by 1930 was doing theatrical work in San Antonio, Texas. Stage work eventually led to Hollywood at age 39 and a 25 year film career. His last role was as Theodore Roosevelt, to whom he bore a resemblance, in "The First Traveling Saleslady" in 1956. He'd played Roosevelt twice before—in "Sun Valley Cyclone" ('46) and "Take Me Out to the Ballgame" ('49).

As was the case with most western character players, Cassidy had numerous roles in serials—over 24 of them—with his best parts coming in "Flaming Frontiers" ('38 Universal) as a henchman, "Deadwood Dick" ('40 Columbia) revealed to be the mysterious Skull, "Son of Zorro" ('47 Republic) playing against type as a crooked Sheriff, and in "Superman" ('48 Columbia) as Clark Kent's Earth father.

Cassidy was married to Dorothy B. McIntosh. They were living at 23041 Friar St. in Woodland Hills, California, when he died of heart failure January 19, 1968, at Hollywood Community Hospital. He'd been under treatment for heart problems since 1953, which was the basic year he left films. He only worked a couple of small jobs after that. Sheriff Cassidy was cremated at Chapel of the Pines in Los Angeles.

Suggested Sampling of Cassidy's Western Heavies:

- Courageous Avenger ('35 Supreme) Johnny Mack Brown
- Sundown Saunders ('36 Supreme) Bob Steele
- Hair Trigger Casey ('36 Atlantic) Jack Perrin
- Feud of the West ('36 Diversion) Hoot Gibson
- Santa Fe Bound ('36 Reliable) Tom Tyler
- Cavalry ('36 Republic) Bob Steele
- Vengeance of Rannah ('36 Reliable) Bob Custer
- Cheyenne Rides Again ('37 Victory) Tom Tyler
- Singing Buckaroo ('37 Spectrum) Fred Scott
- Silver Trail ('37 Reliable) Rex Lease
- Fighting Texan ('37 Ambassador) Kermit Maynard
- Red Rope ('37 Republic) Bob Steele
- Boothill Brigade ('37 Republic) Johnny Mack Brown
- Boots of Destiny ('37 Grand National) Ken Maynard
- Flaming Frontiers ('38 Universal serial) Johnny Mack Brown
- In Early Arizona ('38 Columbia) Bill Elliott
- Man From Music Mountain ('38 Republic) Gene Autry
- Silver On the Sage ('39 Paramount) William Boyd
- Deadwood Dick ('40 Columbia serial) Don Douglas
- Winners of the West ('40 Universal serial) Dick Foran
- Bullets and Saddles ('43 Monogram) Range Busters
- Tucson Raiders ('44) Bill Elliott
- Three In the Saddle ('45 PRC) Tex Ritter/Dave O'Brien
- Roaring Rangers ('46 Columbia) Charles Starrett
- Son of Zorro ('47 Republic serial) George Turner

LANE CHANDLER

Lane Chandler was unique among western actors. He never really became typecast and was able to mix starring roles in early B-westerns with character roles as the brother, assistant mountie, hero's friend, sheriff, cavalryman etc. right along with villainous roles. If you don't think of Chandler as a heavy, watch how effective he can be in Bill Elliott's "Taming of the West" or Bob Livingston's "Wild Horse Rustlers". For over 40 years from 1927 to 1971, the rugged, husky-voiced Chandler made his presence well known in over 300 films and some 60 or more TVers.

Robert Chandler Oakes was born in Walsh County, North Dakota, on June 4, 1899. His parents George W. Chandler and Irene Oakes soon moved to Montana where Robert spent his boyhood riding the range near Culbertson on his father's horse ranch which extended almost to the Canadian border.

He graduated from high school in Helena, Montana, then attended Wesleyan College studying commercial law and accounting for which he quickly found himself unsuited. The strapping 6' 4" young man did find time to play football for Wesleyan who won the state championship in 1921.

After two years of college, he yearned for outdoor life, finding a job driving a tour bus at Yellowstone Park. When Yellowstone shuttered for the winter, he made his way to Los Angeles and found employment driving a bus between Riverside and L.A. Within six months he was driving a gas truck out of Santa Monica for Standard Oil. The job took him to the Douglas Fairbanks-Mary Pickford lot where he became intrigued with movie work.

He found work as an extra in "Dorothy Vernon of Haddon Hall" ('24). Broke and not finding more extra work, he returned to Yellowstone in the Spring. The next winter found him back in Hollywood seeking extra work which he found in a few productions including "The Winning of Barbara Worth" ('26 Paramount).

Paramount saw star possibilities in the Gary Cooperish lad, screen tested him and signed him for the lead in "Open Range" ('27), based on a Zane Grey story. It was at this time he became Lane Chandler. Several more films followed at Paramount in '28 and '29 before he was dropped by the studio due to an overabundance of leading men.

With the coming of sound, Chandler found leads in poverty row westerns for Big 4 and Kent and starred in Universal's "Lightning Express" serial. Along with leads, he was playing supporting roles in westerns and

Rod Cameron teaches Lane Chandler the ways of the "Trigger Trail" ('44 Universal).

serials starring Bob Custer, Harry Carey, Johnny Mack Brown, John Wayne, Jack Hoxie, Tom Tyler, Jack Perrin and others.

By 1936 his starring days were over with two Z-grade "Phantom Rider" epics released by Empire. Lane now concentrated solely on character roles for the rest of his lengthy screen career.

Over the years Lane was seen in over a dozen serials, but the one that stands out is his role as one of the Lone Ranger suspects in Republic's classic "Lone Ranger" serial in 1938. Director William Witney termed Chandler "a very quiet man, a good horseman."

A favorite of Cecil B. DeMille, Chandler worked in ten of the director's epics.

Although parts became harder to come by in the late '50s and '60s, Lane continued with smaller character roles in "Apache Ambush" ('55), "Tall Man Riding" ('55), "Lone Ranger" ('56), "Noose For A Gunman" ('60), "Requiem For a Gunfighter" ('61) and on TV in "Gunsmoke", "Rawhide", "Wagon Train", "Maverick", "Sugarfoot", "Wyatt Earp", "Have Gun Will Travel" and others. He closed out his career with a bit in "One More Train to Rob" in '71.

An astute businessman with industrial and property holdings, Lane Chandler died in Los Angeles at 73 on September 14, 1972, of cardio-vascular disease.

Suggested Sampling of Chandler's' Western Heavies:

- War of the Range ('33 Monarch) Tom Tyler
- Sagebrush Trail ('33 Lone Star) John Wayne
- North of Arizona ('35 Reliable) Jack Perrin
- Two Gun Justice ('38 Monogram) Tim McCoy
- Taming of the West ('39 Columbia) Bill Elliott
- Pioneers of the West ('40 Republic) 3 Mesquiteers
- Last of the Duanes ('41 20th Century Fox) George Montgomery
- Sundown Jim ('42 20th Century Fox) John Kimbrough
- Law of the Saddle ('43 PRC) Bob Livingston
- Wild Horse Rustlers ('43 PRC) Bob Livingston
- Tenting Tonight On the Old Campground ('43 Universal) Johnny Mack Brown
- Trigger Trail ('44 Universal) Rod Cameron
- Riders of the Santa Fe ('44 Universal) Rod Cameron
- Rustler's Hideout ('44 PRC) Buster Crabbe
- Terror Trail ('46 Columbia) Charles Starrett
- Two Fisted Stranger ('46 Columbia) Charles Starrett
- Gunning For Vengeance ('46 Columbia) Charles Starrett
- Prairie Roundup ('51 Columbia) Charles Starrett
- Thunder Over the Plains ('53 Warner Bros.) Randolph Scott

ALDEN (STEPHEN) CHASE

Westerns were not the only type film in which Alden (Stephen) Chase appeared, actually only about a third of the roughly 90 movies he worked in were out on the range. He did also appear in many '50s TV westerns.

Alden Stephen Chase was born April 11, 1902, in Huntington, Long Island, New York. His parents were Arthur E. and Nellie Chase from New York and Vermont respectively. His father was superintendent of public schools for the borough of Fort Lee in New Jersey. The 1930 census reveals Alden, now 28, was first married at 19, although he was then living with his parents in the Bronx doing theatre work in New York.

Although he kept a low profile over the years, it's obvious he had stage experience before he entered films in 1933 with an uncredited role in "Chance at Heaven" with Joel McCrea.

Chase quickly fell into character roles, essaying professors, foremen, detectives, military men, sheriffs, doctors and other professional people.

He first came to westerns in '34 with Tim McCoy's "Prescott Kid" at Columbia. He continued to return frequently to westerns right up until his last film, "Glory Guys" in '65.

Some sort of military service is indicated by his seven year lack of films from '42-'48. This is the point at which he revised his name. Pre-war films he is Alden Chase, post war he is Stephen Chase.

Chase died April 1, 1982, in Santa Monica, California. No other details are known.

Allan "Rocky" Lane runs over Stephen Chase like an "El Paso Stampede" ('53 Republic).

Suggested Sampling of Chase's Western Heavies:

- Cowboy Millionaire ('35 Fox) George O'Brien
- Rogue of the Range ('36 Supreme) Johnny Mack Brown
- Heart of Arizona ('38 Paramount) William Boyd
- Frontier Scout ('38 Grand National) George Houston
- Six Gun Trail ('38 Victory) Tim McCoy
- Code of the Cactus ('39 Victory) Tim McCoy
- Gun Code ('40 PRC) Tim McCoy
- Lone Rider in Ghost Town ('41 PRC) George Houston
- Daring Caballero ('49 United Artists) Duncan Renaldo
- Cisco Kid: Boomerang ('50) Duncan Renaldo
- Frisco Tornado ('50 Republic) Allan "Rocky" Lane
- Lone Ranger: The Outcast ('51) Clayton Moore
- Cisco Kid: Ride On ('51) Duncan Renaldo
- Roy Rogers: Desert Fugitive ('52 Roy Rogers
- Sky King: Stagecoach Robbers ('52) Kirby Grant
- Lone Ranger: Sinner by Proxy ('53) John Hart
- El Paso Stampede ('53 Republic) Allan "Rocky" Lane

GEORGE CHESEBRO

For 39 years in over 400 features and some 33 serials, the lean, nasty, sneering, snarling presence of George Chesebro menaced cowboy stars from silent days on through the demise of the B-westerns in 1954. Chesebro's hatchet-faced badmen knew no boundaries, they were at every studio—Columbia, Republic, Universal, Monogram, PRC down to the lowliest independents.

The 6 ft. 160 lb. Chesebro plied his vile plots in as many as 26 films a year in the '30s, averaging 15-20 per year through the '40s. There is hardly a western star you can name that didn't feel the wrath of George Chesebro in the talkies from '31-'54.

Born July 29, 1888, in Minneapolis, Minnesota, his father, James Chesebro, was from Connecticut and his mother, Margaret Grant, was a native of Kentucky.

George Newell Chesebro started his acting career in a local stock company in 1907. Vaudeville was next, touring the Orient and singing with a musical comedy group from 1911-1913. He continued to perform in vaudeville and stock upon his return to the U. S. in 1913 until coming to Hollywood in 1915 and finding work in an Essanay two-reeler, "Money To Burn," and a feature titled "Mignon". Within a year he had the lead in a Dudley-Unity independent western, "The Land Just Over Yonder".

For the next few years he played male leads opposite popular female performers—Olive Thomas (in "Broadway, Arizona" '17); Texas Guinan (in "Girl of Hell's Agony" '18 and "She Wolf " '19); Ruth Roland ("Hands Up" serial '18).

During the making of "Hands Up" for Astra, George entered the U.S. Army for service in WWI and was replaced for the remainder of the production by George Larkin.

Upon his discharge, he continued as a leading man in serials opposite Eileen Sedgwick in "Diamond Queen" ('21), Juanita Hansen in "Lost City" ('20) and Grace Darmond in "Hope Diamond Mystery" ('21).

In 1921-'22 Chesebro began an association with actor/director/producer Milburn Morante which resulted in George starring in a series of six independent Northwest Mounted Police dramas ("Hate Trail", "The Recoil", etc.). "Wolf Blood" ('25) (which survives on video today) was George's last starring vehicle, a logging camp story which he also helped direct.

Shifting to villainous character roles, Chesebro imperiled silent stars Art Acord, Neal Hart and Bob Curwood, thereby setting the pattern for the rest of his career, rustling cattle, bushwhacking sheriffs, manhandling ladies and plotting all manner of land grabs.

Even after all the badmen he'd played, some of his best roles were afforded to him in those late '40s Durango Kids at Columbia. Don't miss "Riders of the Lone Star" ('47) in which he plays a destitute old outlaw protecting his young son from the truth about his past.

George was *so* associated with loathsome villains that in Roy Rogers' "Trail of Robin Hood" ('50) perhaps the biggest "inside" joke in B-westerns occurred. As Roy rounds up all his B-western star-friends to help get the wagonloads of Christmas trees to market, up rides George, willing to help, extending his hand in friendship, but Tom Keene, Rocky Lane, Tom Tyler and the others give him the cold shoulder. Young Carol Nugent exclaims, "I know you! You're always the meanie!" After George explains he's reformed, Roy and the other cowboy heroes warmly welcome Chesebro into their group. An engaging moment unlike no other in B-western history, and one devout B-western devotees still remember fondly today.

Chesebro capped a 39 year film career with an unbilled part in "Boy From Oklahoma" with Will Rogers Jr. in 1954.

The end of his screen skull-duggery came on May 28, 1959, at 70, when the beloved George Chesebro died at his home (1929 Manhattan Ave. in Hermosa Beach, California) from decompensated left heart failure brought on by hypertension and arteriosclerosis.

Chesebro had suffered from the latter problems 20 years. He was survived by his wife, Sophie G. Chesebro, a stepdaughter and stepson. His remains were cremated and are located at Pacific Coast Cemetery in Redondo Beach, California.

George once remarked, "The picture business is where a guy, who you think is your friend, will stick a knife in your back and then he'll call the police and they'll arrest you for having a concealed weapon."

Chesebro's fellow screen owlhoot, Pierce Lyden, observed, "George Chesebro, with that voice that commanded attention, was always good to work with—and happy to be around—like the time an assistant director said to a group of us one morning, 'What a rotten, no good, tough looking bunch of outlaws.' And George says, 'You ain't seen no outlaws, buddy, until you've seen my in-laws.'"

Suggested Sampling of Chesebro's Western Heavies:

- Rustler's Ranch ('26 Universal) Art Acord
- Mark of the Spur ('32 Big 4) Bob Custer
- Fighting Champ ('32 Monogram) Bob Steele
- Boss Cowboy ('34 Superior) Buddy Roosevelt
- Whirlwind Rider ('34 American) Buffalo Bill Jr.
- Border Guns ('34 Aywon) Bill Cody
- Rawhide Mail ('34 Reliable) Jack Perrin
- Coyote Trails ('35 Reliable) Tom Tyler
- Wolf Riders ('35 Reliable) Jack Perrin
- Defying the Law ('35 American) Ted Wells
- Pals of the Range ('35 Superior) Rex Lease
- Cyclone of the Saddle ('35 Superior) Rex Lease
- Miracle Rider ('35 Mascot serial) Tom Mix
- Silver Bullet ('35 Reliable) Tom Tyler
- Laramie Kid ('35 Reliable) Tom Tyler
- Tumbling Tumbleweeds ('35 Republic) Gene Autry
- Custer's Last Stand ('36 Stage & Screen serial) Rex Lease
- Red River Valley ('36 Republic) Gene Autry
- Pinto Rustlers ('36 Reliable) Tom Tyler
- Vengeance of Rannah ('36 Reliable) Bob Custer
- Roaming Cowboy ('37 Spectrum) Fred Scott
- Westbound Mail ('37 Columbia) Charles Starrett
- Roarin' Lead ('37 Republic) 3 Mesquiteers
- Hills of Old Wyoming ('37 Paramount) William Boyd
- Devil's Saddle Legion ('37 Warner Bros.) Dick Foran
- Springtime In the Rockies ('37 Republic) Gene Autry
- Purple Vigilantes ('38 Republic) 3 Mesquiteers
- Rio Grande ('38 Columbia) Charles Starrett
- Pioneer Days ('40 Monogram) Jack Randall
- Cheyenne Kid ('40 Monogram) Jack Randall
- Pinto Canyon ('40 Metropolitan) Bob Steele
- Land of the Six Guns ('40 Monogram) Jack Randall
- Gun Code ('40 PRC) Tim McCoy
- White Eagle ('41 Columbia serial) Buck Jones
- Pals of the Pecos ('41 Republic) 3 Mesquiteers
- Wrangler's Roost ('41 Monogram) Range Busters
- Lone Rider Ambushed ('41 PRC) George Houston
- The Pioneers ('41 Monogram) Tex Ritter
- Roaring Frontiers ('41 Columbia) Bill Elliott/Tex Ritter
- Thunder River Feud ('42 Monogram) Range Busters
- Jesse James Jr. ('42 Republic) Don Barry
- Rolling Down the Great Divide ('42 PRC) Lee Powell/Art Davis/Bill Boyd
- Perils of the Royal Mounted ('42 Columbia serial) Robert Stevens
- Two Fisted Justice ('42 Monogram) Range Busters
- Fugitive of the Plains ('43 PRC) Buster Crabbe
- Death Rides the Plains ('43 PRC) Bob Livingston
- Black Market Rustlers ('43 Monogram) Range Busters
- Devil Riders ('43 PRC) Buster Crabbe
- Marshal of Gunsmoke ('44 Universal) Tex Ritter
- Arizona Whirlwind ('44 Monogram) Trail Blazers
- Rough Ridin' Justice ('45 Columbia) Charles Starrett
- Gangster's Den ('45 PRC) Buster Crabbe
- Lawless Empire ('45 Columbia) Charles Starrett
- Texas Panhandle ('45 Columbia) Charles Starrett
- Wagon Wheels Westward ('45 Republic) Bill Elliott
- Gunning For Vengeance ('46 Columbia) Charles Starrett
- Terrors on Horseback ('46 PRC) Buster Crabbe
- Stagecoach To Denver ('46 Republic) Allan Lane
- South of the Chisholm Trail ('47 Columbia) Charles Starrett
- Over the Santa Fe Trail ('47 Columbia) Ken Curtis
- Vigilantes of Boomtown ('47 Republic) Allan Lane
- Riders of the Lone Star ('47 Columbia) Charles Starrett
- Stage To Mesa City ('47 PRC) Lash LaRue
- Return of the Lash ('47 PRC) Lash LaRue
- Shadow Valley ('47 PRC) Eddie Dean
- Cheyenne Takes Over ('47 PRC) Lash LaRue
- Fighting Vigilantes ('47 PRC) Lash LaRue
- Check Your Guns ('48 PRC) Eddie Dean
- Trail to Laredo ('48 Columbia) Charles Starrett
- Desert Vigilante ('49 Columbia) Charles Starrett
- Last Bandit ('49 Republic) Bill Elliott
- Gunslingers ('50 Monogram) Whip Wilson
- Streets of Ghost Town ('50 Columbia) Charles Starrett
- Kid From Amarillo ('51 Columbia) Charles Starrett

STEVE CLARK

Steve Clark's 20 year Hollywood career, almost exclusively in westerns from 1933-1953, generally found him as the heroine's kindly father, local banker, ranch owner or sheriff. Those portrayals were a good match for Clark who possessed a mild voice and older-gentleman screen presence. He was often killed off within the first five minutes of the show.

His badman roles were limited to earlier in his screen career as he didn't arrive in pictures til he was 42. Still, he managed to amass nearly 300 film and some 30 TV credits.

Prior to 1933 he had been a stage actor, director and manager since 1909.

Elmer Stephen Clark was born February 26, 1891, on a farm just outside Washington, Indiana (Daviess County). His parents were Wesley Richard Clark and Nancy Eloise Cross.

Clark was educated at the University of Oklahoma, then went East as an actor and director in stock companies for over 20 years. Eventually, Steve gravitated to the film capital.

For some period of time in the '40s, Clark owned and operated a movie theatre in Hollywood which specialized in westerns and fast action pictures, the kind he himself worked in. By the late '40s and on TV in the '50s, Clark was no longer playing badmen, most of his roles now were that of the elderly rancher or sheriff. On TV from '49-'54 he worked primarily on "The Lone Ranger", "Range Rider" and "Cisco Kid" programs.

His last film was at Republic, "El Paso Stampede" in '53 with Allan "Rocky" Lane.

The benevolent white-haired "Pop" of westerns, Steve Clark died June 29, 1954, in Van Nuys, California. He's laid to rest in Valhalla Memorial Park in North Hollywood. He was married at the time to a lady named Ruth.

Johnny Mack Brown hogties badman Steve Clark without using his "Trigger Fingers" ('46 Monogram).

Suggested Sampling of Clark's Western Heavies:

- Prescott Kid ('34 Columbia) Tim McCoy
- No Man's Range ('35 Supreme) Bob Steele
- Rider of the Law ('35 Supreme) Bob Steele
- Where Trails Divide ('37 Monogram) Tom Keene
- Courage of the West ('37 Universal) Bob Baker
- Pinto Canyon ('40 Metropolitan) Bob Steele
- Roll, Wagons, Roll ('39 Monogram) Tex Ritter
- Land of the Six Guns ('40 Monogram) Jack Randall
- Beyond the Sacramento ('40 Columbia) Bill Elliott
- North From the Lone Star ('41 Columbia) Bill Elliott
- Arizona Stagecoach ('42 Monogram) Range Busters
- Lone Prairie ('42 Columbia) Russell Hayden
- Bullets and Saddles ('43 Monogram) Range Busters
- Cattle Stampede ('43 PRC) Buster Crabbe
- Valley of Vengeance ('44 PRC) Buster Crabbe
- Law of the Valley ('44 Monogram) Johnny Mack Brown
- Border Badmen ('45 PRC) Buster Crabbe
- Under Arizona Skies ('46 Monogram) Johnny Mack Brown
- Trigger Fingers ('46 Monogram) Johnny Mack Brown
- Six Gun Serenade ('47 Monogram) Jimmy Wakely
- Crossed Trails ('48 Monogram) Johnny Mack Brown
- Cowboy Cavalier ('48 Monogram) Jimmy Wakely
- Cisco Kid: Newspaper Crusaders ('50) Duncan Renaldo

JOHN CLIFF

"With a kisser like mine," John Cliff used to joke, "what else could I be but a heavy?"

Jack Clifford was born on a minstrel show on November 26, 1918, in Swainsboro, Georgia. His father owned Clifford's Carolina Minstrels. Later his father had a booth called the Grease Store where he sold hotdogs and hamburgers in the Tom Mix Circus, the Hildebrand Circus and various state fairs and rodeos. John handled the soda pop and beer concession for his father.

John's dad also had a stable of prize fighters, so John started at one time to be a fighter. However, before he got going he had a double hernia and the doctors told him to lay off for a year.

John decided to leave carnival life when his father and brother realized the old days were coming to an end and leased out their carnival.

Relocating in California, John started working labor at the movie studios.

Falling in love with aviation, he learned to fly and got a commercial instructor's license. With very little money he bought out a small company and ended up with five airplanes, fully intending to go into the flight instruction business. His timing couldn't have been worse. Within a few weeks it was December 7, 1941, and all private planes were grounded.

John joined the service and spent his time "flying the hump"—the Himalayas.

Coming out of the service a Captain, he wanted to fly commercial airlines but was not qualified due to no college degree—even with all his experience.

1949. John decided to get an agent and try for a career in the movies. Luckily, he signed with a respected agent, Mitch Hamilburg, and his perennial scowl found work on "The Lone Ranger", "Range Rider", "Rin Tin Tin", "Cisco Kid", "My Friend Flicka" and other TVers right away—naturally, as a heavy.

John also was cast in small roles with "Abbott and Costello In the Foreign Legion" ('50) and Gene Autry's "Beyond the Purple Hills" ('50), among others. In 1951 his fledgling career was interrupted by Korea. He'd remained in the reserves and "got sucked into Korea."

Returning in 1953, John lost no time getting back to film work.

Becoming established, the parts got better in westerns with Tim Holt, Dale Robertson, John Payne, Scott Brady and others, as well as on TV's "Cheyenne", "Superman", "Perry Mason", "Wyatt Earp", "Maverick", "Twilight Zone" and dozens more.

"If you're a heavy by nature, I mean the way you deliver," John told interviewers Tom and Jim Goldrup for their FEATURE PLAYERS Vol. 2, "You're a natural heavy. So many people try to lay it on. Give me a guy that can smile at you and cut your throat, you got a heavy."

Retiring from acting after a bit in a 1972 "Kung Fu", John relocated to northern California and went into real estate. Retiring from real estate in 1986, he spent his time traveling and golfing. He was honored at western film festivals in Sonora, California, and Charlotte, North Carolina, in his later years.

A very warm-hearted heavy died at 82 of cancer (which he'd battled hard for 3 years) May 12, 2001, in Hayward, California.

Suggested Sampling of Cliff's Western Heavies:

- Lone Ranger: The Squire ('50) Clayton Moore
- Lone Ranger: Two Gold Lockets ('51) Clayton Moore
- Lone Ranger: Pardon For Curley ('51) Clayton Moore
- Range Rider: Harsh Reckoning ('51) Jock Mahoney
- Law of the Badlands ('51 RKO) Tim Holt
- Best of the Badmen ('51 RKO) Robert Ryan
- Lone Ranger: Triple Cross ('53) John Hart
- Lone Ranger: Woman From Omaha ('53) John Hart
- Jesse James Vs. the Daltons ('54 Columbia) Brett King
- Lone Ranger: Dan Reid's Sacrifice ('55) Clayton Moore
- Rin Tin Tin: Burial Ground ('55) Lee Aaker
- Cisco Kid: Strangers ('56) Duncan Renaldo
- Fury: Stolen Fury ('56) Peter Graves
- Champion: Badmen of the Valley ('56) Jim Bannon
- Cheyenne: Rendezvous at Red Rock ('56) Clint Walker
- Lone Ranger: Counterfeit Mask ('56) Clayton Moore
- Lone Ranger: Code of Honor ('57) Clayton Moore
- Jim Bowie: Bayou Tontine ('57) Scott Forbes
- Cheyenne: Incident at Indian Springs ('57) Clint Walker
- Colt .45: Final Payment ('57) Wayde Preston
- Rin Tin Tin: The Hunted ('57) Lee Aaker
- Gunsmoke In Tucson ('58 Allied Artists) Mark Stevens
- Colt .45: Blood Money ('58) Wayde Preston
- Maverick: Day They Hanged Bret Maverick ('58) James Garner
- Texan: A Tree For Planting ('58) Rory Calhoun
- Wanted Dead or Alive: Drop to Drink ('58) Steve McQueen
- Northwest Passage: Ambush ('59) Keith Larsen
- Bat Masterson: Incident in Leadville ('59) Gene Barry
- Oklahoma Territory ('60 United Artists) Bill Williams
- Lawman: Man From New York ('61) John Russell
- Whispering Smith: Stakeout ('61) Audie Murphy
- Cheyenne: Brahma Bull ('61) Clint Walker
- Tales of Wells Fargo: Trackback ('61) Dale Robertson
- Temple Houston: Siege at Thayer's Bluff ('63) Jeffrey Hunter
- Guns of Will Sonnett: Stopover in a Troubled Town ('68) Walter Brennan
- Virginian: Image of an Outlaw ('68) James Drury

EDMUND COBB

Grim, tight-lipped, droopy-eyed, pudgy and sullen, 6' 1", 170 lb. Edmund Cobb would sometimes be only one of many henchmen at the bottom of the cast, other times he was one of the primary heavies. Earlier, on the silent screen, Cobb starred from '24 to '29 in a popular series of two-reel "Mustang" westerns produced by Universal.

It's doubtful Cobb ever worried about collecting unemployment benefits in a Hollywood career that spanned 56 years from 1912-1966. Counting silents, serials, shorts and TV episodes, it's estimated Cobb was on screen over 550 times in his life.

Edmund Fessenden Cobb was born June 23, 1892, in Albuquerque, New Mexico, to William Henry Cobb (originally from New York) and his wife, Edwinna (Eddie) Ross (originally from Kansas). Edmund F. Cobb's grandfather, Edmund Gibson Ross, served as Governor of the Territory of New Mexico (1885-1889) and was a one-term senator from Kansas (1866-1871), who many contend cast the pivotal vote for acquittal in the impeachment trial of President Andrew Johnson in May, 1868.

Cobb's parents operated Cobb Photography Studio in Albuquerque. Edmund Cobb's siblings, Susan Ross Cobb (1894-1987), Daphne M. Cobb (1898-1928) and Wilfred B. Cobb (1901-1982) remained in Albuquerque, but several Ross cousins resided in California. May Ross, first cousin of Edmund F. Cobb's mother, was married to Meredith Pinxton Snyder (1859-1937), the first Mayor of Los Angeles to be elected to the office four times, his first term beginning in 1897 and his last term ending in 1921.

Young Ed was being prepped by his grandfather for a life in politics, however, he died when Ed was 15. It was at this time Ed got the acting bug with an Albuquerque stock company. After Ed had appeared in several plays for a few years, the St. Louis Motion Picture Company came to New Mexico in 1910 to make a picture (the title of which is lost to the ages) and Ed, who had learned to ride well on his grandfather's ranch, obtained a part in the film.

Over the next couple of years Cobb worked in other films shot in the area, including some for the Romaine Fielding Company in Las Vegas, New Mexico. The only documented Cobb appearance from this era is "A Pueblo Legend" (1912 Biograph) directed by D. W. Griffith and filmed at Isleta Pueblo near Albuquerque.

Cobb first came to California in 1913 to work for Selig in their first serial, "The Adventures of Kathlyn" starring Kathlyn Williams.

In 1914 Cobb married Helen M. Hayes, who was born in 1893 in Tennessee. They had one daughter, Eddie Marie Cobb, who was born in Illinois in 1915 while Cobb was working for the Essanay Company in Chicago in some 35 productions from 1915-1916.

According to a 1920 census, Ed and Helen were living and working as actor and actress in Denver, Colorado. However, their daughter was living with Helen's parents in North Chattanooga, Tennessee.

By the early '20s Cobb was alternating supporting roles with leads in two-reelers.

In 1923 and '24 Ed and Helen worked together in at least two westerns, "Riders of the Range" (Truart) and "A Rodeo Mixup" (Arrow). Also in 1924 Cobb co-starred with Neva Gerber in Arrow's 15 chapter serial "Days of '49".

In 1925 Cobb signed with Universal to star in their two-reel Mustang series along with Fred Gilman, Fred Humes and Ted Wells. One of the first of Cobb's was "The Bashful Whirlwind".

Edmund and Helen divorced around 1925-'27. Helen remarried but died of tuberculosis in 1932. Ed remarried to Vivian Marie Winter who was born in Wisconsin January 16, 1894.

When Ed's Mustang series ended in 1927, he was cast by Universal in several features and then, in 1928, in the Forest Ranger two-reeler series through 1929. He also continued to make serials and co-star with youngsters such as Newton House, Bobby Nelson and Buzz Barton.

As the silent days faded away and talkies were born in 1930, so too did Edmund Cobb's starring days—save for one cheaply made independent, "Racketeer Round-Up" ('34 Aywon) which was reissued a year later by Beaumont with some new footage as "Gunners and Guns". One could also say he "starred" in "Arizona Badman" in 1935 as his role, footage and acting far out shined the real star, Reb Russell. There was also "Rawhide Terror", a Victor Adamson (aka Denver Dixon) cheapie in 1934 which was originally intended to be a serial but was eventually released—or escaped—as a feature starring both Cobb and Art Mix. But none of these did anything to place Cobb at the head of the cast in major B-westerns, so he confidently resigned himself to support roles of all types on through the '60s…mainly as a heavy, but also appearing as sheriffs, fathers, ranchers and townsmen.

As for serials, over the years Cobb appeared in 69. For Essanay there was "The Strange Case of Mary Page", a 1916 15-chapter Henry B. Walthall serial. "Days of '49", in which he was the hero saving Neva Gerber, was released in 1924 by Arrow and "Fighting with Buffalo Bill" came along in '26 from Universal. Cobb was the gallant plainsman aiding Wallace MacDonald for 10 chapters. These were followed by "A Final Reckoning" ('28 Universal) which saw Cobb as a heavy opposing Newton House for 12 chapters and "Scarlet Arrow" ('28 Universal) starring Francis X. Bushman Jr. Cobb played a friend to Tim McCoy in Universal's bridge-over release between silent and sound serials (being released in both versions), "Indians Are Coming" ('30). Cobb continued as a featured player in serials throughout the '30s, '40s and '50s, playing every type of role written—but specializing in heavies. In most of his serials he was only assigned a surname, which gives you some idea of the type of lesser roles he played.

His better sound film cliffhanger roles were as the voice of the Rattler when in disguise, otherwise he is not seen, in "Mystery Mountain" ('34 Mascot), Buck Jones' pal Johnny Snow in "Red Rider" ('34 Universal), crooked horse trainer Jim Luger in "Law of the Wild" ('34 Mascot), crooked animal trainer Craddock in "Darkest Africa" ('36 Republic), cattleman suspect Stockton in "Son of Zorro" ('47 Republic) and industrialist R. J. Cook in "G-Men Never Forget" ('48 Republic). In most of the others he was one of those surname-mainstay-henchmen we so enjoyed seeing week after week in serials (and westerns).

Certainly Cobb is remembered for his scores of westerns, but he also did lots of other film work in Charlie Chan, Falcon, Frankenstein and Ma and Pa Kettle films, as well as an occasional part in a classic film—he's a Senator in "Mr. Smith Goes to Washington" ('39), a reporter in "Citizen Kane" ('41), a tower guard in "Brute Force" ('47) and a detective in "Detective Story" ('51).

In later A-westerns and TV shows of the '40s and '50s Ed played many sheriffs and townsmen. If there was a scene with a group of men on the backlot, you quite often could spot Ed with a line or two ("Comanche Territory" '50, "Kid From Texas" '50, "Carson City" '52, "Gun Belt" '53, "Apache Ambush" '55, etc.). In other words, Cobb continued to work, with his last role being a bit in producer A. C. Lyles' "Johnny Reno" ('66). Producer Alex Gordon had also featured Cobb in several of his productions, including his all-star westerns "Bounty Killer" and "Requiem For a Gunfighter'. Alex told us, "My wife and I, along with Ed and his wife, often had dinner together and became friends. He was a wonderful man—didn't drink—and his wife was very beautiful and so well-dressed. She looked like Theda Bara—but not a vamp. Ed was not a wealthy man and for one of his birthdays in later years we gave him a money tree where all his friends pinned money on it. He was quite moved." By others who knew him, Cobb is described as a quiet, unassuming, down-to-earth, polite, gentleman who lived at 12500 Huston, Apt. 7, in North Hollywood, California.

In poor health, Cobb was admitted to the Motion Picture Hospital in Woodland Hills, California, where he died of congestive heart failure at 82, August 15, 1974.

His wife died there as well, of bronchial pneumonia, barely three weeks earlier. Cobb is buried at Valhalla Cemetery in North Hollywood.

Ed Cobb will be remembered for his starring silent films and his coterie of heavies in sound films in an underrated illustrious career that spanned six decades. But most of all he will be remembered as one of the good guys in real life, a gentleman and a regular guy.

Suggested Sampling of Cobb's Western Heavies:

- Wild Horse ('31 Allied) Hoot Gibson
- Law of the Rio Grande ('31 Syndicate) Bob Custer
- Human Targets ('32 Big 4) Buzz Barton
- Deadwood Pass ('33 Monarch) Tom Tyler
- Rusty Rides Alone ('33 Columbia) Tin McCoy
- Law of the Wild ('34 Mascot serial) Bob Custer
- Tracy Rides ('35 Reliable) Tom Tyler
- Rustler's Paradise ('35 Ajax) Harry Carey
- Danger Trails ('35 Beacon) Big Boy Williams
- Bulldog Courage ('35 Puritan) Tim McCoy
- Cheyenne Tornado ('35 Kent) Reb Russell
- California Mail ('36 Warner Bros.) Dick Foran
- Cherokee Strip ('37 Warner Bros.) Dick Foran
- Call of the Rockies ('38 Columbia) Charles Starrett
- West of Cheyenne ('38 Columbia) Charles Starrett
- Thundering West ('39 Columbia) Charles Starrett
- Blue Montana Skies ('39 Republic) Gene Autry
- Western Caravans ('39 Columbia) Charles Starrett
- One Man's Law ('40 Republic) Don Barry
- Wyoming Wildcat ('41 Republic) Don Barry
- Tonto Basin Outlaws ('41 Monogram) Range Busters
- Lone Star Vigilantes ('42 Columbia) Bill Elliott/Tex Ritter
- Down Rio Grande Way ('42 Columbia) Charles Starrett/Russell Hayden
- Saddles and Sagebrush ('43 Columbia) Russell Hayden
- Silver City Raiders ('43 Columbia) Russell Hayden

- Frontier Fury ('43 Columbia) Charles Starrett
- Six Gun Gospel ('43 Monogram) Johnny Mack Brown
- Texas Kid ('43 Monogram) Johnny Mack Brown
- California Joe ('43 Republic) Don Barry
- Law Men ('44 Monogram) Johnny Mack Brown
- Law of the Valley ('44 Monogram) Johnny Mack Brown
- Song of the Range ('44 Monogram) Jimmy Wakely
- Old Texas Trail ('45 Universal) Rod Cameron
- Navajo Trail ('45 Monogram) Johnny Mack Brown
- Renegades of the Rio Grande ('45 Universal) Rod Cameron
- Man From Oklahoma ('45 Republic) Roy Rogers
- Days of Buffalo Bill ('46 Republic) Sunset Carson
- Roaring Rangers ('46 Columbia) Charles Starrett
- Rustler's Round-up ('46 Universal) Kirby Grant
- Stagecoach to Denver ('46 Republic) Allan Lane
- Oregon Trail Scouts ('47 Republic) Allan Lane
- Riders of the Lone Star ('47 Columbia) Charles Starrett
- Daring Caballero ('49 United Artists) Duncan Renaldo
- Girl From San Lorenzo ('50 United Artists) Duncan Renaldo
- Cisco Kid: Chain Lightning ('50) Duncan Renaldo
- Wild Bill Hickok: Nephew From Back East ('53) Guy Madison
- Sgt. Preston of the Yukon: Crime at Wounded Moose ('56) Richard Simmons

JAMES COBURN

The villainy of lean, gangly James Coburn proved so personable that his suave demeanor and tooth-filled crooked smile thrust him to major stardom.

Coburn was born August 31, 1928, in Laurel, Nebraska. His family moved to California in 1933 after his father's business in Nebraska was wiped out by the Depression.

Following high school, he attended Compton Junior College in 1950 where a classmate recalled Coburn sang in the College glee club. After service as a radio operator during the Korean conflict, Coburn enrolled at Los Angeles City College where he majored in drama. He also studied with Stella Adler in New York City before making his first significant role in a live "Studio One" presentation in 1957.

Beginning in 1958 he was being seen on all the major TV westerns—"Wagon Train", "Rifleman", "Tales of Wells Fargo", "Bronco", "Cheyenne", "Restless Gun", "Bat Masterson", "Have Gun Will Travel", "Lawman" etc.—where his tall, lean, relaxed but tough screen persona kept him in constant demand.

Director Budd Boetticher cast him in his first big screen western, Randolph Scott's "Ride Lonesome" in '59.

A chance meeting with friend Robert Vaughn tipped him that director John Sturges was casting "The Magnificent Seven". Coburn persuaded the director to cast him as Britt, the guy with the knives, in the western version of Kurosawa's "Seven Samurai". From that starmaker role, director Sam Peckinpah hired Coburn for "Major Dundee" ('65) and "Pat Garrett and Billy the Kid" ('73). At the same time, James Bondish spy spoofs "Our Man Flint" ('66) and "In Like Flint" ('67) further elevated his star.

Coburn continued to appear on episodic TV through 1964, including a regular stint as gambler Jeff Durain on NBC's "Klondike" ('60-'61) with co-star Ralph Taeger.

At 60, in 1978, in the middle of an illustrious career, he was stricken with severe rheumatoid arthritis which at times left him completely debilitated. After growing increasingly frustrated with "doctors who didn't know much about it," Coburn found his own relief in dietary supplements. His good friend, R. G. Armstrong, told us, "When he got sick with rheumatoid arthritis was when I got to know him. I had learned from a lady a massage technique about the whole blood flow in the body. I did it with my hands, so I worked on Jim for three months and got him up and moving out of his chair, feeling good and normal. He really came back. He was a wonderful personality. He did a great villain because he had that aplomb, that suavity and style. He carried his great style through to the end."

Jan Merlin remembers, "When James Coburn first

showed up in Hollywood, I owned a little house in Laurel Canyon he rented from me. It had been previously lived in by Robert Mitchum, and the site of some media interest. Being already a well-known actor at the time, I was quite sure Coburn would become a star, and told him so. He grinned and hoped he would be. He was a gentle man…a fine character actor…and I was delighted to see his career leap into what he dreamt of it becoming. I'll always remember his engaging smile."

Don "Johnny Ringo" Durant said, "I will never forget working with James Coburn in 'The Arrival' episode of 'Johnny Ringo'. Not only was he a good actor, he was a gentleman in every way. The characters we have often seen him portray as a heavy or bad guy are exactly opposite of the very man he was. James was always very considerate and courteous with his fellow actors. I remember vividly rehearsing our lines together and the professionalism he showed in making suggestions on any dialogue changes or additions. Also, in blocking out a scene he was always conscious in not 'upstaging' you."

After 10 years of suffering, Coburn began to shun doctors and drugs to find his own relief from the crippling disease through a series of alternative treatments, including electromagnetic therapy and heavy dosage of MSM.

Coburn's health rebounded to where he won the Best Supporting Actor award for "Affliction" in '99.

Coburn was first married to Beverly Kelly from 1959-1979 when they were divorced. They had one son, James, born in 1961. A daughter, Lisa, was born in 1957. He married Paula Murad in 1993.

Coburn, 74, died of a heart attack in his wife Paula's arms at his Beverly Hills home on November 18, 2002.

Suggested Sampling of Coburn's Western Heavies:

- Tales of Wells Fargo: Butch Cassidy ('58) Dale Robertson
- Wanted Dead Or Alive: Reunion For Revenge ('58) Steve McQueen
- Trackdown: Hard Lines ('59) Robert Culp
- Elfego Baca: Move Along, Mustangers ('59) Robert Loggia
- Black Saddle: Client: Steele ('59) Peter Breck
- Restless Gun: The Pawn ('59) John Payne
- Rough Riders: Deadfall ('59) Jan Merlin
- Bat Masterson: Black Pearls ('59) Gene Barry
- Ride Lonesome ('59 Columbia) Randolph Scott
- Johnny Ringo: The Arrival ('59) Don Durant
- Tombstone Territory: The Gunfighter ('59) Pat Conway
- Bonanza: Truckee Strip ('59) Michael Landon, Lorne Greene
- Have Gun Will Travel: One Came Back ('59) Richard Boone
- Lawman: Showdown ('60) John Russell
- Wichita Town: Afternoon In Town ('60) Joel McCrea
- Bat Masterson: Six Feet of Gold ('60) Gene Barry
- Deputy: Truly Yours ('60) Allen Case
- Wanted Dead Or Alive: The Trial ('60) Steve McQueen
- Lawman: The Catcher ('60) John Russell
- Sugarfoot: Blackwater Swamp ('60) Will Hutchins
- Stagecoach West: Come Home Again ('61) Robert Bray
- Tall Man: Best Policy ('61) Barry Sullivan/Clu Gulager
- Outlaws: Culley ('61) Don Collier
- Bonanza: Dark Gate ('61) Pernell Roberts
- Cheyenne: Trouble Street ('61) Clint Walker
- Rifleman: High Country ('61) Chuck Connors
- Tales of Wells Fargo: Wayfarers ('62) Dale Robertson
- Bite the Bullet ('75 Columbia) Gene Hackman
- Last Hard Men ('76 20th Century Fox) Charlton Heston

IRON EYES CODY

Iron Eyes Cody, the movie "Indian" whose career stretched back to 1919, was not a Native American, but of Italian descent. Cody always claimed his mother was a Cree and his father was a Cherokee. However, in tracking Iron Eyes' roots, the key to his past is in the parish records of Louisiana. According to official documents, Iron Eyes' mother was Francesca Salpietra, who sailed from Sicily to New Orleans in 1902 to marry Antonio DeCorti, an Italian immigrant. They ran a small grocery in Gueydan, Louisiana. Iron Eyes was born Oscar DeCorti April 3, 1904, the second of four children. More family history comes from May Abshire, Iron Eyes' half-sister. When Oscar came to California, circa 1924, he changed his name to Iron Eyes Cody and began acting in silent movies.

First Americans in the Arts, Hollywood's leading Native American advocacy group, gave Cody its prestigious Trustee Award in 1992. However, during the presentation, they made it quite clear the award was being presented to Cody as a "non-native". But, Cody's movie legend may long outlive the facts.

In 1936, Cody wed Bertha Parker, a Native American archeologist. They adopted two Indian sons. After her death in 1978, he married again in 1992 to Wendy Foote, but the marriage did not last. They divorced in '93.

His "life" was told in two bios, IRON EYES—MY LIFE AS A HOLLYWOOD INDIAN ('82) and IRON EYES CODY—THE PROUD AMERICAN ('88).

Iron Eyes was in nearly 200 films including over 20 serials like "Wild West Days" ('37), "Flaming Frontiers" ('38), "Scouts to the Rescue" ('39), "Winners of the West" ('40), "Raiders of Ghost City" ('44) and others that called for Indian roles. Often his parts in films and serials were unbilled and brief.

Italian or Indian, whatever the truth, over the years

Iron Eyes became the *symbol* of America's noble Indian hero and was devoted to Native American causes. Iron Eyes was probably more Indian at heart than many Native Americans because he truly loved it and lived it, becoming an authority on Indian culture. He wrote a book on Indian sign language that became a text for the Boy Scouts. Iron Eyes' historic Earth Day 1971 Crying Indian public service spot for Keep America Beautiful made him more recognizable than hundreds of western films were able to do.

Cody, 94, died January 4, 1999, of natural causes at his home in Los Feliz, California.

Iron Eyes Cody in full Indian regalia with Roy Rogers in "North of the Great Divide" ('50 Republic).

Suggested Sampling of Cody's Western Heavies:

- Texas Pioneers ('32 Monogram) Bill Cody
- Miracle Rider ('35 Mascot serial) Tom Mix
- Custer's Last Stand ('36 Stage and Screen serial) Rex Lease
- Crashing Thru ('39 Monogram) James Newill
- Young Buffalo Bill ('40 Republic) Roy Rogers
- Kit Carson ('40 United Artists) Jon Hall
- Pony Post ('40 Universal) Johnny Mack Brown
- Under Nevada Skies ('46 Republic) Roy Rogers
- Bowery Buckaroos ('47 Monogram) Bowery Boys
- Indian Agent ('48 RKO) Tim Holt
- Cherokee Uprising ('50 Monogram) Whip Wilson
- Night Raiders ('52 Monogram) Whip Wilson
- Cisco Kid: Indian Uprising ('53) Duncan Renaldo
- Sitting Bull ('54 United Artists) Dale Robertson
- Wild Bill Hickok: Bold Raven Rodeo ('56) Guy Madison
- Wild Dakotas ('56 Associated) Bill Williams
- Rin Tin Tin: Miracle of the Mission ('58) Lee Aaker
- Lawman: Warpath ('59) John Russell
- Rebel: Burying of Sammy Hart ('61) Nick Adams
- Great Sioux Massacre ('65 Columbia) Joseph Cotten

TRIS (TRISTRAM) COFFIN

Suave and dapper, with wavy, graying hair, Tristram Coffin was one of the best dressed and handsomest heavies to work in westerns. In a Hollywood career spanning 38 years, Coffin's work ran the gamut of all film genres—he even got to be the hero in Republic's "King of the Rocketmen" serial ('49) and TV's "26 Men" ('57-'59), a series which co-starred Kelo Henderson who remembers Tris as "an accomplished veteran actor who knew his theatrical trade and portrayed his role as Ranger Captain with authority. He was pleasant to the various casts he had to work with and to the crew members. Also to the fans who came out to watch the series being filmed."

Tristram Chalkley Coffin was born in the silver mining town of Mammoth, Utah, August 13, 1909. His father, Edwin Coffin, was from Iowa and his mother, Elizabeth Christie, was a Utah native. Tris' father was superintendent of Mammoth Mines, one of the largest silver mines in the world. Tris grew up and received his education in the Salt Lake City, Utah, schools where he started acting in school plays.

Following high school, Tris became a member of a touring stock company with actress Gladys George. He first attended the University of Utah, studying medicine, gave that up to attend, and graduate from, the University of Washington with a major in speech.

Tris had four seasons of stock with Henry Duffy in Seattle and Portland after which he entered radio. After teaching for two years at the Leland Powers School of Dramatics in Boston, Massachusetts, Tris became chief staff announcer on WAB and WNAC radio in Boston. In the mid-'30s in New York, Tris worked on "March of Time" and "Gangbusters" radio programs. While in radio, an RKO Hollywood scout heard him and that, coupled with his good looks, caused the scout to urge Coffin towards Hollywood.

Fittingly, Tris' first film, "The Saint Strikes Back" ('39), saw him playing a radio newscaster, the job he was working at before coming to Hollywood.

From the beginning, Coffin worked in Monogram westerns opposite Jack Randall, Tex Ritter, Range Busters and Rough Riders. By the early '40s he was working at Columbia and Republic menacing Bill Elliott/Tex Ritter, Gene Autry, Roy Rogers and Russell Hayden.

Tris served in the Navy from late '42 to early '46, although he somehow managed to work in a few films during those years, except '45.

Post WWII saw Tris in 10-13 films per year from '46-'51, mostly westerns although he squeezed in a few with Charlie Chan, Jungle Jim and the Bowery Boys...even several major films such as "The Fountainhead" ('49), "Flamingo Road" ('49), "Voice Of the Turtle" ('47) and "The Fat Man" ('51).

But we enjoyed it most when Tris was giving trouble to Johnny Mack Brown, Sunset Carson, Gene Autry, Roy Rogers, Monte Hale, Allan "Rocky" Lane, Charles Starrett, Jimmy Wakely, Whip Wilson, Rex Allen and others.

Tris told Tom and Jim Goldrup (FEATURE PLAYERS VOL. I), "A lot of my (over 300 movie and TV) films I can't remember the titles or having ever worked in them. You made so many, it was almost like being on a roller-skate going from one studio to another. On a couple of occasions I was working in two pictures on the same lot at the same time."

Tris' serial work was prolific as well, with at least 14 credits from "Dick Tracy's G-Men" ('39) to his starring role in "King of the Rocketmen" ('49). He's also in "Holt of the Secret Service" ('41), "Perils of Nyoka" ('42), "Jesse James Rides Again" ('47) and "Pirates of the High Seas" ('50) among others. Republic serial director William Witney wrote, "Tris had ability written all over him."

With the advent of TV, Tris cut his film workload back to only a few a year, concentrating on the multitude of half-hour TV westerns now on the air—"Lone Ranger", "Cisco Kid", "Kit Carson", "Cowboy G-Men", "Wild Bill Hickok", "Judge Roy Bean", "Death Valley Days", "Wyatt Earp" et al. Then came his starring role as Capt. Tom Rynning on "26 Men". He also co-starred on the syndicated "Files of Jeffrey Jones" ('54) with good friend Don Haggerty and Gloria Henry.

Tris continued to work on TV and in films, mostly character parts, until 1971. His last credited role is in the independently made "Father Kino Story" released in '77 but made a few years earlier.

Tris was married to Vera Duke, a petite, red-haired fashion model. They last resided at 2314 Pier Ave., Santa Monica, CA.

At 80, Tris died of cardiac arrest and lung cancer

"Prairie Gunsmoke" is about to erupt as Bill Elliott gets the drop on Tris Coffin ('42 Columbia).

March 26, 1990, at St. John's Medical Center in Santa Monica. His remains were cremated and scattered at sea off the coast of Long Beach.

Describing how he became cast as a badman, Tris said, "I asked for it. I pleaded for it, and fought for it. I was doing leading man and romance roles but I loved westerns. I talked to Scotty Dunlap, who was producing westerns at Monogram, and asked him if I could do some heavies. He said, 'Tris, you're too dignified. You're strictly a leading man and romance type. You can't work in westerns as a heavy.' I said, 'Scotty, have you ever gone to a state penitentiary and looked at some of the inmates? There are lawyers, doctors, and motion picture producers; they're not all mugs.' So he said, 'Well, maybe you've got a point. I've got a script with a heavy that can be played smooth.' So he gave me the part and that was my start playing heavies and I've always loved doing them. I've played many villains and have been so mean that in one picture they even tried to give me to the Indians and they wouldn't take me."

Suggested Sampling of Coffin's Western Heavies:

- Oklahoma Terror ('39 Monogram) Jack Randall
- Rhythm of the Rio Grande ('40 Monogram) Tex Ritter
- West of Pinto Basin ('40 Monogram) Range Busters
- Arizona Bound ('41 Monogram) Rough Riders
- Forbidden Trails ('41 Monogram) Rough Riders
- Prairie Gunsmoke ('42 Columbia) Bill Elliott/Tex Ritter
- A Tornado In the Saddle ('42 Columbia) Russell Hayden
- Silver City Raiders ('43 Columbia) Russell Hayden
- Wyoming Hurricane ('44 Columbia) Russell Hayden
- Gay Cavalier ('46 Monogram) Gilbert Roland
- Gentleman From Texas ('46 Monogram) Johnny Mack Brown
- Rio Grande Raiders ('46 Republic) Sunset Carson
- Under Nevada Skies ('46 Republic) Roy Rogers
- Land of the Lawless ('47 Monogram) Johnny Mack Brown
- Where the North Begins ('47 Screen Guild) Russell Hayden
- Trail To San Antone ('47 Republic) Gene Autry
- California Firebrand ('48 Republic) Monte Hale
- Crashing Thru ('49 Monogram) Whip Wilson
- Lawless Code ('49 Monogram) Jimmy Wakely
- Desert Vigilante ('49 Columbia) Charles Starrett
- Range Justice ('49 Monogram) Johnny Mack Brown
- Cisco Kid: Dog Story ('50) Duncan Renaldo
- Old Frontier ('50 Republic) Monte Hale
- Cisco Kid: Hidden Valley ('51) Duncan Renaldo
- Buckaroo Sheriff of Texas ('51 Republic) Rough Ridin' Kids
- Rodeo King and the Senorita ('51 Republic) Rex Allen
- Kit Carson: Baron of Black Springs ('52) Bill Williams
- Smoky Canyon ('52 Columbia) Charles Starrett
- Cowboy G-Men: Hang the Jury ('53) Russell Hayden
- Cisco Kid: Not Guilty ('54) Duncan Renaldo
- Kit Carson: Powder Depot ('54) Bill Williams
- Wild Bill Hickok: Outlaw's Portrait ('55) Guy Madison
- Champion: Salted Ground ('55) Jim Bannon
- Cisco Kid: Witness ('55) Duncan Renaldo
- Judge Roy Bean: Border Raiders ('56) Edgar Buchanan
- Lone Ranger: The Avenger ('57) Clayton Moore
- Bronco: Yankee Tornado ('61) Ty Hardin

BEN CORBETT

Chubby little Ben Corbett was active in westerns for 41 years as an actor…and sometime stunt double for William Duncan and Antonio Moreno in the silent era and Hoot Gibson and Ken Maynard during their latter day Trail Blazers period in the mid '40s.

Over the years stubby Benny was the co-star of his own series of western comedies (The Bud 'n' Ben films) and a sidekick to Tim McCoy (Magpie in McCoy's Victory series '38-'39), Tom Tyler, Jack Hoxie, Lane Chandler and Jack Perrin. But mostly he was a ranch hand, cook, barfly, prison guard, stagecoach driver, townsman—or—a member of the outlaw band, usually 5th or 6th man through the door.

Benny was most likely born in Hudson, Illinois, February 6, 1892. He went to high school in Hudson, then lied about his age and joined the Cavalry at 17 for a three year hitch, which is where Ben learned to ride. He became an expert Roman rider (standing astride two galloping horses) and bronc buster.

In Ben's own words in a November 17, 1938, document from the Academy of Motion Picture Arts and Sciences, Ben states, "I finished my three-year hitch a top sergeant. The officers seemed to like me because they featured me in all the company horse shows. The Army took me to Manila and Honolulu and all over this country and I got to liking being a trick performer. So from 1910-1919 I entered competitions and won a couple. In 1916 I drove a Roman team a half-mile in 51 seconds in Toppenish, Washington. Then I entered the bronc riding and bulldogging competition at Eugene, Oregon, in 1916 and the same (events) at Ashland, Oregon, in 1918. I had to bulldog a steer in five-and-a-half seconds to win that one." During these formative years Benny also did some work as a rodeo clown.

As for his entry into films, Corbett wrote, "In 1913 they had a rodeo (in Hollywood) and I won the Roman riding contest. I liked the place and kept thinking of going back as I went from one competition to the other. So in 1917 I got a job doubling for Antonio Moreno." Perhaps exaggerating a bit, Ben went on to state, "Since then I've doubled every star in Hollywood."

Hoot Gibson was instrumental in getting Ben started as an actor, casting him in several of his 1920-1921 Universal westerns ("Man With the Punch", "Cactus Kid", etc.).

During the early '20s Ben also appeared in the westerns of Neal Hart, Art Acord, Jack Hoxie and Josie Sedgwick, as well as two smash-hit serials, "Lightning Bryce" ('19 Arrow) with Jack Hoxie and "Riddle Rider" ('24 Universal) with William Desmond.

Benny continues his own story, "After working a while, somebody (at Universal) got the idea of making a batch of two-reelers starring Pee Wee Holmes and me. W. C. Tuttle wrote the series called 'Dirty Shirt and Magpie.' We made 26 two-reelers. We might have gone and got somewhat famous with our series but Pee Wee died, so I drifted into comedy relief and stunting." Indeed, Benny and Pee Wee made a very successful series of 26 Bud 'n' Ben two-reelers from '25-'27, but Pee Wee didn't die until 1936, long after Universal had abandoned the comedy-western duo.

After sound came in, Corbett tried to revive the Bud 'n' Ben idea at Reliable in 1934. Eight of these were produced, running from 20 to 30 minutes, usually co-starring Jack Perrin as Bud but, when he wasn't available, Harry Myers, Fred Humes and Dennis Moore were surrogate co-leads with Ben.

When the silent Bud 'n' Ben (or Dirty Shirt and Magpie as Ben calls it) silent series ended, Ben went on to sidekick with or play roles in the westerns of Ken Maynard ("Red Raiders" '27), Ed Cobb ("One Glorious Scrap" '27), Fred Humes ("Fearless Rider" '28), Ted Wells ("Made To Order Hero" '28) and Don Coleman ("Black Ace" '28). Several of these also featured Pee Wee Holmes.

Benny never missed a beat as sound came in. He certainly wasn't the greatest at delivering dialogue, but his hesitating naturalness beamed through giving him an authentic cowpoke (which he was) feel. From 1930-1956 Benny worked in the westerns of practically every B-western cowboy imaginable. Over 200 films.

When he wasn't acting, he was doing stuntwork ("I like stunting best of all."), especially for director Arthur Rosson. "I guess I made 50 pictures with Arthur Rosson," Ben recalled. "He's directing the location sequences up here (in Utah) for Cecil B. DeMille on 'Union Pacific'. (Rosson) knows his ridin'…he was a stuntman once. He also was one of the best wild horse grabbers in the world." Rosson (1886-1960) began as an actor in 1912. He also wrote several westerns for Hoot Gibson and others between 1913-1937. The multi-talented Rosson also became an assistant director, then a director, helming many silent era westerns and several Hoot Gibson and Ken Maynard talkies in the early '30s. Primarily, he was a terrific second unit action director on big scale westerns such as "The Plainsmen" ('37), "Northwest Mounted Police" ('40), "Kit Carson ('40), "Man From Colorado" ('48), "Red River" ('48), "Cariboo Trail" ('50), among others.

Over the years, Corbett served on the Board of Directors of both the Screen Actors Guild and the Screen Extras Guild.

Stuntman/actor Roydon Clark, who doubled James Garner for years, said, "Ben got me in the business! I was living at Hudkins Ranch, working and taking care of the livestock on my summer vacation. Basically, they raised me. Come time I wanted to get my SAG card in the mid '40s. Ben Corbett was on the SAG Board of Directors that you had to go in front of at that time. He later signed my petition so I could get in the Screen Extras Guild. Over the next many years, he was one of the famous cowboys of that era. He was one of the legends."

Stuntman Whitey Hughes adds, "Ben was a technical advisor on a lot of westerns, especially at Warner Bros., and especially pertaining to the Cavalry. He was one of the old timers that really stood by for the old timers."

Ben's last really noticeable role was as a Cavalry trooper in Guy Madison's 3-D "Charge At Feather River" ('53), but his last known role was a bit in "Great Day In the Morning" ('56 RKO).

Concluding his story, Ben said, "I've had every bone in my body broken several times, but I'd do it all over again. If my daughter were a boy, I'd advise her to be (a stuntman) too."

Corbett died at 69 May 19, 1961, in Hollywood. It's cowboys like Ben who were the true heart and soul of the western movie era.

Suggested Sampling of Corbett's Western Heavies:

- Trailing Trouble ('30 Universal) Hoot Gibson
- In Old Cheyenne ('31 SonoArt–World Wide) Rex Lease
- Guns For Hire ('32 Kent) Lane Chandler
- Haunted Gold ('32 Warner Bros.) John Wayne
- Border Menace ('34 Aywon) Bill Cody
- Lone Bandit ('35 Empire) Lane Chandler
- Circle of Death ('35 Kent) Montie Montana
- Border Vengeance ('35 Kent) Reb Russell
- Silent Code ('35 Stage and Screen) Kane Richmond
- Six Shootin' Sheriff ('38 Grand National) Ken Maynard
- Songs and Saddles ('38 Colony) Gene Austin
- Lightning Carson Rides Again ('38 Victory) Tim McCoy
- Racketeers of the Range ('39 RKO) George O'Brien
- Arizona Bound ('41 Monogram) Rough Riders
- Ghost Town Law ('42 Monogram) Rough Riders
- Cody of the Pony Express ('50 Columbia serial) Jock Mahoney

HARRY CORDING

Harry Cording was one tough customer! Receiving screen billing for only about a third of his over 250 film appearances from 1925-1955, he appeared as a blacksmith, guard, jailer, sergeant, pirate, lumberjack, miner, seamen, brawler, cop, pub keeper—and burly outlaw (often named Bull).

Cording was tall, muscular, balding, with a sort of burly, strong featured Eurasian appearance which made him noticeable even in brief roles, such as one of his best as Bela Lugosi's hulking manservant in '34's Universal horror classic, "The Black Cat".

The gruff-voiced Cording worked for virtually every studio from MGM to Republic, but his work at Universal stands out. He had roles in several other Universal horrors ("Wolf Man", "Son of Frankenstein", "Mummy's Tomb", etc.), four of the six Jon Hall/Maria Montez Technicolor epics, seven of the 12 Basil Rathbone Sherlock Holmes mysteries (including a large role in "House of Fear" ('45), along with many of the action studio's B-westerns.

Born in England, April 29, 1891, Cording was educated at Rugby and served in the English Army in WWI. The six foot, 196 pound Cording bummed around South America before entering films with "Sins of the Father" in 1921. His first billing came four years later in "The Knockout" ('25).

Cording's first western was not until 1930 opposite George O'Brien in "Rough Romance". For the rest of his career he intertwined westerns with not only the above mentioned types of films, but especially swashbuckling costume dramas such as "Count of Monte Cristo" ('34), "Treasure Island" ('34), "The Crusades" ('35), "Adventures of Robin Hood" ('38), "Sea Hawk" ('40), "Raiders of the Desert" ('41), "Forever Amber" ('47) and many more.

Serials did not go wanting, as Cording made seven. He had good roles in "King of the Royal Mounted" ('40 Republic), "Overland Mail" ('42 Universal) and "Great Alaskan Mystery" ('44 Universal).

Harry Cording had completed the role of a bouncer in James Dean's "East of Eden" (released in '55) when he died at 63 in Sun Valley, California, September 1, 1954. Cause and details unknown.

Suggested Sampling of Cording's Western Heavies:

- Texas Cyclone ('32 Columbia) Tim McCoy
- Arizona Legion ('39 RKO) George O'Brien
- Marshal of Mesa City ('39 RKO) George O'Brien
- Destry Rides Again ('39 Universal) James Stewart
- King of the Royal Mounted ('40 Republic serial) Allan Lane
- Law and Order ('40 Universal) Johnny Mack Brown
- Stage to Chino ('40 RKO) George O'Brien
- Bury Me Not On the Lone Prairie ('41 Universal) Johnny Mack Brown
- Rawhide Rangers ('41 Universal) Johnny Mack Brown
- Overland Mail ('42 Universal serial) Lon Chaney Jr.
- Fugitive From Sonora ('43 Republic) Don Barry
- Man From the Rio Grande ('43 Republic) Don Barry
- Dangerous Venture ('47 United Artists) William Boyd
- Marauders ('47 United Artists) William Boyd
- Trail of the Mounties ('49 Screen Guild) Russell Hayden
- Lone Ranger: Sheep Thieves ('50) Clayton Moore
- Night Stage To Galveston ('52 Columbia) Gene Autry
- Hopalong Cassidy: Knife of Carlos Valero ('52) William Boyd
- Wild Bill Hickok: Chain of Events ('53) Guy Madison

JIM COREY

With over 250 films to his credit, silent and sound, in a career that spanned 34 years, 1914-1948, Jim Corey was one busy henchman.

Virtually all of his movies were B-westerns and serials. The outstanding exceptions were an uncredited role in "The Grapes of Wrath" ('40) and his last part, of a priest, in "Joan of Arc" ('48).

Corey's first credited role was in Universal's "Master Key" chapterplay in 1914. After a few with Harry Carey and Eddie Polo, Corey was Hoot Gibson's main antagonist in some 22 Universal two-reelers in 1920-1921. Corey segued right into a badman role in a series of 12 Universal two-reelers with Jack Perrin in '21. He was in the Hooter's first feature length western, "Action" in '21, then supported other silent bronco-busters such as Art Acord, Leo Maloney, Fred Thomson, Pete Morrison, Roy Stewart, Bob Custer and Jack Hoxie.

Having worked with and known Gibson so well in the silent era, it's no surprise Hoot employed Corey in three of his early talkies at Universal in 1930.

From that time on, Corey was seen in nearly 200 sound westerns playing not only unbilled henchmen, but possemen, deputies, cowhands, barflys and townsmen. His parts were often without lines and without even a character name, just the designation "henchman", "ranch hand", "rider" or the like. But it's players like Corey who were the backbone of the B-western industry.

Like many other henchmen-type players of his era, very little background information is available on Corey. And the basic facts of his life have been confused in other research for years with non-actor James Warren Corey of Nebraska.

Corey was lean and lanky with hawk-like features—sunken cheeks, angular face, leering lips and one of his beady eyes seemed to indicate a slight deformity. His clothing appeared seedy and unkempt. He often sported a large mustache.

Born Arthur H. Corey March 22, 1889, in New York, his father's name was Nathan Corey, his mother was Margaret Ford. Corey died March 26, 1950, at 61, at L.A. County General Hospital on N. State Street. Cause of death was due to a retro peritoneal hemorrhage caused by a large abdominal aneurysm. Corey suffered from hypertension and cardiovascular disease. Corey lived in Van Nuys, California, and was divorced from his wife Patrice at the time. The death certificate informant was Clarence Corey. His tombstone in Valhalla Cemetery reads "Beloved Father", so we assume Clarence was his son.

Suggested Sampling of Corey's Western Heavies:

- Cyclone Smith's Partner ('19 Universal) Eddie Polo
- Smilin' Kid ('20 Universal) Hoot Gibson
- Fight It Out ('20 Universal) Hoot Gibson
- Both Barrels ('21 Universal) Jack Perrin
- Action ('21 Universal) Hoot Gibson
- Winners of the West ('21 Universal serial) Art Acord
- Dangerous Coward ('24 FBO) Fred Thomson
- Hair Trigger Baxter ('26 FBO) Bob Custer
- Last Outlaw ('27 Paramount) Gary Cooper
- Courtin' Wildcats ('29 Universal) Hoot Gibson
- Mounted Stranger ('30 Universal) Hoot Gibson
- Red Fork Range ('31 Big 4) Wally Wales
- Clearing the Range ('31 Allied) Hoot Gibson
- Two Gun Man ('31 Tiffany) Ken Maynard
- Red Rider ('34 Universal serial) Buck Jones
- Phantom Rider ('36 Universal serial) Buck Jones
- Feud of the Trail ('37 Victory) Tom Tyler
- Mystery Range ('37 Victory) Tom Tyler
- Gun Lords of Stirrup Basin ('37 Republic) Bob Steele
- Guns In the Dark ('37 Republic) Johnny Mack Brown
- Billy the Kid Returns ('38 Republic) Roy Rogers
- Silver On the Sage ('39 Paramount) William Boyd
- Sheriff of Tombstone ('41 Republic) Roy Rogers
- Desert Bandit ('41 Republic) Don Barry

DON COSTELLO

Don Costello's time in Hollywood was short, less than 40 features from '39-'46 with only nine of those being westerns, but his unusual parts left an indelible mark. In Hopalong Cassidy's "Texas Masquerade" he had the neat penchant for practical jokes. In Bill Elliott's "Great Stagecoach Robbery" he was an abusive school teacher and in Elliott's "Marshal of Laredo" he was the scar-faced-by-fire henchman photographer who is sadistically and constantly tormented with matches by his boss, Roy Barcroft.

Born Don Costell in New Orleans, Louisiana, September 5, 1901, (mother's maiden name was Gillen) Costello was primarily a Broadway stage actor who came to films in 1939 as a gunman in "One Crowded Night."

Costello died in his sleep at only 44 at his Hollywood home October 24, 1945. His last appearance was in "The Blue Dahlia", released after his death in '46.

The "Marshal of Laredo," Bill (Red Ryder) Elliott coerces a gunpoint confession from Don Costello ('45 Republic).

Suggested Sampling of Costello's Western Heavies:

- Ride On Vaquero ('41 20th Century Fox) Cesar Romero
- Last of the Duanes ('41 20th Century Fox) George Montgomery
- Sundown Jim ('42 20th Century Fox) John Kimbrough
- Texas Masquerade ('44 United Artists) William Boyd
- Great Stagecoach Robbery ('45 Republic) Bill Elliott
- Marshal of Laredo ('45 Republic) Bill Elliott

RICHARD CRAMER

The ugly, overbearing, savage, gravel-voiced snarl of Richard (Dick) Cramer scared the beejesus out of front-row kids in the '30s and '40s in dozens of westerns and serials. He's also well remembered by "tents" of Laurel and Hardy devotees for his menace to the comedy duo in "Scram!" ('32), "Pack Up Your Troubles" ('32), "Flying Deuces" ('39) and especially "Saps at Sea" ('40) as the escaped convict.

The bulldog Irish mug of Richard C. Cramer first saw the light of day on July 3, 1890, in Bryan, Ohio.

According to 1910 census records Cramer was employed as an "inspector" in the "movie pictures" industry. By 1920 he listed his occupation as theatrical actor. At some point he graduated from Ohio State University. At 36 Cramer married a lady named Hilda C. whose parents came from Switzerland although she was born in Michigan.

Cramer didn't come to films in the late silent period (1928) until he was 39. But from then until 1952 he worked nonstop in well over 200 films.

Cramer's exaggerated malevolence was ripe for serials, and he appeared in 12 of them, beginning with a silent, "The Tiger's Shadow" (Pathe) in '28. He was prominent as a thug in "The Vanishing Shadow" ('34 Universal) and "Black Coin" ('36 Stage and Screen); trying to steal Rex, King of the Wild Horses, in "Law of the Wild" ('34 Mascot); Joe Portos, Mexican bandit in "Red Rider" ('36 Universal) and as the Apache killer in "Great Adventures of Wild Bill Hickok" ('38 Columbia).

Increasingly, from 1940 on, he began to play grouchy bartenders in the westerns of George O'Brien, Tex Ritter, Range Busters, Bob Steele, George Houston, Tim Holt, Eddie Dean and Lash LaRue. You'd never find Cramer tending bar at Cheers, that's for sure! Matter of fact, he's prominent as the bartender in his next to last film, "Santa Fe" ('52) with Randolph Scott. His bartending actually dates back to serving booze in the independently made "Face On the Barroom Floor" in '32. Totaling up his barkeep pics finds him tending bar in over 30 films…not to count his saloon owner roles as in "Rawhide Mail" with Jack Perrin.

Ironically, Cramer died from cirrhosis of the liver August 9, 1960, in Los Angeles.

Suggested Sampling of Cramer's Western Heavies:

- Lariats and Sixshooters ('31 Cosmos) Jack Perrin
- Pocatello Kid ('31 Tiffany) Ken Maynard
- Red Rider ('34 Universal serial) Buck Jones
- Law of the Wild ('34 Mascot serial) Bob Custer
- Rawhide Mail ('34 Reliable) Jack Perrin
- Defying the Law ('35 American) Ted Wells
- Frontier Justice ('36 Diversion) Hoot Gibson
- Santa Fe Bound ('36 Reliable) Tom Tyler
- Knight of the Plains ('38 Spectrum) Fred Scott
- Great Adventures of Wild Bill Hickok ('38 Columbia serial) Bill Elliott
- Songs and Bullets ('38 Spectrum) Fred Scott
- Legion of the Lawless ('40 RKO) George O'Brien

JAMES CRAVEN

Hard as it is to believe, with nearly 20 years of movie and TV work, there is no record of James Craven…who he was, when he lived and died, no obituaries are to be found in tradepapers…nothing.

We have discerned an early '37 French film credit, possibly indicating Craven's native country. Adding further substance to this belief is the fact his three other credited films in '37-'39 were all made in the United Kingdom. Or perhaps he was British and spoke French.

It was in 1940 he made his stateside debut with major villainous roles in two Columbia serials, "The Green Archer" and "White Eagle". The lean, wavy-haired, thinly-mustached, finely-chiseled features of Craven gave him a look of unqualified integrity. He was suave, sophisticated and cultured, the picture of a gentleman. That look usually belied a cruel scoundrel. In "The Green Archer" ('40 Columbia) he had his own brother kidnapped and thrown in a dungeon. In Buck Jones' "White Eagle" ('41 Columbia) he posed as respectable Dandy Darnell while carrying out his evil deeds. Against "Captain Midnight" ('42 Columbia) he was enemy saboteur Ivan Shark. In "The Purple Monster Strikes" ('45 Republic) Martian invader Roy Barcroft commandeered his lifeless body as an earthly disguise. In "Flying Disc Man From Mars" ('50 Republic) he was a former Nazi collaborator industrialist who attempted to rule the world with Martian Gregory Gay's assistance.

Perhaps with roles becoming less prominent by 1955 (his last is as an oscillator tester in "Francis In the Navy" ('55), and if indeed he was French—or European—Craven decided to return to the Continent.

Suggested Sampling of Craven's Western Heavies:

- White Eagle ('41 Columbia serial) Buck Jones
- Little Joe the Wrangler ('42 Universal) Johnny Mack Brown
- Days of Buffalo Bill ('46 Republic) Sunset Carson
- Sheriff of Redwood Valley ('46 Republic) Bill Elliott
- Desperadoes of Dodge City ('48 Republic) Allan Rocky Lane
- Strange Gamble ('48 United Artists) Hopalong Cassidy
- Gene Autry: Frontier Guard ('51) Gene Autry
- Gene Autry: Outlaw Escape ('51) Gene Autry
- Kit Carson: Golden Trap ('52) Bill Williams
- Lone Ranger: Gold Town ('54) Clayton Moore

DICK CURTIS

Often known as the 'meanest man in Hollywood', there was never any doubt when ox-like Dick Curtis came on screen he was a heavy in the truest sense of the word. He showed no mercy to the heroes on the Columbia lot.

Born Richard D. Dye May 11, 1902, in horse country, Newport, Kentucky, his parents were Frank Dye and Elizabeth Faulkner. They later moved to Los Angeles where Dick received his education. The 6' 3" Curtis started in films as an extra in "The Unpardonable Sin" with Wallace Beery in 1919. He soon left, finding stage work more productive in the East where he had three years of New York stage experience and played stock in New Jersey and Massachusetts.

Curtis returned to Hollywood in 1930 and by 1932 was in First National's "The Famous Ferguson Case" and three other pictures that year.

Several months later, during the making of "King Kong", he was seriously injured and didn't work for over a year. Resuming work at a fever pitch by late 1934, westerns became his main niche with his first several menacing Kermit Maynard at Ambassador followed by Tim McCoy, Johnny Mack Brown and Fred Scott.

Dick seemed to find a home at Columbia in 1937 rustling, robbing and riding hell-for-leather against Charles Starrett and Bill Elliott. Starrett used to refer to his constant on-screen run-ins with the physically menacing Curtis as "the never ending fight".

Even the character names Columbia assigned

Curtis were entertaining: Drag, Link Murdock, Slash Driscoll, Wolf Munro, Lobo Savage, Blaize Carew, Bat Springer, Matt Brawley, Lash Bender, Shoshone Larsen, Mitch Carew—with names like those, you knew he was *bad!*

Columbia kept Curtis busy not only in their B-westerns, but in virtually everything they made from horror films to Blondie movies, short subjects to serials, even bigger budgeted films ("Penitentiary", "You Can't Take It With You", "Man They Could Not Hang", "Behind Prison Gates", etc.) In 1938 Curtis worked in 27 productions…32 in '39!

Over the years Curtis worked on 16 serials, sometimes just a henchman or bit part, but much bigger roles as crippled henchie Korman in "Flying G-Men" ('39 Columbia), Pegleg's right-hand man in "Overland With Kit Carson" ('39 Columbia), the evil Fang in "Terry and the Pirates" ('40 Columbia), a swarthy Tartar in "The Phantom" ('43 Columbia), chief heavy Regan in "Government Agents Vs. Phantom Legion" ('51 Republic) and gunman Campo in "Roar of the Iron Horse" ('51 Columbia).

Constantly busy though the '40s, but less at Columbia, he found work at Universal, MGM, United Artists, even PRC once—"Spook Town" ('44).

His cohort in crime at Columbia, Kenneth MacDonald told an interviewer, "Socially, he was somewhat reclusive. This trait, in fact, was evident in production procedures. He was a thinker regarding his roles, and a strict professional. He found it uneasy to compromise. I felt, at one time, his thinking might lead him to an interest in direction. However, this never occurred. He enjoyed cutting and assembling film clips for whatever purpose."

Oddly, when he came to *The* western thrill factory, Republic, he seemed out of place at times. As Don Miller wrote in HOLLYWOOD CORRAL, "A fine straight menace at Columbia, Curtis was in 'California Gold Rush' and was instructed to make it funny. Curtis was not used to Republic's humorous heavies but did as told. Roy Barcroft could have carried it off in his sleep, but Curtis merely managed to be cute about it. Instead of hitting the whimsical mark, Curtis looked stoned throughout." Still, he was in over a dozen Republics.

There's a notable break in his film work from late '46 to mid '49. It was at this time Curtis discovered what he figured would be a terrific location site in the high desert above Twenty-Nine Palms, California, and, along with Russell Hayden, Roy Rogers, Bud Abbott and some members of the Sons of the Pioneers, 17 partners in all at $500 each, they developed the area for filming of westerns. Gene Autry's Flying-A Productions, ZIV TV's "Cisco Kid" and, eventually, Russell Hayden's production of "Judge Roy Bean" were the primary users of the locale they named Pioneertown.

In the early '50s Curtis found work in television ("Lone Ranger", "Gene Autry", "Wild Bill Hickok") and a couple of good serial roles, "Roar of the Iron Horse"

Charles Starrett and Dick Curtis in another of their "never ending fights" from "Riders of Black River" ('39 Columbia).

('51) and "Government Agents Vs. The Phantom Legion" ('51), just prior to his untimely death January 3, 1952, at only 49. He'd been operated on for a brain tumor at Cedars of Lebanon Hospital in L.A. on Nov. 26, 1951. Cause of death was listed due to respiratory failure, lung cancer and a brain tumor. He is buried at Holy Cross Cemetery in Culver City, California. He was survived by his wife of many years, former silent actress Ruth Sullivan, who also appeared in two low-budget talkies, "Jaws of Justice" ('33) and "Ferocious Pal" ('34).

His last small role was in "Rose of Cimarron" ('52) w/Mala Powers, but it is for his string of Columbia thrillers we will always remember Curtis as one of the Top 10 western screen badmen.

Columbia's Charles Starrett remembered Dick as "…a wonderful fellow. He was really good (in the fight scenes)…well coordinated. His reflex action was good. We had so many fights that we had the routine down perfectly. We had some nice write-ups about our fights."

Fellow badman Pierce Lyden once wrote, "Dick was so bad even the people who worked with him hated him. (Laughs) He was quite a talker, and was always going after the 'big one' (money). When the war was going on in Europe, Dick said, 'I remember the last one (WWI) and all the money people made. If we get into this one, I'm going to make mine.' Well, Dick got his chance—we got into war—and he started a project that was going to make him a millionaire: it was called Pioneertown. It was going to be a western picture location. Several people went in with him. He asked me to join them, but I didn't have the money. The project was a failure because there was not enough water (up on the high desert). Some of the TV shows were shot at Pioneertown, and Russell Hayden spent his retirement years there. Dick did not become the millionaire he had envisioned."

Suggested Sampling of Curtis' Western Heavies:

- Wilderness Mail ('35 Ambassador) Kermit Maynard
- Northern Frontier ('35 Ambassador) Kermit Maynard
- Lion's Den ('36 Puritan) Tim McCoy
- Singing Buckaroo ('37 Spectrum) Fred Scott
- Gambling Terror ('37 Supreme) Johnny Mack Brown
- Bar-Z Badmen ('37 Supreme) Johnny Mack Brown
- A Lawman Is Born ('37 Supreme) Johnny Mack Brown
- Moonlight On the Range ('37 Spectrum) Fred Scott
- Two Gun Law ('37 Columbia) Charles Starrett
- Old Wyoming Trail ('37 Columbia) Charles Starrett
- Outlaws of the Prairie ('37 Columbia) Charles Starrett
- Cattle Raiders ('38 Columbia) Charles Starrett
- Rawhide ('38 20th Century Fox) Smith Ballew
- Call of the Rockies ('38 Columbia) Charles Starrett
- West of Cheyenne ('38 Columbia) Charles Starrett
- South of Arizona ('38 Columbia) Charles Starrett
- West of the Santa Fe ('38 Columbia) Charles Starrett
- Rio Grande ('38 Columbia) Charles Starrett
- Thundering West ('39 Columbia) Charles Starrett
- Overland With Kit Carson ('39 Columbia serial) Bill Elliott
- Riders of Black River ('39 Columbia) Charles Starrett
- Western Caravans ('39 Columbia) Charles Starrett
- Taming of the West ('39 Columbia) Bill Elliott
- Two Fisted Rangers ('40 Columbia) Charles Starrett
- Texas Stagecoach ('40 Columbia) Charles Starrett
- Blazing Six Shooters ('40 Columbia) Charles Starrett
- Pioneers of the Frontier ('40 Columbia) Bill Elliott
- Bullets For Rustlers ('40 Columbia) Charles Starrett
- Three Men From Texas ('40 Paramount) William Boyd
- Ragtime Cowboy Joe ('40 Universal) Johnny Mack Brown
- Across the Sierras ('41 Columbia) Bill Elliott
- Stick to Your Guns ('41 Paramount) William Boyd
- Arizona Cyclone ('41 Universal) Johnny Mack Brown
- Tombstone ('42 Paramount) Richard Dix
- Vengeance of the West ('42 Columbia) Bill Elliott/Tex Ritter
- Pardon My Gun ('42 Columbia) Charles Starrett
- Riders of the Northwest Mounted ('42 Columbia) Russell Hayden
- Cowboy In the Clouds ('43 Columbia) Charles Starrett
- Wagon Wheels Westward ('45 Republic) Bill Elliott
- California Gold Rush ('46 Republic) Bill Elliott
- Song of Arizona ('46 Republic) Roy Rogers
- Lawless Breed ('46 Universal) Kirby Grant
- Santa Fe Uprising ('46 Republic) Allan Lane
- Navajo Trail Raiders ('49 Republic) Allan "Rocky" Lane
- Covered Wagon Raid ('50 Republic) Allan "Rocky" Lane
- Lone Ranger: Bad Medicine ('50) Clayton Moore
- Gene Autry: Sheriff of Santa Rosa ('50) Gene Autry
- Range Rider: Western Fugitive ('51) Jock Mahoney
- Wild Bill Hickok: Lady Mayor ('51) Guy Madison
- Gene Autry: Frame For Trouble ('51) Gene Autry
- Whirlwind ('51 Columbia) Gene Autry
- Roar of the Iron Horse ('51 Columbia serial) Jock Mahoney

DONALD CURTIS

Too often overlooked as a heavy in '40s Columbia B-westerns, Donald Curtis went from badman to ordained minister.

Born Curtis Donald Rudolf February 27, 1915, in Cheney, Washington (near Eugene), Curtis won a scholarship then obtained a B.S. and M.A. in dramatic production from the School of Speech at Northwestern University in Evanston, Illinois. He worked as an associate professor of dramatic Art at Duquesne University in Pittsburgh, Pennsylvania. He won a Rockefeller Fellowship and used it to study acting.

His stage experience includes a role on Broadway in 1949's "Goodbye My Fancy". West Coast productions of "Life with Father", "Outward Bound", "The Male Animal" and numerous others also fill his resume.

He made his screen debut uncredited as an ambulance intern in "Emergency Squad" ('40 Paramount) which starred Bill Henry.

Curtis' next role as Ronal, one of Prince Barin's trusted officers, in Universal's third (and final) Flash Gordon serial, "Flash Gordon Conquers the Universe" ('40), established him further. A small role as a thug in another Universal serial, "Junior G-Men", followed the same year.

Roles in a dozen B-westerns in the '40s led to a

Donald Curtis manhandles his screen sister, Mary Dailey, in Bill Elliott's "Hands Across the Rockies" ('41 Columbia).

contract at prestigious MGM from '43-'46, where his first was "Bataan" ('43) opposite Robert Taylor.

Freelancing again in the late '40s and '50s, Curtis appeared in a few more westerns and made a sci-fi thriller that he called his favorite, "It Came From Beneath the Sea" ('55), because "it was the only time I got the girl at the end of the picture."

In 1953 Curtis changed his life, "I went to Santa Barbara and was ordained a minister in the Church of Religious Science. I made a few more pictures, then retired after 'Night Passage' ('57) with James Stewart. I did go back into acting briefly in the '60s and had a role with David Janssen in 'Warning Shot' ('67)."

For well over 20 years Curtis and his wife, Dorothy, lived in Dallas, Texas, where they were known not for his film career, but as Reverend Donald Curtis and Reverend Dorothy Curtis, pastors of Unity Church on Forest Lane. He established and recorded the five-times-per-week program, "Five Minutes That Will Change Your Life" on WRR radio. The program was also in syndication.

Curtis was the author of 30 books on self improvement, metaphysics and New Thought. He traveled throughout the world giving classes and seminars on meditation and higher dimensions of human potential. He appeared on "Oprah Winfrey" in '87 discussing true meaning of the new age.

Curtis was honored at the Memphis Film Festival in 1989 and a few years later retired to Desert Hot Springs, California.

At 82, he died on May 22, 1997, of unknown causes in Desert Hot Springs.

Suggested Sampling of Curtis' Western Heavies:

- Take Me Back to Oklahoma ('40 Monogram) Tex Ritter
- Hands Across the Rockies ('41 Columbia) Bill Elliott
- Son of Davy Crockett ('41 Columbia) Bill Elliott
- Thunder Over the Prairie ('41 Columbia) Charles Starrett
- Royal Mounted Patrol ('41 Columbia) Charles Starrett
- Code of the Outlaw ('42 Republic) 3 Mesquiteers
- Westward Ho ('42 Republic) 3 Mesquiteers
- Tombstone, The Town Too Tough to Die ('42 Paramount) Richard Dix
- A Tornado In the Saddle ('42 Columbia) Russell Hayden
- Law of the Northwest ('43 Columbia) Charles Starrett
- Stampede ('49 Allied Artists) Rod Cameron
- Stories of the Century: Johnny Ringo ('55) Jim Davis
- Annie Oakley: Western Privateer ('56) Gail Davis
- 7th Cavalry ('56 Warner Bros.) Randolph Scott
- Annie Oakley: Desperate Men ('57) Gail Davis
- Frontier Doctor: Homesteaders ('59) Rex Allen

STEVE DARRELL

Screen, stage and radio actor Steve Darrell first came to films after gaining some stage experience in 1938 as an uncredited gangster in "Angels with Dirty Faces".

By 1945 he'd found his way into Buster Crabbe westerns at PRC. Westerns were either a genre he felt comfortable in, liked or couldn't get out of, because they are primarily all he appeared in for the next 20 years, winding up his career with an episode of "Daniel Boone" in 1964.

J. Stevan Darrell was born November 19, 1904, in Osage, Iowa. His father was Moss David Horsfall of Wisconsin, a railroader, and his mother was Katherine McHugh of Pennsylvania. Playing Abraham Lincoln in a high school play piqued his interest in pursuing a show-biz career.

His first professional work was with the Galloway Players repertory company in Pittsfield, Massachusetts. He came to the west coast in 1937 to study at the famed Pasadena Playhouse. A year later came his first film.

"I enjoyed all kinds of character roles, the more villainous the better," he once corresponded to authors Ken Jones and Arthur McClure, citing his favorite roles as being in "Treasure of Ruby Hills" ('55 Allied Artists) with Zachary Scott and that of a crooked sheriff on a 1959 episode of "26 Men", "Dead or Alive".

Darrell also did a lot of exemplary but wicked roles at Columbia ("West of Sonora" '48 as Black Murphy stands out) and Republic opposite Allan "Rocky" Lane in the late '40s-early '50s.

By the mid '50s, especially on TV, Darrell, now with a leathery, weather-beaten look in his early 50s, turned to portraying lawmen on "Tales of Wells Fargo", "Cheyenne", "Wanted Dead Or Alive", "Rawhide" and others, as well as in films such as "Law Vs. Billy the Kid" ('54).

Darrell is also fondly recalled as an unduly judged Frank James fighting to right the wrongs committed in his and brother Jesse's (Clayton Moore) names in Republic's excellent 1948 serial, "Adventures of Frank and Jesse James".

Married to Gertrude Payette, the Darrells lived at 5624 DeLongpre Avenue in Los Angeles.

Darrell's final legit stand was in "Born Yesterday" at Melodyland theatre in the round in Orange County in 1966 before dying at 65, August 14, 1970, as the result of a brain tumor. Cremated, his remains went to Westwood Memorial Park.

Suggested Sampling of Darrell's Western Heavies:

- Lightning Raiders ('45 PRC) Buster Crabbe
- Terrors on Horseback ('46 PRC) Buster Crabbe
- Valley of Fear ('47 Monogram) Johnny Mack Brown
- Under Colorado Skies ('47 Republic) Monte Hale
- Riders of the Lone Star ('47 Columbia) Charles Starrett
- On the Old Spanish Trail ('47 Republic) Roy Rogers
- Overland Trails ('48 Monogram) Johnny Mack Brown
- West of Sonora ('48 Columbia) Charles Starrett
- Carson City Raiders ('48 Republic) Allan "Rocky" Lane
- Son of God's Country ('48 Republic) Monte Hale
- El Dorado Pass ('48 Columbia) Charles Starrett
- Crashing Thru ('49 Monogram) Whip Wilson
- Challenge of the Range ('49 Columbia) Charles Starrett
- Frontier Outpost ('49 Columbia) Charles Starrett
- Cow Town ('50 Columbia) Gene Autry
- Gene Autry: Gold Dust Charlie ('50) Gene Autry
- Gene Autry: Doodle Bug ('50) Gene Autry
- Gene Autry: Double Switch ('50) Gene Autry
- Rough Riders of Durango ('51 Republic) Allan "Rocky" Lane
- Pecos River ('51 Columbia) Charles Starrett
- Wild Bill Hickok: Outlaw's Son ('52) Guy Madison
- Range Rider: The Chase ('53) Jock Mahoney
- Lone Ranger: Hidden Fortune ('53) John Hart
- Stories of the Century: Quantrill and His Raiders ('54) Jim Davis
- Law Vs. Billy the Kid ('54 Columbia) Scott Brady
- Annie Oakley: Annie's Desert Adventure ('54) Gail Davis
- Treasure of Ruby Hills ('55 Allied Artists) Zachary Scott
- 26 Men: Dead or Alive ('59) Kelo Henderson/Tris Coffin

JIM DAVIS

Many viewers classify Jim Davis as a hero, in actuality, he played heavies as much as heroes in his western films. The "heroic" image no doubt comes from his popular starring series for Republic TV, "Stories of the Century" ('54-'55).

Long respected as an actor and a man by his colleagues, the road to stardom late in his life on TV's "Dallas" was a long, hard one.

Jim O. Davis was born in the small community of Edgerton, Missouri, August 26, 1909, the son of an undertaker. His mother's maiden name was Offutt. He excelled in high school sports and attended William Jewell College in Liberty, Missouri. He held jobs as a railway hand, oil field laborer and circus tent rigger before becoming a salesman for the Quaker State Oil Company headquartered in Kansas City.

In California on a sales trip, the film industry began to interest him. Obtaining an agent, he landed a contract at MGM who cast him in small roles beginning with "Cairo" in '42.

Just as his career was on an upswing, WWII came along and Jim enlisted in the Coast Guard in late '43.

Returning from the war, only a few small parts came his way until he was noticed by Bette Davis who demanded him as her co-star at Warner Bros. for "Winter Meeting" ('48). Unfortunately, the film was a flop for Bette Davis and Jim was made the scapegoat and dropped by Warner Bros.

It was then Jim found his niche in westerns as a heavy at, principally, Republic opposite Bill Elliott, Forrest Tucker, Rod Cameron and others.

It really wasn't until "Stories of the Century" was successful that he began to get leads in B+ westerns such as "Last Stagecoach West" ('57), "Badge of Marshal Brennan" ('57), "Noose For a Gunman" ('60), "Frontier Uprising" ('61), "Gambler Wore a Gun" ('61) and a few others.

In 1949 Jim married Blanche Ellis, a singer and onetime swimmer in Billy Rose's Aquacade. They had one child, Tara, in '53. Unfortunately, she was involved in a tragic car accident on the eve of her high school graduation leaving her in a coma. The Davises were forced to make the tough decision to take her off life support to let her die with dignity.

Jim's co-star on "Stories of the Century", Kristine Miller told us, "Jim Davis was delightful, and in 1955 we won the Emmy for best western series (at the 7th annual event)." The series was cancelled because, "The head of Republic, Herbert J. Yates, decided to change to a Fu Manchu program," Kristine explained. "That was a failure, so both series disappeared—and Republic soon went away—except for leasing its soundstages to other studios. I would have done another 13 episodes very happily. Jim Davis' wife, Blanche, was every bit as tall as me. His daughter, Tara, was absolutely his idol. When she was killed in a car accident at 17 or 18, I thought he'd never get over it. Jim was a round and ready man…sweet, charming and kind. We enjoyed each other. We even had a couple of reunions in Carmel."

By the '60s Jim was working extensively on TV while appearing in cheaper theatrical productions. In '74 he starred in the now forgotten and short-lived "The Cowboys" TV series.

Jim was back on top when "Dallas" debuted to huge ratings in April 1978. The role of oil baron Jock Ewing fit Davis perfectly. Its success brought him not only late in life TV fame but financial security as well.

Unfortunately, Davis had suffered from cluster headaches and ulcers for years and the long, grueling 12 hour TV workdays caused his health to fail. He underwent abdominal surgery for a perforated ulcer and was under treatment for a brain tumor when he died at 71 April 26, 1981, at his home in Northridge, California.

Suggested Sampling of Davis' Western Heavies:

- Fabulous Texan ('47 Republic) William Elliott
- Hellfire ('49 Republic) William Elliott
- Brimstone ('49 Republic) Rod Cameron
- Cariboo Trail ('50 20th Century Fox) Randolph Scott
- California Passage ('50 Republic) Forrest Tucker
- Three Desperate Men ('51 Lippert) Preston Foster
- Oh! Susanna ('51 Republic) Rod Cameron
- Silver Canyon ('51 Columbia) Gene Autry
- Big Sky ('52 RKO) Kirk Douglas
- Woman of the North Country ('52 Republic) Rod Cameron
- Ride the Man Down ('52 Republic) Rod Cameron
- Cowboy G-Men: Silver Shotgun ('52) Russell Hayden
- The Outcast ('54 Republic) John Derek
- Vanishing American ('55 Republic) Scott Brady
- Wild Dakotas ('56 Associated) Bill Williams
- Duel at Apache Wells ('57 Republic) Ben Cooper
- Tales of Wells Fargo: Two Cartridges ('57) Dale Robertson
- Quiet Gun ('57 20th Century Fox) Forrest Tucker
- Raiders of Old California ('57 Republic) Faron Young
- Toughest Gun In Tombstone ('58 U.A.) George Montgomery
- Alias Jesse James ('59 U.A.) Bob Hope
- Yancy Derringer: Two Tickets To Pomentory ('59) Jock Mahoney
- Laramie: Trail Drive ('60) Robert Fuller/John Smith
- Tall Man: Lonely Star ('60) Barry Sullivan
- Tales of Wells Fargo: The Lobo ('61) Dale Robertson
- Gunsmoke: The Imposter ('61) James Arness
- Have Gun Will Travel: The Treasure ('62) Richard Boone
- Death Valley Days: Three Minutes to Eternity ('63) Forrest Tucker
- Branded: One Way Out ('65) Chuck Connors
- Gunsmoke: The Raid ('66) James Arness
- Hondo: War Hawks ('67) Ralph Taeger
- Fort Utah ('67 Paramount) John Ireland
- Cimarron Strip: The Search ('67) Stuart Whitman
- Gunsmoke: The Gun Runners ('68) James Arness
- High Chaparral: New Hostess in Town ('70) Cameron Mitchell
- Five Bloody Graves ('70 Independent International) Scott Brady
- Gunsmoke: Murdoch ('71) James Arness

TED DE CORSIA

Hefty, brash, menacing villain of gangster as well as western films, thick-necked Ted de Corsia was an actor in touring companies and on radio before making a memorable film debut as the killer in 1948's "Naked City". Although he occasionally played such sympathetic roles as a judge or prison warden, de Corsia's size, tough New York street demeanor and raucous, gravelly voice made him perfect casting for street thugs and outlaw gang leaders.

Edward Gildea de Corsia was born September 29, 1905, in Brooklyn, New York, the son of Edward G. de Corsia, a vaudeville actor from Texas, and Helen O'Rielley of New York.

He gained early experience in touring road companies which led to a well noted career in radio beginning around September 1939 when he became Sergeant Velie on CBS' "Adventures of Ellery Queen". Throughout the '40s he was heard on "Big Town", "Cavalcade of America", "The Shadow", "Ford Theatre', "Nightbeat", "Richard Diamond", "Terry and the Pirates" (as Flip Corkin), among others. He starred on two short-lived programs, NBC's "Joe and Mabel" ('41-'42) and CBS' "Pursuit" ('49-'50).

When film and TV work began to occupy more of his time, he dropped out of radio in the early '50s.

Among de Corsia's 60 some film credits are 17 westerns, but among his over 120 TV credits, over half are westerns ranging from "The Lone Ranger" to "Gunsmoke" in type.

One of his vilest, most depraved characters was created in Audie Murphy's "Quick Gun". Leading lady Merry Anders thought, "He was just great though. Just perfect as his character. It helped me in a way because I was supposedly so terrified of him I was speechless."

He may not seem the type, but as he aged, de Corsia became quite adept at portraying Indian Chiefs which he did with regularity on "Sugarfoot", "Rawhide", "Daniel Boone", "High Chaparral" and in Bill Williams' "Oklahoma Territory" ('60).

Ted was first married to Mary Robertson. They divorced in 1935. He married Rachel Thurber in 1939. They had two daughters, one of them was named Deidre.

De Corsia was divorced and living at 320 North Lapeer Ave. in Beverly Hills, California, when he died April 11, 1973, at 67 of cerebral thrombosis. He'd been a patient at West Valley Community Hospital for two weeks prior to his death. His remains were cremated and scattered at sea.

Suggested Sampling of de Corsia's Western Heavies:

- Vengeance Valley ('51 MGM) Burt Lancaster
- Man With the Gun ('55 United Artists) Robert Mitchum
- Frontier: Out of Taos ('56)
- Broken Arrow: Mail Riders ('56) John Lupton/Michael Ansara
- Showdown at Abilene ('56 Universal-International) Jock Mahoney
- Gunfight at the O.K. Corral ('57 Paramount) Burt Lancaster
- Maverick: According to Hoyle ('57) James Garner
- Lawless Eighties ('57 Republic) Buster Crabbe
- Gun Battle at Monterey ('57 Allied Artists) Sterling Hayden
- Casey Jones: Trackwalker ('57) Alan Hale Jr.
- Sugarfoot: Guns For Big Bear ('58) Will Hutchins
- Jefferson Drum: Simon Pitt ('58) Jeff Richards
- Lawman: Short Straw ('58) John Russell
- Rifleman: Young Englishman ('58) Chuck Connors
- Trackdown: Guilt ('58) Robert Culp
- Tales of the Texas Rangers: Ambush ('58) Willard Parker
- 26 Men: False Witness ('58) Kelo Henderson/Tris Coffin
- Mackenzie's Raiders: Scalphunters ('58) Richard Carlson
- Zane Grey Theatre: Trouble at Tres Cruces ('59) Brian Keith
- Frontier Doctor: Gringo Pete ('59) Rex Allen
- Rough Riders: Forty Five Calibre Law ('59) Jan Merlin/Kent Taylor
- Lawman: The Senator ('58) John Russell
- Wanted Dead Or Alive: Chain Gang ('59) Steve McQueen
- Law of the Plainsman: A Question of Courage ('60) Michael Ansara
- Noose For a Gunman ('60 United Artists) Jim Davis
- Deputy: Two-way Deal ('61) Henry Fonda/Allen Case
- Gunsmoke: He Learned About Women ('62) James Arness
- Quick Gun ('64 Columbia) Audie Murphy
- Wild Wild West: Night of the Sabatini Death ('67) Robert Conrad

JOHN DEHNER

When stern-faced John Dehner rode into town with his wide hat brim casting a dark shadow over his steely blue eyes with just his thin mustache and firm grimace showing, you knew Matt Dillon, Paladin, Lucas McCain or whomever was in for trouble.

A consummate actor, he could also bring off comedy equally well, which found him, especially as he grew older, on "Andy Griffith", "Hogan's Heroes", "Beverly Hillbillies", "Love American Style" and as a regular on "The Doris Day Show" ('71-'73).

Also playing against his heavy type, he was crusading newspaper reporter Duke Williams on "The Roaring '20s" ('60-'62) and dramatized many sympathetic roles on various TV westerns—he was never better than on a "Gunsmoke" as lonely Caleb Marr, who, bored with toiling on his farm, decides to live a little and heads for Dodge City.

Born John Forkum November 23, 1915, in Staten Island, New York, the son of an artist, he was educated through grammar schools in Slemdal, Norway, and at the Lycee Carnot in Paris, France. He attended high school at Hastings-on-Hudson, New York, and at the University of California.

Dehner was a man of many talents, not the least of which was a thorough knowledge of four languages. As a radio news editor during WWII he received the Peabody Award for his coverage of the first United Nations Conference in San Francisco.

Unlike many actors, Dehner's career didn't begin on the stage, he started out as an animator for Walt Disney, working on classics like "Bambi" ('42) and "Fantasia" ('40). Previously, as a musician, he was musical director of a touring stock company and a band leader.

In 1944, post WWII service, his rich, well-modulated baritone voice landed him dozens of roles on all the top radio shows—"Escape", "Phillip Marlowe", "Count of Monte Cristo", "Gunsmoke" and dozens more. He starred as CBS' "Frontier Gentleman" in '58 as well as the radio version of "Have Gun Will Travel" from '58-'60. Dehner also starred for a season on "Pursuit" ('51-'52), replacing Ted De Corsia, and "The Truitts" ('50-'51) sit-com.

If this wasn't enough to keep him busy, Dehner began his 150 movie screen career with bit parts in 1944, gradually working up to better parts, such as his first western portraying egotistical, temperamental western

Tim Holt and Richard (Chito) Martin have the drop on renegades John Dehner and Don Harvey in RKO's "Dynamite Pass" ('50).

star Rod Mason in Monte Hale's "Out California Way" for Republic in '46.

Apparently with still not enough to occupy all his time, the obviously workaholic Dehner began doing television in '52, eventually amassing over 160 credits including all the major TV westerns. In 1960 he essayed the role of Burgundy Smith, constantly perplexing Brian Keith on the short-lived "The Westerner" ('60). For half a season in '65, Dehner became Morgan Starr, in charge of Shiloh Ranch on "The Virginian".

Dehner continued to work into the '80s, with his last role that of an admiral on the mini-series "War and Remembrance" in '88.

Whether outlaw leader, crooked banker, dishonest gambler or sympathetic rancher, the tall 6' 3" distinguished John Dehner always gave his all to every role, creating some truly memorable characters.

Director Earl Bellamy told us, "He was a true professional. Came in prepared—knew his part, your part and the next guy's part. A fine actor, old reliable—he could do comedy or heavy villains." Fellow actor Walter Reed said, "He was a hell of an actor with a dry, fey sense of humor. A delightful guy to know."

Dehner died at 76 in Santa Barbara, California, of emphysema and diabetes on February 4, 1992.

Suggested Sampling of Dehner's Western Heavies:

- Out California Way ('46 Republic) Monte Hale
- Riders of the Pony Express ('49 Screencraft) Ken Curtis
- Bandits of El Dorado ('49 Columbia) Charles Starrett
- Horsemen of the Sierras ('49 Columbia) Charles Starrett
- Dynamite Pass ('50 RKO) Tim Holt
- Texas Dynamo ('50 Columbia) Charles Starrett
- Fort Savage Raiders ('50 Columbia) Charles Starrett
- Texas Rangers ('51 Columbia) George Montgomery
- Hot Lead ('51 RKO) Tim Holt
- Desert Passage ('52 RKO) Tim Holt
- Cripple Creek ('52 Columbia) George Montgomery
- Junction City ('52 Columbia) Charles Starrett
- Kit Carson: Bad Man of Marysville ('53) Bill Williams
- Gun Belt ('53 United Artists) George Montgomery
- Stories of the Century: Henry Plummer ('54) Jim Davis
- Man From Bitter Ridge ('55 Universal-International) Lex Barker
- Gunsmoke: Tap Day For Kitty ('56) James Arness
- Cheyenne: Broken Pledge ('57) Clint Walker
- Gunsmoke: Crack-Up ('57) James Arness
- Restless Gun: Quiet City ('58) John Payne
- Apache Territory ('58 Columbia) Rory Calhoun
- Man of the West ('58 United Artists) Gary Cooper
- Wanted Dead Or Alive: The Conquerors ('59) Steve McQueen
- Tales of Wells Fargo: Young Jim Hardie ('59) Dale Robertson
- Rifleman: The Blowout ('59) Chuck Connors
- Law of the Plainsman: Clear Title ('59) Michael Ansara
- Laramie: Company Man ('60) John Smith/Robert Fuller
- Rawhide: Incident at Sulphur Creek ('60) Eric Fleming
- Maverick: Greenbacks Unlimited ('60) James Garner
- Tales of Wells Fargo: Day of Judgment ('60) Dale Robertson
- Gunsmoke: The Badge ('60) James Arness
- Bat Masterson: Prescott Campaign ('61) Gene Barry
- Rawhide: Incident of the New Start ('61) Eric Fleming
- Rifleman: The Prisoner ('61) Chuck Connors
- Maverick: Devil's Necklace (Pt. 1-2) ('61) Jack Kelly
- Lawman: Long Gun ('62) John Russell
- Gunsmoke: Ash ('63) James Arness
- Virginian: Echo From Another Day ('63) Doug McClure
- Wild Wild West: Night of the Casual Killer ('65) Robert Conrad
- Branded: One Way Out ('65) Chuck Connors
- Big Valley: The Invaders ('65) Lee Majors
- Wild Wild West: Night of the Steel Assassin ('66) Robert Conrad
- Monroes: Gun Bound ('67) Michael Anderson Jr.
- Winchester 73 ('67 TVM) Tom Tryon
- High Chaparral: The Legacy ('69) Leif Ericson

BRUCE DERN

He killed John Wayne on-screen in "The Cowboys". Alone, that's enough to qualify Bruce Dern for inclusion into the Heavies Hall of Fame. But his 25 nasty appearances on TV westerns like "Bonanza", "Big Valley", "Wagon Train", "Gunsmoke" and others, along with several movies, lend even more credence to Dern's qualifications among the best of the badmen.

When Dern was awarded a Golden Boot in 2002 for his many westerns, he related his encounter with John Wayne. Dern was apprised by the director that Mr. Wayne had a strong personality and for Dern not to take any guff from him for fear it might diminish Dern's on-screen killing of Wayne. Just before the scene was to be filmed, Wayne brusquely confronted Dern face to face and, staring into his eyes, said gruffly, "They're going to hate you out there for this." Calmly standing his ground, Dern glared back, "Yeah, but they'll love me in Berkeley."

Although he's played some likable characters in his still ongoing 40 year career (such as Jack Lord's rodeo buddy E. J. Stocker on the '62 "Stoney Burke" series), Dern is best thought of as an intense actor whose quiet demeanor often belies a hint of madness seething beneath the surface. Dern himself admits, "I've played more psychotics, freaks and dopers than anyone."

Born Bruce Macleish June 4, 1936, in Chicago, Illinois, he is the nephew of poet Archibald Macleish. His prominent American family connected with the law and politics, he graduated New Tier Township High School in Winnetka, Illinois, attended the University of Pennsylvania in Philadelphia, then studied at the renown Actors Studio in 1959, then plunged into TV and movie work in 1960, honing his craft first on stage then on a variety of shows which eventually culminated in a best supporting actor award nomination for "Coming Home" in '78 as Jane Fonda's troubled husband.

But it seems Dern's best work was then behind him. He'd given up TV guest shots as of 1970 to concentrate on films, but after the nomination he drifted into art-house films and other projects that no one ever saw, essentially crippling his career. In recent years he has emerged as an older, wiser character actor in more mainstream films, "The Haunting" ('99), "All the Pretty Horses" ('00), "Glass House" ('01) and "Monster" ('03).

Dern was first married to Marie Dean (years unknown). When they divorced he married actress Diane Ladd in 1960. They had two daughters, including actress Laura Dern. Divorced in '69, Bruce married Andrea Beckett later that same year.

Suggested Sampling of Dern's Western Heavies:

- Wagon Train: Eli Bancroft Story ('63) Robert Fuller
- Wagon Train: Those Who Stay Behind ('64) John McIntire
- Virginian: The Payment ('64) Clu Gulager
- Wagon Train: Indian Girl Story) ('65) Terry Wilson
- Laredo: Rendezvous at Arillo ('65) Peter Brown/William Smith/Neville Brand
- Gunsmoke: Ten Little Indians ('65) James Arness
- A Man Called Shenandoah: The Verdict ('65) Robert Horton
- Gunsmoke: South Wind ('65) James Arness
- Branded: The Wolfers ('65) Chuck Connors
- Big Valley: Under a Dark Star ('66) Richard Long
- Loner: To Hang a Dead Man ('66) Lloyd Bridges
- Big Valley: By Force and Violence ('66) Barbara Stanwyck
- Big Valley: Lost Treasure ('66) Lee Majors
- Gunsmoke: The Jailer ('66) James Arness
- War Wagon ('67 Universal) John Wayne
- Big Valley: Four Days to Furnace Hill ('67) Barbara Stanwyck
- Bonanza: The Trackers ('68) Lorne Greene/Dan Blocker
- Lancer: Julie ('68) James Stacy
- Big Valley: The Prize ('68) Lee Majors
- Will Penny ('68 Paramount) Charlton Heston
- Hang 'Em High ('68 United Artists) Clint Eastwood
- Support Your Local Gunfighter ('69 United Artists) James Garner
- Gunsmoke: Long Night ('69) James Arness
- High Chaparral: Only the Bad Come to Sonora ('70) Henry Darrow
- The Cowboys ('72 Warner Bros.) John Wayne
- Posse ('75 Paramount) Kirk Douglas

RICHARD DEVON

Badman Richard Devon's deadly, thin-lipped evil smile became a TV western staple at Four Star during the late '50s and early '60s. Four Star used Devon relentlessly on all their series, "Law of the Plainsman", "Zane Grey Theatre', "Johnny Ringo", "Big Valley", "Rifleman", "Trackdown", "Wanted Dead Or Alive", "Stagecoach West" and others. If Devon wasn't to be found rustling cattle at Four Star, he was robbing stages on the Universal backlot.

Richard Devon was born December 11, 1931, in Glendale, California. He wanted to be an actor from the time he played a small part in a first grade grammar school production.

Among all the odd jobs Devon did as a youngster was a part time job at a riding academy at the Griffith Park stable. He learned to ride so well they made him an alternate instructor on weekends.

Graduating high school, Devon worked as a mail boy at Monogram, as a nurseryman, a mechanic's helper and at the Hollywood Palladium as a bouncer.

Answering a newspaper ad which offered training to the novice, Stage 8 drama school allowed Devon to work his way through as he didn't have tuition money.

During this time he made his first live TV appearance for experimental W6XAO atop Mt. Lee in the Hollywood Hills. Additional work came from Armed Forces radio, the Video Players little theatre and KTLA-TV.

After studying with Richard Boone's acting class for about six months, Devon began to find employment on live TV shows such as "Space Patrol", "Marshal of Gunsight Pass", "Tim McCoy Show" and "Matinee Theatre". It was this training that brought him into better quality TV shows and films by 1955.

He also did radio, including a short stint as Batman on the "Superman" radio series. In between all this, he worked on stage, including "Country Girl" in Tustin, California.

In 1959 Richard had the semi-regular role of Jody Barker on "Yancy Derringer". In Devon's own words the character was "frightened all the time, always looking for a buck, and wanted everyone to be happy. It was a delight, nothing but kicks. They wanted to sign me up for the whole series. Everything was looking rosy and then (the sponsor) didn't pick up the series."

For 30 years the ominous, imposing Devon worked steadily. Then in 1985 he moved from Los Angeles to Mill Valley in northern California where he continued to do a lot of voice work, including commercials, a spoken word religious album in which he played Jesus, and work on George Lucas' animated "The Ewoks". 1988 saw him as a Cardinal in his last film to date, "The Seventh Sign".

Richard's wife Pat retired from United Airlines and they now make ample opportunities to travel.

Suggested Sampling of Devon's Western Heavies:

- Rin Tin Tin: Bugle Call ('55) Lee Aaker
- Wyatt Earp: Time for All Good Men ('57) Hugh O'Brian
- Sgt. Preston: Rebel Yell ('57) Richard Simmons
- Tales of Wells Fargo: Dr. Alice ('58) Dale Robertson
- Trackdown: The Brothers ('58) Robert Culp
- Wanted Dead Or Alive: Giveaway Gun ('58) Steve McQueen
- Wyatt Earp: Reformation of Doc Holliday ('58) Hugh O'Brian
- Badman's Country ('58 Warner Bros.) George Montgomery
- Wanted Dead Or Alive: Eager Man ('59) Steve McQueen
- Rifleman: Blood Brothers ('59) Chuck Connors
- Law of the Plainsman: Prairie Incident ('59) Michael Ansara
- Johnny Ringo: The Posse ('59) Don Durant
- Colt .45: Yellow Terror ('59) Wayde Preston
- Riverboat: Landlubbers ('60) Darren McGavin
- Rifleman: The Grasshopper ('60) Chuck Connors
- Rifleman: Miss Milly ('60) Chuck Connors
- Sugarfoot: Vinegaroon ('60) Will Hutchins
- Laramie: Saddle and Spur ('60) Robert Fuller/John Smith
- Law of the Plainsman: Stella ('60) Michael Ansara
- Overland Trail: Sour Annie ('60) Doug McClure/William Bendix
- Stagecoach West: A Fork In the Road ('60) Robert Bray
- Gunfighters of Abilene ('60 United Artists) Buster Crabbe
- Stagecoach West: Songs My Mother Taught Me ('61) Robert Bray/Wayne Rogers
- Stagecoach West: Renegades ('61) Robert Bray/Wayne Rogers
- Whispering Smith: Stakeout ('61) Audie Murphy
- Rifleman: Stand-In ('61) Chuck Connors
- Rifleman: Most Amazing Man ('62) Chuck Connors
- Laramie: Gun Duel ('62) Robert Fuller
- Rawhide: Incident of the Buryin' Man ('63) Eric Fleming/Clint Eastwood
- Wagon Train: Emmett Lawton Story ('63) Denny (Scott) Miller
- Gunsmoke: Quest For Asa Janin ('63) James Arness
- Gunsmoke: Ex-Con ('63) James Arness
- Cattle King ('63 MGM) Robert Taylor
- Destry: Big Deal at Little River ('64) John Gavin
- A Man Called Shenandoah: Onslaught ('65) Robert Horton
- Laredo: The Jinx ('65) Peter Brown/William Smith/Neville Brand
- Virginian: No Drums. No Trumpets ('66) Doug McClure
- Iron Horse: Shadow Run ('67) Dale Robertson
- High Chaparral: A Quiet Day In Tucson ('67) Cameron Mitchell
- Guns of Will Sonnett: End of the Rope ('68) Walter Brennan
- Big Valley: A Stranger Everywhere ('68) Lee Majors
- Lancer: Warburton's Edge ('69) James Stacy

JOHN DOUCETTE

With a hefty build, menacing sneer, and a booming bass voice, balding John Doucette was the perfect western badman and was equally adept in gangster roles.

John Arthur Doucette Sr. was born January 21, 1921, the son of Arthur Doucette and Nellie Bishop, both natives of Massachusetts, in Brockton, Massachusetts.

His father was a shoemaker and moved the family constantly from town to town, resulting in John being educated in 32 different grammar schools, eventually graduating in Haverhill at which time the family moved to California where he attended Lincoln High School in Los Angeles. By the time John graduated he'd been in three light operas, four Shakespearean plays and done 48 radio shows.

Next stop was the Pasadena Playhouse where he performed in 27 plays in two years. During that time he appeared in his first film, "Two Tickets to London" ('43).

The draft during WWII interrupted John's studies. He spent three years in Europe during WWII, first with the Air Corps driving a forklift in a warehouse, then in the infantry in Northern Germany including the Battle of the Bulge. He was also with General Patton in the final sweep.

A chance meeting with actor Don Harvey led to a role in Mae West's cross-country tour of "Come On Up, Ring Twice" in 1947.

By now John was beginning to work regular in films and, with a little money, he was married in 1948. Over the years he fathered eight children, five daughters and three sons.

In films and on TV Doucette played gruff heavies, sheriffs, ranchers and townsmen. His characters were varied, both serious and comic.

As the half-hour TV western metamorphosized into hour long dramas, producers and directors began to see the softer side of Doucette, casting him in more sympathetic roles on "Wagon Train", "Rawhide", "Bonanza", "Virginian" and "Big Valley".

Doucette also distinguished himself as a teacher of drama at the University of Portland where, in 1971, he was given an honorary degree in Fine Arts. He also was presented Lecturer of Communications Arts at Loyola and Professional Training Instructor in Theatre Arts for the California Educational Development Corporation at Palo Alto, California.

Summing up his career, Doucette told writers Tom and Jim Goldrup for their book FEATURE PLAYERS Vol. 2, "I'd do the same thing over again. I wouldn't have done anything different. I miss my friends in it, all the actors…those fellows were just great, warm human beings."

Widowed at the time of his death, John died of cancer at his home in Cabazon, Riverside County, California, at 73 on August 16, 1994. His remains were cremated and returned to the custody of his daughter, Nicole Bulaich.

Suggested Sampling of Doucette's Western Heavies:

- Lone Ranger: Masked Rider ('49) Clayton Moore
- Lone Ranger: Gold Fever ('49) Clayton Moore
- Bandits of El Dorado ('49 Columbia) Charles Starrett
- Border Treasure ('50 RKO) Tim Holt
- Gene Autry: The Posse ('50) Gene Autry
- Gene Autry: Devil's Brand ('50) Gene Autry
- Lone Ranger: Hooded Men ('51) Clayton Moore
- Thunder In God's Country ('51 Republic) Rex Allen
- Texas Rangers ('51 Columbia) George Montgomery
- Roy Rogers: Shoot to Kill ('52) Roy Rogers
- Roy Rogers: Hunting For Trouble ('52) Roy Rogers
- Rose of Cimarron ('52 20th Century Fox) Mala Powers
- Sky King: One For the Money ('52) Kirby Grant
- Desert Pursuit ('52 Allied Artists) Wayne Morris
- Range Rider: Border City Affair ('53) Jock Mahoney
- Range Rider: Bullets and Badmen ('53) Jock Mahoney
- Lone Ranger: Bandits in Uniform ('53) John Hart
- Kit Carson: Savage Outpost ('53) Bill Williams
- Gene Autry: Dry Gulch at Devil's Elbow ('53) Gene Autry
- Cisco Kid: Pancho and the Wolf Dog ('53) Duncan Renaldo
- Annie Oakley: Escape From Diablo ('54) Gail Davis
- Lone Ranger: The Fugitive ('54) Clayton Moore
- Roy Rogers: Backfire ('54) Roy Rogers
- Forty Niners ('54 Allied Artists) Bill Elliott

- Annie Oakley: Trouble Shooter ('55) Gail Davis
- Buffalo Bill Jr.: Six Gun Symphony ('55) Dick Jones
- Ghost Town ('56 United Artists) John Smith
- Phantom Stagecoach ('57 Columbia) William Bishop
- Lawless Eighties ('57 Republic) Buster Crabbe
- Gunfire at Indian Gap ('57 Republic) Anthony George
- Tales of Wells Fargo: Alder Gulch ('57) Dale Robertson
- Sheriff of Cochise: Approach With Caution ('57) John Bromfield
- Man Without A Gun: Fugitive ('57) Rex Reason
- Gunsmoke: Liar From Blackhawk ('57) James Arness
- Tombstone Territory: Geronimo ('58) Pat Conway
- Broken Arrow: War Trail ('58) John Lupton/Michael Ansara
- Mackenzie's Raiders: Dream of an Empire ('58) Richard Carlson
- Tales of Wells Fargo: The Renegade ('58) Dale Robertson
- Rough Riders: Murderous Sutton Gang ('58) Jan Merlin/Kent Taylor
- Lawman: The Prisoner ('58) John Russell
- Colt .45: Dead Aim ('59) Wayde Preston
- Tombstone Territory: Surrender at Sunglow ('59) Pat Conway
- Bat Masterson: A Grave Situation ('60) Gene Barry
- Laramie: Naked Steel ('63) John Smith
- Wild Wild West: Night of the Flaming Ghost ('66) Robert Conrad

CURLEY DRESDEN

Curley Dresden is probably the ultimate henchman. Looked tough. Always on hand. Stayed in the background. Said little. Followed orders. Apart from a couple of bit roles early on, all Curley ever appeared in were B-westerns and serials, over 150 of them from 1935-1945, an average of 15 a year—with 1941 being his peak year, 32 films.

Albert J. Dresden (the original spelling of the family name was Drezden) was born July 17, 1900, in Chicago, Illinois. His parents both immigrated from Germany. He had two older brothers, August and Frank, both of whom were teenagers when he was born, and a younger sister, Francis, seven years his junior. All these children were born in Illinois. Albert's father's name is unknown.

He died shortly after his last child was born sometime around 1907 or 1908 with Albert raised by his mother, Anna.

Exactly how he came to Hollywood and got into films is unknown, but an April 1930 California census shows Albert J. Dresden, age 29, as an actor in motion pictures.

Albert was at first a stunt double—for Edmund Lowe in "The Cisco Kid" ('31 Fox with Warner Baxter) and "Women of all Nations" ('31 Fox) and for Leo Carrillo in "Four Frightened People" ('34 Paramount).

By 1935 he was accepting bit roles in films like "Hard Rock Harrigan" with George O'Brien and "The Lost City" serial.

In all, Albert—who assumed the moniker Curley about this time—worked in 16 serials for Republic, Columbia, Mascot and Universal.

Dresden seemed to find a home at PRC in the early '40s bedeviling George Houston, Bob Steele, Robert Livingston and the Art Davis/Lee Powell/Bill Boyd threesome.

Curley left films in 1945 after yet one more unbilled henchman role in Jimmy Wakely's "Lonesome Trail".

When he left the movies he settled in Spokane, Washington. His latter years were not the best of times. Curley had a serious drinking problem, was a welfare recipient and was reduced to working as a newsboy delivering papers for the Spokane SPOKESMAN-REVIEW.

Dresden died June 7, 1953, at 52. He was found in his hotel room at the Norland Hotel and died several days later at Sacred Heart Hospital in Spokane of liver failure due to severe cirrhosis.

Dresden was single, never served in the Armed Forces and had never married. He was buried at Holy Cross Cemetery in Spokane in what amounts to an unmarked pauper's grave. Not a fitting end for a black-hat badman who gave us all so much enjoyment.

Suggested Sampling of Dresden's Western Heavies:

- Rough Riding Rhythm ('37 Ambassador) Kermit Maynard
- Roaring Six Guns ('37 Ambassador) Kermit Maynard
- Outlaws of Sonora ('38 Republic) 3 Mesquiteers
- Pals of the Saddle ('38 Republic) 3 Mesquiteers
- Gun Packer ('38 Monogram) Jack Randall
- Adventures of the Masked Phantom ('39 Equity) Monte Rawlins
- Zorro's Fighting Legion ('39 Republic serial) Reed Hadley
- Arizona Gangbusters ('40 PRC) Tim McCoy
- Lone Rider Rides On ('41 PRC) George Houston
- Lone Rider Crosses the Rio ('41 PRC) George Houston
- Billy the Kid's Fighting Pals ('41 PRC) Bob Steele
- Lone Rider In Cheyenne ('42 PRC) George Houston
- Sheriff of Sage Valley ('42 PRC) Buster Crabbe
- Border Roundup ('42 PRC) George Houston
- Carson City Cyclone ('43 Republic) Don Barry
- Law of the Saddle ('43 PRC) Bob Livingston
- Carson City Cyclone ('43 Republic) Don Barry
- Westward Bound ('44 Monogram) Trail Blazers

DOUGLASS DUMBRILLE

With penetrating eyes and hawk nose peering out over a dark, thin mustache, Douglass Dumbrille's charming demeanor, resonant voice and conspiratorial smile were perfect for slick screen villains, and he played them all from mobster and mad scientist to corrupt politician and western badman. Better yet, he could play them straight or farcefully.

Douglass R. Dumbrille was born October 13, 1889, in Hamilton, Ontario, Canada. His father, Richard Willie Dumbrille, and his mother, Elizabeth Coulter, were both natives of Canada. Douglass later became a U.S. citizen.

Following his early education, where he excelled in athletics, primarily hockey, he worked as a bank clerk, onion farmer, sold auto accessories, insurance, books, haberdashery, real estate and manufactured plows.

Apparently tiring of the many changes in occupation, he at last gravitated to acting, finding an extensive career on the legit stage, including Broadway turns in "Three Musketeers" in 1928 and "A Month in the Country" in 1930.

Arriving in Hollywood in 1931, his first film role

Roy Rogers has the drop on Douglass Dumbrille (seated), and LeRoy Mason in "Under Nevada Skies" ('46 Republic). George J. Lewis is the Indian in the background.

was an unbilled bit as an Indian at a party in the Marx Brothers' "Monkey Business". His real debut was as Alisandroe opposite Claudette Colbert in "His Woman" ('31). At last, Dumbrille had found a career that suited him. He continued pleasing audiences in a wide variety of roles for the next 35 years.

Dumbrille married Jessie Lawson in 1910. The marriage lasted 47 years until her death on January 12, 1957. She briefly appeared on eastern legit stages. Three years after Jessie's passing, Dumbrille married actress Patricia Mowbray, the daughter of his friend and fellow actor, Alan Mowbray. Dumbrille was 71 and his bride was 28. The marriage endured until his death at 84.

On April 1, 1974, Dumbrille was rushed from his home on North Fuller Street in Los Angeles to the Motion Picture and TV Hospital in Woodland Hills, where, the following day, April 2, he died from cardiac arrest.

No indication of any military service in his life. He was buried at Valhalla Cemetery in North Hollywood.

When you add up the number of westerns (26) and serials (2) this fine supporting actor appeared in compared to his total number of films, close to 200, the ratio weighs heavily non-western. But in the westerns in which he did appear, his performances were of the highest caliber, obviously a nod to his stage training.

Undoubtedly, his most memorable westerns were Paramount's Zane Grey adaptation of "The Mysterious Rider" in which Dumbrille has the lead in a William S. Hart good-badman type role as masked avenger Pecos Bill. In Johnny Mack Brown's departure from the norm as a doctor in "Flame of the West", Dumbrille again acquits himself as good-badman Sheriff Tom Nightlander. Dumbrille's performance elevated this Monogram B to near A status.

Suggested Sampling of Dumbrille's Western Heavies:

- Rustler's Roundup ('33 Universal) Tom Mix
- End of the Trail ('36 Columbia) Jack Holt
- Mysterious Rider ('38 Paramount) Russell Hayden
- Rovin' Tumbleweeds ('39 Republic) Gene Autry
- King of the Mounties ('42 Republic serial) Allan Lane
- False Colors ('43 United Artists) William Boyd
- Lumberjack ('44 United Artists) William Boyd
- Forty Thieves ('44 United Artists) William Boyd
- Flame of the West ('45 Monogram) Johnny Mack Brown
- Under Nevada Skies ('46 Republic) Roy Rogers
- Fabulous Texan ('47 Republic) William Elliott
- Riders of the Whistling Pines ('49 Columbia) Gene Autry
- Kangaroo Kid ('50 Allied Artists) Jock Mahoney
- Bat Masterson: Wanted Alive Please ('60) Gene Barry

BOB DUNCAN

Virtually nothing is known about badman Bob Duncan who arrived late in the B-western era. His mother's maiden name was Spencer. Born December 7, 1906, in Topeka, Kansas, he was nearly 40 when he landed his first role as a deputy in "The Cisco Kid Returns" ('45 Monogram).

His stay in Hollywood was limited strictly to westerns at Monogram and PRC with roles in a couple of Columbia serials, "The Vigilante" ('47) and "Sea Hound" ('47).

He apparently had aspirations to be a scriptwriter and penned the low-budget Hoot Gibson swan-song, "The Marshal's Daughter" ('53), in which he wrote in a juicy outlaw role for himself. He also wrote a couple of "Iron Horse" and "Riverboat" TV episodes. He often co-wrote scripts with his then wife Wanda.

Police officers reported on March 13, 1967, Duncan phoned the North Hollywood Police Department early in the morning and stated he intended to kill himself. Four minutes later when police arrived, he was found dead still grasping a rifle. Duncan had been despondent over ill health recently and left a note asking his accountant be contacted to dispose of his belongings. He was 62.

Suggested Sampling of Duncan's Western Heavies:

- Moon Over Montana ('46 Monogram) Jimmy Wakely
- Caravan Trail ('46 PRC) Eddie Dean
- Colorado Serenade ('46 PRC) Eddie Dean
- Tumbleweed Trail ('46 PRC) Eddie Dean
- Song of the Sierras ('46 Monogram) Jimmy Wakely
- Wild West ('46 PRC) Eddie Dean
- Range Beyond the Blue ('47 PRC) Eddie Dean
- Border Feud ('47 PRC) Lash LaRue
- Rainbow Over the Rockies ('47 Monogram) Jimmy Wakely
- Westward Trail ('48 PRC) Eddie Dean
- Son of Billy the Kid ('49 Western Adventure) Lash LaRue
- Marshal's Daughter ('53 United Artists) Hoot Gibson

KENNE DUNCAN

Gene Autry called Kenne Duncan "the meanest man in the movies" for Dell publication WHO'S WHO IN WESTERN MOVIES #3 in '53. "For my money," Gene continued, "He's the most convincing of all the badmen. Off screen, Kenne is a close personal friend of mine and nothing at all like the villain he's played in 14 of my pictures."

Veteran heavy Pierce Lyden stated, "Kenne was white-haired and handsome; the pictures did not do his looks justice. He was an expert marksman and in demand making personal appearances throughout the south. They would show one of his pictures, and then a music group would perform. Next, would be Kenne and his shooting exhibition." Incidentally, that trick shooting act was filmed and released circa 1949 as "The Face", a 10 minute color short directed by the notorious Ed Wood, for whom Duncan did many films late in his career.

Stuntman and Bob Steele double Rex Rossi stated Kenne was one of the most enjoyable actors he worked with in film.

Kenne's best friend over the years was Roy Barcroft. "Kenne Duncan is my pal—friends on and off the set for more years than I care to remember. We used to gang up on the hero in the serials. Kenne is a hardened bachelor. He doesn't change much—to give you an idea of this, he's lived at the same place for over 30 years."

Kenneth Duncan MacLachlan was born February 17, 1902, in Chatham, Ontario, Canada, of Scottish parents Duncan MacLachlan and Jane Elder (whose nickname was Duchess), both Canadian natives. Kenne later became a U. S. citizen.

Prior to entering films Duncan was a successful gentleman jockey who won races at Canada's Bluebonnet tracks and rode with the hounds in England. He later owned a brood farm "somewhere near where the Equestrian Center in Los Angeles is now" according to actor Dale Berry who recalls it being named the Silver D. "As I recall, Dale thought, "Kenne had around 11 thoroughbreds. He loved horses but hated to ride." Between pictures, Kenne often trained horses at the Riviera Country Club.

Duncan was well educated, attending both St. Andrews College in Toronto and the Royal School of Infantry at Wolseley Barracks, London, Ontario. However there is no evidence Duncan ever served in the Armed Forces for either Canada or the U.S.

Duncan reportedly made his stage debut shortly after he finished school. Although the play closed after a week, acting was in Kenne's blood and, after a brief fling as an accountant, he found his way to Hollywood at the end of the silent era, managing to work in two Universal two-reelers with George Chandler and Bob Curwood and a Jack Hoxie feature "Man From Wyoming" ('30).

Possessed of a solid, husky voice, Kenne moved easily into talkies with several uncredited bit parts.

In 1934 he co-starred opposite Charles Starrett in the Canadian made "Undercover Man," for which he also contributed the original story.

From then until the late '50s Duncan worked continually, and often—some 225 westerns and serials—through 1959, primarily at Monogram, Republic and, later, with Gene Autry at Columbia and for his various Flying A TV series as well as essaying sheriffs, military officers and businessmen on "Cisco Kid", "Kit Carson" and "Lone Ranger". His last work was on a "Rawhide" in '60.

Sunset Carson towers over Kenne Duncan in Republic's "Oregon Trail" ('45).

In 1948 Kenne even got the chance to star in a western. "Powder River Gunfire" was a 25 minute short released by Universal-International who were also experimenting with short westerns starring Tex Williams. Sadly, a series did not materialize and the film seems lost to the ages. Kenne did take this film on tour with him in the '50s for showing along with his trick shooting exhibition.

In 1954 Duncan made a tour of Japan where he was quite popular and even starred in a Japanese "western" titled "Onna Jariocha Wachu Wachu Dochu" ("Tokaida Road" in English). Kenne spoke phonetic Japanese in the Oriental version and had to be cued by hand signals. The story had Keene in Japan's feudal days battling the evil Samurai villains. So popular was Kenne in Japan, he rode Emperor Hirohito's white horse down the Ginza in Tokyo.

Serials were always a strong part of Kenne's career and he made an even two dozen beginning with "Flash Gordon's Trip To Mars" ('38 Universal). He was chief aide to the nefarious Scorpion in Republic's "Adventures of Captain Marvel" in '41. Becoming one of Republic's main henchmen he teamed with Bud Geary and Roy Barcroft in "Haunted Harbor" in '44 and was the right hand man of Captain Mephisto in "Manhunt On Mystery Island" in '45. He made a few departures in serials (and several westerns) from the usual henchman role such as when he played Ram Singh in Columbia's two Spider serials ('38 and '41).

Musician/actor Dale Berry first met Kenne Duncan in 1947 at the Ervay Theatre on Ervay St. in Dallas, Texas. "I went to see his personal appearance show. I had a five piece band, went backstage, told him about my band. Said we'd do a show the next night for him and if he liked us, we'd like to tour with him. He did and we toured with him on up into the '50s. And I stayed in touch with him practically every week after that. Personality wise, he was grumpy and grouchy. Not with me, but he was constantly being mistaken for Hopalong Cassidy, because of his white hair, and that irritated him! He wasn't grouchy with everybody…if it was a good lookin' girl he was the friendliest, nicest, sweetest person that ever was. If it was some guy he really didn't want to be bothered with…he was kind of a Pat Buttram type. He could be nice in one breath and testy the next. Later, we made the movie 'Natchez Trace' in late '59, and we hooked up in Natural Bridge, Tennessee. Kenne said he had us booked on a tour, sponsored by Remington. That's when he did the fancy trick shooting. Rodd Redwing was working at Stembridge gun rentals at the time and developed the act for Kenne. Kenne used .22 caliber lead bullets. When that lead would hit that steel target board it would splatter, so no matter what target you had hung up in there, no matter where, it broke it. It's the same basic act Sunset Carson later picked up. I'd often ask Kenne how he was doin', and he'd use the quotation, 'As the jockeys say at the track, I'm scufflin' for groceries.' When we were on the road on tour, he'd call his mother, who he called Duchess, he'd call her most every night. Also, you talk about a guy that was thrifty with a buck, he was tight. He wouldn't buy brand name beer. He'd buy off brand beer that tasted like…(Laughs) When he went to a restaurant, he'd grab up all those little bags of sugar. (Laughs) He *was* frugal! Kenne had an apartment at 1842 N. Edgemont St. in Hollywood where he'd lived forever, the Edgemont Arms, apartment #2."

In 1957, now 55, parts were harder to come by for Duncan and regretfully, he hooked up with cheapo producer/director Ronnie Ashcroft to make "The Astounding She-Monster". That wouldn't have been so bad, but somehow Kenne and Ashcroft hooked up with the notorious Ed Wood. Needing work, Kenne worked in several of Wood's no-budget epics ("Night of the Ghouls", "Sinister Urge") and worse yet, began to party with Wood.

Wood makeup man Harry Thomas speaks of Kenne's "risqué parties" in the book about Ed Wood, NIGHTMARE OF ECSTASY. Thomas says Kenne was a "lover of the female gender" and "had all he could." Thomas also states, "I was looking at Kenne…and you know, all men are not created equal." Dale Berry concurs that Kenne was "well endowed."

In NIGHTMARE OF ECSTASY Ashcroft tells, "Kenne had a book, and it was quite thick, of the women he had in bed. He said there was over a thousand in there."

Again in NIGHTMARE—, Ed Wood's widow, Kathy, recalls Kenne's 36 ft. wooden hull boat, Oil Ken, and some of the drinking that went on there, "It was real crazy." Dale Berry also recalls the Oil Ken and says, Kenne and Kathy had quite an affair that even Ed was aware of but unconcerned about. "There was no secret about it," Dale stated.

Duncan died at 69, February 7, 1972, at a Los Angeles hospital. He'd suffered a stroke a year earlier and many sources state, incorrectly, that was the cause of his death. Upon his demise, an investigation ensued with actual cause of death ruled a suicide from an overdose of barbiturates and alcohol. Friend Dale Berry disagrees, "I just do not believe that! He loved life. He loved living. Every day was a new adventure to him. And every day was gonna be a little bit better than the day before. Kenne did like to drink, and he'd had a light stroke and developed a little bit of a speech impediment. He was on whatever medication they gave you back then for strokes. So I think what happened, the booze mixed with the medication…I don't think he deliberately committed suicide. Statements in books that he was 'tired of living' are wrong…each day was a new conquest to him, especially if she was good looking. (Laughs)"

At any rate, it was a sad end for a fabulous B-western badman. Of his career, Kenne once stated, "I didn't mind being typecast as a badman. In fact, I enjoyed it. Me, Roy Barcroft, Jack Ingram, and all of us heavies worked all the time. We made good money because we would finish up a day's work on one set, walk right across the lot to another and get paid for two jobs in one day."

Suggested Sampling of Duncan's Western Heavies:

- Undercover Man ('34 Booth Dominion) Charles Starrett
- Colorado Kid ('37 Republic) Bob Steele
- Murder On the Yukon ('40 Monogram) James Newill
- Pinto Canyon ('40 Metropolitan) Bob Steele
- Land of the Six Guns ('40 Monogram) Jack Randall
- Frontier Crusader ('40 PRC) Tim McCoy
- White Eagle ('41 Columbia serial) Buck Jones
- Dynamite Canyon ('41 Monogram) Tom Keene
- King of the Texas Rangers ('41 Republic serial) Sammy Baugh
- Riding the Sunset Trail ('41 Monogram) Tom Keene
- A Missouri Outlaw ('41 Republic) Don Barry
- Billy the Kid's Roundup ('41 PRC) Buster Crabbe
- Raiders of the West ('42 PRC) Lee Powell/Art Davis/Bill Boyd
- Law and Order ('42 PRC) Buster Crabbe
- Sundown Kid ('42 Republic) Don Barry
- Days of Old Cheyenne ('43 Republic) Don Barry
- Avenging Rider ('43 RKO) Tim Holt
- Wolves of the Range ('43 PRC) Bob Livingston
- Red River Robin Hood ('43 RKO) Tim Holt
- Trail of Terror ('43 PRC) Dave O'Brien/James Newill
- Wagon Tracks West ('43 Republic) Bill Elliott
- Raiders of Sunset Pass ('43 Republic) Eddie Dew
- Pride of the Plains ('44 Republic) Bob Livingston
- Mojave Firebrand ('44 Republic) Bill Elliott
- Hidden Valley Outlaws ('44 Republic) Bill Elliott
- Outlaws of Santa Fe ('44 Republic) Don Barry
- Marshal of Reno ('44 Republic) Bill Elliott
- Song of Nevada ('44 Republic) Roy Rogers
- Stagecoach to Monterey ('44 Republic) Allan Lane
- Cheyenne Wildcat ('44 Republic) Bill Elliott
- Vigilantes of Dodge City ('44 Republic) Bill Elliott
- Corpus Christi Bandits ('45 Republic) Allan Lane
- Santa Fe Saddlemates ('45 Republic) Sunset Carson
- Trail of Kit Carson ('45 Republic) Allan Lane
- Oregon Trail ('45 Republic) Sunset Carson
- California Gold Rush ('46 Republic) Bill Elliott
- Sheriff of Redwood Valley ('46 Republic) Bill Elliott
- Home On the Range ('46 Republic) Monte Hale
- Rainbow Over Texas ('46 Republic) Roy Rogers
- Red River Renegades ('46 Republic) Sunset Carson
- Rio Grande Raiders ('46 Republic) Sunset Carson
- Hidden Danger ('48 Monogram) Johnny Mack Brown
- Gun Runner ('49 Monogram) Jimmy Wakely
- West of El Dorado ('49 Monogram) Johnny Mack Brown
- Roaring Westward ('49 Monogram) Jimmy Wakely
- Western Courage ('50 Universal) Tex Williams
- Lone Ranger: Greed For Gold ('50) Clayton Moore
- Blazing Sun ('50 Columbia) Gene Autry
- Gene Autry: Six Shooter Sweepstakes ('50) Gene Autry
- Wanted Dead or Alive ('51 Monogram) Whip Wilson
- Badman's Gold ('51 Eagle Lion) Johnny Carpenter
- Hills of Utah ('51 Columbia) Gene Autry
- Texans Never Cry ('51 Columbia) Gene Autry
- Range Rider: Diablo Pass ('51) Jock Mahoney
- Range Rider: Stage to Rainbow's End ('51) Jock Mahoney
- Wild Bill Hickok: Lumber Camp Story ('52) Guy Madison
- On Top of Old Smoky ('53 Columbia) Gene Autry
- Pack Train ('53 Columbia) Gene Autry
- Gene Autry: Boots and Ballots ('54) Gene Autry
- Lawless Rider ('54 United Artists) Johnny Carpenter
- Wild Bill Hickok: Sagebrush Manhunt ('55) Guy Madison
- Champion: Deer Hunters ('55) Jim Bannon
- Sky King: Golden Burro ('56) Kirby Grant
- Annie Oakley: Renegade's Return ('56) Gail Davis
- Wild Bill Hickok: Great Obstacle Race ('56) Guy Madison
- Sgt. Preston: Border Action ('56) Richard Simmons

DAN DURYEA

The sneering presence of Dan Duryea on screen indicated the female of the film was in for a rough time. Duryea himself once commented, "My fan mail goes up every time I tee off on a girl." Duryea was also the screen's number one "heel", he'd doublecross a pal then brag about it. It was often the wry amusement with which Duryea viewed his own misdeeds that made him so enjoyable. Duryea used his trademark semi-deranged laugh—sometimes a cackle—to effectively project his sadistic badman image. Duryea stated, "You can't make a picture without a villain…it pays well and you last." Constantly employed, in over 65 films and that many or more TV shows, he was usually the bad guy. That's what his public expected of him.

However, his 1952 TV series "China Smith" (revived in '54 as "New Adventures of China Smith") saw him as an Irish soldier of fortune in, at first, the Far East, then San Francisco.

The real Dan Duryea could not be further from his evil screen persona. He was a model citizen and devout family man, married for 35 years to Helen Duryea who died in '67 of a heart ailment. They had two sons, Peter, born in '39 and Richard, born in '42. Those who knew Dan loved him and always remark on his wonderful sense of humor. He loved gardening and was a member of the PTA and was a scout master.

The slim 6' 1" Duryea was born January 23, 1907, in White Plains, New York, to Richard Hewlett Duryea, a textile salesman, and his wife Mabel.

Dan was a member of the drama club at White Plains High and majored in English at Cornell University. After graduation, Dan opted for the advertising profession. During his six years in advertising he met Helen Bryan and they were married April 15, 1932.

It was a heart attack that derailed Dan from the hectic advertising world. Deciding now to pursue acting, after some summer stock jobs, he contacted old Cornell classmate Sidney Kingsley whose new play "Dead End" was about to be produced on Broadway. Dan obtained a bit part in the hit play which ran from October '35-June '37.

He was also in "Many Mansions" and played Bob Ford in the Jesse James play "Missouri Legend" on Broadway in '37 and '38. Then came the play that made him a star and took him to Hollywood, "The Little Foxes", for which he got rave reviews playing the weasel-like nephew. The play ran on Broadway from February '39 to February '40 and Dan transferred the part to the screen in '41. "That picture started me off on the road to Hell as a badman and ever since then I've been portraying the most hateful screen characters you can think of," Duryea observed.

With his slicked-back blonde hair and malicious smile he became the premier louse of the movies, playing gangsters, pimps, cheats and doublecrossers in such films as "Mrs. Parkington" ('44), "Woman In the Window" ('44), "Scarlet Street" ('45), "Valley of Decision" ('45), "Johnny Stool Pigeon" ('49), "Manhandled" ('49) and "Criss Cross" ('49).

He first came to westerns by shooting Gary Cooper in "Along Came Jones" in '45. It would not be his last. At first, under a profitable contract to Universal for five years, he bought a home on Mulholland Drive, then moved to Lake Arrowhead where he built and raced speedboats. In 1948 his Universal contract was revised to where he would do one film a year for them for the next four years and be able to freelance at other studios.

Fellow badman Tom Reese told us he found Duryea, "A very nice man. Worked with him in 'Taggart' and later in 'Stranger On the Run'. Great laugh. He wasn't well the second time I worked with him, but he invited me over to his dressing room and we hung out. A real nice man. (Chuckles) Heavies (in person) are usually nice guys."

After his wife died, Dan underwent surgery for a malignancy but recovered enough to play villainous Eddie Jacks on TV's "Peyton Place". On June 7, 1968, he was found dead in his home, a victim of cancer. He left his estate to his sons while his movie memorabilia was donated to USC's Library for Performing Arts. He is buried at Forest Lawn, Hollywood Hills.

Friendly rivals Audie Murphy and Dan Duryea come together for the final shootout in "Ride Clear of Diablo" ('54 Universal-International).

Suggested Sampling of Duryea's Western Heavies:

- Along Came Jones ('45 RKO) Gary Cooper
- Black Bart ('48 Universal-International) Dan Duryea
- River Lady ('48 Universal-International) Rod Cameron
- Winchester 73 ('50 Universal-International) James Stewart
- Al Jennings of Oklahoma ('51 Columbia) Dan Duryea
- Ride Clear of Diablo ('54 Universal-International) Audie Murphy
- Rails Into Laramie ('54 Universal-International) John Payne
- The Marauders ('55 MGM) Jeff Richards
- Night Passage ('57 Universal-International) James Stewart
- Zane Grey Theatre: This Man Must Die ('58)
- Cimarron City: Terror Town ('58) George Montgomery
- Texas John Slaughter: Showdown at Sandoval ('59) Tom Tryon
- Rawhide: Incident With An Executioner ('59) Eric Fleming
- Wagon Train: The Last Man ('59) Robert Horton
- Laramie: Stage Stop ('59) Robert Fuller/John Smith
- Wagon Train: Joshua Gilliam Story ('60) Ward Bond
- Bonanza: Badge Without Honor ('60) Pernell Roberts/Lorne Greene
- Laramie: Long Riders ('60) Robert Fuller/John Smith
- Laramie: Mountain Men ('61) Robert Fuller/John Smith
- Six Black Horses ('62 Universal-International) Audie Murphy
- He Rides Tall ('64 Universal-International) Tony Young
- Taggart ('64 Universal-International) Tony Young
- Wagon Train: Race Town Story ('64) Robert Fuller
- Bonanza: Logan's Treasure ('64) Lorne Greene
- Daniel Boone: Sound of Fear ('65) Fess Parker
- Bounty Killer ('65 Embassy) Dan Duryea
- Incident at Phantom Hill ('66 Universal-International) Robert Fuller
- Monroes: Gold Fever ('66) Michael Anderson Jr.

EARL DWIRE

Pencil thin with a distinct, easily recognizable drone to his voice, Earl D. Dwire was born October 3, 1883, in Rockport, Missouri. His parents were Dumont Dwire, a native of Ohio, and Alice Sparks of Missouri.

Dwire was a frequent companion at the home of director Robert North Bradbury and his son Bob Steele. Dwire accompanied them on hunting and fishing trips according to Steele's younger brother, Jim Bradbury, who speculates the relationship may have evolved when the senior Bradbury was active on the vaudeville circuit. The close personal relationship saw Bradbury utilizing Dwire's talents in 17 of Steele's early films as well as several Bradbury-directed John Wayne and Johnny Mack Brown titles. Bradbury is pretty much responsible for Dwire's career.

Besides a snaky badman, Dwire could just as easily turn soft, gray his hair, don a mustache and play a girl's father, a rancher, sheriff or doctor. He was a good actor—except when it came to his portrayals of Mexicans (as in "Lawless Frontier"). His attempt at the accent was horrible.

Following roles in the Universal serial "Flash Gordon Conquers the Universe" and "King of the Lumberjacks", one of the best western screen scoundrels of the '30s died at 56 January 16, 1940, at the Veteran's Administration Hospital in Los Angeles where he'd been a patient since December 13, 1939. Surgery was performed December 29 from which he did not recover. Cause of death was attributed to chronic gastric pre-pyloric ulcer (obstructing, perforated) and peritonitis.

Dwire was at one time married to a lady named Beth, but when he died he was divorced and living at the National Military Home in Los Angeles, indicating he'd spent some years in the Armed forces, most likely during WWI.

Suggested Sampling of Dwire's Western Heavies:

- Man From Hell's Edges ('32 SonoArt-World Wide) Bob Steele
- Son of Oklahoma ('32 SonoArt-World Wide) Bob Steele
- Riders of Destiny ('33 Lone Star) John Wayne
- Star Packer ('34 Lone Star) John Wayne
- Lawless Frontier ('34 Lone Star) John Wayne
- No Man's Range ('35 Supreme) Bob Steele
- Tombstone Terror ('35 Supreme) Bob Steele
- Saddle Aces ('35 Resolute) Rex Bell
- Rider of the Law ('35 Supreme) Bob Steele
- Between Men ('35 Supreme) Johnny Mack Brown
- Alias John Law ('35 Supreme) Bob Steele
- Last of the Clintons ('35 Ajax) Harry Carey
- Fighting Pioneers ('35 Resolute) Rex Bell
- Wildcat Saunders ('36 Atlantic) Jack Perrin
- Pinto Rustlers ('36 Reliable) Tom Tyler
- Cavalcade of the West ('36 Diversion) Hoot Gibson
- Headin' For the Rio Grande ('36 Grand National) Tex Ritter
- Kid Ranger ('36 Supreme) Bob Steele
- Gun Ranger ('37 Republic) Bob Steele
- Trouble in Texas ('37 Grand National) Tex Ritter
- Lightnin' Crandall ('37 Republic) Bob Steele
- Trusted Outlaw ('37 Republic) Bob Steele
- Hittin' the Trail ('37 Grand National) Tex Ritter
- Riders of the Rockies ('37 Grand National) Tex Ritter
- Doomed at Sundown ('37 Republic) Bob Steele
- Riders of the Dawn ('37 Monogram) Jack Randall
- Six Shootin' Sheriff ('38 Grand National) Ken Maynard

"Your outlaw days are over," Tex Ritter tells Earl Dwire in "Hittin' the Trail" ('37 Grand National).

JACK ELAM

"The heavy today is usually not my kind of guy. In the old days, Rory Calhoun was the hero because he was the hero and I was the heavy because I was the heavy—and nobody cared what my problem was. And I didn't either. I robbed the bank because I wanted the money. I've played all kinds of weirdoes but I've never done the quiet, sick type. I never had a problem—other than the fact I was just bad." In his own words Jack Elam, the man with the off-kilter eye, described the type of heavy that made him one of the top five screen heavies in a career that spanned nearly 50 years with his rich repertoire of badmen, scoundrels, gangsters and loveable bumblers. Even an occasional hero.

Jack Elam was born November 13, 1920, in Miami, Arizona, a tiny mining community 100 miles from Phoenix, then grew up in Phoenix. His mother died when Jack was about two and he lived with various families who made him earn at least part of his keep. He remembered picking cotton at six. When Jack was nine he was reunited with his father, a building and loan appraiser who suffered from a serious eye ailment which made it difficult for him to work. He had Jack fill out forms for him at night.

When Jack was 12, he, himself, suffered the loss of vision in his left eye when he was involved in a fight at a Boy Scout meeting and was jabbed in the eye with a pencil by another boy.

Elam had no control over his wandering eye, "It does whatever the hell it wants," Jack laughed. But the handicap became an asset when he later turned to movie work. His eyes conveyed villainy as surely as Durante's nose suggested humor," Doug Martin wrote. "One eye squinted and the other was open. One pointed one way and the other another. It all seemed malevolent." As he changed from thugs to humorous characters, so followed the eye to comic situations.

After high school, Jack moved to California and attended Santa Monica Junior College and Modesto Junior College where he met his future wife, Jean Hodgert. Married in 1937, they had two children, Scott and Jeri.

Jack had a third child, Jacqueline, with his second wife, Margaret (Jenny) Jennison whom he married in 1961 after his first wife passed away.

Exempt from WWII military service because of his eye, Jack worked as a civilian for the Navy in Culver City.

During his 20s and early 30s, Jack took a position as both auditor and manager of the famed Bel Air Hotel. When the Bel Air sold, Jack proved himself to be a 'Jack of all Trades' working as an accountant, purchasing agent, business manager and controller at Hopalong Cassidy Productions. Working as an auditor looking at numbers put a strain on Jack's good eye. His eye doctor told him to find a new line of work.

Because of his contacts in the picture business, he was able to help establish financing for three films (two of which were "High Lonesome" and "The Sundowners", both '50) in exchange for a small role in each.

Jack's big break came in 1949 filming "Rawhide" for director Henry Hathaway. With strong encouragement from star Tyrone Power, Jack played one of the nastiest, most sadistic villains ever on the screen. Power urged Darryl Zanuck to put Elam under contract, which resulted in a seven year contract at 20th Century Fox.

Jack was off and running and never stopped being in huge demand until his last film ("Bonanza: Under Attack" for TV) in '95…119 movies and 260 television appearances.

Jack's career falls into three phases—in the '50s and '60s he was the meanest of screen heavies, that is, with the exception of being on the right side of the law as reformed gunfighter, J. D. Smith, now deputy to Marshal Frank Ragan (Larry Ward) for 19 episodes of Warner Bros.' "The Dakotas" in '63. When that series failed, WB put Jack into "Temple Houston" ('63-'64) as Jeffrey Hunter's sidekick, George Taggart, another reformed gunfighter.

In the late '60s, beginning with "Support Your Local Sheriff" ('69) starring James Garner, Elam drifted into comedic portrayals, often playing a self parodying western heavy such as Sam Urp on "F-Troop: Dirge of the Scourge" ('65). The star of "Gunsmoke", James

Arness, said, "He played a rogue kind of guy, but not a real mean heavy, although he could certainly do that. What made him distinctive was the fact he could play unusual characters and he had this marvelous face—it was one of a kind. Also he was a great card player, great at all kinds of gambling. He always took everybody's money when he was on the set. He was a wonderful guy."

When, as Elam put it, "I grew too old and too fat to jump on a horse," he grew a long beard and settled into loveable old coot characterizations on "Father Murphy", "Alias Smith and Jones", "Paradise" and in "Hawken's Breed" ('87), "Big Bad John" ('90), "Once Upon a Texas Train" ('88) and "Lucky Luke" ('95).

Pinned down as to his favorite film, it's "Support Your Local Gunfighter". King Vidor and Burt Kennedy were directors Elam admired. His work in "Ransom of Red Chief" led to a 1977 daytime Emmy nomination. In 1983 Jack received the Golden Boot Award and in 1994 he was inducted into the Cowboy Hall of Fame in Oklahoma City.

Cards were always one of Jack's passions. An avid poker player and a proponent of Liar's Poker, the stories about Jack's gambling are legendary. Another terrific heavy, Gregg Palmer, remembers, "I kept bills in my wallet just for Jack Elam! We always played Liar's Poker on the lot. He had that one bad eye. Well, I had one bill tucked away just for Jack. I'm over at CBS doing a 'Gunsmoke' and Jack's in there playing Liar's Poker with Paul 'Tiny' Nichols, the first assistant director, and Bob Totten, the director. Jack says to me, 'Get your money out.' Now, the crew would always come in and give Jack bills with four numbers (alike) on it or five numbers for Liar's Poker. So I pulled out *my* bill and the game went to four fours and five of these. Finally, I got up and said 'Six sevens.' There's only four of us playing. Nichols says, 'Pass.' Totten passed. Jack looked at me with that big smile of his and says, 'Gotcha cowboy.' I looked at him and said, 'I called seven sevens.' I knew I'd only called six. Nichols said, 'No, you only called six, Gregg.' Jack said, 'He called seven sevens!' I said, 'How many sevens do you have Paul?' 'None.' Totten? 'None.' Elam? 'None.' So I took the money and said, 'Thank you, just made it.' Elam said, 'Whatcha talkin' about?' I said, 'I called seven sevens you said.' Elam growls, 'Lemme see that bill!' I had seven sevens on this bill. Jack's eye, from the side, went all the way down to the center and back up again! He says, 'You got me, didn't you? You got me.' Jack was the only one who ever had in his contract at Warner Bros. (on "Temple Houston" and "Dakotas") the right to gamble on the set. Everybody else they closed down. You couldn't play Pitch or Hearts or anything like that. But we had the understanding if they called you to the set, you threw your cards in. God love him."

Will ("Sugarfoot") Hutchins recalls, "The leisure moments on the set were great sport with Jack at a convenient card table. With that great smile and those enlightened eyes that had seen and knew it all, he'd gently glean his winnings in sociable gatherings of Hi-Low Jack and *the game*. He doesn't have a poker face—too much expression. No, that grin, that glint let you know that it's adios to your lunch money. One day we were outside on the Western Street ready to go into our dance. Beautiful day. A bit hot. On the WB back lot it was either ten degrees hotter or colder than anywhere else in Burbank. Jack looked up at that blue, August sky and allowed as how it was going to snow the next day. No way, said I. 'Tell you what,' he said, 'If it doesn't snow I'll pay you a dollar. If it does snow you pay me a thousand dollars.' Whatta sucker bet. I took it. I won the dollar, but it wasn't worth the sleepless night, the constant trips to the window to check the skies. Next day as Jack placed the buck onto my sweaty palm he told me, 'You know, I make a lot of bets like that. Usually lose, but once in a while I win, and when I do, I *collect!*'"

Will summed up the Jack Elam he knew, "He was the brother I'd never had; my long-lost uncle who once blew into town with gifts and wild tales; my dad who died too soon. I liked Jack straight off, the way I liked his acting. The abiding intelligence and humanity of the man overwhelmed me. Today I see a lot of sensational actors on screen showing off, but where's the humanity? Jack Elam doesn't show off. He doesn't *show* you anything. He lets you discover it for yourself. Whether he plays the good bad guy or the bad good guy, he has the ability to take us along with him, so we seem to be working things out together."

"I drank scotch and played poker." That's what Jack Elam always said he wanted on his tombstone. Jack died at 82, October 20, 2003, of congestive heart failure at his home in Ashland, Oregon, where he'd lived since 1990.

Suggested Sampling of Elam's Western Heavies:

- Rawhide ('51 20th Century Fox) Tyrone Power
- Bushwhackers ('52 Realart) John Ireland
- Montana Territory ('52 Columbia) Lon McCallister
- Gun Belt ('53 Columbia) George Montgomery
- Stories of the Century: Black Jack Ketchum ('54) Jim Davis
- Lone Ranger: Outlaw's Trail ('54) Clayton Moore
- Cattle Queen of Montana ('55 RKO) Ronald Reagan
- Gunfight at the O. K. Corral ('57 Paramount) Burt Lancaster
- Tales of Wells Fargo: Hijackers ('57) Dale Robertson
- Night Passage ('57 Universal) James Stewart
- Bronco: The Besieged ('58) Ty Hardin
- Rifleman: Duel of Honor ('58) Chuck Connors
- Gunsmoke: Jayhawkers ('59) James Arness
- Lawman: The Senator ('59) John Russell
- Texan: South of the Border ('59) Rory Calhoun
- Tombstone Territory: Day of the Amnesty ('59) Pat Conway
- Lawman: Thirty Minutes ('60) John Russell
- Bonanza: Spitfire ('61) Michael Landon
- Rebel: Helping Hand ('61) Nick Adams
- Gunslinger: Hostage Fort ('61) Tony Young

- Laramie: Tumbleweed Wagon ('61) John Smith
- Lawman: The Four ('61) John Russell
- Bronco: The Equalizer ('61) Ty Hardin
- Cheyenne: Durango Brothers ('62) Clint Walker
- Legend of Jesse James: Three Men From Now ('65) Christopher Jones
- Gunsmoke: Clayton Thaddeus Greenwood ('65) James Arness
- Gunsmoke: My Father, My Son ('66) James Arness
- Rare Breed ('66 Universal) James Stewart
- Fire Creek ('68 Warner Bros.) James Stewart
- Once Upon A Time In the West ('68 Paramount) Henry Fonda
- Outcasts: Glory Wagon ('69) Don Murray
- Gunsmoke: Murdoch ('71) James Arness
- Hannie Caulder ('72 Paramount) Robert Culp

GEORGE ELDREDGE

The older of the two acting Eldredge brothers, George Eldredge's 26 years in Hollywood and his over 150 films and nearly as many TV shows were not limited to westerns and serials, but like his brother John, embodied a perfect sort of general-purposeness, usually urbane and presumably well-educated, too indefinite to be termed a stereotype, but George could be poured into several different kinds of stereotypes—urbane dress heavy, judge, business executive, attorney, police official or town doctor.

George was born in San Francisco, California, on September 10, 1898. His father's name was also George. No record of the brothers' mother's name.

Although not known for sure, it is assumed he first worked in New York repertory theatre, as younger brother John did. Even though older, for whatever reason, George entered films three years later than John with his first being as a prosecuting attorney in Syndicate's spy-drama "Special Agent K–7" ('37).

He was noticeable as the ultimately treacherous Allen Kendall in Republic's action-packed serial "Hawk of the Wilderness" in '38. The next few years saw him in

In Universal's "Lone Star Trail" ('43), Johnny Mack Brown rounds up the badmen (L-R) Earle Hodgins, Robert Mitchum, and George Eldredge.

nine more serials— "Gang Busters" ('42 Universal), "Adventures of Smilin' Jack" ('43 Universal), "Raiders of Ghost City" ('44 Universal) as the gang's saloon manager, "Jungle Queen" ('45 Universal) as a Nazi, "Secret Agent X-9" ('45 Universal), and one of his best as gold raider Grail in "Royal Mounted Rides Again" ('45 Universal), the boss heavy role of the Baron in "Roar of the Iron Horse" ('51 Columbia), mysterious scientist Dr. Tobor in "Captain Video" ('51 Columbia) and finally a bit in "Man With the Steel Whip" ('54 Republic).

A tall, handsome man with a calm demeanor, George was talented enough to never confine himself to just westerns (most of which were at Universal) but was seen in character roles in a variety of B and A features throughout his career: "Ghost of Frankenstein" ('42), "Voodoo Man" ('44), "Story of Dr. Wassell" ('44), "Mom and Dad" ('45), "Dark Alibi" ('46), "Angel's Alley" ('48), "Shanghai Chest" ('48), "Bad Boy" ('49), "Jungle Jim In the Forbidden Land" ('52), "Monkey Business" ('52), "It Came From Outer Space" ('53) and "Psycho" ('60), among dozens more. Work on TV was also plentiful, appearing frequently on "Spin and Marty", "Wild Bill Hickok", "Cisco Kid", "Loretta Young Show", "Science Fiction Theatre", "Superman" and "M-Squad", but now cast in elderly good-guy roles.

Eldredge retired in '63 after a bit in "Johnny Cool" and died on March 12, 1977, in Los Angeles after suffering a stroke.

Suggested Sampling of Eldredge's Western Heavies:

- Buzzy Rides the Range ('40 Ziehm) Buzz Henry
- Raiders of San Joaquin ('43 Universal) Johnny Mack Brown
- Lone Star Trail ('43 Universal) Johnny Mack Brown
- Frontier Law ('43 Universal) Russell Hayden
- Oklahoma Raiders ('44 Universal) Tex Ritter
- Raiders of Ghost City ('44 Universal serial) Dennis Moore
- Trigger Trail ('44 Universal) Rod Cameron
- Song of the Range ('44 Monogram) Jimmy Wakely
- Old Texas Trail ('44 Universal) Rod Cameron
- Rustlers of the Badlands ('45 Columbia) Charles Starrett
- Royal Mounted Rides Again ('45 Universal serial) Bill Kennedy
- Quick On the Trigger ('48 Columbia) Charles Starrett
- Wild Bill Hickok: Hepsibah ('51) Guy Madison
- Roar of the Iron Horse ('51 Columbia serial) Jock Mahoney
- Brave Warrior ('52 Columbia) Jon Hall
- Overland Pacific ('54 United Artists) Jock Mahoney

JOHN ELDREDGE

Although six years younger than his actor brother George Eldredge, John Eldredge entered films three years earlier and was no doubt the better actor of the pair.

John was a quite capable actor, possessed of the subtly of suggestion—the eyebrow raised querulously or humorously, a voice that often sounded impatient or superior, a soft face with dark eyes and a thin mustache that enhanced his sophisticate image. Although he frequently played villains, he was not sinister enough to be cast except in the proper role, just as his sympathetic roles had also to be properly cast. In many "other man" roles he was disqualified because he was too "stuffy" for the girl as in "Flirtation Walk" ('34), "His Brother's Wife" ('36) and "Blossoms in the Dust" ('40).

Eldredge's best parts came in "Oil For the Lamps of China" ('35), "High Sierra" ('41), "Charlie Chan at the Olympics" ('37), "Black Cat" ('41) "Mad Doctor of Market Street" ('42) and Republic's "Lonely Heart Bandits" ('50) as the male half of a pair of grifters who swindle middle-aged people looking for companionship.

In the late '40s Eldredge relied more and more on B-pictures with Charlie Chan, the Bowery Boys and Republic mysteries for his livihood. Then in 1954, early TV found him as Corliss Archer's father on the syndicated "Meet Corliss Archer".

Many early TV viewers also remember him well for the suave criminal masterminds he essayed to perfection on four episodes of "Superman"—seemed like a dozen more he was so memorable. He was on "Crime Wave" ('53), "Shot in the Dark" ('53), "Girl Who Hired Superman" ('56) and "Superman's Wife" ('58).

John Eldredge was born August 30, 1904, in San Francisco, California.

He was part of Eva LeGallienne's Civic Repertory Theatre in New York, seeing successful runs in "The Cherry Orchard" and "Three Cornered Moon". His first film, under contract to Warner Bros. from the outset, was "Man With Two Faces" starring Edward G. Robinson.

Working in bigger budgeted films during the heyday of the chapterplay, he only saw duty in three serials: "The Master Key" ('45 Universal), "Lost City of the Jungle" ('46 Universal) and a bit in "Great Adventures of Captain Kidd" ('53 Columbia).

His westerns were sporadic (he didn't make his first until 1940), but he always turned in a notable performance.

Retiring after "Five Guns to Tombstone" ('61 United Artists) with James Brown, he died shortly thereafter of a heart attack at Treasure Island Trailer Park in Laguna Beach, California, on September 23, 1961. He was only 57. Married to Virginia Eldredge, their home was at 8163 Gould Ave. in Hollywood. Eldredge's remains were cremated and stored at Melrose Abbey in Orange, California.

Suggested Sampling of Eldredge's Western Heavies:

- Son of Roaring Dan ('40 Universal) Johnny Mack Brown
- Song of Nevada ('44 Republic) Roy Rogers
- Bad Men of the Border ('46 Universal) Kirby Grant
- Square Dance Jubilee ('49 Lippert) Don Barry
- Rustlers On Horseback ('50 Republic) Allan "Rocky" Lane
- Lone Ranger: Outlaw Town ('50) Clayton Moore
- Lone Ranger: Black Hat ('50) Clayton Moore
- Lone Ranger: One Jump Ahead ('50) Clayton Moore
- Sky King: Danger Point ('52) Kirby Grant
- Annie Oakley: Annie Gets Her Man ('54) Gail Davis

FRANK ELLIS

Like so many Gower Gulch badmen that worked in hundreds of B-westerns, there's oddly very little personal information known about Frank Ellis. The primary thing is, among his peers, he was recognized off screen as a real nice guy. Not untypical of all the men who played heavies on screen. "A big blustering working heavy," Pierce Lyden called him.

Like dozens of others who found steady employment in western and serial productions, Ellis' dour, sour-faced, droopy-mustached puss became a familiar fixture to B-western watchers over a 34 year career that stretched from his (apparently) first role in "Elmo the Fearless" (Universal) serial in 1920 opposite Elmo Lincoln to his final showdown in "Silver Lode" ('54) with John Payne. Ellis worked in well over 450 films, including some 40 serials. He was nearly always one of the henchmen, but did manage to play the boss heavy in Jack Randall's "Covered Wagon Trails" ('40).

Frank Birney Ellis was born February 29, 1897, in Oklahoma Territory (it became a state in 1907), near what is now Newkirk, not too far from the famous Miller Brothers 101 Ranch which was in full glory. He spent much of his youth hanging around the celebrated outfit, becoming acquainted with the show world. His earliest credited western is "King's Creek Law" ('23) with Leo Maloney.

For the next 30 years the prolific Ellis seldom strayed away from western badman or bully roles (except in Sam Katzman scrials). Frank, and other cowboys of the era, could actually work in several productions at a time or quickly move from one to another within a week's time, because their acting assignments did not limit them to a long period of time as it did the principal actors.

In silents Frank imperiled Buffalo Bill Jr., Ken Maynard, Al Hoxie, Bob Custer, Wally Wales, Buddy Roosevelt and Bill Cody. With the dawn of talkies, Ellis' first roles were in "Trails of Peril" with Wally Wales, "Cheyenne Kid" with Buffalo Bill Jr. and "Shadow Ranch" with Buck Jones...all 1930. From there on, in well over 300 westerns (and over 30 serials), the burly frame, prominent roman nose, and stomach paunch of Frank Ellis was a permanent fixture in the B-westerns of nearly every cowboy who ever starred at any studio...although Ellis seemed to find a home of sorts at PRC and Monogram in the mid '40s. One of his memorable scenes is in "Texas Troubleshooters" where Range Buster "Crash" Corrigan forces Ellis to drink...milk!

Frank was widowed at the time of his death, from respiratory failure, February 23, 1969, in a Santa Clarita, California, hospital in Saugus where he'd been a patient for over two weeks. He was six days shy of his 72nd birthday. His wife had died February 11, 1964.

Stuntman Whitey Hughes says Ellis was one of the first heavies he met when Whitey got in the business, "A real nice old man. I knew his kid real well. I later used Frank's boy, Frank Jr., in 'Wild Wild West' when I was stunt coordinator on that series. Frank was a nice, nice man and his boy came up in the business. He was a clown and a bullfighter too…talented kid but he didn't seem to take hold in the stunt business. I remembered Frank as somebody I hated when I was younger going to the movies, then when I met him he was such a nice, friendly man."

Pierce Lyden remembered Ellis "liked to talk about the early westerns and 'poverty row'. Ellis said the King Brothers could make a picture cheaper than anyone in the business."

In his off time, Ellis took pleasure in managing a baseball team that won the San Fernando Valley championship in 1944.

Frank's growley voice and tough demeanor were probably taken little note of by the "A" film world, but we knew him well—and he's fondly recalled wherever B-westerns are screened.

Sheriff Ed Cassidy puts the cuffs on badman Frank Ellis with approving looks from Tim McCoy and Jack Rockwell in "Roarin' Guns" ('36 Puritan).

Suggested Sampling of Ellis' Western Heavies:

- Fighting Sheriff ('25 Independent) Bill Cody
- Law of the Mounted ('28 Syndicate) Bob Custer
- Whistlin' Dan ('32 Tiffany) Ken Maynard
- Silent Valley ('35 Reliable) Tom Tyler
- North of Arizona ('35 Reliable) Jack Perrin
- Fast Bullets ('36 Reliable) Tom Tyler
- Gambling Terror ('37 Supreme) Johnny Mack Brown
- Sundown On the Prairie ('39 Monogram) Tex Ritter
- Westbound Stage ('39 Monogram) Tex Ritter
- Two Fisted Justice ('39 Monogram) Range Busters
- Covered Wagon Trails ('40 Monogram) Jack Randall
- Lone Rider Fights Back ('41 PRC) George Houston
- Outlaws of the Rio Grande ('41 PRC) Tim McCoy
- Land of the Open Range ('42 RKO) Tim Holt
- Rock River Renegades ('42 Monogram) Range Busters
- Border Roundup ('42 PRC) George Houston
- Cowboy Commandos ('43 Monogram) Range Busters
- Law of the Saddle ('43 PRC) Bob Livingston
- Cattle Stampede ('43 PRC) Buster Crabbe
- Raiders of Red Gap ('43 PRC) Bob Livingston
- Devil Riders ('43 PRC) Buster Crabbe
- Whispering Skull ('44 PRC) Tex Ritter/Dave O'Brien
- Wild Horse Phantom ('44 PRC) Buster Crabbe
- Outlaw Roundup ('44 PRC) Dave O'Brien/James Newill
- Arizona Whirlwind ('44 Monogram) Trail Blazers
- Westward Bound ('44 Monogram) Trail Blazers
- Frontier Fugitives ('45 PRC) Tex Ritter/Dave O'Brien
- Border Badmen ('45 PRC) Buster Crabbe
- Lightning Raiders ('46 PRC) Buster Crabbe
- Ambush Trail ('46 PRC) Bob Steele
- Vigilante ('47 Columbia serial) Ralph Byrd
- Cody of the Pony Express ('50 Columbia serial) Jock Mahoney

DOUGLAS EVANS

Urbane, refined badmen were the forté of dapper dress-heavy Douglas Evans. But beneath his well-trimmed mustache lay evil plans.

Evans was born in Virginia January 26, 1904.

He began his entertainment career in the late '30s as an announcer at KFI radio in Los Angeles. This led to a role of—an announcer—in Gene Autry's "Public Cowboy No. 1" for Republic in '37. With his well modulated voice, several more announcer roles followed as well as uncredited bit parts, including four serials.

His career was put on hold in '42 for service during WWII as an Army Captain.

Following the war, he appeared in several Broadway plays before reentering pictures in 1946, now receiving featured billing.

Evans worked as a heavy in many B-westerns from '47-'52, and TVers from '50-'54, then pretty much abandoned horsebackers altogether for character roles in non-western films and TV shows although he did appear unbilled as a saloon owner on "Sugarfoot" in '58. His last role was as a mayor in '68's "Panic In the City".

Evans died in Hollywood at 64 on March 25, 1968. A daughter was the only survivor listed.

Suggested Sampling of Evans' Western Heavies:

- Dangerous Venture ('47 United Artists) William Boyd
- Flashing Guns ('47 Monogram) Johnny Mack Brown
- Gun Talk ('47 Monogram) Johnny Mack Brown
- California Firebrand ('48 Republic) Monte Hale
- Cowboy Cavalier ('48 Monogram) Jimmy Wakely
- Crossed Trails ('48 Monogram) Johnny Mack Brown
- Trail's End ('49 Monogram) Johnny Mack Brown
- Powder River Rustlers ('49 Republic) Allan "Rocky" Lane
- Golden Stallion ('49 Republic) Roy Rogers
- Cisco Kid: Medicine Flats ('50) Duncan Renaldo
- Range Rider: Hidden Gold ('51) Jock Mahoney
- Wild Bill Hickok: Hepsibah ('51) Guy Madison
- Roy Rogers: Jailbreak ('51) Roy Rogers
- Sky King: Winged Justice ('52) Kirby Grant
- South Pacific Trail ('52 Republic) Rex Allen
- Lone Ranger: Stage For Mademoiselle ('53) John Hart

GENE EVANS

Describing Gene Evans, Leonard Maltin wrote, "He displayed the kind of talent and screen presence that would, in other players, be key requisites for stardom. But as a burly, harsh-voiced, not particularly handsome man, Evans settled for a career as a very busy character actor."

Eugene Barton Evans was born in lonely Holbrook, Arizona, on July 11, 1922. His dad was a grocer on the Navajo Indian reservation and Gene and his mother worked in the grocery store. Soon they moved to Colton, California.

Gene did some acting in high school, but preferred to play football.

In junior college, although an intelligent person, Gene was "drifting" until a Dean suggested he apply for a working scholarship at the Pasadena Playhouse. Gene worked there in '41 and '42 building sets, sweeping up and working the main stage show at night.

WWII interrupted this activity. In the Army Engineers he built camouflage for airplane factories and anti-aircraft installations on the coast.

On his GI bill Gene returned to the Playhouse for a while as well as working in theatre-in-the-round with a friend in Altadena, California. From this, Gene connected in 1947 with a bit in "Larceny" at Universal with John Payne and a solid role in Republic's "Under Colorado Skies" starring Monte Hale. It was this role that more or less established him as a western heavy.

Other small roles followed, including three "Lone Ranger" episodes in 1950 which paid, Gene said, $40 apiece.

It was firebrand director Sam Fuller who realized Gene's potential and starred him in unforgettable roles, as the brutish Sgt. Zack in "The Steel Helmet" ('51 Lippert) and as the crusading, cigar-chomping newspaper editor in "Park Row" ('52 United Artists).

From those excellent breakthrough roles, Gene went on to a healthy career as a character man in many worthy pictures—"Ace In the Hole" ('51), "Fixed Bayonets" ('51), "Long Wait" ('54), "Helen Morgan Story" ('57), "The Bravados" ('58), "Giant Behemoth" ('59), "Shock Corridor" ('63)—as well as guest shots on all the major TV westerns. He was especially proud of two outstanding "Gunsmoke" episodes—"A Hat" and "Thirty a Month and Found". The latter earned the Western Heritage Award at the Cowboy Hall of Fame Awards.

In 1955 Gene signed on to play youngster Johnny Washbrook's Montana rancher father on "My Friend Flicka". The series only ran for one season, 38 episodes, and Gene felt it was just as well due to co-star Anita Louise's demanding nature.

His only other cracks at series regularity were brief, "Matt Helm" ('75-'76) and "Spencer's Pilots" ('76), due to the failure of both to catch on with the public.

In the '70s, Gene broke through with excellent character portrayals in "The Sacketts" ('79 TVM), "Wild Times" ('80 TVM), "Shadow Riders" ('82 TVM), "Travis McGee" ('83 TVM) and "Alamo: 13 Days to Glory" ('87 TVM).

In 1972, Gene went on location to Tennessee to film "Walking Tall" and fell in love with the wooded areas. He returned in 1976 and purchased 40 acres of out-of-the-way woodlands with a seven acre lake and small house near Jackson, Tennessee.

Although Evans often played tough, snarling sergeants, gunslingers or cops, in reality he had very poor eyesight and could barely see without his glasses. Only in "Donovan's Brain" ('53) did Evans' character, a boozy scientist, get to wear glasses, and, at the time, Evans remarked it was a revelation for him to be able to actually see the actors he was working with.

Because of his obvious liking of all people and his fabulous sense of humor, the affable Evans was a very popular guest at western film festivals in the '80s and '90s. He was awarded a Golden Boot Award in 1988, a recognition from his peers for 42 years of screen work.

At 75, Gene died in a Jackson hospital April 1, 1998, after suffering a heart attack on his farm in February.

His best friend was Jack Elam, who told us, "I wouldn't say Gene Evans and I crossed paths a lot. It's more like we walked the same path for over forty years. Even after he retired to Tennessee ten years ago, he managed to spend a few days every year or so with us at our home in Oregon. I was privileged to be best man at his first marriage, present him his Golden Boot, present him his Rusty Horseshoe award and speak at his funeral. Most of all, I was privileged to share his companionship and great sense of humor for over forty years, working together and playing together. Gene Evans was a whole,

Marshal Matt Dillon (James Arness) tries to prevent bloodshed as powerful rancher Gene Evans holds back water rights from small ranchers on "Gunsmoke: Iron Blood of Courage" ('74).

complete, one of a kind. The best kind! When I finally accept I can't pick up the phone and call him with my latest story, an aching reality will set in!"

Johnny Washbrook who played his son Ken on "My Friend Flicka" said, "Working with Gene Evans was one of the most memorable and exciting times of my life. Gene was one of the reasons why the company was so bonded and worked so well together." Washbrook, now a New England banker, also remembers Evans' generosity. "Near the end of the series, I said something to my Mom about getting rid of all my scripts. I didn't want to keep them because they took up too much space. Gene secretly intervened and arranged to have them all bound in leather and individually engraved. He gave them to me as a Christmas gift. I still treasure them today."

Suggested Sampling of Evans' Western Heavies:

- Under Colorado Skies ('47 Republic) Monte Hale
- Lone Ranger: Devil's Pass ('50) Clayton Moore
- Lone Ranger: Star Witness ('50) Clayton Moore
- Wyoming Mail ('50 Universal-International) Stephen McNally
- Sugarfoot ('51 Warner Bros.) Randolph Scott
- Wyoming Renegades ('54 Columbia) Phil Carey
- Cattle Queen of Montana ('55 RKO) Ronald Reagan
- Restless Gun: The Coward ('57) John Payne
- Rawhide: Incident at the Buffalo Smokehouse ('59) Eric Fleming
- Johnny Ringo: Die Twice ('60) Don Durant
- Bonanza: Fear Merchants ('60) Lorne Greene/Michael Landon
- Riverboat: The Quota ('60) Darren McGavin
- Outlaws: The Quiet Killer ('60) Don Collier
- Rawhide: Incident On the Road Back ('61) Eric Fleming
- Gunslinger: The Recruit ('61) Tony Young
- Temple Houston: Find Angel Chavez ('63) Jeffrey Hunter
- Rawhide: Incident at El Crucero ('63) Eric Fleming/Clint Eastwood
- Gunsmoke: Extradition (Pt. 1-2) ('63) James Arness
- Rawhide: Moment In the Sun ('65) Eric Fleming/Clint Eastwood
- Branded: The Bounty ('65) Chuck Connors
- Legend of Jesse James: Vendetta ('65) Christopher Jones
- Iron Horse: Pride at the Bottom of the Barrel ('66) Dale Robertson
- Apache Uprising ('66 Paramount) Rory Calhoun
- Cimarron Strip: Battle of Bloody Stones ('67) Stuart Whitman
- Gunsmoke: A Hat ('67) James Arness
- Custer: Breakout ('67) Wayne Maunder
- Gunsmoke: First People ('68) James Arness
- Daniel Boone: The Man ('69) Fess Parker
- The Intruders ('70 TVM) Don Murray
- Gunsmoke: Tatum ('72) James Arness
- Gunsmoke: Thirty A Month and Found ('74) James Armess
- The Shadow Riders ('82 TVM) Tom Selleck/Sam Elliott

FRANK FENTON

Frank Fenton made a name for himself as a stage actor years before he began in films in 1942.

Born Frank Fenton Moran in Hartford, Connecticut, April 9, 1905, after graduation from Georgetown University, he made his Broadway bow in "Dead End" which began its run in October 1935. In January 1936 he was cast in the original comedy "O Evening Star". A year later he was appearing in "Susan and God" followed by "The Philadelphia Story" opposite Joseph Cotten, Van Heflin and Katharine Hepburn which ran on Broadway from March 28, 1939, til March 30, 1940.

He then toured the country with Katherine Cornell in "Alien Corn", "Romeo and Juliet" and "The Barretts of Wimpole Street".

His first film was "The Navy Comes Through" in 1942 with Pat O'Brien at RKO. He first came to westerns with 1944's "Buffalo Bill" starring Joel McCrea but didn't return to westerns on a regular basis as a heavy until 1947.

Fenton had just completed a role in James Arness' "Gun the Man Down" when he died September 26, 1957, of a pulmonary embolism. He was only 52.

There has been much confusion over the years with a writer also named Frank Fenton, apparently born in 1906 in Liverpool, England. This Fenton was a novelist/playwright/screenwriter first credited onscreen with the story idea for "Behind Jury Doors" at Mayfair in 1932. He continued to develop story ideas and write screenplays until his death in 1971. Part of the confusion between the two stems from the fact that the writer Fenton worked on several westerns beginning in 1948, just about the time the actor Fenton turned heavily to westerns. The writer Fenton penned "Station West" ('48), "Ride Vaquero" ('53), "Escape From Fort Bravo" ('54) (based on a story by Michael Pate), "River of No Return" ('54), "Garden of Evil" ('54) as well as many non-westerns and several TV episodes of "The Virginian", "Man Without A Gun", "Bus Stop" etc.

When badmen confer—Frank Fenton and Barton MacLane in "Relentless" ('48 Columbia.)

Suggested Sampling of Fenton's Western Heavies:

- Adventures of Don Coyote ('47 United Artists) Richard Martin
- Relentless ('48 Columbia) Robert Young
- Rustlers ('49 RKO) Tim Holt
- Ranger of Cherokee Strip ('49 Republic) Monte Hale
- Doolins Of Oklahoma ('49 Columbia) Randolph Scott
- Streets of Ghost Town ('50 Columbia) Charles Starrett
- Lone Ranger: Gold Train ('50) Clayton Moore
- Prairie Roundup ('51 Columbia) Charles Starrett
- Wild Bill Hickok: Wild White Horse ('52) Guy Madison
- Lone Ranger: Treason At Dry Creek ('52) John Hart
- Stories of the Century: Clay Allison ('55) Jim Davis
- Sgt. Preston: Trouble At Hogback ('55) Richard Simmons
- Tales of the Texas Rangers: Bandits of El Dorado ('56) Willard Parker
- Annie Oakley: Front Trail ('56) Gail Davis

AL FERGUSON

With over 265 films, silent and sound, to his credit over a 45 year period, husky-voiced, 6 ft., 185 lb. Al "Fergie" Ferguson made a profitable career out of playing badmen. A staggering 55 of those films were serials!

Alfred George Ferguson was born in Rosslarre, Ireland, April 19, 1888. His parents, James Ferguson and Nancy Collins, were both Irish nationals.

Ferguson was educated in London, England. Exactly how and when he came to the U.S. is unknown, but he was in films by age 24 with 1912's "Whiskey Runners" (Selig) with Myrtle Stedman being his earliest credited appearance. There are no more credits til 1916's "With Life At Stake", an Art Acord western in which Al played the girl's father.

In the silent era Ferguson worked in nine silent chapterplays, with his best roles coming in "Haunted Island" ('28 Universal) opposing Jack Daugherty, "Tarzan the Mighty" ('28 Universal) as Black John, ruler of a tribe descended from pirates, "Tarzan The Tiger ('29 Universal) tricking Tarzan (Frank Merrill) by posing as a friendly scientist, and "Pirates of Panama" ('29 Universal) trying to beat Jay Wilsey (later Buffalo Bill Jr.) to a buried treasure.

When not toiling in serials, Al rode silent western trails trying to outsmart William Russell, Tom Tyler, Jack Perrin, Buzz Barton, Bill Patton, Franklyn Farnum, Yakima Canutt, Ted Wells, Dick Hatton, Bob Steele, Cheyenne Bill, Ken Maynard and others.

Al made a brief stab at stardom himself in 1924-'25 when he starred in four westerns (or Mountie/northwoods pictures) for Davis. He also directed three of these. Evidently, he quickly realized he belonged on the wrong side of the law, and stayed there right on through a 1958 TV episode of "Sky King", "Note For a Dam", in which he played a crazed old hermit. Oddly, it was his only TV work. With that, at 70, he retired.

During the sound era, "Fergie" (as his friends called him) threatened cowboy heroes from Bob Steele, Tim McCoy, Tom Tyler and Buck Jones on through William Boyd, Buster Crabbe, Eddie Dean and Tim Holt.

Forty-six sound serials provided Ferguson plenty of employment. He was railroad detective Whispering Smith helping Lane Chandler in "Lightning Express" ('30 Universal), a French-Canadian outlaw in "Mystery Trooper" ('31 Syndicate), the Wrecker's pilot in "Hurricane Express" ('32 Mascot), and one of many thugs in "Galloping Ghost" ('31 Mascot), "Lost Special" ('32 Universal), "Pirate Treasure" ('34 Universal), "Vanishing Shadow" ('34 Universal), "Tailspin Tommy" ('34 Universal), "Secret Agent X-9" ('37 Universal), "Green Ar-

Range rats Al Ferguson (L) and George Chesebro have the upper hand on Bob Steele in Monogram's "Death Valley Rangers" ('43).

cher" ('40 Columbia), and plenty more. Sam Katzman cast him as outlaw "Fergie" in *his* last serial, and the last serial made, "Blazing the Overland Trail" ('56 Columbia).

Married to Narcissus M. Weston and living at 300 N. Screenland Dr. in Burbank, researcher John Brooker met him and found Ferguson's wife didn't like him talking about his old westerns. Al had an old shed out back with a few crumbling stills on the wall. Maybe his wife didn't appreciate him, but we did. One of the best of the badmen died at 83 on December 4, 1971, at Burbank Community Hospital from prostate cancer. His cremated remains were inurned at Forest Lawn, Glendale.

Suggested Sampling of Ferguson's Western Heavies:

- Hi-Jacking Rustlers ('26 Rayart) Jack Perrin
- Grit Wins ('29 Universal) Ted Wells
- Smiling Terror ('29 Universal) Ted Wells
- Saddle King ('29 Anchor) Cliff Lyons
- Near the Rainbow's End ('30 Tiffany) Bob Steele
- Red Fork Range ('31 Big 4) Wally Wales
- Mystery Trooper ('31 Syndicate serial) Robert Frazer
- Sign of the Wolf ('31 Metropolitan serial) Rex Lease
- One Way Trail ('31 Columbia) Tim McCoy
- Arizona Nights ('34 Reliable) Bud 'n' Ben (Jack Perrin, Ben Corbett)
- Red Rider ('34 Universal serial) Buck Jones
- Desert Trail ('35 Lone Star) John Wayne
- Laramie Kid ('35 Reliable) Tom Tyler
- Roamin' Wild ('36 Reliable) Tom Tyler
- North of the Rio Grande ('37 Paramount) William Boyd
- Frontiers of '49 ('39 Columbia) Bill Elliott
- Billy the Kid's Gun Justice ('40 PRC) Bob Steele
- White Eagle ('41 Columbia serial) Buck Jones
- Perils of the Royal Mounted ('42 Columbia serial) Robert Stevens
- Devil Riders ('43 PRC) Buster Crabbe
- Arizona Whirlwind ('44 Monogram) Trail Blazers
- Outlaw Trail ('44 Monogram) Trail Blazers
- Harmony Trail ('44 Mattox) Ken Maynard
- Rustler's Hideout ('44 PRC) Buster Crabbe
- Wildfire ('45 Screen Guild) Bob Steele
- God's Country ('46 Screen Guild) Robert Lowery
- Overland Riders ('46 PRC) Buster Crabbe
- Wild West ('46 PRC) Eddie Dean
- Fighting Mustang ('48 Yucca) Sunset Carson
- Blazing the Overland Trail ('56 Columbia serial) Lee Roberts/Dennis Moore
- Sky King: Note For a Dam ('58) Kirby Grant

FRANK FERGUSON

Tall, lean, leathery-faced character actor Frank S. Ferguson was in his mid 30s before he brought his talent to the screen. Prior to that he was a prominent performer in stock and on Broadway and was an original director with the acclaimed Pasadena Playhouse where he coached up and coming actors. He broke into films himself in 1940 usually playing minor supporting roles. It was another 10 years before he fully broke into playing western heavies. On through 1977 he played hundreds of ranchers, bankers, reporters, lawyers, doctors, sheriffs, preachers and quite a share of wily, unassuming badmen, often the one you'd least expect because of his seemingly gentle nature, broad smile and bedraggled mustache. Ferguson also quite often came fully equipped with a chaw of tobacco firmly planted in his cheek. No matter what movie (over 180) or TV show (over 200) he was in, his talent always enhanced the quality of the film.

He became familiar on a weekly basis as Gus, the ranch foreman on "My Friend Flicka" ('56-'57) and even more familiar as the family patriarch, Eli Carson (Tim O'Connor's father) on the popular ABC nighttime soap opera, "Peyton Place" ('64-'69). He also became a staple playing every type of role on TV westerns in the late '50s and early '60s.

Ferguson was born Christmas Day, 1906, in Ferndale, California.

He'd just played the semi-regular role of Grandpa Macahan on "How the West Was Won" with James Arness in '77-'78 when he died of cancer at 71 on September 12, 1978, in Los Angeles.

Suggested Sampling of Ferguson's Western Heavies:

- Under Mexicali Stars ('50 Republic) Rex Allen
- Oklahoma Annie ('52 Republic) Judy Canova
- Hopalong Cassidy: Ghost Trails ('52) William Boyd
- Wagons West ('52 Monogram) Rod Cameron
- Marksman ('53 Allied Artists) Wayne Morris
- Texas Bad Man ('53 Allied Artists) Wayne Morris
- Lone Ranger: The Globe ('54) Clayton Moore
- Lone Ranger: Enfield Rifle ('55) Clayton Moore
- Lone Ranger: Death Goes To Press ('55) Clayton Moore
- Lone Ranger: Trapped ('55) Clayton Moore
- Trackdown: Law in Lampasas ('57) Robert Culp
- Tales of the Texas Rangers: Deadfall ('58) Willard Parker
- Bronco: Trail to Taos ('58) Ty Hardin
- Tales of Wells Fargo: Toll Road ('59) Dale Robertson
- Colt .45: Law West of the Pecos ('59) Wayde Preston
- Texan: Quarantine ('60) Rory Calhoun
- Sugarfoot: Vinegaroon ('60) Will Hutchins
- Bronco: Ordeal at Dead Tree ('61) Ty Hardin
- Lawman: Grubstake ('61) John Russell
- Lawman: A Friend of the Family ('62) John Russell

ROBERT FISKE

Obviously more intelligent than the average badman, coldhearted, smooth schemer Robert Fiske was nearly always cast as a well-dressed banker, saloon owner or slick businessman out to steal the ranch, trick immigrant settlers or swindle someone out of something.

With a thin mustache, high brow and black hair center-parted, Fiske reeked of treachery. Columbia realized his potential and put his smarmy talents to best use.

Born in Griggsville, Missouri, October 20, 1889, (his mother's maiden name was Lawrence), Robert L. Fiske didn't come to films until 1936 at age 47. Prior to films he was a theatrical actor employed in touring stock companies. The 1930 census locates him in Pittsburgh, Pennsylvania, with his wife Catherine J., 26, and daughter Gloria, 8.

After a few uncredited roles he was cast as a heavy in five of the eight Tom Keene historical "westerns" made for E. B. Derr's Crescent Pictures in '37. The die was forever cast.

Fiske also worked in nine serials during his brief nine years in Hollywood. He was seen to best advantage as the Phantom Raider chief in "Great Adventures of Wild

Bill Hickok" ('38 Columbia) with Bill Elliott, as henchman Savini in "The Green Archer" ('40 Columbia), as evil Dr. Daka's assistant in "Batman" ('43 Columbia) and revealed to be the Black Tiger in "The Shadow" ('40 Columbia).

Fiske made two westerns, one with Charles Starrett, one with Russell Hayden, the year he died just short of his 55th birthday, September 12, 1944, from congestive heart failure in Sunland, California. He's buried at Forest Lawn Cemetery in Glendale.

Note: there is no relation between Robert Fiske and Columbia contract player Richard Fiske whose real name was Thomas Richard Potts. Potts, born November 20, 1915, in Shelton, Washington, was killed in action during WWII.

Suggested Sampling of Fiske's Western Heavies:

- Battle of Greed ('37 Crescent) Tom Keene
- Raw Timber ('37 Crescent) Tom Keene
- Cassidy of the Bar 20 ('38 Paramount) William Boyd
- Purple Vigilantes ('38 Republic) 3 Mesquiteers
- Great Adventures of Wild Bill Hickok ('38 Columbia serial) Bill Elliott
- South of Arizona ('38 Columbia) Charles Starrett
- Colorado Trail ('38 Columbia) Charles Starrett
- Sunset Trail ('39 Paramount) William Boyd
- North of the Yukon ('39 Columbia) Bill Elliott/Tex Ritter
- Racketeers of the Range ('39 RKO) George O'Brien
- Timber Stampede ('39 RKO) George O'Brien
- Carolina Moon ('40 Republic) Gene Autry
- Along the Rio Grande ('41 RKO) Tim Holt
- Apache Kid ('41 Republic) Don Barry
- Vengeance of the West ('42 Columbia) Bill Elliott/Tex Ritter
- Texas Kid ('43 Monogram) Johnny Mack Brown
- Cyclone Prairie Rangers ('44 Columbia) Charles Starrett

PAUL FIX

One of the busiest character actors in the business, Paul Fix, appeared in over 400 films, movies and TV, of which dozens were westerns and a fair share cast him as one of the heavies.

Peter Paul Fix was born in Dobb's Ferry, New York, March 13, 1901. His father, William Fix, a brewmeister, was from Germany and his mother, Francis Amelia Drayton (who added the name Harvey when she was adopted) was a native of Ohio. She nicknamed herself Taddy.

Paul's only child, daughter Marilyn Fix (born in 1925), tells us, "My Dad joined the National Guard, hated it, left, joined the Army, hated it, left, and then he joined the Navy. When they found out he was only 16, they said, 'Oh well.' (Laughs) His service career is absolutely hysterical, you wouldn't believe what he got away with. But he always had a mentor who got him through it. Dad's sister lived in Kent, Ohio, so after his Dad died he went out there to stay with her and met my mother at the local soda shop. She and her girlfriends had a bet on who could get a date with him first 'cause he was a snappy dresser, and pretty cute. (Laughs) Dad was married in 1924, I believe he was a free spirit, so he said, 'Let's go out to California where it's warm.' They lived it up in California for awhile til the money ran out. There was a photographer who became famous named Bruno. He came up to my parents and said we'll take your picture and get it around. It was really sort of a scam. He took your picture in sort of a (movie) set. At first you were sort of at the back. As Bruno got more guys who wanted to be actors, you'd move forward in the picture. Eventually, Dad got a few jobs from that and started to work in pictures." Paul's first film in 1926 was a western for Artclass with Buddy Roosevelt, "Hoodoo Ranch".

Marilyn continued, "Dad thought it was a dumb kinda thing to be doing, but he decided, you know, so he did some stage work (in stock and local theatre) and did quite a lot."

Fix was extremely versatile, playing everything in his 53 year career from a gabby Irish railroad engineer to a cold-eyed killer to a sniveling squealer.

Early in his career Fix became friends with John Wayne and the two remained close the rest of their lives. When Wayne began acting, he told Fix he felt awkward in front of the camera, unnatural. When John Ford cast Wayne in "Stagecoach", Wayne was fearful he wouldn't be able to carry it off. Going to Paul for help, the pair worked together at Fix's house every night without Ford's knowledge. As Harry Carey Jr. relates, "Because Duke was kind of heavy footed and used to trudge more than walk, Paul told Duke to point his toes when he walked, and the 'John Wayne walk' was born. As the Wayne legend began to form, the walk became more pronounced." Most people give John Ford credit for formulating the John Wayne image, but it was much more Paul Fix.

In addition to his acting, Paul "always liked to write" Marilyn remembers. Fix co-wrote "Tall In the Saddle" ('44), "Ring of Fear" ('54) and "Notorious Mr. Monk" ('58). Marilyn continues, "When I was growing up in Hollywood, there was the little Las Palmas Theatre, and he put on a lot of stage plays which he'd written…Mom was in a couple of them. Also, with Batjac (Wayne's production company), or whatever it was called before that, he was basically a script doctor. So he was always writing."

Two famous acting families became one when Marilyn Fix married Harry Carey Jr. on August 12, 1944. Harry stated, "Paul Fix was one of those guys my friend Wendell Corey called 'a blue-shirt' actor. To him that signified an old pro who could do it all on a moment's notice." Marilyn added, "My Dad was the actor everyone called when the actor they'd hired got either drunk or sick, 'cause he could step right in."

In the early '30s Fix mixed heavies with juvenile roles. By the late '30s on into the '40s he was cast in lots of gangster films. Better roles in bigger pictures began to develop in the mid '40s. By the mid '50s he was essaying older man character roles. From September '58 to April '63, Fix was TV's Marshal Micah Torrance on "The Rifleman", a role he will be forever associated with. But according to daughter Marilyn, he was most proud of his role as Judge Taylor in the Academy Award winning "To Kill A Mocking Bird" ('62)—"but he never much talked about it."

Fix was divorced in 1945 and remarried in 1949 to Beverly Pratt who died in 1979, the year Paul played his last role in "Wanda Nevada".

For about the last three years of his life he was on dialysis three times a week for diabetes. The immortal Paul Fix, 82, died of kidney failure October 14, 1983, at St. John's Hospital in Los Angeles. He's buried at Woodlawn Cemetery in Santa Monica.

Suggested Sampling of Fix's Western Heavies:

- Fighting Sheriff ('31 Columbia) Buck Jones
- South of the Rio Grande ('32 Columbia) Buck Jones
- Gun Law ('33 Majestic) Jack Hoxie
- Somewhere In Sonora ('33 Warner Bros.) John Wayne
- Fargo Express ('33 World Wide) Ken Maynard
- The Westerner ('34 Columbia) Tim McCoy
- Desert Trail ('35 Lone Star) John Wayne
- His Fighting Blood ('35 Ambassador) Kermit Maynard
- Eagle's Brood ('35 Paramount) William Boyd
- Valley of Wanted Men ('35 Conn) Grant Withers
- Bar 20 Rides Again ('35 Paramount) William Boyd
- Bulldog Courage ('35 Puritan) Tim McCoy
- Phantom Patrol ('36 Ambassador) Kermit Maynard
- Triple Justice ('40 RKO) George O'Brien
- Fargo Kid ('40 RKO) Tim Holt
- Down Mexico Way ('41 Republic) Gene Autry
- A Missouri Outlaw ('41 Republic) Don Barry
- South of Santa Fe ('42 Republic) Roy Rogers
- War of the Wildcats (aka In Old Oklahoma) ('43 Republic) John Wayne
- Dakota ('45 Republic) John Wayne
- Red River ('48 United Artists) John Wayne
- The Plunderers ('48 Republic) Rod Cameron
- Hellfire ('49 Republic) Bill Elliott
- Fighting Man of the Plains ('49 20th Century Fox) Randolph Scott
- Lone Ranger: Million Dollar Wallpaper ('50) Clayton Moore
- Cahill, U. S. Marshal ('73 Warner Bros.) John Wayne

ROBERT FOULK

Big, well over 6 ft. tall, overpowering Robert Foulk came to Hollywood not as an actor, but as a dialogue coach, serving on many top-drawer pictures such as "Flight Angels" ('40), "River's End" ('40), "Sea Hawk" ('40), "Bad Men of Missouri" ('41), "Maltese Falcon" ('41) and others before WWII. This work was interrupted in 1942 by military service (1943-1946).

After WWII, Foulk resumed dialogue work ("Unconquered" '48 and others) and began to act, with his first work being as a cop in "Road House" ('48). Foulk's first western roles came on four episodes of "The Lone Ranger" from '52-'55.

With his overbearing size, Foulk played many rough house heavies, but as time went on, especially for

TV, he became the one to call when you needed an insurgent or rebellious townsman to lead the lynch mob or stir up the townsfolk, i. e. "Restless Gun: The Pawn" or "Deputy: Hang the Law".

Perhaps a bit of insight into Foulk's demeanor comes from Wright King who worked with him in Audie Murphy's "Cast A Long Shadow" ('59 United Artists). "The heavyset guy—Robert Foulk, who played a character part—got on the wrong side of Jimmy Best, and Best just terrorized him. His eyes would get big and he'd just look at him. Foulk was just in terror of him. I'd never met Jim Best before—he seemed like just a regular guy until this happened. He was just gonna tear this guy apart. And for no real reason. Foulk was an unassuming simple guy. Best just showed himself to be so irate...he just wanted to terrorize Foulk. I always respected Best's acting, he was a good actor, but it was so surprising that he would take on, probably, the weakest guy on the set. Foulk was a guy who didn't want any trouble from anybody, didn't really talk to anybody, and Best just terrorized him."

Foulk retired after voice-over work in the feature cartoon "Pete's Dragon" ('77) as an old sea captain.

Robert C. Foulk was born May 5, 1908, in Philadelphia, Pennsylvania. His parents, Miller Foulk and Alice Casselberry, were both Pennsylvania natives. He was married to minor '40s actress Barbara Slater.

Foulk died at 80 February 25, 1989, of a heart attack at San Pedro and Peninsula Hospital in San Pedro, California. He was cremated and is buried at Green Hills Memorial park in San Pedro.

Suggested Sampling of Foulk's Western Heavies:

- Lone Ranger: Stage to Tishomingo ('54) Clayton Moore
- Lone Ranger: Sawtelle Saga's End ('55) Clayton Moore
- Broken Arrow: The Doctor ('57) John Lupton/Michael Ansara
- Last of the Badmen ('57 Allied Artists) George Montgomery
- Maverick: Point Blank ('57) James Garner
- Tales of Wells Fargo: John Wesley Hardin ('57) Dale Robertson
- Tombstone Territory: Gunslinger From Galeville ('57) Pat Conway
- Trackdown: Easton, Texas ('57) Robert Culp
- Man Without a Gun: Decoy ('57) Rex Reason
- 26 Men: Montezuma's Cave ('58) Kelo Henderson/Tris Coffin
- Colt .45: The Deserters ('48) Wayde Preston
- 26 Men: Hoax at Globe ('48) Kelo Henderson/Tris Coffin
- 26 Men: Brief Glory ('58) Kelo Henderson/Tris Coffin
- Colt .45: The Pirate ('49) Wayde Preston
- Texan: Town Divided ('60) Rory Calhoun
- Bat Masterson: Welcome to Paradise ('60) Gene Barry
- Rifleman: Lost Treasure of Canyon Town ('61) Chuck Connors
- Cheyenne: Pocketful of Stars ('62) Clint Walker
- Destry: Destry Had a Little Lamb ('64) John Gavin
- Guns of Will Sonnett: The Trap ('68) Walter Brennan

DOUGLAS FOWLEY

From debonair dress heavy to toothless old coot, Douglas Fowley did it all on screen from 1933-1981, a fabulous nearly 50 year career in over 400 film and TV shows, including a memorable stint as Doc Holliday on Hugh O'Brian's popular ABC "Wyatt Earp" series from '57-'58 and again from '59-'61.

Daniel Vincent Fowley was born in Greenwich Village, New York, on May 30, 1911, and aspired to an acting career from childhood. His father was an Irishman, John Fowley of New York, and his mother, from Ireland, was Annie O'Connor. After attending St. Francis Xavier Military Academy where he was active in school plays, he appeared in nightclubs as a song and dance man and acquired experience in stock. He even sang in backyards for change. Additionally, Fowley was a barker for theatres, a Wall St. runner, an athletic coach at a summer camp and worked in the shipping department of a silk house. For a time, later on, he ran his own drama school in Hollywood.

Fowley eventually gravitated to Hollywood where he made his movie debut opposite Spencer Tracy in "The Mad Game" ('33).

Soon the fast talking, sharp-tongued, handsomely mustached Fowley was seen playing everything from gangsters to reporters to military men to western heavies. His chameleon-like talent allowed him to immerse himself in a role. Always in demand throughout his career, Doug was able to mix major films like "Dodge City",

"It Could Happen to You", "Riding High", "Mighty Joe Young", "Singin' In the Rain" and "The High and the Mighty" with dozens of B-melodramas and comedies: Charlie Chan, Mr. Moto, Tarzan, Hopalong Cassidy, Laurel and Hardy, Kitty O'Day, Maisie, Gas House Kids, Joe Palooka, Blondie, and many more. He occasionally played leads as in "Lady In the Death House" ('44) and "Yankee Fakir" ('47). He even co-starred in one serial with Lyle Talbot, "Chick Carter, Detective" ('46 Columbia).

At the beginning of WWII Doug was 30, married and had one child, so was exempt from the draft until late in the war, 1944. He then served with the U.S. Navy in San Diego until the war was over in 1945.

When he took out his upper plate to play the memorable role of smart-aleck Private "Kipp" Kippton who entertains his fellow GI's by constantly clicking his poorly fitted GI issue false teeth in "Battleground" ('49), Doug reinvented himself. As the years went by and he grew older, he often played a toothless old codger, both on film and TV. He was Grandpa Hanks on CBS' western comedy "Pistols 'n' Petticoats" ('66-'67).

As for "Wyatt Earp", before he was Doc Holliday, he played the part of Doc Fabrique in Wichita during the first season ('55-'56). In 1994 Doug told us through his wife Jean, "I had a false upper plate, having lost my upper teeth prematurely in mid-life. I started playing old character roles by removing my false upper plate, adding a beard, voice, and gait to match my interpretation. Fabrique was one of those characters. It was the part and association on the series that helped me (later) get the Holliday role." (Episode #67 in '57). During the third year of the series Doug got a deal to do a picture in Europe while "Earp" wasn't filming. The shoot went long and Doug wasn't able to get back. Producers replaced him for episodes #105-150 ('58-'59) with Myron Healey.

Fowley returned with episode #151 as the series switched from Dodge City to Tombstone and finished off the last two years of the popular series.

The star of the series, Hugh O'Brian, told us, "Doug was one of the most professional people I ever worked with. He not only always knew what he was going to say, he also had a very definite feeling about how he was going to handle it physically. He never sloughed off anything. When it came to delivery of his work he was very focused. It was a pleasure to have him on the set because he was a real pro. As in his famous 'Battleground' role, when he played Doc Fabrique he'd take his teeth out…let his beard grow, whiten his hair and play the old wizened doctor with a lotta humor. He was quite versatile. To me he was an older performer who'd been around, so I looked up to him. He was very kind to me and very generous."

Dirk London, Morgan Earp on the series, remembers, "Doug used to drop in at our place every once in a while. We were around him at many parties. One especially I remember. Towards the end of the evening…he'd been kinda keeping an eye on everybody throughout the whole party…he went into a rhythm and rhyme type of thing about everybody that was there, about the whole evening. It wasn't anything written down, he just picked each individual person and made a rhyme out of it. It was really unusual. He encouraged me to stick around and be an actor after the war was over. Doug was an up front guy. It was like an old shoe to be with him later on 'Wyatt Earp'."

Jan Shepard (actress and wife of Dirk London) said, "He was really Mr. Showbiz…ever since the movies started. I did a pilot with him…'Yankee Privateer.' He was a real actor and a real mimic and one of the greatest story tellers ever. When we lived in Hollywood he used to come over to our place and that's when the storytelling would start for hours and hours."

Myron Healey, who replaced Doug as Doc Holliday for a year, smiled, "When I did the Doc Holliday thing, Doug was in Germany doing a movie and he couldn't get loose, so they used me. Doug said, 'The only reason they hired Myron Healey was they were trying to find somebody as ugly as Doug Fowley!' (Chuckles) He was a hell of a man with a good sense of humor. I enjoyed him when I was a little kid growing up back in the '30s at the Mystic Theatre. Wonderful man."

Walter Reed, a co-worker for years at RKO and star of the only movie Fowley directed, "Macumba Love", recalled Doug as, "…a wonderful actor who really knew his craft. He could do anything. Doug asked me if I'd star in a picture he was gonna do in Brazil. 'Macumba Love' turned into a little sleeper. Doug was a fine director as well as an actor. I wish he'd directed more. An all around good guy."

Doug was married several times and had five children. With his pre-war romance and marriage to Shelby Payne (daughter of composer Rudolf Friml), there was son Kim, who has been quite successful in his field of music writing and producing. After a break-up with Shelby, there was a wartime marriage to Mary Hunter in 1944 which produced a daughter, Gretchen, and a son, Douglas Jr. After the war there was a divorce and a romance and marriage in 1947 to Vivian Chamber and a son, Kip. Following their break-up, Doug married Joyce Torstup in 1950 and had a son, Danny. All short-lived marriages, as were his marriages to Mary Ann Walsh (1954-1955), then Maria; with no children in either of these marriages. Only after not being married for a few years did Doug settle down and marry his long time dear friend Jean Louise Paschall in 1961. This happy marriage endured until his death.

Doug and Jean had been living in Murrieta, California, but moved into the Motion Picture Television Fund's retirement community in Woodland Hills as Doug's health began to fail. One of our greatest character players and western badmen died a few days shy of his 87th birthday on May 21, 1998, of heart disease at the Motion Picture Hospital. He is buried at Laurel Cemetery in Murrieta.

Suggested Sampling of Fowley's Western Heavies:

- Wild and Wooly ('37 Fox) Jane Withers
- Dodge City ('39 Warner Bros.) Errol Flynn
- Wagons Westward ('40 Republic) Chester Morris
- Cherokee Strip ('40 Paramount) Richard Dix
- Secrets of the Wasteland ('41 Paramount) William Boyd
- Sunset on the Desert ('42 Republic) Roy Rogers
- Lost Canyon ('42 United Artists) William Boyd
- Colt Comrades ('43 United Artists) William Boyd
- Bar 20 ('43 United Artists) William Boyd
- Along the Navajo Trail ('45 Republic) Roy Rogers
- Drifting Along ('46 Monogram) Johnny Mack Brown
- 'Neath Canadian Skies ('47 Screen Guild) Russell Hayden
- Wild Country ('47 PRC) Eddie Dean
- Ridin' Down the Trail ('47 Monogram) Jimmy Wakely
- Coroner Creek ('48 Columbia) Randolph Scott
- Denver Kid ('48 Republic) Allan "Rocky" Lane
- Gun Smugglers ('48 RKO) Tim Holt
- Susanna Pass ('49 Republic) Roy Rogers
- Satan's Cradle ('49 United Artists) Duncan Renaldo
- Renegades of the Sage ('49 Columbia) Charles Starrett
- Rider From Tucson ('50 RKO) Tim Holt
- Rio Grande Patrol ('50 RKO) Tim Holt
- South of Caliente ('51 Republic) Roy Rogers
- Wild Bill Hickok: Wrestling Story ('52) Guy Madison
- Wild Bill Hickok: Nephew From Back East ('53) Guy Madison
- Red River Shore ('53 Republic) Rex Allen
- Wild Bill Hickok: Boy and the Hound Dog ('55) Guy Madison
- State Trooper: Prettiest Dress In Goldfield ('59) Rod Cameron

OLIN FRANCIS

Olin Francis, a big, beefy man, 6' 2", 225 lbs., with gray eyes, mustache and black hair, never reached his potential as a screen heavy for whatever reason. To see him at his ruthless best watch "Rough Riding Rhythm" ('37) with Kermit Maynard. Even after this outstanding job, his roles continued to be relegated to fifth man through the door henchies. He shone again as Mule Bates, hired to kill Tex Ritter in "Take Me Back to Oklahoma" in 1940, but by then he was nearing 50, his best days behind him.

Born Olin Caldwell Francis in Mooreville, Mississippi, September 13, 1891, he graduated from the University of Mississippi with a degree in engineering. Prior to films he was a locomotive fireman, engineer and Air Corps pilot. He also gained some stage experience before arriving in Hollywood during the heyday of silent westerns, 1921.

Francis started off "at the top", starring in "A Knight of the West" in '21 for independent Blanchfield and Sanford's "Fightin' Devil" in '22.

He soon found his true calling playing heavies opposite Jack Hoxie, Tom Tyler, Buddy Roosevelt, Buffalo Bill Jr., Dick Carter and others.

His voice transferred well to talkies, but he seemed stuck in low-budget independents from poverty row.

In the mid '30s, Francis was one of the founding members of the Screen Actors Guild.

His final film was a bit role as an express man in the prestigious "Citizen Kane" in '41.

Francis, only 60, died June 30, 1952, in Hollywood. The tradepaper VARIETY afforded him only four lines. He deserved better.

Suggested Sampling of Francis' Western Heavies:

- Rarin' To Go ('24 Action) Buffalo Bill Jr.
- Let's Go Gallagher ('25 FBO) Tom Tyler
- Pioneers of the West ('27 Sanford) Dick Carter
- Flying U Ranch ('27 FBO) Tom Tyler
- Battling Buckaroo ('32 Kent) Lane Chandler
- Lightning Range ('34 Superior) Buddy Roosevelt
- Gun Grit ('36 Atlantic) Jack Perrin
- Irish Gringo ('36 Keith) Pat Carlyle
- Rough Riding Rhythm ('37 Ambassador) Kermit Maynard
- Two Gun Justice ('38 Monogram) Tim McCoy
- Pals of the Saddle ('38 Republic) 3 Mesquiteers
- Red River Range ('38 Republic) 3 Mesquiteers
- Overland With Kit Carson ('39 Columbia serial) Bill Elliott
- Riders of Black River ('39 Columbia) Charles Starrett
- Take Me Back to Oklahoma ('40 Monogram) Tex Ritter
- Man From Tumbleweeds ('40 Columbia) Bill Elliott

ROBERT FRAZER

Robert Frazer was not particularly tall and was slightly built but he gave the impression of tremendous nervous energy with his flashing black eyes.

Born Robert William Browne June 29, 1889, in Worcester, Massachusetts, his parents, John Browne and Mary Frazer, were both born in Nova Scotia.

Frazer was educated at Boston High School and received a "special course in college." While working as a grocery store clerk during his high school years he acquired the reputation as an amateur actor.

He began his theatrical career around age 19 with many small barnstorming repertoire companies. Some of the plays he appeared in over the next few years were "Squaw Man", "Brewster's Millions", "Quincey Adams Sawyer" and "Call of the North". Frazer finally connected with a New York stock company and played 52 weeks a year, the bill changed twice a week. He hit it "big" opposite Julia Arthur in "Seremonda" at the Criterion Theatre.

From 1912 to 1921 Frazer combined both stage and screen acting, having entered that medium in 1912 at Eclair in Fort Lee, New Jersey. For the next few years he made many two and three reelers for Eclair including his first western "The Squatter" in 1914.

On stage he played in "Ben Hur" for two years, opposite Florence Reed in "The Mirage" in 1920, and succeeded Douglas Fairbanks in "The Show Shop" when Fairbanks went into film full time in 1915.

In 1913 Frazer married actress Mildred Bright with whom he appeared in "Rob Roy" in 1913, "The Renunciation" in 1914, both for Eclair. Bright was born in New York City April 30, 1892, and died September 27, 1967, in Woodland Hills, California. As far as could be traced, the couple were childless. They worked together again in 1922's Allene Ray western "Partners of the Sunset".

To this point Frazer had not fully accepted the film media over the stage, but he finally took the leap and moved to Hollywood in 1923. By 1924 he was ranked among the first half dozen leading men in pictures earning around $1,000 a week. He was a man of high intelligence who preferred romantic roles.

However, there were westerns among his dozens of silent screen roles…he starred in "Scarlet West" ('25 First National), "Splendid Road" ('25 First National) and "Silent Hero" ('27 Rayart) as well as supporting Tim McCoy in "Sioux Blood" ('29 MGM).

Frazer was considered one of the finest amateur portrait photographers, a chemist, an oil portrait painter and an inventor. He adapted his Victrola to play 12 records one after the other long before you could buy an automatic changer. His house held the largest radio receiving set in Los Angeles in 1924. A radio engineer stated Frazer knew as much about radio as any man west of Chicago.

Through the '20s he continued to work steadily in major films opposite Clara Bow, John Bowers, Pola Negri, Billie Dove and other major stars of the era.

Frazer's voice was quite well adapted for sound but like so many silent screen matinee idols, now 41, he was doomed to secondary or supporting roles. He did star in a cheap western, "Beyond the Law" for Syndicate in 1930, as well as Syndicate's 10 chapter "Mystery Trooper" serial in 1931. He then began a career of supporting roles, mostly as the dress-heavy (crooked lawyer, banker) who had his henchmen do the dirty work.

Serials remained part of Frazer's repertoire throughout his career. Besides "Mystery Trooper" he threatened and glowered his way through 12 other chapterplays, with good roles in "Mystery Squadron" ('33 Mascot), "Three Musketeers" as the masked El Shaitan, ('33 Mascot), "Fighting Marines" ('35 Mascot), "Black Coin" ('36 Stage & Screen), "Clutching Hand" ('36 Stage & Screen), "Dick Tracy Vs. Crime Inc." ('41 Republic), "Daredevils of the West" ('43 Republic) and "Tiger Woman" ('44 Republic).

Frazer had worked in two Republic serials, two Johnny Mack Brown Monograms, a Hoppy and a Bill Elliott the year he died—August 17, 1944, of leukemia at St. Vincent's Hospital in Los Angeles. He was a patient there for 17 days.

His glowering expression and modulated deep authoritative voice will long be with us on screen.

Suggested Sampling of Frazer's Western Heavies:

- Saddle Buster ('32 RKO) Tom Keene
- Trail Beyond ('34 Lone Star) John Wayne
- Fighting Trooper ('34 Ambassador) Kermit Maynard
- Miracle Rider ('35 Mascot serial) Tom Mix
- Silverspurs ('36 Universal) Buck Jones
- Left Handed Law ('37 Universal) Buck Jones
- Black Aces ('37 Universal) Buck Jones
- Renfrew On the Great White Trail ('38 Grand National) James Newill
- Pals of the Pecos ('41 Republic) 3 Mesquiteers
- Gangs of Sonora ('41 Republic) 3 Mesquiteers
- Gunman From Bodie ('41 Monogram) Rough Riders
- Riders of the West ('42 Monogram) Rough Riders
- Daredevils of the West ('43 Republic serial) Allan Lane
- Law Men ('44 Monogram) Johnny Mack Brown
- Wagon Tracks West ('44 Republic) Bill Elliott

TERRY FROST

Believe it or not—Terry Frost's first "performance" was reciting poetry in a house of prostitution. Seems most who frequent such establishments are not there to listen to poetry, but that is what Frosty claimed.

Terry Lawrence Frost was born October 26, 1906, in Bemidji, Minnesota, a northern Minnesota logging town. His father, Frank Frost, a one-time lumberjack, also owned a "saloon" where Terry sold newspapers and recited poetry. Terry's mother was Minnie Williams.

With the advent of prohibition in 1919, Terry's father went from being a successful barkeeper to a flourishing bootlegger. His untimely death a few years later created an economic burden for the family while Minnie struggled as a seamstress. So, upon graduation, following the example of his older brother, Terry struck out for the open road.

Arriving in Oregon by freight car, he was completely broke. Offering to do odd jobs in a local brothel, he was given a place to eat and sleep. With his great memory for poetry, Frost nightly provided interpretations of well known pieces such as "The Ballad of Yukon Jake". According to Frost, he "kept waiting customers occupied while the girls were busy." He set out a bowl and was allowed to keep all the donations he collected. Frost actually did the same in houses of ill repute in Spokane and Seattle before returning home with a nest egg of $7,000.

Employed in yet another whorehouse in Minneapolis, a local stock company producer threw a party, asking Frost to entertain. The producer was impressed and cast Terry as a drunken bum at $35 a week at the Shubert Theatre. However, he maintained his "other" job as it was by now earning him $200 a week.

For years Terry traveled throughout the midwest in stock companies and vaudeville shows. When his wife, a dancer, became pregnant, Terry decided to try settling down as a movie actor.

At first his film aspirations failed and he opened a restaurant, Terry Gene's, on Wilshire Blvd.

Eventually, his agent began to find work for him in westerns. Regarding the person who helped him on his first film, Terry said, "He was a very friendly person, so I got to know him on the first day, and I said, 'You know, I don't know a thing about motion pictures; I'm from the theatre…can you help me?' Well, he helped me all week in the first motion picture I made—(it was) Ray Whitley." The film was Tim Holt's "Cyclone On Horseback" ('41).

From there, the film and TV work, mostly westerns, never let up until the late '50s with over 120 movies and serials and some 150 TV shows to his credit. In the '40s Terry was primarily associated with Monogram and PRC for westerns, and Sam Katzman's Columbia serials. "I told them (studio heads) to give me a black hat, not the white one. I wanted to be a heavy; the guy who ran the saloon, robbed the widows, and stole the money. That was the best part since you worked all the time. I never wanted a contract either because I wanted to be free. I free-lanced all the time. I was kind of an adventurous guy. I always thought Monogram made the best westerns—story-wise for one thing—and had the best directors."

Frost worked in 15 serials for producer Katzman, with good roles in "Hop Harrigan" ('46), "Jack Armstrong" ('47), "Tex Granger" ('48), "Superman" ('48), "Bruce Gentry" ('49), "Pirates of the High Seas" ('50), "Mysterious Island" ('51), "Great Adventures of Captain Kidd" ('53), "Gunfighters of the Northwest" ('54) and "Perils of the Wilderness" ('56).

In the '60s as film parts faded away, Frost turned to teaching, conducting a drama course at Patricia Stevens Career College in Pasadena for a year. After that he worked for a travel agency as a tour director for nine years, visiting remote parts of the world. In 1973 he elected to spend more time with his wife of 40 years who, unfortunately, died the Christmas Eve following his retirement.

Frost next put together a handbook for aspiring actors, ACTORS ONLY, published in '77. He then did eight or ten stage shows including a tour of "Come Blow Your Horn" with Sylvia Sidney along the east coast into Canada.

On November 20, 1983, Terry married former actress Marion Carney who appeared with him at several western film festivals in the '80s and early '90s.

Terry was fond of saying, "When I hear the expression 'Crime Doesn't Pay,' I think to myself, I did pretty well by it."

Those that worked with Frost recall, while sitting around locations between scenes, Terry would carve a little wooden fist with a hole in it to be used to cinch up a neck handkerchief. He carved these and gave them to various friends.

Terry was well liked as witnessed by the comments we received at his death. Myron Healey: "Lots of laughter. Always had a funny story to tell. Always carried his carving knife…he always whistled and whittled. He was a sturdy son of a gun. Wonderful man." Gregg Barton: "When I worked with him in pictures, he was a heavy drinker but he was never abusive with it…and it never interfered with his work. He always performed. He was a delightful guy to work with. I used to die laughing at him…every time he had one of those death scenes he would flip-flop like a fish out of water. (Director) Jack (John) English said to him one time, 'C'mon Terry…die already, will ya…we only got a two reeler here.' I liked working with him, he was fun, he relieved the pressure, he had endless energy. I don't know how he did it, drinking as much as he did, but he was great." House Peters Jr.: "He was a boisterous sort of a person and he let you know he was around, that's for dang sure. He had a million stories." Lois Hall: "Terry was fun and funny always during shootings. He always had a million stories to tell. He was always out to enjoy life and have fun. He certainly wasn't afraid to do stunts and jump into the middle of any fracas." Walter Reed: "I thought he was a very competent actor. He had a good background on the stage. He did a lot of work and was very well liked. He drank too much but I never saw Terry nasty…and I never saw him drink while working. He was a very rugged man." John Hart: "I knew Terry since the late '40s with Katzman. He was quite likable. He had a unique style of acting. It was a little…well, if you've seen his films, he was great at popping his eyeballs. But his unique style of acting fit into those westerns. He worked all the time and made a good living at it. Then he became a tour guide for cruises and traveled all over the world doing that. He was competent with a great sense of humor and a great deal of perseverance."

Terry died as an in-patient at Valley Medical Center in Los Angeles March 1, 1993, of congestive heart failure. He was 86. His remains were cremated and scattered around his birthplace.

Suggested Sampling of Frost's Western Heavies:

- Cyclone on Horseback ('41 RKO) Tim Holt
- Border Bandits ('46 Monogram) Johnny Mack Brown
- Moon Over Montana ('46 Monogram) Jimmy Wakely
- Haunted Mine ('46 Monogram) Johnny Mack Brown
- Caravan Trail ('46 PRC) Eddie Dean
- Gentleman From Texas ('46 Monogram) Johnny Mack Brown
- Trail to Mexico ('46 Monogram) Jimmy Wakely
- Shadows On the Range ('46 Monogram) Johnny Mack Brown
- Wild West ('46 PRC) Eddie Dean
- Pioneer Justice ('47 PRC) Lash LaRue
- Ghost Town Renegades ('47 PRC) Lash LaRue
- Stage to Mesa City ('47 PRC) Lash LaRue
- Black Hills ('47 PRC) Eddie Dean
- Check Your Guns ('48 PRC) Eddie Dean
- Tornado Range ('48 PRC) Eddie Dean
- Hawk of Powder River ('48 PRC) Eddie Dean
- Dead Man's Gold ('48 PRC) Lash LaRue
- Lawless Code ('49 Monogram) Jimmy Wakely
- Son of Billy the Kid ('49 Western Adventure) Lash LaRue
- West of El Dorado ('49 Monogram) Johnny Mack Brown
- Dalton's Women ('50 Western Adventure) Lash LaRue
- Outlaws of Texas ('50 Monogram) Whip Wilson
- Stage to Blue River ('51 Monogram) Whip Wilson
- Range Rider: Sealed Justice ('51) Jock Mahoney
- Cisco Kid: Foreign Agent ('51) Duncan Renaldo
- Gene Autry: Heir to the Lazy L ('51) Gene Autry
- Roy Rogers: Desert Fugitive ('52) Roy Rogers
- Texas City ('52 Monogram) Johnny Mack Brown
- Night Raiders ('52 Monogram) Whip Wilson
- The Gunman ('52 Monogram) Whip Wilson
- Fargo ('52 Monogram) Bill Elliott
- Roy Rogers: Blind Justice ('52 Roy Rogers)
- Range Rider: Convict at Large ('53) Jock Mahoney
- Roy Rogers: Mingo Kid ('53) Roy Rogers
- Gene Autry: Cold Decked ('53) Gene Autry
- Wild Bill Hickok: Chain of Events ('53) Guy Madison
- Kit Carson: Outlaw's Justice ('54) Bill Williams
- Hopalong Cassidy: Renegade Press ('54) William Boyd
- Roy Rogers: Deputy Sheriff ('54) Roy Rogers
- Annie Oakley: Annie Makes a Marriage ('54) Gail Davis
- Gene Autry: Santa Fe Raiders ('54) Gene Autry
- Kit Carson: Frontier Empire ('54) Bill Williams
- Wild Bill Hickok: Gorilla of Owlhoot Mesa ('54) Guy Madison
- Gunfighters of the Northwest ('54 Columbia serial) Jock Mahoney
- Cisco Kid: Kidnapped Cameraman ('55) Duncan Renaldo
- Stories of the Century: Rube Burrows ('55) Jim Davis
- Buffalo Bill Jr.: Empire Pass ('55) Dick Jones
- Cisco Kid: Witness ('55) Duncan Renaldo
- Wild Bill Hickok: Hideout ('55) Guy Madison
- Champion: A Bugle For Ricky ('55) Jim Bannon
- Buffalo Bill Jr.: Trouble Thompson ('56) Dick Jones
- Annie Oakley: Annie and the Leprechauns ('56) Gail Davis
- Sgt. Preston: Pack Ice Justice ('56) Richard Simmons
- Perils of the Wilderness ('56 Columbia serial) Dennis Moore
- Wild Bill Hickok: Jingles Wins a Friend ('56) Guy Madison
- Rin Tin Tin: Racing Rails ('56) Lee Aaker
- Roy Rogers: Junior Outlaw ('57) Roy Rogers
- Rin Tin Tin: Stagecoach Sally ('57) Lee Aaker
- Roy Rogers: End of the Trail ('57) Roy Rogers
- 26 Men: Run No More ('58) Kelo Henderson/Tris Coffin
- Man Without A Gun: Hangtree Inn ('59) Rex Reason

BUD GEARY

Bud Geary, one of the most recognizable of the Saturday matinee sluggers in the '40s, appeared to be a man with the attitude "I'm rough and I'm tough and I can prove it." That made him an excellent badman.

One of Republic's so called "stock players", Geary was born Sigsbee Maine Geary in Salt Lake City, Utah, Feb. 15, 1898. His parents, Charles Geary and Jennie Helen, were both born in Ireland and migrated to the U.S.

Following service in WWI, Bud apparently made his screen debut in the silent feature "What Would You Do?" ('20) which starred Charles French and Madlaine Traverse. This was soon followed by "Everyman's Place" in '21 starring Grace Darling. In '22, billed as Maine Geary, he was Will Scarlett in Douglas Fairbanks Sr.'s "Robin Hood".

Western credits during the silent era include "Smoking Trails" ('24) with Bill Patton and "Arizona Romeo" ('25) with Buck Jones.

Bud worked continuously in mostly unbilled parts in picture after picture, easily making a transition to sound. He was 6 ft. 1 in., beefy, and athletic so was cast as a cop, cowboy, sea captain, henchman and gangster. Despite scores of mainly uncredited roles, especially at 20th Century Fox, it wasn't until a string of 12 Columbia and then Republic serials from '38-'41 that his days as a tough henchman took off and he found a home at Republic on through 1946. The stuntman/actor slugged it out in 18 serials at the Thrill Factory—from "Daredevils of the Red Circle" ('39) through "King of the Forest Rangers" ('46)—and dozens of westerns opposite 3 Mesquiteers, Gene Autry, Don Barry, Bill Elliott, Bob Livingston, Sunset Carson, and Allan Lane.

He became a real "workhorse" in westerns, grinding out 28 films in '44…20 B-westerns, 3 serials and a few other action films, such as "Fighting Seebees" with John Wayne.

The main body of Geary's work was at Republic because the studio put he, along with Roy Barcroft, LeRoy Mason, Kenne Duncan, Jack Kirk and Tom London, under contract in 1943. Geary's contract ran from July 22, 1943 til July 21, 1945.

Republic action director Bill Witney said of him, "Bud Geary thought he was the baddest of bad guys. One night, while with his drinking buddies, Geary bragged that no one had ever knocked him off his feet. Suddenly, there was a loud crash, and Bud's feet were on the bar and his body had disappeared behind it. Ace stuntman Davy Sharpe had just demonstrated to Bud that someone could knock him off his feet. When Geary started for the door, another stuntman named Duke Taylor called out Bud's name. When Bud turned around, Taylor knocked him across a table and shrugged, 'I just wanted Bud to know I could do it, too.'"

With the cessation of his Republic contract, Bud was just getting his feet wet in a few Durango Kid B's at Columbia when he was involved in a car wreck on a rural highway in San Fernando, California, February 22, 1946. He died at Newhall Community Hospital after a 10 hour stay. Actual cause of death was listed as intracranial hemorrhage and a fractured skull. He'd just turned 48. Investigators determined Geary was driving at an excessive speed when the car left the road and overturned. It was the cliffhanger he didn't walk away from. His final film, "California" with Ray Milland, was released after his death. Geary is buried at Forest Lawn in Glendale. Survivors included his wife and two sons.

Only a handful of stuntmen/actors have gained the recognition of Bud Geary, even though many of his over 200 roles were uncredited. This talented and athletic man richly deserves our praise and admiration.

Suggested Sampling of Geary's Western Heavies:

- Gangs of Sonora ('41 Republic) 3 Mesquiteers
- King of the Texas Rangers ('41 Republic serial) Sammy Baugh
- Home In Wyomin' ('42 Republic) Gene Autry
- Sundown Kid ('42 Republic) Don Barry
- Overland Mail Robbery ('43 Republic) Bill Elliott
- Death Valley Manhunt ('43 Republic) Bill Elliott
- Pride of the Plains ('44 Republic) Bob Livingston
- Beneath Western Skies ('44 Republic) Bob Livingston
- Mojave Firebrand ('44 Republic) Bill Elliott
- Laramie Trail ('44 Republic) Bob Livingston
- Outlaws of Santa Fe ('44 Republic) Don Barry
- Tucson Raiders ('44 Republic) Bill Elliott
- Marshal of Reno ('44 Republic) Bill Elliott
- Silver City Kid ('44 Republic) Allan Lane
- Code of the Prairie ('44 Republic) Sunset Carson
- Sheriff of Sundown ('44 Republic) Allan Lane
- Vigilantes of Dodge City ('44 Republic) Bill Elliott
- Firebrands of Arizona ('44 Republic) Sunset Carson
- Topeka Terror ('45 Republic) Allan Lane
- Great Stagecoach Robbery ('45 Republic) Bill Elliott
- Lone Texas Ranger ('45 Republic) Bill Elliott
- Santa Fe Saddlemates ('45 Republic) Sunset Carson
- Trail of Kit Carson ('45 Republic) Allan Lane
- Oregon Trail ('45 Republic) Sunset Carson
- Phantom of the Plains ('45 Republic) Bill Elliott
- Marshal of Laredo ('45 Republic) Bill Elliott
- Cherokee Flash ('45 Republic) Sunset Carson
- Wagon Wheels Westward ('45 Republic) Bill Elliott
- Sheriff of Redwood Valley ('46 Republic) Bill Elliott
- Thunder Town ('46 PRC) Bob Steele
- Under Arizona Skies ('46 Monogram) Johnny Mack Brown
- Heading West ('46 Columbia) Charles Starrett
- Landrush ('46 Columbia) Charles Starrett

LEO GORDON

Leo Gordon's hulking, muscular physique and deep set hard eyes combined with his raucous, menacing growl of a voice certified this man was a sadistic heavy. Director Don Siegel ("Riot In Cell Block 11") claimed, "Leo Gordon was the scariest man I have ever met." Gordon came by his toughness through life experiences, serving time in San Quentin for armed robbery.

Leo Vincent Gordon Jr. was born December 2, 1922, in Brooklyn, New York, to Leo Vincent Gordon Sr. and Ann Qualy. He left school in the 8th grade, went to work in construction and demolition, then the CCC (Civilian Conservation Corps) after which Leo enlisted in the Army in 1941 where he served two years.

It was after the war he was arrested for armed robbery in southern California and was shot by arresting officers when he pulled a gun. Leo served five years in San Quentin where he read nearly every book in the library. He put his life back together and attended the American Academy of Dramatic Arts on the GI Bill of Rights.

Leo married one of his classmates, actress Lyn Cartwright, in 1950 and was soon cast as a boatswain mate in the London and Canadian companies of "Mr. Roberts".

Then, as Leo tells it, "I replaced Jack Palance in (the play) 'Darkness At Noon' in New York. A Hollywood agent got me the first film ("China Venture" in '53). I came back to New York and three months later I got another call. They asked if I could ride a horse. I said, 'If I can't ride, I'll carry it.' I went out and rented a horse in Central Park. I couldn't walk for two days. Anyway, they put me on a horse and I was there for 35 years. But I have a good foundation for a western background. I was born in the same town as Billy the Kid…Brooklyn." That first western which started Leo on a lengthy career in film and TV westerns was "City of Badmen".

Gordon was not just a one-note villain. He played sympathetic parts on occasion, notably in "Black Patch" (which he wrote), in Roger Corman's Civil Rights drama "The Intruder", and on episodic TV, "Gunsmoke" in particular. He always turned in first rate performances. He was recognized for his abilities with a Golden Boot Award in 1997.

Gordon was also a screenwriter. For TV he wrote for "Bonanza", "Gunsmoke", "Maverick", "Cheyenne", "Colt .45" and "Adam 12". His big screen entries include "Escort West", "Wasp Woman", "Attack of the Giant Leeches", "The Terror", "Bounty Killer" and the big budget WWII film, "Tobruk". As to how he started writing, Leo explained, "When Charles Marquis Warren was directing the pilot for "Gunsmoke" ("Hack Prine"—filmed first but not aired until eight months later), I told him I had an idea for an episode. 'Don't tell me, write it,' he answered. I went home and the next thing I knew I had 110 pages. I showed it to my agent. Next thing I know, George Montgomery wanted to buy it. That was 'Black Patch'. Gene Corman negotiated the deal. That's how I came into contact with him and Roger Corman. In writing, conflict is the thing. Take a normal person and put him in an abnormal situation and you got a story. Take an abnormal person and put him in a normal situation and you've got a story. Writing is more rewarding than acting, but look at my face. Nobody believes I'm a writer. I should be 5' 8", 142 pounds, wear patches on my elbows and horn-rimmed glasses and smoke a pipe. That's a writer. (Laughs)"

Two of his most memorable heavies were with John Wayne in "McLintock!" and "Hondo". Leo recalled, "In the scene in 'Hondo' where he kills me down by the stream, I reach for my gun and he shoots me. I buckled up and pitched forward. Wayne hollered, 'Cut! Cut!' even though John Farrow was directing. Wayne says to me, 'What was that? When you get hit in the gut with a slug you go flying backwards.' I pulled up my shirt to show him where I'd really been shot in the gut (back when he was arrested for armed robbery). 'Yeah? I got hit point blank and I went forward.'"

On the right side of the law, Leo was a semi-regular as Hank Miller on "Circus Boy" ('56-'57) and had a recurring role on "Maverick" as Big Mike McComb. "I liked Jim Garner. I thought he was an honest guy. I would have liked to have gone further with that role, but they brought in Jack Kelly for a sidekick and Roger Moore as a cousin and made it a family affair."

Leo guested on "Cheyenne" with Clint Walker several times. Their fight in "Vengeance Is Mine" is legendary. Clint told us, "Leo was a serious and intense actor, but I appreciated that working with him. Leo co-starred in my favorite film, 'Night of the Grizzly'. I was so glad when Leo was cast in that film. I knew it would make a better picture."

Incidentally, "Night of the Grizzly" was Leo's favorite role. "It just had a quality to it. It was something Disney might have done. Basically, a clean story with no rotten nastiness about it. The whole concept of the thing was good."

The fast gun star of "26 Men", Kelo Henderson, remembers Leo. "Very few actors could out heavy Leo, he was the ultimate on-screen bad guy, as his long successful career has proven. But in reality, he was a nice guy on and off the set. I remember him sitting in the shade of a Saguaro cactus, out on location with his portable typewriter, working on some movie or TV script when he wasn't needed in front of the camera."

Another heavy, George Keymas, told us, "I worked

with Leo several times. We were in 'Santa Fe Passage' and the remake of 'Beau Geste,' then we did another TV show together. He was a gentleman all the time and a hell of an actor. I don't think people really realize the amount of talent this man had. I say that because he was used primarily as a bad guy all the time, but I remember a film he made where he played a very sensitive kind of character. He was excellent."

And Gregory Walcott said, "We worked on 'Rifleman' ("Angry Gun"). He had a menacing presence and was a valuable asset to our industry. He also was successful as a writer of screenplays. I remember on 'Rifleman', between each set-up, he'd retreat rapidly to his dressing room where he had a portable typewriter set up. He'd peck away on a script until he was called back to the set. I admired that ability."

And the late producer Alex Gordon provided this insight into Gordon. "Leo submitted a script to me in '63 which he had written for Mickey Rooney. The role was that of a timid young man who becomes a tough killer and is involved with two girls. I liked the central role and bought the script with the understanding we could do a rewrite as we wished. R. Alexander (my wife, Ruth Gordon) had done some previous script writing and outlines for me like 'Underwater City' and 'Masque of the Red Death'. She re-wrote 'The Bounty Killer', combining the two female roles into one and coming up with a new script though we gave Leo original story credit. Leo wanted to play the Rod Cameron role, but we explained we needed Rod for the foreign co-financing and I preferred Buster Crabbe in the villain's part. He understood. Leo was a nice guy but slightly intimidating in size and appearance."

As for Leo's own assessment of acting and being typecast as a heavy, "Actors should never have speeches that run more than four or five lines consecutively. Westerns are fundamental…the morality play. There's a good guy and a bad guy. You know which is which. You don't have to go into the psyche to find out his parents were abusive. (And the heavy is) the guy people remember. You get more recognition. After all, I look like a heavy. I'm 6' 2", 200 pounds. Got a craggy-ass face. I was walking down the street in Morocco when a little kid steps out of the alley and looks at me. He runs a few feet ahead of me—turns around and looks again—he puts his hands down like he's drawing two pistols. He goes 'bip, bip, bip!' Y'know? Like he's shooting. You figure, here you are, a world away from anything you're familiar with, and some little kid in an alley in Morocco recognizes you? Once, coming down the street in Madrid with my wife a car slides up and these guys jump out. They were a couple of photographers from the Spanish press. They spent the whole afternoon with us."

After a brief illness, one of the top five screen/TV western badmen died in his sleep at his home on Warnom Ave. in Sunland, California, on December 26, 2000. Cause of death according to the department of health services was respiratory failure and chronic obstructive pulmonary disease. He was 78. Leo was buried at Hollywood Forever Cemetery in Santa Monica.

Leo's wife of 50 years, Dora Lyn Cartwright, the daughter of a congressman, died at 76 on January 2, 2004, of dementia related disease following a hip fracture. A daughter, Tara, survives.

Suggested Sampling of Gordon's Western Heavies:

- City of Bad Men ('53 20th Century Fox) Dale Robertson
- Gun Fury ('53 Columbia) Rock Hudson
- Hondo ('53 Warner Bros.) John Wayne
- Yellow Mountain ('54 Universal) Lex Barker
- Stories of the Century: Doolin Gang ('54) Jim Davis
- Ten Wanted Men ('55 Columbia) Randolph Scott
- Santa Fe Passage ('55 Republic) John Payne
- Rin Tin Tin: White Buffalo ('55) Lee Aaker
- Cheyenne: Outlander ('55) Clint Walker
- Man With the Gun ('55 United Artists) Robert Mitchum
- Red Sundown ('56 Universal) Rory Calhoun
- Gunsmoke: Hack Prine ('56) James Arness
- Cheyenne: Death Deals the Hand ('56) Clint Walker
- Broken Arrow: The Raiders ('56) John Lupton/Michael Ansara
- Black Patch ('57 Warner Bros.) George Montgomery
- Tall Stranger ('57 Allied Artists) Joel McCrea
- Tales of Wells Fargo: Hasty Gun ('57) Dale Robertson
- Have Gun Will Travel: Winchester Quarantine ('57) Richard Boone
- Tombstone Territory: Guns of Silver ('57) Pat Conway
- Quantrill's Raiders ('58 Allied Artists) Steve Cochran
- Apache Territory ('58 Columbia) Rory Calhoun
- Ride A Crooked Trail ('58 Universal) Audie Murphy
- Tales of the Texas Rangers: Desert Fury ('58) Willard Parker
- Bat Masterson: Dude's Folly ('58) Gene Barry
- 26 Men: Showdown ('59) Kelo Henderson/Tris Coffin
- Have Gun Will Travel: Fifth Man ('59) Richard Boone
- Bonanza: Death On Sun Mountain ('59) Lorne Greene/Michael Landon
- Rawhide: Incident of the Valley in Shadow ('59) Eric Fleming
- Bat Masterson: Law of the Land ('60) Gene Barry
- Outlaws: Rape of Red Sky ('60) Don Collier
- Gunsmoke: No Chip ('60) James Arness
- Noose For a Gunman ('60 United Artists) Jim Davis
- Deputy: The Border Between ('60) Allen Case/Henry Fonda
- Wyatt Earp: The Shooting Starts ('61) Hugh O'Brian
- Lawman: Whiphand ('61) John Russell
- Tales of Wells Fargo: Trackback ('61) Dale Robertson
- Cheyenne: Vengeance Is Mine ('62) Clint Walker
- Bonanza: Deadly Ones ('62) Michael Landon
- McLintock! ('63 United Artists) John Wayne
- Hostile Guns ('67 Paramount) George Montgomery
- High Chaparral: Gold Is Where You Leave It ('68) Leif Erickson
- Gunsmoke: A Quiet Day In Dodge ('73) James Arness

FRED GRAHAM

One of the greatest "fight" men ever in the film business was Fred Graham. His screen fights are legend amongst his peers and film buffs alike. Although not always a perfect stunt double for such stars as John Wayne, Clark Gable or Robert Taylor, because of different builds, Fred always managed a slugfest that kept actor and director alike completely satisfied.

Born Charles 'Fred' Graham October 26, 1908 (not 1918 as is widely reported), baseball gave Fred his start in the motion picture business. Back in 1928 he worked for MGM in the sound department, while playing ball on the side for semi-professional teams. MGM made a baseball picture starring Robert Young, "Death On the Diamond" in 1934, for which Fred was hired to tutor Young in the finer points of the game. Fred also doubled for actor Nat Pendleton in the catching scenes, thus beginning his stunt career.

Fred stayed at MGM several years doubling Clark Gable ("Mutiny on the Bounty"), Nelson Eddy ("Rosemarie") and Charles Bickford ("The Storm" at Universal).

In 1938 Fred moved over to Warner Bros. becoming a staff stuntman for them. His first assignment was "Adventures of Robin Hood" where he doubled for Basil Rathbone, and on his first job at his new studio, broke an ankle jumping off a battlement. He was part of the classic barroom brawl in Errol Flynn's "Dodge City" and did work in "Roaring '20s" and "Valley of the Giants".

Work at Paramount ("Reap the Wild Wind") and other studios followed. He doubled Harry Woods in Universal's "Winners of the West" serial in '40.

In 1943 Fred hit his stride when he moved (non-exclusively) to the action factory known as Republic. Fred was battered hither and yon in many of their classic serials ("Masked Marvel", "Captain America", "Tiger Woman", "Haunted Harbor", "Zorro's Black Whip", "Trader Tom of the China Seas"—17 in all) and over 40 B-westerns with everyone from Rex Allen, Roy Rogers and Allan Lane to Bill Elliott, Monte Hale and Sunset Carson. Director Bill Witney once proclaimed Graham "…the best screen brawler I ever used." It was about this time he gained the nickname "Slugger".

His other serials are "Brick Bradford", "Congo Bill" and "Perils of the Wilderness" in '47, '48 and '56 respectively at Columbia, and "Don Winslow of the Coast Guard" ('43) at Universal. Fred once stated, "Katzman's budgets and conceptions were considerably less."

Fred did A-films in the '40s as well…"Buffalo Bill", "Murder My Sweet", "Dakota", "Fort Apache", "Wake of the Red Witch", "Asphalt Jungle", "She Wore A Yellow Ribbon".

He was involved in the classic fight from "Seven Sinners" ('40) with his friend John Wayne. He began doubling for Wayne in '42 despite the marked difference in size between the two men. In his later years, with his reputation firmly established as one of the stunt greats, Fred was queried about his very realistic fights on screen. He answered, "Fights came easy to me. My ideas to make

Saloon owner Roy Barcroft restrains Allan "Rocky" Lane while his burly henchman Fred Graham prepares to take a swing at "The Bold Frontiersman" ('48 Republic).

fights look good on screen were to stay loose and relaxed, a little distance from your opponent, and throw punches. Never throw a punch at chin level because a good take makes it look like a miss. Throw (the punch) at the opponent's eye level because a good take makes it appear like it's right on the chin. Design your routines for 30 to 40 seconds of screen time, leaving room for closeups on the stars."

During the '50s, Fred's work was in evidence in "Dallas", "Samson and Delilah", "Rear Window", "20,000 Leagues Under the Sea", "Seven Men From Now", "Badman's Country", "Giant Gila Monster", "Horse Soldiers", "Rio Bravo", "Seven Ways From Sundown", "North To Alaska" and "Arizona Raiders".

After nearly 40 years in the stunt and acting profession, Fred moved to Arizona in 1968 and did more to encourage film location work in that state than almost anyone while heading up the Department of Economic Planning and Development of Motion Pictures. He was also vice president and general manager of Cine Logistics, a subsidiary of Southwest Research and Development, operators of the Graham Studios in Carefree, Arizona, now known as Carefree at Southwest Studios. Fred kept active til the end in parts on films shot around Phoenix and Scottsdale.

Just shy of 71, Fred died in Scottsdale, Arizona, October 10, 1979. Stuntman Neil Summers said, "A measure of your success in the stunt profession is how much you are admired by your colleagues. Fred Graham had nothing to worry about. He was one of the most admired and respected stuntmen ever."

Suggested Sampling of Graham's Western Heavies:

- Bandits of the Badlands ('45 Republic) Sunset Carson
- Colorado Pioneers ('45 Republic) Bill Elliott
- Cherokee Flash ('45 Republic) Sunset Carson
- Out California Way ('46 Republic) Monte Hale
- Bells of San Angelo ('47 Republic) Roy Rogers
- On the Old Spanish Trail ('47 Republic) Roy Rogers
- Bold Frontiersman ('48 Republic) Allan "Rocky" Lane
- Timber Trail ('48 Republic) Monte Hale
- Son of God's Country ('48 Republic) Monte Hale
- Lone Ranger: Pete and Pedro ('49 Republic) Clayton Moore
- Range Rider: Grand Fleece ('50) Jock Mahoney
- Overland Telegraph ('51 RKO) Tim Holt
- Fort Osage ('52 Monogram) Rod Cameron
- Colorado Sundown ('52 Republic) Rex Allen
- Roy Rogers: Haunted Mine of Paradise Valley ('52) Roy Rogers
- Roy Rogers: Death Medicine ('52) Roy Rogers
- Kit Carson: Trail to Fort Hazard ('52) Bill Williams
- Old Oklahoma Plains ('52 Republic) Rex Allen
- Lone Ranger: Dan Reid's Sacrifice ('55) Clayton Moore
- Roy Rogers: Violence in Paradise Valley ('55) Roy Rogers
- 26 Men: Slaughter Trail ('58) Kelo Henderson/Tris Coffin
- Badman's Country ('58 Warner Bros.) George Montgomery
- Tales of Wells Fargo: Deadwood ('58) Dale Robertson
- Casey Jones: Lethal Journey ('58) Alan Hale Jr.
- Lawman: Intruders ('58) John Russell
- Jim Bowie: Ursula ('58) Scott Forbes
- Arizona Raiders ('65 Columbia) Audie Murphy

DUANE GREY

Too many name changes probably prevented husky, strong Duane Grey from becoming a bigger badman on-screen than he was. Born Duane Edwin Thorsen, when he got into films in 1952 he was planning on using the name Duke Thorsen but agents told him it sounded too much like a Chicago gangster. So for the first 3-4 years he went under Duane Thorsen. His agent talked him into Rex Thorsen for a brief period. As directors could not remember or pronounce his last name and checks often misspelled it, he finally decided on Duane Grey as his mother had named him after Zane Grey's "Last of the Duanes".

Born October 4, 1921, in Chicago, Illinois, Duane was raised there until he was 15. His father, Eddie Thorsen, was nicknamed The Flying Norwegian because he was a long-track and half-mile motorcycle racer. Taken out of school at 15, the family covered the East Coast racing circuits. Duane became the youngest short-track motorcycle racer in the world.

A bit older, he went to welding school in Ohio and

learned the trade of arc welding, working at Greevey Shipyards in Chicago.

Following WWII as a Marine Raider, Duane went to a radio dramatic arts school in Chicago on his GI bill. His training eventually led to parts in industrial films for Wilding Pictures in the windy city. From there he began doing stock around Chicago, branching out to Connecticut, and other venues.

A few years and many plays later, Duane headed west for Hollywood. Struggling for a while, he eventually obtained small roles in "Yankee Buccaneer" and "Willie and Joe Back at the Front" (both '52). While getting a foothold early on in Hollywood, Duane caught the tail end of the serial era and appeared in small roles in two of Republic's last, "Canadian Mounties Vs. Atomic Invaders" ('53) and "Trader Tom of the China Seas" ('54).

His rugged good looks and 6' 2" size made him a natural for westerns and he worked as heavies (as well as townsmen, ranchers and sheriffs later on) on "Kit Carson", "Hopalong Cassidy", "Annie Oakley", "Rin Tin Tin", "Circus Boy", "Casey Jones", "Cisco Kid", "Death Valley Days", "Cheyenne", "Have Gun Will Travel", "Lone Ranger", "Lawman" and dozens more through the early '70s.

Medical problems slowed him down but he continued to work sporadically, with his last role coming in Oliver Stone's "JFK" in '91 after which Duane moved to Eugene, Oregon, and continued to do local commercial work. Duane once told Tom and Jim Goldrup for their FEATURE PLAYERS Vol. 2, "I always enjoyed the heavies when there was a little variation on them instead of a snarl. When I was doing a Hopalong Cassidy Edgar Buchanan said, 'Hey, we have a smiling heavy this time!' I had enough stage work that I'd make the guy somewhat of a human being."

The big man with the big heart died October 13, 2002, of cancer in Eugene.

Suggested Sampling of Grey's Western Heavies:

- Kit Carson: War Whoop ('52) Bill Williams
- Kit Carson: Trouble at Ft. Mojave ('53) Bill Williams
- Hopalong Cassidy: Death By Proxy ('53) William Boyd
- Kit Carson: Powdersmoke Law ('53) Bill Williams
- Hopalong Cassidy: Black Sombrero ('54) William Boyd
- Annie Oakley: Outlaw Mesa ('54) Gail Davis
- Annie Oakley: Annie and the Outlaw's Son ('54) Gail Davis
- Lone Ranger: Homer With the High Hat ('54) Clayton Moore
- Cisco Kid: Cisco and the Giant ('55) Duncan Renaldo
- Rin Tin Tin: Rusty Goes To Town ('55) Lee Aaker
- Champion: Mystery Mountain ('56) Jim Bannon
- Champion: Brand of the Lawless ('56) Jim Bannon
- Steve Donovan, Western Marshal: Missouri Outlaws ('56) Douglas Kennedy
- Circus Boy: White Eagle ('56) Mickey Braddock
- Rin Tin Tin: Old Soldier ('57) Lee Aaker
- Casey Jones: Night Mail ('57) Alan Hale Jr.
- Casey Jones: Prison Train ('57) Alan Hale Jr.
- Sugarfoot: Dead Hills ('58) Will Hutchins
- Wild Bill Hickok: Clem's Reformation ('58) Guy Madison
- Iron Horse: Man From New Chicago ('66) Dale Robertson
- Charro ('69 National General) Elvis Presley

JAMES GRIFFITH

Hungry looking, spindly-lean James Griffith portrayed many roles on screen that were a far cry from his real, warm human being persona.

James Jeffrey Griffith was born February 13, 1916, in Los Angeles, California, the son of a boat builder who worked at Fellows and Stewart in Wellington. His mother's father was pure Scotch, his mother's mother pure Irish, his father's father was pure Welsh and his father's mother was the daughter of a British admiral.

Jim's early childhood was spent in San Pedro, California, where he appeared in his first play at a Methodist Church before he was even in kindergarten.

When the family moved to Balboa, Jim worked at the Newport Harbor Yacht Club as a bellhop. With the crash of '29, hard times hit the Griffith family so they sailed away in 1930 to Tahiti where they lived for a time.

Returning to Balboa in 1931, his parents were divorced and Jim and his sister moved with his mother to Santa Monica to live with his grandmother.

In his junior and senior years of high school Jim played clarinet in the orchestra. He also played in the Santa Monica Symphony in the winter season.

After high school, Jim joined the Marine Corps intending to go in as a musician, instead spending a year and a half in a howitzer outfit. He was later transferred to Pearl Harbor as a member of a 28 piece band. During this period he performed in many community theatres.

Following his hitch in the Marines he was hired by the San Diego Sun as a reporter while he performed in plays with the Barn Players. This brief career was interrupted near the close of WWII when Jim was recalled into the Marines until his discharge in 1947.

Jim found work pumping gas at a Standard Oil station in Westwood. A chance encounter with customer Spike Jones found Jim performing with Jones' wacky musicians.

Still working with Jones and holding down a shift at the gas station, Jim made his first film, "Blonde Ice", in 1948. From this time on film roles and TV work kept Jim busy.

His first western was "Daughter of the West" ('49), the script of which Jim and his friend Jack Daley re-wrote to make it serviceable.

In 1950, Jim became a regular performer on most of Gene Autry's Flying-A Productions—"Range Rider", "Gene Autry", "Annie Oakley", "Buffalo Bill Jr.".

In 1958, Jim played the role of Aaron Adams, a barber, and second lead on "Trackdown" with Robert Culp. At the same time, '58-'59, Jim was playing deputy Tom Ferguson on John Bromfield's "U.S. Marshal". John, frequent director Earl Bellamy, and Jim all formed a lasting relationship from that series. Bromfield told us, "Jim loved good humor while we were setting the scene up. He always could find some humor about it and he'd keep everybody in stitches most of the time. Great personality. It's amazing in the years that we'd go places and do things together, people would recognize him—didn't know his name because very few people know character actor's names—but they knew his face. We had a lot of fun together. He was blessed in that he had two wonderful wives. He had a good life, a fun life."

Besides his busy acting schedule over the years, Jim collaborated with Hal Hopper (who once sang with the Pied Pipers) on scripts and title tunes for a couple of movies. Jim worked on the scripts of "Shalako" ('68) and "Catlow" ('71) under the name J. J. Griffith. Over time he also penned the story for "Motor Psycho" ('65) and scripted certain episodes of "The Fugitive" and "Mission Impossible".

Papillary cancer and a subsequent operation in 1978 left Jim without the strong voice he'd once possessed, so he concentrated on writing.

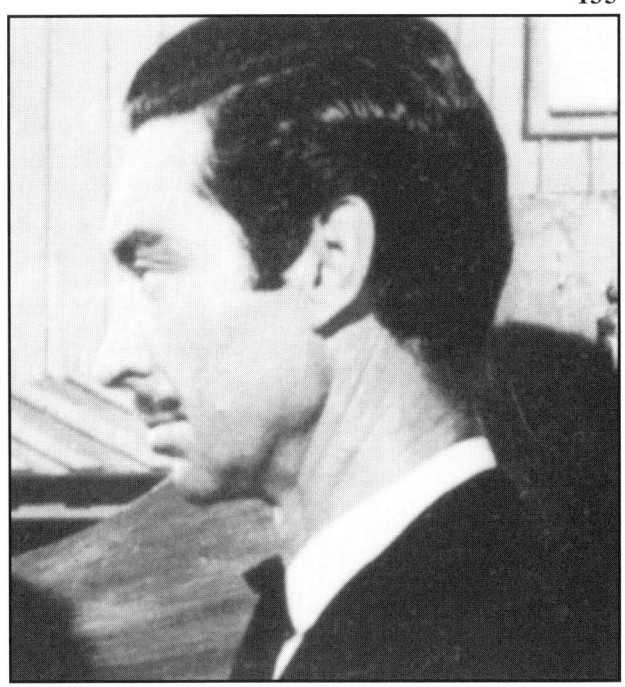

One of filmdom's best character actors succumbed to cancer at 77, September 17, 1993, at his home in Avila Beach, California. In his farewell letter to his friends in August, Jim wrote, "I have lived a wonderfully full life. You name it, I've done it. I've made a living doing what I wanted to do. Best of all, look at all of you who are my friends."

Suggested Sampling of Griffith's Western Heavies:

- Daughter of the West ('49 Film Classics) Phillip Reed
- Fighting Man of the Plains ('49 20th Century Fox) Randolph Scott
- Cariboo Trail ('50 20th Century Fox) Randolph Scott
- Indian Territory ('50 Columbia) Gene Autry
- Lone Ranger: Mission Bells ('50) Clayton Moore
- Gene Autry: Gray Dude ('50) Gene Autry
- Range Rider: Fatal Bullet ('51) Jock Mahoney
- Range Rider: Blind Trail ('51) Jock Mahoney
- Hopalong Cassidy: Alien Range ('52) William Boyd
- Lone Ranger: Delayed Action ('52) John Hart
- Lone Ranger: Durango Kid ('53) John Hart
- Kansas Pacific ('53 Allied Artists) Sterling Hayden
- Jesse James Vs. the Daltons ('54 Columbia) Brett King
- Black Dakotas ('54 Columbia) John Bromfield
- Masterson of Kansas ('54 Columbia) George Montgomery
- Lone Ranger: Lost Chalice ('55) Clayton Moore
- Buffalo Bill Jr.: Runaway Renegade ('55) Dick Jones
- Annie Oakley: Powder Rock Stampede ('55) Gail Davis
- Gunsmoke: Kite's Reward ('55) James Arness
- Cheyenne: Land Beyond the Law ('57) Clint Walker
- Guns of Fort Petticoat ('57 Columbia) Audie Murphy
- Man Without a Gun: Dark Road ('58) Rex Reason
- Jefferson Drum: Return ('58) Jeff Richards
- Wagon Train: Sakae Ito Story ('58) Ward Bond
- Return to Warbow ('58 Columbia) Phil Carey
- Seven Guns to Mesa ('58 Allied Artists) Charles Quinlivan
- Bullwhip ('58 Allied Artists) Guy Madison
- Maverick: Duel at Sundown ('59) James Garner
- Deputy: The Deputy ('59) Henry Fonda/Allen Case
- Texan: No Way Out ('59) Rory Calhoun
- Wichita Town: Bullet For a Friend ('59) Joel McCrea
- Two Faces West: The Return ('60) Charles Bateman
- Cheyenne: Frightened Town ('61) Clint Walker
- Tall Man: A Kind of Courage ('61) Barry Sullivan/Clu Gulager
- Wagon Train: Duke Shannon Story ('61) Denny Miller
- Wyatt Earp: Hiding Behind a Star ('61) Hugh O'Brian
- Have Gun Will Travel: The Waiting Room ('62) Richard Boone
- Tales of Wells Fargo: Angry Sky ('62) Dale Robertson
- Virginian: Gentle Tamers ('68) Charles Bickford
- Gunsmoke: Gunrunners ('68) James Arness
- Guns of Will Sonnett: Time Is the Rider ('69) Walter Brennan

WILLIAM HAADE

When the part called for a likeable or dimwitted comic badman, they usually called on William Haade. Witness his comic badmen in "In Old Cheyenne" with Roy Rogers, "Stage to Chino" with George O'Brien, "Red River Shore" with Rex Allen, "Robin Hood of the Pecos" with Roy Rogers, or "Old Frontier" with Monte Hale. An excellent natural actor, Haade always seemed to bring more to the role than was called for. Republic even utilized him once as Roy's titular sidekick in "Yellow Rose of Texas" ('44).

Non-western producers exploited his light comedic talents, as well, in such films as "You're In the Army Now" ('41), "Maisie Gets Her Man" ('42), "Buck Privates Come Home" ('47), "Joe Palooka In Squared Circle" ('50), "Stop That Cab" ('51) and many more.

Appearing in over 240 films from 1937's "Kid Galahad" as the boxing champion managed by Humphrey Bogart to a small lumberjack role in Rod Cameron's "Spoilers of the Forest" in '57, Haade also played dozens of hoods, cops, doormen, truck drivers, Army sergeants, MPs and various blue collar workmen.

Perhaps Republic put his true acting talents to work best in several Don Barry B's, "Desert Bandit", "Kansas Cyclone" and especially "Days of Old Cheyenne".

The brawny, tow-haired, gruff voiced, tough-looking Haade, who writer David Quinlan termed a cross between Harry Carey and Bruce Cabot, was born of Dutch extraction March 2, 1903, in New York, New York.

He was a structural steel worker before becoming an actor in 1936. Hired as a technical advisor for the play "Iron Man", he wound up playing the lead in producer Norman Bel Geddes' play which led to film work.

Interestingly, Haade raised mink as a hobby since 1928.

His first western was as a Cavalry sergeant in "The Texans" ('38). As good an actor as he was, he found work in many classic films ("Grapes of Wrath", "They Drive By Night", "Shepherd of the Hills", "Honky Tonk", "Pittsburgh", "Hangmen Also Die", "Incendiary Blonde", "Secret Life of Walter Mitty", "Unconquered", "Good Sam", "The Fountainhead", "Rancho Notorious" and many more.) Because of this he only returned to westerns sporadically. For the same reason, his serial appearances were few, only five, with his best role coming as the right hand thug of boss heavy Robert Frazer in Republic's "Daredevils of the West" ('43) with Allan Lane.

Haade was only 63 when he died (of unknown causes) in Los Angeles on November 15, 1966. Survived by his wife, Anna, he's buried at San Fernando Mission Cemetery in Mission Hills, California.

Another confrontation between badmen William Haade and George J. Lewis and the "Daredevils of the West", Allan Lane and Eddie Acuff ('43 Republic).

Suggested Sampling of Haade's Western Heavies:

- Bullet Code ('40 RKO) George O'Brien
- Stage to Chino ('40 RKO) George O'Brien
- Robin Hood of the Pecos ('41 Republic) Roy Rogers
- The Round Up ('41 Paramount) Richard Dix
- In Old Cheyenne ('41 Republic) Roy Rogers
- Pirates on Horseback ('41 Paramount) William Boyd
- Desert Bandit ('41 Republic) Don Barry
- Kansas Cyclone ('41 Republic) Don Barry
- Man From Cheyenne ('42 Republic) Roy Rogers
- Heart of the Rio Grande ('42 Republic) Gene Autry
- Heart of the Golden West ('42 Republic) Roy Rogers
- Daredevils of the West ('43 Republic serial) Allan Lane
- Days of Old Cheyenne ('43 Republic) Don Barry
- Song of Texas ('43 Republic) Roy Rogers
- Sheriff of Las Vegas ('44 Republic) Bill Elliott
- Phantom of the Plains ('45 Republic) Bill Elliott
- Royal Mounted Rides Again ('45 Universal serial) Bill Kennedy
- Under Colorado Skies ('47 Republic) Monte Hale
- Last of the Wild Horses ('48 Screen Guild) James Ellison
- Wyoming Bandit ('49 Republic) Allan "Rocky" Lane
- Outcast of Black Mesa ('50 Columbia) Charles Starrett
- Lone Ranger: Beeler Gang ('50) Clayton Moore
- Old Frontier ('50 Republic) Monte Hale
- Gene Autry: Doublecross Valley ('50) Gene Autry
- Lone Ranger: Outlaw's Revenge ('50) Clayton Moore
- Range Rider: Blind Canyon ('51) Jock Mahoney
- Buckaroo Sheriff of Texas ('51 Republic) Rough Ridin' Kids
- Range Rider: Bandit Stallion ('52) Jock Mahoney
- Kit Carson: Wild Horses of Pala ('52) Bill Williams
- Lone Ranger: Outlaw's Son ('52) John Hart
- Lone Ranger: Sheriff's Son ('53) John Hart
- Wild Bill Hickok: Monster In the Lake ('53) Guy Madison
- Red River Shore ('53 Republic) Rex Allen
- Hopalong Cassidy: Outlaw's Reward ('54) William Boyd
- Lone Ranger: Rendezvous at Whipsaw ('54) Clayton Moore
- Wild Bill Hickok: Sheriff's Secret ('55) Guy Madison
- Tales of the Texas Rangers: Shooting of Sam Bass ('55) Willard Parker
- Sergeant Preston: Tobacco Smugglers ('56) Richard Simmons
- 26 Men: Killer's Trail ('58) Kelo Henderson/Tris Coffin

HERMAN HACK

Riding with the gang or posse…lounging in the background…hanging out or playing cards in the saloon…going along with the lynch mob…stubby little Herman Hack was the ultimate badman "extra". If he ever

Buster Crabbe (R) and Al "Fuzzy" St. John (L) round-up the "Stagecoach Outlaws"—John Cason, Bob Kortman, Kermit Maynard and Herman Hack. Frances Gladwin approves ('45 PRC).

had more than two lines in a row, I'd be surprised. Usually his lines, if he had any at all, consisted of "Right," Okay," "Over there" or some such.

In a calculated 400 plus westerns beginning in 1931, he was virtually uncredited on-screen in any of them. So insignificant were his parts that he very seldom was even assigned a character name. He was just another henchman…6th man through the door in a five member gang. Townsman. Barfly. Mine Guard. Raider #3. Trail herder. Stage passenger. Gang member. Card player. But 'ol Herman Hack was there with the best of them…Tim McCoy, Tom Tyler, Johnny Mack Brown, Bob Steele, John Wayne, Ken Maynard, Hoot Gibson, Bob Allen, Tom Keene, Gene Autry, Roy Rogers, Charles Starrett, 3 Mesquiteers, Don Barry, Range Busters, Buster Crabbe, Hopalong Cassidy, Russell Hayden, Allan Lane, Jimmy Wakely, Sunset Carson, Lash La Rue, Monte Hale, Cisco Kid, Bill Elliott and many more.

Producer Alex Gordon honored Hack by casting him, naturally as a townsman, in his 1965 all-star roundup, "The Bounty Killer", some 10 years after Hack had made his "final" film, "Reprisal!" in '56 with Guy Madison.

Herman H. Hackenjos was born in Illinois, June 15, 1899. His mother's maiden name was Gramm. Hack died in Hollywood at 68, October 19, 1967, from a heart attack. Prior to going to Hollywood Hack was a horse wrangler in Wyoming and Oregon. Herman and his wife, Signe, also a movie extra, spent all their money as they went along trying to get a foothold in producing religious films. However, it never quite jelled.

Hack was survived by Signe and two daughters, Dorothy and Dolly Kay. Signe died on January 6, 1973, at 74. Their daughter Dorothy married Smiley Burnette's son Stephen in 1959.

Suggested Sampling of Hack's Western Heavies:

- Range Riders ('34 Superior) Buddy Roosevelt
- Paradise Canyon ('35 Lone Star) John Wayne
- Gangs of Sonora ('41 Republic) 3 Mesquiteers
- Lone Prairie ('42 Columbia) Russell Hayden
- Cherokee Flash ('45 Republic) Sunset Carson
- Return of the Durango Kid ('45 Columbia) Charles Starrett
- Two Fisted Stranger ('46 Columbia) Charles Starrett
- Jesse James Rides Again ('47 Republic serial) Clayton Moore
- Marshal of Cripple Creek ('47 Republic) Allan Lane

KARL HACKETT

Karl Hackett was in so many PRC westerns, over 40, one might assume he owned stock in the Gower Gulch studio. Certainly, Hackett worked for others, but PRC was his bread and butter. While most producers used Hackett strictly as a badman, at least PRC cast him as a father, governor, banker, judge, rancher, assayer and sheriff, as well as an outlaw.

With over 150 film credits, mainly B-westerns, in just a 12 year stay in Hollywood, Hackett was one of the busiest of the badmen from '35-'47.

During that time, the smallish, well-dressed Hackett (often in a black coat with a string tie) was seldom involved in the fisticuffs; he was the saloon owner/crooked banker/outlaw leader who directed the dog-heavies to perform his dirty tricks.

Hackett employed his dire deeds on most of the cowboys of the time, in particular Johnny Mack Brown, Tim McCoy, Bob Steele, Rex Bell, Kermit Maynard, Buster Crabbe, Tex Ritter, Fred Scott, George Houston, Lee Powell/Art Davis/Bill Boyd, Tom Keene, Tim Holt, Bob Livingston and the Trail Blazers. For whatever reason, Hackett worked mostly for PRC and other independents and seldom for Republic, Universal, Columbia, RKO and Paramount.

Like most of his contemporaries, his roles became more sympathetic with age.

Hackett was born Carl Ellsworth Germain in Carthage, Missouri, on September 5, 1893. His father,

Crooked Karl Hackett and Tex Ritter are about to come to blows in "Starlight Over Texas" ('38 Monogram).

William G. Germain, was from Colorado and his mother, Anna Scott, was a Missouri native.

Upon graduation from high school, he went directly into Chicago dramatics and stock, finally coming to Hollywood at 42. He was a member of the Armed Forces during WWI.

Hackett was married at least once, but at the time of his death he was divorced from Ruby Germain, indicating Hackett was simply his screen name.

Hackett died at only 55 on October 24, 1948, at the VA's National Military Hospital in Los Angeles County where he'd been a patient for nearly five months. His cause of death was due to bronchopneumonia aggravated greatly by cirrhosis of the liver, indicating Hackett had been a heavy drinker. He's buried at the Veterans Administration Cemetery in Los Angeles.

Truly, one of the knaves we loved to hate.

Suggested Sampling of Hackett's Western Heavies:

- Bulldog Courage ('35 Puritan) Tim McCoy
- Roarin' Guns ('36 Puritan) Tim McCoy
- Cavalry ('36 Republic) Bob Steele
- Stormy Trails ('36 Colony) Rex Bell
- Trail of Vengeance ('37 Supreme) Johnny Mack Brown
- Whistling Bullets ('37 Ambassador) Kermit Maynard
- Gun Lords of Stirrup Basin ('37 Republic) Bob Steele
- Sing, Cowboy, Sing ('37 Grand National) Tex Ritter
- Arizona Gunfighter ('37 Republic) Bob Steele
- Tex Rides With the Boy Scouts ('37 Grand National) Tex Ritter
- Ranger's Round-Up ('38 Spectrum) Fred Scott
- Phantom Ranger ('38 Monogram) Tim McCoy
- Feud Maker ('38 Republic) Bob Steele
- Songs and Saddles ('38 Colony) Gene Austin
- Rollin' Plains ('38 Grand National) Tex Ritter
- Six Gun Trail ('38 Victory) Tim McCoy
- Sundown On the Prairie ('39 Monogram) Tex Ritter
- Murder On the Yukon ('40 Monogram) James Newill
- Frontier Crusader ('40 PRC) Tim McCoy
- Take Me Back to Oklahoma ('40 Monogram) Tex Ritter
- Lone Rider Rides On ('41 PRC) George Houston
- Billy the Kid's Range War ('41 PRC) Bob Steele
- Outlaws of the Rio Grande ('41 PRC) Tim McCoy
- Billy the Kid In Santa Fe ('41 PRC) Bob Steele
- Texas Marshal ('41 PRC) Tim McCoy
- Lone Rider in Frontier Fury ('41 PRC) George Houston
- Man From Montana ('41 Universal) Johnny Mack Brown
- Death Valley Outlaws ('41 Republic) Bill Elliott
- Texas Manhunt ('42 PRC) Lee Powell/Art Davis/Bill Boyd
- Western Mail ('42 Monogram) Tom Keene
- Jesse James Jr. ('42 Republic) Don Barry
- Come On Danger ('42 RKO) Tim Holt
- Outlaws of Boulder Pass ('42 PRC) George Houston
- Thundering Trails ('43 Republic) 3 Mesquiteers
- Wolves of the Range ('43 PRC) Bob Livingston
- Death Valley Rangers ('43 Monogram) Trail Blazers
- Sonora Stagecoach ('44 Monogram) Trail Blazers
- His Brother's Ghost ('45 PRC) Buster Crabbe

KEVIN HAGEN

Beneath the quiet, calm exterior of lanky Kevin Hagen breathed a cool viciousness that erupted on TV's "Have Gun Will Travel", "Gunsmoke", "Laramie", "Rifleman", "Lawman" and others in the late '50s and '60s. But just as often as not, Hagen was a put-upon peaceful settler, preacher or shopkeeper on other TV westerns. Perhaps his best big screen badman role was that of a conniving bounty hunter in Allied Artists' "Rider On a Dead Horse" ('62).

Hagen is no doubt best remembered early in his career as New Orleans Civil Administrator John Colton who gave Jock Mahoney his undercover orders on "Yancy Derringer" ('58-'59). Perhaps even more remembered is his recurring role from '77-'81 as kindly Doc Hiram Baker on Michael Landon's warm-hearted "Little House On the Prairie".

Kevin Hagen was born April 3, 1928, in Chicago, Illinois. Hagen told Boyd Magers, "My father had several names. The one he was born with was Haakon Olaf Hagen. He changed it as quick as he could. Both Haakon and Olaf were Norwegian kings. His parents were born and lived in Oslo, Norway, and migrated to America and Chicago in the early 1900's. He became Herbert Hagen and met my mother at a ballroom dance studio. Her name was Marvel Lucile Wadsworth, and they became a ballroom dancing act, Herbert and Lucile, touring fairs and amusement parks. When I turned five and was ready for school, my parents opened a dance studio in Joliet, some 40 miles west of Chicago, where my uncle had recently established a medical practice."

"My father deserted my mother when I was about 5. My mother tried running the dance studio for several years but it didn't work out. She moved in with her mother and two sisters and they all took care of Donnie, as I was known in those childhood days. My uncle filled much of the void left behind by the departure of my father. There was probably a lot of my Uncle Harold in my role as Doc Baker so many years later on 'Little House.'"

"During WWII, the ladies moved to Portland, Oregon, along with me, a very fat kid of 250 lbs. ready to enter his junior year in high school. My aunt Alverteen, a teacher, had answered a notice for a teaching position in

Vanport, Oregon, a temporary city with prefabs for the people who built the Liberty and Victory ships that carried the men and equipment that were needed to fight the war."

"I lost weight, played football and baseball, pitched a 2-0 shutout in the state championship game, was the sports editor of the school paper and the tenor in the choir and quartet. Those two years made it for me."

"I went to Oregon State College (as it was known then) for my freshman year, enlisted in the U.S. Navy for two years and played baseball and football at the San Diego Naval Training Center and the North Island Naval Air Station, came home to Portland and, on my G.I. bill, went to Lewis and Clark College for two years, transferred to the University of Southern California, changed majors and graduated with a B.A. degree in International Relations. Traveled to Wiesbaden, Germany, lived with the family of a former German soldier who had attended USC and with whom I had shared a room and found a job as a supervisor with the Marshall Plan, which rebuilt Europe. After two years I returned to America in 1953, taught ballroom dancing at Arthur Murray's while waiting for the fall semester of UCLA Law School to begin, but discovered law was not what I wanted. I cared for my mother who had breast cancer and didn't catch it soon enough. It was shortly after my mother's untimely death at 54 that I discovered little theatre, specifically in Pacific Palisades at Buddy Ebsen's sister's dance studio that doubled as a theater on weekends. I found that acting was what I wanted, that I was good at it, attended acting workshops, acted in little theaters in Santa Monica, Westwood, and in Hollywood. Got an agent who saw me in Eugene O'Neill's 'Desire Under the Elms' in which I played the 70 year old lead, Ephraim Cabot, at the age of 28, got a SAG card by appearing in Jack Webb's 'Dragnet' and began 30 years of freelancing, with an occasional regular series role. In between roles I sold cars and insurance, hung wallpaper and worked in a bank until Michael Landon gave me a steady role on 'Little House'."

"It was fun (playing the heavy), you could be as mean as you wanted to be. There's a heavy in all of us. I tapered off with nine years on 'Little House on the Prairie', after which the fire in the belly was no longer there for the Hollywood scene and its rejection of 'Little House' and its series actors who were nevertheless loved and admired by the world."

In 1991, Kevin escaped Hollywood's mean streets and settled down amongst the lush green of Grant's Pass in the Rogue Valley of Oregon. Since moving to Oregon he has performed at South Oregon's Rogue Music Theatre in several musicals, finding at this time of life he'd much rather sing than act. For several years Kevin rode atop the Valley of the Rogue Bank stagecoach in commercials which he also wrote.

He has developed and presented his original one-man show, "A Playful Dose of Prairie Wisdom", for theatres, dinner shows, conventions and pageants throughout the country. In words and music, as Doc Baker he paints for his audience an amusing, informative picture of the life and profession of a turn of the century prairie doctor. Included in his CD, "A Kid on the Hood of a '29 Chevy" and on his audio cassette, "Just an Ordinary Man", are his favorite songs of the 20th Century and personal favorites by Harry Chapin, Billy Joel and others.

As for marriages, Kevin told us, "Four. My second wife died tragically a few years after we met on the set of 'Perry Mason'. Her name was Suzanne Cramer and she was well known in the German films of the early '60s, a kind of German Brigitte Bardot. My third wife, who was born in Brazil, became the mother of my one and only son, Kristopher Hagen. He is a Special Education teacher and the baseball coach at Highland High School in Bakersfield, California. I'm very proud of him. For almost 20 years I was a single parent and Kristopher lived with me in Thousand Oaks, California, during the years of 'Little House'."

"My fourth and final wife is Jan. We met while I was doing 'A Playful Dose of Prairie Wisdom' at a dinner theatre here in Grants Pass. She is also a Special Ed teacher and a woman of great beauty and wisdom. We have been married for going on ten years (as of May 2004)."

Hagen, 77, died July 9, 2005, of esophageal cancer at his home in Grants Pass, Oregon.

Suggested Sampling of Hagen's Western Heavies:

- Tales of Wells Fargo: Shotgun Messenger ('57) Dale Robertson
- Have Gun Will Travel: Half Brother ('58) Richard Boone
- Gunsmoke In Tucson ('58 Allied Artists) Mark Stevens
- Gunsmoke: Love of a Good Woman ('59) James Arness
- Laramie: Run to Tumavaca ('59) Robert Fuller
- Riverboat: Jessie Quinn ('59) Darren McGavin
- Sugarfoot: Blackwater Swamp ('60) Will Hutchins
- Deputy: Final Payment ('60) Henry Fonda/Allen Case
- Rifleman: The Prodigal ('60) Chuck Connors
- Hotel de Paree: Fallen Sparrow ('60) Earl Holliman
- Gunsmoke: Brother Love ('60) James Arness
- Have Gun Will Travel: Quiet Night In Town (Pt. 1-2) ('61) Richard Boone
- Outlaws: Assassin ('61) Don Collier
- Bat Masterson: Fourth Man ('61) Gene Barry
- Laramie: Killer Legend ('61) Robert Fuller
- Rider On a Dead Horse ('62 Allied Artists) John Vivyan
- Rawhide: Long Count ('62) Eric Fleming/Charles Gray
- Lawman: The Vintage ('62) John Russell
- Gunsmoke: Wagon Girls ('62) James Arness
- Lawman: Cort ('62) John Russell
- Have Gun Will Travel: A Place For Abel Hix ('62) Richard Boone
- Laramie: Renegade Brand ('63) John Smith
- Gunsmoke: No Hands ('64) James Arness
- Branded: Mightier Than the Sword ('65) Chuck Connors
- A Man Called Shenandoah: The Reward ('65) Robert Horton
- High Chaparral: Shadow on the Land ('67) Lief Erickson
- Bonanza: Showdown at Tahoe ('67) David Canary
- Wild Wild West: Night of the Amnesiac ('68) Robert Conrad
- Cimarron Strip: Blue Moon Train ('68) Stuart Whitman

DON HAGGERTY

Don Haggerty alternated most of his 36 year film career between honest portrayals and hateful heavies. But viewers found him most effective when he was wicked.

Don Haggerty was born July 3, 1914, in Poughkeepsie, New York. Always active in sports of all kinds, Don attended two prep schools as well as Brown University where he boxed and became a Golden Gloves champion.

Oddly, his start was at Vassar College, the famous school for girls. In Vassar's summer school for theatre Don was selected as one of three guys to act among 350 girls.

From there Don worked at the famed Federal Theatre and did summer stock in Woodstock, New York, for two seasons, and in Suffield, Connecticut, Cumberland Hills, Rhode Island…wherever he could to gain experience.

After serving three and a half years with Military intelligence in the Army during WWII, Don made a "March of Time" film extolling the virtues of Alcoholics Anonymous. Off of that, he went to California in 1945. Struggling, he managed to land roles in five of the last 12 Hopalong Cassidy westerns for United Artists in 1948.

Several sheriff roles in Tim Holt RKO B-westerns followed as well as the 12 week exposure of being henchman Tony Dirken in Republic's excellent "King of the Rocketmen" serial ('49) which is where Don formed a lifelong friendship with Tris Coffin.

Don starred in early TV's private eye show "The Cases of Eddie Drake" in '52, then, with pal Tris Coffin, in the similar "The Files of Jeffrey Jones" in '54.

Coffin told Boyd Magers in 1988, "Don was one of the most well liked men that ever worked in films…a fine actor…admired by everyone. It was a great loss to me personally…'King of the Rocketmen' was the first time I met Don. He'd never done a serial before. We had choreographed a fight, but something went wrong and he didn't throw a punch when he should have—or maybe I threw one when I shouldn't have…anyway, I hit him on the chin and he went right down. He got up—shook his head and said 'Ok, let's go.' Don started after me and I yelled 'cut-cut.' We stopped and got things straightened out and were very close friends from then on...for 40 years professionally and personally."

Now established, work was plentiful—character roles in major films and plenty of heavies to keep him more than busy on TV. He had the semi-regular role of newspaper editor Marsh Murdock for the first year of "Wyatt Earp" ('55-'56).

However, his favorite role was a sympathetic one, that of a blind rancher in Joel McCrea's "Cattle Empire" ('58 20th Century Fox).

His last role was in "Legend of the Wild" in '81 with old pals John Dehner and Ken Curtis.

Retired, Don moved to Florida in 1986 where he died in Cocoa Beach, August 19, 1988.

Richard (Chito) Martin told us in '88, upon hearing of Don's passing, "Elaine (Riley/Martin) and I were just talking about him the other day. We used to have him and his wife over to the house...he was a fun guy, always laughing...pretty comical guy offscreen even though he played heavies...(you'd) never suspect him of being a heavy."

"Many, many things you look back on," Don said, "and I will say I thoroughly enjoyed the westerns more than anything. It's more freedom and you're out of doors. The guys are all fine—a nice bunch of people."

Suggested Sampling of Haggerty's Western Heavies:

- False Paradise ('48 United Artists) William Boyd
- Sinister Journey ('48 United Artists) William Boyd
- South of Rio ('49 Republic) Monte Hale
- Lone Ranger: Six Gun Legacy ('49) Clayton Moore
- Lone Ranger: Matter of Courage ('50) Clayton Moore
- Vanishing Westerner ('50 Republic) Monte Hale
- Kid From Texas ('50 Universal-International) Audie Murphy
- Vigilante Hideout ('50 Republic) Allan "Rocky" Lane
- Spoilers of the Plains ('51 Republic) Roy Rogers
- Wild Stallion ('52 Monogram) Ben Johnson
- Phantom Stallion ('54 Republic) Rex Allen
- Stories of the Century: Sam Bass ('54) Jim Davis
- 26 Men: The Recruit ('57) Kelo Henderson/Tris Coffin
- 26 Men: Legacy of Death ('58) Kelo Henderson/Tris Coffin
- Californians: Alice Pritchard Case ('58) Adam Kennedy
- Sugarfoot: Mule Team ('58) Will Hutchins
- Rough Riders: Electioneers ('59) Jan Merlin/Kent Taylor
- Have Gun Will Travel: Maggie O'Bannion ('59) Richard Boone
- Frontier Doctor: Superstition Mountain ('59) Rex Allen
- Bat Masterson: Lady Luck ('59) Gene Barry
- Sugarfoot: Highbinder ('60) Will Hutchins
- Riverboat: Wichita Arrows ('60) Dan Duryea
- Rawhide: Incident of the Silent Web ('60) Eric Fleming
- Texan: The Accuser ('60) Rory Calhoun
- Sugarfoot: Shepherd With a Gun ('61) Will Hutchins
- Bronco: Yankee Tornado ('61) Ty Hardin
- Lawman: The Promise ('61) John Russell
- Gunsmoke: Quint's Trial ('63) Burt Reynolds/Dennis Weaver

FRANK HAGNEY

Plug-ugly Frank Hagney had quite a life. Born in Sydney, New South Wales, Australia, March 20, 1884, he worked in vaudeville, on the stage, as a stuntman and was in over 300 silent and sound movies and some 20 TVers. He also obviously had some pugilistic background as his entrance into films was in "The Battler" in 1919 along with 7-10 other boxing films (including "The Champ" in '31) over the years.

From 1919 to 1967, for 48 years, Hagney labored in the film industry in westerns, comedies, dramas, serials and crime films. He played lead heavies at PRC, henchmen/ranchers/sheriffs at Ambassador, Columbia, Republic, etc. and character roles or bit parts in major westerns such as "Along Came Jones" ('45), "Sea of Grass" ('47), "River Lady" ('48), "The Paleface" ('48), "Hangman's Knot" ('52), "Ride Clear of Diablo" ('54), "Gunfight at the O.K. Corral" ('57), "3:10 to Yuma" ('57) and "McLintock!" ('63).

His thuggish tough-looking demeanor was also put to use in major non-westerns: "Pack Up Your Troubles" ('32), "Treasure Island" ('34), "Night Key" ('37), "Robin

Hood" ('38), "Seven Sinners" ('40), "Dr. Jekyll and Mr. Hyde" ('41), "Glass Key" ('42), "Corregidor" ('43), "Crazy House" ('43), "Wild Harvest" ('47), "My Favorite Spy" ('51), "Invasion of the Body Snatchers" ('56) and "Friendly Persuasion" ('56), among many others.

Hagney was in 16 serials, including four silents— "The Whirlwind" ('19) and "Go Get 'Em Hutch" ('22) both with Charles Hutchison, "Fighting Marine" ('26) with boxer Gene Tunney and "Vultures of the Sea" ('28) with Johnnie Walker. With sound, Hagney was usually just a thug or hireling with his best roles in "Black Coin" ('36 Stage & Screen) and "Airmail Mystery" ('32 Universal).

At 83 Hagney called it quits in 1967 after being in three episodes of "Daniel Boone" with Fess Parker.

Hagney died at 89 in Los Angeles on June 25, 1973. His wife's name was Edna Shephard.

Suggested Sampling of Hagney's Western Heavies:

- Galloping Gallagher ('24 FBO) Fred Thomson
- Lone Hand Saunders ('26 FBO) Fred Thomson
- Last Trail ('27 Fox) Tom Mix
- Rawhide Kid ('28 Universal) Hoot Gibson
- Ride Him, Cowboy ('32 Warner Bros.) John Wayne
- Western Frontier ('35 Columbia) Ken Maynard
- Thunderbolt ('35 Regal) Kane Richmond
- Valley of the Lawless ('36 Supreme) Johnny Mack Brown
- Heroes of the Range ('36 Columbia) Ken Maynard
- Ghost Town Gold ('36 Republic) 3 Mesquiteers
- Wild Horse Round-Up ('37 Ambassador) Kermit Maynard
- Lone Rider Rides On ('41 PRC) George Houston
- Lone Rider in Ghost Town ('41 PRC) George Houston
- Lone Rider Ambushed ('41 PRC) George Houston
- Lone Rider Fights Back ('41 PRC) George Houston
- Texas Manhunt ('42 PRC) Lee Powell/Art Davis/Bill Boyd
- Tumbleweed Trail ('42 PRC) Lee Powell/Art Davis/Bill Boyd
- The Renegades ('43 PRC) Buster Crabbe
- Blazing Frontier ('43 PRC) Buster Crabbe
- Where the North Begins ('47 Screen Guild) Russell Hayden
- Cisco Kid: Powder Trail ('54) Duncan Renaldo
- A Lawless Street ('55 Columbia) Randolph Scott
- Lone Ranger: Uncle Ed ('55) Clayton Moore

KENNETH HARLAN

Sober-faced, square-jawed Kenneth Harlan belonged to the dress heavy group of western badmen, crooked lawyers, judges and saloon owners.

The man who would become an important matinee idol in silent films was born July 26, 1895, in Boston, Massachusetts, the son of Rita W. and George W. Harlan.

Educated at St. Francis High School in Brooklyn and Fordham University in New York, the brown-haired, blue-eyed, 185 lb., 5' 11" Harlan received his initial acting experience in vaudeville and on the stage beginning at the age of seven, no doubt helped by his mother who was an actress and his plump character actor uncle, Otis Harlan (1865-1940). At 18 the dashing Harlan made his debut in an Eastern stock company.

By 1917 he was in the movies with almost immediate stardom appearing with top leading ladies like Constance Talmadge, Clara Bow, Mary Pickford, Bessie Love and his second wife Marie Prevost.

Harlan saw military service (circa 1918-1919) during WWI, often joking later about his K.P. experiences with fellow actor George Chesebro.

Upon his return from the service, he quickly resumed his movie career. He only starred in one major western among his over 75 silents, "The Virginian" ('23).

Insight into Harlan's personality comes from PHOTO DRAMA MAGAZINE (8/21). "He is young, good-looking and clever at a quiet, innocent type of characterization. He portrays, with excellent result, the self-sacrificing hero with the big heart and the gentle manners and the way with the ladies. Kenneth Harlan has had a wide experience. At one time or other, he has played lead to almost all the better known movie queens. That is because he is adaptable, ready to lend himself to any part; working with ease and pleasantness in the studio; preserving a patience in the face of problems that is constantly commendable; taking himself seriously because he means to do his best; taking his associates seriously and to earning their respect. Harlan dresses well, but not strikingly. He has no spontaneous, eager smile like the famous Wally Reid smile; he has none of the dreamy, poetic quality of Dick Barthelmess. He has none of the vivaciousness of Charles Ray or the distinguished presence of Percy Marmont. But, he has a winning smile that is just a hint sad, a slow manner that earns regard for its very precision; his appeal is to the heart rather than to the eyes, and he makes a better martyr than a conqueror."

With the advent of sound, Harlan's starring days were all but over. He managed the lead in Tiffany's odd "Under Montana Skies" and Universal starred him in two early talkie serials, "Finger Prints" and "Danger Island" (both '31). Harlan quickly turned to all sorts of character roles—police chiefs, G-Men, lawyers, judges, cattle buyers, bankers—and heavies.

Married seven times, former Follies dancer Florence Hart was his first wife from June 26, 1920 to 1922. Divorced, he was married to actress Marie Prevost from 1924-1927. A son was born during that marriage but it ended in a well publicized divorce. His later wives were Massachusetts socialite Doris Booth (1930-?), actress Emily McLaughlin, actress Helene Stanton, screenwriter Phyllis McClure (1932-?) and dancer Rhea Walker (1957-1959).

Harlan was seen in 15 serials, besides the two starrers mentioned, in particular a good supporting role in John Wayne's "Shadow of the Eagle" ('32 Mascot) and as the murderous Carter Snowden in "Mysterious Pilot" ('37 Columbia) opposite air ace Frank Hawks and Rex Lease.

Incidentally, Harlan co-authored a book with Lease, WHAT ACTORS EAT—WHEN THEY EAT.

At 48, following nine films and two serials released in 1943, Kenneth Harlan retired from acting turning briefly to the restaurant business before becoming a Hollywood agent, a career he followed for about 20 years.

Harlan lived in Sacramento for about four years after his retirement from agency work.

He died of an acute aneurysm March 6, 1967, at 71 at Sutter Memorial Hospital in Sacramento, California. He'd entered the hospital the day before for abdominal surgery.

Suggested Sampling of Harlan's Western Heavies:
- Renfrew of the Royal Mounted ('37 Grand National) James Newill
- Gunsmoke Ranch ('37 Republic) 3 Mesquiteers
- Mysterious Pilot ('37 Columbia serial) Frank Hawks
- Whirlwind Horseman ('38 Grand National) Ken Maynard
- Pride of the West ('38 Paramount) William Boyd
- Law of the Texan ('38 Columbia) Buck Jones
- Prairie Schooners ('40 Columbia) Bill Elliott
- Fighting Bill Fargo '(41 Universal) Johnny Mack Brown
- Perils of the Royal Mounted ('42 Columbia serial) Robert Kent
- Deep In the Heart of Texas ('42 Universal) Johnny Mack Brown/Tex Ritter
- Bandit Ranger ('42 RKO) Tim Holt
- Law Rides Again ('43 Monogram) Trail Blazers
- Death Valley Rangers ('43 Monogram) Trail Blazers

DON HARVEY

Handsome, mustached, deep-voiced Don Harvey was one of the post-WWII group of B-western and TV badmen who quickly rose to prominence in the late '40s and early '50s, especially on TV where he made well over 100 westerns. Sometimes dress heavy, sometimes one of the gang, he was a regular face on "Gene Autry", "Wild Bill Hickok", "Range Rider", "Annie Oakley", "Roy Rogers", "Sky King" and others. As TV issued in the adult western, Harvey began playing character roles on "Rawhide" (a semi-regular drover, Collins), "Restless Gun", "Texan", "Sugarfoot", "Wyatt Earp", "Tall Man", "Laramie" and others.

After making his first movie in '45 at Universal, "That Night with You" which starred Franchot Tone, Don quickly became a regular in producer Sam Katzman's band of serial performers. Don's first for Sam was "Batman and Robin" ('49) and he appeared in seven more up through "Blazing the Overland Trail" ('56 Columbia), having the dubious distinction of being the last lead heavy in the last serial made.

Don Carlos Harvey was born December 12, 1911, in Marquette, Kansas, and was raised by his parents John and Frances Harvey in the historic Kansas township of Council Grove, the last supply stop on the Old Santa Fe Trail before heading west. Don's father (from California) was a railroader for the Missouri Pacific, his mother (born in Nebraska) worked as a laundress at home.

The old Last Chance store on West Main Street was later converted into a residence, and this is where his divorced mother raised Don, who was known as Carlos in his younger days. Don began acting in high school plays and also served as assistant editor of the school year book. In 1928 he was a member of the football team.

After graduation in 1929, Don attended Salt College Business College in Hutchinson, KS, where he graduated in '32.

Don returned to Council Grove where he was invited to be Master of Ceremonies at the weekly amateur night at the Stella Theater. At this time there was a traveling theater troupe called the Model Players. They had a circuit, playing five nights a week, each night in a different town, with the Friday night performance being at the Stella Theater in Council Grove. The owner of this stock company, Harry Clark, spotted Don at one of the amateur nights, was impressed with his ability, and invited him to join the troupe.

Clark's step-daughter, Jean Bartness, was the ingénue in their plays while Don became their leading man. Falling in love, Don and Jean were married on March 5, 1934. They continued to perform together in

Rare 1958 candid photo of Don Harvey and his actress wife, Jean, with thir horse, Goldie, who was ridden by Bill Williams as TV's "Kit Carson."

midwest tent shows, Chautauqua and repertory companies until they moved to Sioux Falls, South Dakota, where Don was an announcer for KSCO and KELO radio stations in 1941. Frankie Prather, a boyhood friend, told writers Tom and Jim Goldrup, "He was in South Dakota and Iowa in radio. He knew Ronald Reagan who was on the same radio station. His mother told me the public couldn't understand his name (Carlos) so he went to his first name of Don. After that, all his credits went by Don C. Harvey."

Don worked several years in radio, then the couple went to Hollywood in '44.

Praiseworthy comments about Don come from several of his co-stars: Gregg Barton: "Don was a serious thespian—He walked proud." House Peters Jr.: "He was such an easy going chap and a much finer actor than given credit for. He also gave of his time to entertain at the Actor's home. He was one of the most giving people in the business." Terry Frost: "I worked with both Don and Jean. They were confident actors and nice people." Pierce Lyden knew Don well. "Don was a good actor, a good friend. He was serious, had his dialogue memorized and was always ready to work. I think I first heard the expression from Don—'never let 'em see ya sweat.' When he went on an interview for a picture, he walked into the casting office like he already had the job. He was the kind of guy that when they asked him what he had done he'd say, 'I must be in the wrong place, I thought you wanted to know what I can do.' He was always smiling and enthusiastic about everything. He was one of the 'spark plugs' of the Hollywood Christian Group, on the Steering Committee and an officer. Harvey could play convincing good guys as well as baddies, probably because of his experience on the stage and as a radio announcer. If he had landed in Hollywood at an earlier time, I'm sure he could have promoted himself into something big. His wife, Jean, a character lady in pictures, was a princess. They didn't have any children. They were a very happy, loving couple."

So well liked was Don, he was named honorary mayor of Pacoima.

Incidentally, Don and Jean were the owners of the movie horse Goldie, ridden by Bill Williams on his "Kit Carson" TV series.

Don had completed an episode of "McHale's Navy" and was a policeman in Stanley Kramer's madcap, "It's a Mad, Mad, Mad, Mad World" when he died suddenly of a heart attack at his Studio City home on April 24, 1963.

Don's wife Jean Harvey also worked as an actress in movies. "They were devoted to each other and she got to a point where she just couldn't go on," a friend told the Goldrup brothers. "She just died from a broken heart on Dec. 14, 1966, in Studio City."

Suggested Sampling of Harvey's Western Heavies:

- Trail of the Rustlers ('50 Columbia) Charles Starrett
- Gunmen of Abilene ('50 Republic) Allan "Rocky" Lane
- Girl From San Lorenzo ('50 United Artists) Duncan Renaldo
- Dynamite Pass ('50 RKO) Tim Holt
- Gene Autry: Poisoned Waterhole ('50) Gene Autry
- Cisco Kid: Chain Lightning ('50) Duncan Renaldo
- Prairie Roundup ('51 Columbia) Charles Starrett
- Night Riders of Montana ('51 Republic) Allan "Rocky" Lane
- Texans Never Cry ('51 Columbia) Gene Autry
- Range Rider: Marked Bullets ('51) Jock Mahoney
- Gene Autry: Revenge Trail ('51) Gene Autry
- Wild Bill Hickok: Mexican Rustlers Story ('51) Guy Madison
- Range Rider: Pale Horse ('52) Jock Mahoney
- Roy Rogers: Treasure of Howling Dog Canyon ('52) Roy Rogers
- Gene Autry: Hot Lead and Old Lace ('52) Gene Autry
- Wild Bill Hickok: Schoolteacher Story ('52) Guy Madison
- Roy Rogers: Ghost Town Gold ('52) Roy Rogers
- Hopalong Cassidy: Devil's Idol ('53) William Boyd
- Annie Oakley: Annie Makes a Marriage ('54) Gail Davis
- Gunfighters of the Northwest ('54 Columbia serial) Jock Mahoney
- Roy Rogers: Last of the Larabee Kid ('54) Roy Rogers
- Wild Bill Hickok: Ol' Pardner Rides Again ('54) Guy Madison
- Roy Rogers: Dead End Trail ('55) Roy Rogers
- Roy Rogers: Quick Draw ('55) Roy Rogers
- Buffalo Bill Jr.: Boomer's Blunder ('55) Dick Jones
- Annie Oakley: Annie Takes A Chance ('55) Gail Davis
- Wild Bill Hickok: Buckshot Comes Home ('55) Guy Madison
- Champion: Stone Heart ('55) Jim Bannon
- Sky King: Boomerang ('56) Kirby Grant
- Perils of the Wilderness ('56 Columbia serial) Dennis Moore

- Champion: Deadly Double ('56) Jim Bannon
- Blazing the Overland Trail ('56 Columbia serial) Lee Roberts
- Wild Bill Hickok: Steamwagon ('56) Guy Madison
- Wyatt Earp: Hanging Judge ('56) Hugh O'Brian
- Buchanan Rides Alone ('58 Columbia) Randolph Scott
- Casey Jones: Silk Train ('58) Alan Hale Jr.
- Sky King: Bullet Bait ('58) Kirby Grant
- Bronco: Last Resort ('59) Ty Hardin
- Laramie: Trail Drive ('60) John Smith/Robert Fuller
- Riverboat: Path of an Eagle ('60) Darren McGavin
- Tales of Wells Fargo: New Orleans Trackdown ('61) Dale Robertson

MYRON HEALEY

Beginning with "Hidden Danger" at Monogram in 1948 opposite Johnny Mack Brown, Myron Healey instantly became one of the best, most recognizable and most frequently seen heavies in the waning days of the B-western and the burgeoning days of the TV western. His stern good looks and rich deep voice made him a memorable western heavy.

Myron Daniel Healey was born June 8, 1923, in Petaluma, California, the son of Robert and California (Penney) Healey. His father was a noted proctologist and sportsman who numbered among his friends renowned horticulturist Luther Burbank who became Myron's godfather. Myron's mother was head of the local Red Cross during WWI, a three term president of the Petaluma Women's Club, a two term president of California's 14th District PTA and a writer on education and medicine.

Aspiring at a young age to show business, Myron appeared on various radio programs, even as a singer. He also performed as a dancer and instrumentalist, giving piano and violin concerts. He became quite interested in acting while in high school and participated in plays in high school and in junior college in Santa Rosa, California.

From '40-'41, under sponsorship of the Victory Committee (later known as the USO), Myron acted in roadshow productions as well as legitimate theatre.

It's "Trail's End" for Myron Healey in another Johnny Mack Brown Monogram thriller.

Soon he was studying acting with noted teacher and Russian actress Maria Ouspenskaya. In 1943 he was signed to a term contract by MGM.

Later in '43, Myron volunteered for training as an Air Force Cadet, graduating from the U.S. Army Aviation Corps. During WWII, Myron served with the Air Corps, seeing combat in France and Germany while flying with the 323rd Medium Bomber Group and B-26 Martin Marauders. He was a navigator and bombardier being twice awarded the Air Medal and Nominated DFC. After the war he served in the U.S. Air Force Reserve as Motion Picture Technical Officer, Aerial Observer and Information Services Staff Officer. He retired as a Captain in 1962.

Myron resumed his film career in 1946 with Abbott and Costello's "The Time of Their Lives" and "Crime Doctor's Manhunt". His first western role was a bit in Glenn Ford's "Man From Colorado" ('48 Columbia).

The same year he made "Hidden Danger" with Johnny Mack Brown and immediately became a staple in the Monogram westerns of Brown, Whip Wilson and Jimmy Wakely.

As the TV western entered the western landscape, Myron was there, working in over 225 shows from '50-'85. He was a "regular" heavy on all of Gene Autry's Flying-A productions—"Gene Autry Show", "Range Rider", "Annie Oakley", "Buffalo Bill Jr.", "Champion". He also fought the law on "Roy Rogers", "Kit Carson", "Wild Bill Hickok", "Cisco Kid", "Rin Tin Tin", "Judge Roy Bean", "Cowboy G-Men", "Lone Ranger" and others, easily graduating to the adult westerns of "Bat Masterson", "Wagon Train", "Cimarron City", "Rawhide", "Deputy", "Riverboat", "Tales of Wells Fargo", "Laramie" and others—gradually sliding into more character oriented roles. When Douglas Fowley was unavailable for a year, Myron took up the role of Doc Holliday on "The Life and Legend of Wyatt Earp" from '58-'59. His final TV role was on "Fame" in 1985, spoofing the B-westerns slightly as Broncho Bob.

As to playing badmen, Myron told us, "There's much more leeway in playing a heavy, you can get more out of the role. With the existing dialogue, you get more of a chance to pull things out of it…character and personality. With a heavy, you just play it straight and it's just plain interesting, the fact that you're not a nice guy. (Laughs) I enjoyed that much more than playing a hero."

During his B-western days, Myron found time to write several screenplays including "Texas Lawmen" ('51), and "Colorado Ambush" ('51).

Myron only worked in two serials, as a heavy in "Roar of the Iron Horse" ('51 Columbia) and as the co-star, with Phyllis Coates, in Republic's "Panther Girl of the Kongo" ('55).

In between film and TV assignments, Myron served as a director for the Ebell Playhouse and Santa Monica Playhouse. He also appeared in a number of plays in the L.A. area, including "Of Mice and Men".

Healey once told me he was married and divorced "several" times but is currently a bachelor again. His documented wives include Ann Sumney ('40-'49) with daughters Christine and Ann; Elizabeth Mary Erric ('66-'68) with a daughter Mikel; and Adair Jameson ('71-'72).

Myron Healey, one of the Top 10 western screen badmen, received a Golden Boot Award in 2000. Myron died December 21, 2005, of natural causes in Simi Valley, California.

Suggested Sampling of Healey's Western Heavies:

- Hidden Danger ('48 Monogram) Johnny Mack Brown
- Gun Law Justice ('49 Monogram) Jimmy Wakely
- Trail's End ('49 Monogram) Johnny Mack Brown
- Haunted Trails ('49 Monogram) Whip Wilson
- Western Renegades ('49 Monogram) Johnny Mack Brown
- Lawless Code ('49 Monogram) Jimmy Wakely
- Fence Riders ('50 Monogram) Whip Wilson
- Trail of the Rustlers ('50 Columbia) Charles Starrett
- West of Wyoming ('50 Monogram) Johnny Mack Brown
- Short Grass ('50 Allied Artists) Rod Cameron
- Lone Ranger: Dead Man's Chest ('50) Clayton Moore
- Cisco Kid: Postal Inspector ('50) Duncan Renaldo
- Colorado Ambush ('51 Monogram) Johnny Mack Brown
- Roar of the Iron Horse ('51 Columbia serial) Jock Mahoney
- Bonanza Town ('51 Columbia) Charles Starrett
- Longhorn ('51 Monogram) Bill Elliott
- Cisco Kid: Kid Sister Trouble ('51) Duncan Renaldo
- Fargo ('52 Monogram) Bill Elliott
- Apache War Smoke ('52 MGM) Robert Horton
- The Maverick ('52 Allied Artists) Bill Elliott
- Range Rider: Silver Blade ('52) Jock Mahoney
- Gene Autry: Sheriff Is a Lady ('52) Gene Autry
- Sky King: Deadly Cargo ('52) Kirby Grant
- Roy Rogers: Hunting For Trouble ('52) Roy Rogers
- Lone Ranger: Condemned Man ('52) John Hart
- Saginaw Trail ('53 Columbia) Gene Autry
- Vigilante Terror ('53 Allied Artists) Bill Elliott
- Range Rider: Bullets and Badmen ('53) Jock Mahoney
- Cisco Kid: Devil's Deputy ('53) Duncan Renaldo
- Cowboy G-Men: Rawhide Gold ('53) Russell Hayden
- Kit Carson: Outlaw Trail ('53) Bill Williams
- Gene Autry: Gypsy Wagon ('53) Gene Autry
- Hopalong Cassidy: Jinx Wagon ('53) William Boyd
- Roy Rogers: M Stands for Murder ('53) Roy Rogers
- Son of Belle Starr ('53 Allied Artists) Keith Larsen
- Kit Carson: Copper Town ('54) Bill Williams
- Roy Rogers: Deputy Sheriff ('54) Roy Rogers
- Annie Oakley: A Gal For Grandma ('54) Gail Davis
- Rails Into Laramie ('54 Universal) John Payne
- Stories of the Century: Dalton Gang ('54) Jim Davis
- Gene Autry: Outlaw Warning ('54) Gene Autry
- Lone Ranger: Gold Town ('54) Clayton Moore
- Cisco Kid: Pot of Gold ('54) Duncan Renaldo
- Wild Bill Hickok: Masquerade at Moccasin Flats ('54) Guy Madison
- Man From Bitter Ridge ('55 Universal) Lex Barker
- Roy Rogers: Uncle Steve's Finish ('55) Roy Rogers
- Rin Tin Tin: Babe In the Woods ('55) Lee Aaker

- Annie Oakley: Dead Man's Bluff ('55) Gail Davis
- Buffalo Bill Jr.: Devil's Washbowl ('55) Dick Jones
- Champion: Medicine Man Mystery ('55) Jim Bannon
- Gene Autry: Law Comes to Scorpion ('55) Gene Autry
- Cheyenne: Border Showdown ('55) Clint Walker
- Judge Roy Bean: Checkmate ('56) Edgar Buchanan
- Sky King: Plastic Ghost ('56) Kirby Grant
- Annie Oakley: Joker on Horseback ('56) Gail Davis
- Lone Ranger: Blind Witness ('57) Clayton Moore
- Jim Bowie: Hare and the Tortoise ('57) Scott Forbes
- Casey Jones: Lost Train ('57) Alan Hale Jr.
- Tombstone Territory: Johnny Ringo's Last Ride ('58) Pat Conway
- Jim Bowie: Pirate on Horseback ('58) Scott Forbes
- Colt .45: Deserters ('58) Wayde Preston
- State Trooper: Crisis at Comstock ('58) Rod Cameron
- 26 Men: Judge Not ('58) Kelo Henderson/Tris Coffin
- Apache Territory ('58 Columbia) Rory Calhoun
- Bronco: Baron of Broken Lance ('59) Ty Hardin
- Bat Masterson: To the Manner Born ('59) Gene Barry
- Sugarfoot: MacBrewster the Bold ('59) Will Hutchins
- Cimarron City: Runaway Train ('59) George Montgomery
- Laramie: Three Roads West ('60) Robert Fuller
- Deputy: Jason Harris Story ('60) Henry Fonda/Allen Case
- Rebel: The Pit ('61) Nick Adams
- Laramie: Dynamiters ('62) Robert Fuller
- Outlaws: Farewell Performance ('62) Don Collier
- Laramie: Beyond Justice ('62) John Smith
- Laredo: Which Way Did They Go ('65) Peter Brown/Neville Brand/William Smith

EDWARD HEARN

Edward Hearn's career was certainly not limited to westerns. The versatile character actor kept a career going for an amazing 40 years, from 1915 to 1955, all through the silent era, on into talkies and even a few TV episodes in the late stages of his career. Besides western badmen in the '30s, Hearn (also billed as Guy Edward Hearn, Eddie Hearn and Ed Hearn) played policemen, ranchers, military officers, sheriffs, various types of businessmen, thugs, detectives—you name it, and could be seen in dramas, short subjects, westerns, comedies and serials. It seems no role was too small for Hearn—obviously he loved acting and loved being in the movies.

Guy Edward Hearn was born September 6, 1888, in Dayton, Washington.

Prior to entering the movies in 1915, he had nine years of stage experience with various stock companies.

When he started his film career he was a leading man in dozens of films. The westerns he did make in the silent era were opposite Harry Carey, Tom Tyler, Buzz Barton, Josie Sedgwick, Buffalo Bill Jr., Tim McCoy and a few others. A longtime associate and friend of director Robert North Bradbury, the pair were active in vaudeville together then in the early days at Kalem where the two of them appeared regularly in acting roles in the "American Girl" two-reelers starring Marin Sais. In 1921 Bradbury, now a director, starred Hearn in a couple of westerns at Pathé, including "Beyond the Trail". Hearn also won acclaim for roles in two of Bradbury's 1926 Sunset epics, "With Daniel Boone Thru the Wilderness" and "With Davy Crockett at the Fall of the Alamo".

Hearn played male lead to Ruth Roland in Pathé's "Avenging Arrow" serial in 1921, and the same to Allene Ray in "The Yellow Cameo" ('28 Pathé). He also is in the cast of Helen Holmes' "Lost Express" serial ('17 Signal). In the sound era, Hearn appeared in at least 18 chapterplays, with his best roles coming at Mascot as Frankie Darro's accused father in "Vanishing Legion" ('31), as Colonel Munro in "Last of the Mohicans" ('32) and as prime suspect Emil Janss in "The Miracle Rider" ('35).

With the advent of sound, now a middle aged man of 43, he was mostly relegated to supporting roles, often uncredited. The heavies he did play were all done for the independent studios who were wise enough to realize the marquee value still left in his name.

Extremely well liked, Hearn became a favorite of classic director Frank Capra and had small roles in several of Capra's productions.

Hearn's last really decent roles were as cattleman Terry Moran, killed by businessman Mauritz Hugo in Tim Holt's "Pistol Harvest" ('51 RKO), and as the

Tom Tyler, our "Fighting Hero", grabs Edward Hearn by the collar. ('34 Reliable).

Sheriff in Holt's "Road Agent" ('52 RKO). After an unbilled role in Randolph Scott's "Tall Man Riding" ('55 Warner Bros.), Hearn retired to play golf, his favorite pastime.

The 6 ft., 185 lb. actor was married to actress Tryna Saindon. At least one child was born in 1917.

Hearn died April 15, 1963, in Los Angeles, California at 74.

Suggested Sampling of Hearn's Western Heavies:

- Pals in Peril ('27 Pathé) Buffalo Bill Jr.
- Hero on Horseback ('27 Universal) Hoot Gibson
- Desert Pirate ('27 FBO) Tom Tyler
- Son of the Plains ('31 Syndicate) Bob Custer
- Cheyenne Cyclone ('31 Kent) Reb Russell
- Local Bad Man ('32 Allied) Hoot Gibson
- Texas Tornado ('32 Kent) Lane Chandler
- Fighting With Kit Carson ('33 Mascot serial) Johnny Mack Brown
- Fighting Hero ('34 Reliable) Tom Tyler
- Fighting Through ('34 Kent) Reb Russell
- In Old Santa Fe ('34 Mascot) Ken Maynard
- Miracle Rider ('35 Mascot serial) Tom Mix
- Tumbling Tumbleweeds ('35 Republic) Gene Autry
- Bulldog Courage ('35 Puritan) Tim McCoy
- Springtime In the Rockies ('37 Republic) Gene Autry

CAROL HENRY

Often confused in some books with being the leading lady in a particular B-western, Oklahoma rodeo cowboy Carol Henry was anything but.

Henry came to Hollywood off the rodeo circuit as a steer wrestler at 25 in 1943 and started doing stunts and small bit roles at Monogram in particular, but also at Columbia and Republic on Sunset Carson, Allan Lane and Durango Kid pictures. One of his showiest roles was in a "respectful" gunfight with Johnny Mack Brown in "Hidden Danger" ('48).

Over the years he doubled for Bill Elliott, Charles Starrett, Russell Hayden, Johnny Mack Brown and Richard Martin as Chito in Tim Holt's RKO B's.

When the B-westerns died out at Monogram, Henry found plenty of work with Gene Autry's Flying-A Productions and was seen on all Gene's series ("Annie Oakley", "Range Rider", "Buffalo Bill Jr.", "Gene Autry") driving stage, playing sheriffs, townsmen—and outlaws. Dick Jones ("Range Rider", "Buffalo Bill Jr.") remembers, "He was a real fun guy. Good stuntman, darn good fight man, could drive a wagon like crazy, good saddlefall. He doubled a lot of people. He had a sense of humor that just wouldn't quit. I used to go deer hunting with him up above Bishop (California) at Bridgeport. We had a two horse trailer in the back. He'd take his horse, I'd take mine. I remember one time we were coming down the

Scoundrels Carol Henry (L) and House Peters Jr. momentarily have the upper hand on Johnny Mack Brown who is "Gunning for Justice" ('48 Monogram).

hill up there and he said, very slowly (speaking in a drawn out monotone), "You know, if you'd slow this gentleman down to about a hundred, I'd step off and get us a beer." (Laughs) That's the way he talked—real slow. I liked him a bunch. Nice guy. He could tell some great stories. We'd go up to Bridgeport before venison season opened and we'd fish. Carol says, 'I got this old horse that's real good at hunting. He'll pack our venison out for us.' The first deer we got, he rode up there and goes to step off the horse to field dress this deer, and that horse just came unglued! Bucked…threw Carol about 10 miles high. Carol says, 'You son of a bitch!' Down the hill the horse ran and Carol had to hike out after him. My old horse, I'd never been hunting with him, never shot off of him or anything like that…he just walked up there, laid his ears back, put his head down and just stood there while we field dressed this deer, loaded him up, took him out. (Chuckles) Carol's horse was sure well trained!"

Stuntman Whitey Hughes said Henry had been a bareback and bronc rider in rodeo, terming him "a good soul." When Hughes stunt coordinated "Wild Wild West in the '60s he would find work for Henry.

Henry's last known work was on an episode of "Mission Impossible" in '72. Prior to that, in addition to the Flying A shows, Henry could be seen doing bits and stunts on "Kit Carson", "Cisco Kid", "Wild Bill Hickok", "Tales of Wells Fargo", "Sergeant Preston", "Cheyenne", "Restless Gun", "Shane", "Wagon Train", "Rough Riders", "Riverboat", "Cimarron Strip", "Buckskin", "Have Gun Will Travel" and "Hotel de Paree".

Carol D. Henry was born in Oklahoma July 14, 1918, to Noah Henry of Oklahoma and Evla Howard of Illinois. Henry did not serve in the military. He was married at least once, but was divorced at the time of his death at his home on Archwood St. in North Hollywood on September 17, 1987, of cardiovascular disease. He had a daughter, Colleen Schwab of Woodland Hills. He is buried at Valhalla Memorial Cemetery.

Suggested Sampling of Henry's Western Heavies:

- Belle Starr's Daughter ('47 20th Century Fox) George Montgomery
- Rangers Ride ('48 Monogram) Jimmy Wakely
- Back Trail ('48 Monogram) Johnny Mack Brown
- Sheriff of Medicine Bow ('48 Monogram) Johnny Mack Brown
- Hidden Danger ('48 Monogram) Johnny Mack Brown
- Shadows of the West ('49 Monogram) Whip Wilson
- Gun Runner ('49 Monogram) Jimmy Wakely
- Gun Law Justice ('49 Monogram) Jimmy Wakely
- Trail's End ('49 Monogram) Johnny Mack Brown
- Across the Rio Grande ('49 Monogram) Jimmy Wakely
- Range Land ('49 Monogram) Whip Wilson
- Gunslingers ('50 Monogram) Whip Wilson
- Arizona Territory ('50 Monogram) Whip Wilson
- Outlaw Gold ('50 Monogram) Johnny Mack Brown
- Cisco Kid: Railroad Land Rush ('50) Duncan Renaldo

WILLIAM "BILL" HENRY

Bill Henry was born in Los Angeles, California, November 10, 1914, but spent much of his youth in Hawaii where he became a well respected surfer and swimmer.

Bill's parents, Leslie A. Henry and Madge Irene Sink, had a close family alliance with the Kahanamoku Royal family of Hawaii. Duke Kahanamoku, born in 1890, was an Olympic swimming champion. Bill stayed with the Kahanamoku family during some of his high school years. As a matter of fact, William Henry Avenue in Honolulu is named after Bill Henry. For years, crowded among the high rise hotels in Honolulu, there was an old canoe club that displayed one of Bill's longboards.

It was through his association with Duke Kahanamoku that, Bill, at age 11, and Duke appeared in Paramount's 1925 film "Lord Jim" based on the famous Joseph Conrad south seas novel.

During his schooling at the University of Hawaii, Bill served as a stage technician and appeared in a number of plays.

There were no more films until, at 19, he worked in "Adorable" ('33).

Bill's second wife, actress Barbara Knudsen, told us, "Bill had been quite an up and coming actor with Robert Taylor, Loretta Young and that whole group. He'd been with 20th Century Fox and MGM. He was thirteen years older than me. Bill was quite a surfer and swimmer. I think a lot of that came from Les Henry, his father, who was with the Los Angeles Athletic Club years and years ago. They had connections with the Olympics and Bill was kind of in that atmosphere as a young boy and actually lived in Hawaii for several years."

From '33-'44 Bill was seen in over 60 films including "The Thin Man" ('34) (as the obnoxious, teenage expectant heir and dilettante crime solver), "China Seas" ('35), "Tarzan Escapes" ('36), "Madame X" ('37), "Blossoms In the Dust" ('41), "Pardon My Stripes" ('42), "Nearly Eighteen" ('43), "Adventures of Mark Twain" ('44) and others, including a few westerns—"Geronimo" ('39), "Cherokee Strip" ('40), "Calaboose" ('43) and Gene Autry's "Stardust On the Sage" ('42) as a young misguided embezzler.

Henry took time out to accompany the U.S. Olympic Swimming Team to Europe as their mascot in 1938.

Barbara Knudsen picks up Bill's story in mid-1944, "Bill went in the Navy and when he came back (in 1946) things weren't the same. But whatever it was in his life, he at least accepted things like that. So that's where I met him. We were in a stock company together at the Birdcage Theatre in the Last Frontier Casino in Las Vegas. I got my professional dollar bill from them and of course, joined SAG. Bill's brother was Thomas Browne Henry, who looked nothing like Bill as they had different fathers. Thomas Browne resembled his mother (Madge Irene) very, very much. He was older than Bill but I don't know how many years. But they certainly were not similar in appearance." (Thomas Browne Henry was born in 1907 and died in 1980.)

Bill had previously been married to Grace Durkin and they had two children, Michael and Michele.

Bill met Barbara while he was working in Vegas after the war in 1946 and they became friends. Talent scouts spotted Barbara with Bill attending the Pasadena Playhouse in Hollywood and she was signed by Paramount in January 1950.

In late 1948 John Ford was making "She Wore a Yellow Ribbon" and wanted Bill for a small role which he turned down, and according to Barbara, "Ford made Bill pay his penance. I remember Bill was here in Las Vegas, now this is before I went down to Hollywood. Ford wanted him to do a part in "She Wore a Yellow Ribbon" and he didn't want to do it. He didn't and John Ford made him pay for it later. Ford was very rude to Bill and me when I first met him on the set one night but John Wayne came over and took care of it right away. He came over and babied me, kind of, and John Ford wasn't mean to me after that. He would see me, and call me 'the little one' and he'd be kind. Bill was very happy in Las Vegas. He never wanted to go back to Hollywood. If it hadn't been for my career, Bill Henry would never have gone back down there. He was perfectly happy and settled in here. He loved just being local. He was a lifeguard at the Last Frontier Hotel pool and he probably would have done great things in Vegas. He was so personable and everybody loved him. He would have been perfectly happy to stay here in Las Vegas. But when I went to Hollywood, he felt compelled to follow me." However, Henry did split his time between Vegas and Hollywood in the late '40s which is the time he began appearing in many Republic westerns with Allan "Rocky" Lane and Monte Hale.

Bill and Barbara believed John Ford's vindictive "penance" came into play in mid 1949. "Bill was called back and drafted into the Navy. Being thirty-six years of age and drafted back into the Navy, that was quite a political move, I'm sure. I do believe it was done through his family. His mother had quite a bit of pull and was very close friends with John Ford and John Ford had a lot of military pull."

Bill returned to Hollywood after about a year, which is when he started working steadily in the new medium of television. He went from one TV western to the next on through the late '60s. He also did more work at Republic including a starring role in "Canadian Mounties Vs. Atomic Invaders" ('53), his only serial.

Barbara and Bill were married in Hawaii in 1952. The marriage lasted just a few months over ten years. They had one son in 1958. "When I left Bill, our son Billy was two and a half. Bill Senior never visited or played the role of father, ever. In fact, he would send any literature he had or anything to me, under Barbara Knudsen instead of Barbara Henry. So Bill Junior never did know his dad at all." Bill's drinking problem was the reason for the break-up of the marriage. "He didn't have a problem, as far as he was concerned. Took a whole bunch of vitamin B and he was going to be fine. It just was one of those things, where I just had to leave…one day I realized he didn't really know what planet he was on. That was scary to me and I decided then I had to save one of them, either Bill Senior or Bill Junior and I decided to save my son. I feel badly, because all of us in the family still loved him as a person, he was really sick. He was his own worst enemy. It got to be where, truly, you could not live with that. I couldn't see raising a child and having him be afraid to bring people home. It's really very sad."

Obviously, at some point, John Ford and Bill Henry came to an understanding as Bill worked small roles in Ford's "Last Hurrah" ('58), "Horse Soldiers" ('59), "Sergeant Rutledge" ('60), "Two Rode Together" ('61), "Man Who Shot Liberty Valance" ('62), "How the West Was

Won" ('62) and "Cheyenne Autumn" ('64). He's also in John Wayne's "The Alamo" ('60) and "El Dorado" ('67).

Bill's last work was on an episode of "Emergency" in 1972. As film work became sparse in the '70s, Henry was working as a landscape designer around Lake Arrowhead.

Barbara Knudsen added, "Over the years, I kept wanting Bill Junior to want to find his father. I had a neighbor who had quite a few connections and was going to do that when we read in VARIETY that he'd died. He'd been transferred from the Motion Picture Home to another hospital within 24 hours before he passed away."

Henry was 68 when he died of pneumonia August 10, 1982, at West Hills Medical Center in Canoga Park, California. His remains were cremated at Chapel of the Pines Cemetery in Los Angeles.

Suggested Sampling of Henry's Western Heavies:

- Stardust on the Sage ('42 Republic) Gene Autry
- Gene Autry: Poisoned Waterhole ('50) Gene Autry
- Cisco Kid: Performance Bond ('51) Duncan Renaldo
- Thundering Caravans ('52 Republic) Allan "Rocky" Lane
- Hopalong Cassidy: Frontier Law ('53) William Boyd
- Cisco Kid: Powder Trail ('54) Duncan Renaldo
- Wild Bill Hickok: Masquerade at Moccasin Flats ('54) Guy Madison
- Annie Oakley: The Runaways ('54) Gail Davis
- Masterson of Kansas ('54 Columbia) George Montgomery
- Kit Carson: Renegades of Rejo ('54) Bill Williams
- Buffalo Bill Jr.: Black Ghost '(55) Dick Jones
- Buffalo Bill Jr.: Red Hawk ('55) Dick Jones
- Adventures of Champion: Stone Heart ('55) Jim Bannon
- Judge Roy Bean: The Fugitive ('56) Edgar Buchanan
- Judge Roy Bean: Sunburnt Gold ('56) Edgar Buchanan
- Sky King: Manhunt ('56) Kirby Grant
- Wyatt Earp: It's a Wise Calf ('56) Hugh O'Brian
- Champion: Andrew and the Deadly Double ('56) Jim Bannon
- Sky King: Geiger Detective ('56) Kirby Grant
- Buffalo Bill Jr.: Angelo Goes West ('56) Dick Jones
- Annie Oakley: Showdown at Diablo ('56) Gail Davis
- Lone Ranger: Twisted Track ('56) Clayton Moore
- Brave Eagle: Papoose ('56) Keith Larsen
- Annie Oakley: Annie and the Miser ('57) Gail Davis
- Sergeant Preston of the Yukon: Out of the Night ('57) Richard Simmons
- Tales of Wells Fargo: The Witness ('57) Dale Robertson
- Wild Bill Hickok: Marvin's Mix-up ('58) Guy Madison
- 26 Men: Montezuma's Cave ('58) Kelo Henderson/Tris Coffin
- 26 Men: Hoax at Globe ('58) Kelo Henderson/Tris Coffin
- Lone Ranger and the Lost City of Gold ('58 Warner Bros.) Clayton Moore
- Bat Masterson: A Noose Fits Anybody ('58) Gene Barry
- 26 Men: Ranger Without a Badge ('59) Kelo Henderson/Tris Coffin
- Rough Riders: The Holdout ('59) Jan Merlin/Kent Taylor/Peter Whitney

WELDON HEYBURN

If you were watching B-westerns at the theatre from 1940-1944 you probably know who Weldon Heyburn was. Otherwise, you may not.

After a promising start on the Broadway stage at a young age in "Pagan Lady" in 1930 and a revival of the dramatic triumph "Rain", Heyburn arrived in California late in 1930 ready to conquer Hollywood. Sadly it was not to be.

After a couple of films, Heyburn was signed by 20th Century Fox in 1932, co-starring with Joan Bennett in "Careless Lady". He was also seen in "Chandu the Magician", "Call Her Savage" and others.

However, within a year he was freelancing at low-rent studios like Monogram ("West of Singapore" '33), First Division ("Convention Girl" '35) and Imperial ("Dynamite Delaney" '36).

He returned to form in MGM's "Speed" in '36 co-starring with James Stewart, but then it was right back to Republic ("Git Along Little Dogies" '37), Monogram ("Atlantic Flight" and "Saleslady" '37 and '38) and Grand National ("Panama Patrol" '39).

Again, a decent support role at Warner Bros. in '38's "Crime School" came his way, but overall it was a downward spiral.

Heyburn turned to B-westerns heavily in 1940 and made a strong impression in films with the Trail Blazers, Bill Elliott and Sunset Carson—especially in "Code of the Prairie" ('44) as Sunset's misguided friend running against him for sheriff.

Then just as suddenly as he'd come to westerns, he abandoned them in 1944. He had WWII military service, 1945 was probably this period. Heyburn only returned briefly in '46 for one film (a Charles Starrett western) not to be seen again until five uncredited bit roles from late '48 to '50.

What caused such inconsistencies in Heyburn's career? Why did such promise crash and burn? Badman Pierce Lyden may have had the answer, "Weldon Heyburn was one of the most handsome actors with whom I worked. Great things were expected of him. Some thought he might be a challenger to Clark Gable, but he was a heavy drinker, and the word got around. The last time I saw him, he seemed disillusioned, discouraged and down on his luck. He said he was through with Hollywood, and was going back to New York. I never saw him again."

The "going back to New York" period was probably circa 1946. Obviously, when that didn't work out either, he briefly returned to Hollywood in late '48.

He'd been under treatment as a patient, possibly for alcoholism, for nearly a year ('50-'51) at the Veteran's Administration Hospital in West Los Angeles when he died May 18, 1951. Cause of death was listed as bronchopneumonia as well as cancer of the mouth, right adrenal and kidney.

Contrary to widely published reports, Heyburn was not born in Selma, Alabama, and was not a football star at the University of Alabama.

Weldon (or Welden according to his death certificate—likely misspelled) was born September 19, 1910, in Washington, D.C., the son of Wyatt Heyburn, an Alabama native, and Marie Pierce of Pennsylvania.

Heyburn was twice married, first in 1932, to silent screen star Greta Nissen (who died in 1988 at 82). They separated in 1934. The blonde leading lady had once been under contract to Paramount ('25-'27) and later co-starred with Heyburn in "Silent Witness" ('32 Fox) and "Hired Wife" ('34 Universal). Heyburn was later married to socialite Jane Eichelberger and a Virginia Haggard.

Heyburn's tale is indeed a sad one, but we thank him for the western cads he gave us.

Badmen Weldon Heyburn (L), Herbert Heyes (center) and Bud Geary (R) have Wild Bill Elliott at a disadvantage in Republic's "Death Valley Manhunt" ('43).

Suggested Sampling of Heyburn's Western Heavies:

- Git Along Little Dogies ('37 Republic) Gene Autry
- Mysterious Rider ('38 Paramount) Douglass Dumbrille
- Gaucho Serenade ('40 Republic) Gene Autry
- Trail Blazers ('40 Republic) 3 Mesquiteers
- In Old Colorado ('41 Paramount) William Boyd
- Stick To Your Guns ('41 Paramount) William Boyd
- Code of the Outlaw ('42 Republic) 3 Mesquiteers
- Rock River Renegades ('42 Monogram) Range Busters
- Blazing Guns ('43 Monogram) Trail Blazers
- Overland Mail Robbery ('43 Republic) Bill Elliott
- Death Valley Manhunt ('43 Republic) Bill Elliott
- Death Valley Rangers ('43 Monogram) Trail Blazers
- Westward Bound ('44 Monogram) Trail Blazers
- Bordertown Trail ('44 Republic) Sunset Carson
- Yellow Rose of Texas ('44 Republic) Roy Rogers
- Frontier Gun Law ('46 Columbia) Charles Starrett

RILEY HILL

Riley Hill might well be referred to as the "Camille Cowboy" as once his film career ended, he effectively disappeared, apparently preferring to be left alone. Some who knew him attribute his alienation from society to personal problems with alcohol.

Little is known of his background, other than he was most likely born on either March 12, 1920, or March 20, 1914, in Fort Worth, Texas. Spotted by a talent scout while Riley was on the stage, his first film role was as a young lieutenant in "The Firefly" ('37 MGM).

Under contract to Universal as of 1939, his first western was an uncredited role in Johnny Mack Brown's "Oklahoma Frontier". It appears Universal was giving him a slow build up, casting him in various types of pictures through mid-1942 when his career was interrupted by WWII service in the Air Corps.

During his Universal period he was billed as Roy Harris with his best roles coming in a pair of Johnny Mack Browns—memorable as the Wolverine Kid in "Law of the Range" ('41), and "Rawhide Rangers" ('41).

He was off the screen for 1943 and most of 1944 (military service) and returned in late '44 for a role in Johnny Mack's "Ghost Guns", now using the Riley Hill moniker.

For the rest of the B-western era he primarily worked at Monogram, often playing the hot-headed juvenile lead or heavy.

Badman Pierce Lyden remarked, "Riley was a little wild at times and 'quick on the draw,' but good natured."

When TV arrived, Hill found plenty of work on "Cisco Kid", "Lone Ranger", "Range Rider", "Gene Autry", "Roy Rogers" and other B-western styled TVers. After Eddie Dean left the "live" series, Hill was briefly the lead on ABC's "Marshal of Gunsight Pass" in 1950.

When B-westerns effectively died in the mid-'50s, so did Hill's career. He found only sporadic bit parts in big budget titles like "The Lusty Men" ('52), "The Raiders" ('52) and "Kansas Pacific" ('53). Hill more or less quit the business in '54 after a nothing role in Columbia's "Riding with Buffalo Bill" serial in '54.

Hill resurfaced briefly in '58 for a recurring role as a trooper on ZIV TV's "Mackenzie's Raiders" with Richard Carlson and a single role for an episode of "26 Men".

A puffy, overweight Hill reemerged for a bit role in John Wayne's "Rio Bravo" in '59 made at Old Tucson in Arizona. Hill apparently continued to live in the Tucson area for several years and appeared in small roles in movies made in Arizona such as "Deadly Companions" ('61), "El Dorado" ('67), "Trial of Billy Jack" ('74), "Last Hard Men" ('76), "Wanda Nevada" ('79) and other straight-to-video lowbudgeters on into the '80s. By this time he was nearly unrecognizable, having gained considerable weight.

At some point Hill was reported living in Truth or Consequences, New Mexico, then in obscurity and anonominity in Las Cruces, New Mexico, according to stuntman Rodd Wolff.

Dick Jones, who worked with Hill on several "Range Rider" episodes, noted he was "handy and straightforward" recalling how "erect" he sat in the saddle, "almost military—like Tim McCoy."

According to Social Security records a Riley O. Hill (born 3/12/20) died on April 20, 1992, in Cherokee County, Texas. Definitively, this may or may not be "our" Riley Hill.

Jimmy Wakely issues a stern warning to Riley Hill in Monogram's "Lawless Code" ('49).

Suggested Sampling of Hill's Western Heavies:

- Law of the Range ('41 Universal) Johnny Mack Brown
- Overland Mail ('42 Universal serial) Lon Chaney Jr.
- Sheriff of Cimarron ('45 Republic) Sunset Carson
- Desert Horseman ('46 Columbia) Charles Starrett
- Range Renegades ('48 Monogram) Jimmy Wakely
- Cheyenne Cowboy ('49 Universal-International) Tex Williams
- Law of the West ('49 Monogram) Johnny Mack Brown
- Lawless Code ('49 Monogram) Jimmy Wakely
- Fence Riders ('50 Monogram) Whip Wilson
- Short Grass ('50 Allied Artists) Rod Cameron
- Lone Ranger: Double Jeopardy ('50) Clayton Moore
- Range Rider: Golden Peso ('51) Jock Mahoney
- Kit Carson: Riders of Capistrano ('51) Bill Williams
- Gene Autry: Killer's Trail ('51) Gene Autry
- Wild Bill Hickok: Silver Stage Holdup ('51) Guy Madison
- Canyon Raiders ('51 Monogram) Whip Wilson
- Nevada Badmen ('51 Monogram) Whip Wilson
- Valley of Fire ('51 Columbia) Gene Autry
- Roy Rogers: Jailbreak ('51) Roy Rogers
- Night Stage to Galveston ('52 Columbia) Gene Autry
- Gene Autry: Melody Mesa ('52) Gene Autry
- Roy Rogers: Badman's Brother ('52) Roy Rogers
- Roy Rogers: Desert Fugitive ('52) Roy Rogers
- Range Rider: Outlaw's Double ('52) Jock Mahoney
- Target ('52 RKO) Tim Holt
- Outlaw Women ('52 Lippert) Marie Windsor
- Cowboy G-Men: Silver Fraud ('53) Russell Hayden
- Roy Rogers: Phantom Rustlers ('53) Roy Rogers
- Cisco Kid: Bodyguard ('53) Duncan Renaldo
- Wild Bill Hickok: Heading For Trouble ('53) Guy Madison
- 26 Men: Gun Hand ('58) Kelo Henderson/Tris Coffin

REX HOLMAN

Lanky and sneering, with a sarcastic voice, Rex Holman was one of TV western's last classic heavies. His scary, skeletal, scarecrow-like look enhanced nearly 100 TV westerns from 1960-1985, 99% of the time as the nastiest, most contemptible member of the outlaw gang. Only once can I recall Holman in a sympathetic role, that of John Hoyt's non-violent pacifist son in "No Chip", a December 1960 episode of "Gunsmoke". Primarily, in Holman's 16 episodes of "Gunsmoke" and dozens more he effectively portrayed twisted outlaw pond scum. Holman was a deviant we loved to hate.

Holman was born in 1935 in Tulsa, Oklahoma. His real name may be Roy(e) Baker, a name he used in a couple of early screen credits including "Ma Barker's Killer Brood" ('60), but this is unconfirmed. His family came to California during the depression years seeking employment "ala 'Grapes of Wrath'" as Holman once put it. He graduated from Canoga Park High School and attended Pierce Junior College in Woodland Hills, California.

His first thought of theatre work was to "rid myself of complexes." Holman worked in little theatre, college theatre, community theatre and summer stock, all of which gave him a good background for his screen work which began with several TV episodes in 1959.

On a cast information questionnaire in 1959,

Walter Sande (L) and Rex Holman (R) have Audie Murphy's "Quick Gun" at a disadvantage ('64 Columbia).

Holman stated his ambition was "to use my talents to the fullest," with his hobbies listed as flamenco guitar playing and dancing.

Beside westerns, Holman worked on "Thriller", "Twilight Zone", "Ben Casey", "Man From U.N.C.L.E.", "Outer Limits", "Star Trek", "Mannix"…in other words all the top shows of the '60s and early '70s.

His last TV work seems to be on the short-lived "Wildside" western in '85 and his last film was "Star Trek V: The Final Frontier" in '89.

Suggested Sampling of Holman's Western Heavies:

- Deputy: The Choice ('60) Allen Case
- Overland Trail: High Bridge ('60) Doug McClure
- Gunsmoke: Small Water ('60) James Arness
- Young Jesse James ('60 20th Century Fox) Willard Parker
- 13 Fighting Men ('60 20th Century Fox) Grant Williams
- Laramie: Killer Without Cause ('61) John Smith
- Lawman: The Inheritance ('61) John Russell
- Tales of Wells Fargo: Who Lives by the Gun ('62) Dale Robertson
- Rifleman: Death Never Rides Alone ('62) Chuck Connors
- Bonanza: The Last Haircut ('63) Michael Landon
- Rifleman: Old Man Running ('63) Chuck Connors
- Dakotas: Return to Drydock ('63) Jack Elam, Larry Ward
- Quick Gun ('64 Columbia) Audie Murphy
- Big Valley: Hazard ('66) Richard Long
- Legend of Jesse James: 1863 ('66) Christopher Jones
- Road West: This Savage Land ('66) Barry Sullivan
- Laredo: Legend of Midas Mantee ('66) William Smith/Peter Brown/Neville Brand
- Iron Horse: High Devil ('66) Dale Robertson
- Monroes: The Hunter ('66) Michael Anderson Jr.
- Guns of Will Sonnett: Guns of Will Sonnett ('67) Walter Brennan
- Gunsmoke: The Wreckers ('67) James Arness
- Big Valley: Ambush ('67) Barbara Stanwyck
- Gunsmoke: Zavala ('68) James Arness
- Guns of Will Sonnett: Chapter and Verse ('68) Walter Brennan
- Lancer: Child of Rock and Sunlight ('69) Wayne Maunder
- Lancer: Buscaderos ('70) Wayne Maunder
- Gunsmoke: Luke ('70) James Arness
- Gunsmoke: Sarah ('72) James Arness
- Bounty Man ('72 TVM) Clint Walker
- Gunsmoke: Town Tamers ('74) James Arness

REED HOWES

Strikingly handsome Reed Howes was a mid-range silent star in the '20s who managed to star in a few early talkie quickies and serials. However, it quickly became apparent neither Howes' voice (very monotonish) nor dramatic ability (stiff with not much zip) were as well suited for sound as they were for silents, and he soon drifted into supporting roles, often as one of the boss' henchmen in close to 100 westerns and some 25 serials.

Born Hermon Reed Howes July 5, 1900, in Washington, D.C., the son of Edwin L. Howes and Grace Messerse, he served as an apprentice seaman in the Navy during the final year of WWI. During this time he captained the swimming team of the Pacific fleet. Discharged a junior grade lieutenant, he graduated from the University of Utah and the School of Business Administration at Harvard. It was then he began to appear in small parts in stock and vaudeville shows.

Handsome, with a near perfect physique, Howes was selected to be a model for artist J.C. Leyendecker's famous Arrow Collar print ads along with John Barrymore, Brian Donlevy, Jack Mulhall and Fredric March. But it was Howes who gained the most publicity, being referred to as "the handsomest man in America".

By 1923, both producers Ben Wilson and Harry Joe Brown took note of the handsome model and signed him to star in fast action/adventure films like "High Speed Lee", "Super Speed", "Geared to Go", "Danger Quest", "Night Owl", "Rough House Rosie", "Racing Fool" and others.

Among these were leads in several westerns for W. Ray Johnston's Rayart Pictures from '24-'26 ("Lightning Romance", "Cyclone Cavalier", "Dangerous Dude",

"Moran of the Mounted"). Howes also supported Buck Jones in "Gentle Cyclone" at Fox in '26.

Other than that, Howes made no other westerns until the start of the sound era, 1931's poverty row "White Renegade" starring Tom Santschi (another popular name from the silent era).

Howes managed to star in Universal's "Terry of the Times" 10 chapter serial in 1930, the low-budget "Queen of the Jungle" serial for Screen Attractions in '35 and a couple of fastly forgotten independent quickies, but other than that he was swiftly relegated to supporting roles in action films and, predominately, dozens of B-westerns. Every now and then, down through the years, he got to be on the right side of the law, supporting John Wayne in "Dawn Rider" ('35 Lone Star), Whip Wilson in "Silver Raiders" ('50 Monogram) and in Republic's "Zorro Rides Again" serial ('37).

Fellow western henchman Pierce Lyden offered a revealing view of Howes, "Reed had some stormy times during his career, due to his drinking problem, which he freely talked about. He was president of the Hollywood Alcoholics Anonymous. He said he had gone through three million dollars. He told me he woke up one time and found his mother had visited him for three weeks, and he didn't know it. She left, heartbroken, and he never saw her again—that was when he said, 'I quit.'"

Howes hung in there on through the early '60s, finding bit roles in many A-westerns, especially those with Randolph Scott produced by his old friend from the silent era, Harry Joe Brown. For a while in the '50s he played the Sheriff on the "Roy Rogers" TV series.

Howes' health declined in the early '60s and, at 64, he died August 6, 1964, of prostate cancer at the Motion Picture Country Home and Hospital in Woodland Hills, California, where he'd been confined for several months.

He was cremated and is buried at the Fort Rosecrans National Cemetery in San Diego, California.

Suggested Sampling of Howes' Western Heavies:

- Paradise Canyon ('35 Lone Star) John Wayne
- Custer's Last Stand ('36 Stage and Screen serial) Rex Lease
- Feud of the West ('36 Diversion) Hoot Gibson
- Lightning Carson Rides Again ('38 Victory) Tim McCoy
- Ghost Town Riders ('38 Universal) Bob Baker
- Six Gun Rhythm ('39 Grand National) Tex Fletcher
- Riders of the Sage ('39 Metropolitan) Bob Steele
- Straight Shooter ('40 Victory) Tim McCoy
- Flaming Lead ('39 Colony) Ken Maynard
- Westbound Stage ('39 Monogram) Tex Ritter
- Cheyenne Kid ('40 Monogram) Jack Randall
- Billy the Kid Outlawed ('40 PRC) Bob Steele
- Roll, Wagons, Roll ('40 Monogram) Tex Ritter
- Lone Rider In Ghost Town ('41 PRC) George Houston
- Fugitive Valley ('41 Monogram) Range Busters
- Lone Star Law Men ('41 Monogram) Tom Keene
- Down Texas Way ('42 Monogram) Rough Riders
- Thundering Trails ('43 Republic) 3 Mesquiteers
- Border Buckaroos ('43 PRC) Dave O'Brien/James Newill
- Red River Robin Hood ('43 RKO) Tim Holt
- Saddle Leather Law ('44 Columbia) Charles Starrett
- Under Arizona Skies ('46 Monogram) Johnny Mack Brown
- Range Land ('49 Monogram) Whip Wilson
- Gene Autry: The Peacemaker ('50) Gene Autry
- Cisco Kid: Stolen Bonds ('51) Duncan Renaldo
- Cisco Kid: Protective Association ('51) Duncan Renaldo
- Kit Carson: Fury at Red Gulch ('51) Bill Williams
- Wild Bill Hickok: Fortune Telling Story ('52) Guy Madison
- Kit Carson: Thunder Over Inyo ('52) Bill Williams
- Hangman's Knot ('52 Columbia) Randolph Scott
- Cisco Kid: Black Terror ('53) Duncan Renaldo
- Wild Bill Hickok: Gorilla of Owl Hoot Mesa ('54) Guy Madison
- Blazing the Overland Trail ('56 Columbia serial) Lee Roberts/ Dennis Moore

MAURITZ HUGO

Swedish born Mauritz Hugo found his way into a handful of latter day B-westerns as a thin mustached, usually well dressed, dapper, sharp-tongued boss heavy. A smallish man, he often wore a coat and tie and used a thin cigar or cigarette as a prop.

Born in Sweden January 12, 1909, it's unclear how or when he came to the U.S., but he gained some stage experience here and found his way to Hollywood in 1938 for a role in Frankie Darro's "Wanted By the Police".

Hugo is absent from the screen until 1943 at which time he began to work constant through 1964. At that time he became semi-retired, only accepting a few film parts again from '68-'71. His last role was in "The Love Machine" in '71.

Hugo appeared in nine serials but only in "Man With the Steep Whip" ('54 Republic) did he have a showy lead heavy role. His best western roles came opposite Tim Holt.

Director Earl Bellamy, who turned producer once for "Stagecoach to Dancer's Rock" in '62, used Hugo whenever he could, terming him a "solid, dependable character player."

Hugo was 65 when he died in North Hollywood, California on June 16, 1974.

Suggested Sampling of Hugo's Western Heavies:

- Outlaws of Stampede Pass ('43 Monogram) Johnny Mack Brown
- Marked Trails ('44 Monogram) Bob Steele/Hoot Gibson
- Blazing the Western Trail ('45 Columbia) Charles Starrett
- Rustler's Round-Up ('46 Universal) Kirby Grant
- Homesteaders of Paradise Valley ('47 Republic) Allan Lane
- Renegades of Sonora ('48 Republic) Allan "Rocky" Lane
- Death Valley Gunfighter ('49 Republic) Allan "Rocky" Lane
- Frisco Tornado ('50 Republic) Allan "Rocky" Lane
- Cisco Kid: Water Well Oil ('51) Duncan Renaldo
- Saddle Legion ('51 RKO) Tim Holt
- Gunplay ('51 RKO) Tim Holt
- Yukon Gold ('52 Monogram) Kirby Grant
- Road Agent ('52 RKO) Tim Holt
- Lone Ranger: Gun Powder Joe ('53) Clayton Moore
- Man With the Steel Whip ('54 Republic serial) Richard Simmons
- Kit Carson: Frontier Empire ('54) Bill Williams
- Wild Bill Hickok: Sheriff's Secret ('55) Guy Madison
- Tales of the Texas Rangers: Blood Trail ('55) Willard Parker
- Champion: Hangman's Noose ('55) Jim Bannon
- Lone Ranger: Message From Abe ('57) Clayton Moore
- Sky King: Double Trouble ('57) Kirby Grant
- 26 Men: Sundown Decision ('58) Kelo Henderson/Tris Coffin
- Rough Riders: Scavengers ('59) Jan Merlin/Kent Taylor

JACK INGRAM

Jack Ingram was one of the top heavies in B-westerns for 20 years from the mid '30s to the mid '50s. Ingram was also featured in at least 49 serials, becoming one of Sam Katzman's "regulars" at Columbia in the late '40s.

When the cameras were rolling he rustled, robbed, cheated and killed with wild abandon, yet in real life he felt everything had a right to live and would not even harm an ant or bee. He felt it was his duty to set a good example off screen and conducted himself accordingly. He constantly laughed and joked. Researcher Lee Koonce of Colorado found Ingram to be a "religious fanatic."

John Samuel Ingram was born November 15, 1902, in Chicago, Illinois, to Irish parents, Jacob Ingram (born in Ireland) and Ann Fitzgerald, an Illinois native. Orphaned as an infant, he spent his boyhood on his uncle's farm in Wisconsin where he acquired his love of animals and his riding abilities. Then the family moved to Dallas, Texas.

At the young age of 15 he was tall for his age and anxious to join the Army. With consent he lied about his age and enlisted, serving with the 8th Field Artillery overseas where he was wounded and gassed. He spent two years recuperating at a French hospital.

Because he lied about his age, saying he was born in 1900, many records to this day still reflect that incorrect birth year, including Social Security records. However, his California death certificate testified to by his widow indicates the correct 1902 date.

Although he found a natural ability to make others laugh while in WWI service, he did not immediately gravitate to showbiz upon his discharge. Jack enrolled at the University of Texas to study law, but eventually became more interested in performing. He became a regular member of a successful traveling minstrel show and later joined and toured the country with Mae West's stage shows. He also traveled with the Donald MacGregor Shows out of Ft. Worth, Texas.

Jack was spotted on Broadway in West's "Diamond Lil" ('28) and signed by Paramount in '29 because of his knowledge of horses and his ability to perform difficult stunts.

New to the business, he learned everything he could behind and in front of the camera as he performed stunts and even worked as an assistant director on several films through the early '30s.

While performing a leap from a high rock onto a horse in "Charge of the Light Brigade" ('36), the horse shied, throwing Jack's timing off. When he fell he broke his arm. He'd begun doing bit roles in Republic westerns in '35 but by '36 moved seriously into acting fulltime. He appeared in at least 10 films and two serials in '36.

In '37 he gave a try to being a comedy sidekick as Kermit Maynard's half-wit pal, Spud, in "Valley of Terror". This wasn't right for Jack and it was back to heavies, completing some 14 other films and three serials in '37.

Throughout the '30s and '40s Jack worked

freelance at Republic, PRC, Universal, Monogram and Columbia. Many years he made as many as 25 films.

Fellow badman Pierce Lyden had high praise for Jack, "We had a lot of fun working together. He had a great sense of humor although dry and sometimes not too real. He was liked by everyone. Jack was a hard worker and producers never had any trouble with him. He and good friend Kenne Duncan talked all the time about sailing."

1944 was a banner year for Jack. Not only did he make 22 movies and three serials, he found time to marry Eloise (Lou) Fullerton, a Hollywood columnist and publicist. They purchased 200 acres of what had been part of the old Charlie Chaplin estate. The property had previously been purchased by Dave O'Brien and James Newill (The Texas Rangers at PRC) with ulterior motives. The two actors bought the property in an effort to avoid being inducted into WWII service by passing themselves off as goat farmers in the belief the government would assign them a deferment for raising farm animals. The subterfuge wasn't necessary as the cowboys were soon both classified 4-F. Free of their wartime fears, and perhaps tired of getting up early to tend nearly 100 goats; they sold the property to Ingram, whom they knew well from his many badman roles in their series.

Ingram purchased an old bulldozer and, with the help of several badfellow pals (Pierce Lyden, Kenne Duncan, Lane Bradford), built a western street set. The property included a well-landscaped house that became Ingram's home. (It can be seen in the background of "Mark of the Lash" with Lash LaRue.) Dozens of westerns and TV episodes were lensed at Ingram's ranch. In filming days, the entrance was reached from a side road off Topanga Canyon, but now you can drive by the property (the house is still there although the western streets are gone) on Mulholland (on the right about a half mile after you turn off Topanga going west). The open fields next to the house are where the western streets once were.

Failing health caused Jack to sell the ranch in 1956 to 4 Star Productions who continued to use the site for a number of years in their various western TV series.

Moving to Encino, Jack bought a 55 ft. yacht, berthed at Long Beach Harbor, on which he enjoyed himself during his retirement. He also rented the yacht to film companies, including ZIV's "Sea Hunt".

While fishing at their lodge in Oregon, Jack suffered a heart attack and was hospitalized for a month. Returning to California, his recovery was slow and one of the nicest and one of the busiest men in westerns and serials (with or without his mustache) suffered a second heart attack and died at West Hills Doctor's Hospital in Canoga Park, California, February 20, 1969. Ingram is buried at Oakwood Memorial Park in Chatsworth.

Gene Autry struggles with Jack Ingram in "Colorado Sunset" ('39 Republic).

Suggested Sampling of Ingram's Western Heavies:

- Wild Horse Rodeo ('37 Republic) 3 Mesquiteers
- Riders of the Black Hills ('38 Republic) 3 Mesquiteers
- Where the West Begins ('38 Monogram) Jack Randall
- Durango Valley Raiders ('38 Republic) Bob Steele
- Frontier Scout ('38 Grand National) George Houston
- Western Jamboree ('38 Republic) Gene Autry
- Shine On Harvest Moon ('38 Republic) Roy Rogers
- Feud of the Range ('39 Metropolitan) Bob Steele
- Down the Wyoming Trail ('39 Monogram) Tex Ritter
- Colorado Sunset ('39 Republic) Gene Autry
- Saga of Death Valley ('39 Republic) Roy Rogers
- Adventures of the Masked Phantom ('39 Equity) Monte Rawlins
- Ghost Valley Raiders ('40 Republic) Don Barry
- Deadwood Dick ('40 Columbia serial) Don Douglas
- Ridin' the Trail ('40 Ziehm) Fred Scott
- White Eagle ('41 Columbia serial) Buck Jones
- Prairie Pioneers ('41 Republic) 3 Mesquiteers
- King of Dodge City ('41 Columbia) Bill Elliott/Tex Ritter
- Lone Rider Ambushed ('41 PRC) George Houston
- Lone Rider and the Bandit ('41 PRC) George Houston
- South of Santa Fe ('42 Republic) Roy Rogers
- Mysterious Rider ('42 PRC) Buster Crabbe
- Arizona Roundup ('42 Monogram) Tom Keene
- Along the Sundown Trail ('42 PRC) Lee Powell/Art Davis/Bill Boyd
- Riders of the Northwest Mounted ('42 Columbia) Russell Hayden
- Perils of the Royal Mounted ('42 Universal serial) Robert Stevens
- Boss of Rawhide ('43 PRC) Dave O'Brien/James Newill
- Frontier Law ('43 Universal) Russell Hayden
- Devil Riders ('43 PRC) Buster Crabbe
- Silver City Raiders ('43 Columbia) Russell Hayden

- Arizona Trail ('43 Universal) Tex Ritter
- Lone Star Trail ('43 Universal) Johnny Mack Brown
- Wolves of the Range ('43 PRC) Bob Livingston
- Man From Thunder River ('43 Republic) Bill Elliott
- Fugitive of the Plains ('43 PRC) Buster Crabbe
- Gunsmoke Mesa ('44 PRC) Dave O'Brien/James Newill
- Oath of Vengeance ('44 PRC) Buster Crabbe
- Trigger Law ('44 Monogram) Bob Steele/Hoot Gibson
- Raiders of Ghost City ('44 Universal serial) Dennis Moore
- Range Law ('44 Monogram) Johnny Mack Brown
- Boss of Boomtown ('44 Universal) Rod Cameron
- Outlaw Roundup ('44 PRC) Dave O'Brien/James Newill
- Oklahoma Raiders ('44 Universal) Tex Ritter
- Mojave Firebrand ('44 Republic) Bill Elliott
- Valley of Vengeance ('44 PRC) Buster Crabbe
- Marked For Murder ('45 PRC) Tex Ritter/ Dave O'Brien
- Bandits of the Badlands ('45 Republic) Sunset Carson
- Rough Ridin' Justice ('45 Columbia) Charles Starrett
- Beyond the Pecos ('45 Universal) Rod Cameron
- Saddle Serenade ('45 Monogram) Jimmy Wakely
- Frontier Feud ('45 Monogram) Johnny Mack Brown
- Scarlet Horseman ('46 Universal serial) Paul Guilfoyle
- Moon Over Montana ('46 Monogram) Jimmy Wakely
- South of the Chisholm Trail ('47 Columbia) Charles Starrett
- Pioneer Justice ('47 PRC) Lash LaRue
- Tex Granger ('48 Columbia serial) Robert Kellard
- Whirlwind Raiders ('48 Columbia) Charles Starrett
- Blazing Across the Pecos ('48 Columbia) Charles Starrett
- Law of the West ('49 Monogram) Johnny Mack Brown
- Son of a Badman ('49 Western Adventure) Lash LaRue
- Gold Strike ('50 Universal) Tex Williams
- Cody of the Pony Express ('50 Columbia serial) Jock Mahoney
- Texan Meets Calamity Jane ('50 Columbia) James Ellison
- Gene Autry: Doublecross Valley ('50) Gene Autry
- Cisco Kid: Railroad Land Rush ('50) Duncan Renaldo
- Range Rider: Baron of Broken Bow ('51) Jock Mahoney
- Roar of the Iron Horse ('51 Columbia serial) Jock Mahoney
- Kit Carson: Curse of the Albas ('52) Bill Williams
- Range Rider: West of Cheyenne ('53) Jock Mahoney
- Son of the Renegade ('53 United Artists) Johnny Carpenter
- Riding with Buffalo Bill ('54 Columbia serial) Marshall Reed
- Hopalong Cassidy: Emerald Saint ('54) William Boyd
- Buffalo Bill Jr.: Fight For Texas ('55) Dick Jones

ARCH JOHNSON

Tall and husky, semi-balding Arch Johnson had his share of castings as bullies, brutes and forceful ranchers during the heyday of TV westerns.

Johnson was born Archible W. Johnson in Minneapolis, Minnesota, on March 14, 1922.

After appearing in several stage plays, Johnson entered films with a role as a cab driver in Marilyn Monroe's "Niagara" ('53). His first western was "Gun Glory" ('57) with Stewart Granger.

No sooner had his film career taken hold than he was tapped for the role of the bigoted NYPD detective in the Broadway smash "West Side Story" which ran from September 26, 1957, to June 27, 1959. Arch was also in the cast of the revival in 1980.

With his strong versatility and a hit Broadway production backing him, Arch now moved heavily into TV and film.

Not only was he seen on "Gunsmoke", "Bonanza", "Bat Masterson" and dozens of other TV westerns of the era, he also essayed tough guy roles on "Alfred Hitchcock Presents", "Roaring '20s", "Twilight Zone", "Hawaiian Eye", "Perry Mason", "The Fugitive", "The F.B.I." and other popular series.

He continued to work heavily through the '70s, including a role as Buddy Holly's father in "The Buddy Holly Story" ('78). His appearances in the '80s were sporadic with his last role coming in the 1990 TV movie "Murder In Black and White".

The prolific Johnson died October 9, 1997. He married his last wife, Jean, in '94. He had five children from a previous marriage.

Suggested Sampling of Johnson's Western Heavies:

- Johnny Ringo: A Killing For Cully ('59) Don Durant
- Law of the Plainsman: Dangerous Barriers ('60) Michael Ansara
- Bronco: Tangled Trail ('60) Ty Hardin
- Bat Masterson: Big Gamble ('60) Gene Barry
- Lawman: Old War Horse ('60) John Russell
- Maverick: A Bullet For the Teacher ('60) Roger Moore
- Lawman: Lords of Darkness ('61) John Russell
- Lawman: Hold-Out ('62) John Russell
- Gunsmoke: Wagon Girls ('62) James Arness
- Tales of Wells Fargo: Angry Sky ('62) Dale Robertson
- Dakotas: A Man Called Ragan ('62) Larry Ward
- Rawhide: Incident at Crooked Hat ('63) Eric Fleming
- Rawhide: Incident at Paradise ('63) Clint Eastwood
- Gunsmoke: Hammerhead ('64) James Arness
- Virginian: Timberland ('65) James Drury
- Bonanza: Judgement at Olympus ('67) Michael Landon/Dan Blocker
- Big Valley: 25 Graves of Midas ('69) Barbara Stanwyck

I. STANFORD JOLLEY

Black-hatted, black-mustached, black-hearted I. Stanford Jolley was a busy badman in close to 300 features, primarily portraying the sophisticated "dress-heavy" bossing around his "dog-heavy" henchmen. The lean, intellectual-looking Jolley was a fixture at PRC in the '40s, then at Monogram when PRC went out of the cowboy biz. Jolley was also featured in 25 serials from '37-'54 with his best roles coming in "Perils of the Royal Mounted" ('42 Columbia) as thug Pierre, "Black Arrow" ('44 Columbia) as one of a trio of carpetbaggers, "Jungle Raiders" ('45 Columbia) as henchman Brent, "Crimson Ghost" ('46 Republic) as the spooky voice of the skeletal-cloaked villain and another totally unrelated character, "Black Widow" ('47 Republic) as henchman scientist Jaffa, "Tex Granger" ('48 Columbia) as the town boss, "Congo Bill" ('48 Columbia) as a crooked circus manager, and, especially, "Desperadoes of the West" ('50 Republic) as stovepipe hat-wearing chief heavy Dude Dawson. Besides all this, Jolley was in over 160 TVers, playing heavies in the early juvenile westerns ("Lone Ranger", "Cisco Kid", "Roy Rogers", "Gene Autry") then, like most of the "vintage" movie badmen, now in his mid 50s, switched to character roles circa 1955.

Jolley set a standard for himself with his second B-western role of any consequence, playing the mysterious killer "The Jingler", wearer of ominously noisy spurs, in the Range Busters' "Trail of the Silver Spurs" ('41 Monogram).

Isaac (after his grandfather) Stanford Jolley was born October 24, 1900, in Elizabeth, New Jersey. His father, Robert B. Jolley, was a New Jersey native who was the owner of a circus and carnival, hence, much of Jolley's formative years were spent on tour as a kid clown with the family enterprise up and down the east coast. His mother, Minnie Smith, was also a Jersey native.

As the years went by, Jolley's father became an electrical contractor in New Jersey. Jolley went to school in Morristown.

Jolley's career started around 1916-1917 in vaudeville, achieving the dream of every vaudeville performer by playing the Palace Theatre in New York with Vera Gordon. Jolley played a blind juvenile in a sketch called "America". Later he was successful on the Broadway stage in "Sweet Seventeen" in 1924, then on to radio where he was one of the voices for Cecil B. DeMille's "Lux Presents Hollywood". That opened the way for a film career starting in '35 with an unbilled role in "Front Page Woman".

Slowly, Jolley's status as an actor rose over the next five years until he found his niche as a usually well-dressed boss heavy in westerns with 1940's "Trail of the Silver Spurs". Fellow badman Pierce Lyden said, "He was one of everybody's favorites! Always turning in a good performance. Stan was always quietly promoting himself, knew everyone in the business, and with his big home, was able to entertain. Of course, this never hurt you with the stars, producers and directors. He wasn't the physical stuntman of most badmen, but one of the better actors."

As for Jolley's approach to acting, "I don't try to

Whip Wilson corrals one of Monogram's "Nevada Badmen", I. Stanford Jolley.

act. I just try to play the individual and all this comes out in the performance. You get the part, study the part, absorb it, you walk in front of the camera and you've got it."

Jolley was married in about 1920 to Emily Mae Hacker. They had two children, Stan, who became a successful motion picture art designer and production designer, and Sandra, a one-time Earl Carroll showgirl, who was at one time married to actors Forrest Tucker and later Jack Carson. Son Stan has an Academy Award nomination to his credit.

Jolley's last film was an episode of TV's "The Macahans" in 1976. He had also done several Purina Pet Food commercials.

On December 6, 1978, at 78, Jolley died of congestive heart failure due to arteriosclerosis while a patient at the Motion Picture and TV Hospital in Woodland Hills, California.

His widow lived to be 102, spending the last 12 years of her life at the Motion Picture Home. She died October 18, 2003, and was buried next to her husband on a steep slope at Forest Lawn Cemetery, Hollywood Hills.

Stan's marker reads, "A gentle man and as Jolley by nature as he was by name—loved by all, especially his family."

Suggested Sampling of Jolley's Western Heavies:

- Rolling Home to Texas ('40 Monogram) Tex Ritter
- Trail of the Silver Spurs ('41 Monogram) Range Busters
- Arizona Roundup ('42 Monogram) Tom Keene
- Boot Hill Bandits ('42 Monogram) Range Busters
- Perils of the Royal Mounted ('42 Columbia serial) Robert Stevens
- Prairie Pals ('42 PRC) Lee Powell/Art Davis/Bill Boyd
- Border Roundup ('42 PRC) George Houston
- Rangers Take Over ('42 PRC) Dave O'Brien/James Newill
- Bad Men of Thunder Gap ('42 PRC) Dave O'Brien/James Newill
- Wolves of the Range ('42 PRC) Bob Livingston
- Frontier Fury ('43 PRC) George Houston
- Blazing Frontier ('43 PRC) Buster Crabbe
- Frontier Law ('43 Columbia) Russell Hayden
- Oklahoma Raiders ('44 Universal) Tex Ritter
- Brand of the Devil ('44 PRC) Dave O'Brien/James Newill
- Gangsters of the Frontier ('44 PRC) Tex Ritter/Dave O'Brien
- Black Arrow ('44 Columbia serial) Robert Scott
- Whispering Skull ('44 PRC) Tex Ritter/Dave O'Brien
- Frontier Fugitives ('45 PRC) Tex Ritter/Dave O'Brien
- Gangster's Den ('45 PRC) Buster Crabbe
- Fighting Bill Carson ('45 PRC) Buster Crabbe
- Outlaws of the Rockies ('45 Columbia) Charles Starrett
- Stagecoach Outlaws ('45 PRC) Buster Crabbe
- Six Gun Man ('46 PRC) Bob Steele
- Ambush Trail ('46 PRC) Bob Steele
- 'Neath Canadian Skies ('46 Screen Guild) Russell Hayden
- Wild Country ('47 PRC) Eddie Dean
- West of Dodge City ('47 Columbia) Charles Starrett
- Land of the Lawless ('47 Monogram) Johnny Mack Brown
- Check Your Guns ('48 PRC) Eddie Dean
- Oklahoma Blues ('48 Monogram) Jimmy Wakely
- Tex Granger ('48 Columbia serial) Robert Kellard
- Gunning For Justice ('48 Monogram) Johnny Mack Brown
- Gun Law Justice ('49 Monogram) Jimmy Wakely
- Rimfire ('49 Lippert) James Millican
- Haunted Trails ('49 Monogram) Whip Wilson
- Roll, Thunder, Roll ('49 Equity) Jim Bannon
- Desperadoes of the West ('50 Republic serial) Richard Powers (Tom Keene)
- Lone Ranger: Eye For an Eye ('50) Clayton Moore
- Gene Autry: Twisted Trails ('50) Gene Autry
- Cisco Kid: Confession for Money ('51) Duncan Renaldo
- Texans Never Cry ('51 Columbia) Gene Autry
- Canyon Raiders ('51 Monogram) Whip Wilson
- Texas Lawmen ('51 Monogram) Johnny Mack Brown
- Waco ('52 Monogram) Bill Elliott
- Leadville Gunslinger ('52 Republic) Allan "Rocky" Lane
- Man From the Black Hills ('52 Monogram) Johnny Mack Brown
- Cisco Kid: Quarter Horse ('52) Duncan Renaldo
- Wild Bill Hickok: A Joke on Sir Anthony ('52) Guy Madison
- Roy Rogers: Unwilling Outlaw ('52) Roy Rogers
- Rebel City ('53 Allied Artists) Bill Elliott
- Range Rider: Hideout ('53) Jock Mahoney
- Lone Ranger: Hidden Fortune ('53) John Hart
- Hopalong Cassidy: Renegade Press ('54) William Boyd
- Annie Oakley: Annie Gets Her Man ('54) Gail Davis
- Gene Autry: Civil War in Deadwood ('54) Gene Autry
- Cisco Kid: Montezuma's Treasure ('55) Duncan Renaldo
- Tales of the Texas Rangers: West of Sonora ('55) Willard Parker
- 26 Men: Panic In Bisbee ('58) Kelo Henderson/Tris Coffin

L. Q. JONES

L. Q. Jones' cunning, wolf-like looks—a thatch of dingy, straw blond hair, thick mustache, and feral smile lurking beneath the surface—were right at home on a sheriff's office wanted poster.

Justus Ellis McQueen was born August 19, 1927, in Beaumont, Texas, the son of Justus Ellis McQueen Sr. and Pat Stephens.

Growing up in Texas, he was educated at Lamar Junior College until 1944 and Lon Morris College until 1949. After serving with the Navy from '45-'46 he studied law at the University of Texas from '50-'51. He was sidetracked into being a standup comic and did some 800 shows in the area. He once joked, "I am but several hours away from three degrees—one in law, one in business, one in journalism."

Heavily into competitive sports at a young age, he

played "a little professional baseball, football until I had both legs broken. I like sports of all kinds."

The actor-to-be was ranching in Nicaragua when an old college roommate, Fess Parker, who had come to Hollywood, sent him a copy of the book BATTLE CRY. Brash and innocent, McQueen thought he'd like to play the part of L. Q. Jones in the film, it seemed to fit him. Through luck, circumstance and pure bravado swagger, director Raoul Walsh took a liking to "the kid," took a wild chance and cast him in "Battle Cry" ('55) as Texan L. Q. Jones—a name that stuck, he's used it ever since.

Explaining his take on being a heavy, Jones told author William R. Horner for his BAD AT THE BIJOU book, "Different parts call for different heavies. I have a certain presence. I play *against* that presence a lot of times. One school of heavy that kind of came in vogue, I use it, Warren Oates used it for a while, Jack Elam did with his own twist—and that's of a heavy that is not crazy or deranged—although we play those, of course—but rather someone who is a heavy because he *enjoys* being a heavy. I've done 25, 30, 50 different types of heavies, a shade here, a shade there…it's really hard to say what they're looking for when they pick me. A lot of times your heavy is not that well presented in the script. Most times he's too one-sided. So we look for things to bring to being a heavy: a certain softness; a vulnerability that makes him human; a quiet moment when he's a screamer most of the time; a look; the way he dresses; the way he walks into a room. There are many things that contribute to why a casting director will choose me over someone else…or someone else over me."

1962 saw L. Q. team up with violent director Sam Peckinpah for "Ride the High Country", the first of five films with the maverick director.

In 1975 Jones produced and directed his own film, the post-apocalyptic "A Boy and His Dog", which has become a cult film. Through his production company, L. Q. Jones and Friends, he produced and directed several horror films in the '60s and '70s.

He's flirted with being "on" various TV series over the years. He was Clint Walker's sidekick Smitty on a few early episodes of "Cheyenne" in '55, but Warner Bros. soon abandoned the character and let Walker ride alone. He had the recurring role of ranch hand Andy Belden on "The Virginian" from '64-'67, but the character was never fully developed. He was Joe Teal on a few early episodes of "Klondike" in '60, but that character was also quickly dropped, as was the series after 17 episodes. Lastly, Jones played the when-needed sheriff on "The Yellow Rose" series in '83.

Jones married Sue Helen Lewis on October 10, 1950. After she died, he remarried in '74 but divorced after 21 years.

Jones has continued to work on into the new century, as the lines in his craggy face have deepened, he turns up more frequently as crusty old westerners as in "Lightning Jack" ('94), "Tornado" ('96), "Mask of Zorro" ('98), "Jack Bull" ('99) and "Route 666" ('01).

Suggested Sampling of Jones' Western Heavies:

- Annie Oakley: Dilemma at Diablo ('56) Gail Davis
- Jefferson Drum: Keeney Gang ('58) Jeff Richards
- Buchanan Rides Alone ('58 Columbia) Randolph Scott
- Black Saddle: Client: Banks ('59) Peter Breck
- Johnny Ringo: Four Came Quietly ('60) Don Durant
- Rebel: Earl of Durango ('60) Nick Adams
- Rebel: Explosion ('60) Nick Adams
- Two Faces West: Last Man ('60) Charles Bateman
- Wyatt Earp: Casey and the Clowns ('61) Hugh O'Brian
- Laramie: Cactus Lady ('61) John Smith
- Wagon Train: Christopher Hale Story ('61) Robert Horton/John McIntire
- Two Faces West: The Noose ('61) Charles Bateman
- Laramie: Siege at Jubilee ('61) John Smith
- Laramie: The Replacement ('62) John Smith/Robert Fuller
- Ride the High Country ('62 MGM) Joel McCrea/Randolph Scott
- Rifleman: Day of Reckoning ('62) Chuck Connors
- Laramie: Among the Missing ('62) Robert Fuller
- Wagon Train: Charlie Wooster–Outlaw ('63) Frank McGrath
- Showdown ('63 Universal) Audie Murphy
- Apache Rifles ('64 Columbia) Audie Murphy
- A Man Called Shenandoah: Rope's End ('66) Robert Horton
- Big Valley: By Force and Violence ('66) Barbara Stanwyck
- Big Valley: Court Martial ('67) Peter Breck
- Big Valley: Showdown in Limbo ('67) Lee Majors

- Big Valley: Ambush ('67) Barbara Stanwyck
- Cimarron Strip: The Search ('67) Stuart Whitman
- Hondo: Death Drive ('67) Ralph Taeger
- Hang 'Em High ('68 United Artists) Clint Eastwood
- Wild Bunch ('69 Warner Bros.) William Holden
- Gunsmoke: Good Samaritans ('69) James Arness
- Lancer: Blind Man's Bluff ('69) James Stacy
- Gunsmoke: Albert ('70) James Arness
- Alias Smith and Jones: Stagecoach Seven ('71) Ben Murphy/Peter Duel
- Gunsmoke: Tara ('72) Buck Taylor
- Pat Garrett and Billy the Kid ('73 MGM) James Coburn
- Kung Fu: Last Raid ('75) David Carradine
- Winterhawk ('75 Howco) Michael Dante

VICTOR JORY

Victor Jory relished playing villains. His commanding presence made him perfect as an in-charge heavy. His mesmerizing coal-black eyes could hold you in a trance when combined with his distinctive, fascinating clipped manner of speaking with dramatic pauses. Jory was a unique actor indeed whose career took on many facets over 50 years.

Jory was born November 23, 1902, in Dawson City, Yukon Territory, Canada, the son of Edwin Jory, a horse trader who was a native of Oregon. Jory's mother was a native of Virginia who was one of the few working newspaperwomen in the Canadian wilderness. Actually, his parents were divorced before Vic was born. Born into a very poor environment, an uncle on his mother's side got him a job at $4 a day in a paper mill in Astoria, Oregon.

While working at the Hammond Lumber Company he accidentally received a terrific electrical shock from a huge electrical turbine that generated power for 18 surrounding towns. The current passed through his left arm, across his chest and came out his foot. Doctors, concerned he might lose the use of his left arm, advised the exercise of boxing.

With no place in Astoria where he could learn to box, the now 14 year old Jory moved to Vancouver, British Columbia, where his mother owned some property. Learning the rudiments of the fight game, he soon defeated four opponents to become the cruiser-weight golden gloves champion of that province.

While he was 14 to 17 he spent a goodly amount of time in the ring, earning from $7.50 to $15 a bout.

When he also found he could earn an extra one dollar by doing "walk on" bits at Vancouver's Empress Theatre, the acting bug bit Jory. Turning 18, he attended the Pasadena Community Playhouse, and attended the University of California for a semester. Vic then began a 10 year roving theatrical apprenticeship that included work in various stock companies across the U.S.

Jory eventually made his Broadway debut in 1929 in "Berkeley Square" with Leslie Howard.

Jory was playing the lead in the Norman Krasna comedy "Louder, Please" in California when he was approached by a Fox talent scout. His first film was "Renegades" in 1930 with Warner Baxter.

On December 23, 1928, Jory had married actress Jean Inness. They appeared on stage a number of times over the years. Inness made many films ("Gun Fever", "The Gunfighter', "Rosemary's Baby") and TV episodes ("Big Valley', "Gunsmoke", "Peter Gunn", "Rawhide", "Twilight Zone", "Virginian: Return of Golden Tom" with her husband, "Dragnet", etc.) as well as directing 31 plays at the Pasadena Playhouse. Born December 18, 1900, Inness died December 27, 1978.

The Jorys had two children, a son Jon who became the director of the Actors Theatre of Louisville, Kentucky, and a daughter Jean Jory Anderson, a public relations director of the theatre department at Utah State University.

Jory was never more at his menacing best than as Injun Joe, one of the meanest, most brutish villains the movies ever gave us pursuing Tommy Kelly and Ann Gillis in "The Adventures of Tom Sawyer" ('38).

Although he made many good films, it seems 1939 was a banner year for Jory, the year he "arrived". Among his 10 films that year were the gangster classic "Each Dawn I Die", Shirley Temple's "Susannah of the Mounties", his first big western "Dodge City" and as the carpetbagger overseer in the immortal "Gone With the Wind".

Oddly enough, after these prestigious pictures, the next year of 1940 saw him playing the lead in two Columbia serials ("The Shadow" and "The Green Archer") and joining the ranks of producer Harry "Pop" Sherman's stock company in two medium-budget westerns ("Knights of the Range" and "Cherokee Strip"). Jory would eventually make 12 pictures for Sherman, including seven Hopalong Cassidy entries.

In 1943, just before WWII military service in the Coast Guard, Jory made one of his favorite films, director Kurt Neumann's suspense thriller for Monogram, "Unknown Guest".

Just because he was now in pictures, Jory did not turn his back on the stage. Besides "Unknown Guest", Jory co-starred on Broadway in "The Two Mrs. Carrolls". Post war, in 1945 Jory did "Therese" with Dame May Whitty and in 1946 was a member of the fledgling American Repertory Theatre in New York.

The war and Broadway gave Jory a four year break from the B-westerns he'd been doing, so when he returned

"The Kansan", Richard Dix (R), and an interested Eddy Waller demand a monetary explanation from Victor Jory ('43 United Artists).

to Hollywood in 1948 he began to be featured in bigger pictures once again. Dramatic television also became a part of his life in 1950 ("Philco Television Playhouse", "Studio One", "Broadway Television Theatre", etc.).

In 1958 Vic filmed 78 episodes of the San Diego based "Dragnet"-like cop series, "Manhunt" co-starring Patrick McVey. Screen Gems syndicated the show in '59.

In '59, filmed in Milton, New York, Jory acted in what he termed his favorite role, that of a Mississippi general store owner who is dying of cancer and who is afraid of losing his no-good wife (Anna Magnani) to drifter Marlon Brando. "The Fugitive Kind", the Tennessee Williams story, based on his "Orpheus Descending", was poorly received.

Jory took a filming break '60-'62 and returned that year to play Helen Keller's father in "The Miracle Worker". He also began to work hard in episodic television.

In 1964, now a craggy-faced 62, Jory essayed the part of Indian Chief Tall Tree in John Ford's adieu to westerns, "Cheyenne Autumn". The role opened up another facet of Jory's career as he began to play elderly Indians in other films ("Flap", "Papillon") and on TV ("Nakia", "Gunsmoke", "Virginian", "Young Maverick"). It was the role of a 109 year old Indian, Iron Belly, in "Mountain Men" that brought the end to Jory's illustrious career in 1980.

Jory died February 12, 1982, at 79, at his home in Santa Monica of a heart attack. He had a long history of coronary trouble.

On screen Jory played heavies with all the vigor he could muster, but in real life he was known by his broad smile, and calm, astute, charming manner.

Suggested Sampling of Jory's Western Heavies:

- Dodge City ('39 Warner Bros.) Errol Flynn
- River's End ('40 Warner Bros.) Dennis Morgan
- Cherokee Strip ('40 Paramount) Richard Dix
- Knights of the Range ('40 Paramount) Russell Hayden
- Border Vigilantes ('41 Paramount) William Boyd
- Bad Men of Missouri ('41 Warner Bros.) Dennis Morgan
- Wide Open Town ('41 Paramount) William Boyd
- Tombstone ('42 Paramount) Richard Dix
- Hoppy Serves a Writ ('43 United Artists) William Boyd
- Buckskin Frontier ('43 United Artists) Richard Dix
- Leather Burners ('43 United Artists) William Boyd
- The Kansan ('43 United Artists) Richard Dix
- Colt Comrades ('43 United Artists) William Boyd
- South of St. Louis ('49 Warner Bros.) Joel McCrea
- Canadian Pacific ('49 20th Century Fox) Randolph Scott
- Cariboo Trail ('50 20th Century Fox) Randolph Scott
- Cave of Outlaws ('51 Universal-International) Macdonald Carey
- Flaming Feather ('52 Paramount) Sterling Hayden
- Toughest Man In Arizona ('52 Republic) Vaughn Monroe
- Blackjack Ketchum, Desperado ('56 Columbia) Howard Duff
- Last Stagecoach West ('57 Republic) Jim Davis
- Wanted Dead Or Alive: The Legend ('59) Steve McQueen
- Rawhide: Incident of the Dry Drive ('59) Eric Fleming
- Temple Houston: Twisted Rope ('63) Jeffrey Hunter
- Bonanza: Ride the Wind (Pt. 1-2) ('66) Michael Landon
- Loner: Burden of the Badge ('66) Lloyd Bridges
- Virginian: Return of Golden Tom ('66) James Drury
- Iron Horse: Pride at the Bottom of the Barrel ('66) Dale Robertson
- Virginian: A Bad Place to Die ('67) Doug McClure

IAN KEITH

With his distinct speech, his stage presence and bearing, Ian Keith always gave the impression of a western gangster in his handful of B's in the '40s.

Ian Keith was born Keith Macaulay Ross on February 27, 1899, according to his WWI draft registration in 1918. His mother's name was Mary Wilson Ross. The 1930 census lists him as Ian Keith Ross. INTERNATIONAL FILM NECROLOGY has him named Ian Sylvester Ross. Whatever the name, Keith's forte was clearly the legitimate stage. The famous Castle Square theatre in Boston was the scene of his stage debut. He afterward spent several years in Eastern stock companies before he came to Broadway in 1921 when William Faversham engaged him to appear in "The Silver Fox".

Ian Keith's pickaxe is no match for Wild Bill Elliott, "The Man from Thunder River" ('43 Republic).

The following season he created the role of the French Ambassador in Gilbert Miller's production of "The Czarina". His first leading role, Orlando in "As You Like It" in 1923, was under the aegis of David Belasco. That same year saw him in the lead role for Belasco's "Laugh, Clown, Laugh". A series of tours followed when he starred or co-starred in the Theatre Guild productions of "He Who Gets Slapped", "Reunion in Vienna" and "Elizabeth the Queen".

In his 43 years in the theatre, Keith appeared in more than 350 parts. These included a number of Shakespearean roles, Macbeth, Lear, Hamlet, Othello and Bolingbroke in the Maurice Evans production of "Richard II". He afforded himself the opportunity to combine his Shakespearean talents with the wide open spaces as a playwright spouting showman in Universal's musical comedy western, "Under Western Skies" ('45).

His screen career began in 1925 but his only silent western was as the star of the 1929 version of "The Great Divide".

He played John Wilkes Booth in "Abraham Lincoln" ('30) and had a role in John Wayne's breakthrough "Big Trail" in '30, but then relegated himself to other types of roles until 1942 with Don Barry's "Sundown Kid".

He didn't play heavies in a lot of B-westerns, but in the ones where he did, his stage presence, mannered speech and lean look made him quite noticeable.

At one time, after the death of Lon Chaney, he was one of the actors considered by Universal for the title role in "Dracula" ('31), which finally went to Bela Lugosi. Keith eventually portrayed a Dracula-like Ormond Murks in Republic's B-scarer "Valley of the Zombies" ('46).

Keith also made a terrific right-out-of-the-comic-strip Vitamin Flintheart in two of RKO's Dick Tracy features in the mid '40s.

Throughout his screen career he always maintained a presence on the legit stage, almost as if films were simply a way to pay the bills. Other appearances were in "Touchstone", "The Leading Lady", Cauchon in "St. Joan", as Prospero in "The Tempest" and in "Volpone". He was also co-starred with Helen Hayes in "Mary of Scotland".

In 1958, after he'd left films altogether in 1956, he began an association with Jose Ferrer, appearing with him in "Edwin Booth" as Junius Brutus Booth the elder. He followed this engagement with a national touring company production of Eugene O'Neill's "Long Day's Journey Into Night".

Keith was married four times, or five depending upon how you view it. He was first married in the '20s to actress Blanche Yurka. The union ended in divorce in 1925 and she was awarded $125 a week alimony. In late 1926 Yurka sued Keith as he was $6,050 in arrears. The court ordered him to pay up or go to jail. Keith next married actress Ethel Clayton sometime prior to 1930. No dates, but they too were divorced. Then came his third and fourth marriages, both to Fern Andra. After being married in 1932 in Tijuana, Mexico, there arose some doubt as to its legality, so they repeated their nuptials on February 20, 1934, in the U.S. Apparently, this marriage dissolved in divorce at some point also, as Keith was wed at the time of his death to Hildegarde Pabst.

Keith died at 61, March 26, 1960, following a heart attack in New York City. His last performance was March 24 in the Broadway production of "The Andersonville Trial".

Suggested Sampling of Keith's Western Heavies:

- Big Trail ('30 Fox) John Wayne
- Sundown Kid ('42 Republic) Don Barry
- Wild Horse Stampede ('43 Monogram) Trail Blazers
- Man From Thunder River ('43 Republic) Bill Elliott
- Bordertown Gunfighters ('43 Republic) Bill Elliott
- Arizona Whirlwind ('44 Monogram) Trail Blazers
- Cowboy From Lonesome River ('44 Columbia) Charles Starrett
- Song of Old Wyoming ('45 PRC) Eddie Dean
- Singing On the Trail ('46 Columbia) Ken Curtis
- Border Feud ('47 PRC) Lash LaRue

DeFOREST KELLEY

DeForest Kelley was known to millions of TV viewers as Dr. Leonard "Bones" McCoy on the original "Star Trek" series ('66-'69) but prior to that, in the '50s and early '60s, he was one of the vilest skunks on western TV, often bordering on the psychotic.

Born DeForest Jackson Kelley in Atlanta, Georgia, on January 20, 1920, the son of a Baptist minister, his career dream was to become a doctor like the uncle who delivered him, but his family did not have the wherewithal to send him to medical school.

He graduated from high school at 16 and sang at the church where his father was a minister. He got a job on WSB radio in Atlanta which in turn led to an engagement with Lew Forbes and his orchestra at the renowned Paramount Theatre. At 17 he made his first trip outside Georgia to visit an uncle in Long Beach, California. Intending to stay for two weeks, he ended up staying a year and acting in a play with the Long Beach Theatre Group.

Kelley acted in the evening while roughnecking for Richfield Oil during the day. It was at this time he met his wife-to-be, blonde Carolyn Dowling.

Upon returning home he informed his parents he was moving to California to become an actor. His mother encouraged him but the idea didn't sit well with his father.

With WWII on the horizon, Kelley served with the Army Air Corps, appearing in a handful of training films at "Fort Roach" (the former Hal Roach studio) in Culver City. From these training films he was spotted by a Paramount talent scout and was a finalist with Alan Ladd to play the lead in "This Gun for Hire". Kelley lost the role to Ladd but was signed by Paramount with his first film being "Fear In the Night" ('47).

Kelley's first westerns were three episodes of "The Lone Ranger" in '49. Through the '50s and '60s he was as contemptible as could be, often putting to use a heavy southern accent to enhance his detestable manner. He was also featured in several major big-screen westerns. Paramount producer A. C. Lyles cast Kelley in four of his westerns in the '60s, "I always used him as a heavy, a mean man, and he was marvelous at that. In real life, Kelley was known for his great sense of humor and his skill at growing roses."

Once Kelley got the role of "Bones" on "Star Trek" he was typecast for life. For 33 years he lived in the shadow of Dr. McCoy, finding later TV work in the '70s quite scarce.

De, as his friends called him, entered the Motion Picture convalescent home in March of '99 suffering from emphysema, colon cancer and a collapsed colon. Kelley's wife of 55 years, Carolyn Dowling, who was recuperating from a broken leg at the Motion Picture Home, was by his side the entire period.

Kelley, 79, died June 11, 1999.

Leonard Nimoy stated, "He represented humanity. He was a decent, loving and caring partner."

William Shatner said, "De was a Southern gentleman all of his life and a kind, wonderful friend."

Suggested Sampling of Kelley's Western Heavies:

- You Are There: Gunfight at the O.K. Corral ('55)
- Gunsmoke: Indian Scout ('56) James Arness
- Trackdown: End of an Outlaw ('57) Robert Culp
- Trackdown: The Jailbreak ('58) Robert Culp
- Rough Riders: Nightbinders ('58) Jan Merlin/Kent Taylor
- Mackenzie's Raiders: The Hawk ('58) Richard Carlson
- Man From Blackhawk: Station 6 ('59) Robert Rockwell
- 26 Men: Trail of Revenge ('59) Kelo Henderson/Tris Coffin
- Northwest Passage: Death Rides the Wind ('59) Keith Larsen
- Wanted Dead or Alive: Secret Ballot ('59) Steve McQueen
- Warlock ('59 20th Century Fox) Richard Widmark
- Trackdown: Quiet Night in Porter ('59) Robert Culp
- Black Saddle: Apache Trail ('59) Peter Breck
- Rawhide: Incident at Barker Springs ('59) Eric Fleming/Clint Eastwood
- Lawman: The Thimblerigger ('60) John Russell
- Two Faces West: Fallen Gun ('60) Charles Bateman
- Tales of Wells Fargo: Captain Scoville ('61) Dale Robertson
- Lawman: Squatters ('61) John Russell
- Stagecoach West: Image of a Man ('61) Wayne Rogers
- Deputy: The Means and the End ('61) Henry Fonda/Allen Case
- Bonanza: Honor of Cochise ('61) Lorne Greene
- Laramie: Gun Duel ('62) Robert Fuller
- Have Gun Will Travel: The Treasure ('62) Richard Boone
- Dakotas: Reformation at Big Nose Butte ('63) Larry Ward/Jack Elam
- Gunfight at Comanche Creek ('63 Allied Artists) Audie Murphy
- Bonanza: Ride the Wind (Pt. 1-2) ('66) Lorne Greene/Michael Landon
- Apache Uprising ('66 Paramount) Rory Calhoun
- Waco ('66 Paramount) Howard Keel

CY KENDALL

Serial writer Bill Cline described Cy Kendall perfectly as "a big, stout, lumbering man whose first impression of drowsiness or laziness was disarmingly deceptive. He portrayed with finesse the sly, crafty, insinuating gang boss who badgered those around him with guile and deceit, praising them with a sarcastic display of oily supercilious charm while constantly nagging them with a cynical sneer of thinly disguised contempt. He was so easy to hate."

Cyrus Willard Kendall, a large man of 6 ft. weighing some 225 lbs. during his acting days, was born in St. Louis, Missouri, March 10, 1898, the son of John W. Kendall and Clara Elizabeth Brunan. Early in life, Kendall worked as a traveling salesman.

Kendall was a charter member of the Pasadena Playhouse's 18 Actors Inc., becoming active in over 100 plays from 1920-1949. He became well known on radio with his earliest known role that of Capt. Tracy on the syndicated "Tarzan" serial from '32-'34.

He entered films in 1935 but continued to find work over the years in radio—"Big Town", "Remarkable Miss Tuttle", "One Man's Family", "Cinnamon Bear", "Lux Radio Theatre", "Aunt Mary", "Charlie Chan" and others.

He also continued to act in plays on the East and West Coasts.

Only a handful of his nearly 140 movies were westerns, but when he did turn to that genre he was the ultimate carpetbagger or shady politician.

Kendall appeared in six Universal serials, notably as a gang lieutenant who turned out to be the master criminal in "The Green Hornet" ('40), as the leader of the Flaming Torch gang in "Junior G-Men" ('40), and as Lucky Kamber, boss of Shadow Island in "Secret Agent X-9" ('45). In his THOSE ENDURING MATINEE IDOLS serial journal, Robert Malcomson noted, "He didn't even have to open his mouth, you just knew he was going to be an s.o.b."

Leaving films in 1950, Kendall died at 55 on July 22, 1953, following a confinement of five weeks at the Motion Picture Hospital. Cause of death was cerebral thrombosis with hypertension as a contributing factor.

He was survived by his wife, Margaret, and three children. His remains are at the Mountain View Mausoleum in Altadena, California.

There's trouble in the "Land Beyond the Law" as Dick Foran learns from heavyset Cy Kendall (L) and Harry Woods (R) ('37 Warner Bros.).

Suggested Sampling of Kendall's Western Heavies:

- King of the Pecos ('36 Republic) John Wayne
- Lonely Trail ('36 Republic) John Wayne
- Land Beyond the Law ('37 Warner Bros.) Dick Foran
- Rawhide ('38 20th Century Fox) Smith Ballew
- Trouble In Sundown ('39 RKO) George O'Brien
- Prairie Law ('40 RKO) George O'Brien
- Fargo Kid ('40 RKO) Tim Holt
- Robin Hood of the Pecos ('41 Republic) Roy Rogers
- Outlaw Trail ('44 Monogram) Trail Blazers
- Cisco Kid Returns ('45 Monogram) Duncan Renaldo

BILL KENNEDY

All of actor Bill Kennedy's plentiful badman roles came within a seven year period from '48-'55 as the B-westerns moved from film to TV. His western work was primarily at Monogram and then with the Lone Ranger and the Cisco Kid on TV.

Willard Kennedy was born June 27, 1908, in Cleveland Heights, Ohio. Attending films as a child, he knew he wanted to be an actor. He prepared his voice by reading novels aloud, over and over, sometimes going several pages without a fluff.

While making a living as a stockbroker, Bill began to audition for a job in radio, eventually landing a staff announcer job on WTAM, Cleveland. From there he moved to WWJ, Detroit, Michigan, as staff announcer, sports announcer and Hollywood commentator.

Some years later, now married, Bill was working at KHJ radio in Los Angeles when producer Hal Wallis heard him on the air and offered him a screen test. Accepted, he signed a five year contract with Warner Bros. in 1941. His first bit was as a cop in "Highway West" ('41).

This being war years, Bill appeared in many training films and propaganda shorts. "The Busses Roar" ('42) was his first decent role as an FBI man in disguise.

Dropped by Warner Bros. in '46, Bill began to freelance at Monogram and Republic including a good role in the Bowery Boys' "News Hounds" ('47) and a lead in "Web of Danger" ('47).

Prior to playing western heavies at Monogram beginning in '48, Bill's only experience in a western had been as the lead on loan-out from Warner Bros. in Universal's "Royal Mounted Rides Again" serial in '45.

Bill has since stated, "I loved westerns. If you knew your words and knew how to do a fight scene and you knew about a fast mount and dismount, they liked you and hired you."

One of the routine, at the time, jobs Bill did was the voice-over narration for the opening credits of the "Superman" TV series. When the series became so popular over the years, Bill wished he had insisted on screen credit.

After an unhappy experience making "I Died a Thousand Times" ('55), Bill left Hollywood and moved to Windsor, Ontario, Canada, hosting a TV interview show, "Bill Kennedy's Showtime" on CLKW (now CBET).

Running for 13 years, he showed movies and talked about all the people in them, often personally interviewing various actors. Moving across the river to WKBD-TV in Southfield (Detroit), Michigan, Bill was at Channel 50 for fourteen and a half more years with "Bill Kennedy at the Movies". He finally wrapped it all up in 1983. Dennis Vaughn of Toledo, Ohio, a regular viewer over the years, tells us, "His show was warmly received in the Detroit/Toledo/Windsor area and is missed years after he signed off. I don't believe I'm overstating the issue that he probably laid the groundwork for such movie hosts as AMC's Bob Dorian and Nick Clooney. Kennedy set a standard for motion picture enjoyment that didn't talk down to viewers or treat them as uneducated, uninformed idiots. Kennedy's own personal knowledge didn't reek of fan mag fluff. Duncan Renaldo made one of his last appearances on Bill's show shortly before his death and spoke warmly of Bill's appearances on his 'Cisco Kid' series."

In later years, Kennedy retired to Palm Beach, Florida, where he died at his home at 88 on January 27, 1997.

Suggested Sampling of Kennedy's Western Heavies:

- Overland Trails ('48 Monogram) Johnny Mack Brown
- Sheriff of Medicine Bow ('48 Monogram) Johnny Mack Brown
- Shadows of the West ('49 Monogram) Whip Wilson
- Law of the West ('49 Monogram) Johnny Mack Brown
- Gunslingers ('50 Monogram) Whip Wilson
- Storm Over Wyoming ('50 RKO) Tim Holt
- Marshal of Trail City: unsold pilot ('50) Bill Elliott
- Lone Ranger: Barnaby Boggs, Esquire ('50) Clayton Moore
- Lone Ranger: Drink of Water ('50) Clayton Moore
- Cisco Kid: Wedding Blackmail ('50) Duncan Renaldo
- Border Outlaws ('50 Eagle Lion) Spade Cooley/Bill Edwards
- Abilene Trail ('51 Monogram) Whip Wilson
- Silver City Bonanza ('51 Republic) Rex Allen
- Nevada Badmen ('51 Monogram) Whip Wilson
- Range Rider: The Range Rider ('51) Jock Mahoney
- Cisco Kid: Haven For Heavies ('51) Duncan Renaldo
- Gene Autry: Bandits of Boulder Bluff ('51) Gene Autry
- Cisco Kid: Haunted Stage Stop ('54) Duncan Renaldo
- Lone Ranger: Code of the Pioneers ('55) Clayton Moore
- Buffalo Bill Jr.: Empire Pass ('55) Dick Jones
- Sky King: Boomerang ('56) Kirby Grant

DOUGLAS KENNEDY

Lean, curly-haired, ruggedly good-looking Douglas Kennedy should have been a major western star, all the ingredients were there. At 6' 1" he was the type of handsome, personable actor TV was looking for. Unfortunately, the stardom that finally came his way in 1955 was "Steve Donovan, Western Marshal", a cheaply produced B-western type half-hour TV western from ex-Lone Ranger producer Jack Chertok that did nothing to enhance Kennedy's star status. His roles in films in the late '50s became less and less noteworthy.

Douglas Richards Kennedy was born in New York City, September 16, 1917, the son of Dion W. Kennedy and Alice Frances Richards. His father was a musical composer and organist. Doug attended Larchmont, New York, high school then graduated from prestigious Deerfield Academy and Amherst College in Massachusetts.

At one time he held aspirations to enter diplomatic service but instead took his first job with a New York advertising agency. A lyric baritone, he picked up a few occasional singing jobs then finally journeyed to California where he taught English at the Thatcher School for Boys in Ojai while he attempted to find work in the film industry.

Eventually, he began to obtain bit parts in films in 1940 often using the name Keith Douglas. He'd done some 18 small roles when any momentum he'd built up was interrupted by WWII.

Doug enlisted as a private in the Army, rising with distinction to the rank of Major in the Signal Corps working with the O.S.S. and Army Intelligence.

Upon his discharge in late 1946, he signed a contract with Warner Bros. with the promise of leading man status. Somehow, the right part and stardom eluded him.

His first "real" role in a major western was as one of the three partners of the Three Bell Ranch along with Joel McCrea and Zachary Scott in "South of St. Louis" in '49.

Kennedy had an auto accident in the early '50s. He had his left hand hanging out an open window and the car rolled over his hand. As a result of the accident he couldn't close that hand and his little finger was permanently bent.

By the '50s he was playing nasty heavies in many westerns (it seemed like he was in every other George Montgomery starrer) and on TV with the Lone Ranger, Annie Oakley and others.

Kennedy went on in the '50s and '60s to guest star on all the major TV westerns, eventually portraying Sheriff Fred Madden of Stockton, California, for the last two seasons of "Big Valley" ('67-'69) after which he retired to Kailua, Oahu, Hawaii.

His last several roles were on the Hawaii lensed "Hawaii Five-0" which were shown after his death.

Kennedy died at only 55 August 10, 1973, at Straub Hospital in Honolulu of a massive hemorrhage. The heavy who should have been a star was cremated. He was survived by three daughters and a son by an earlier marriage and two daughters by his second wife, Betty Lou Howell.

Suggested Sampling of Kennedy's Western Heavies:

- South of Rio ('49 Republic) Monte Hale
- Ranger of Cherokee Strip ('49 Republic) Monte Hale
- Montana ('50 Warner Bros.) Errol Flynn
- Cariboo Trail ('50 20th Century Fox) Randolph Scott
- Texas Rangers ('51 Columbia) George Montgomery
- Lone Ranger: A Pardon For Curley ('51) Clayton Moore
- Indian Uprising ('52 Columbia) George Montgomery
- Fort Osage ('52 Monogram) Rod Cameron
- Lone Ranger: Ranger In Danger ('52) John Hart
- Jack McCall, Desperado ('53 Columbia) George Montgomery
- Gun Belt ('53 United Artists) George Montgomery
- Lone Gun ('54 United Artists) George Montgomery
- Stories of the Century: Bill Longley ('54) Jim Davis
- Annie Oakley: Annie Takes a Chance ('55) Gail Davis
- Wyoming Renegades ('55 Columbia) Phil Carey
- Last of the Badmen ('57 Allied Artists) George Montgomery
- Cheyenne: Spanish Grant ('57) Clint Walker
- Tales of Wells Fargo: Silver Bullets ('57) Dale Robertson
- State Trooper: Crisis At Comstock ('58) Rod Cameron
- Tombstone Territory: Gatling Gun ('58) Pat Conway
- Bronco: Four Guns and a Prayer ('58) Ty Hardin
- Lone Ranger and the Lost City of Gold ('58 Warner Bros.) Clayton Moore
- Cimarron City: Kid On a Calico Horse ('58) George Montgomery
- Restless Gun: Shadow of a Gunfighter ('59) John Payne
- Bat Masterson: License To Cheat ('59) Gene Barry
- Wagon Train: Charlie Wooster, Wagon Master ('59) Frank McGrath
- Wyatt Earp: Trail to Tombstone ('59) Hugh O'Brian
- Have Gun Will Travel: Misguided Father ('60) Richard Boone
- Gunsmoke: Speak Me Fair ('60) James Arness
- Gunsmoke: Cherry Red ('60) James Arness
- Legend of Jesse James: One Too Many Mornings ('65) Christopher Jones
- Gunsmoke: Prime of Life ('66) James Arness

GEORGE KEYMAS

Renegade Indians. Double-crossing badmen. Ruthless killers. Hired gunmen. Savage bushwhackers. George Keymas played all to loathsome perfection in the late '50s and the '60s.

Born Constantine Keymas November 18, 1925, in Springfield, Ohio, to George Keymas and Penelope Toloutis, both of whom were born in Greece.

George first saw a stage play when he was 17. They made people laugh and cry and he decided that's what he wanted to do. After becoming involved in little theatre and radio in his hometown, as well as winning several speech contests in high school, George received a scholarship with a professional stock company in Milwaukee, Wisconsin, for one year.

In 1944 George enlisted in the Air Force and was stationed at Truex Field, Wisconsin; Chanute Field, Illinois; Boca Raton, Florida and Columbia Air Force Base, South Carolina. He was sent to school to study airborne radar and they made him an instructor. While in the service he produced a couple of plays for GI's at various bases.

Returning to civilian life in 1947, George got back into stock at Plymouth, Massachusetts. Becoming a member of Actor's Equity with professional stock companies in Lynn and Cambridge, Massachusetts, George went to New York and studied with the American Theatre Wing on his GI bill for two and a half years. George performed in some 30 legitimate plays while he was back east.

Coming close, but failing to connect with a Broadway play, George headed west and quickly wound up as his first heavy in Don Barry's "Border Rangers" ('50 Lippert). He adopted his father's name as his professional name.

Other minor roles followed while George became involved with the Players Ring, *the* theatre in Los Angeles. Performing plays there, he was spotted by an agent and started working one television western after another, as well as some 35 movies.

After being cast as Chief Crazy Horse on "Stories of the Century" in '54, and doing such an excellent job as an Indian, many casting agents and directors saw him as a native American and cast him as such on "Rin Tin Tin", "Wagon Train", "Cimarron Strip", "Rawhide", "Law of the Plainsman", "Maverick", "Wyatt Earp", "Tall Man", "Bonanza" and others, including films like "Santa Fe Passage", "White Squaw" and "Apache Warrior".

In 1971, at 46, just as he was coming into another bracket of his career, George had his aortic valve close down. Surgeons replaced the faulty valve with a plastic valve.

Then around 1980, with a vision problem in his right eye, George had three surgeries but lost the sight of his right eye. On top of that, due to a cataract, his vision was blurred in his left eye, and still is. Without depth perception, and because his right eye was cockeyed due to the blindness, and also because he could no longer face the bright lights of the cameras, George was forced to leave the acting profession many years before he normally would have.

A friend of his was an art auctioneer and got George (and his excellent voice) involved with a company that held art auctions all over the world…fund raising for non-profit organizations, supplying all the art, a cocktail party and the auctioneer. Being an auctioneer, George was fortunate to travel to Greece, Alaska, Hawaii, all over Europe.

When the art market collapsed, George worked for Beverly Hills Art Gallery in Hawaii.

Homesick, George returned to California circa 1990 and became an apartment manager for a large L.A. company for 13 years, only retiring in 2003 and living in Burbank.

George was married around 1966-'67 for six years and then divorced.

Had it not been for the eye problems, we would have been privileged to see one of the best of the '50s-'60s badmen, George Keymas, as a despicable heavy in films and TV for another 15 or 20 years. Keymas died of a heart attack in Lantana, Florida, January 17, 2008.

Suggested Sampling of Keymas' Western Heavies:

- Border Rangers ('50 Lippert) Don Barry
- Hopalong Cassidy: Masquerade For Matilda ('54) William Boyd
- Stories of the Century: Chief Crazy Horse ('54) Jim Davis
- Wyoming Renegades ('54 Columbia) Phil Carey
- Santa Fe Passage ('55 Republic) John Payne
- Vanishing American ('55 Republic) Scott Brady
- Fury at Gunsight Pass ('56 Columbia) Richard Long
- Maverick Queen ('56 Republic) Barbara Stanwyck
- Ford Television Theatre: Black Jim Hawk ('56) John Derek
- Rin Tin Tin: Boone's Grandpappy ('56) Lee Aaker
- White Squaw ('56 Columbia) David Brian
- Utah Blaine ('57 Columbia) Rory Calhoun
- Storm Rider ('57 20th Century Fox) Scott Brady
- Gunfire at Indian Gap ('57 Republic) Anthony George
- Tales of Wells Fargo: Belle Starr ('57) Dale Robertson
- Restless Gun: Rink ('57) John Payne
- Apache Warrior ('57 20th Century Fox) Keith Larsen
- Jim Bowie: Apache Silver ('58) Scott Forbes
- Colt .45: Manbuster ('58) Wayde Preston
- Restless Gun: Outlander ('58) John Payne
- 26 Men: Killer's Trail ('58) Kelo Henderson/Tris Coffin

- Texas John Slaughter: Ambush in Laredo ('58) Tom Tryon
- Trackdown: Day of Vengeance ('58) Robert Culp
- Bronco: Brand of Courage ('58) Ty Hardin
- Yancy Derringer: Marble Fingers ('58) Jock Mahoney
- Tales of the Texas Rangers: Fifth Plague ('58) Willard Parker
- Gunsmoke In Tucson ('58 Allied Artists) Mark Stevens
- U.S. Marshal: Grandfather ('59) John Bromfield
- Rin Tin Tin: Pillajohn's Progress ('59) Lee Aaker
- Black Saddle: Client: Vardon ('59) Peter Breck
- Tales of Wells Fargo: Cole Younger ('60) Dale Robertson
- Deputy: Lawman's Blood ('60) Allen Case/Henry Fonda
- Overland Trail: Westbound Stage ('60) Doug McClure/ William Bendix
- Texan: Borrowed Time ('60) Rory Calhoun
- Shotgun Slade: Charcoal Bullet ('60) Scott Brady
- Wyatt Earp: Miss Sadie ('60) Hugh O'Brian
- Johnny Ringo: Shoot the Moon ('60) Don Durant
- Laramie: Lost Dutchman ('61) Robert Fuller
- Gunsmoke: Old Faces ('61) James Arness
- Wagon Train: Dr. Denker Story ('62) Robert Horton
- Laramie: The Runt ('62) John Smith
- Gunsmoke: Durham Bull ('62) James Arness
- Wagon Train: Lisa Rain Cloud Story ('62) Terry Wilson
- Gunsmoke: Quest for Asa Janin ('63) James Arness
- Gunsmoke: Friend ('64) James Arness
- Arizona Raiders ('65 Columbia) Audie Murphy
- Bonanza: The Last Mission ('66) Lorne Greene
- Shane: Killer In the Valley ('66) David Carradine
- Laredo: Leave it to Dixie ('66) Peter Brown/William Smith/ Neville Brand
- Big Valley: The Long Ride ('68) Barbara Stanwyck
- Gunsmoke: Sarah ('72) James Arness
- Gunsmoke: A Family of Killers ('74) James Arness

CHARLES KING

Charles King is, without a doubt, the preeminent badman of '30s and '40s B-westerns. In the early years, Charlie alternated between wearing a thick black mustache or being clean shaven. It was quite obvious he was always fighting the 'battle of the bulge' but still maintained a good figure until the late '30s when he must have decided to 'let it all hang out'. His paunchy potbelly, ever growing mustache (which flowered to full old-west droopiness in many PRC titles), and often baggy-pants western garb endeared him to several generations of front row kids. In his nearly 300 westerns he had the opportunity to play every type of villain from suave banker or saloon owner to the nastiest, black-hearted, dog-kicker of them all.

Charles Lafayette King Jr. was born February 21, 1895, in Hillsboro, TX, the son of Charles Lafayette King Sr., a Kentucky born physician, and Evelyn King. Charlie had three sisters, Ruth, Maurgeriet, and Hilda. His father wanted Charles to follow in his footsteps but Charlie chose acting instead.

By age 20 Charlie was in Hollywood with his earliest supposed work as an extra in "Birth of a Nation" (1915). Some reports assert a Universal film unit had filmed a silent epic in Texas where King was assigned a minor role, after which he came to the film capital. His first recorded film work came in 1921 as a bartender in the comedy "A Motion To Adjourn" with Roy Stewart, and supporting William Russell in "Singing River". "The Price of Youth" and "The Black Bag" followed in 1922.

One of his earliest, if not his first, western roles was opposite Lester Cuneo in "Hearts of the West" ('25). From there he was seen menacing Fred Humes and Bill Cody in silent oaters.

But before Charlie really became established in westerns he had a run at being a comedian in Universal's popular Mike and Ike two-reel comedy shorts of the late '20s. Researcher Ken Weiss found this notice in the September 1928 UNIVERSAL WEEKLY, a studio in-house publication. "Charles King Arrives in New York For First Visit: Charles King, better known on screen as Mike of the Stern Brothers' 'Mike and Ike, They Look Alike' comedies, is visiting New York for the first time. Accompanied by his wife, whose stage name is Dorothy Murray, they are visiting relatives in her hometown, Brooklyn. King plans to remain here for 10 days before returning to Universal City to start a new series of the Ike and Mike comedies. His wife has been engaged for a tour of the Publix Theaters in a song and dance act under the title 'The Little Girl With the High Silk Hat'. When not clowning in Universal comedies, King plays leading roles in dramatic productions, having recently completed 'Sisters of Eve' with Betty Blythe."

Incidentally, Charlie's early screen credits are often confused with those of an English actor by the same name who died in 1944.

Charlie's comedic flair was often later demonstrated in westerns—especially the Dave O'Brien/ Tex Ritter PRC series (in particular "Enemy of the Law"), much earlier in Ken Maynard's "Lone Avenger" ('33) and Hoot Gibson's "Lucky Terror" ('36), then in "Caravan Trail" with Eddie Dean and Al (Lash) LaRue ("Rabbits, rabbits, rabbits!").

With the advent of sound, Charlie found himself solidly ensconced and well-received in hordes of B-westerns opposite Ken Maynard, Buck Jones, Bob Steele, Tim McCoy, Rex Bell, Hoot Gibson, Gene Autry, Kermit Maynard, Tom Tyler and others.

His barroom brawls with, first, Bob Steele then Tex Ritter became legendary screen battles we all eagerly anticipated. In an interview with writer Grant Lockhart, Ritter referred to Charlie as a "lovely guy. He lived hard and played hard. Married, had a couple of kids. Very sentimental. He liked to drink. He was from Texas. He told me his father was a doctor. Now you take for instance an actor from New York, comes out, tries to get in a western so he'll have some film to show, 'Can you shoot?' 'Yes,' 'Can you ride?' 'Yes.' You get him in a picture and he can't do either one. Charlie King could handle a gun well, he was a good horseman and possibly the best fighter in Hollywood. He taught me all my tricks about fistfights. I owe a lot to Charlie because we had some pretty good fistfights. And he would never fight with my double, he always insisted on fighting with me. He said, 'Wally fights like a woman!' He would wake me up a lot of the time at night—or I would be with him—and he'd want to rehearse the fight for the next day. This is maybe two or three o'clock in the morning. The director would usually leave it to us to routine it. Maybe in the longer shots you'd start mixing it but in the close-ups we knew who was hitting and from which side it was coming. Charlie was my rough heavy—you usually had a dress heavy and a rough heavy. The main trouble was, unfortunately, a lot of the other stars used him, and at Monogram they got to the point where they said, 'Charlie's just in too many westerns. You whup him and in the next picture somebody else whups him.' And I said, 'Well, I don't care about that. Every time I use somebody else, they don't seem to be as good. I don't care how many he's been in, I'd like to keep using him as much as I can.' Columbia didn't use Charlie much and neither did Universal. They had their own people."

Bob Steele once stated, "I took Black Jack O'Shea on most of my personal appearances. I know everyone was used to seeing me mix it up with Charlie King, but Charlie drank too much for me to take him on the road with me. Charlie left no room for doubt; he always let you know how he felt. He was a great guy. In fact, many other heavies and some heroes learned a lot from Charlie King. He was so much fun in real life. In those days when we were all together so much, we became one happy family. If there was any larking around off-screen, you can be sure Charlie was in the middle of it. He was a big man—not too tall—but he weighed over 200 pounds. He was great to do fights with—so agile for a man his size."

Buster Crabbe remembered Charlie much the same way. "Charlie was a big man, but he was as agile as a cat. He moved like a gazelle. He fought a lot of the movie cowboys and always lost, but I doubt any of them could have whipped him in a real fight. I know I wouldn't have wanted to take him on. He was not only agile; he was very fast for a big man, and as strong as an ox. If he had been more serious about his career, and laid off the booze, he might have been a big star. He certainly had the talent."

Although all the studios employed him, PRC and Monogram kept Charlie the busiest in the '40s in feature after feature, daunting the likes of Buster Crabbe, Lee Powell, James Newill, Dave O'Brien, George Houston, Johnny Mack Brown, the Rough Riders, Tom Keene, Lash LaRue, Trail Blazers, Range Busters and others.

Older (now in his early 50s) and heavier, always fighting a well-known battle with booze, Charlie found work harder to come by as the B-westerns which had been his steady form of income faded from the screen. A role in "Oklahoma Blues" ('48) with Jimmy Wakely seems to be his last B-western although he can be spotted in smaller roles in bigger budget films such as "Wyoming" and Abbott and Costello's "Wistful Widow of Wagon Gap" (both '47) and several Sam Katzman Columbia serials from '47-'53, "Great Adventures of Captain Kidd" being his last.

Charlie had found work in serials since "What Happened to Jane" back in 1926 and continued to do so with "Mystery Trooper" ('31 Syndicate), "Hurricane Express" ('32 Mascot), "Miracle Rider" ('35 Mascot), "Shadow of Chinatown" ('36 Victory), "Flaming Frontiers" ('38 Universal), "Deadwood Dick" ('40 Columbia), "White Eagle" ('41 Columbia), "Iron Claw" ('41 Columbia), "Jungle Raiders" ('45 Columbia), "Chick Carter, Detective" ('46 Columbia), "Superman" ('48 Columbia), "Congo Bill" ('48 Columbia), "Adventures of Sir Galahad" ('49 Columbia) (again displaying his true comic talent) and "Bruce Gentry" ('49 Columbia) among quite a few others.

Despondent and out of work, Charlie attempted suicide on February 15, 1951, only days before his 56th birthday. According to an L.A. EVENING HERALD AND EXPRESS 2/16/51 article, Charlie "gazed upon the peaceful scene of his family gathered in the living room at 539 North Arden Blvd. watching television. Tears coursed down his cheeks as he entered the room and announced, 'I love you all—goodbye!' Then he stalked dramatically out and, a few moments later, the family heard a (gunshot) report and rushed into the bathroom to discover Charlie had shot himself in the chest with his son's .22 caliber rifle. He was too rugged for that, however. Police said the bullet coursed around his ribs and out his back and that his injury was not critical. No reason was given (to police) for his act."

He was known to "hit on" his friends for loans that they knew would never be repaid. Movie badman, Terry Frost said, "Charlie was a great guy, but he was an alcoholic. He tried to kill himself twice. One time, he shot himself with a .22, and another time he climbed a tree and tried to hang himself. Either the limb or the rope broke, and Charlie ended up with a broken leg. The last time I saw him, he said, 'Terry, can you help me out?' I gave him a five-spot. I knew I would never see it again, and that he was going to buy a bottle with it, but I thought, oh, what the hell."

During his final years, Charlie appeared as an extra on early episodes of "Gunsmoke" (watch for him right behind James Arness as a courtroom observer in "Custer", drinking a beer in the barroom in "Man Who Would Be Marshal" and "Jealousy", sitting in a chair in "Liar From Blackhawk".)

To supplement his income during this period,

Charlie is known to have worked as a security guard at Menasco Steel Company in the San Fernando Valley.

It's often been said King died while playing a corpse on the James Arness series, or minutes thereafter. However, this is the stuff of which western "urban legends" are born as I've personally never seen a "Gunsmoke" where King played a corpse. The other fact that makes this a myth is the time of his death on May 7, 1957—7:45pm. Not that they *couldn't* have been filming this late, it's just more unlikely. In truth, Charlie died at 62 of a hepatic coma brought on by cirrhosis and chronic alcoholism at John Wesley County Hospital in North Hollywood. At the time Charlie was divorced and living at 4914 Bellaire Ave. in N. Hollywood. He was cremated at Grandview Crematory in Glendale, California, and his ashes were apparently sent to a funeral home in Charlie's hometown of Hillsboro, Texas, although the funeral home has no record of receiving the ashes. Therefore Charlie's "final" resting place is unknown.

Much earlier Charlie was married to Pauline Dorothy Nelson of Arizona. After they divorced he married a lady named "Babs", but she left him due to his drinking.

Charlie had three sons. William and Charles "Chuck" L. King III, a film sound recorder and sound mixer, were with Dorothy. Chuck married Helene Patricia "Pat" Stengel in the mid '50s who had formerly been married to actor Eddie Hall from 1944 until the early '50s. Both were working at Technicolor at the time. Chuck and Stengel later divorced. King III remarried but was murdered on June 29, 1990, by an intruder in his Hollywood apartment. He'd worked in the industry from 1950-1989 on such TV series as "Lone Ranger", "Wagon Train", "Six Million Dollar Man", "Bionic Woman" and films like "Somewhere In Time". He was training as an apartment manager at the complex where he was killed. His sons (Charlie's grandsons) were Clark (a sound mixer) and Billy who was killed in a motorcycle accident when he was about 21. Charlie King's third son was Bobby, "Babs" was his mother.

All in all, Charlie worked in over 400 films, 350 of them in the sound era (including serials). If only Charlie had lived to realize he was *the* heavy we loved to hate, I think he would have been pleased. He truly was among the top five Best of the Badmen.

Jack Randall (L) and Sheriff Steve Clark (R) have finally stopped Charles King and Tom London from plundering Monogram's "Wild Horse Range" ('40).

Suggested Sampling of King's Western Heavies:

- Oklahoma Cyclone ('30 Tiffany) Bob Steele
- Beyond the Law ('30 Syndicate) Robert Frazer
- Two Gun Man ('31 Tiffany) Ken Maynard
- Branded Men ('31 Tiffany) Ken Maynard
- Ghost City ('32 Monogram) Bill Cody
- A Man's Land ('32 Allied) Hoot Gibson
- Outlaw Justice ('32 Majestic) Jack Hoxie
- Young Blood ('32 Monogram) Bob Steele
- Crashin' Broadway ('33 Monogram) Rex Bell
- Fighting Parson ('33 Allied) Hoot Gibson
- Mystery Ranch ('34 Reliable) Tom Tyler
- Prescott Kid ('34 Columbia) Tim McCoy
- Silver Bullet ('35 Reliable) Tom Tyler
- Outlawed Guns ('35 Universal) Buck Jones
- Singing Vagabond ('35 Republic) Gene Autry
- Lawless Nineties ('36 Republic) John Wayne
- Last of the Warrens ('36 Supreme) Bob Steele
- Law Rides ('36 Supreme) Bob Steele
- Crooked Trail ('36 Supreme) Johnny Mack Brown
- Idaho Kid ('36 Colony) Rex Bell
- Brand of the Outlaws ('36 Supreme) Bob Steele
- Phantom of the Range ('36 Victory) Tom Tyler
- Gambling Terror ('37 Supreme) Johnny Mack Brown
- Trouble In Texas ('37 Grand National) Tex Ritter
- Lightnin' Crandall ('37 Republic) Bob Steele
- Rootin', Tootin' Rhythm ('37 Republic) Gene Autry
- Sing, Cowboy, Sing ('37 Grand National) Tex Ritter
- Riders of the Rockies ('37 Grand National) Tex Ritter
- Red Rope ('37 Republic) Bob Steele
- Mystery of the Hooded Horsemen ('37 Grand National) Tex Ritter
- Ridin' the Lone Trail ('37 Republic) Bob Steele
- God's Country and the Man ('37 Monogram) Tom Keene
- Danger Valley ('37 Monogram) Jack Randall
- Fighting Deputy ('37 Spectrum) Fred Scott
- Thunder In the Desert ('38 Republic) Bob Steele
- Songs and Bullets ('38 Spectrum) Fred Scott
- Flaming Frontiers ('38 Universal serial) Johnny Mack Brown
- Rollin' Plains ('38 Monogram) Tex Ritter
- Gun Packer ('38 Monogram) Jack Randall
- Starlight Over Texas ('38 Monogram) Tex Ritter
- Feud of the Range ('39 Metropolitan) Bob Steele
- Frontiers of '49 ('39 Columbia) Bill Elliott
- Sundown On the Prairie ('39 Monogram) Tex Ritter
- Lone Star Pioneers ('39 Columbia) Bill Elliott
- Lightning Strikes West ('40 Colony) Ken Maynard
- Cheyenne Kid ('40 Monogram) Jack Randall
- One Man's Law ('40 Republic) Don Barry
- Deadwood Dick ('40 Columbia serial) Don Douglas
- Billy the Kid in Texas ('40 PRC) Bob Steele
- White Eagle ('41 Columbia serial) Buck Jones
- Outlaws of the Rio Grande ('41 PRC) Tim McCoy
- Lone Rider Crosses the Rio ('41 PRC) George Houston
- Billy the Kid's Fighting Pals ('41 PRC) Bob Steele
- Texas Marshal ('41 PRC) Tim McCoy
- Gunman From Bodie ('41 Monogram) Rough Riders
- Billy the Kid's Roundup ('41 PRC) Buster Crabbe
- Lone Star Lawmen ('41 Monogram) Tom Keene
- Raiders of the West ('42 PRC) Lee Powell/Art Davis/Bill Boyd
- Where Trails End ('42 Monogram) Tom Keene
- Tumbleweed Trail ('42 PRC) Lee Powell/Art Davis/Bill Boyd
- Riders of the West ('42 Monogram) Rough Riders
- Law and Order ('42 PRC) Buster Crabbe
- Arizona Stagecoach ('42 Monogram) Range Busters
- Overland Stagecoach ('42 PRC) Bob Livingston
- Pirates of the Prairie ('42 RKO) Tim Holt
- Outlaws of Boulder Pass ('42 PRC) George Houston
- Trail Riders ('42 Monogram) Range Busters
- Land of Hunted Men ('43 Monogram) Range Busters
- Western Cyclone ('43 PRC) Buster Crabbe
- Riders of the Rio Grande ('43 Republic) 3 Mesquiteers
- Border Buckaroos ('43 PRC) Dave O'Brien/James Newill
- Stranger From Pecos ('43 Monogram) Johnny Mack Brown
- Cattle Stampede ('43 PRC) Buster Crabbe
- Raiders of Red Gap ('43 PRC) Bob Livingston
- Blazing Guns ('43 Monogram) Trail Blazers
- Devil Riders ('43 PRC) Buster Crabbe
- Death Valley Rangers ('43 Monogram) Trail Blazers
- Guns of the Law ('44 PRC) Dave O'Brien/James Newill
- Spook Town ('44 PRC) Dave O'Brien/James Newill
- Sonora Stagecoach ('44 Monogram) Trail Blazers
- Law of the Valley ('44 Monogram) Johnny Mack Brown
- Dead or Alive ('44 PRC) Tex Ritter/Dave O'Brien
- Rustler's Hideout ('44 PRC) Buster Crabbe
- Thundering Gunslingers ('44 PRC) Buster Crabbe
- His Brother's Ghost ('45 PRC) Buster Crabbe
- Marked For Murder ('45 PRC) Tex Ritter/Dave O'Brien
- Shadows of Death ('45 PRC) Buster Crabbe
- Enemy of the Law ('45 PRC) Tex Ritter/Dave O'Brien
- Both Barrels Blazing ('45 Columbia) Charles Starrett
- Border Badmen ('45 PRC) Buster Crabbe
- Navajo Kid ('45 PRC) Bob Steele
- Ambush Trail ('46 PRC) Bob Steele
- Ghost of Hidden Valley ('46 PRC) Buster Crabbe
- Prairie Badmen ('46 PRC) Buster Crabbe
- Lawless Breed ('46 Universal) Kirby Grant
- Outlaws of the Plains ('46 PRC) Buster Crabbe

JACK KIRK

Jack Kirk was one of the busiest men in westerns—identified in over 325 of them from 1930-1948. He actually began a bit earlier, doing uncredited bit roles and stuntwork in the late silent period. He can be glimpsed in "Stolen Ranch" ('26 Universal) with Fred Humes.

Born John Kirkhuff in 1895 in Nickerson, Kansas, he entered films sometime in the '20s. Quickly identified as a dependable, versatile actor they could always rely on, he was employed at one time or another by nearly every studio churning out B-western films. Constantly busy—he made 28 westerns in '35, 27 in '37, seldom less than 20 a year in the '30s and early '40s—he was seldom off the range in any other type of picture. Some 180 of his westerns were at Republic although he was only officially under contract to the studio for one year, from July 12, 1943 to July 11, 1944. It was during this time he had one of his best roles as a cold-blooded killer in "Marshal of Reno". Kirk played many a badman role but was often seen as the rancher, sheriff, cattleman, storekeeper or stage driver.

Kirk had a nice voice, liked to sing and in the early '30s formed a musical group with Chuck Baldra and Glenn Strange. Their group vocalizing—or sometimes just Kirk alone—can be heard in "Freighters of Destiny" ('31 RKO), "Partners" ('32 RKO), "Beyond the Rockies" ('32 RKO), "Saddle Buster" ('32 RKO), all with Tom Keene; "Headin' for Trouble" ('31 Big 4) and "Mark of the Spur" ('32 Big 4) with Bob Custer; "Fiddlin' Buckaroo" ('33 Universal) with Ken Maynard; "Outlaw Justice" ('32 Majestic) and "Gun Law" ('33 Majestic) with Jack Hoxie; "Sundown Rider" ('33 Columbia) with Buck Jones; "Telegraph Trail" ('33 Warner Bros.), "Westward Ho" ('35 Republic), "New Frontier" ('35 Republic), "Lawless Range" ('35 Republic) all with John Wayne; "No Man's Range" ('35 Supreme) with Bob Steele; "Fighting Through" ('34 Kent) and "Outlaw Rule" ('35 Kent) with Reb Russell; "Law of 45s" ('35 First Division) with Big Boy Williams; and "Ghost Rider" ('35 Superior) with Rex Lease, among others. It should also be noted it was Jack Kirk who warbled off-screen for John Wayne in "Westward Ho" and "Lawless Range".

Sammy McKim worked with Kirk in several 3 Mesquiteers Republic westerns and recalled, "Sometimes on location Jack Kirk would get up and sing. He had a pretty good voice. On one of the Mesquiteers films, Jack was doubling for Max Terhune. He was tearing across the landscape and was to be shot and fall from the galloping horse in this long shot. When Jack took the fall he knocked the breath out of himself. The first-aid Doc took Jack behind a rock to revive him with a fifth of whiskey. Jack's coworkers kidded him by asking how many nips he got out of the bottle. Jack asked, 'What bottle?' The Doc had used the bottle himself."

Besides Terhune, Kirk often stunt-doubled for Smiley Burnette in Gene Autry's late '30s-early '40s Westerns.

Jack was nicknamed "Pappy" for good reason; he and his wife had eight children.

It's rather surprising Kirk decided to leave Hollywood, and his family, to go to work in Alaska on a fishing boat, but he did just that in 1948. He was still very active as an actor (although the roles were becoming skimpier) with the work on the boat extremely strenuous for a nearly 53-year-old man. It could be that, as his children were getting older, he needed more money, and perhaps the pay was better in Alaska than it was in B-westerns. For whatever reason, Kirk departed sunny California for frigid Alaska.

He was working at shoveling fish on a boat when he suffered a massive heart attack and died on September 3, 1948. He is buried at the Valhalla Cemetery in Glendale, California.

Suggested Sampling of Kirk's Western Heavies:

- Gun Law ('33 Majestic) Jack Hoxie
- Fiddlin' Buckaroo ('33 Universal) Ken Maynard
- Rider of the Law ('35 Supreme) Bob Steele
- Lawless Range ('35 Republic) John Wayne
- Kid Ranger ('36 Supreme) Bob Steele
- Song of the Gringo ('36 Grand National) Tex Ritter
- Prairie Justice ('38 Universal) Bob Baker
- Ghost Town Riders ('38 Universal) Bob Baker
- Honor of the West ('39 Universal) Bob Baker
- Prairie Pioneers ('41 Republic) 3 Mesquiteers
- Kansas Cyclone ('41 Republic) Don Barry
- Jesse James At Bay ('41 Republic) Roy Rogers
- Jesse James Jr. ('42 Republic) Don Barry
- Sheriff of Sage Valley ('42 PRC) Buster Crabbe
- Border Roundup ('42 PRC) George Houston
- Carson City Cyclone ('43 Republic) Don Barry
- Vigilantes Ride ('43 Columbia) Russell Hayden
- Pride of the Plains ('44 Republic) Bob Livingston
- Marshal of Reno ('44 Republic) Bill Elliott
- Bordertown Trail ('44 Republic) Sunset Carson
- Firebrands of Arizona ('44 Republic) Sunset Carson
- Gunning for Vengeance ('46 Columbia) Charles Starrett
- Terrors On Horseback ('46 PRC) Buster Crabbe

FRED KOHLER JR.

Fred Kohler Jr. tried to emulate his father's evil ways on screen but didn't have the menacing, snarling look of his illustrious father. Nevertheless, although overshadowed by his dad, Fred Jr. piled up a respectable amount of badman roles after a brief attempt at becoming a lead in "Toll of the Desert" and "Pecos Kid", both made in '35 for William Steiner's Commodore Pictures.

His best role came in one of his father's last films, "Lawless Valley" ('38 RKO) as they played the corrupt father-son rulers of Shadow Valley.

Born September 4, 1911, in Hollywood, to actor Fred Kohler Sr. and his wife, Kohler Jr. was 18 when he entered films in 1930 with an uncredited part as a football player in "Maybe It's Love".

Following his aborted starring attempt in 1935, he played undistinguished small roles in 25 or so mostly B-films, including two serials, "Flash Gordon" ('36 Universal) and "Jungle Menace" ('37 Columbia), before making "Lawless Valley" with his father.

Kohler Jr. worked steadily through the '40s and '50s but the roles were, for the most part, small and unimportant, failing to really gain him a solid foothold in the business. By '67 he was out of films, save for an uncredited role in "Ruby", a '77 horror picture.

Kohler Jr. made news in April 1949 when columnist Louella Parsons reported Kohler had been secretly wed for several months to model Carol Janis. Janis made front page news circa 1947 when a semi-nude portrait of her was reportedly slashed to ribbons by her then employer, actor/magician John Calvert. However, Janis told Parsons Calvert only *advised* her to destroy the painting. Janis later said she'd only posed for the subject's face. Artist Edward Withers added the semi-nude body later. The portrait made news when it was awarded a gold medal by the Southern California Painters and Sculptors Club.

Kohler Jr. died January 7, 1993, at 81 in Scottsdale, Arizona. He was survived by a son, Frederick.

Suggested Sampling of Kohler's Western Heavies:

- Lawless Valley ('38 RKO) George O'Brien
- Texas Stampede ('39 Columbia) Charles Starrett
- Two Gun Sheriff ('41 Republic) Don Barry
- Nevada City ('41 Republic) Roy Rogers
- Western Mail ('42 Monogram) Tom Keene
- Raiders of the Range ('42 Republic) 3 Mesquiteers
- Lone Star Ranger ('42 20th Century Fox) John Kimbrough
- Loaded Pistols ('48 Columbia) Gene Autry
- Gay Amigo ('49 United Artists) Duncan Renaldo
- Range Justice ('49 Monogram) Johnny Mack Brown
- Cisco Kid: Big Switch ('50) Duncan Renaldo
- Cisco Kid: Railroad Land Rush ('50) Duncan Renaldo
- Cisco Kid: Renegade Son ('50) Duncan Renaldo
- Twilight In the Sierras ('50 Republic) Roy Rogers
- Wild Bill Hickok: Pony Express Vs. Telegraph ('51) Guy Madison
- Spoilers of the Plains ('51 Republic) Roy Rogers
- Wild Bill Hickok: Medicine Show ('52) Guy Madison
- Judge Roy Bean: Lone Star Killer ('56) Edgar Buchanan

FRED KOHLER SR.

Fred Kohler Sr., a brute of a man standing 6' 2" and weighing 200 pounds, had the perfect build and features, including a truly evil sneer, to portray screen badmen. His glowering look "spoke" more than any amount of dialogue. He was one of the Best of the Badmen, beginning in the early silent era until his untimely death at only 50.

Author Buck Rainey described Kohler best, "On screen he was the most contemptible, ill-tempered badman, committing his evil deeds without a shade of remorse. He was ruthless and cunning. One could almost hear him grinding his teeth in his silent roles. Kohler always relished showing a total disregard for the rights of others, and if he had any pangs of conscience he never bothered to reveal them."

Dick Alexander once remarked of Kohler (and Noah Beery Sr.), "They were so rotten, mean, filthy, sneering characters that if they even looked at you when you passed them, you felt they had accepted you as a friend! This is what they wanted the public to believe, actually they were very nice, regular guys, just making a living doing what they did best, being an actor."

Off-screen Kohler was just the opposite … researcher Lee Koonce described him as "one of the most loving fathers I have seen."

Kohler was born in Dubuque, Iowa (not Kansas City as often reported), April 21, 1888. His father, Frederick L. Kohler, an inventor, was born in Germany.

Fred left home as a teenager, working various jobs. During this time, according to his son, Fred Kohler Jr., his Dad was employed by a mining company. Working with explosives he lost two fingers and part of his right hand in a mining accident. According to Fred Jr., his father was of an age where it was illegal to work with explosives, so the mining company, to protect itself, paid Kohler $100 not to report the incident and fabricate a hunting accident story.

Shortly after, circa 1907, an actor friend of Kohler's, William Carleton, offered Fred an opportunity to go with a touring theatrical company performing "When Johnny Comes Marching Home". Fred accepted and began his stage career with the Willis Wood Theatre in Kansas City, Missouri. He toured the vaudeville circuit and tent shows for about four years.

Going to see old friend Jim McGee at the Selig Company gained him a role in his first film in 1911; a one-reeler entitled "Code of Honor".

His on-stage and screen nastiness quickly found him a niche as a western villain. Perhaps the role that cemented his career of corruptness was as the renegade Indian Three Fingers in John Ford's classic "Iron Horse" in which he and George O'Brien battle to the death after Kohler has murdered George's father.

Kohler was married to Marjorie Prole and they had one son, Fred Jr., who followed in his father's footsteps as an actor and screen badman.

Fred Kohler Sr. died in his sleep of an apparent heart attack on October 18, 1938, at his home at 1354 N. Harper Ave. in West Hollywood, California. His wife was vacationing in the Sierras at the time. The body was discovered by a visiting nephew.

Kohler is buried at Inglewood Park Cemetery in Inglewood, California.

Suggested Sampling of Kohler's Western Heavies:

- Cyclone Bliss ('21 Arrow) Jack Hoxie
- Trimmed ('22 Universal) Hoot Gibson
- Red Warning ('23 Universal) Jack Hoxie
- Iron Horse ('24 Fox) George O'Brien
- Riders of the Purple Sage ('25 Fox) Tom Mix
- Shootin' Irons ('27 Paramount) Jack Luden
- Open Range ('27 Paramount) Lane Chandler
- Vanishing Pioneer ('28 Paramount) Jack Holt
- Light of Western Stars ('30 Paramount) Richard Arlen
- Fighting Caravans ('31 Paramount) Gary Cooper
- Rider of Death Valley ('32 Universal) Tom Mix
- Texas Bad Man ('32 Universal) Tom Mix
- Fourth Horseman ('32 Universal) Tom Mix
- Wild Horse Mesa ('32 Paramount) Randolph Scott
- Fiddlin' Buckaroo ('33 Universal) Ken Maynard
- Honor of the Range ('34 Universal) Ken Maynard
- Man From Hell ('34 Kent) Reb Russell
- West of the Pecos ('35 Paramount) Richard Dix
- Wilderness Mail ('35 Ambassador) Kermit Maynard
- Border Brigands ('35 Universal) Buck Jones
- Trail's End ('35 Beaumont) Conway Tearle
- Lightning Triggers ('35 Kent) Reb Russell
- For the Service ('36 Universal) Buck Jones
- Vigilantes Are Coming ('36 Republic serial) Bob Livingston
- Forbidden Valley ('38 Universal) Noah Beery Jr.
- Billy the Kid Returns ('38 Republic) Roy Rogers
- Lawless Valley ('38 RKO) George O'Brien
- Painted Desert ('38 RKO) George O'Brien

BOB KORTMAN

With the face the Lord bestowed on Bob Kortman, he couldn't play anything but a mean, nasty heavy. His skeletal high cheekbones, hollow cheeks, crooked evil smile and glaring eyes definitely branded him an outlaw. The scowl and sneer were perpetual from the days of William S. Hart silents on through the '50s in some 250 films, 90% of them westerns.

Robert F. Kortman was born December 24, 1887, in the state of New York, not in Philadelphia as is widely reported. His parents were Henry Kortman and Lina Thiel.

According to the 1931 Motion Picture Almanac, he was educated in England and Germany, then spent six years in the U.S. Cavalry. He entered films in 1911 as a horse trainer for filmmaker Thomas H. Ince, however his earliest known film is "Desert Gold" ('14 Kay-Bee) with Charles Ray. This led to several westerns from 1915-1919 opposite the illustrious William S. Hart.

During the silent era Kortman also appeared in various comedies, utilizing his villainous looks. Work included major films like "Hunchback of Notre Dame" ('23), "Godless Man" ('20) and "Sunrise" ('27). There was also one serial, "The Great Radium Mystery" ('20).

Kortman moved easily into talkies, continuing to send shivers up the spines of Buck Jones, Ken Maynard, Tim McCoy, Rex Bell, Tom Mix, Harry Carey, John Wayne, Bob Steele, Bob Allen, Roy Rogers, George O'Brien, Johnny Mack Brown, William Boyd, Tim Holt, Buster Crabbe and others.

Kortman etched out a career in serials as well, appearing in some 20 cliffhangers with his treacherous role as Magua in "Last of the Mohicans" ('32 Mascot), Ravenhead warrior Longboat in "Miracle Rider" ('35 Mascot), and his black-eye-patched One Eye in "Adventures of Red Ryder" ('40 Republic) heading the list.

Well respected as an actor, he gained credits not only in B-westerns but in classics such as "The Virginian" ('29), "Trader Horn" ('31), "Trail of the Lonesome Pine" ('36), "Oklahoma Kid" ('39), "Beau Geste" ('39), "Sullivan's Travels" ('42), "Along Came Jones" ('45), "The Paleface" ('48) and "Mating Season" ('51), among others.

Although early television probably beckoned, he

What's Buster Crabbe to do with these tough "Stagecoach Outlaws", Bob Kortman (R) and I. Stanford Jolley (L) ('45 PRC).

apparently wanted no part of the small screen. He continued to work though '52 with his last role coming in "Aaron Slick From Punkin Crick".

Following that, he'd been spotted working as a janitor in the Directors Guild offices.

Widowed, Bob Kortman, truly one of the best of the badmen, died March 13, 1967, at 79, as a result of cancer at the VA Hospital in Long Beach, California, where he'd been a patient for three months. His death certificate indicates military service in WWI, apparently circa mid-1917-mid 1919 judging by his lack of screen credits during that period. Kortman's remains were cremated and are at rest at Montecito Park in Colton, California.

Suggested Sampling of Kortman's Western Heavies:

- The Ruse ('15 Broncho) William S. Hart
- Narrow Trail ('17 Artcraft) William S. Hart
- Montana Bill ('21 Pioneer) William Fairbanks
- Devil Horse ('26 Pathe) Yakima Canutt
- Lone Rider ('29 Universal) Bob Curwood
- Lone Defender ('30 Mascot serial) Walter Miller
- Branded ('31 Columbia) Buck Jones
- Fighting Fool ('32 Columbia) Tim McCoy
- Last of the Mohicans ('32 Mascot serial) Harry Carey
- Night Rider ('32 Artclass) Harry Carey
- Come On Tarzan ('32 World Wide) Ken Maynard
- Gold ('32 Majestic) Jack Hoxie
- Terror Trail ('33 Universal) Tom Mix
- Phantom Thunderbolt ('33 World Wide) Ken Maynard
- King of the Arena ('33 Universal) Ken Maynard
- The Fugitive ('33 Monogram) Rex Bell
- Mystery Mountain ('34 Mascot serial) Ken Maynard
- Crimson Trail ('35 Universal) Buck Jones
- Miracle Rider ('35 Mascot serial) Tom Mix
- Arizonian ('35 RKO) Richard Dix
- Wild Mustang ('35 Ajax) Harry Carey
- Heroes of the Range ('36 Columbia) Ken Maynard
- Feud of the West ('36 Diversion) Hoot Gibson
- Lonely Trail ('36 Republic) John Wayne
- Vigilantes Are Coming ('36 Republic serial) Bob Livingston
- Romance Rides the Range ('36 Spectrum) Fred Scott
- Unknown Ranger ('36 Columbia) Bob Allen
- Ghost Town Gold ('36 Republic) 3 Mesquiteers
- Sandflow ('37 Universal) Buck Jones
- Zorro Rides Again ('37 Republic serial) John Carroll
- Texas Trail ('37 Paramount) William Boyd
- West of Rainbow's End ('38 Monogram) Tim McCoy
- Stagecoach Days ('38 Columbia) Jack Luden
- Law of the Texan ('38 Columbia) Buck Jones
- Oklahoma Frontier ('39 Universal) Johnny Mack Brown
- Adventures of Red Ryder ('40 Republic serial) Don Barry
- Lone Rider Rides On ('41 PRC) George Houston
- Fugitive Valley ('41 Monogram) Range Busters
- Thundering Hoofs ('41 RKO) Tim Holt
- Jesse James Jr. ('42 Republic) Don Barry
- Sundown Kid ('42 Republic) Don Barry
- Days of Old Cheyenne ('43 Republic) Don Barry
- Avenging Rider ('43 RKO) Tim Holt
- Vigilantes Ride ('44 Columbia) Russell Hayden
- Pinto Bandit ('44 PRC) Dave O'Brien/James Newill
- Forty Thieves ('44 U.A.) William Boyd
- Whispering Skull ('44 PRC) Tex Ritter/Dave O'Brien
- Wyoming Hurricane ('44 Columbia) Russell Hayden
- Rough Ridin' Justice ('45 Columbia) Charles Starrett
- Stagecoach Outlaws ('45 PRC) Buster Crabbe
- Gunning For Vengeance ('46 Columbia) Charles Starrett
- Landrush ('46 Columbia) Charles Starrett

FRANK LACKTEEN

Thin and shifty-eyed with a rough, chiseled, pock-marked or scarred high-cheekboned face and a scowling look, Frank Lackteen portrayed menacing half-breed, oriental, Arab, Mexican and Indian villains for five decades beginning in 1916.

Arriving in Hollywood in 1916, his first film role was as a Chinese heavy in the "Yellow Menace" serial. His beak-nosed, rodent-like features instantly provoked suspicion and distrust. His searing, savage eyes left no doubt he was up to some dastardly deed. His face alone was of screen value in depicting evil visually in silent serials. Lackteen went from one serial to another in the silent period, an astounding 21 serials in all through 1929. Basically, that's all he did in the silent era, other than a scant nine other films.

When sound arrived, his hoarse, thickly accented Lebanese voice made him a favorite in another 21 sound serials, with his best-remembered roles coming as

Buckskin Joe in "Heroes of the West" ('32 Universal), Abdul, High Priest Aide in "Tarzan the Fearless" ('33 Principal), top spy Fang in "Perils of Pauline" ('34 Universal), henchman Yoroslaf in "Mysterious Pilot" ('37 Columbia), Iranian Mr. Tahata in "Radio Patrol" ('37 Universal), Chinatown racketeer Quong Lee in "Red Barry" ('38 Universal), and witch doctor Shamba in "Jungle Girl" ('41 Republic).

In between sound serials he played henchmen, Indians, Mexicans, French-Canadians and more in B-westerns while essaying practically every nationality possible in A-films like "Cimarron" ('31), "Escape From Devil's Island" ('35), "Charge of the Light Brigade" ('36), "I Cover the War" ('37), "Suez" ('38), "Union Pacific" ('39), "Sea Hawk" ('40), "Reap the Wild Wind" ('42), "Arabian Nights" ('42), "Mask of Dimitrios" ('44), "Amazon Quest" ('49), "King of the Khyber Rifles" ('53) and many more. Producer Alex Gordon used him for his last screen role in "Requiem For a Gunfighter" in '65.

Playing against type, he could often be on the side of right, as in "Frontier Badmen" ('43 Universal) as one of Robert Paige's hands, "Son of a Badman" ('49 Western Adventure) as Noel Neill's protector and in "Cowboy and the Indians" ('49 Columbia) as Gene Autry's reservation Indian friend.

Frank Samuel Lackteen was born in Kubber-Ilias, Asia Minor (now Lebanon) on August 29, 1895. His father, Samuel Lackteen, was born in Persia (now Iran) and his mother, Mariam, was a native of Syria. Lackteen attended a protestant American school in Kubber-Ilias, immigrated to the U.S. in 1908, then attended an American school in Lawrence, Massachusetts. He had visited Spain, Puerto Rico and Jamaica before coming to the U.S. to live.

He soon went to Canada, obtaining motion picture work there. He played in New York in comedies and with Universal. Other early screen work was with Pathe, PDC, Paramount and Vitagraph.

After a nearly 50 year career, 1916-1965, Lackteen retired. Fellow badman Pierce Lyden recalls, "He was always walking. He walked to work, he walked home from work, and usually barefooted. Frank was always alone. I never saw him ride in a car or walk with anyone else."

1920 and 1930 census records indicate Lackteen was briefly married then divorced during this period.

Lackteen passed away at the Motion Picture Home in Woodland Hills on July 8, 1968, at 72, of respiratory failure. He is buried at Valhalla Cemetery in North Hollywood. His widow's name was Muriel Dove.

Suggested Sampling of Lackteen's Western Heavies:

- Last Frontier ('26 PDC) William Boyd
- Unknown Cavalier ('26 First National) Ken Maynard
- Hawk of the Hills ('27 Pathé serial) Allene Ray
- Heroes of the West ('32 Universal serial) Onslow Stevens
- Last Frontier ('32 RKO serial) Lon Chaney Jr.
- Come On Danger ('32 RKO) Tom Keene
- Treason ('33 Universal) Buck Jones
- Clancy of the Mounted ('33 Universal serial) Tom Tyler
- Mysterious Pilot ('37 Columbia serial) Frank Hawks
- Left Handed Law ('37 Universal) Buck Jones
- Great Adventures of Wild Bill Hickok ('38 Columbia serial) Bill Elliott
- Kansas Terrors ('39 Republic) 3 Mesquiteers
- Stagecoach War ('40 Paramount) William Boyd
- Under Western Skies ('45 Universal) Noah Beery Jr.
- Hopalong Cassidy: Gypsy Destiny ('53) William Boyd
- Casey Jones: Fire Eater ('58) Alan Hale Jr.

ETHAN LAIDLAW

Big, burly, not so pretty Ethan Laidlaw fit the prescribed role of heavy in westerns as well as anyone…no wonder he worked so steadily in silent and sound westerns (as well as serials and TV shows) for 38 years (1925-1963).

Born Ethan Allen Laidlaw November 25, 1899, in Butte, Montana, the son of Charles P. Laidlaw and Mary Olas, he had one brother, Byron E. Laidlaw.

Before entering movies, possibly as early as 1923 in uncredited roles, Ethan Allen Laidlaw worked as a bus driver, mechanic, steam fitter, painter, policeman and salesman. He'd also obtained an engineering degree. With that background, what brought him to Hollywood and movies is unknown, but his 6' 1", 180 lb. frame and menacing looks—a long straight nose protruding over his upper lip which held a thick, trimmed black mustache over a short chin—gave him a hawkish look that automatically branded Laidlaw as a badman.

His earliest traceable movie is "Crack O' Dawn" ('25), an action drama with Reed Howes. His first credited westerns were "No Man's Law" with Bob Custer and "Wyoming Wildcat" with Tom Tyler, both in '25. The pair started him on the path of western villains.

Laidlaw traded silent gunfire with Tom Tyler, William Russell, Tom Mix, Buzz Barton, Hoot Gibson, Jack Perrin and others. He slid easily into early talkies, appearing in "The Virginian" ('29) as a posse member and "Pardon My Gun" ('30) with Tom Keene. From there, he appeared in over 220 films, of which more than half were westerns, and over 20 serials.

Although he worked steadily, he seemed usually to have little dialogue, with his roles seldom more than that of a henchman. Over the B-western decades he shot at and fought with Charles Starrett, Johnny Mack Brown, Tex Ritter, 3 Mesquiteers, Tim McCoy, Buck Jones, Richard Dix, George O'Brien, Gene Autry, Cisco Kid, Don Barry, Tim Holt, Kirby Grant, Rod Cameron, Bill Elliott and others.

Amidst his B-western and serial work, Laidlaw essayed smaller roles in many A-westerns: "Allegheny Uprising" ('39) w/John Wayne, "Jesse James" ('39) w/ Tyrone Power, "Union Pacific" ('39) w/Joel McCrea, "Texas" ('41) w/William Holden, "Desperadoes" ('43) w/Randolph Scott, "Relentless" ('48) w/Robert Young, "Winchester 73" ('50) w/James Stewart, "Powder River" ('53) w/Rory Calhoun, "Great Missouri Raid" ('51) w/ Macdonald Carey/Wendell Corey, and more.

Laidlaw's threatening countenance was used in comedies also—such as "Goofs and Saddles" ('37) with the 3 Stooges, "Westward Ho-Hum" ('41) with Edgar Kennedy, "Sillie Billies" ('36) with Wheeler and Woolsey, "Alias Jesse James" ('59) with Bob Hope, "Wistful Widow of Wagon Gap" ('47) with Abbott and Costello and "Behind the Eight Ball" ('42) with the Ritz Brothers.

Gangster films such as "Crime School" ('38), "Invisible Stripes" ('39) and "The Killers" ('46) also fit his looks.

Entering his 60s, Laidlaw's work on TV was relegated to fewer and lesser roles on "Bat Masterson", "Wild Bill Hickok", "Destry" and "Wyatt Earp". (In fact, he's seen in the standard barroom opening segment of "Destry" which aired for 13 episodes in '64...obviously filmed just prior to his passing.) In short, Laidlaw did it all!

Previously married to a Mildred Carter, Laidlaw was married to Marie V. Laidlaw, a registered nurse, at the time of his death from a heart attack May 25, 1963, at only 63. They were living on Wedgewood Place in Los Angeles. He is buried at Forest Lawn Cemetery. His death certificate credits him with service in WWII. This is suspect. It isn't often 42 year olds are drafted or enlist. Then too, during the war years (1942-1945) Laidlaw is credited with dozens of films. The death certificate may be in error. On the U.S. entry into WWI, Laidlaw would have been of draft age. But then, Hollywood actors often joined the California National Guard, assuming they would not be called to action, continuing their careers, and getting credit for military service.

Ethan Laidlaw's menacing features and strong presence were always a welcome sight in his 35 years of film work.

Note: He is no relation to silent screen heavy Roy Laidlaw (1883-1936) born in Canada.

Ethan Laidlaw (R) is confronted by Don "Red" Barry on "Fugitive from Sonora" ('43 Republic). Kenne Duncan watches with interest.

Suggested Sampling of Laidlaw's Western Heavies:

- Silent Rider ('27 Universal) Hoot Gibson
- Sonora Kid ('27 FBO) Tom Tyler
- Thunderbolt's Tracks ('27 Rayart) Jack Perrin
- Outlawed ('29 FBO) Tom Mix
- Dugan of the Badlands ('31 Monogram) Bill Cody
- Gordon of Ghost City ('33 Universal serial) Buck Jones
- Powdersmoke Range ('35 RKO) Harry Carey
- Rhythm of the Saddle ('38 Republic) Gene Autry
- Home On the Prairie ('39 Republic) Gene Autry
- Western Caravans ('39 Columbia) Charles Starrett
- Cowboys From Texas ('39 Republic) 3 Mesquiteers
- Son of Roaring Dan ('40 Universal) Johnny Mack Brown
- Tulsa Kid ('40 Republic) Don Barry
- Law and Order ('40 Universal) Johnny Mack Brown
- Law of the Range ('41 Universal) Johnny Mack Brown
- Last of the Duanes ('41 20th Century Fox) George Montgomery
- Riders of the Badlands ('41 Columbia) Charles Starrett/Russell Hayden
- Lone Star Vigilantes ('42 Columbia) Bill Elliott/Tex Ritter
- Stagecoach Express ('42 Republic) Don Barry
- Little Joe the Wrangler ('42 Universal) Johnny Mack Brown/Tex Ritter
- Fugitive From Sonora ('43 Republic) Don Barry
- Border Buckaroos ('43 PRC) Dave O'Brien/James Newill
- Marshal of Gunsmoke ('44 Universal) Tex Ritter/Russell Hayden
- Lawless Empire ('45 Columbia) Charles Starrett
- Rustler's Roundup ('46 Universal) Kirby Grant
- Six Gun Law ('48 Columbia) Charles Starrett
- Trail of the Rustlers ('50 Columbia) Charles Starrett
- Powder River ('53 20th Century Fox) Rory Calhoun

JACK LAMBERT

Jack Lambert studied to be an English professor but, after gaining a degree from a Colorado college, aspired to be an actor. Following a successful career in stock and on Broadway, the toughest, meanest looking heavy west of Yonkers, New York (where he was born), arrived in Hollywood in 1942 for his first film, "About Face", one of the William Tracy/Joe Sawyer service comedies.

It took a few years before he set foot on the range, but when he did, in "Abilene Town" ('46) opposite Randolph Scott, he left an indelible impression of a gangster or hood come west. In future westerns through the '40s and '50s he often portrayed a dim-witted badman.

The slit-eyed, jut-toothed menace of Lambert was equally at home in stark film-noir gangster films like "The Killers" ('46) as Dum-dum Clarke, "Dick Tracy's Dilemma" ('47) as The Claw, "The Enforcer" ('51) and Mickey Spillane's "Kiss Me Deadly" ('55).

For whatever reason, Lambert never quite reached the popular heights of mean contemporaries like Lee Van Cleef, Bob Wilke, Warren Oates and Leo Gordon.

The surly Lambert started working the TV screen in '51, appearing on "Rin Tin Tin", "Jim Bowie", "Wagon Train", "Lawman", "Tales of Wells Fargo", "Deputy", "Texan", "Sugarfoot", "Gunsmoke", "Have Gun Will Travel", "Bonanza", "Virginian", "Loner", Branded", "Daniel Boone" and others.

He turned honest—but still tough—as Joshua, first mate of "Riverboat" Captain Grey Holden (Darren McGavin), on NBC ('59-'60).

His last work was a "Gunsmoke" two-parter, "The Badge" in 1970, after which John Taylor Lambert, born April 13, 1920, in Yonkers, retired and eventually moved to affluent Carmel, California, where he operated a small shop of some sort for the final 20 years of his life.

Lambert was of Scottish descent; his father, John Lambert, was born in Scotland. His mother's name was Elizabeth.

He never served in the Armed Forces.

At 79 Lambert died February 18, 2000, at Carmel Convalescent Hospital of heart problems. He was widowed at the time of his death and living with his son, Lee, on Highland Dr. in Carmel. Lambert's remains were cremated and returned to his son.

Suggested Sampling of Lambert's Western Heavies:

- Abilene Town ('46 United Artists) Randolph Scott
- Vigilantes Return ('47 Universal) Jon Hall
- Belle Starr's Daughter ('48 20th Century Fox) George Montgomery
- Brimstone ('49 Republic) Rod Cameron
- Dakota Lil ('50 20th Century Fox) George Montgomery
- North of the Great Divide ('50 Republic) Roy Rogers
- Bend of the River ('52 Universal) James Stewart
- Montana Belle ('52 RKO) Jane Russell
- Vera Cruz ('54 United Artists) Gary Cooper
- At Gunpoint ('55 Universal) Fred MacMurray
- Rin Tin Tin: Return of the Chief ('56) Lee Aaker
- Jim Bowie: Plot to Assassinate Jackson ('57) Scott Forbes
- Wagon Train: Sakae Ito Story ('58) Ward Bond
- Lawman: Short Straw ('58) John Russell
- Tales of Wells Fargo: Cow Town ('58) Dale Robertson
- Sugarfoot: Extra Hand ('59) Will Hutchins
- Frontier Doctor: Bittercreek Gang ('59) Rex Allen
- Gunsmoke: There Never Was a Horse ('59) James Arness
- Deputy: Back to Glory ('59) Allen Case/Henry Fonda
- Rifleman: Spiked Rifle ('59) Chuck Connors
- Have Gun Will Travel: Never Help the Devil ('60) Richard Boone
- Bonanza: Showdown ('60) Lorne Greene
- Bat Masterson: Bullwhacker's Bounty ('61) Gene Barry
- Gunsmoke: Stolen Horses ('61) James Arness
- Loner: Escort For a Dead Man ('65) Lloyd Bridges
- Daniel Boone: The Trap ('66) Fess Parker

HARRY LAUTER

Harry Lauter started out his quarter century in film playing juvenile leads in non westerns in 1947. By 1949 he was doing the same in the westerns of Allan "Rocky" Lane, Monte Hale, Rex Allen and TV's "Lone Ranger". But Harry soon found his niche playing bushwhackers, rustlers and just plain no goods in several B-westerns but primarily on TV in the '50s and '60s. Gene Autry's Flying A Productions was his most frequent employer with every series Gene produced.

Lauter came to be a very familiar presence in TV films, serials and B films, coming close to stardom on several occasions in the mid '50s. He co-starred as Ranger Clay Morgan with Willard Parker (as Jace Pearson) on TV's "Tales of the Texas Rangers" for 52 episodes from '55-'58. He had the lead in two of Republic's last serials, "Trader Tom of the China Seas" ('54) and "King of the Carnival" ('55). He'd earlier been a henchman heavy in Republic's "Flying Disc Man from Mars" ('50) starring Walter Reed and had running parts on two other TV series, "Rocky Jones, Space Ranger" ('54) and "Waterfront" ('53-'56). Even as late as 1965 he had the lead in "Convict Stage" for 20th Century Fox.

There's no doubt, judging from his well over 300 TV episodes and some 150 movies plus commercials and other work, Harry was a popular and effective workaholic.

Herman Arthur Lauter was born June 19, 1914, in White Plains, New York. His grandparents were circus people, the world famous trapeze act, The Flying Lauters. Harry's father was also involved in the act as well as being a graphic artist, and his uncle was one of the foremost church stained-glass window artists in the country. His mother, who died when Harry was four, wrote for the LITERARY DIGEST. His parents moved to Colorado when Harry was quite young which is where he learned to ride. They later moved to San Diego. When Harry was 13 he established California State Junior records in the 100 yard and 220 yard free style swimming sprints.

In San Diego Harry attended grammar school and San Diego High.

While still in high school, he began working at radio station KGB as an announcer and general handyman. Whenever time would permit, he appeared in plays at the Globe Theatre in Balboa Park. This theatre experience convinced Harry he wanted an acting career and it led to his joining the Elitch Garden Theatre Group in Denver, Colorado, one of the oldest stock companies in the country.

Harry's first wife was named Dorothy; they had a son named Bill.

In 1946 Harry married Barbara Ayres whom he met while appearing at Elitch Gardens. They had a daughter, Brooke. The couple were later divorced.

Harry soon went to New York, where he worked in several radio dramas, and to New England for summer stock. He toured the country with Lillian Gish in "The Story of Mary Suratt" in 1947 and was doing "The Voice of the Turtle" at Martha's Vineyard in Maine when Hollywood producer Frank Seltzer spotted him.

Drafted for the duration of WWII, upon his discharge 20th Century Fox brought him out to California but never used him so he asked for a release. It was then he began to work, with his first film being "Hit Parade of 1947" in 1946.

After bit roles in a few other films, Harry asked himself what movies would always be doing. Westerns. Being a good rider and with television coming on, westerns are what he concentrated on.

Harry told Tom and Jim Goldrup for their FEATURE PLAYERS Vol. 1, he liked playing heavies, "because every part you do is a challenge. You got to watch yourself that you don't get into a set character. I used to like to work with makeup, not go overboard on it, but play with a scar, or the character itself. I like to play the heavy because they pretty well leave you alone, unless you go overboard. I love the heavies, and I love the reaction I get from people. 'Why are you so mean on screen? You're not a mean guy at all.' Most of the people I know that played really nasty heavies, Bob Wilke, Mickey Simpson…they are the nicest guys in the world."

In another interview Harry smiled, "I loved to play villains, especially in horse operas. That's what I'm best in and what I like most. I can ride anything that moves on four legs and it never bothered me one teeny bit that I didn't get to wear the white hat or win the girl at the end. When I was a kid I always remembered the varmint better than the hero anyway."

The artist's blood from his family came through in Harry also. When he worked on location, he'd often spend time in between takes painting the Tetons, the Sierras, the Rockies, the Alabams at Lone Pine. Harry's widow Doris (Gilbert) wrote in 1999, "Harry became an accomplished artist, painting mostly beautiful oil landscapes, with lakes, trees, and mountains. His father, also an artist, was a great influence on him as a child. The Favell Museum of Western Art (in Klamath Falls, Oregon) has one of his landscapes on display in their permanent collection (alongside those of Remington and Russell). Being an artist myself, we met in 1970 at various art functions. He had a gallery in Studio City, California, 'Lauters Gallery Row,' and also ran an art show on La Cienega on Sundays. After we married, we had a small gallery in Ojai where we did our paintings. We exhibited together in professional art shows and two-man shows all over the country. He sold everything he painted, and was pleased that his art would be around long after he was gone."

As the westerns began to fade from view, Harry wound his career with an episode of "How the West Was Won" in '79 and concentrated more on artistic endeavors. "It's been a marvelous business and it's been very kind to me. I have no regrets over it at all."

Harry attended several western film festivals until his health began to fail. One of the nicest western heavies—one of the best of the badmen—died October 30, 1990, of heart failure at his home in Ojai, California.

Myron Healey remembers, "Harry probably saved my life. We were up at Big Bear for a week's location shoot with Autry; Harry and I were doing heavies. I'm supposed to ride by a rock, Gene follows and bulldogs me into the lake for a fight in that cold water. Harry has to ride by with Pat Buttram pursuing him—Pat bulldogs him and he succumbs to Pat—on dry ground. Now, I had a bad cold all week—real sick, coughing, no medication. Unbeknownst to me, Harry talked to director George Archainbaud and said, 'What's the difference who goes in the water? Let us switch places.' So we did—If I'd gone in the water I would have come down with pneumonia and possibly died. To this day, I say Harry probably saved my life. He was always good for a laugh—take a bad situation and make it fun."

Chris Alcaide had a similar experience, "Harry was always willing to help another actor. I hurt my back the first day we were shooting…so in fight scenes Harry went out of his way to make sure I didn't hurt myself further—he did all the hard stuff. Doing a 'Kit Carson' episode, Harry told me 'Never roll your sleeves up 'cause then you can't wear armpads, and get a pair of gloves so your hands won't get ripped up in the dirt.' He was good at comedy too—just never got the chance."

Suggested Sampling of Lauter's Western Heavies:

- Gene Autry: Doublecross Valley ('50) Gene Autry
- Gene Autry: Hot Lead ('50) Gene Autry
- Gene Autry: Bandits of Boulder Bluff ('51) Gene Autry
- Range Rider: Shotgun Stage ('51) Jock Mahoney
- Whirlwind ('51 Columbia) Gene Autry
- Hills of Utah ('51 Columbia) Gene Autry
- Valley of Fire ('51 Columbia) Gene Autry
- Range Rider: Ambush In Coyote Canyon ('52) Jock Mahoney
- Gene Autry: Western Way ('52) Gene Autry
- Kit Carson: Border City ('52) Bill Williams
- Cowboy G-Men: Frontier Smugglers ('52) Russell Hayden
- Roy Rogers: Doublecrosser ('52) Roy Rogers
- Apache Country ('52 Columbia) Gene Autry
- Yukon Gold ('52 Monogram) Kirby Grant
- Range Rider: Convict at Large ('53) Jock Mahoney
- Cowboy G-Men: Silver Fraud ('53) Russell Hayden
- Gene Autry: Bandidos ('53) Gene Autry
- Hopalong Cassidy: Illegal Entry ('53) William Boyd
- Kit Carson: Army Renegades ('53) Bill Williams
- Topeka ('53 Allied Artists) Bill Elliott
- Fighting Lawman ('53 Allied Artists) Wayne Morris
- Gene Autry: Civil War In Deadwood ('54) Gene Autry

- Forty-Niners ('54 Allied Artists) Bill Elliott
- Lone Ranger: Code of the Pioneers ('55) Clayton Moore
- Buffalo Bill Jr.: Fugitive From Injustice ('55) Dick Jones
- Lone Ranger: Counterfeit Redskins ('55) Clayton Moore
- Gene Autry: Million Dollar Fiddle ('55) Gene Autry
- Wyatt Earp: Assassins ('56) Hugh O'Brian
- Fury: Tungsten Queen ('56) Peter Graves
- Annie Oakley: A Tall Tale ('56) Gail Davis
- Buffalo Bill Jr.: Rough-Shod ('56) Dick Jones
- Lone Ranger: White Hawk's Decision ('56) Clayton Moore
- Steve Donovan, Western Marshal: Missouri Outlaws ('56) Douglas Kennedy
- Annie Oakley: Tuffy ('57) Gail Davis
- Jim Bowie: Intruder ('57) Scott Forbes
- Sergeant Preston: Gold Rush Patrol ('58) Richard Simmons
- Jefferson Drum: Hanging of Joe Lavett ('58) Jeff Richards
- Colt .45: Sanctuary ('59) Wayde Preston
- Laramie: Run to Tumavaca ('59) Robert Fuller
- Fury: Timber Whackers ('59) Peter Graves
- Gunsmoke: Big Tom ('60) James Arness
- Colt .45: Impasse ('60) Wayde Preston
- Deputy: The Lesson ('61) Henry Fonda/Allen Case
- Laramie: Deadly Is the Night ('61) Robert Fuller/John Smith
- Laramie: Fall Into Darkness ('62) John Smith
- Rifleman: The Bullet ('63) Chuck Connors
- Fort Utah ('67 Paramount) John Ireland
- Guns of Will Sonnett: Pariah ('68) Walter Brennan
- Guns of Will Sonnett: A Town In Terror (Pt. 1-2) ('69) Walter Brennan
- Cade's County: Slay Ride (Pt. 1-2) ('72) Glenn Ford

GEORGE J. LEWIS

Neither completely suave nor completely savage, yet possessing a modicum of both, George J. Lewis was one of the best known henchmen of the '40s in westerns and serials, moving right into the TV era on all the action oriented juvenile TVers from '49-'54.

But he was equally at home on the right side of the law in westerns and serials whether as an Indian Chief ("Under Nevada Skies" '46 Republic with Roy Rogers, "Renegades of Sonora" '48 Republic with "Rocky" Lane, "Dalton Gang" '49 Lippert with Don Barry, etc.), some sort of Latin rurale or official ("South of Monterey" '46 Monogram with Gilbert Roland, "Saddle Legion" '51 RKO with Tim Holt, "Kid From Amarillo" '51 Columbia with Charles Starrett, etc.) or often as the second lead or friend of the hero ("Ride Ranger Ride" '36 Republic with Gene Autry, "Zorro's Black Whip" '44 Republic serial with Linda Stirling, "Silver Trails" '48 Monogram with Jimmy Wakely, "Ghost of Zorro" '49 Republic serial with Clayton Moore, "Radar Patrol Vs. Spy King" '50 Republic serial with Kirk Alyn and the "Zorro" TV series, '57-'61, on which he played Don Alejandro de Vega, Zorro/Guy Williams' stately father.)

The dashing, black-haired actor was born December 10, 1903, in Guadalajara, Mexico. Lewis' American parents (Victor Courtney Lewis of New York and Marie De La Luz Garcia from Spain) moved to Brazil to evade the Mexican revolution when George was only six. Only two years later they moved on to Green Bay, Wisconsin.

His father, formerly a typewriter company exec, now an Army officer, was guarding shipyards in Long Beach, California, during WWI and was later in charge of patrolling the U.S. Mexican border, being stationed at Nogales, Arizona. By 1919 George's father was out of the service and living in Coronado, California, where George finished high school and became interested in dramatics.

Soon after (1923), he was in Hollywood appearing in small roles for silent films. His first significant billed role was in '25's "His People", a prizefight story, after which Universal signed him to a six-year contract. During this time he co-starred with serial-heroine-to-be Dorothy Gulliver in 46 Collegians short subjects between '26-'29 as well as working in many features.

Universal released George after only four years but Fox quickly put his Latin speaking talent to work in Spanish versions of their films, including the John Wayne role in "The Big Trail".

George began to freelance and found himself with a small role in his first serial, "Whispering Shadow" ('33) at Mascot, followed by the adult lead (behind Rin Tin Tin Jr. and Frankie Darro) in Mascot's "Wolf Dog" serial ('33).

Disenchanted with the roles he was getting, George left Hollywood in '36 for the stage lights of New York where he appeared in numerous plays and on radio.

At one point George added the initial J. (for Joseph) to his name to avoid confusion with two other George Lewises prominent in show biz at the time, one a burlesque comic and the other a jazz musician.

By 1939 he was back on the west coast—this time to stay. He found work in several Republic westerns opposite Don Barry and became a serial mainstay at Republic and Columbia, following a part in "Gangbusters" ('42), his only Universal serial. He was in three serials in '42, five in '43, seven in '44, and at least one every year after that (except '47) on through 1950.

Often his vivid black mustache lent a cunning note to his evil undertakings as in "Federal Operator 99" ('45), a boss heavy role he thoroughly enjoyed.

It was due to a shortage of leading men during WWII that George found himself back in the good guy column aiding Linda Stirling in "Zorro's Black Whip"

('44). He did turn up again on the side of right as the hero's pal in "Phantom Rider", "Ghost of Zorro" and "Radar Patrol Vs. Spy King", but the bulk of his roles were mean heavies as in "G-Men Vs. the Black Dragon" ('43) as a spy named Lugo; "Daredevils of the West" ('43) as a henchman; "Captain America" ('44) as Lionel Atwill's lieutenant; more henchmen in "Tiger Woman" ('44), "Haunted Harbor" ('44), "Adventures of Frank and Jesse James" ('48) and back to boss saloon heavy for "Cody of the Pony Express" ('50).

George had high compliments for the stuntmen. "They were professionals who knew exactly what they were doing. They taught me a lot about timing. They made me look good on those fights even when I wasn't being doubled. Dale Van Sickel and Ken Terrell were two of the very best in the business. For me, the difficult part of working in serials was the dialogue. It was geared for a young audience and trying to make dialogue sound believable that might be a little stilted was a challenge."

Besides the serials there were the westerns with the 3 Mesquiteers, Johnny Mack Brown, Cisco Kid, Roy Rogers, Gene Autry, Jimmy Wakely, Jimmy Ellison, Lash LaRue and others.

As the B-westerns and serials ended, George continued to work steadily on TV westerns and in A-films, both western ("Shane", "Cow Country", "Drum Beat", "Big Land" etc.) and non-western ("Desert Legion", "Phantom of the Rue Morgue", "Santiago", "Jeanne Eagels" etc.).

George ended a 40 year career in 1966 after an episode of "Family Affair", devoting fulltime to his thriving real estate business from which he retired by 1980, living a quiet life until his death December 8, 1995, two days shy of his 92nd birthday at his home in Rancho Santa Fe, California, near San Diego. Cause of death was congestive heart failure and aortic stenosis. He also suffered from Parkinson's disease. He was survived by his wife, Mary Louise Lohman. His remains were cremated.

Of his career, George once mused, "I was always going to the movies (as a youngster) and had in the back of my mind that I'd like to try it. I liked all the western stars: Buck Jones, Tom Mix, and then there was another one, way back there, Broncho Billy Anderson. I remember him when I was a kid, and used to watch his pictures. There was a shortage of leading men during the war years, and producer Ronald Davison thought that without my mustache, I could play the hero in 'Zorro's Black Whip'. Besides, I had played so many heavies that the friends of my daughter Maylo used to pity her. They would see me in films where I was so mean, and believe I was actually that way at home."

Republic leading lady Peggy Stewart told us, "Georgie was well-loved by everybody. Handsome, good-looking man. He was a favorite at Republic, he worked in everything. He was a lot of fun. My galfriend, Catalina Lawrence, John Wayne's right hand gal for 17 years—and in between those shows she was script girl for Roy's shows—George was her Godfather. He lived only about three blocks from me. Being Spanish they had a lot of fun talking together."

In his book, IN A DOOR, INTO A FIGHT, OUT A DOOR, INTO A CHASE, director William Witney remembers his 'old friend.' George used to take Bill's sisters to a ballroom in Coronado, California, where he was raised. Witney laughs, "I'm a little (kid) George had to take along to the dance as a chaperone. I remember (George) carrying me home half asleep."

Don Diamond played Corporal Reyes in 50 of the 70 "Zorro" Disney TVers with Lewis ('57-59). "He was a very, very, nice sociable person. Laughed a lot…good sense of humor. I was able to speak Spanish with him because he was of Mexican extraction before coming to California. I looked forward to seeing him."

Fellow badman Pierce Lyden said, "I wondered why George never attained reel stardom. Maybe, like a lot of us, he did too many westerns, too many heavies, and too much Republic. The ways of producers are sometimes strange. He had a great career with over 300 pictures (movie and television). He was always a gentleman, dapper, well-dressed and friendly. Much too good-looking to be a badman. He was a handsome and fine actor."

Suggested Sampling of Lewis' Western Heavies:

- Outlaws of Pine Ridge ('42 Republic) Don Barry
- Black Hills Express ('43 Republic) Don Barry
- Daredevils of the West ('43 Republic serial) Allan Lane
- Laramie Trail ('44 Republic) Robert Livingston
- Black Arrow ('44 Columbia serial) Robert Scott
- South of the Rio Grande ('45 Monogram) Duncan Renaldo
- Wagon Wheels Westward ('45 Republic) Bill Elliott
- Rainbow Over Texas ('46 Republic) Roy Rogers
- Oklahoma Blues ('48 Monogram) Jimmy Wakely
- Sheriff of Medicine Bow ('48 Monogram) Johnny Mack Brown
- Adventures of Frank and Jesse James ('48 Republic serial) Clayton Moore
- Crashing Thru ('49 Monogram) Whip Wilson
- Lone Ranger: Enter the Lone Ranger ('49) Clayton Moore
- Gene Autry: Head for Texas ('50) Gene Autry
- Gene Autry: Star Toter ('50) Gene Autry
- Gene Autry: Gun Powder Range ('50) Gene Autry
- Hostile Country ('50 Lippert) Jimmy Ellison/Russell Hayden
- Colorado Ranger ('50 Lippert) Jimmy Ellison/Russell Hayden
- Crooked River ('50 Lippert) Jimmy Ellison/Russell Hayden
- Cody of the Pony Express ('50 Columbia serial) Jock Mahoney
- King of the Bullwhip ('50 Western Adventure) Lash LaRue
- Lone Ranger: Trouble at Black Rock ('51) Clayton Moore
- Wild Bill Hickok: Homer Atchison ('51) Guy Madison
- Range Rider: Silver Blade ('52) Jock Mahoney
- Range Rider: Romeo Goes West ('52) Jock Mahoney
- Gene Autry: Melody Mesa ('52) Gene Autry
- Roy Rogers: Ghost Gulch ('52) Roy Rogers
- Wagon Team ('52 Columbia) Gene Autry
- Annie Oakley: Dude Stagecoach ('54) Gail Davis
- Annie Oakley: Annie and the Lily Maid ('54) Gail Davis
- Buffalo Bill Jr.: Death of Johnny Ringo ('55) Dick Jones
- Champion: Salted Ground ('55) Jim Bannon
- Champion: Canyon of Wanted Men ('55) Jim Bannon
- Sgt. Preston of the Yukon: Crime at Wounded Moose ('56) Richard Simmons
- Buffalo Bill Jr.: A Diamond For Grandma ('56) Dick Jones
- Lone Ranger: Return of Don Pedro O'Sullivan ('56) Clayton Moore

ARTHUR LOFT

Rotund-faced, heavy-set, balding Arthur Loft played politicos, bankers and other fast talking scam artist business types while masquerading as a respectable citizen.

Of Loft's 225 or so films from 1932-1948 only three dozen were westerns, but his appearance in one always signaled underhanded deeds for Gene or Roy.

Loft was an accomplished, and busy, actor, averaging nearly 20 pictures a year from '36-'46...with a high of 28 films in '42.

He was seen in five serials, all at Universal, with his most notable being that of the good Mongolian priest in "Ace Drummond" ('36).

Hans Peter Loft was born May 25, 1897, in Ouray, Colorado. His father, Arthur Christian Loft, was born in Danneborg, Nebraska, while his mother, Marguerite Nissen, was from Denmark.

Loft served in the Armed Forces during WWI and one suspects stage training prior to coming to Hollywood in 1932 where his first film was "Behind Jury Doors".

As is the case with so many other working actors, little is known about his life. He was dependable, did his work and made a good living entertaining us for many years until his untimely death at 49 due to a heart attack January 1, 1947, at the home of he and his wife, Daisy Del Loft, 3917 Cumberland Ave. in Los Angeles. Loft is buried at Forest Lawn.

Suggested Sampling of Loft's Western Heavies:

- Western Justice ('35 Supreme) Bob Steele
- King of the Royal Mounted ('36 20th Century Fox) Robert Kent
- Public Cowboy No. 1 ('37 Republic) Gene Autry
- Rawhide ('38 20th Century Fox) Smith Ballew
- Southward Ho ('39 Republic) Roy Rogers
- Days of Jesse James ('39 Republic) Roy Rogers
- Riders of Pasco Basin ('40 Universal) Johnny Mack Brown
- Colorado ('40 Republic) Roy Rogers
- Texas Terrors ('40 Republic) Don Barry
- Back In the Saddle ('41 Republic) Gene Autry
- North From the Lone Star ('41 Columbia) Bill Elliott
- Down Mexico Way ('41 Republic) Gene Autry
- Frontier Badmen ('43 Universal) Robert Paige
- Man From Oklahoma ('45 Republic) Roy Rogers
- Sheriff of Redwood Valley ('46 Republic) Bill Elliott
- Lone Star Moonlight ('46 Columbia) Ken Curtis

TOM LONDON

During a movie career that spanned 48 years beginning in 1915, Tom London had a face everyone recognized from his nearly 550 movies and close to 100 TV episodes.

Then there's dispute of Tom being in the "first" western, "The Great Train Robbery" in 1903. Some filmographies list it, some don't. Some western film historians say he was, some dispute it. However, freelance writer Jack Lewis (who wrote screenplays for "King of the Bullwhip", "Outlaw Gold", "Cisco Kid" episodes and others, as well as owning and publishing such magazines as GUN WORLD) interviewed Tom in 1954 during the filming of "Gunfighters of the Northwest" serial. Tom indicated to Jack he was in the picture, but offered a sly chuckle about his birth year as he did so. If he was in "The Great Train Robbery", he was only 14 at the time. Certain facts indicate otherwise.

London was born Leonard Clapham August 24, 1889, in Louisville, Kentucky. Both of his parents, Harry R. Clapham and Mary J. Huesman, were Kentucky natives.

As soon as he was old enough to leave home, Tom went to work as a salesman. Obviously, he couldn't have done this as a young teenager and made his way to the east coast where "The Great Train Robbery" was filmed. However, he did work as a salesman in New York, then Chicago. It was in the Windy City that he went to work as a prop man for the film company owned by William Selig. He did everything from sweeping stages to working as a stunt rider during this time in the early teens. Tom told Jack Lewis, "When I first tried to get on with Selig, I was afraid they'd say I was too young for the kind of work they were offering. That's the reason I backed up my birth date on job applications (to 1882), I needed the job."

When Selig had enough of making films in the Chicago area, having to sit out the harsh winters, he moved his operation to sunny California, and Leonard Clapham went along with him.

"Out of (those Selig shorts) came a friendship with a Universal star named J. W. Kerrigan," Tom continued. "He got me on at Universal and I worked there from 1916 until 1923 or '24. Until then I was Leonard Clapham. It was the next year (1925) that I changed my name to Tom London."

Throughout the silent era of the teens and '20s London rustled cattle, shot sheriffs in the back, ran sheepmen off their land and every other rotten deed as he functioned as a badman opposite Fred Church, Tom Mix, Eddie Polo, Hoot Gibson, Leo Maloney, Jack Perrin, Ken Maynard, Pete Morrison, Lefty Flynn, Fred Humes, William Desmond and others. As Leonard Clapham, he even achieved star status in a host of two-reelers co-starring Virginian Browne-Faire at Universal in 1920.

When sound came in, Tom's hearty, slightly nasal, but deep baritone voice made the transition easily. Developing a reputation as a true professional, he was cast constantly in westerns and serial after serial. Speaking of serials, we count Tom being in at least 60.

Republic was utilizing London so much in their westerns that they signed him (and fellow freelancers Roy Barcroft, Bud Geary, Kenne Duncan, Jack Kirk and LeRoy Mason) to term contracts in July 1943. Tom stayed under contract til July '47 playing sheriffs, sidekicks (especially to Sunset Carson), ranchers, fathers—and badmen.

As he turned more to character roles when his Republic contract ended, three of his best are as tough old Marshal Blackjack Flint in Jimmy Wakely's "Brand of Fear" ('49 Monogram), as Jocko Mahoney's weathered sidekick Doc Laramie in "Cody of the Pony Express" ('50 Columbia serial) and as "ghost rider" old man Roberts in "Riders In the Sky" ('49 Columbia) starring Gene Autry.

When TV came along, it was just another medium in which Tom could work. Now 61 in 1950, he left the owlhoot roles to a younger group of bushwhackers and concentrated on playing grizzled old-timers, sheriffs, scouts and the like. Gene Autry respected his talent and used Tom on close to 20 of his Flying A TV productions. Tom also worked on "Roy Rogers", "Kit Carson", "Lone Ranger", "Laramie", "Cisco Kid", "Death Valley Days", "Fury", "Wyatt Earp", "Have Gun Will Travel", "Bat

Jack Randall ropes one of the best of the badmen, Tom London, with a little help from Steve Clark (R) and his deputies (unknown with gun, Foxy Callahan holding London). "Wild Horse Range" ('40 Monogram).

Masterson", "Tall Man" and others.

Although the ideal western character actor on screen, off-screen Tom was a different person. He had an uncle who owned a clothing store, enabling him to buy all his clothes wholesale. Seen around town, he was a well-dressed man, especially when he went out dancing in the ballrooms, which he loved to do.

Tom lived in later years with his sister Anita J. Pearcy. However, contrary to published accounts, he *was* married at one time to silent screen actress Edith Stayart who preceded him in death. This is proven by the word "widowed" on Tom's California death certificate.

When Jack Lewis asked Tom who he most enjoyed acting with, he thought for a moment and replied, "Mae West. I worked with her in 'I'm No Angel' in '32. She was a fun lady." Asked who his least favorite in a working environment might be gave cause for a scowl, "Ken Maynard. I did six pictures with him, then refused offers after that. He was mean to his horses and mean to the people he thought he could buffalo. He was often half drunk on a picture and sometimes didn't even show up."

Queried in another interview about the number of pictures he'd been in, Tom mused, "I don't know how many I've been in. (London is in the GUINNESS BOOK OF RECORDS for appearing in the most films.) It's like asking how many pair of socks you've worn in your life. If you put on socks every day for 50 years, well that's a lot of socks. I've been in movies for more than 50 years, and that's a lot of pictures. I got along with all of them (the cowboy stars), with the exception of one (Maynard). I especially liked Wild Bill Elliott, and although a lot of people found 'Rocky' Lane too hard to work with because he was too much of a perfectionist, I enjoyed working with him on around 12 pictures, and respected that he tried to make his films stand out over the usual little western. One of my favorites was Sunset Carson. He encouraged me by giving me his sidekick role in some of his pictures. A star I owe lot to is Gene Autry. I made around 18 pictures with him and he was one of the nicest guys to work with. He always saw I got decent characters to play, and, in 'Riders In the Sky' ('49 Columbia), I got a great part playing a cowpoke in a big death scene. I've been told this was the best acting of my whole career. Later on, when I auditioned for some television work, I would bring along a 16mm print of that scene and show it on a casting agent's wall. Most of the time, I got the part."

Known affectionately by his showbiz friends as Ol' Tom, Max Terhune said, "He was a good actor, and could portray almost any character from villain to comic to lovable person. Off the screen he was a gentleman."

As for what others thought of London, it's best summed up by Jock Mahoney, "The most underrated actor in town. The most patient, most professional actor I've ever known, as well as a kind, giving man. He's one I feel lucky to be able to call a close friend."

London wound up his career in 1961 with a bit role in "Underworld U.S.A." and an episode of TV's "Miami Undercover".

According to his death certificate, he served with the armed forces during WWI, probably circa 1917-1918 when his film credits are quite sparse.

The beloved Tom London, 74, passed away at his home at 4368 Camellia Ave. in North Hollywood on December 5, 1963.

Suggested Sampling of London's Western Heavies:

- Wolf Tracks ('20 Universal) Hoot Gibson
- Luck and Sand ('25 Clarion) Leo Maloney
- Long Loop On the Pecos ('27 Pathé) Leo Maloney
- Mystery Rider ('28 Universal serial) William Desmond
- Border Wildcat ('29 Universal) Ted Wells
- Under Texas Skies ('30 Syndicate) Bill Cody
- Two Gun Man ('31 Tiffany) Ken Maynard
- Westward Bound ('31 Syndicate) Buffalo Bill Jr.
- Lightnin' Smith Returns ('31 Syndicate) Buddy Roosevelt
- Without Honor ('32 Artclass) Harry Carey
- Beyond the Rockies ('32 RKO) Tom Keene
- Night Rider ('32 Artclass) Harry Carey
- Ferocious Pal ('34 Principal) Kazan (the dog)
- Outlaw's Highway ('34 Regal) Jack King
- Prescott Kid ('34 Columbia) Tim McCoy
- Mystery Mountain ('34 Mascot serial) Ken Maynard
- Miracle Rider ('35 Mascot serial) Tom Mix
- Law Beyond the Range ('35 Columbia) Tim McCoy
- Wildcat Saunders ('35 Atlantic) Jack Perrin
- Tumbling Tumbleweeds ('35 Republic) Gene Autry
- Last of the Clintons ('35 Ajax) Harry Carey
- Gun Play ('35 Beacon) Big Boy Williams
- Courage of the North ('35 Stage and Screen) John Preston
- Lawless Nineties ('36 Republic) John Wayne
- Avenging Waters ('36 Columbia) Ken Maynard
- Border Patrolman ('36 Fox) George O'Brien
- Guns and Guitars ('36 Republic) Gene Autry
- Bar-Z Badmen ('37 Supreme) Johnny Mack Brown
- Law of the Ranger ('37 Columbia) Bob Allen
- Springtime In the Rockies ('37 Republic) Gene Autry
- Mysterious Pilot ('37 Columbia serial) Frank Hawks
- Lone Ranger ('38 Republic serial) Lee Powell
- Six Shootin' Sheriff ('38 Colony) Ken Maynard
- Riders of the Black Hills ('38 Republic) 3 Mesquiteers
- Prairie Moon ('38 Republic) Gene Autry
- Southward Ho ('39 Republic) Roy Rogers
- Westbound Stage ('39 Monogram) Tex Ritter
- Covered Wagon Days ('40 Republic) 3 Mesquiteers
- Kid From Santa Fe ('40 Monogram) Jack Randall
- Wild Horse Range ('40 Monogram) Jack Randall
- Stage to Chino ('40 RKO) George O'Brien
- Roll, Wagons, Roll ('40 Monogram) Tex Ritter
- Trailing Double Trouble ('40 Monogram) Range Busters
- Riders From Nowhere ('40 Monogram) Jack Randall
- Robbers of the Range ('41 RKO) Tim Holt
- Lone Rider in Frontier Fury ('41 PRC) George Houston
- Twilight On the Trail ('41 Paramount) William Boyd
- Underground Rustlers ('41 Monogram) Range Busters
- West of Tombstone ('42 Columbia) Charles Starrett/Russell Hayden
- Ghost Town Law ('42 Monogram) Rough Riders
- Land of the Open Range ('42 RKO) Tim Holt
- Valley of Vanishing Men ('42 Columbia serial) Bill Elliott
- Fighting Frontier ('43 RKO) Tim Holt
- Wild Horse Stampede ('43 Monogram) Trail Blazers
- Santa Fe Scouts ('43 Republic) 3 Mesquiteers
- West of Texas ('43 PRC) Dave O'Brien/James Newill
- The Renegades ('43 PRC) Buster Crabbe
- Stranger From Pecos ('43 Monogram) Johnny Mack Brown
- Beneath Western Skies ('44 Republic) Bob Livingston
- Call of the Rockies ('44 Republic) Sunset Carson
- Cheyenne Wildcat ('44 Republic) Bill Elliott
- Wagon Wheels Westward ('45 Republic) Bill Elliott
- Corpus Christi Bandits ('45 Republic) Allan Lane
- Phantom Rider ('46 Republic serial) Robert Kent
- Son of Zorro ('47 Republic serial) George Turner
- Marshal of Cripple Creek ('47 Republic) Allan Lane
- Blue Canadian Rockies ('52 Columbia) Gene Autry

WALTER LONG

Scowling Walter Long looked like a bulldog. Most often an unlikable bulldog. His shaved-head bulldog look portrayed some of the most heinous villains on the screen...embezzlers, gangsters, Mexicans, Indians, Arabs, thugs, rustlers...on and on.

Long's career began because of a donkey. W. S. Van Dyke, who became an ace director at MGM, was in a stock company of players (circa 1908-1909) somewhere in Michigan. They were prodding a donkey through the streets to the playhouse where they were to perform "Michael Strogoff". Many bystanders were jeering the actors and applauding the donkey for its passive resistance when one spectator, husky young Walter Long, stepped forward and informed them he could get the donkey to the theatre if they'd let him stay backstage during the performance. According to the story, Long actually picked the donkey up and carried him to the theatre. Stage-struck, Long joined the company as a bit player, eventually becoming sure enough of himself to head for Hollywood where the infant film industry was burgeoning. He got a job as an extra the first day he applied in 1909.

From 1910 ("The Fugitive") to 1930 he appeared in over 100 silent features, including some of the biggest—in "The Birth of a Nation" ('15) he was the bad Negro Gus, for "Intolerance" ('16) he was the Musketeer of the Slums and in Rudolph Valentino's "The Sheik" ('21) he was Omar the bandit. At this time Long was earning as much as $1,250 a week. (Compared to $10,000 a week for Lillian Gish and $4,000 a week for Tom Mix.) Very good pay at that time.

Although Long saw action in about a dozen westerns in the silent era, they were of the A variety and not B's, except for Hoot Gibson's "Ridin' Kid From Powder River" ('24). Long was the sheriff in Cecil B. DeMille's "Romance of the Redwoods" ('17) and supported Neil Hamilton in Zane Grey's "Desert Gold" ('19).

His growling voice and demeanor gave him an easy transition into talkies where he became a perfect foil for Laurel and Hardy in "Pardon Us" ('31), "Any Old Port" ('32), "Live Ghost" ('34) and others. He was Miles Archer in the '31 version of "The Maltese Falcon" and appeared in major films like "I Am A Fugitive From a Chain Gang" ('32), "Thin Man" ('34), "Naughty Marietta" ('35) and "Annie Oakley" ('35).

However by 1936, now 57, his "star" began to fade and he was accepting roles in more and more B films, but still giving it his all. One of his best performances is a dual role as good and bad twin brothers in Jack Randall's "Man's Country" ('38).

Long's last screen appearance was in one of Edgar Kennedy's last two-reel comedies, "No More Relatives" (Feb. '48).

Walter Huntley Long was born in Milford, New Hampshire, a hamlet a short distance from Nashua, on March 5, 1879.

Long was married to Luray Roble, born 1890 in Wisconsin, a silent screen actress who worked under the name Luray Huntley until her untimely death at 28 on January 6, 1919, of pneumonia and influenza. There was a son, John Huntley Long.

Long was a second lieutenant in the Pacific Coast Artillery during WWI circa mid-1917-mid 1919. There is also unsubstantiated information that Long was Captain of the Military Police during WWII in Washington, D.C., and Virginia—although at the time he would have been 62. It *is* known he made no films from 1942-mid 1945.

The great screen villain died July 4, 1952, of a heart attack while watching a Fourth of July fireworks display in Los Angeles, California.

Suggested Sampling of Long's Western Heavies:

- Ridin' Kid From Powder River ('24 Universal) Hoot Gibson
- Glory Trail ('36 Crescent) Tom Keene
- North of the Rio Grande ('37 Paramount) William Boyd
- Painted Trail ('38 Monogram) Tom Keene
- Six Shootin' Sheriff ('38 Grand National) Ken Maynard
- Bar 20 Justice ('38 Paramount) William Boyd
- Man's Country ('38 Monogram) Jack Randall
- Wild Horse Canyon ('38 Monogram) Jack Randall
- Flaming Lead ('39 Colony) Ken Maynard
- Fighting Mad ('39) Monogram) James Newill
- Silver Stallion ('41 Monogram) Dave Sharpe

THEODORE (TED) LORCH

Large, six foot, hulking Ted Lorch always stood out because of his size…even his nose and chin seemed outsized. One 1935 writer called him "As repulsive a specimen of malignant manhood as ever committed crime on screen."

Born Theodore A. Lorch September 29, 1880, in Springfield, Illinois, of German and English parents, he spent 20 years with legit road and stock companies. He acted in "The Crowded Hour", "Sherlock Holmes", "Dr. Jekyll and Mr. Hyde" and other dramas. He was also in vaudeville with Frank Tinney before coming to Hollywood in 1920 as Chingachgook in the 1920 silent version of "Last of the Mohicans".

According to the 1920 census he was married to a lady named Cesil who was listed as an actress in movies. At the time of the census in January 1920, the couple was living in Chicago.

Ted continued his stage work while working in some 23 silent films, including several westerns with Buck Jones and Ken Maynard.

In silents and when sound came in, Lorch's acting talents were definitely not limited to westerns and serials. He appeared in musicals like "Showboat" (both '29 and '36 versions) "Whoopee!" ('30), big budget dramas ("Mad Love" '35, "Madame X" '37, "Pride of the Yankees" '42), comedy shorts ("Uncivil Warriors" '35, "We Want Our Mummy" '39, "Spook Louder" '43, "Micro-Phonies" '45 and others with the Three Stooges; "Half Shot at Sunrise" '41 with Roscoe Karns), horror films ("The Sphinx" '33, "Mysterious Mr. Wong" '34, "Voodoo Man" '44)…in other words, his talents ran the gamut.

Lorch was noted in seven serials. He was the hunched, mysterious crippled stranger in Red Grange's "Galloping Ghost" ('31 Mascot), Pierre La Forge suspected of being the Wolf Man in "Lightning Warrior" ('31 Mascot), Ming the Merciless' High Priest in "Flash Gordon" ('36 Universal), the skulking butler Daggett in "Blake of Scotland Yard" ('37 Victory), the pilot of the flying Wing in "Fighting Devil Dogs" ('38 Republic) and was also in "Dick Tracy" ('37 Republic) and "Zorro's Fighting Legion" (39 Republic).

It seems, as an actor, Lorch actively sought out unusual, creative and diverse parts, be it in poverty row or A-budget films.

Perhaps his most interesting western role is not as a villain but as a medicine show pitchman with a ventriloquist dummy in "Orphan of the Pecos" ('37 Victory). At one point, to aid Tom Tyler, Lorch throws his ghostly voice, pretending to be heroine Jeanne Martel's dead father to spook a confession out of wicked Forrest Taylor.

Then the same year, in Tyler's "Cheyenne Rides Again", Lorch was as nasty a skunk as can be.

It's "Aces Wild" when Harry Carey confronts slippery Ted Lorch ('36 Commodore).

Lorch's many talents left us November 11, 1947, at Camarillo, California, following a long illness. He was 67.

Lorch, a member of the Screen Extras Guild board of directors, was survived by his wife, Jeannette.

Suggested Sampling of Lorch's Western Heavies:

- Black Jack ('27 Fox) Buck Jones
- Canyon of Adventure ('28 First National) Ken Maynard
- Wild Blood ('29 Universal) Jack Perrin
- Royal Rider ('29 First National) Ken Maynard
- Tonto Kid ('35 Resolute) Rex Bell
- Gunfire ('35 Resolute) Rex Bell
- Rustler's Paradise ('35 Ajax) Harry Carey
- Wildcat Trooper ('36 Ambassador) Kermit Maynard
- Romance Rides the Range ('36 Spectrum) Fred Scott
- Aces Wild ('36 Commodore) Harry Carey
- Cheyenne Rides Again ('37 Victory) Tom Tyler
- Lost Ranch ('37 Victory) Tom Tyler

PIERCE LYDEN

Named "Villain of the Year" in a 1944 Photo Press fan poll, Pierce Lyden became one of the best known and beloved badmen in western films, a lot of it due to his longevity and numerous western film festival appearances.

Republic leading lady Peggy Stewart said, "Pierce Lyden was a real professional. He always knew his lines and gave his all to a particular scene. He was a fine gentleman—and he knew how to handle horses. Believe me, Pierce is no badman—just when playing the role. In later years I think Pierce found and knew more love than he had ever known. Everyone liked and knew Pierce, but it wasn't like a Charlie King or Bud Osborne—'cause Pierce is a quiet guy. But in later years at the festivals, he just couldn't believe it. Then to have streets in his own hometown named after him, to go to England and be on the BBC, Golden Boot award—just all the recognition he got was awesome to him and thrilled him to death. He was quite talented…a loving person, always thinking of the other person."

One of the sweetest, most humble, thoughtful human beings you could ever meet was born on a ranch in a sod house January 8, 1908, in Hildreth, Nebraska. Pierce learned to ride as a boy—his father (Albert Lyden) was a horse buyer for the U.S. Army. His mother, Ida Pearson, was from Illinois. As a youngster he was bitten by the acting bug when he saw traveling tent shows.

Attending the University of Fine Arts in Lincoln,

Nebraska, he managed to gain stage and radio experience which led to six years of stock company work in the Midwest and New England.

In late 1931 he headed west to Los Angeles, appearing in several plays there before his expert horsemanship broke him into westerns at 24 in 1943. Sporting a mustache, he was forever typed as a heavy.

Reflecting on work as a badman, Pierce wrote, "The heavies always worked. There was always room for them. The good-looking boys they would hire for one picture, then they didn't want them again for a while. But the heavies and stuntmen, who did stuff I did, worked all the time. So I got stuck on westerns. I made up my mind that's the way it was going to be. Some say the western will come back. I, too, would like to think so, but I cannot imagine the audience of today cheering and worshipping the hero in the white hat, week after week, year after year. This was the lot that fell to Gene and Roy, and I, for one, do not see this kind of audience coming again."

Pierce was a regular serial badman as well, beginning with a small role in "Green Hornet Strikes Again" at Universal in 1941. Some of his better serial parts came in "The Vigilante" ('47 Columbia), "Sea Hound" ('47 Columbia), "Cody of the Pony Express" ('50 Columbia), "Roar of the Iron Horse" ('51 Columbia), "Government Agents Vs. Phantom Legion" ('51 Republic) and "Gunfighters of the Northwest" ('54 Columbia). After appearing in "Wild Westerners", Pierce left films in 1962 and got into stagecraft, manning spotlights at Disneyland and later joining Johnson's Ice Follies as property master.

Discovered by western film festivals in the '80s, Pierce was overwhelmed by the fact people still remembered "this old black hat" and revered his work. Since then, he's received countless honors and awards. He was most proud of those bestowed on him by his native Nebraska, his Golden Boot award and his star on the Palm Springs Walk of Fame.

In the '80s Pierce authored five books about his Hollywood experiences. For a thorough picture of Pierce's career, read THE MOVIE BAD MAN; CAMERA! ROLL 'EM! ACTION!!; FROM B'S TO TVS; MOVIE BADMEN I RODE WITH and THOSE SATURDAY SERIALS.

Pierce Lyden (sans his customary mustache) tries to make a getaway holding Virginia Belmont hostage in Jimmy Wakely's "The Rangers Ride" ('48 Monogram).

Pierce also found time to get involved with the Meals On Wheels program in 1978 and was on their advisory board as its president. Besides being active in the Elks Club, he was very involved in various religious activities. He was a Mason and received several honors from that organization.

Lyden's domestic life was not tranquil. He was once divorced, twice widowed (his last wife was Hazel who accompanied him to many festivals) and his only child, a son, died in 1988.

Pierce last resided on North Olive Street in Orange, California.

One of the most respected Best of the Badmen died at 90 on October 10, 1998, in an Orange County hospice following a six month bout with cancer.

Tributes came in from many of his fellow badmen which were printed in Boyd Magers' WESTERN CLIPPINGS. *Gregg Barton:* "Pierce loved the picture business and was proud of his part in it. Whether it was one or 100 in his audience, he was happy to pass on stories of the good old days. He was very serious about his career and enjoyed being the black hat baddie. In his quiet and sincere way he made you proud to have been a part of it too." *House Peters Jr.:* "I never really got to *know* Pierce until we started going to these festivals. That's when we became much better acquainted. It's strange—sometimes we never saw each other on a set, even though we were on the same picture. Maybe we came in for a day or so…small part…just didn't work the same days. And when we did, sometimes we never saw each other for another year before we got in another picture together. He was one of the steadfast black hat heavies; he sure did a whale of 'em." *Walter Reed:* "He was one of the nicest, most humble gentlemen I ever knew in the business." *John Hart:* "He was a real gentleman. I've known him on and off for nearly 50 years. He worked in the Lone Rangers…he worked for Katzman. I've enjoyed knowing him and sharing memories of working together." *Chris Alcaide:* "He was a nice man—for a bad guy!" *Myron Healey:* "Pierce was one of the most vital, energetic, fantastic men I've ever known. I just pray many of us can equal his mark in longevity." *John Mitchum:* "I first met Pierce when I was working on the serial, 'Perils of the Wilderness'. I was totally a greenhorn as to westerns—riding horses and all of that. Pierce kind of 'fathered' me. He took me aside, told me little things, helped me from going over the side of the mountain and all that kinda thing. He was so gentle and so kind that he's been a dear friend of mine ever since…over 40 years. This is a strangely unique man. He played heavies but has not an evil bone in his body. Basically, there's no way in real life this man could do what he's done on the screen. If you really care about somebody for almost half a century, they have to have something most people don't have. Pierce was one of the true gentlemen of the screen."

Suggested Sampling of Lyden's Western Heavies:

- Undercover Man ('42 U.A.) William Boyd
- Blocked Trail ('43 Republic) 3 Mesquiteers
- False Colors ('43 U.A.) William Boyd
- Canyon City ('43 Republic) Don Barry
- California Joe ('43 Republic) Don Barry
- San Fernando Valley ('44 Republic) Roy Rogers
- Trail to Vengeance ('45 Universal) Kirby Grant
- Cherokee Flash ('45 Republic) Sunset Carson
- Rainbow Over Texas ('45 Republic) Roy Rogers
- Wild Beauty ('46 Universal) Buzz Henry
- Shadows on the Range ('46 Monogram) Johnny Mack Brown
- Bad Men of the Border ('46 Universal) Kirby Grant
- Six Gun Serenade ('47 Monogram) Jimmy Wakely
- Rustlers of Devil's Canyon ('47 Republic) Allan Lane
- Overland Trails ('48 Monogram) Johnny Mack Brown
- Back Trail ('48 Monogram) Johnny Mack Brown
- Rangers Ride ('48 Monogram) Jimmy Wakely
- Silver Trails ('48 Monogram) Jimmy Wakely
- Dead Man's Gold ('48 Western Adventure) Lash La Rue
- Shadows of the West ('49 Monogram) Whip Wilson
- Twilight In the Sierras ('50 Republic) Roy Rogers
- Cody of the Pony Express ('50 Columbia serial) Jock Mahoney
- Covered Wagon Raid ('50 Republic) Allan "Rocky" Lane
- Kid From Texas ('50 Universal International) Audie Murphy
- Roar of the Iron Horse ('51 Columbia serial) Jock Mahoney
- Lawless Cowboys ('51 Monogram) Whip Wilson
- Cisco Kid: Stolen Bonds ('51) Duncan Renaldo
- Wagon Team ('52 Columbia) Gene Autry
- Wild Bill Hickok: Wild White Horse ('52) Guy Madison
- Roy Rogers: The Feud ('52) Roy Rogers
- Hopalong Cassidy: Vanishing Herd ('52) William Boyd
- Range Rider: Cherokee Roundup ('53) Jock Mahoney
- Cowboy G-Men: Rawhide Gold ('53) Russell Hayden
- Roy Rogers: The Run-A-Round ('53) Roy Rogers
- Gene Autry: Outlaw Stage ('53) Gene Autry
- Hopalong Cassidy: Death By Proxy ('53) William Boyd
- Gene Autry: Talking Guns ('54) Gene Autry
- Kit Carson: Renegades of Rejo ('54) Bill Williams
- Gunfighters of the Northwest ('54 Columbia serial) Jock Mahoney
- Riding With Buffalo Bill ('54 Columbia serial) Marshall Reed
- Rin Tin Tin: Iron Horse ('55) Lee Aaker
- Judge Roy Bean: Horse Thief ('56) Edgar Buchanan
- Cisco Kid: Mr. X ('56) Duncan Renaldo
- Wild Bill Hickok: Blind Alley ('56) Guy Madison
- Roy Rogers: His Weight in Wildcats ('56) Roy Rogers
- Perils of the Wilderness ('56 Columbia serial) Dennis Moore
- Blazing the Overland Trail ('56 Columbia serial) Lee Roberts
- Lone Ranger: Slim's Boy ('57) Clayton Moore
- Sgt. Preston: Jailbreaker ('57) Richard Simmons
- 26 Men: Bells of St. Thomas ('58) Kelo Henderson/Tris Coffin

FRANK McCARROLL

Stone-faced rodeo rider, stuntman and henchman (95% of the time uncredited), Frank McCarroll was one of Hollywood's real cowboys.

One of 17 children, he was born Frank Leo McCarroll September 5, 1892, in Minnesota, his father, James William McCarroll, was from Canada and his mother, Anna L. Hartrick, was a Minnesota native.

It's unknown just how McCarroll came to the rodeo world, but he did, and in 1916 and again in 1931 was Champion Steer Wrestler at the Pendleton, Oregon, Round-Up. He also won steer wrestling championships in New York and Chicago rodeos. He was clocked bulldogging a steer in eight seconds.

In 1929, his wife, Bonnie McCarroll, was killed during bucking horse competition. After that, women were forbidden to ride bucking broncs in Pendleton.

By 1934, McCarroll, now 42, was getting a bit old for the rough licks of the rodeo arena and decided to try his hand in Hollywood as a stuntman and actor in westerns.

Over the years he doubled in Dick Foran films, for Fuzzy Knight at Universal, Dub Taylor at Columbia and Monogram, among many others.

He also started doing bit parts, primarily as 4th or 5th henchie through the door in the westerns of Reb Russell, Kermit Maynard, Dick Foran, Tim McCoy, Roy Rogers, Johnny Mack Brown, Hopalong Cassidy, Bill Elliott, Range Busters, Buster Crabbe, Tim Holt, Sunset Carson, Jimmy Wakely, Charles Starrett, Whip Wilson and others.

Another heavy, Pierce Lyden, remembers, "Frank and I mixed it up several times for the camera, but never when I wasn't scared to death, it was that face and build. He was big, heavy and strong enough to break a man in two. But one of the nicest guys you could ever work with. He was a great stuntman, especially in fights."

McCarroll supplemented his movie work income as a painting contractor.

He was married to Lorrie McCarroll when he decided to retire at 60 in 1952 with his last film role being a Cavalryman in "Laramie Mountains", a 1952 Durango Kid.

A little over a year later, March 8, 1954, he suffered a coronary (according to his death certificate) at his home at 623 Whitnall Hwy. in Burbank, California. Tradepaper obits stated his cause of death was due to a fall at his home, however the death certificate disputes this, not mentioning any fall whatsoever.

McCarroll's remains were cremated and are at Forest Lawn Memorial Park.

Some 150 films and several Cisco Kid TV episodes over 18 years testify to McCarroll's popularity and abilities.

Jack Ingram (L) gets the drop on Jimmy Wakely as he tries to rescue tied-up Alan Foster and Claire James. In the middle are Dee Cooper, Frank McCarroll (with rope) and Bob Duncan. "Saddle Serenade" ('45 Monogram).

Suggested Sampling of McCarroll's Western Heavies:

- Blazing Guns ('34 Kent) Reb Russell
- Fighting Through ('34 Kent) Reb Russell
- His Fighting Blood ('35 Ambassador) Kermit Maynard
- Big Calibre ('35 Supreme) Bob Steele
- West of Nevada ('36 Colony) Rex Bell
- Valley of Terror ('37 Ambassador) Kermit Maynard
- Land of Hunted Men ('43 Monogram) Range Busters
- Outlaws of Santa Fe ('44 Republic) Don Barry
- Guns of the Law ('44 PRC) James Newill/Dave O'Brien
- Hidden Valley Outlaws ('44 Republic) Bill Elliott
- Wild Horse Phantom ('44 PRC) Buster Crabbe
- Lonesome Trail ('45 Monogram) Jimmy Wakely
- Lost Trail ('45 Monogram) Johnny Mack Brown
- His Brother's Ghost ('45 PRC) Buster Crabbe
- Heading West ('46 Columbia) Charles Starrett
- Conquest of Cheyenne ('46 Republic) Bill Elliott
- Buckaroo From Powder River ('47 Columbia) Charles Starrett
- Brand of Fear ('49 Monogram) Jimmy Wakely
- West of Wyoming ('50 Monogram) Johnny Mack Brown
- Gunslingers ('50 Monogram) Whip Wilson
- Cisco Kid: Water Rights ('51 Duncan Renaldo

MERRILL McCORMICK

For 37 years, from 1916 to 1953, the lean, angular, usually unshaven Merrill McCormick played henchmen-type heavies in over 215 movies, 98% of them westerns.

William Merrill McCormick was born in Denver, Colorado, February 5, 1892. He had a brief fling on the stage prior to holding up the stage over and over again.

McCormick, about whom virtually nothing is known, usually wore a rather large black hat and dressed in a vest and rumpled, checkered shirt, often torn at the elbows. With his bewhiskered face, it gave him a true outlaw look beginning with his first western, "Hands Off" ('21 Fox) with Tom Mix.

However, one time, in 1923, McCormick elected to write, direct and star in a western—"A Son of the Desert", released by American. It was his only fling at "stardom", although he did write and direct another for American, "Good Men and Bad", but he took the "bad" part in it to the unknown Steve Carries' "good" role.

Although he was in 15 sound (and one silent) serials, his only really prominent role was in "The New Adventures of Tarzan" ('35).

McCormick continued to work in film ("Salome" and "The Robe" both '53) and TV ("Ramar of the Jungle" '53) right up until the time of his death following a heart attack in San Gabriel, California, August 9, 1953.

McCormick was often billed as W. M. McCormick or William Merrill McCormick. His last name is often misspelled in credits as McCormack.

Outlaws Merrill McCormick (L) and Al Ferguson (R) have a falling out "Near the Rainbow's End", a 1930 Bob Steele Tiffany.

Suggested Sampling of McCormick's Western Heavies:

- Red Courage ('21 Universal) Hoot Gibson
- Flashing Steeds ('25 Chesterfield) Bill Patton
- Arizona Nights ('27 FBO) Fred Thomson
- Born to the Saddle ('29 Universal) Ted Wells
- Nevada Buckaroo ('31 Tiffany) Bob Steele
- Border Devils ('32 Artclass) Harry Carey
- Deadwood Pass ('33 Freuler) Tom Tyler
- Range Riders ('34 Superior) Buddy Roosevelt
- Boss Cowboy ('34 Superior) Buddy Roosevelt
- Call of the Coyote ('34 Imperial) Ken Thomson
- Winds of the Wasteland ('36 Republic) John Wayne
- Old Corral ('36 Republic) Gene Autry
- Cheyenne Rides Again ('37 Victory) Tom Tyler
- Ghost Town Riders ('38 Universal) Bob Baker
- Riders of the Frontier ('39 Monogram) Tex Ritter
- Lone Star Pioneers ('39 Columbia) Bill Elliott
- Desert Bandit ('41 Republic) Don Barry
- Below the Border ('42 Monogram) Rough Riders
- Fighting Stallion ('50 Eagle-Lion) Bill Edwards

PHILO McCULLOUGH

Disreputable, smug and smarmy, often with an imposing creepiness to his physique as his evil mind plotted how to steal the gal's ranch or rustle the rancher's herd, Philo McCullough found his best western roles opposite Hoot Gibson and Tom Mix in the '20s. The '30s found him playing heavies primarily in the B's and serials ground out on Poverty Row. Even though his 57 year career on screen lasted until 1969, by the '40s he was reduced to playing uncredited character parts, although the parts were primarily in A films ("Tennessee Johnson" '43; "Life With Father" '47; "Fountainhead" '49; "Stars In My Crown" '50; "Bedtime For Bonzo" '51; "Destry" '54; "Cheyenne Autumn" '64 and his last, "Great Bank Robbery" '69).

Philo McCoullough (original spelling) was born in San Bernardino, California, June 16, 1893. The son of Mary S. McCoullough of Iowa, a non-professional, (his father unknown, but from Texas), he was educated at Los Angeles High School then started his career at a very young age during stage training with the Burbank Stock Company. He entered films in 1912 at 19 with his first credit in 1914, "While Wifey Is Away".

Of his well over 100 silent films, 15 were westerns (five with Hoot Gibson at Universal, four with Tom Mix at Fox and others with Dustin Farnum, Vola Vale and Buck Jones). McCullough enjoyed serials as well—appearing in six silent chapterplays and 11 talkie cliffhangers. He had good roles in "A Dangerous Adventure ('22 WB), "Bar-C Mystery" ('27 Pathe), "Phantom of the West" ('31 Mascot), "Heroes of the West" ('32 Universal), "Jungle Mystery" ('32 Universal) and "Tarzan the Fearless" ('33 Principal).

In the '30s he made over 60 films, 34 of them serials and westerns, mostly for poverty row outfits such as Mascot, Resolute, Grand National, Kent, Reliable, Artclass, Tiffany, Imperial and Empire.

During the '40s he was a contract player at Warner Bros.

McCullough's wife of many years was Laura Anson (1892-1968), a silent actress in several Fatty Arbuckle comedies. Apparently, McCullough remarried as his tradepaper obituaries state he was survived by a wife when he died at his Burbank, California, home June 5, 1981, just short of his 88th birthday.

"Unhand that girl," Ken Maynard tells slimy Philo McCullough as Ruth Hiatt cowers in fear on the "Sunset Trail" ('32 Tiffany).

Suggested Sampling of McCullough's Western Heavies:

- Primal Law ('21 Fox) Dustin Farnum
- Arizona Sweepstakes ('26 Universal) Hoot Gibson
- Bar-C Mystery ('26 Pathe serial) Wallace MacDonald
- Chip of the Flying U ('26 Universal) Hoot Gibson
- Silver Valley ('27 Fox) Tom Mix
- Clearing the Trail ('28 Universal) Hoot Gibson
- Painted Post ('28 Fox) Tom Mix
- Spurs ('30 Universal) Hoot Gibson
- Phantom of the West ('31 Mascot serial) Tom Tyler
- Vanishing Legion ('31 Mascot serial) Harry Carey
- Sunset Trail ('32 Tiffany) Ken Maynard
- South of the Rio Grande ('32 Columbia) Buck Jones
- Heroes of the West ('32 Universal serial) Onslow Stevens
- Wheels of Destiny ('34 Universal) Ken Maynard
- Ridin' Thru ('34 Reliable) Tom Tyler
- Twisted Rails ('35 Imperial) Jack Donovan
- Gunfire ('35 Resolute) Rex Bell
- Gun Smoke ('35 Kent) Buck Coburn
- Renfrew On the Great White Trail ('38 Grand National) James Newill

FRANCIS McDONALD

A veteran of 53 years before motion picture cameras, Francis McDonald made his first appearance in 1912 for a number of short subjects and was last seen as a Russian in Blake Edwards' "The Great Race" in 1965.

McDonald's nearly 300 films and nearly 100 TV episodes are far from all western, although that is primarily all he made from 1951 on when, now 60, he turned to chiefly portraying old-timers, fathers, stablemen, aged Indian Chiefs and the like. A great deal of his work in the '50s was for Gene Autry's Flying A Pictures on "Range Rider", "Gene Autry", "Annie Oakley", etc. Many western moviegoers envision McDonald as a wiry, hard-lined-faced, mustachioed heavy in many silents and at various times in talkies opposite Tom Mix, Bob Steele, Hopalong Cassidy, Richard Dix, Roy Rogers and Allan "Rocky" Lane.

McDonald was born August 22, 1891, in Bowling Green, Kentucky, according to his 1917 WWI Draft Registration card which he himself filled out. At the time he was married. He was the son of non-professionals John Francis McDonald and Catherine Ashlue. 5' 9", 150 lbs, with dark black hair and brown eyes, McDonald was educated at St. Xavier School in Cincinnati.

He started his theatrical career with the Forepaugh Stock Company in Cincinnati, moving to the Pacific Coast after eight months to fill a season's engagement with the Lois Stock Company in Seattle, Washington. This led to three years engagement with the Virginia Brissac Company in San Diego and Honolulu. He followed that up with a season with the American Stock Company in Spokane.

His earliest movies were shorts in 1912 for the Monopole Company. In the early years he also worked at Reliance, Triangle, Imperial and other independents as well as Universal, Fox and First National. McDonald made over 100 silents, even starring in a couple at MGM—"Desert's Toll" ('26) and "Valley of Hell" ('27).

Nearly 40 when sound arrived, McDonald was relegated to supporting roles, with only one starring chance in a cheapie from B. F. Ziedman, "Trailing the Killer", upstaged by canine star Caesar.

As for serials, he made two silents, "Voice On the Wire" ('17 Universal) with Ben Wilson and "The Gray Ghost" ('17 Universal) with Harry Carter. In 1934 Mascot cast him as crooked race car driver Ridpath up against Jack Mulhall in "Burn 'Em Up Barnes". In 1937 he was a member of the outlaw Secret Seven in Johnny Mack Brown's "Wild West Days" at Universal. He was shifty Cajun Batiste in "Mystery of the Riverboat ('44 Universal), then had his top serial role as "leading citizen" outlaw boss in "Zorro's Black Whip" ('44) at Republic.

McDonald was married and divorced three times, first to popular actress Mae Busch in December 1915. They divorced in 1922. His second wife was Bella Roscoe, and his last was Irene Mary Schuck. No children resulted from any of his marriages.

McDonald was an active member of the Masquers since 1925. It was the Masquers who arranged his funeral service and burial when he died, as a resident of the Motion Picture Hospital, of bronchopneumonia resulting from cardiovascular disease on September 18, 1968. The pneumonia resulted when McDonald fell to the floor getting out of bed on September 14 and fractured his first lumbar vertebra. At the time he was living at 1749 N. Sycamore Ave. in Hollywood. He was interred at Valhalla Cemetery.

Once named "Hollywood's Prettiest Man" by a jury of magazine editors, McDonald rebelled, and later stated, "To counteract the publicity, I shaved off my mustache and had my agent book me as a villain. In 1928 I worked in 'Underworld', the first great gangster picture. Through picture after picture I was jailed and strung up. I slugged and was slugged by the best—from Tom Mix on."

Francis McDonald has Hopalong Cassidy in a bad position in "Bar-20" ('43 United Artists).

Suggested Sampling of McDonald's Western Heavies:

- Call of the North ('21 Paramount) Jack Holt
- Trooper O'Neil ('22 Fox) Buck Jones
- Yankee Senor ('26 Fox) Tom Mix
- Outlaws of Red River ('27 Fox) Tom Mix
- In Line of Duty ('31 Monogram) James Murray
- Hidden Valley ('32 Monogram) Bob Steele
- Texas Buddies ('32 World Wide) Bob Steele
- Terror Trail ('33 Universal) Tom Mix
- Wild West Days ('37 Universal serial) Johnny Mack Brown
- Gun Law ('38 RKO) George O'Brien
- Range War ('39 Paramount) William Boyd
- Carson City Kid ('40 Republic) Roy Rogers
- Men of the Timberland ('41 Universal) Richard Arlen
- The Kansan ('43 U.A.) Richard Dix
- Bar 20 ('43 U.A.) William Boyd
- Lumberjack ('44 U.A.) William Boyd
- Zorro's Black Whip ('44 Republic serial) Linda Stirling
- South of the Rio Grande ('45 Monogram) Duncan Renaldo
- Roll On Texas Moon ('46 Republic) Roy Rogers
- Devil's Playground ('46 U.A.) William Boyd
- Dead Don't Dream ('48 U.A.) William Boyd
- Rim of the Canyon ('49 Columbia) Gene Autry
- Powder River Rustlers ('49 Republic) Allan "Rocky" Lane
- Lone Ranger: Finders Keepers ('49) Clayton Moore
- Kit Carson: Counterfeit Country ('54) Bill Williams
- Kit Carson: Powder Depot ('54) Bill Williams
- Lone Ranger: Courage of Tonto ('57) Clayton Moore
- Trackdown: Day of Vengeance ('58) Robert Culp

IAN MacDONALD

In the minds of western devotees, Ian MacDonald will always be thought of as Frank Miller, the fierce killer set to arrive in Hadleyville at high noon and take revenge on newly-wed sheriff Gary Cooper in Fred Zinnemann's superbly directed, masterfully constructed "High Noon" ('52 Columbia).

Born Ulva William Pippy, June 28, 1914, in Great Falls, Montana, his father, William Pippy, was a Methodist minister. His mother was Sara Ann MacDonald—obviously the source for part of his professional name change.

During his school years he was athletic, playing high school football and basketball, yet still expressing an early interest in drama.

After graduating from a small parochial college in Helena, Montana, where he served as president of the drama club, Ian worked at various jobs: clerk in a bank, on a highway construction gang and school teacher in an authentic ghost town where he was superintendent, repairman, and taught all high school classes. Coming to California, he studied at the Pasadena Playhouse.

Ian entered films as a heavy in a pair of Hopalong Cassidys, "Secrets of the Wasteland" and "Stick To Your Guns" (both '41 Paramount).

MacDonald struggled along in small, often uncredited roles for the next several years. By the late '40s, better parts had begun to come his way, eventually cinching a career by beating out Royal Dano, Peter Mamakos, G. Pat Collins and Bob Wilke for the choice role of Frank Miller in "High Noon". (Wilke ended up as one of his henchmen along with Sheb Wooley and Lee Van Cleef.)

MacDonald is credited with serving in the Armed Forces during WWII, explaining the gap in his film credits from mid '42 through 1946.

By the mid '50s Parkinson's disease began to have an effect on MacDonald. It is noticeable by the ever increasing non-use of his right arm in films of this period. It's often quite interesting to see how he "protects" this weak arm in various scenes.

It is obviously for medical reasons MacDonald began to hone his behind the camera skills in 1955. He was writer/producer and actor in "The Silver Star" ('55 Lippert) with Earle Lyon; writer, associate producer and actor for "Lonesome Trail" ('55 Lippert) with John Agar and associate producer and actor for "Two Gun Lady" ('56 Associated) with Peggie Castle as well as "Stagecoach to Fury" ('56 Regal/20th Century Fox) with Forrest Tucker.

MacDonald continued to work until 1959 when he and his wife, Shirley Kannegaard Pippy, returned to their Montana roots. They were living at 1103 N. Cedarview in Bozeman, Montana, when one of the screen's ultimate badmen died April 11, 1978, of cardiac arrest and the late stages of Parkinson's disease. He is buried at Wilsall Cemetery in Wilsall, Montana.

Rex Allen isn't concerned about Ian MacDonald's warnings in "Thunder in God's Country" ('51 Republic).

Suggested Sampling of MacDonald's Western Heavies:

- Stick to Your Guns ('41 Paramount) William Boyd
- Lone Ranger: Stage to Estacado ('49) Clayton Moore
- Colt .45 ('50 Warner Bros.) Randolph Scott
- Comanche Territory ('50 Universal) Macdonald Carey
- Thunder In God's Country ('51 Republic) Rex Allen
- Texas Rangers ('51 Columbia) George Montgomery
- High Noon ('52 United Artists) Gary Cooper
- Toughest Man In Arizona ('52 Republic) Vaughn Monroe
- Taza, Son of Cochise ('54 Universal) Rock Hudson
- Johnny Guitar ('54 Republic) Sterling Hayden
- Two Gun Lady ('56 Associated) Peggie Castle
- Zane Grey Theatre: Stage For Tucson ('56) Eddie Albert

KENNETH MacDONALD

Smooth, dapper, thin-mustached Kenneth MacDonald dates his acting career back to 1909 when he was a child actor at eight on the legitimate stage.

Born Kenneth Royce Dollins September 8, 1901, in Portland, Indiana, where his father was an auctioneer and his mother was a teacher. He grew up in Richmond, Indiana, where he earned seven letters at Richmond High School as a member of its football, basketball and track squads. He was the first president of the Richmond Athletic Association. His last appearance in Richmond was in 1970 when he returned for the 50th anniversary of his high school graduating class.

He discovered the name MacDonald in his family background and changed his name accordingly (making it legal in 1930). Possessed of a fine singing voice, he often performed solos at various churches in the area. Upon graduation, his interest turned to acting and music.

MacDonald went on the stage in the early '20s, appearing in some 3,000 performances before American and Canadian audiences. Finding entrance into films tough, he wrote and published a pamphlet, "The Case for Kenneth MacDonald". This self promoting booklet was distributed to all the studios and finally landed him a part in "Slow as Lightning" in '23 followed by "What Love Will Do", "Dynamite Dan", "Yankee Speed", "After A Million" and others including a series of two reelers (co-starring Milburn Morante) under the "Fortune Hunter" designation. His last silent was "Little Buckaroo" with Buzz Barton. In 1931 Kenneth claimed a small role in Jack Holt's "Dirigible". By the mid '30s on into the '40s, MacDonald was the suave crook with black manicured mustache menacing western stars Charles Starrett and Bill Elliott at Columbia.

Serials were a big part of MacDonald's work in the late '30s and '40s as he menaced Robert Stevens in "Perils of the Royal Mounted" ('42 Columbia), Bill Elliott in "Valley of Vanishing Men" ('42 Columbia), Tom Tyler in "The Phantom" (43 Columbia), Gilbert Roland in "The Desert Hawk" ('44 Columbia) and Robert Scott in "Black Arrow" ('44 Columbia). He also had roles in Columbia's "Mandrake the Magician" ('39), "Overland With Kit Carson" ('39) and "Monster and the Ape" ('45). After an 11 year serial hiatus, MacDonald returned to the genre for Columbia's next to last, "Perils of the Wilderness" ('56), matching some of his stock from "Perils of the Royal Mounted".

According to another veteran heavy, Pierce Lyden, MacDonald refused to do fights or stunts saying, "Make them double you. They'll have respect for you then as an actor." Pierce said Mac always carried a VIP attaché case. "It attracts attention. People ask questions. They notice you." Pierce remembered Mac always wanted to be a director for stage or movies but never attained that goal, "He was an intelligent, serious-minded actor, though."

Maturing by the mid '40s on into the '50s, MacDonald became more of a character player, turning up as cops, doctors, military officers and as quite a few sheriffs in westerns with Tim Holt, Allan "Rocky" Lane and on TVers like "The Lone Ranger", "Cowboy G-Men", "Annie Oakley", "Stories of the Century", "Cheyenne", "Wanted Dead or Alive". He had a recurring role for a while on Warner Bros.' "Colt .45" as Colonel Parker.

Saloon boss Kenneth MacDonald temporarily restrains his henchmen, Roy Barcroft (L) and Ed Cobb (center) from preaching "Six Gun Gospel" to Johnny Mack Brown ('43 Monogram).

MacDonald gained great notoriety in the late '40s and early '50s as a comic foil in several Three Stooges Columbia shorts including westerns like "Shot In the Frontier" ('54) and "Punchy Cowpunchers" ('50).

It was his work with the Stooges that landed him the recurring role as a Superior Court judge for 32 appearances on TV's popular "Perry Mason" ('57-'66). It seems Sam White, whose brother Jules was in charge of many of the Three Stooges comedies, was a member of the Mason Production team. Sam remembered MacDonald and suggested him for the role of the judge.

MacDonald's last role is an uncredited bit in "Which Way To the Front" ('70).

He was married to La Mee Nave MacDonald. His parents were John Wesley Dollins of Kentucky and Mary Tate of Indiana.

MacDonald died at 70 of a brain tumor and a tumor in his left lung at the Motion Picture Country Hospital in Woodland Hills, California, on May 5, 1972. At the time of his death the MacDonalds were living on North Griffith Park Drive in Burbank. The suave badman is buried at Forest Lawn Memorial Park, Hollywood Hills, California.

Suggested Sampling of MacDonald's Western Heavies:

- Border Vengeance ('35 Kent) Reb Russell
- Spoilers of the Range ('39 Columbia) Charles Starrett
- Outpost of the Mounties ('39 Columbia) Charles Starrett
- Taming of the West ('39 Columbia) Bill Elliott
- Bullets For Rustlers ('40 Columbia) Charles Starrett
- Texas Stagecoach ('40 Columbia) Charles Starrett
- Wildcat of Tucson ('40 Columbia) Bill Elliott
- Frontier Vengeance ('40 Republic) Don Barry
- Durango Kid ('40 Columbia) Charles Starrett
- Son of Davy Crockett ('41 Columbia) Bill Elliott
- Prairie Pioneers ('41 Republic) Three Mesquiteers
- Perils of the Royal Mounted ('42 Columbia serial) Robert Stevens
- Valley of Vanishing Men ('42 Columbia serial) Bill Elliott
- Six Gun Gospel ('43 Monogram) Johnny Mack Brown
- Pride of the Plains ('44 Republic) Bob Livingston
- Black Arrow ('44 Columbia serial) Robert Scott
- Lost Trail ('45 Monogram) Johnny Mack Brown
- That Texas Jamboree ('46 Columbia) Ken Curtis
- False Paradise ('48 United Artists) Hopalong Cassidy
- Kit Carson: Range Master ('51) Bill Williams
- Kit Carson: Roaring Challenge ('52) Bill Williams
- Cisco Kid: Trouble in Tonopah ('54) Duncan Renaldo
- Cisco Kid: Vendetta ('55) Duncan Renaldo
- Cisco Kid: Doorway to Nowhere ('55) Duncan Renaldo
- Rough Riders: Wilderness Trace ('59) Jan Merlin/Kent Taylor

J. P. McGOWAN

Certainly J. P. McGowan deserves the title of film pioneer, coming to the fledgling industry in 1909. Certainly he deserves the title jack of all trades as he was an editor, writer, producer, director and actor. Problem is, he was master of none, perhaps doing his best work as an actor.

John Patterson McGowan was born February 24, 1880, in Terowie, Australia. He left his homeland as part of the Australian Army to serve in South Africa during the Boer War. He later made his way around the world, embarking on a successful career on the legitimate stage, performing with such stars as William Faversham.

McGowan first came to America in 1904 as a stage actor at the St. Louis world fair.

He was hired by police departments to train their horses, then tried ranching in Texas and traveled throughout Mexico for a year. He joined Robert Mantell's Traveling Show and by 1909 he was working for Kalem, the pioneer motion picture company. As a director of silent films, he was responsible for over 125 features and serials, including two with his serial queen wife Helen Holmes whom he married in 1912. (They later divorced.) As a silent screen actor he appeared in over 100 features and serials, many of which he also directed and starred in such as "Ruse of the Rattlesnake" ('12 Playgoers). He also wrote screenplays during this period.

When sound came in, McGowan found his demand in decline with only poverty row studios providing work for him. He cranked out low-budget dreck at an alarming rate, with little concern for quality. His workaholic disposition led him to no budget independents like Empire, Kent, Syndicate, Big 4, Freuler and Ambassador. At these "studios" there was simply no budget for his ambitious attitude, so much of his directorial work with Tom Tyler, Bob Custer, Buzz Barton, Lane Chandler and Bob Steele is hurried and crudely fashioned. Sometimes writer/actor/director/editor Jack of all trades on the same picture, he often tried to do too much and is brought down by the lack of budget and his own inadequacies. McGowan's pictures as a director are often filled with mismatched shots, odd reaction takes, stilted dialogue that doesn't seem to relate and other shortcomings such as the terribly unfunny padding of Ben Corbett "humor" in "Lone Bandit" ('35 Empire) with Lane Chandler. In Chandler's final slugfest with Slim Whitaker you can even hear director McGowan say "Cut" after one particular knockdown.

As a director, his one talkie serial was "Hurricane Express" starring John Wayne, co-directed with Armand (Mandy) Schaefer. He retired from directing in '38 after Jack Randall's "Where the West Begins" for Monogram.

As an actor in talkies, he played small parts in many

of the lowbudgeters he directed…outlaws, sheriffs, fathers. It was the same in films directed by others, he even played Hopalong Cassidy's boss Buck Peters in "Bar 20 Rides Again" ('35 Paramount).

Giving up directing in '38, he continued to act for another year or so ("Great Adventures of Wild Bill Hickok" '38 Columbia serial, John Ford's "Stagecoach" '39) then retired to serve as executive secretary of the Screen Director's Guild from '39-'50. Director William Witney wrote, "When the Depression hit the country in the late '20s, Mack became an actor to keep body and soul together. We had worked together a few times; he was a wonderful, smart gentleman. I still think without Mack's and Frank Capra's dedication to the Guild during the first stormy years the Guild might not have survived." He also served as the group's press representative up until the time of his death at his home on March 26, 1952, at age 72. He was survived by his wife (name unknown) so obviously he'd remarried after his divorce from Helen Holmes.

Sheriff Gene Autry corrals "Guns and Guitars" schemers J. P. McGowan (L) and Tom London (center) ('36 Republic).

Suggested Sampling of McGowan's Western Heavies:

- Senor Daredevil ('26 First National) Ken Maynard
- Gun Gospel ('27 First National) Ken Maynard
- Arizona Days ('28 Syndicate) Bob Custer
- Bad Men's Money ('29 Bell) Yakima Canutt
- Lawless Valley ('32 Kent) Lane Chandler
- Deadwood Pass ('33 Freuler/Monarch) Tom Tyler
- Somewhere In Sonora ('33 Warner Bros.) John Wayne
- Fighting Hero ('34 Reliable) Tom Tyler
- Secret Patrol ('36 Columbia) Charles Starrett
- Three Mesquiteers ('36 Republic) 3 Mesquiteers
- Guns and Guitars ('36 Republic) Gene Autry
- Hit the Saddle ('37 Republic) 3 Mesquiteers
- Heart of the Rockies ('37 Republic) 3 Mesquiteers

JOE McGUINN

From a stand-in at Fox for John Boles and Gilbert Roland to a hefty career playing dozens of heavies (and not a few Sheriffs), ruggedly handsome Joe McGuinn had a good 28 year run in westerns beginning with Charles Starrett's "Two Gun Law" (Columbia '37) on through a TV episode of "Legend of Jesse James" in 1965.

Joseph Ford McGuinn was born in Brooklyn, New York, January 21, 1904. Educated at Clason Point Military Academy in New York, he later graduated from Villanova University in Pennsylvania. He worked in a law office as a title searcher and oil lease purchaser, then had a brief fling on Broadway before coming to Hollywood circa 1930.

The athletic McGuinn was "discovered" by a Fox talent scout while playing handball at the Hollywood YMCA. He spent his early years learning the business as a stand-in and stuntman at Fox for John Boles ("Wild Gold" '34; "Orchids To You" '35) and Gilbert Roland ("Mystery Woman" '35).

His A-film career stymied in the late '30s, except for a bit in the classic "Gunga Din" ('39 RKO), McGuinn put his athletic prowess to work in westerns and serials as of 1937. His eight serial roles, all at Republic and Columbia, usually casting him simply as a thug or henchman, include "Great Adventures of Wild Bill Hickok" ('38), 'Zorro's Fighting Legion" ('39), "Daredevils of the Red Circle" ('39), "Dick Tracy's G-Men" ('39), "Mysterious Dr. Satan" ('40), "Spider Returns" ('41) and his biggest serial role as Crimp Evans in "Holt of the Secret Service" ('41).

Joe told authors Arthur F. McClure and Ken D. Jones for their HEROES, HEAVIES AND SAGEBRUSH ('72), "I liked to work and enjoyed it all." And work he did, but ofttimes uncredited and seldom rising above the rank of henchman in westerns with George O'Brien, Gene Autry, Bill Elliott, Don Barry, George Montgomery and others, as well as bits in A-films such as "Meet John Doe" ('41), "Talk of the Town" ('42), "Glass Key" ('42) and "Jailhouse Rock" ('57). Perhaps his best role is as the store-owning big boss opposing Bob Steele in "Billy the Kid Outlawed" ('40 PRC).

Notably there is a five year gap in McGuinn's film career (mid '45-'50) with no film credits. Unfortunately, it is unknown what he was doing during that time.

As big screen westerns became fewer, Joe turned to TV appearing on "Gene Autry", "Wagon Train", "Wichita Town", "Texan" and others.

A charter member of the Screen Actors Guild and a member of AFTRA, Joe died of a heart attack at 67, September 22, 1971, following surgery a week earlier. He was survived by his wife, Alice, a brother, sister and a stepson (Edward N. Patton). (Sometimes credited as Joseph F. McGuinni or Joe McQuinn.)

There's "Prairie Gunsmoke" when Tex Ritter meets range rats Tris Coffin (L) and Joe McGuinn ('42 Columbia).

Suggested Sampling of McGuinn's Western Heavies:

- Marshal of Mesa City ('39 RKO)—George O'Brien
- Billy the Kid Outlawed ('40 PRC)—Bob Steele
- Ride, Tenderfoot, Ride ('40 Republic) Gene Autry
- Pioneers of the West ('40 Republic) 3 Mesquiteers
- Roaring Frontiers ('41 Columbia)—Bill Elliott/Tex Ritter
- Prairie Gunsmoke ('42 Columbia)—Bill Elliott/Tex Ritter
- Bullets For Bandits ('42 Columbia)—Bill Elliott/Tex Ritter
- Cyclone Kid ('42 Republic)—Don Barry
- Saddles and Sagebrush ('43 Columbia)—Russell Hayden
- Cherokee Flash ('45 Republic)—Sunset Carson

BARTON MacLANE

One of the screen's best heavies, Barton MacLane was at his vilest in "Relentless", a vastly overlooked 1948 western chase drama with Robert Young from Columbia.

MacLane was a staple in films from the '30s to the '60s, always a tough guy, usually bad, but sometimes good such as when he teamed with feisty newspaper reporter Glenda Farrell as hard-bitten detective Steve McBride in Warner Bros.' Torchy Blane series ('37-'39).

MacLane was tall and stocky with a square, rugged face. He had mean-looking, menacing eyes and a hard, raspy voice.

"I don't think it's my face—at least I don't think I look like a heel," MacLane chortled. "I suppose the real reason I was originally cast as a villain is because I'm a big man. You'll notice villains are usually brawny, a fact which explains the slang term the heavy."

Born in Columbia, South Carolina, on Christmas Day 1902, his parents (Waldon MacLane, Caroline O'Brien) were both from South Carolina. Growing up in the South, he attended Wesleyan University where he was a football and basketball star. After being observed in a football game, he was asked to audition for the 1926 Richard Dix film, "The Quarterback".

Bitten by the acting bug, MacLane enlisted at the American Academy of Dramatic Arts in New York as well as attending a community theatre in Brooklyn. He soon debuted on Broadway in such plays as "Subway Express", "Trial of Mary Dugan", "Steel", "The Tree" and even put his talent for writing to work for the drama "Rendezvous" in which he starred.

By 1929 he was back in Hollywood where he worked steadily in some 150 films and dozens of TV shows until 1968.

MacLane was twice married, first to a Martha Stewart. This union produced a son, William, and a daughter, Marlane. He next wed actress Charlotte Wynters.

At one time MacLane owned a 2,000 acre cattle ranch in Madera, California.

MacLane died January 1, 1969, at 66 at a Santa Monica, California, hospital of intracranial hemorrhage, cardio-vascular disease and pneumonia—not cancer as often reported. He is buried at Valhalla Cemetery in North Hollywood.

Besides his numerous western roles, MacLane was often seen in gangster films such as "Bullets or Ballots" ('36), "Mutiny In the Big House" ('39), "High Sierra" ('41), "Maltese Falcon" ('41) and "San Quentin" ('46). Most, but not all, of his westerns came late in his career—from '46 on.

For TV, MacLane turned good guy as head U.S. Marshal Frank Caine on the first season of NBC's "The Outlaws" ('60). Co-star Don Collier told us, "MacLane was great. I'd been an admirer of his for years when I was a youngster in the '30s and he was a heavy at Warner Bros. What a treat to work with a guy like that!"

Suggested Sampling of MacLane's Western Heavies:

- Thundering Herd ('33 Paramount) Randolph Scott
- Melody Ranch ('40 Republic) Gene Autry
- Western Union ('41 20th Century Fox) Randolph Scott
- Song of Texas ('43 Republic) Roy Rogers
- Santa Fe Uprising ('46 Republic) Allan Lane
- Cheyenne (Wyoming Kid) ('47 Warner Bros.) Dennis Morgan
- Dude Goes West ('48 Allied Artists) Eddie Albert
- Relentless ('48 Columbia) Robert Young
- Bandit Queen ('50 Lippert) Barbara Britton
- Kansas Pacific ('53 Allied Artists) Sterling Hayden
- Cow Country ('53 Allied Artists) Edmond O'Brien
- Jack Slade ('53 Allied Artists) Mark Stevens
- Last of the Desperadoes ('55 Allied Artists) James Craig
- Cheyenne: Storm Riders ('55) Clint Walker
- Silver Star ('55 Lippert) Earle Lyon
- Gunfighters of Abilene ('60 United Artists) Buster Crabbe
- Noose For a Gunman ('60 United Artists) Jim Davis
- Laramie: Street of Hate ('60) John Smith
- Elfego Baca: Friendly Enemies at Law ('60) Robert Loggia
- Overland Trail: Lawyer in Petticoats ('60) Doug McClure
- Laramie: High Country ('62) John Smith
- Arizona Bushwhackers ('68 Paramount) Howard Keel

GEORGE MACREADY

If he'd made only his four well-remembered westerns with Randolph Scott and nothing else, George Macready would be respected and highly regarded in the annals of great screen villains. But you can add to that over 20 other TV and film heavies to which he brought his aristocratic arrogance coupled with disdainful meanness. And that distinctive scar on his right cheek, which resulted from a road accident, didn't harm his evilness either. "At heart," claimed Macready, "I'm really a harmless and calm person."

Though specializing in playing hissable heavies, the tall, slender 6' 1" blond, blue-eyed George Peabody Macready was actually a cultured and expert art collector, as was his good friend Vincent Price with whom Macready was partners in a Los Angeles art gallery.

Born August 29, 1899, in Providence, Rhode Island, he claimed (probably correctly) to be a descendant of the great 19th century Shakespearean actor William Charles Macready. George's parents were George Peabody and Grace Clark, both of Rhode Island, which begs the question was Peabody his true surname? Where then does William Macready fit into the name equation?

Whatever the true heritage, George acquired an Ivy League education by attending Brown University studying Greek and mathematics.

His first job was as a reporter in the early '20s for the New York DAILY NEWS. He later studied at the Boleslawski Theatre in New York and pursued a career on the legitimate stage, commencing with the Jesse Bonstell Theatre in Detroit, Michigan. He made it to Broadway with appearances in plays such as "The Barretts of Wimpole Street" and "Romeo and Juliet". Making a name for himself in "Victoria Regina" in 1937 with Vincent Price and Helen Hayes, his next stop was Hollywood in 1942 under contract to Columbia for "Commandos Strike at Dawn". Macready remained at Columbia for four years during which time he essayed scheming prime ministers, haughty politicians and—the scheming Professor Ernst in "The Monster and the Ape" serial ('45).

It was 1948 before he came to westerns, but who can forget his portrayal in "Coroner Creek" of renegade Younger Miles who led a band of Indians in a stagecoach raid in which Randolph Scott's fiancée is killed. By the time Scott's long trail reaches Macready he is now a greedy freight line owner who readily abuses his wife. He's ripe for killing—as he was for the next 15 years in film and on TV.

In addition to westerns he was memorable in "I Love A Mystery" as Jefferson Monk, "My Name Is Julia Ross", "The Big Clock" as Charles Laughton's toady, "Gilda" as Rita Hayworth's despicable husband and "Paths of Glory" as a cold-blooded French general. He was also among the regular cast of TV's "Peyton Place" ('65-'68).

Once married to actress Elizabeth Dana, they divorced in '42, but the marriage lasted long enough to produce a son and two daughters, including minor producer Michael Macready who featured his father in Macready's last film in '71, "Return of Count Yorga".

One of the classic screen heavies died at 73 July 2, 1973, of heart-failure while at the University of California Hospital in L.A. where he'd been a patient for two days.

His remains were donated to the U.C.L.A. Hospital Pathology Department for medical research.

Suggested Sampling of Macready's Western Heavies:

- Coroner Creek ('48 Columbia) Randolph Scott
- Doolins of Oklahoma ('49 Columbia) Randolph Scott
- The Nevadan ('50 Columbia) Randolph Scott
- Stranger Wore a Gun ('53 Columbia) Randolph Scott
- Thunder Over Arizona ('56 Republic) Skip Homeier
- Rifleman: Eight Hours to Die ('58) Chuck Connors
- Gunsmoke: Lynching Man ('58) James Arness
- Wanted Dead Or Alive: Rawhide Breed ('58) Steve McQueen
- Texan: A Time of Year ('58) Rory Calhoun
- Rough Riders: Last Rebel ('58) Jan Merlin
- Bonanza: A Rose For Lotta ('59) Michael Landon
- Rebel: Vicious Circle ('59) Nick Adams
- Tall Man: Counterfeit Law ('60) Barry Sullivan
- Laramie: Handful of Fire ('61) John Smith
- Dakotas: Mutiny at Ft. Mercy ('63) Chad Everett

RORY MALLINSON

Rory Mallinson's stiff, reserved, unexciting acting style usually relegated him to lesser roles, especially sheriffs, and even though a latecomer, he did manage to play a few lead heavies during Republic's latter days and on early juvenile TV westerns.

Charles Joseph Mallinson (often spelled Mallison) was born in Atlanta, Georgia, October 27, 1913 (not 1903 as sometimes reported). His parents were Charles A. Mallinson from England and Mary Hayes, a Georgia native.

Although he would have preferred to be an actor, Mallinson had a new wife to support so he started life working at a railroad express agency in Atlanta. In his free time he appeared in local plays, only leaving his secretarial job when he got a part in a minstrel show. He trouped with the show winding up in Miami where he found work as a master of ceremonies in a night club.

Never giving up his acting ambitions, Mallinson moved to Los Angeles, taking a job at Douglas Aircraft in order to attend dramatic school by night. His director there arranged a screen test for him at Warner Bros. who put him under contract in 1944. WWII service interrupted his blossoming career, but he restarted it in 1947.

Unfortunately, no other information is known about his life. Divorced from two wives, Eileen McNulty and Helen Mallinson, he was living alone on North Vine St. in Los Angeles when he died of a heart attack at Los Angeles' Fox Hills Hospital March 26, 1976. He is apparently buried in Atlanta, Georgia. His last film work was in 1963.

Suggested Sampling of Mallinson's Western Heavies:

- Frontier Days ('45 Warner Bros.) Robert Shayne
- Denver Kid ('48 Republic) Allan "Rocky" Lane
- Last of the Wild Horses ('48 Lippert) James Ellison
- Prince of the Plains ('49 Republic) Monte Hale
- Wild Bill Hickok: Indian Pony Express ('51) Guy Madison
- Three Desperate Men ('51 Lippert) Preston Foster
- Laramie Mountains ('52 Columbia) Charles Starrett
- Kit Carson: Curse of the Albas ('52) Bill Williams
- Roy Rogers: Death Medicine ('52) Roy Rogers
- Montana Belle ('52 Republic) Jane Russell
- Jesse James Vs. the Daltons ('54 Columbia) Brett King
- Gene Autry: Holdup ('54) Gene Autry
- Cisco Kid: Stolen River ('55) Duncan Renaldo
- Roy Rogers: Violence in Paradise Valley ('55) Roy Rogers

TED MAPES

Stuntman Ted (Tyler) Mapes worked in the halcyon days of Hollywood when film-making was fun and adventurous. Ted was born in St. Edward, Nebraska, November 25, 1901, and grew up on his father's wheat farm where they also ran a small herd of 75 to 100 head of cattle. Eventually, the 6' plus Ted decided there must be more than wheat farming for a strapping young man.

In his 20s, he headed west to California to seek his fame and fortune. He worked as a truck driver for the Signal Hills Oil Fields in Long Beach. Then at 28, driving a moving van for a Los Angeles storage company, he was assigned to move actor John Barrymore's baggage and equipment off the Goldwyn lot. While on the lot Ted discovered the grips were making twice what his salary was as a driver so, within six months, Ted was hired on as a grip, his first film being "Taming of the Shrew" in '29.

Stuntman/badman Ted Mapes tussles with Wild Bill Elliott in "Topeka" ('53 Allied Artists).

In later interviews Ted stated he was the head grip on Tom Mix's last film, "Miracle Rider" ('35 Mascot serial), and the head grip on Gene Autry's serial, "Phantom Empire" ('35 Mascot) and Gene's first B-western, "Tumbling Tumbleweeds" ('35 Republic).

Ted's first screen role was as a Mountie in Stage and Screen's "Silent Code" in '35 with Kane Richmond, on which Ted also did stuntwork.

It was director Joe Kane who first saw the possibilities in Ted as far as a career in front of the camera. Armed with some footage Kane had shot of the virile Mapes, it was suggested he try his luck over at Columbia as a possible new western star. Timing was bad as the studio had just signed Charles Starrett. The studio asked Ted to start doubling for Starrett, thus began his stunt career. Ted doubled for Starrett for over 10 years besides picking up some nice featured roles along the way. Also at Columbia, he worked in Russell Hayden and Bill Elliott features. During this period Ted can also be spotted in many Range Busters B's at Monogram.

Teaming up with ace director William Witney and others at Republic in '37, Ted also worked at that valley studio in a whole slew of their serials including "Hawk of the Wilderness", "Daredevils of the Red Circle", (stunt double for Herman Brix in both), "Lone Ranger Rides Again", "Dick Tracy's G-Men", "Zorro's Fighting Legion", "King of the Royal Mounted", "Adventures of Capt. Marvel", "Phantom Rider", "Daughter of Don Q", "Son of Zorro", "Black Widow" and others as well as western features with Gene Autry, 3 Mesquiteers, Roy Rogers, Bill Elliott, Monte Hale, Rod Cameron and Allan "Rocky" Lane. Mapes managed to work in Columbia serials such as "Iron Claw", "Monster and the Ape", "Valley of Vanishing Men", "The Vigilante", etc. as well.

In 1938, Ted was tested for one of the leads in "The Lone Ranger" serial and in 1940 he was seriously considered for the lead in Republic's "Red Ryder" serial but studio boss Herbert J. Yates oddly went with the shorter Don Barry. A tough break for Mapes as it meant stardom for Barry and back to the rigors of stunts for Ted.

Ted also has the distinction of being in Wayne Morris' "Two Guns and A Badge", considered by many the last B-western series film.

Ted started a 17 picture stunt association with Gary Cooper on "For Whom the Bell Tolls" that only ended with Cooper's death in '61.

In 1950, Ted began a stint with another giant of the screen, James Stewart. Director Delmar Daves asked Ted to come to Sedona, AZ, to double for Stewart on "Broken Arrow". Mapes went on to work with Stewart on over 30 films.

After hundreds of films and thousands of stunts, Mapes called it a day in '69 after Stewart's "Firecreek" and "Bandolero".

However, he was not done with the film industry for he now started another career, monitoring animal action on film sets for the American Humane Association.

Mapes enjoyed his 40 year career in films and stated he loved working for Bill Witney and Joe Kane the best and liked doing fights with Johnny Mack Brown more than any other actor. Johnny was "just super", he said. Mapes is in "Law Men", "Partners of the Trail", "Flame of the West", "Frontier Feud" and others with Johnny Mack.

Mapes was married to Ruth Ensign on October 12, 1931. James Stewart inducted Ted into the Stuntman's Hall of Fame in 1978, Ted died Sept. 9, 1984, at 82, in Burbank, California, after a long illness. His stunt and badman legacy lives on for all of us to witness in countless films and TV shows.

Suggested Sampling of Mapes' Western Heavies:

- Thunder River Feud ('42 Monogram) Range Busters
- Texas Trouble Shooters ('42 Monogram) Range Busters
- Vengeance of the West ('42 Columbia) Bill Elliott/Tex Ritter
- Pardon My Gun ('42 Columbia) Charles Starrett
- Land of Hunted Men ('43 Monogram) Range Busters
- Dead or Alive ('44 PRC) Tex Ritter/Dave O'Brien
- Black Arrow ('44 Columbia serial) Robert Scott
- Law Men ('44 Monogram) Johnny Mack Brown
- Last Horseman ('44 Columbia) Russell Hayden
- Rustlers of the Badlands ('45 Columbia) Charles Starrett/Russell Hayden
- Texas Panhandle ('45 Columbia) Charles Starrett
- Two Fisted Stranger ('46 Columbia) Charles Starrett
- Terror Trail ('46 Columbia) Charles Starrett
- Stranger From Ponca City ('47 Columbia) Charles Starrett
- Riders of the Lone Star ('47 Columbia) Charles Starrett
- El Dorado Pass ('48 Columbia) Charles Starrett
- Hopalong Cassidy: Black Sheep ('52) William Boyd
- Kit Carson: Roaring Challenge ('52) Bill Williams
- Cisco Kid: Jewelry Holdup ('52) Duncan Renaldo
- Hopalong Cassidy: Ghost Trails ('52) William Boyd
- Cisco Kid: Canyon City Kid ('52) Duncan Renaldo

LEE MARVIN

Rugged, rough-hewn and prematurely gray-haired, Lee Marvin was 27 years old when he made his first movie, "You're In the Navy Now" ('51 20th Century Fox) and 40 when he first starred in a film, "The Killers" ('64 Universal). Previously, Marvin had starred on TV's "M-Squad" for 37 episodes in '57-'58.

After "The Killers", Marvin's popularity in Hollywood suddenly exploded and he, surprised as anyone, found himself an Academy Award recipient for 1965's "Cat Ballou" for his dual role as drunken Kid Shelleen and his evil, black-clad, silver-nosed brother. Accepting, Marvin said, "I think half of this belongs to a horse somewhere out in the Valley."

From there, a succession of hit films ("Dirty Dozen", "Monte Walsh", "Professionals", etc.) kept Marvin at the top of the boxoffice, but an equal succession of failures in the '70s diminished Marvin's status.

But on his way to stardom, his vicious demeanor was expertly exploited in a host of badman roles in westerns.

Born February 19, 1924, in New York City to advertising exec Lamont Marvin and his wife Courtenay, a fashion writer, the young Marvin was thrown out of dozens of schools for incorrigibility. His parents took him to Florida where he attended St. Leo's Preparatory School near Dade City, but he was dismissed there as well.

Marvin enlisted in the Marines at the beginning of WWII. Severely wounded at Iwo Jima, he earned the Navy Cross. Pvt. Marvin was invalided with a severed sciatic nerve and discharged.

Finding work in Woodstock, New York, as a plumber's apprentice, he was asked to replace an ailing actor in a rehearsal while he was repairing a toilet at a local community theatre. Caught up with the acting bug, he went to New York City where he studied and found small roles in stock and off-Broadway. He made his Broadway debut in "Billy Budd" in 1951.

Quickly moving to Hollywood, he found work on TV in "Dragnet", "Biff Baker, U.S.A." and in films, including his first western, "Duel at Silver Creek" ('52) with Audie Murphy.

Marvin was first married to Betty Ebeling in February 1951. They had four children, Christopher born 1952, Courtenay born 1954, Cynthia born 1956 and Claudia born 1958. The couple divorced in 1967.

In 1979 he was dragged into court by his "companion" Michele Triola in the now infamous "palimony" suit in which Triola claimed half of Marvin's income as her own.

Marvin remarried in October 1970 to Pamela Feeley. It lasted until his death from a heart attack on August 29, 1987 in Tucson, Arizona. He is buried at Arlington National Cemetery in a grave alongside three and four star generals.

Suggested Sampling of Marvin's Western Heavies:

- Hangman's Knot ('52 Columbia) Randolph Scott
- Stranger Wore a Gun ('53 Columbia) Randolph Scott
- Gun Fury ('53 Columbia) Rock Hudson
- The Raid ('54 20th Century Fox) Van Heflin
- Bad Day at Black Rock ('55 MGM) Spencer Tracy
- Seven Men From Now ('56 Warner Bros.) Randolph Scott
- Wagon Train: Jose Morales Story ('56) Terry Wilson
- The Comancheros ('61 20th Century Fox) John Wayne
- Wagon Train: Christopher Hale Story ('61) Robert Horton/John McIntire
- Bonanza: The Crucible ('62) Pernell Roberts
- Virginian: It Tolls For Thee ('62) Lee J. Cobb
- Man Who Shot Liberty Valance ('62 Paramount) John Wayne
- Cat Ballou ('65 Columbia) Jane Fonda
- The Professionals ('66 Columbia) Burt Lancaster

LeROY MASON

Handsome and usually well dressed, LeRoy Mason was the perfect "dress heavy" or "big boss" in B-westerns throughout the '30s and '40s. There was bad blood all the way through his veins. So much in demand was Mason that Republic put his slick, conniving abilities under exclusive contract as of July 1943. He remained with Republic until his untimely death in '47.

LeRoy Franklin Mason was born in Larimore, North Dakota, on July 2, 1903. Mason's death certificate indicates no information was available as to the name and place of birth of Mason's father. His mother, Bertha Nelson, was born in Norway.

It's also unknown how this North Dakota boy came to California and entered films at 21 in 1924, working in several Tom Tyler/Frankie Darro FBO silent westerns.

He had a brief fling at leading man roles in latter day silents but by the time sound arrived in 1930, he seldom veered away from B-westerns and serials.

Speaking of serials, Mason worked in 13 of them with his best roles coming as heavies in "Last Frontier" ('32 RKO), "Phantom of the Air" ('33 Universal), "Painted Stallion" ('37 Republic), "Jungle Menace" ('37 Columbia), "Tiger Woman" ('44 Republic), "Phantom Rider" ('46 Republic) and "Daughter of Don Q" ('46 Republic).

During WWII Mason was in the Signal Corps in 1942 but was discharged after a year due to poor health.

Mason married silent screen actress Rita Carewe (born 1909 in New York City) in 1928. However, at the time of Mason's death, he was married to a Bernice Mason whose age was listed as 27.

During the filming of one of Republic's westerns Mason lost the sight in one eye. Fellow badman Tris Coffin once told researcher John Brooker, "He was doing a fight scene with Bill Elliott and Bill's glove grazed his eye. An infection set in and he had to lose it…he died of a heart attack while we were working together on a Monte Hale picture."

Mason suffered a heart attack while filming Hale's "California Firebrand" and was taken to Birmingham VA Hospital in Van Nuys, California, on September 12, 1947. He died at the VA hospital on October 13, 1947, of an acute myocardial infarction and coronary thrombosis.

He was buried at Forest Lawn Cemetery in Glendale. The Masons had been living at 10342 Zelzah Ave. in Northridge.

The boss, LeRoy Mason (right, seated) tells (L-R) Bud Geary, Hal Taliaferro and Kenne Duncan, "You know what to do," in Bill Elliott's Red Ryder thriller "Vigilantes of Dodge City" ('44 Republic).

Suggested Sampling of Mason's Western Heavies:

- Texas Pioneers ('32 Monogram) Bill Cody
- Last Frontier ('32 RKO serial) Lon Chaney Jr.
- Dude Ranger ('34 Fox) George O'Brien
- Fighting Trooper ('34 Ambassador) Kermit Maynard
- When A Man Sees Red ('34 Universal) Buck Jones
- Texas Terror ('35 Lone Star) John Wayne
- Rainbow Valley ('35 Lone Star) John Wayne
- Comin' Round the Mountain ('36 Republic) Gene Autry
- Border Patrolman ('36 20th Century Fox) George O'Brien
- Ghost Town Gold ('36 Republic) 3 Mesquiteers
- Round-Up Time In Texas ('37 Republic) Gene Autry
- Painted Stallion ('37 Republic serial) Ray "Crash" Corrigan
- Western Gold ('37 20th Century Fox) Smith Ballew
- Singing Outlaw ('38 Universal) Bob Baker
- Gold Mine In the Sky ('38 Republic) Gene Autry
- Santa Fe Stampede ('38 Republic) 3 Mesquiteers
- Lure of the Wasteland ('39 Al Lane Pictures) Grant Withers
- Mexicali Rose ('39 Republic) Gene Autry
- Wyoming Outlaw ('39 Republic) 3 Mesquiteers
- Fighting Gringo ('39 RKO) George O'Brien
- Ghost Valley Raiders ('40 Republic) Don Barry
- Rocky Mountain Rangers ('40 Republic) 3 Mesquiteers
- Range Busters ('40 Monogram) Range Busters
- Across the Sierras ('41 Columbia) Bill Elliott
- Robbers of the Range ('41 RKO) Tim Holt
- Apache Kid ('41 Republic) Don Barry
- Riders of the Purple Sage ('41 20th Century Fox) George Montgomery
- Western Mail ('42 Monogram) Tom Keene
- Silver Bullet ('42 Universal) Johnny Mack Brown
- Bandit Ranger ('42 RKO) Tim Holt
- Blazing Guns ('43 Monogram) Trail Blazers
- California Joe ('43 Republic) Don Barry
- Raiders of Sunset Pass ('43 Republic) Eddie Dew
- Beneath Western Skies ('44 Republic) Bob Livingston
- Mojave Firebrand ('44 Republic) Bill Elliott
- Hidden Valley Outlaws ('44 Republic) Bill Elliott
- Outlaws of Santa Fe ('44 Republic) Don Barry
- Tucson Raiders ('44 Republic) Bill Elliott
- Song of Nevada ('44 Republic) Roy Rogers
- Stagecoach to Monterey ('44 Republic) Allan Lane
- Vigilantes of Dodge City ('44 Republic) Bill Elliott
- Phantom Rider ('46 Republic serial) Robert Kent
- Home On the Range ('46 Republic) Monte Hale
- Red River Renegades ('46 Republic) Sunset Carson
- Under Nevada Skies ('46 Republic) Roy Rogers
- Apache Rose ('47 Republic) Roy Rogers
- Under Colorado Skies ('47 Republic) Monte Hale
- Gay Ranchero ('48 Republic) Roy Rogers
- California Firebrand ('48 Republic) Monte Hale

CARL MATHEWS

Carl Mathews is one of the unsung background henchman that had a 20 year career in films ('34-'55) but of whom little is known. He also worked from '34-'51 as a stuntman beginning with the Kermit Maynard series for Ambassador. He doubled Fred Scott throughout his series for Spectrum, as well as having some of his better acting parts in those films. He also doubled Ray Corrigan in the Mesquiteers a bit, Ken Maynard at Colony and did a lot of work at PRC and Monogram in the '40s doubling various actors in Bob Steele, Range Busters, George Houston, Buster Crabbe, Eddie Dean and Johnny Mack Brown titles. His last stuntwork was in the six Jimmy Ellison/Russell Hayden Lippert pictures as the '50s rolled around.

Fellow stuntman Bill Catching refers to Mathews as "…Ol' Cherokee. He had some Indian blood in him. He played lead heavies in some early pictures. But old Johnny Barleycorn got ahold of him. (Stuntman) Troy Melton and I used to find parts for him. Eddie Davis, who started as an assistant director at ZIV, and then became head of production and later switched to directing…he directed some of the best 'Cisco Kid' TVs we ever made…anyway, Cherokee was one of Eddie's favorite guys 'cause he'd known him back in the '30s. Eddie brought him to the Ciscos, then Troy and I adopted him. We tried to bump into him in a fight. He got an extra bit of money if you happened to sail into him and knock him down during the fight. We'd always put ol' Cherokee in a spot where he'd get an extra check, but we had to tell him the day before or he'd have a little barley corn in him. So many of those guys were at the top of the class in the '30s, then in the '40s or '50s they were nothin'. But Carl was a great guy. Easy goin' guy, very quiet. He never got too far from the set. If you called him, he'd say, 'Yes,' and he'd be right behind you. He got to doin' nothin' but extra work. You never had to look too far to find him. A pleasant guy."

If you believe studio publicity, in 1942 Monogram stated, "When the government in Washington allotted each member of Carl's Oklahoma tribe a piece of land in their native state, Mathews hurried back to the Sooner State to view his real estate. Imagine his joy, his elation, his overflowing happiness to find Uncle Sam had given him an untenable strip atop a rock covered hill. It seems Mathews is the only holder of non-oil producing land in Oklahoma."

Carl's last film was a western, "Treasure of Ruby Hills" ('55 Allied Artists) with Zachary Scott and Carole Mathews (no relation). Mathews can be seen in at least 18 "Cisco Kid" episodes.

Carl Davis "Cherokee" Mathews, born February 19, 1899, in Oklahoma Territory, came to the end of his trail on May 3, 1959, in Los Angeles at 60.

Carl Mathews lays in wait for Jack Randall at the edge of the oft-used Walker Cabin in "Wild Horse Range" ('40 Monogram).

Suggested Sampling of Mathews' Western Heavies:

- Silent Code ('35 Stage & Screen) Kane Richmond
- Rough Riding Ranger ('35 Superior) Bill Cody
- Boots of Destiny ('37 Grand National) Ken Maynard
- Ranger's Roundup ('38 Spectrum) Fred Scott
- Songs and Bullets ('38 Spectrum) Fred Scott
- Six Shootin' Sheriff ('38 Colony) Ken Maynard
- Outlaw's Paradise ('39 Victory) Tim McCoy
- Two Gun Troubadour ('39 Spectrum) Fred Scott
- Code of the Fearless ('39 Spectrum) Fred Scott
- Phantom Rancher ('40 Colony) Ken Maynard
- Covered Wagon Trails ('40 Monogram) Jack Randall
- Range Busters ('40 Monogram) Range Busters
- Thunder River Feud ('42 Monogram) Range Busters
- Rock River Renegades ('42 Monogram) Range Busters
- Lawless Plainsmen ('42 Columbia) Charles Starrett/Russell Hayden
- Arizona Stagecoach ('42 Monogram) Range Busters
- Rangers Take Over ('42 PRC) Dave O'Brien/James Newill
- Haunted Ranch ('43 Monogram) Range Busters
- Fighting Valley ('43 PRC) Dave O'Brien/James Newill
- Bad Men of Thunder Gap ('43 PRC) Dave O'Brien/James Newill
- Frontier Fugitives ('45 PRC) Tex Ritter/Dave O'Brien
- Tumbleweed Trail ('46 PRC) Eddie Dean
- Stars Over Texas ('46 PRC) Eddie Dean
- Stage to Mesa City ('47 PRC) Lash LaRue
- Gun Talk ('47 Monogram) Johnny Mack Brown
- Song of the Drifter ('48 Monogram) Jimmy Wakely
- Haunted Trails ('49 Monogram) Whip Wilson
- West of Wyoming ('50 Monogram) Johnny Mack Brown
- Six Gun Mesa ('50 Monogram) Johnny Mack Brown
- Crooked River ('50 Lippert) Jimmy Ellison/Russell Hayden
- Arizona Territory ('50 Monogram) Whip Wilson
- Cisco Kid: Newspaper Crusaders ('50) Duncan Renaldo
- Cisco Kid: Marriage By Mail ('54) Duncan Renaldo

KERMIT MAYNARD

If you were a youngster in the '30s, you remember Kermit Maynard as a starring cowboy hero at Ambassador, but if you grew up in the '40s, you think of him as a villain in a whole lot of films, especially at PRC. He was well liked, much more so than his hard drinking, often troublesome brother, Ken Maynard, for whom Kermit frequently doubled on horseback, and this enabled Kermit to keep working for a very long time.

The younger brother of Ken, they both were born in Vevay, Indiana—Ken in 1895 and Kermit Roosevelt Maynard on September 20, 1897 (there were also three Maynard sisters—Bessie, Trixie and Willa). Their parents were William H. Maynard and Emma May Stewart. Their father was a carpenter who worked on construction of riverboats and houses.

A few years after the turn of the century, due to economic conditions, the family moved to Columbus, a less rural community. It was there Ken began to show an interest in horsemanship, subsequently leaving home two years later to join a traveling show.

Kermit graduated Garfield High School in 1916 and a year later enrolled at Indiana University in Bloomington taking a pre-law curriculum while lettering in football, basketball, track and baseball. He left in 1921 prior to receiving a degree to work for the Hormel Packing Company in Austin, Minnesota. Entering a management training program, within two years Kermit advanced from department assistant to department manager. The reasoning for this move was that he played on Hormel's football and basketball teams.

Kermit was married to Edith Jessen of Denmark in 1924. By 1926 brother Ken was starring in westerns for First National, and would occasionally write his brother espousing the wonders of sunny California and the possibility of Kermit getting work in films. Kermit decided to heed his brother's advice, and he and Edith headed west to California.

A natural athlete, Kermit taught himself to become an experienced horsebacker through countless hours of practice at Fat Jones Stables.

Kermit got some stuntwork and bit parts while continuing to hone his riding skills. Toward the end of the silent era, in 1927, he signed with W. Ray Johnston's Rayart Pictures to star in a series billed as Tex Maynard.

When talkies came in, Kermit reverted back to stuntwork, becoming Fox's "main man," doubling George O'Brien, Victor McLaglen and others. He also worked with brother Ken in some of his early '30s Tiffany and Universal B's and appeared in several Mascot serials.

During this period Kermit purchased a three year old dapple grey, named him Rocky, and personally trained the horse. In 1933, on Rocky, Kermit won the trick and fancy roping competition at the National Competition Rodeo in Salinas, California.

In 1934 Maurice Conn signed Kermit to star in a series of Northwest Mountie adventures for his fledgling Ambassador Pictures. Under Conn's guidance, the pictures were a cut above the other independent fare of the time. Between 1934 and 1937 Kermit starred in 18 for Ambassador, the first group as an RCMP officer and the latter group being strict westerns.

With the end of Ambassador, Republic wanted to sign Kermit as a contract player, but he chose to freelance rather than be in servitude to one company.

During the '40s Kermit was in dozens of films as a heavy, practically a regular at PRC and Monogram, but also working at Republic, Universal, Columbia, etc. At the same time he did scores of stunt jobs in not only B-westerns but big budget A's as well.

As for his on going relationship with brother Ken, Kermit once stated, "I've never approved of him drinking. I don't drink. Never have. And I don't smoke. I play nine holes of golf every day I'm not working."

The Maynards purchased a ranch in the San Fernando Valley and made it their home for 20 years until the state highway expansion program forced them to move to a smaller place in N. Hollywood. A son, William Frederick Maynard, was born in 1943.

As major roles became less and less, Kermit continued to work extra in dozens of the TV westerns being filmed in the mid to late '50s.

In 1962, now 65, Kermit began to serve as representative of the Screen Extras' Guild. He retired in 1969.

Kermit Maynard's long, varied and honorable career came to a close on January 16, 1971, when he died suddenly of a heart attack at 73 at his Valley Village, N. Hollywood home.

Perhaps Buster Crabbe summed it up most succinctly, "The difference between Ken and Kermit Maynard was like comparing night and day. Kermit was always the gentleman, excellent horseman, and a real pleasure to work with. He never had an unkind word for anyone, and above all, he was my friend."

Suggested Sampling of Maynard's Western Heavies:

- The Showdown ('40 Paramount) William Boyd
- The Range Busters ('40 Monogram) Range Busters
- Stick to Your Guns ('41 Paramount) William Boyd
- Texas Troubleshooters ('42 Monogram) Range Busters
- Prairie Pals ('42 PRC) Lee Powell/Art Davis/Bill Boyd
- Arizona Stagecoach ('42 Monogram) Range Busters
- Along the Sundown Trail ('42 PRC) Lee Powell/Art Davis/Bill Boyd
- Mysterious Rider ('42 PRC) Buster Crabbe
- Trail Riders ('42 Monogram) Range Busters
- Blocked Trail ('43 Republic) 3 Mesquiteers
- Fugitive of the Plains ('43 PRC) Buster Crabbe
- Western Cyclone ('43 PRC) Buster Crabbe
- Blazing Frontier ('43 PRC) Buster Crabbe
- Devil Riders ('43 PRC) Buster Crabbe
- Death Rides the Plains ('43 PRC) Bob Livingston
- Texas Kid ('43 Monogram) Johnny Mack Brown
- Gunsmoke Mesa ('44 PRC) Dave O'Brien/James Newill
- Frontier Outlaws ('44 PRC) Buster Crabbe
- Wild Horse Phantom ('44 PRC) Buster Crabbe
- Thundering Gunslingers ('44 PRC) Buster Crabbe
- Enemy of the Law ('45 PRC) Tex Ritter/Dave O'Brien
- Gangster's Den ('45 PRC) Buster Crabbe
- Stagecoach Outlaws ('45 PRC) Buster Crabbe
- Fighting Bill Carson ('45 PRC) Buster Crabbe
- Galloping Thunder ('46 Columbia) Charles Starrett
- Prairie Badmen ('46 PRC) Buster Crabbe
- Stars Over Texas ('46 PRC) Eddie Dean
- 'Neath Canadian Skies ('46 Screen Guild) Russell Hayden
- Ridin' Down the Trail ('47 Monogram) Jimmy Wakely
- Range Land ('49 Monogram) Whip Wilson
- Silver Raiders ('50 Monogram) Whip Wilson
- Gene Autry: The Peacemaker ('50) Gene Autry
- Gene Autry: Ghost Town Raiders ('51) Gene Autry
- Cisco Kid: Fool's Gold ('54) Duncan Renaldo

LEW MEEHAN

Lew Meehan looked like a man who had been hit in the face with a shovel, or had his nose flattened in a prizefight. You had to see him only once, and that flat, pointed nose that dipped menacingly down into his black mustache and upper lip left its impression on you forever. He looked mean and untrustworthy—and usually was, from his silent era beginning in 1921 throughout the '30s. By 1940, then 50, his parts became less frequent and more character oriented—saloon keeper, deputy, voting official—until he retired in 1944.

Born James Lew Meehan in Minnesota, September 7, 1890, his parents, James L. Meehan and Margaret Dougherty, were both from Wisconsin.

Like so many "henchies", how and why he migrated to Hollywood and entered films is lost to the ages, but beginning with Pete Morrison's "Crossing Trails" ('21 Associated Photoplays) he became a foreboding presence in the silent westerns of Lester Cuneo, Bill Patton, Jack Perrin, Jack Hoxie, Buffalo Bill Jr., Bob Custer, Tom Mix, Tom Tyler, Art Acord and others.

Moving into talkies, he found his best roles with the independent poverty row producers, with lesser "fourth man through the door" roles at Columbia, Republic and Universal. Meehan is in at least a dozen serials, including "Mystery Squadron" ('33 Mascot), "Burn 'Em Up Barnes" ('34 Mascot), "Black Coin" ('36 Stage & Screen) and "Great Adventures of Wild Bill Hickok" ('38 Columbia).

Never a member of the Armed Forces, Meehan was married to Dolores Meehan but was divorced and living on North Ivar Street in Los Angeles when he died at 60 on August 10, 1951, at Rancho Los Amigos, some sort of hospital or rest home where he'd been for four months and six days before his death. Cause of death was congestive heart failure aggravated by heart disease and emphysema.

His death certificate indicates his remains were turned over to the University of Southern California, possibly for research.

Suggested Sampling of Meehan's Western Heavies:

- Ace of the Law ('24 Anchor) Bill Patton
- Red Blood ('26 Rayart) Al Hoxie
- Cactus Trails ('27 FBO) Bob Custer
- King Cowboy ('28 FBO) Tom Mix
- Gun Law ('29 RKO) Tom Tyler
- Hunted Men ('30 Syndicate) Bob Steele
- Silver Bullet ('34 Reliable) Tom Tyler
- Rawhide Mail ('34 Reliable) Jack Perrin
- Range Riders ('34 Superior Talking Pictures) Buddy Roosevelt
- Prescott Kid ('34 Columbia) Tim McCoy
- Man Trailer ('34 Columbia) Buck Jones
- Gunfire ('35 Resolute) Rex Bell
- Texas Jack ('35 Reliable) Jack Perrin
- Lawless Nineties ('36 Republic) John Wayne
- Reckless Buckaroo ('36 Spectrum) Bill Cody
- Gunlords of Stirrup Basin ('37 Supreme) Bob Steele
- Melody of the Plains ('37 Spectrum) Fred Scott
- Rangers Step In ('37 Columbia) Bob Allen
- Arizona Gunfighter ('37 Republic) Bob Steele
- Whirlwind Horseman ('38 Grand National) Ken Maynard
- Thunder In the Desert ('38 Republic) Bob Steele
- Bullet Code ('40 RKO) George O'Brien

DON MEGOWAN

In the '50s and '60s, when the script called for a *big* man, producers and directors inevitably turned to Don Megowan. Just witness his character name in some of the roles he played—Big Charlie, Big Hardy, big longshoreman, Big Mike, The Beast, the Frankenstein monster—and he even played (uncredited) the Creature From the Black Lagoon (on land) in "The Creature Walks Among Us" ('56). His imposing 6' 6" frame made him ideal for westerns, a great opponent for the equally impressive Clint Walker on "Cheyenne" where Don appeared in six episodes.

Clint Walker told us, "Don was an inch taller than I am, and I'm 6' 5". Big, good lookin' guy, curly black hair, had a good voice. A rather imposing guy because he was so big. He was kind of a quiet guy, didn't talk a whole lot. Don had a little bar over in Sunland for quite a while. I did several 'Cheyenne' with Don. In one he's supposed to be a very good friend of mine and gets framed for a murder he didn't commit. They had him in jail and the crowd had formed in the town and was coming to lynch him. He says, 'Cheyenne, gimmie my guns so I can at least protect myself.' So I was moving him out of the jail to somewhere else in town. He takes his two Colt .45s and sticks 'em in his belt, in his pants, in the front with the handles stickin' out. I've got a shotgun and here comes the mob. Now, as you know, the single action Colt, you've got to cock that hammer back to fire it. Well, as Don is pulling the guns out, he cocks them—with full loads in there. Lo and behold, as he cocks them, both guns go off while they're still in his trousers. (Laughs) They had to take what was left of his manhood to the hospital for about four days. It's funny, but I felt very sorry for him because he got burned fairly good."

At Universal Gregg Palmer recalls, "Don wore the suit in 'The Creature Walks Among Us' but he didn't do any of the water stuff. Let me tell you how big he was. We were doing a 'Gunsmoke'. Don and I were supposed to be from the back hills of Kentucky or someplace. There's a gunfight and so forth in the street and I had to go out and pick up Don, put him over my shoulder and walk out of camera range. My vertebras were damn near crushed. He says, 'Oh I only weight about 202 pounds.' I laughed, 'Your shoes weigh that much!' His hands and feet were dragging on the ground and I'm standing up at 6' 2". His size limited him; he couldn't work with Alan Ladd for instance."

But Don was such a good actor that he could expose a softer, gentler side as well, which often worked favorably behind his massive frame. This side of the man was never more apparent than in the cult classic family film "Snowfire" ('58 Allied Artists) in which he plays the rancher father of two young girls who befriend a wild horse.

Megowan was born May 24, 1922, in Inglewood, California, the son of Robert E. Megowan of Kentucky and Leila D. Hunter of Texas.

It's unknown how Don came to films, but his first role was as a longshoreman in "The Mob" ('51). He quickly found his niche in westerns as a heavy—but, as in "Snowfire", sometimes was on the right side of the law as when he played Col. William Travis in Disney's "Davy Crockett" or as Sheriff Haines tracking down "The Werewolf" in '56, and he almost co-starred in a series called "Men of Defiance", the unsold pilot of which aired on "Laramie" in '60.

Like many others of the time, Megowan traveled to Europe to star in a couple of films in '60-'61.

Roles began to slow down as to where Don did nothing in '66, '71 and '72. Sadly, his final roles in the mid '70s, such as the gum chewer in "Blazing Saddles", were but small reminders of what his career had once been.

A once important part of the TV western era died at his home in Panorama City, California, of throat cancer June 26, 1981, at only 59. Forgotten by the industry, there was not even an obit in VARIETY. But those of us who grew up in the TV western era remember Don with much respect.

Suggested Sampling of Megowan's Western Heavies:

- Kid From Amarillo ('51 Columbia) Charles Starrett
- Lone Ranger: Stage to Tishomingo ('54) Clayton Moore
- A Lawless Street ('55 Columbia) Randolph Scott
- Gun the Man Down ('56 United Artists) James Arness
- Cheyenne: Star In the Dust ('56) Clint Walker
- Cheyenne: Hired Gun ('57) Clint Walker
- Tales of Wells Fargo: Hide Jumpers ('57) Dale Robertson
- Hell Canyon Outlaws ('57 Republic) Dale Robertson
- Trackdown: Chinese Cowboy ('57) Robert Culp
- Cimarron City: Beast of the Cimarron ('58) George Montgomery
- U. S. Marshal: Grandfather ('58) John Bromfield
- Cheyenne: The Reprieve ('59) Clint Walker
- Laramie: Bare Knuckles ('59) John Smith
- Gunsmoke: Big Tom ('60) James Arness
- Deputy: Bitter Root ('59) Henry Fonda/Allen Case
- Lawman: The Post ('60) John Russell
- Cheyenne: The Beholden ('61) Clint Walker
- Two Faces West: Trail to Indian Wells ('61) Charles Bateman
- Gunsmoke: Phoebe Strunk ('62) James Arness
- A Man Called Shenandoah: Town On Fire ('65) Robert Horton
- Death Valley Days: Halo For a Badman ('67)

JAN MERLIN

Jan Merlin brought nasty, grinning, near psychotic cads to perfection in films and TV throughout the '50s.

Jan more or less bookended these contemptible roles by playing good guys—first as Cadet Roger Manning in "Tom Corbett, Space Cadet" starting in 1950 and then in '58-'59 as Lt. Colin Kirby on ABC's "Rough Riders", co-starring Kent Taylor and Peter Whitney.

Jan was born April 3, 1925, on the lower east side of New York City where his parents were caretakers of a Russian Orthodox Church on East 4th Street. Jan's father was Peter Wasylewski, a Russian who came to America in 1912. His mother, Theresa, was an Austrian Polish lady who arrived here in 1913. They met and were married in 1914. At age 10, when his father died, Jan entered Grace Church School for boys, a choir school where he sang in the choir until his voice changed at 15, which is how he paid to attend a private school.

Enlisting in the Navy in 1942 after WWII broke out, Jan served on destroyers as a torpedo man, spending most of his time in the South Pacific. They fought battles from Wake Island, New Guinea, Tarawa, up through the Gilbert and Marshal Islands and Okinawa.

Leaving the Navy after the war in 1946 without a trade to follow, a chance meeting with the owner of a summer theatre in Fishkill, New York, found Jan putting his artistic talents to work designing and building sets.

Believing he could do what he was seeing the actors do, Jan enrolled a year later in the Neighborhood Playhouse School of the Theatre and studied under the renowned Sanford Miesner. Frank Butler, the actor who told him of the famous school, also suggested he change his Slavic name to Jan Merlin.

After being taught how to speak, dance, and the rudiments of acting, Jan returned to summer stock as an actor in Fishkill, doing as many plays as he could. He then returned for a second semester at the Neighborhood Playhouse and another season of summer stock.

Down to his last nickel when the season was over, and wondering how he'd make a living, Jan answered a cattle call casting for Josh Logan's "South Pacific". Interviewed by Logan, he was told one of the boys was leaving the big hit "Mr. Roberts" and which play would he rather be in? Stunned, Jan chose "Mr. Roberts" because, as he told Logan, "I can't sing." He stayed with the Broadway play for two years.

About the end of the second year, they were casting for TV's "Tom Corbett, Space Cadet". Jan's cocky, self-assured attitude won him the role of sassy Roger

Manning.

Feeling typed with the same character, Jan left after three and a half years, spending time in Africa, a county he's always studied and loved ever since he read TARZAN OF THE APES as a child. When he returned to the states, he also returned to "Corbett" for six months, then did several off-Broadway shows including "Rope". During the run of "Rope", he was contacted by Universal and cast in "Six Bridges to Cross" ('55).

Jan worked non-stop in film and TV for 41 years, doing two plays in Hollywood as well, with his last role on a TV movie shown in 1992. Jan believes, "The 'heavy' is the engine which actually runs the film…he's the reason for stirring up all the action and leads the rest of the cast on a merry chase until the end, when he generally gets his just desserts. It's always the most interesting role in the film and it's a challenge to find different ways to die. The 'good guy' gets top billing and the girl, but he's only reacting to whatever the 'bad guy' has done. The audience already knows how the hero will end up, but never knows what or how the bad guy is going to do something next at any point in the film."

"I did happen to get cast as a dashing romantic hero for my TV series, 'The Rough Riders', and had a hard time adjusting at first. My directors were constantly telling me to lighten up, until I began to enjoy surviving each time, often getting to smooch the girl before riding off with my horse."

"I was a likeable fellow in the movie 'Screaming Eagles' but would have preferred not to have changed roles with Tom Tryon—but he wanted to be a 'heavy' for a change, and I wanted to try being a 'hero'…and anyway, the 'heavy' had to lug the blinded hero around for most of the movie…and Tom had more muscle and height than I did—so it worked out for the best."

"One of the disadvantages of being a good guy is having to look heroic and clean cut, while the heavy can be as grungy as he pleases…or sometimes wears far more fancy duds than his pursuer…maybe even be better looking! I guess I loved playing westerns most for being able to just play the role and not fuss with a comb and makeup checks all the time."

One of his most interesting, yet torturesome, film roles was being made-up for and wearing all the mask disguises for cast members of "The List of Adrian Messenger" in '63, for which he received *no* screen credit. Now, Jan has written a fictionalized account about his painstaking experiences making the film, SHOOTING MONTEZUMA, published in 2001.

Jan first became a novelist in '82 with BROCADE, a war novel recently republished by Xlibris as AINOKO.

An old friend who was now head writer on the "Another World" soap opera persuaded Jan to join his group of writers. Jan worked for that series for about five years, earning an Emmy in '75 and an Emmy nomination in '79.

Jan was first married to actress Patricia Ann Datz in 1951. His son Peter, now co-founder and co-owner of Aerospace Archeology Field Research Team, commonly known as an "X-Hunter", was born in 1964. Jan's wife Pat died of cancer in 1986.

Nowadays, from his home with his second wife Barbara Doyle (whom he married in 1988) in Burbank, California, Jan writes to please himself, including his African novel, GUNBEARER—PART ONE and GUNBEARER—PART TWO, both published in '99 and GYPSIES DON'T LIE published in 2000. He also recently completed CRACK POTS and THE PAID COMPANION OF JOHN WILKES BOOTH with co-author William Russo in '03. "As I gradually began to write more and more, I realized I loved doing something without any interference whatever…all my novels are completely my own work, and no one can make changes to the stories or the characters or the plots. There's much reward in using past life situations, past acquaintances and past travels as the basis for books. Sometimes a character can be identified; most times, not…since many are created from combinations of people I've known…and some are merely invented."

"Writing novels became another form of reaching an audience for me, touching them far more intensely than from a stage. I sometimes drew tears or laughter from a theatre audience…now I do it with my pages…pages which contain far more depth than any TV or film performance can express due to the limited length of a script…half hour…one hour or two or more…mini series…all suffer the lack of exposition a novel grants the reader. I choose whatever is to be kept in the story; nothing gets cut unless I do it myself. Which is why I don't write scripts anymore. Far too restricting! And too many fingers in the pie after submission."

Suggested Sampling of Merlin's Western Heavies:

- A Day of Fury ('56 Universal) Jock Mahoney
- The Peacemaker ('56 United Artists) James Mitchell
- Wyatt Earp: Vengeance Trail ('57) Hugh O'Brian
- Broken Arrow: Apache Girl ('57) John Lupton/Michael Ansara
- Trackdown: Marple Brothers ('57) Robert Culp
- Casey Jones: Way Station ('57) Alan Hale Jr.
- Cole Younger, Gunfighter ('58 Allied Artists) Frank Lovejoy
- Tombstone Territory: Guilt of a Town ('58) Pat Conway
- Tales of Wells Fargo: Great Bullion Robbery ('60) Dale Robertson
- Bat Masterson: Last Stop to Austin ('60) Gene Barry
- Hell Bent For Leather ('60 Universal) Audie Murphy
- Tall Man: First Blood ('61) Barry Sullivan, Clu Gulager
- Laramie: Stolen Tribute ('61) Robert Fuller
- Whispering Smith: Blind Gun ('61) Audie Murphy
- Bonanza: The Ride ('62) Michael Landon
- Laramie: Among the Missing ('62) Robert Fuller
- Rawhide: Incident at Crooked Hat ('63) Eric Fleming
- Laramie: The Fugitives ('63) Robert Fuller/John Smith
- Virginian: Ryker ('64) Doug McClure
- Legend of Jesse James: The Celebrity ('65) Christopher Jones

JOHN MERTON

Big boss or henchman, the square-jawed, glint-eyed, huskily-built John Merton was one of B-westerns' baddest renegades in over 200 pictures and 22 serials from 1933-1956.

In Seattle, Washington, on February 18, 1901, Myrtland F. LaVarre was born to William J. LaVarre and Lelia Hayes, both from Virginia. Why his birth was here seems lost to the ages, as he was raised on the east coast with three brothers—Claude LaVarre who later lived in Santiago, Cuba, and was somehow involved with Singer Sewing Machines; William LaVarre, a traveler and explorer in South America and author of several books; and Franklin LaVarre (known as Andre de LaVarre of Austria), a travelogue photographer with the noted Burton Holmes who took over as headliner when Holmes died. Becoming an actor displeased the family, causing Myrtland to be blackballed from the family.

Look out, Smiley. That's a knife John Merton is holding to your gut in "The Blazing Trail" ('49 Columbia).

Myrtland served in the Navy during WWI and made 13 trips across the Atlantic to France.

After the war, he went to New York to try his hand at acting. In 1919 he began with the New York Theatre Guild. He soon acted on Broadway and up and down the eastern seaboard with various stock companies.

Circa 1926-'27 he worked at Paramount's Astoria Pictures on Long Island in a couple of W. C. Fields films. Those films drew on stage players who could work in a movie during the day and still make the curtain for a play's performance in the evening.

In 1932, with 12 years of stage experience, LaVarre, his wife (Ellen) and four children came west in his Ford delivery van to become a "movie star".

He settled first in Glendale, then on Romaine Avenue in Hollywood, finally on Lankershim in what is today North Hollywood.

He found work in "Captured" ('33 Warner Bros.) as a prisoner of war, then in Laurel and Hardy's "Sons of the Desert" ('33), then (billed as Mert LaVarre) in Buck Jones' "Red Rider" Universal serial in '34.

At this time, he was chosen by Cecil B. DeMille, who liked his husky look, for a bit in "Cleopatra". DeMille used Merton in every one of his films right on through "The Ten Commandments" in 1956, Merton's last film (which, incidentally, also features his son, Bob LaVarre as a task master).

It was DeMille who suggested to LaVarre that Myrtland LaVarre was a "New York actor name" and that he change it. LaVarre selected John Merton, of which De Mille approved.

Opposite Hopalong Cassidy, Tim McCoy and Kermit Maynard over the next few years, one of the vilest cads of the B-western screen emerged. His ramrod-straight bearing and determined, grim expression were perfect, barking out orders to his underlings.

In addition to film after film, as many as 18 a year, Merton was a member of the Henry Wilcoxen Group Players of Santa Monica, a theatre group.

According to his son, in Tom and Jim Goldrup's

FEATURE PLAYERS Vol. 1, Merton's all consuming drive to get ahead in the business brought on family hardships. "He was a handsome buzzard," Bob LaVarre said, "and the women were always after him and he started giving in. He was playing the game...socializing and parties. He (hung out) at the famous Garden of Allah on Crescent Heights and Sunset Blvd. It was gorgeous and was just as the name denotes, a great big lascivious, let's-have-a-ball, get-the-broads place. He would stay away three or four days. It just got to be a little too much. He had six children and a wife, and in 1941 my mother left him. He was a scoundrel, but I loved him dearly. He was a hell of a man, strong as a bull."

Merton became typecast in westerns and serials as a heavy, but he loved the work. In his autobiography, director William Witney wrote, "John Merton usually played heavies, he could fight, ride and act. Because he had five kids, he was always at the top of the panic list. I watched them all grow up. A couple of them were in the picture business as crew members, and one of them turned out to be as good an actor and fight man as his dad. Lane Bradford was also as quiet and gentlemanly as his old man."

In the mid-'50s as it became increasingly difficult to find employment in films, Merton drove a truck for Wholesale Supply Company delivering raw materials to the big studio labs. This led to a job in negative cutting as an IATSE technician at MGM circa mid '56 til his death in '59.

Besides the westerns, Merton embraced the serials, 22 of them. He was the meanest son of rotten Pa Stark (Charles Middleton) in "Dick Tracy Returns" ('38 Republic); a councilman suspected of being power mad Don Del Oro in "Zorro's Fighting Legion" ('39 Republic); a mindless Dacoit slave in "Drums of Fu Manchu" ('40 Republic); foreign spy chief Baroda in "Radar Patrol Vs. Spy King" ('50 Republic); and a gunny assistant in "Vigilantes Are Coming" ('36 Republic), "White Eagle" ('41 Columbia), "Lone Ranger" ('38 Republic) and "Zorro's Black Whip" ('44 Republic). In the '40s he became a member of producer Sam Katzman's stock company of heavies in "Hop Harrigan" ('46) as eccentric bald-headed Dr. Tobor; "Jack Armstrong" ('47) as crooked Gregory Pierce (this serial, incidentally, gave Merton's son Lane Bradford his first big role); "Brenda Starr, Reporter" ('45) as a big city gangster; "Brick Bradford" ('47) as mad inventor Dr. Tymak; and "Adventures of Sir Galahad" ('49) as Saxon King Ulric.

One of the best of the badmen, John Merton died of a heart attack September 18, 1959, at his home at 7629 Coldwater Canyon in Los Angeles. He's buried at Valhalla Memorial Park in North Hollywood.

Suggested Sampling of Merton's Western Heavies:

- Eagle's Brood ('35 Paramount) William Boyd
- Border Caballero ('36 Puritan) Tim McCoy
- Call of the Prairie ('36 Paramount) William Boyd
- Lightnin' Bill Carson ('36 Puritan) Tim McCoy
- Crooked Trail ('36 Supreme) Johnny Mack Brown
- Vigilantes Are Coming ('36 Republic serial) Bob Livingston
- Three Mesquiteers ('36 Republic) 3 Mesquiteers
- Wild Horse Round-Up ('36 Ambassador) Kermit Maynard
- Valley of Terror ('37 Ambassador) Kermit Maynard
- Gun Ranger ('37 Republic) Bob Steele
- Law of the Ranger ('37 Columbia) Bob Allen
- Blazing Sixes ('37 Warner Bros.) Dick Foran
- Gunsmoke Ranch ('37 Republic) 3 Mesquiteers
- Roaring Six Guns ('37 Ambassador) Kermit Maynard
- Lone Ranger ('38 Republic serial) Lee Powell
- Land of Fighting Men ('38 Monogram) Jack Randall
- Knight of the Plains ('38 Spectrum) Fred Scott
- Two Gun Justice ('38 Monogram) Tim McCoy
- Gunsmoke Trail ('38 Monogram) Jack Randall
- Songs and Saddles ('38 Colony) Gene Austin
- Where the Buffalo Roam ('38 Monogram) Tex Ritter
- Code of the Fearless ('39 Spectrum) Fred Scott
- In Old Montana ('39 Spectrum) Fred Scott
- Renegade Trail ('39 Paramount) William Boyd
- Covered Wagon Days ('40 Republic) 3 Mesquiteers
- Frontier Crusader ('40 PRC) Tim McCoy
- Billy the Kid In Texas ('40 PRC) Bob Steele
- Under Fiesta Stars ('41 Republic) Gene Autry
- Gunman From Bodie ('41 Monogram) Rough Riders
- Arizona Terrors ('42 Republic) Don Barry
- Boot Hill Bandits ('42 Monogram) Range Busters
- Law and Order ('42 PRC) Buster Crabbe
- Sheriff of Sage Valley ('42 PRC) Buster Crabbe
- Along the Sundown Trail ('42 PRC) Lee Powell/Art Davis/ Bill Boyd
- Lone Prairie ('42 Columbia) Russell Hayden
- Mysterious Rider ('42 PRC) Buster Crabbe
- Land of Hunted Men ('43 Monogram) Range Busters
- Law Rides Again ('43 Monogram) Trail Blazers
- Fighting Valley ('43 PRC) Dave O'Brien/James Newill
- Black Market Rustlers ('43 PRC) Range Busters
- Devil Riders ('43 PRC) Buster Crabbe
- Zorro's Black Whip ('44 Republic serial) Linda Stirling
- Stranger From Santa Fe ('45 Monogram) Johnny Mack Brown
- Oregon Trail ('45 Republic) Sunset Carson
- Rustler's Hideout ('45 PRC) Buster Crabbe
- Bandits of the Badlands ('45 Republic) Sunset Carson
- Cherokee Flash ('45 Republic) Sunset Carson
- Border Bandits ('46 Monogram) Johnny Mack Brown
- Haunted Mine ('46 Monogram) Johnny Mack Brown
- Gay Cavalier ('46 Monogram) Gilbert Roland
- Desert Horseman ('46 Columbia) Charles Starrett
- Heading West ('46 Columbia) Charles Starrett
- Cheyenne Takes Over ('47 PRC) Lash LaRue
- Riders of the Dusk ('49 Monogram) Whip Wilson
- Arizona Territory ('50 Monogram) Whip Wilson
- Border Rangers ('50 Lippert) Don Barry
- Bandit Queen ('50 Lippert) Barbara Britton
- Lone Ranger: Banker's Choice ('50) Clayton Moore
- Gold Raiders ('51 United Artists) George O'Brien
- Cisco Kid: Foreign Agent ('51) Duncan Renaldo
- Wild Bill Hickok: Boy and the Bandit ('52) Guy Madison
- Blue Canadian Rockies ('52 Columbia) Gene Autry
- Cisco Kid: Bodyguard ('53) Duncan Renaldo
- Roy Rogers: Last of the Larabee Kid ('54) Roy Rogers
- Wild Bill Hickok: Blake's Kid ('55) Guy Madison

EMILE MEYER

If Emile Meyer played no role other than that of vicious, land-grabbing cattle baron Rufus Ryker in Alan Ladd and director George Stevens' immortal "Shane", he would still be forever immortalized in the annals of screen heavies.

But the big, burly, rough-spoken Meyer took this role and used it to good advantage for the next quarter century.

Emile G. Meyer was born in New Orleans, Louisiana, August 10, 1910.

Before acting he had been a longshoreman, paymaster, truck driver, insurance salesman, safety engineer and cab driver.

He was performing in "The Petrified Forest" on the stage in New Orleans in 1948 at the Le Petit Theatre du Vieux Carre, a local little theatre company, when he was observed by director Elia Kazan who was in New Orleans preparing to direct "Panic In the Streets". Meyer was hired by Kazan as the Nile Queen Captain and from there Meyer went to Hollywood, obtaining roles in prestigious pictures like "The People Against O'Hara" ('51), "The Mob" ('51) and "Carbine Williams" ('52) as well as Bob Tansey's lowbudget "Cattle Queen" ('51), his first and only western prior to "Shane".

Over the years his drawn-back dark hair, furrowed brow, disgruntled look and cutting, nasal voice were seen and heard as prison wardens, sheriffs, detectives, fight managers and western heavies.

Films of note include "Blackboard Jungle" ('55), "Riot In Cell Block 11" ('54), "Paths of Glory" ('57), "The Lineup" ('58) and "The Outfit" ('74).

Meyer returned to his native Louisiana following his Hollywood days, dying in Covington, Louisiana, of Alzheimer's disease on March 19, 1987. He was survived by a son, three daughters. No mention of a wife.

Suggested Sampling of Meyer's Western Heavies:

- Cattle Queen ('51 United-International) Maria Hart
- Shane ('53 Paramount) Alan Ladd
- Annie Oakley: Dead Man's Bluff ('55) Gail Davis
- Gene Autry: Ride Ranchero ('55) Gene Autry
- Raw Edge ('56 Universal-International) Rory Calhoun
- Badlands of Montana ('57 Fox) Rex Reason
- Broken Arrow: Water Witch ('58) John Lupton/Michael Ansara
- Northwest Passage: Bound Woman ('58) Keith Larsen
- King of the Wild Stallions ('59 Allied Artists) George Montgomery
- Young Jesse James ('60 Fox) Willard Parker
- Wichita Town: The Avengers ('60) Joel McCrea
- Lawman: Belding's Girl ('60) John Russell
- Outlaws: Outlaw Marshals ('61) Don Collier
- Taggart ('64 Universal-International) Tony Young
- Legend of Jesse James: A Real Tough Town ('66) Christopher Jones

CHARLES MIDDLETON

Although he made over 200 movies from 1920-1949, the tall, thinly built, dour speaking Charles Middleton will always be remembered for his role as the satanic purveyor of evil, Ming the Merciless, in three Universal Flash Gordon serials opposite Buster Crabbe.

A decision by Middleton along about 1913 to spurn an offer from fledgling producer Thomas Ince to leave the legitimate Eastern stage and journey west to star in westerns instead elevated William S. Hart to stardom. Middleton recalled an earlier experience with Ince that resulted in no money and, besides that, he'd just purchased a new $25,000 home on Long Island. He turned down Ince's offer and suggested Hart who was then barely surviving at the American Music Hall in a wobbly western stage play. You know the rest of the story, Hart became a major star and Middleton eventually did decide in 1929 that movies could make him a living.

Middleton was born October 7, 1879, in Elizabethtown, Kentucky, the son of Hugh Middleton and Mary Carter.

With a rich theatrical voice, Middleton's first taste of show business was in carnivals and circuses and then vaudeville where he was one half of the team of Middleton and (Leora) Spellmeyer. The team later became permanent when the couple married.

Spellmeyer was her actual maiden name which she later changed to Spellman for acting purposes. She worked with her husband in his first two silent films. Born in Missouri July 13, 1888, she was several years younger than her husband but preceded him in death, passing away in Los Angeles September 4, 1945, of a heart attack. Less than a year later he was appearing on Broadway in "January Thaw".

Middleton's deeply lined, cruel visage was perfect for heavies in all types of films, not just westerns. Look for Middleton in "Beau Hunks" ('31) with Laurel and Hardy, "Safe In Hell" ('31) as lawyer Jones, "Road Gang" ('36) as a mine warden, "Grapes of Wrath" ('40), "Strangler of the Swamp" ('46), among others.

Middleton's high cheekboned scowl proved effective in serials other than the Flash Gordon triology. He was Zaroff pitted against Tom Mix in Mascot's "Miracle Rider" ('35), saloon owner Ace Daggett in Universal's "Flaming Frontiers" ('38) with Johnny Mack Brown, the evil Pa Stark in Republic's "Dick Tracy Returns", criminal mastermind known only by his prison number 39-0-13 in "Daredevils of the Red Circle" (Republic '39), villainous Arab Cassib in "Perils of Nyoka" ('42 Republic), and treacherous Jason Grood in "Jack Armstrong" ('47 Columbia). He also has roles in four other Columbia cliffhangers—"Black Arrow" ('44), "Who's Guilty" ('45), "Desert Hawk" ('44) and "Batman" ('43). Undoubtedly, one of the top serial heavies.

Of his roles, Middleton once said, "I believe my mean roles had a definite influence for good among those who saw my pictures. It is a warning to folks not to be the kind of man I play in the film. Their hatred prevents them from doing the outrageous tricks I do on screen."

In describing Middleton's personality, veteran heavy himself, Tris Coffin explained, "Square is not exactly the word for him but it's pretty near—and I don't mean to be depreciating because that was his personality. He was very quiet and, as I recall, he didn't mix too much with the rest of us. If there was anything going on that was fun, he was most likely not in it. There was nothing unfriendly about him but he was sort of a loner—on the set at least; I don't know anything about his private life."

Every now and then Middleton could be seen in sympathetic roles such as "Empty Saddles" ('36) with Buck Jones, "Sunset Pass" ('33) with Randolph Scott, "Cowboys From Texas" ('39) with 3 Mesquiteers. He even broke into song in the Marx Brothers' "Duck Soup" ('33) and was Hopalong Cassidy's boss, Buck Peters, in "Hop-A-Long Cassidy" ('35).

Middleton never served in the Armed Forces.

He died of heart disease April 22, 1949, after a five day stay at Jared-Sidney Torrance Memorial Hospital. Three days earlier he had his right foot amputated due to gangrene.

He was survived by the couple's daughter, also named Leora, later Mrs. William F. Ladd. Middleton is the grandfather of actor Burr Middleton who has perpetuated his grandfather's work in writing and at various film gatherings.

Middleton was a member of the actors' Masquers Club and the Comedy Club.

He is buried at Hollywood Forever Cemetery in California.

Suggested Sampling of Middleton's Western Heavies:

- Beau Bandit ('30 RKO) Rod La Rocque
- Mystery Ranch ('32 RKO) George O'Brien
- Square Shooter '(35 Columbia) Tim McCoy
- Miracle Rider ('35 Mascot serial) Tom Mix
- Song of the Saddle ('36 Warner Bros.) Dick Foran
- Two Gun Law ('37 Columbia) Charles Starrett
- Hollywood Cowboy ('37 RKO) George O'Brien
- Yodelin' Kid From Pine Ridge ('37 Republic) Gene Autry
- Flaming Frontiers ('38 Universal serial) Johnny Mack Brown
- Stick to Your Guns ('41 Paramount) William Boyd
- Wagon Wheels West ('43 Warner Bros.) Robert Shayne

ROBERT MIDDLETON

Despite the fact the glowering, hulking, balding, beetle-browed Robert Middleton was known as a portrayer of oily villains capable of the most contemptible of crimes, in real life he was a hearty gentleman who apparently loved to play practical jokes, especially on his family.

Middleton was born Samuel G. Messer, May 13, 1911, in Cincinnati, Ohio, the son of a building contractor. From 1928-1933 he attended the Cincinnati College of Music, the Cincinnati Conservatory of Music and Carnegie Institute of Technology.

His voice quality was such it earned him a position as a radio announcer before the Army made him a First Sergeant. Discharged, his work in radio sparked an interest in acting and a stage career flourished, taking him to Broadway in 1954 for "Ondine" with Audrey Hepburn and Mel Ferrer.

By then he'd already worked in several TV shows, including appearances on "The Honeymooners" as Jackie Gleason's boss.

His first film was "The Silver Chalice" in '54, then he solidified his evil image in "The Desperate Hours" ('55) with Humphrey Bogart and "Friendly Persuasion" ('56) with Gary Cooper.

One of the meanest heavies, Chris Alcaide, was Middleton's henchie in "Day of the Badman" in '58 with Fred MacMurray and recalled, "Middleton went through a divorce just as he was hitting it big after 'Friendly Persuasion'. He was impressive as an actor with those powerful vocal chords. The doctor told him once his vocal chords were like two hunks of liver laying down. Powerful, beautiful voice. Even if the lines were stilted, he found a way to make them believable. The guy *owned* his parts."

In television and on film Middleton, the western equivalent of Sydney Greenstreet, afforded us a wide array of memorable, cigar-chomping town bosses, loutish mountain men, hateful lynch mob leaders and generally repulsive knaves, often reminiscent of Edward Arnold's characterizations of a decade or so earlier.

Heart problems beset the august Middleton in the late '60s, causing him to severely curtail his acting chores.

He died at 66 on June 14, 1977, of congestive heart failure at St. Joseph's Hospital in Burbank. His survivors included two sons, two brothers and a sister.

"Cattle King" Robert Middleton (L) and his henchman Richard Devon issue a strong warning to rancher William Windom ('63 MGM).

Suggested Sampling of Middleton's Western Heavies:

- Gunsmoke: Word of Honor ('55) James Arness
- Red Sundown ('56 Universal-International) Rory Calhoun
- Friendly Persuasion ('56 United Artists) Gary Cooper
- Lonely Man ('57 Paramount) Tony Perkins
- Day of the Bad Man ('58 Universal-International) Fred MacMurray
- Law and Jake Wade ('58 MGM) Robert Taylor
- Bat Masterson: Double Showdown ('58) Gene Barry
- Texas John Slaughter: Ambush in Laredo ('58) Tom Tryon
- Hell Bent For Leather ('60 Universal-International) Audie Murphy
- Wagon Train: Tom Tuckett Story ('60) Ward Bond
- Tales of Wells Fargo: Threat of Death ('60) Dale Robertson
- Bonanza: Death at Dawn ('60) Lorne Greene
- Wrangler: A Time For Hanging ('60) Jason Evers
- Tall Man: Garrett and the Kid ('60) Barry Sullivan/Clu Gulager
- Tales of Wells Fargo: Man of Another Breed ('61) Dale Robertson
- Rebel: Road to Jericho ('61) Nick Adams
- Gunsmoke: The Hunger ('62) James Arness
- Cattle King ('63 MGM) Robert Taylor
- Rawhide: Brush War at Buford ('65) Clint Eastwood
- Monroes: Incident at Hanging Tree ('66) Michael Anderson Jr.
- Daniel Boone: The Gun ('66) Fess Parker
- Big Valley: Down Shadow Street ('67) Barbara Stanwyck
- Alias Smith and Jones: Bounty Hunter ('71) Ben Murphy/Peter Duel
- The Lincoln Conspiracy ('77 Sunn Classic) Bradford Dillman

JOHN MILFORD

Rugged appearing, the educated John Milford was ideal for arrogant, sarcastic badman roles on TV, however seldom rose to the position of top-billed guest star, remaining usually as one of the gang.

Born September 7, 1929, in Johnstown, New York, he received a bachelor's degree in civil engineering at Union College in Schenectady, New York, and a master's degree in drama at Yale.

Milford made his acting debut on the early TV series "What's My Name?" at KGRB in Albany, New York, and his film debut in "Marty" in '55.

Over the years he had recurring famous-outlaw roles on two series. He was Ike Clanton on "Wyatt Earp" from '59-'60 (recast with Rayford Barnes '60-'61) and Cole Younger on the short-lived "Legend of Jesse James" ('65).

Milford also had regular non-western roles on "The Lieutenant" ('63-'64) and "Enos" ('80-'81).

Perhaps "The Rifleman" made best use of Milford's talents, employing him 11 times over its five season run.

In later years, Milford was a member of the so-called Johnny Carson Players, playing Leonid Brezhnev to Carson's Ronald Reagan in late night skits.

When acting didn't pay the bills, Milford went back to civil engineering for which he'd been schooled. In that capacity he created the original design for the Hollywood Walk of Fame which now has over 2,000 engraved bronze stars. But Milford may be best remembered for what he did for the theatre business in Los Angeles. In 1957, he helped build a venue at 3759 Cahuenga Blvd., once known as the REP Playhouse, then Studio Theatre. In 1969, with partners, it was changed to the 45 seat Chamber, the first of the city's equity waiver theatres. The little theatre helped launch the careers of such actors as Richard Chamberlain and Vic Morrow.

At 72, Milford collapsed and died August 14, 2000, en route to his Brentwood, California, home following outpatient care for skin cancer at the John Wayne Cancer Institute in Santa Monica. He'd recently appeared on "Melrose Place" and "Chicken Soup For the Soul".

He was married to film and TV producer Susan Graw for many years.

Suggested Sampling of Milford's Western Heavies:

- Mackenzie's Raiders: Lost Raider ('58) Richard Carlson
- Wyatt Earp: Death For a Stolen Horse ('59) Hugh O'Brian
- Wanted Dead or Alive: Call Your Shot ('59) Steve McQueen
- Tales of Wells Fargo: The Daltons ('59) Dale Robertson
- Texan: Trail Dust ('59) Rory Calhoun
- Fury: Trail Drive ('59) Peter Graves
- Bonanza: Vendetta ('59) Lorne Greene
- Rifleman: The Coward ('59) Chuck Connors
- Wichita Town: The Avengers ('60) Joel McCrea
- Rifleman: Horse Traders ('60) Chuck Connors
- Two Faces West: The Operation ('60) Charles Bateman
- Sugarfoot: Man From Medora ('60) Will Hutchins
- Tales of Wells Fargo: Frightened Witness ('60) Dale Robertson
- Have Gun Will Travel: Long Way Home ('61) Richard Boone
- Outlaws: Culley ('61) Don Collier
- Rifleman: Dark Day at North Fork ('61) Chuck Connors
- Cheyenne: Man Alone ('62) Clint Walker
- Rifleman: The Assailants ('62) Chuck Connors
- Laramie: Vengeance ('63) Robert Fuller
- Virginian: Fatal Journey ('63) James Drury
- Destry: Red Brady's Kid ('64) John Gavin
- Gunsmoke: Winner Take All ('65) James Arness
- Virginian: Shadows of the Past ('65) Clu Gulager
- Big Valley: Forty Rifles ('65) Lee Majors
- Man Called Shenandoah: Young Outlaw ('65) Robert Horton
- Iron Horse: Man From New Chicago ('66) Dale Robertson
- High Chaparral: A Quiet Day in Tucson ('67) Henry Darrow/Cameron Mitchell
- Bonanza: A World Full of Cannibals ('68) Lorne Greene
- Daniel Boone: Road to Freedom ('69) Fess Parker
- Gunsmoke: The Badge ('70) James Arness

WALTER MILLER

Walter Miller had been one of the top paid leading men in silent serials before changing lanes to become a dastardly villain in talkies during the '30s. He and heroine Allene Ray were the most famous team in ten silent serials for Pathe between 1925-1929, including "Hawk of the Hills", "Man Without a Face" and "Black Book". In addition he co-starred at Pathe with boxer Gene Tunney in "Fighting Marine" ('26) and "Queen of the Northwoods" ('29) with Ethlyne Clair. During the same period he made "Mysterious Airman" ('28) and "Police Reporter" ('28) with Eugenia Gilbert for Artclass. Always on the right side of the law.

Born Walter Corwin Miller, March 9, 1892, in Dayton, Ohio, (his parents were George E. Miller of Dayton and Isabelle Corwin of Hillsdale, Michigan) he apparently spent a portion of his youth in Atlanta, Georgia, before being educated at Manual Training High School in Brooklyn, New York, where he began a stage career at 17 playing juvenile leads with stock companies and in Vaudeville.

In 1910, after closing a short season with a stock company in Troy, New York, he was offered a leading man role in films by small independent Reliance. He remained with them only a year before returning to stage work with the Hall Stock Company.

By 1912 he was back in Hollywood, briefly with D. W. Griffith before moving to some class features at Fox and Metro as well as work at a handful of independents.

Writer Ken Weiss found an article in the February 1918 MOTION PICTURE MAGAZINE titled "Where Have They Gone?" by Sue Roberts wondering what had happened to Walter Miller, "Biograph's one best bet as a leading man three years ago," who has vanished from the screen. She had sent a letter to Miller's last known address and received a reply from his wife, Lillian, who explained, "Two years ago illness made it impossible for me to remain in this climate. Walter gave up everything for me and now that I've recovered he's returning to the screen." The story offers a glimpse into Miller's measure as a person.

Never really becoming a major star, it was Miller's ten serials with Allene Ray that endeared him to a legion of fans in the '20s. He was earning $1,000 a week, top pay for a serial star at the time.

When sound came in he was quickly signed in '29 by Nat Levine at Mascot for the lead in "King of the Kongo" which was released in both sound and silent versions. In all, Miller made six for Mascot: "King of the Wild" ('30); "Lone Defender" ('30); "Last of the Mohicans" ('32); "Shadow of the Eagle" ('32) and "Galloping Ghost" ('31). In all he was still on the right side of the law except for "Galloping Ghost" in which he challenged gridiron star Red Grange. That switch seemed to set the tone and harken the future as a heavy for Miller as he moved to Universal for "Danger Island" ('31); "Gordon of Ghost City" ('33); "Tailspin Tommy" ('34); "Vanishing Shadow" ('34); "Pirate Treasure" ('34); "Red Rider" ('34); "Call of the Savage" ('35); "Roaring West" ('35), "Wild West Days" ('37) and Columbia for "Great Adventures of Wild Bill Hickok" ('38). In only one at

Boss Walter Miller (L) gives henchman Al Bridge some underhanded orders in Johnny Mack Brown's Universal serial, "Wild West Days" ('37).

Universal, "Rustlers of Red Dog" ('35), was he a good guy once again—as Deacon, Johnny Mack Brown's pal.

These were followed by a great role in "Secret of Treasure Island" ('38) at Columbia. "Dick Tracy's G-Men" ('39) and "Dick Tracy Vs. Crime Inc." ('41) at Republic finished out Miller's serial appearances. As a matter of fact, the latter was released after his death March 30, 1940, at only 48.

Miller was initially married to Lillian Louise Coffin and later to onetime headline vaudeville dancer (and actress) Eileen Schofield (who has a minor role in his "King of the Wild" serial). There was at least one child.

While filming Gene Autry's "Gaucho Serenade" on a Thursday, he and a fellow actor agreed to pull no punches in a fight scene. Over the next two days he continued to complain of a pain in his back during the filming when, while doing some closeups on Saturday March 30, 1940, Walter Miller suffered a massive heart attack and collapsed on the Republic backlot. He died a short time later at the Hollywood Receiving Hospital. His wife took his body to Calvary Cemetery in Evanston, Illinois. He was also survived by a son, Richard.

It was an all too early end for Miller, as during his heyday he'd stayed fit working out at Sullivan's Gym where he was friendly with Joe Bonomo, Cliff Lyons, Richard Talmadge and others.

Suggested Sampling of Miller's WesternHeavies:

- Hurricane Horseman ('31 Kent) Lane Chandler
- Riding For Justice ('32 Columbia) Buck Jones
- Ghost City ('32 Monogram) Bill Cody
- Gordon of Ghost City ('33 Universal serial) Buck Jones
- Gun Justice '(33 Universal) Ken Maynard
- Red Rider ('34 Universal serial) Buck Jones
- Rocky Rhodes ('34 Universal) Buck Jones
- Ivory Handled Gun ('35 Universal) Buck Jones
- Roaring West ('35 Universal serial) Buck Jones
- Stormy ('35 Universal) Noah Beery Jr.
- Desert Gold ('36 Paramount) Tom Keene
- Fugitive Sheriff ('36 Columbia) Ken Maynard
- Ghost Patrol ('36 Puritan) Tim McCoy
- Ranger Courage ('37 Columbia) Bob Allen
- Boss of Lonely Valley ('37 Universal) Buck Jones
- Wild Horse Rodeo ('37 Republic) 3 Mesquiteers
- Home On the Prairie ('39 Republic) Gene Autry
- Bullet Code ('40 RKO) George O'Brien

MORT MILLS

Ex-Marine paratrooper Mort Mills made his screen debut in 1952 as a thug in the Bowery Boys' "No Holds Barred".

Although Mills co-starred (with Rex Reason) as Marshal Frank Talman on TV's "Man Without A Gun" ('57-'59) and certainly simulated the part of other sheriffs, bartenders, reporters, etc., it is as a stern, sour-faced badman that we best remember him on over 150 TV shows and in nearly 50 films for almost 20 years from '52-'71.

Mortimer Michael Mills, whose true surname might have been Kaplan, as his father, Hyman Kaplan, was from Russia, was born in New York City, January 11, 1919. His mother's name was Florence, state of birth unknown.

Following his Marine paratrooper career in WWII ('41-'45), Mills more than likely came to the screen via his cousin, comic actress Mary Treen who began in 1934. His abilities as a badman were quickly put to use, especially in the burgeoning TV medium where new faces were being sought. Moving from the half-hour juvenile westerns to the more adult westerns, Mills was ever in demand. Following "Man Without a Gun", the "Perry Mason" series hired him for the recurring role of Lt. Ben Landau. He also had a recurring role as Sheriff Fred Madden on "Big Valley" in '65.

During his career, Mills managed some significant character roles in several classic films…he was a deputy in Marlon Brando's "Wild One" ('53), a soldier in Audie Murphy's "To Hell and Back" ('55), a reporter in Bogart's "The Harder They Fall" ('56), a highway patrolman in "Psycho" ('60) and a farmer in another Hitchcock film, "Torn Curtain" ('66).

With the TV western era ending, Mills dropped from public life after a small role in an "Alias Smith and Jones" episode ('71). Fellow screen badman Chris Alcaide recalls, "Mort wanted out of 'Man Without a Gun'. He felt he was doing a stupid job and wanted to do more important things. But from the moment he got out of the series, it never seemed to happen for him. The next time I ran into him he was selling nuts and bolts…wholesale manufacturing. A friend of Mort's was a manufacturer and Mort was an agent representing him going all over."

Mills suffered a heart attack at his home on Pierpont Blvd. in Ventura, California, while in bed and died June 6, 1993. Since he was allegedly smoking in bed, it was first reported he fell asleep with a lighted cigarette and died from "Thermal burns and inhalation of noxious products of combustion." Saner heads prevailed, and an amended death certificate was filed stating the cause of death to be a heart attack. His remains were cremated and deposited at sea offshore in the Santa Barbara Channel by the Neptune Society.

Mills was widowed at the time of his death from a woman named Mary. There was at least one child, a son named Michael G. Mills of Malibu.

Suggested Sampling of Mills' Western Heavies:

- Lone Ranger: Six Gun Artist ('49) Clayton Moore
- Hopalong Cassidy: Arizona Trouble Shooters ('53) William Boyd
- Kit Carson: Badman's Escape ('53) Bill Williams
- Cisco Kid: Sky Sign ('54) Duncan Renaldo
- Gunsmoke: How to Die For Nothing ('55) James Arness
- Broken Arrow: Black Moment ('57) John Lupton
- Iron Sheriff ('57 United Artists) Sterling Hayden
- Wanted Dead Or Alive: The Bounty ('58) Steve McQueen
- Bronco: Long Ride Back ('58) Ty Hardin
- Rifleman: The Sister ('58) Chuck Connors
- Ride A Crooked Trail ('58 Universal) Audie Murphy
- Trackdown: Bad Judgment ('59) Robert Culp
- Gunsmoke: Murder Warrant ('59) James Arness
- Have Gun Will Travel: Hunt the Man Down ('59) Richard Boone
- Tales of Wells Fargo: The Bounty Hunter ('59) Dale Robertson
- Wichita Town: Man On the Hill ('59) Joel McCrea
- Bat Masterson: Who'll Bury My Violence ('59) Gene Barry
- Bonanza: Vendetta ('59) Lorne Greene
- Man From Blackhawk: Station 6 ('59) Robert Rockwell
- Sugarfoot: Journey To Provision ('60) Will Hutchins
- Texan: Thirty Hours to Kill ('60) Rory Calhoun
- Stagecoach West: The Marker ('61) Wayne Rogers
- Quick Gun ('64 Columbia) Audie Murphy
- Outlaws Is Coming ('65 Columbia) 3 Stooges
- Return of the Gunfighter ('67 TVM) Robert Taylor
- Guns of Will Sonnett: A Town In Terror (Pt. 1-2) ('69) Walter Brennan

STEVE MITCHELL

Steve Mitchell resembled a New York gangster who'd somehow been dropped into the middle of the Wild West. So naturally, it's not surprising to learn this screen tough guy (who really has a heart of gold) was born in Brooklyn, New York, December 15, 1926, and brought up in New York and Detroit, Michigan (where he graduated high school) and Amarillo, Texas. His parents (Harry Mitchell and Celia Simmons) were restaurateurs, owning restaurants and nightclubs at various times in all three cities.

After high school, with WWII raging, Mitchell was in the Navy from 1944-'46. Serving as a gunner on destroyers and destroyer escorts in the North Atlantic and the Pacific, Steve tells it, "I got a little beat up in the war and was a patient at St. Albans Naval Hospital in Long Island. I didn't talk too well on account of getting clobbered, so basically had to learn to talk again."

Not knowing where to go with his life, Mitchell drifted from job to job—bus driver, produce business with A&P, private detective with the Burns Agency, in charge of the Astor Bar in New York's theatre district. A wild weekend with some Army buddies found him in Kitty Hawk, North Carolina. Stranded, he went to work for Carolina Power and Light as a lineman.

Tired of drifting, and on advice from the V.A., Steve enrolled in dramatic school in New York using his GI education bill. That training led to roles on various live TV shows being made in New York at the time. Meanwhile he drove a cab to pay the bills.

Eventually the blood, sweat, tears and callbacks paid off with a kidnapper's role in producer Louis de Rochemont's "Walk East on Beacon" ('52 Columbia) with George Murphy.

Up for a role in "Pat and Mike", Uncle Sam squashed that when Mitchell was recalled in 1952 for the Korean Conflict, but a medical discharge cut his time to three months. By the time of his discharge, the role had gone to Aldo Ray, but director George Cukor assigned Steve the part of Katharine Hepburn's caddy, although he wound up on the cutting room floor.

The days of the serials were about over, but Mitchell managed to connect in "Jungle Drums of Africa" ('53 Republic) as Gauss, one of dress-heavy Henry Rowland's two plug-ugly henchmen (the other was John Cason).

With his 'New Yawk' accent, and shifty-lout look,

Mitchell was perfect for gangster roles in "The Killing", "Big Combo", "Most Dangerous Man Alive" and TV's "Sea Hunt", "Public Defender", "Harbor Command", "Alfred Hitchcock Presents", "Tightrope" and others.

But even with the accent, plenty of western work came his way on "26 Men", "Lone Ranger", "Mackenzie's Raiders", "Death Valley Days", "Annie Oakley", "Tales of Wells Fargo", "Wild Wild West", "Have Gun Will Travel" and others.

Having a disc taken out of his back following an accident about 1968 more or less curtailed his finding strenuous work in action films. Lesser roles in a few films such as the Sheriff in "Bloody Mama" ('70) and a thug on TV's "Wonder Woman" ('74) followed, but Steve changed directions and, although remaining in California, he became the forerunner of the Arkansas State Film Commission by helping to bring Hollywood movies to Arkansas. "Bloody Mama" for Roger Corman was one such film.

Married to Glenda Bullock in 1969, their one son, Stephen, was born in 1972.

Steve applied for his actor's retirement in 1982 and stayed in the San Fernando Valley until 1993. At that time he moved to Santa Fe, New Mexico, then Albuquerque for about a year. After a short stint in Las Vegas, Nevada, he returned to the Valley. Mitchell died at 80 on January 23, 2007, in an L.A. medical facility.

Suggested Sampling of Mitchell's Western Heavies:

- Lone Ranger: Mrs. Banker ('53) John Hart
- Annie Oakley: A Gal For Grandma ('54) Gail Davis
- Buffalo Bill Jr.: Rails Westward ('55) Dick Jones
- Tales of the Texas Rangers: Prairie Raiders ('55) Willard Parker
- Sergeant Preston: Love and Honor ('56) Richard Simmons
- Seven Men From Now ('56 Warner Bros.) Randolph Scott
- Gunsight Ridge ('56 U.A.) Joel McCrea
- Terror In a Texas Town: ('58 U.A.) Sterling Hayden
- 26 Men: Cattle Embargo ('58) Kelo Henderson/Tris Coffin
- 26 Men: Sundown Decision ('58) Kelo Henderson/Tris Coffin
- Rawhide: Incident of the Calico Gun ('59) Eric Fleming/Clint Eastwood
- Tales of Wells Fargo: Little Man ('59) Dale Robertson
- Deputy: The Border Between ('60) Henry Fonda/Allen Case
- Bat Masterson: Last of the Night Raiders ('60) Gene Barry
- Nevada Smith ('66 Paramount) Steve McQueen
- Hondo: Hanging Town ('67) Ralph Taeger
- Wild Wild West: Night of the Headless Woman ('68) Robert Conrad

ART MIX

Art Mix could be called "the man in the hat". The rather large, unusual cowboy hat, worn by the balding cowboy, became his trademark for over 20 years in westerns. Art Mix (George Kesterson) was another of the familiar, usually in the background, B-western performers. He starred in a few films early on, then slipped into supporting roles and bit parts, and was seen as a henchman/gang member, townsman, etc. Don't confuse this Art Mix, real name George Kesterson, with the Art Mix persona of ultra low-budget film creator Victor Adamson, also known as Denver Dixon.

Before becoming a full-fledged sound western henchie, Mix/Kesterson was a talkies range hero…for a very brief time. He starred in "West of the Rockies" ('29 Davis), "Sagebrush Politics" ('30 Hollywood) and "The Rawhide Terror" ('34 Security) (which was originally intended as a serial), the latter two for Victor Adamson/Denver Dixon…you know, the "other" Art Mix.

Confusing matters more, there was a lawsuit in January 1939—or at least some legal wrangling—between a Bob Roberts (real name Leon Joseph Roberts) and Kesterson over the use of the "Art Mix" name. Roberts was another actor whom Adamson used as "Art Mix" in some late silent low-budget westerns. He then made personal appearances in the middle west under that name until he pled guilty to a bigamy charge in Little Rock, Arkansas, in late 1938. At that time Kesterson (Mix) stated, "I have to take action to keep him from using my name, at least, in California. I can't sue him in every state. I am happily married to Inez Gomez and have been for the past 12 years." Kesterson continued to use the name til the end.

George Kesterson was born in Atlas, Illinois, June 18, 1896. Shortly thereafter, his parents moved to Alberta, Canada, where his father owned a string of stables. This is where Art learned to ride. Before coming to films, sports-oriented Kesterson was a pitcher for the Edmonton, Canada, baseball team and in 1915 won the lightweight boxing championship of Canada in the amateur division.

He somehow hooked up with writer/producer/director/actor Victor Adamson who had grown tired of acting under the Art Mix name he'd devised (obviously to cash in on the very popular Tom Mix moniker) and hired Kesterson to assume the role for five low-budget sagebrush silents in 1924, the first of which was "Ace of Cactus Range" for Aywon. Adamson directed and acted in the film under his other alias, Denver Dixon. The pair went on to make six more silents, but now our star reverted to George Kesterson for "Salt Lake Trail" and the others (all in '25-'26).

A few other roles were interspersed with these, then came the starring talkies, after which Art stuck with the henchman-type roles in some 150 films (except for the "Rawhide Terror" abomination). His most fertile period was at Columbia from '36-'43, most often as one of lead heavy Dick Curtis' henchies trying to do away with Charles Starrett or Bill Elliott.

After 1946's "Moon Over Montana" with Jimmy Wakely, Art Mix disappeared from public view. Kesterson—Art Mix—died December 7, 1972, at 76. He's buried at Forest Lawn Cemetery in Glendale, California.

Looks like dress-heavy Norman Willis needs a little help from gunman Art Mix in Wild Bill Elliott's "Beyond the Sacramento" ('40 Columbia).

Suggested Sampling of Mix's Western Heavies:

- Pueblo Terror ('31 West Coast/Cosmos) Buffalo Bill Jr.
- Young Blood ('32 Monogram) Bob Steele
- Treason ('33 Columbia) Buck Jones
- Sagebrush Trail ('33 Lone Star) John Wayne
- Way of the West ('34 Superior) Wally Wales
- Prescott Kid ('34 Columbia) Tim McCoy
- Lucky Terror ('36 Diversion) Hoot Gibson
- Call of the Rockies ('38 Columbia) Charles Starrett
- West of Cheyenne ('38 Columbia) Charles Starrett
- South of Arizona ('38 Columbia) Charles Starrett
- Spoilers of the Range ('39 Columbia) Charles Starrett
- Taming of the West ('39 Columbia) Bill Elliott
- Overland with Kit Carson ('39 Columbia serial) Bill Elliott
- Thundering West ('39 Columbia) Charles Starrett
- Bullets For Bandits ('42 Columbia) Bill Elliott/Tex Ritter
- Overland Stagecoach ('42 PRC) Bob Livingston
- Outlaws of Stampede Pass ('43 Monogram) Johnny Mack Brown
- Silver City Raiders ('43 Columbia) Russell Hayden

GERALD MOHR

Sleek and dark, with a wolfish smile that could portray extreme sophistication or out and out villainy, Gerald Mohr did it all, heroic and heavy. From Broadway to radio. From serial villain to crime thriller lead. Top screen narrator and cartoon voiceover artist. And a western heavy, particularly on the Warner Bros. TV westerns of the late '50s and early '60s.

Born in New York City June 11, 1914, Mohr was the son of Gerald Mohr Sr. and Henrietta Noustadt, a Viennese singer. His father died when he was quite young so Gerald was primarily raised by his grandfather, a psychologist and close associate of Dr. Sigmund Freud, the famed psychoanalyst. Because of this association, Mohr became a fervent student of Freud, studies which he later employed on screen.

Mohr was taught piano at an early age and attended the prestigious Dwight Preparatory School in New York, however medicine interested him more at the time. But while in medical school at Columbia University, due to his laconic, resonant voice he was asked to make an audition at CBS. Shortly thereafter he was made the network's youngest special events reporter.

Urged to try for the Broadway stage, he played a minor gangster in "The Petrified Forest" which began its run in '35 and made a star out of Humphrey Bogart.

In 1937 Mohr joined Orson Welles' Mercury Theatre Company on radio.

From there it was an easy step into films in 1939 where his voice served him well as the mysterious Dr. Zodiac in "Charlie Chan at Treasure Island" ('39 20th Century Fox). However, on screen, Zodiac is revealed to be Caesar Romero. Again, in Republic's top serial, "Adventures of Captain Marvel" ('41), he was the uncredited voice of The Scorpion. Republic rewarded him later in the year, top casting him as the vicious Slick Latimer in "Jungle Girl".

Other roles followed, but radio was Mohr's real meal ticket throughout the '40s and '50s. He was the Lone Wolf on Mutual in '48 (after starring on screen as Michael Lanyard in three Columbia thrillers in '46-'47). He was the star of "The Adventures of Phillip Marlowe" from '48-'51 on CBS. Mohr was also heard on "Nero Wolfe", "Burns and Allen", "Damon Runyan Theatre", "Eddie Cantor Show", "Judy Canova", "Our Miss Brooks", "The Whistler" and other programs.

Mohr began working in television in '51 and was

Gerald Mohr and Sheriff Stephen McNally strike up an uneasy friendship in Audie Murphy's "Duel at Silver Creek" ('52 Universal-International).

cast as Christopher Storm, the American owner of a hotel in Vienna and a fast man with a gun and dame, in the final revamped incarnation of "Foreign Intrigue" ('54-'55).

It was then he hooked up with Warner Bros. TV to portray some terrific badmen, charming con men and slick heavies on "Cheyenne", "Bronco", "Sugarfoot", "Maverick" and "Alaskans". Other TV westerns used him also, but never as well as Warner Bros.

In '67 he was the cartoon voice of The Green Lantern on the animated "Superman/Aquaman Hour of Adventure" as well as the voice of Reed Richards, Mr. Fantastic, on the animated "Fantastic Four".

Following an excellent role in Barbara Streisand's "Funny Girl" ('68), Mohr was overseas in Stockholm, Sweden, producing and starring in a TV series when he died suddenly of a heart attack at 54 on November 9, 1968.

Mohr was first married to Rita Deneau in 1939. They had one child but were divorced in 1957. In 1958 he married Swedish born Mai Dietrich which endured until his death.

Suggested Sampling of Mohr's Western Heavies:

- King of the Cowboys ('43 Republic) Roy Rogers
- Duel at Silver Creek ('52 Universal-International) Audie Murphy
- Cheyenne: Rendezvous at Red Rock ('56) Clint Walker
- Maverick: Quick and the Dead ('57) James Garner
- Buckskin Lady ('57 United Artists) Patricia Medina
- Maverick: Burning Sky ('58) Jack Kelly
- Sugarfoot: Guns for Big Bear ('58) Will Hutchins
- Tombstone Territory: Doc Holliday in Durango ('58) Pat Conway
- Maverick: Escape to Tampico ('58) James Garner
- Wanted Dead or Alive: Til Death Do Us Part ('58) Steve McQueen
- Texan: Duchess of Denver ('59) Rory Calhoun
- Rough Riders: The Injured ('59) Jan Merlin/Kent Taylor
- Bat Masterson: Promised Land ('59) Gene Barry

- Maverick: You Can't Beat the Percentage ('59) Jack Kelly
- Sugarfoot: Outlaw Island ('59) Will Hutchins
- Johnny Ringo: Love Affair ('59) Don Durant
- Tales of Wells Fargo: The Easterner ('60) Dale Robertson
- Deputy: Final Payment ('60) Henry Fonda/Allen Case
- Overland Trail: Baron Comes Back ('60) Doug McClure/William Bendix
- Maverick: Mano Nera ('60) Jack Kelly
- Outlaws: Rape of Red Sky ('60) Don Collier
- Bonanza: The Abduction ('60) Dan Blocker/Michael Landon
- Bronco: The Invaders ('61) Ty Hardin
- Bat Masterson: Run For Your Money ('61) Gene Barry
- Outlaws: No Luck On Friday ('61) Don Collier
- Bronco: Then the Mountains ('62) Ty Hardin
- Rifleman: Squeeze Play ('62) Chuck Connors
- Iron Horse: Golden Web ('67) Dale Robertson

TOM MONROE

No pretense on trying to fool anyone into believing he was a respected citizen, rough and tough-looking Tom Monroe was a badman-outlaw through and through, a sort of TV counterpart to the big-screen likes of John Cason, Lane Bradford, Dick Curtis and Bud Geary.

Alfred Thomas Monroe was born in Waco, Texas, on September 2, 1919, the fifth son of six boys. His father was a Baptist minister.

Attending high school, Tom played football, baseball and basketball and attended Baylor University on a scholarship. While in college he sang with and fronted a dance band.

After playing a little pro football, Tom went into the service where he also had a dance band.

Discharged from the service, he hooked up with an old friend who was now an actor, James Brown (later star of "Rin Tin Tin"). By chance, an agent heard Tom sing and helped him get into pictures, with his initial outing being Henry Hathaway's "The Dark Corner" ('46 20th Century Fox).

A hefty guy with an angular scowling face made Tom perfect for westerns. His first was a bit in Rod Cameron's "Panhandle" ('48 Allied Artists), quickly followed by others with Allan "Rocky" Lane, Don Barry, Randolph Scott and Bill Elliott—plus small roles in three latter day Republic serials, "G-Men Never Forget" ('48), "Invisible Monster" ('50) and "Man With the Steel Whip" ('54).

According to Monroe, "I never got back to singing. Work in movies was so much fun and so easy for me, I never did sing."

Tom entered the business at just the right time to be one of the "new" TV heavies, and he worked all the shows, especially "Gene Autry", "Range Rider", "Cowboy G-Men", "Buffalo Bill Jr.", "Wyatt Earp", "Cheyenne", "Judge Roy Bean", "26 Men", among others.

One of Monroe's last roles was with golfing buddy James Garner in "Skin Game" ('71 Warner Bros.).

Tom's longtime friend, late actor Allan Nixon told Boyd Magers, "I met Tom right after the war—1946 or so, through Bob Lowery. We had a little group who hung out—Tom, Lowery, Fred Clark, Jack Beutel, William Tracy. We had golf and barroom socializing in common…the now gone Cock 'n' Bull and Scandia, among others. Tom was one of the best golfers in the business, along with Jim Garner, Bob Wilke and John Agar, each of whom he beat at times. He taught Jason Evers how to play and they became close friends. Whenever the rent was due, Tom said, 'I'd call ol' Jason and we'd go out as a team to play another twosome for money and we seldom lost.' In recent years Tom was on a downhill spiral, healthwise. He managed an apartment house in Hollywood and kept an apartment there. I think he had to turn down a few jobs. His strength was pretty well gone. He was through with golf maybe 10 or 12 years before. But he kept up a big front, entertained friends and enjoyed his cocktails. Tom had lots of girlfriends and, as you may guess, loved 'partying'. I think in his last few years Tom was depressed…most of his buddies had died…James Brown, Fred Clark, Beutel, Lowery, Tracy, Sonny Tufts, Tim Holt, Russell Hayden, Alan Hale, Neville Brand, etc. He was in and out of the Veterans Hospital, and fading away from the 235 pound giant of a man I met in '46. At one point (in 1992), before going in for an operation for prostate cancer, he invited me and six other regular friends and gave each a carefully wrapped present from his belongings and said 'so long.'

But he survived that and came home again, for awhile."

Monroe, 74, died December 4, 1993, of cancer and congestive heart failure at a California VA hospital.

Suggested Sampling of Monroe's Western Heavies:

- I Shot Billy the Kid ('50 Lippert) Don Barry
- Border Treasure ('50 RKO) Tim Holt
- Border Rangers ('50 Lippert) Don Barry
- Gene Autry: Gray Dude ('50) Gene Autry
- Range Rider: Stage to Rainbow's End ('51) Jock Mahoney
- Gene Autry: Frontier Guard ('51) Gene Autry
- Range Rider: Secret of Superstition Peak ('52) Jock Mahoney
- Wild Bill Hickok: Medicine Show ('52) Guy Madison
- Cowboy G-Men: Gunslingers ('52) Russell Hayden
- Cisco Kid: Face of Death ('52) Duncan Renaldo
- Half Breed ('52 RKO) Robert Young
- Range Rider: West of Cheyenne ('53) Jock Mahoney
- Cowboy G-Men: Spring the Trap ('53) Russell Hayden
- Cowboy G-Men: Rawhiders ('53) Russell Hayden
- El Paso Stampede ('53 Republic) Allan "Rocky Lane
- The Homesteaders ('53 Allied Artists) Bill Elliott
- Stories of the Century: Cattle Kate ('54) Jim Davis
- Annie Oakley: Alias Annie Oakley ('54) Gail Davis
- Annie Oakley: Hard Luck Ranch ('55) Gail Davis
- Buffalo Bill Jr.: Apache Raid ('55) Dick Jones
- Wild Bill Hickok: Golden Rainbow ('55) Guy Madison
- Cheyenne: Julesburg ('55) Clint Walker
- Broken Arrow: The Captive ('56) Michael Ansara/John Lupton
- Judge Roy Bean: Lone Star Killer ('56) Edgar Buchanan
- Wyatt Earp: The Pinkertons ('56) Hugh O'Brian
- Cheyenne: Deadline ('57) Clint Walker
- Cheyenne: Hard Bargain ('57) Clint Walker
- 26 Men: Trouble at Pinnacle Peak ('57) Kelo Henderson/ Tris Coffin
- Casey Jones: Dutch Clock ('57) Alan Hale Jr.
- 26 Men: Violent Land ('57) Kelo Henderson/Tris Coffin
- Wyatt Earp: Wyatt Rides Shotgun ('58) Hugh O'Brian
- Wyatt Earp: Frontier Woman ('58) Hugh O'Brian
- Frontier Doctor: Double Boomerang ('58) Rex Allen
- Tall Man: Where Is Sylvia ('61) Barry Sullivan/Clu Gulager
- Lawman: Hold-out ('62) John Russell
- Hondo: Hondo and the Savage ('57) Ralph Taeger

MONTE MONTAGUE

One of the early western support players that kept his lariat in the loop for 34 years from the silent era in 1920 on through small character roles ending in 1954 is Walter H. "Monte" Montague.

Born in Somerset, Kentucky, April 23, 1891, he started in the world of entertainment as an aerialist with Ringling Brothers Circus. His parents were Oliver H. Montague and Nanny Davis, both originally from Virginia.

Monte came to the movies in 1920 with a role in Universal's "Flaming Disc" serial starring Elmo Lincoln. Becoming a close friend of Lincoln's, he often doubled for the star.

During the silent era Monte worked in the westerns of Fred Humes, William Fairbanks, Neal Hart, Jack Hoxie, Hoot Gibson, Ken Maynard, Art Acord and Bill Cody. The majority of Montague's silent work was at Universal.

Monte easily made the transition to sound, appearing in over 150 films, including at least 25 serials.

Never more than 3rd or 4th henchman through the door, his best roles as a badman came at RKO in the early '40s.

He was absent from the screen for unknown reasons for the most of '43, '44 and '45. Since these were war years, it is surmised Montague was connected with the war effort in some manner. When he returned, now in his mid '50s, his roles were much smaller and character oriented, but he continued to work on through "Border River" ('54 Universal) with Joel McCrea.

Monte served in the military in WWI. His wife's name was Mary. She was employed as a stroller assembler.

Montague died of coronary problems at Behrne's Memorial Hospital in Burbank, California, April 6, 1959. He was a few weeks shy of his 68th birthday.

Tim Holt has a grip on bushwhacker Monte Montague "Along the Rio Grande" ('41 RKO).

Suggested Sampling of Montague's Western Heavies:

- Ace of Spades ('25 Universal serial) William Desmond
- Rough and Ready ('27 Universal) Jack Hoxie
- Danger Rider ('28 Universal) Hoot Gibson
- Trigger Tricks ('30 Universal) Hoot Gibson
- Lonesome Trail ('30 Syndicate) Charles Delaney
- Quick Trigger Lee ('31 Big 4) Bob Custer
- Red Rider ('34 Universal serial) Buck Jones
- Rustlers of Red Dog ('35 Universal serial) Johnny Mack Brown
- Song of the Saddle ('36 Warner Bros.) Dick Foran
- Guns of the Pecos ('37 Warner Bros.) Dick Foran
- Renegade Ranger ('38 RKO) George O'Brien
- Law West of Tombstone ('38 RKO) Harry Carey
- Trouble In Sundown ('39 RKO) George O'Brien
- Legion of the Lawless ('40 RKO) George O'Brien
- Fargo Kid ('40 RKO) Tim Holt
- Along the Rio Grande ('41 RKO) Tim Holt
- Thundering Hoofs ('41 RKO) Tim Holt
- Cyclone Kid ('42 Republic) Don Barry
- Phantom Plainsmen ('42 Republic) 3 Mesquiteers
- Fighting Frontier ('43 RKO) Tim Holt

DENNIS MOORE

Dennis (Smoky) Moore almost made the transition from screen badman to B-western hero. In fact, he did just that—several times.

Early on, in 1934, he was Bud of Bud 'n' Ben (with Ben Corbett) in Reliable's "West On Parade". But only once. Then in 1942 he was second lead to George Houston in five Lone Rider PRC westerns. In 1943 he joined the Range Busters trio for their last four films as well as supporting Tex Ritter in two at Universal ("Oklahoma Raiders", "Arizona Trail"). In 1944 Moore was second lead to Jimmy Wakely in his first two Monograms. Also in 1944, "Wells Fargo Days" was released in Cinecolor by Warner Bros., a 20 minute short that had been made in 1940. It starred Moore. Also that year Moore starred in Universal's "Raiders of Ghost City" serial. In 1945 he co-starred with Milburn Stone as the heroes battling "The Master Key", another Universal serial. Over at Republic, still in 1945, he fought Roy Barcroft for 15 chapters as "The Purple Monster Strikes". 1946–he was the hero of Universal's last serial, "The Mysterious Mr. M". It was 10 more years before he starred again, this time in Columbia's last two serials, "Perils of the Wilderness" and "Blazing the Overland Trail", both '56.

In between all these attempts at real stardom, Dennis Moore played hundreds of heavies in movies and on TV. He also played juvenile roles—the girl's brother type—in many B-westerns.

Dennis Moore was born in Fort Worth, Texas, January 26, 1908, but schooled in El Paso, Texas. His true name was apparently Dennis Meadows, the name he acted under early in his career, however his California death certificate refers to his father as Dennis Moore. Puzzling, yes! His mother's name was Bessie Price.

Studio publicity, which can often be discounted as hype, suggests several things about Moore's early life prior to entering films at 24. The best scenario is that he traveled the world extensively as a child with his parents who were financially stable. He later performed in both stock and stage drama. Having an avid interest in aviation, he received his pilots license and flew about four years until a bad crackup severely injured him. For an unspecified amount of time, Dennis found activity as a physical director.

More to the point from three other heavies that knew him: Pierce Lyden wrote, "He loved flying and was an instructor at Whitman Airport in the San Fernando Valley." As to his personality, Myron Healey said, "He was never what you'd call a team player. I don't know whether he didn't like the business or was just a private man." Gregg Barton described him as "a loner who limited his personal associations." For greater insight into the personality of Dennis Moore, reference is made to the book SEE YA UP THERE BABY, by Linda Lee Wakely, daughter of singing cowboy star Jimmy Wakely, in which she relates, that in the '40s, Moore was selected, along with "Lasses" White, to play sidekick roles in a Wakely series at Monogram. Moore's ego was such that he apparently felt it demeaning to play second banana to a singing cowboy. One night (8/29/45) during a drinking session with Foy Willing and some other lesser known Hollywood cowboys in one of Hollywood's cantinas, Moore was bemoaning his fate when, drunk as a skunk, he announced he was going out to Wakely's ranch to "kill that singing cowboy son of a bitch." After midnight, Moore arrived at the Wakely home (at 7600 Lankershim Blvd.), called Jimmy outside and, armed with a knife, stabbed Jimmy in the head. The police arrived, took Moore into custody, but in court, Wakely refused to press charges. (LOS ANGELES TIMES 9/1/45). According to the book, the judge's words were, "My God, Mr. Wakely, this man tried to kill you and it could happen again. He should be put away." Wakely still refused to press charges, and the judge ruled thusly, "If Mr. Wakely won't have you jailed, you will have to leave town for 60 days. If you come back to Los Angeles, I'll have you jailed." John James replaced Moore as the third member of the star trio.

A stable fixture in westerns from '32-'58, 26 years, Moore's co-workers referred to him as "Dinty" while on screen he was often "Denny" or "Smoky".

The L.A. TIMES of July 28, 1952, reported Dennis received legal permission from a superior judge to drop his given name of Meadows and change it permanently to Moore. At the time, Dennis had been married for several years and was the father of an infant daughter. His wife, Marilyn Estelle Moore, only 25, and little girl, Linda, 2, also changed their names to Moore. At this time, Dennis was employed as a flying instructor, obviously to supplement his acting income.

It was also around mid 1952, flying as a transport pilot, that he went into a spin at 3,299 feet. The crash left him with every bone in his body broken and small hope for him to live. Fourteen months in the hospital and nearly two more years of rest and recovery made him as good as new. He returned to film and TV work in 1954 where he found plenty of work, especially in TV series such as "Annie Oakley", "Kit Carson", "Lone Ranger", "Stories of the Century", "Buffalo Bill Jr.", "Roy Rogers", "Gene Autry", "Judge Roy Bean", "Sky King", "Wild Bill Hickok" and "Wyatt Earp". And he starred in those last two Columbia serials.

As the '50s rolled on, with his hair thinning, Moore found character roles on "Cimarron City", "Dragnet", "Black Saddle", "Have Gun Will Travel", "Buckskin", "Laramie" and "Wagon Train". Moore essayed recurring roles on "Tombstone Territory" (as a deputy) and "MacKenzie's Raiders" (as a Cavalry sergeant), both in '58 for ZIV TV. His last two parts were on "Bat Masterson" and "Tales of Wells Fargo" episodes in '61. (He only earned $700 that year as an actor.)

Moore and his wife moved to Big Bear Lake (where so many westerns were filmed) where they resided on Pine Knot Blvd. and operated a gift shop for four years until one of the best of the badmen, Dennis Moore, died of acute circulatory failure...rheumatic heart disease...and rheumatic fever on March 1, 1964. He's buried at Mountain View Cemetery.

The next time you watch a film with Dennis Moore, notice his unique gun belt. It had a buckle on each side instead of having one buckle in the middle. The belt was obviously made expressly for Moore since we never saw anyone else with this design.

Suggested Sampling of Moore's Western Heavies:

- Dawn Rider ('35 Lone Star) John Wayne
- Valley of the Lawless ('36 Supreme) Johnny Mack Brown
- Trigger Smith ('39 Monogram) Jack Randall
- Across the Plains ('39 Monogram) Jack Randall
- Rocky Mountain Rangers ('40 Republic) 3 Mesquiteers
- Pirates on Horseback ('41 Paramount) William Boyd
- Lone Rider Fights Back ('41 PRC) George Houston
- Billy the Kid In Santa Fe ('41 PRC) Bob Steele
- Raiders of the Range ('42 Republic) 3 Mesquiteers
- Frontier Law ('43 Universal) Russell Hayden
- Driftin' River ('46 PRC) Eddie Dean
- Colorado Serenade ('46 PRC) Eddie Dean
- Frontier Agent ('48 Monogram) Johnny Mack Brown
- Tioga Kid ('48 PRC) Eddie Dean
- Across the Rio Grande ('49 Monogram) Jimmy Wakely
- Navajo Trail Raiders ('49 Republic) Allan "Rocky" Lane
- Roaring Westward ('49 Monogram) Jimmy Wakely
- Gunslingers ('50 Monogram) Whip Wilson
- Colorado Ranger ('50 Lippert) Jimmy Ellison/Russell Hayden
- King of the Bullwhip ('50 Western Adventure) Lash LaRue
- Marshal of Heldorado ('50 Lippert) Jimmy Ellison/Russell Hayden
- West of Wyoming ('50 Monogram) Johnny Mack Brown
- Cisco Kid: Newspaper Crusaders ('50) Duncan Renaldo
- Abilene Trail ('51 Monogram) Whip Wilson
- Range Rider: Ten Thousand Reward ('51) Jock Mahoney
- Cisco Kid: Performance Bond ('51) Duncan Renaldo
- Gene Autry: Revenge Trail ('51) Gene Autry
- Man From Sonora ('51 Monogram) Johnny Mack Brown
- Gene Autry: Ruthless Renegade ('52) Gene Autry
- Wild Bill Hickok: Heading For Trouble ('53) Guy Madison
- Kit Carson: Hermit of Indian Ridge ('54) Bill Williams
- Cisco Kid: Six Gun for No Pain ('54) Duncan Renaldo
- Annie Oakley: Thunder Hill ('55) Gail Davis
- Buffalo Bill Jr.: Hooded Vengeance ('55) Dick Jones
- Roy Rogers: Brothers O'Dell ('55) Roy Rogers
- Roy Rogers: Three Masked Men ('55) Roy Rogers
- Judge Roy Bean: Gunman's Bargain ('56) Edgar Buchanan
- Roy Rogers: Ambush ('56) Roy Rogers
- Sky King: Showdown ('56) Kirby Grant
- Buffalo Bill Jr.: The Assassins ('56) Dick Jones
- Lone Ranger: The Avenger ('57) Clayton Moore
- Rin Tin Tin: Stagecoach Sally ('57) Lee Aaker
- Lone Ranger: Angel and the Outlaw ('57) Clayton Moore
- Roy Rogers: Johnny Rover ('57) Roy Rogers

LEE MORGAN

Lee Morgan was strictly a low-rent end of the trail B-western badman. According to co-workers, his roles never matched his own egotistical beliefs about his status as a "badman".

Morgan started off at PRC in '47 playing sheriffs in several Eddie Dean and Lash LaRue pics, then graduated to a few meaty "heavies" roles at the very end of the B-western cycle. Most of his parts from '52 on were brief uncredited bits in A-westerns such as "Duel At Silver Creek" ('52), "Drums Across the River" ('54), "Man From Bitter Ridge" ('55) and "Villa" ('58).

Raymond Lee Morgan was born June 12, 1902, in the Texas border country and died of heart disease January 30, 1967, leaving many questions unanswered about his life, in particular what he'd done before arriving in films at the age of 45?

Morgan gave it a good try at the end of an era. Had he come along 10 years earlier his contributions would have, no doubt, been much greater.

Suggested Sampling of Morgan's Western Heavies:

- Fighting Vigilantes ('47 PRC) Lash LaRue
- Cheyenne Takes Over ('47 PRC) Lash LaRue
- Dangers of the Canadian Mounted ('48 Republic serial) Jim Bannon
- Roll, Thunder, Roll ('49 Eagle Lion) Jim Bannon
- Rio Grande ('49 Lautem/Astor) Sunset Carson
- Raiders of Tomahawk Creek ('51 Columbia) Charles Starrett
- Border Fence (aka Cactus Barrier) ('51 Astor) Walt Wayne
- Vanishing Outpost ('51 Western Adventure) Lash LaRue
- Gene Autry: Return of Maverick Dan ('51) Gene Autry
- Cowboy G-Men: Koniackers ('52) Russell Hayden
- Blazing the Overland Trail ('56 Columbia serial) Lee Roberts
- Cisco Kid: Tangled Trails ('56) Duncan Renaldo
- Hidden Guns ('56 Republic) Faron Young
- Last of the Fast Guns ('58 Universal) Jock Mahoney
- Sierra Baron ('58 20th Century Fox) Brian Keith

CHUCK MORRISON

Looking like a barracuda, the jut-jawed, chunky, large-framed Chuck Morrison only had an eight year, 50-plus film career, principally as a henchman in B-westerns and five serials.

No information is available as to date, place of birth, or death. But one wonders about a possible relationship to brothers Chick Morrison (1878-1924), George "Pete" Morrison (1890-1973) (who had two sons Douglas and Clifford) and Carl Morrison (dates unknown) who were all employed in silent films. As a matter of fact, Chick's real name was Chuck. Coincidence? Or relationship? In searching Social Security records, the most likely candidate is a Charles "Chuck" Morrison born March 24, 1911, who died May 6, 1982, in Santa Clara, California.

More speculation. Charles "Chuck" Morrison entered films in 1934 and his last film was a bit as a guard in Jackie Gleason's "Tramp, Tramp, Tramp" which finished filming in January '42. It seems likely Morrison entered WWII and was either killed, stayed in the service or returned to seek employment in another line of work.

At this point, Morrison's life remains a mystery.

Suggested Sampling of Morrison's Western Heavies:

- Wild Mustang ('35 Ajax) Harry Carey
- Aces Wild ('36 Commodore) Harry Carey
- Ghost Town ('36 Commodore) Harry Carey
- Law For Tombstone ('37 Universal) Buck Jones
- Chip of the Flying U ('39 Universal) Johnny Mack Brown
- Return of Wild Bill ('40 Columbia) Bill Elliott
- Golden Trail ('40 Monogram) Tex Ritter
- Rainbow Over the Range ('40 Monogram) Tex Ritter
- Winners of the West ('40 Universal serial) Dick Foran
- North From the Lone Star ('41 Columbia) Bill Elliott
- Pals of the Pecos ('41 Republic) 3 Mesquiteers
- Arizona Terrors ('42 Republic) Don Barry
- Code of the Outlaw ('42 Republic) 3 Mesquiteers

Fred "Snowflake" Toones and Harry Carey listen carefully at the barn door to the plotting of Chuck Morrison (L) and Roger Williams (R) in "Aces Wild" ('36 Commodore).

ZON MURRAY

Big, mustached, rugged and intimidating looking with his Stetson always worn in a half-cocked manner, Zon Murray played virtually nothing but nasty western heavies during his 20 year screen career which began with Monogram's "Lonesome Trail" in 1945 opposite Jimmy Wakely.

Born Emery Zon Murray April 13, 1910, he capitalized on his unusual middle name, making it a very memorable screen moniker.

Both of his parents, Franklin Lafayette Murray and Dora Edwards, were natives of Missouri. The Murray family migrated from Missouri to California as many people did in the '30s. Zon labored as a carpenter, specializing in building swimming pools, before he got into pictures, as well as after.

"He was one of the wildest, non-conformist persons you could meet," close friend Pierce Lyden exclaimed. "I've had a lot of unpredictable Irish friends, but he was the greatest. He could and would tell off the biggest in the business; they would have blacklisted me, but they loved Zon. Make no mistake about it, he was tough, rough and serious. But he did have a heart of gold and maybe the people we dealt with knew it."

Pierce remembers Zon being a jack-of-all-trades. He said Zon built a home in Laurel Canyon all by himself. The house included everything, even a pool. Lyden also recalls Murray was a lot of fun. He and his wife even served as foster parents for some boys after the Murray's own children left home.

Actually, before the Wakely film, Zon played two small uncredited parts in two serials, "The Secret Code" ('42 Columbia) and "Secret Agent X-9" ('45 Universal). The time gap between the two and the years indicate possible military service.

At any rate, with the Wakely film his badman screen persona was in constant view in B-westerns and on TV.

Zon also managed good roles in several A-westerns as well— "Dallas" ('50), "Along the Great Divide" ('51), "Blood On the Moon" ('48), "Carson City" ('52),

"Powder River ('53), "Calamity Jane" ('53), "Passion" ('54) and his final fling, producer Alex Gordon's "all star roundup", "Requiem For a Gunfighter" in '65.

Zon also worked in six latter day serials for Sam Katzman whom he reportedly wasn't fond of due to his cheapness.

According to Zon's great nephew, Zon (like most men who played heavies) had a completely different nature off screen—where he was fun and outgoing. Having acquired some property on Laurel Canyon in the '40s, he put his carpentry knowledge to use in the '60s to build a second house on the acreage which he rented out. Unfortunately, he wound up renting to some rock groups who trashed his property.

Pierce Lyden recalled, "Zon was cracked up pretty bad in the mid '60s during a riding scene (while filming a "Virginian" episode) where a horse fell on him. He couldn't do much after that and was in litigation a long time over it."

Fed up with the changing Hollywood atmosphere, Zon moved to 35215 Cielo Vista in Palm Springs in the '70s. Pierce continued, "Zon called me once and said 'I've bought a 20-foot trailer, we're taking off for a year and touring the U.S.' I never saw or heard from him again!"

Murray was married to Dorothy J. Sands and they had one son, Gary Zon Murray.

Previous reports indicate Murray died in his armchair after having finished lunch on March 2, 1979. Fact is, according to the official California death certificate, Murray died April 30, 1979, of acute myocardial infarction due to atherosclerotic heart disease at Desert Hospital in Palm Springs, California. He was 69. Murray's remains were cremated and placed in Forest Lawn Memorial Park in Glendale, California.

The movie camera responded to Zon's unique brand of nastiness—as did we the viewers—and thankfully we have it all to watch and recall on film and video.

There's trail tension between Zon Murray (L) and Bill Elliott in "The Longhorn" ('51 Monogram).

Suggested Sampling of Murray's Western Heavies:

- Lonesome Trail ('45 Monogram) Jimmy Wakely
- El Paso Kid ('46 Republic) Sunset Carson
- Ghost of Hidden Valley ('46 PRC) Buster Crabbe
- Terror Trail ('46 Columbia) Charles Starrett
- Rainbow Over the Rockies ('47 Monogram) Jimmy Wakely
- West of Dodge City ('47 Columbia) Charles Starrett
- West to Glory ('47 PRC) Eddie Dean
- Law Comes to Gunsight ('47 Monogram) Johnny Mack Brown
- Gun Talk ('47 Monogram) Johnny Mack Brown
- Oklahoma Blues ('48 Monogram) Jimmy Wakely
- Crossed Trails ('48 Monogram) Johnny Mack Brown
- False Paradise ('48 U.A.) William Boyd
- Grand Canyon Trail ('48 Republic) Roy Rogers
- Trail's End ('49 Monogram) Johnny Mack Brown
- Son of a Badman ('49 Western Adventure) Lash LaRue
- Dallas ('50 Warner Bros.) Gary Cooper
- Lone Ranger: Pay Dirt ('50) Clayton Moore
- Gene Autry: Six Shooter Sweepstakes ('50) Gene Autry
- Cisco Kid: Dog Story ('50) Duncan Renaldo
- Wanted Dead or Alive: ('51 Monogram) Whip Wilson
- Oklahoma Justice ('51 Monogram) Johnny Mack Brown
- Longhorn ('51 Monogram) Bill Elliott
- Pecos River ('51 Columbia) Charles Starrett
- Kit Carson: Spoilers of California ('51) Bill Williams
- Cisco Kid: Water Rights ('51) Duncan Renaldo
- Wild Bill Hickok: Rock Springs Rustlers ('51) Guy Madison
- Border Saddlemates ('52 Republic) Rex Allen
- Laramie Mountains ('52 Columbia) Charles Starrett
- Cripple Creek ('52 Columbia) George Montgomery
- Desperadoes Outpost ('52 Republic) Allan "Rocky" Lane
- Son of Geronimo ('52 Columbia serial) Clayton Moore
- Roy Rogers: Set-Up ('52) Roy Rogers
- Cisco Kid: Ghost Town ('52) Duncan Renaldo
- Kit Carson: Border City ('52) Bill Williams
- Roy Rogers: Mayor of Ghost Town ('52) Roy Rogers
- Lone Ranger: Trader Boggs ('53) John Hart
- Old Overland Trail ('53 Republic) Rex Allen
- On Top of Old Smoky ('53 Columbia) Gene Autry
- Powder River ('53 20th Century Fox) Rory Calhoun
- Down Laredo Way ('53 Republic) Rex Allen
- Hopalong Cassidy: Masquerade For Matilda ('54) William Boyd
- Lone Ranger: Frightened Woman ('54) Clayton Moore
- Gunfighters of the Northwest ('54 Columbia serial) Jock Mahoney
- Cisco Kid: Stolen River ('55) Duncan Renaldo
- Rin Tin Tin: Rusty Meets Mr. Nobody ('56) Lee Aaker
- The Lone Ranger ('56 Warner Bros.) Clayton Moore
- Lone Ranger: Dead-Eye ('57) Clayton Moore
- Wyatt Earp: Nice Ones Always Die First ('57) Hugh O'Brian
- Colt .45: Gypsies ('57) Wayde Preston
- Casey Jones: Marauders ('57) Alan Hale Jr.
- Tales of the Texas Rangers: Panhandle ('57) Willard Parker
- Maverick: Point Blank ('57) James Garner
- Lawman: Brand Release ('59) John Russell
- Bronco: Red Water North ('59) Ty Hardin
- Rawhide: Incident of the Roman Candles ('59) Eric Fleming/Clint Eastwood

JAY NOVELLO

Jay Novello, a smallish Italian-American character actor with a big talent, didn't do many westerns, but he made a huge impact on western audiences of the early '40s in six Roy Rogers pictures, especially his dual role in "Sheriff of Tombstone" as a foppish Wells Fargo manager and a Mexican bandit.

Novello was born in Chicago, Illinois, August 22, 1904. He learned to speak Italian before learning English. He later spoke fluent German and Greek. His mother's maiden name was Salemme.

Jay began his lengthy career with stock companies around Chicago, coming to Hollywood with the advent of sound in 1930 for a bit in Universal's 10 chapter "Jade Box" serial.

His immense talent and versatility when it came to playing a variety of characters, especially shady-like foreigners and cringing cowards, kept him busy in films, on radio and on TV for 47 years through 1977.

His radio credits begin around 1942 and continue til the end of dramatic radio in the late '50s. He was heard on "Escape", "Rocky Jordan", "I Love a Mystery", "Lone Wolf", "One Man's Family" and others.

Besides "Jade Box", Novello worked in seven serials in the early '40s with perhaps his best role in "Adventures of Smilin' Jack" ('43 Universal).

His comedic talents did not go unnoticed either, especially by Lucille Ball who used Novello frequently on her TV shows. Especially memorable is the classic 1951 "I Love Lucy" episode, "The Séance", in which he played a prissy, overwrought man trying to contact his late wife Tillie.

Also memorable is his portrayal of gangster Willie Sutton on a three part "Gangbusters" TVer in 1952 and the title role of "Small Man" on a 1957 "Colt .45".

Distinguished radio actress Barbra Fuller remembers the talented Novello as, "A little man with an unusual face and a big talent—very good at dialects. I liked him a lot. He wasn't a meanie in real life, he was a pussycat to be around, a very likable person."

Novello's wife's name was Patricia and they had one daughter, Yvonne.

The giant talent of Jay Novello left us September 2, 1982, when he succumbed to lung cancer in North Hollywood.

Suggested Sampling of Novello's Western Heavies:
- Bandits and Ballads ('39 RKO) Ray Whitley
- Two Gun Sheriff ('40 Republic) Don Barry
- Border Legion ('40 Republic) Roy Rogers
- Robin Hood of the Pecos ('41 Republic) Roy Rogers
- Sheriff of Tombstone ('41 Republic) Roy Rogers
- Bad Man of Deadwood ('41 Republic) Roy Rogers
- King of the Mounties ('42 Republic serial) Allan Lane
- Man From Music Mountain ('43 Republic) Roy Rogers
- Rin Tin Tin: Gentle Kingdom ('54) Lee Aaker
- Colt .45: Small Man ('57) Wayde Preston
- Maverick: Plunder of Paradise ('58) Jack Kelly
- Zorro: five part "Eagle" serial ('58) Guy Williams
- Lawman: Big Hat ('59) John Russell
- Maverick: The Marquessa ('60) Jack Kelly
- Wichita Town: Brothers of the Knife ('60) Joel McCrea
- The Rebel: Unsurrendered Sword ('60) Nick Adams

WHEELER OAKMAN

Most movie fans these days remember Wheeler Oakman as a crooked gambler, corrupt official or dishonest rancher opposing, primarily, Tim McCoy and Kermit Maynard. Some recall him as a nasty heavy in 18 serials between 1932-1948. However, during the silent era of the late teens and early '20s, Oakman was extremely popular in heroic roles.

He was born Vivian Eichelberger February 21, 1890, in Washington, D.C., the third of four children. His father, Fred Eichelberger, a native of the District, was a clerk in the War Department and a veteran of the Civil War. He was a distant relative of General Joe Wheeler. His mother was Mildred Watkins of Virginia.

With a nonchalant manner and sly smile, Oakman stood 5' 11" and weighed around 170. He had brown hair and eyes, with a muscular build. He engaged in competitive sports for recreation and was a life-long baseball fan.

Following education in Washington, D.C., graduating from high school at 17, in 1908 he joined a repertory theatre group at the suggestion of his sister, Sara, who was in the company. His sister was known by the stage name of Gertrude Oakman. For obvious reasons, Vivian Eichelberger became Wheeler Oakman.

With about three years of stage experience, he began to do extra work in films produced by Lubin and Selig. Credited roles in Selig's stock company of screen actors came in 1912 with his first film being "Millionaire Vagabonds". The handsome actor alternated heroic and villainous roles.

Cast as the Broncho Kid in the original "Spoilers" (with William Farnum and Thomas Santschi) in 1914, Oakman attracted the attention of producers who began to cast him in leading roles at Selig ("Uphill Climb" '14, "Shotgun Jones" '14 etc.).

After Selig closed, and while working at Universal in 1917, he met New York actress Priscilla Dean whom he married on January 10, 1920, in Reno, Nevada. But, prior to that, Oakman enlisted in the artillery branch of the Army, serving from February 13, 1918 til January 26, 1919, during WWI. He was discharged with the rank of corporal.

Returning to film, one of his major roles in 1919 was with Nell Shipman (mother of noted screenwriter Barry Shipman) in "Back to God's Country". Other hits were "Outside the Law' ('20) with wife Priscilla Dean and "Peck's Bad Boy" ('21).

By the end of 1923, marital problems had set in and Wheeler left Hollywood to return to the New York stage. Shortly thereafter, Priscilla sold their home and announced a separation. Some time later they were divorced.

Wheeler was married twice thereafter, both ended in divorce. He had at least one child, Wheeler Jr. Priscilla subsequently married an Eastern Air Lines executive. She died on December 27, 1987, at 91.

Disappointed in his return to the stage, Oakman was back on film by mid 1925, mostly playing con men, fixers and heavies.

When sound hit, his excellent voice proved a boon. He was cast in the first all-talkie, Warner's "Lights of New York" ('28).

Oakman worked tirelessly in B-films throughout the '30s. Heart problems that began in 1940 slowed his pace to fewer films per year in the '40s.

His last seven films from '45-'48 were all serials for good friend and producer Sam Katzman. ("Brenda Starr, Reporter", "Who's Guilty", "Hop Harrigan", "Son of the Guardsman", "Jack Armstrong', "Brick Bradford' and "Superman").

In all, Oakman worked in 19 cliffhangers and was memorably villainous in "Airmail Mystery" ('32 Universal), "Lost Jungle" ('34 Mascot), "Phantom Empire" ('35 Mascot), "Adventures of Rex and Rinty" ('35 Mascot), "Darkest Africa" ('36 Republic), "Flash Gordon's Trip to Mars" ('38 Universal), "Brenda Starr, Reporter" ('45 Columbia), "Hop Harrigan" ('46 Columbia), "Jack Armstrong" ('47 Columbia) and "Brick Bradford" ('47 Columbia).

During these later years, Oakman also worked as an assistant manager of the El Portal Theatre in North Hollywood.

On March 19, 1949, at 59, he suffered a fatal heart attack at his home at 13021 Chandler Blvd. in North Hollywood. He is buried at Valhalla Cemetery in Burbank, California.

Wheeler Oakman ranks as one of the screen's best heavies of the '30s.

Suggested Sampling of Oakman's Western Heavies:

- In the Days of the Thundering Herd ('14 Selig) Tom Mix
- Hey! Hey! Cowboy ('27 Universal) Hoot Gibson
- Texas Cyclone ('32 Columbia) Tim McCoy
- Two Fisted Law ('32 Columbia) Tim McCoy
- End of the Trail ('32 Columbia) Tim McCoy
- Boiling Point ('32 Universal) Hoot Gibson
- Sundown Rider ('33 Columbia) Buck Jones
- Rusty Rides Alone ('33 Columbia) Tim McCoy
- Frontier Days ('34 Spectrum) Bill Cody
- In Old Santa Fe ('34 Mascot) Ken Maynard
- Square Shooter ('35 Columbia) Tim McCoy
- Phantom Empire ('35 Mascot serial) Gene Autry
- Man From Guntown ('35 Puritan) Tim McCoy
- Timber War ('35 Ambassador) Kermit Maynard

- Mysterious Avenger ('36 Columbia) Charles Starrett
- Roarin' Guns ('36 Puritan) Tim McCoy
- Song of the Trail ('36 Ambassador) Kermit Maynard
- Ghost Patrol ('36 Puritan) Tim McCoy
- Land of Fighting Men ('38 Monogram) Jack Randall
- Code of the Rangers ('38 Monogram) Tim McCoy
- Fighting Buckaroo ('43 Columbia) Charles Starrett
- Saddles and Sagebrush ('43 Columbia) Russell Hayden
- Sundown Valley ('44 Columbia) Charles Starrett

ARTIE ORTEGO

Little Artie Ortego (often billed Artie Ortega, Art Ardigan or variations thereof) was one of those frequently seen background henchmen who seldom received any billing or spoke many lines.

Born in Shasta County, California, February 9, 1890, his mother was one of the Digger Indian tribe originally found in the Mt. Lassen, California, district. His father was of Mexican and Irish decent. Artie was baptized by the fathers of the Santa Clara Mission near where his parents owned a stock ranch in that fertile valley.

Hearing that motion picture companies were hiring riders, Artie coaxed his parents into letting him go to Hollywood. He started his 45 year career riding for the Bison Company in 1909.

Child star "Baby Peggy", Diana Serra Cary, whose father was actor Jack Montgomery, in her book HOLLYWOOD POSSE, refers to Ortego as "a short, stocky California Indian" and one of her father's closest friends.

He was soon married to Mona Darkfeather (real name Josephine Mona Workman) (1886-1977), a popular "Indian" actress of the time who was actually of Spanish heritage. Artie played Indians in many of her silent two-reelers.

Divorced, Ortego married Billie Mack, a cowgirl with the Wild West at Luna Park. They made their wedding part of the show in an old-fashioned ceremony on horseback on June 26, 1917.

A hiatus during Ortego's busy schedule during the years of WWI indicates he may have seen military service.

Artie made the transition to sound and worked until 1955, his last western was Bill Elliott's "Forty-Niners" in '54. His roles were usually so small as to not only not receive billing, but seldom receive a cast name. For most of his credits he is designated simply as henchman, barfly, posse rider, stage driver, deputy, Indian, townsman, etc. Nevertheless, he worked in over 200 silent and sound westerns, including 14 serials such as "Rustlers of Red Dog" ('35 Universal) and "Custer's Last Stand" ('36 Stage and Screen).

According to Cary's book. Ortego had been working at newly opened Disneyland driving a miniature stagecoach when "whoever was serving in that capacity for Artie failed to keep idle spectators safely away from the docks when the highstrung ponies were brought in to be loaded. On this particular afternoon as Artie was coming in to pick up passengers, the noisy onlookers terrified his team, and they bolted. In an effort to keep the runaways from charging through the crowd and injuring hundreds of bystanders, Artie risked trying to turn them sharply out onto the track. The unwieldy little coach would not maneuver properly and heeled over on top of its driver. As it turned out, Artie was on crutches for months and remained crippled for the rest of his life."

Ortego died July 24, 1960.

Suggested Sampling of Ortego's Western Heavies:

- Juanita ('13 Nestor) Mona Darkfeather
- Stacked Cards ('26 Circle) Fred Church
- Nevada Buckaroo ('31 Tiffany) Bob Steele
- Man Trailer ('34 Columbia) Buck Jones
- Star Packer ('34 Lone Star) John Wayne
- Fighting Trooper ('34 Ambassador) Kermit Maynard
- 'Neath the Arizona Skies ('34 Lone Star) John Wayne
- Northern Frontier ('35 Ambassador) Kermit Maynard
- West of Nevada ('35 Colony) Rex Bell
- The Test ('35 Reliable) Rin Tin Tin Jr.
- Custer's Last Stand ('36 Stage and Screen serial) Rex Lease
- Ghost Patrol ('36 Puritan) Tim McCoy
- Ghost Rider ('43 Monogram) Johnny Mack Brown
- Prairie Express ('47 Monogram) Johnny Mack Brown
- Where the North Begins ('47 Screen Guild) Russell Hayden

BUD OSBORNE

Considered one of the finest six-up drivers in westerns, Lennie B. (Bud) Osborne was born in Claymore, Indian Territory (now Oklahoma), July 20, 1884. Available records indicate his father's name and place of birth are unknown and the only info on his mother is that her name was Betty.

At one time a rancher in Indian Territory, Bud later appeared in various wild west shows including Buffalo Bill's famous outfit (where he became assistant arena director) and the 101 Ranch Wild West Show. He made his first film, "For the Cause", in 1912. Unknown whether this was a western, but "Sheep Herder" (1914 Universal) was, starring J. Warren Kerrigan.

In a 6/10/48 HOLLYWOOD CITIZEN-NEWS interview Bud explained, "I came out to Hollywood from Indian Territory in 1912 with a consignment of horses and cattle for the Thomas H. Ince movie outfit. The studio was located on the beach front at the foot of Santa Inez Canyon, four miles north of Santa Monica. There were just a few sets, and interiors were built outdoors just the same as exteriors. Transportation from the end of the trolley line was the stagecoach and ranch wagon we used in the pictures. And it wasn't the smoothest riding in the world. We found it took too much time traveling back and forth from Santa Monica so Ince decided to build a tent city at the studio. I put up the 24 tents, including a cook and mess tent. The place became known as Inceville. And I became an actor. Our bathtub was the Pacific. Our recreation hall was the beach. When we went on location we used horses and stagecoachs and wagons. We had sandwiches and cold coffee for lunch. In the old days, we didn't draw salaries. We got wages. Five dollars a day. Leading men and women sometimes got $60 a week. And no limit on working hours. Overtime? Everything was overtime. But there were compensations. You could get a room at the swank Hollywood Hotel for three dollars a week. A good meal from soup to nuts cost two bits. A drink was a dime instead of a dollar."

By 1916-1917 Bud was playing supporting roles in Harry Carey ("Knight of the Range", "Texas Sphinx") and Neal Hart ("Bill Brennan's Claim", "Squaring It") westerns at Universal. Throughout the teens and '20s Bud played (mostly) heavies opposite Leo Maloney, Don Coleman, Bob Custer, Dick Hatton, Bob Curwood, Fred Thomson, Franklyn Farnum, Jack Perrin, Bob Steele, Jack Hoxie, Buddy Roosevelt, Fred Gilman, Dick Carter and Fred Humes, among others, even a role in John Ford's prestigious "Three Bad Men" ('26).

Bud starred, at least once, in "Prairie Mystery" for director George Edward Hall at Truart in 1922.

Bud easily made the transition into sound and played everything from the boss heavy to 5th man through the door opposite virtually *every* cowboy star. He even got to saddle up a couple of times as a sidekick—to Big Boy Williams in "Big Boy Rides Again" ('35 Beacon) and in Sam Katzman's "Son of Geronimo" ('52 Columbia) serial with Clayton Moore. He was particularly fond of Tim McCoy's serial, "The Indians Are Coming", in which he's featured in a dagger duel with McCoy.

Bud's serial output stretched to over 40 cliffhangers, counting silent epics, and about a third of them were other than western serials. His first serial was in 1919 at Pathe opposite Ruth Roland in "Tiger's Trail". At least six more silents followed including "White Eagle" ('22 Pathe) with Ruth Roland; "Ghost City" ('23 Universal) with Pete Morrison and "Mystery Rider" and "Vanishing Riders" (both '28 Universal) with William Desmond. Like features, western sound serials were his forte—"Rustlers of Red Dog", "Son of Geronimo", "Deadwood Dick", "Vigilantes Are Coming", "White Eagle", "Winners of the West", "Law of the Wild", "Lone Ranger", "Red Rider", "Riders of Death Valley", "Black Arrow" and others, but he also had good roles in a dozen or more non-western chapterplays such as "Adventures of Capt. Africa", "Batman", "Batman and Robin", "Great Adventures of Capt. Kidd", "Heroes of the Flames", "Monster and the Ape", "Phantom of the Air", "Tailspin Tommy", "Shadow of the Eagle" and others.

Working in a calculated 584 films and serials and close to 100 TV shows from 1912-1962, an amazing 50 years, Bud's output gives him the record for screen appearances of any actor in history.

As Bud began to age you'd spot him driving the stage or essaying the part of the Sheriff more and more.

Besides his scores of B's, Bud appeared in some major A's—"The Plainsman", "Allegheny Uprising", "Virginia City", "Blood On the Moon", "Winchester 73" and "Hanging Tree". His greatest talent was the ability he displayed in handling six-up stagecoaches, buckboards or any type of wagon regardless of the terrain. His friend Glenn Strange said, "When I first met Bud Osborne, he was a broncobuster and all-around hand. He was one of the best four and six-up drivers in the business, and when the story called for some wild driving, Bud usually got the job. He was big-hearted, forever ready for a good time, and well liked by all who knew him. He liked to joke a lot." Some good examples of Bud's driving are in "Texas City" ('52 Monogram), "Bonanza Town" ('51 Monogram), "Fighting Frontier" ('43 RKO), "Border Buckaroos" ('43 PRC) and many TV episodes of "Lone Ranger", "Gene Autry", "Hopalong Cassidy". One of the best is in "Cisco Kid: Stolen Bonds".

His last work was apparently on a "Have Gun Will Travel" episode ("Darwin's Man" 4/21/62) and a "Rawhide" ("The Pitchwagon" 3/2/62).

Osborne died at the Motion Picture Hospital February 2, 1964, of a heart attack at 79. He was survived by his wife, Elderine C. Osborne, a receptionist. They resided at 18646 Malden Dr. in Northridge, California. Bud had a son and daughter. His remains were cremated and are now in niche #60688 right above the ashes of Bob Steele and his twin brother, Dr. Bill Bradbury, in the Columbarium of Remembrance at Hollywood Hills, Forest Lawn Cemetery.

Tris Coffin remembered, "Bud Osborne was a close friend; I worked with him many times. He was a heavy drinker, but I never saw him louse up a scene because of it."

Roy Barcroft, Charlie King, Jack Elam, Lee Van Cleef and others may have a bigger "name" in the annals of screen badmen, but as to longevity and number of films, Bud Osborne is the "King of the Badmen".

Suggested Sampling of Osborne's Western Heavies:

- A Knight of the Range ('16 Universal) Harry Carey
- Galloping Devil ('20 Canyon) Franklyn Farnum
- Cactus Trails ('27 FBO) Bob Custer
- Cowboy and the Outlaw ('29 Syndicate) Bob Steele
- Call of the Desert ('30 Syndicate) Tom Tyler
- Red Fork Range ('31 Big 4) Wally Wales
- One Way Trail ('31 Columbia) Tim McCoy
- Diamond Trail ('32 Monogram) Rex Bell
- Sunset Trail ('32 Tiffany) Ken Maynard
- Riding Speed ('34 Superior) Buffalo Bill Jr.
- Prescott Kid ('34 Columbia) Tim McCoy
- Gun Smoke ('35 Kent) Buck Coburn
- Crimson Trail ('35 Universal) Buck Jones
- Outlaw Deputy ('35 Puritan) Tim McCoy
- Pinto Rustlers ('36 Reliable) Tom Tyler
- Law of the Ranger ('37 Columbia) Bob Allen
- Mexicali Kid ('38 Monogram) Jack Randall
- In Early Arizona ('38 Columbia) Bill Elliott
- Utah Trail ('38 Grand National) Tex Ritter
- Law Comes To Texas ('39 Columbia) Bill Elliott
- Beyond the Sacramento ('40 Columbia) Bill Elliott
- Pioneer Days ('40 Monogram) Jack Randall
- Robbers of the Range ('41 RKO) Tim Holt
- Arizona Terrors ('42 Republic) Don Barry
- Rangers Take Over ('42 PRC) James Newill/Dave O'Brien
- Riders of the West ('42 Monogram) Rough Riders
- Haunted Ranch ('43 Monogram) Range Busters
- Avenging Rider ('43 RKO) Tim Holt
- Devil Riders ('43 PRC) Buster Crabbe
- Stranger From Pecos ('43 Monogram) Johnny Mack Brown
- Range Law ('44 Monogram) Johnny Mack Brown
- Arizona Whirlwind ('44 Monogram) Trail Blazers
- Harmony Trail ('44 Mattox) Ken Maynard
- Marshal of Gunsmoke ('44 Universal) Tex Ritter
- Terrors on Horseback ('46 PRC) Buster Crabbe
- Six-Gun Man ('46 PRC) Bob Steele
- Wild West ('46 PRC) Eddie Dean
- Colorado Ranger ('50 Lippert) Jimmy Ellison/Russell Hayden
- Crossroad Avenger: Adventures of the Tucson Kid ('53) Tom Keene

JACK O'SHEA

Black Jack O'Shea was short, heavy, wore a mustache and could look mean enough to make a baby cry—just what was needed for a B-western badman. He could, and sometimes did, have other roles, but because he was so short he was seldom called on to mix it up with the taller heroes in fight scenes.

O'Shea was born John Martin Rellaford April 6, 1906, in San Francisco, California. His parents were John Rellaford of Kentucky and Mary Watts of California. Twelve days after Jack's birth (April 18, at 5:13am), a devastating earthquake hit the city killing some 700 persons and destroying 497 city blocks. Fortunately, baby John survived, but his nurse perished in the disaster. Even after the terrible scare, his family remained living in the city.

In his teens, O'Shea, like many youngsters of his time, sought work on the ship docks. It was often backbreaking labor, but provided employment at a time when jobs were difficult to find. Jack must have done his job well because he was noticed by a group of San Francisco socialites and offered work as a cabin boy on a two year trip to the South Seas. When the boat reached Hawaii, the cruise's entertainment director was suddenly struck with appendicitis. Desperate for someone to entertain, Jack, the cabin boy, was thrust into the role of cruise entertainer. Thus, began his career in show business.

After the cruise, Jack decided he'd try to continue in the entertainment field. George Raft was sponsoring a dance contest to find new talent. Jack teamed up with actor Michael O'Shea and entered the event. They won the event and began in vaudeville billed as the "O'Shea Brothers". Obviously, O'Shea was a far better stage name than Rellaford.

We now know how Jack got the name O'Shea, but even his family doesn't know how he acquired the handle "Black Jack". It is, however, rather commonplace for a man called Jack to be referred to as "Black Jack".

Jack eventually made his way to Hollywood circa 1932. His first film seems to be "Guns For Hire" ('32 Kent) with Lane Chandler.

Jack became such a superb dancer that Dale Evans once told his son, Alan, that his dad was one of the finest dancers she'd ever met. The O'Shea family was close friends with Dale Evans and Roy Rogers; Jack's second wife was Dale's secretary for seven years.

Because of his coordination and agility, he found work as a stuntman. In addition to stuntwork in westerns, he doubled big stars like Lou Costello and Orson Welles, but it was his work as a B-western badman where he made his mark. His best roles came at PRC circa '46-'47.

Jack befriended many of the people with whom he worked. In addition to Roy and Dale, other frequent visitors to the O'Shea home were Lash LaRue, Bob Steele and Mr. and Mrs. Roy Barcroft. Jack worked for several different studios and with most of the leading cowboy stars.

After many years and scores of films, Jack's screen career came to a halt when he was injured in a stagecoach scene in 1949. Pierce Lyden remembered the incident this way, "O'Shea came barreling down the street in a buckboard, pulled up in front of the hitching rack, jumped down to run in and warn the marshal of some danger. When he landed, it sounded like two fast rifle shots—both his ankles were broken, and another stunting career ended. He hadn't taken the time to change his high-heeled boots." Another version has Jack's foot almost amputated when it got caught in one of the wheels. In any event, a long and painful recovery followed. Good friend Roy Rogers saw to it Jack found employment, utilizing Jack in various roles on his TV series from '53-'56. Although Jack continued to essay small roles until late '56, he decided to seek other employment.

For a period he worked in a Reno, Nevada, casino dealing—appropriately enough—blackjack. While working there, in 1949, Jack met his second wife, Patricia Elizabeth Garry. The marriage lasted until his death and produced three children: Gary, born in 1950, and twin boys, Alan and Barry, born in 1960.

Jack's first marriage to Viola Hasson had ended in divorce. A son, Jack, was born from that union.

While making films, and even after, Jack toured for a number of years with some of the cowboy stars—especially Bob Steele and Lash LaRue. On these tours, he was billed as "Black Jack O'Shea—The Man You Love to Hate". Bobby Copeland was privileged to see Black Jack and Bob Steele when they visited his hometown, Oak Ridge, Tennessee, in the late '40s. Steele came on stage and started addressing the audience. While he was talking, there was a loud pounding on one of the side doors. Bob kept trying to speak but the pounding grew louder and louder. Finally, Bob asked one of the kids to see what was going on. When the kid opened the door, in charged Black Jack screaming at the top of his lungs and firing his pistol. It took some time for the startled kid to get over that incident! Black Jack proceeded to the stage where he and Bob staged a terrific mock battle. And just as he always did on the screen, Battling Bob whipped old Black Jack once again. Of course, Bob was cheered loudly while Black Jack drew a lusty chorus of boos.

Tiring of life on the road, Jack opened an antique store, JR Trading Post, in Chatsworth, California. In 1966, he moved his family and the store to Paradise, California, where he was honored as Grand Marshal at the local Gold Nugget Days celebration. While in Chatsworth and Paradise, one could often go into Jack's store and run into some old western film performers. Reportedly, western badman Art Dillard of Texas (2/20/07-3/30/60) died of a heart attack in Jack's Chatsworth store.

Only 61, Black Jack died October 1, 1967, of heart failure at Feather River Hospital in Paradise, Butte

County, California. He is buried in the Paradise Cemetery.

Although a screen badman, Jack *must* have been a nice man in real life. Bob Steele said of him, "I toured the country with Black Jack O'Shea. At every little theater, we put on a fight demonstration for the fans. Old Black Jack was a pretty mean guy on the screen, but in real life he was one of the nicest fellows you ever met."

Lash LaRue said, "Black Jack and I made a lot of tours. We didn't make much money, but we made a *lot* of tours. He was a good friend and I miss him."

Sunset Carson remembered, "I shot old Black Jack a few times, but we didn't mix it up too much. It wouldn't look good for me to whip up on a short guy like Jack."

The greatest compliment came from Jack's son Barry, "Perhaps one of the best things that can be said about him is that he loved his family. He had a hard life, even with all the glamour, but I think I've always known how he felt about us."

Glowing praises, indeed, for "Black Jack O'Shea—The Man You Love to Hate."

Suggested Sampling of O'Shea's Western Heavies:

- Sons of the Pioneers ('42 Republic) Roy Rogers
- Riders of the Rio Grande ('43 Republic) 3 Mesquiteers
- Outlaws of Santa Fe ('44 Republic) Don Barry
- Overland Riders ('46 PRC) Buster Crabbe
- Outlaws of the Plains ('46 PRC) Buster Crabbe
- Rio Grande Raiders ('46 Republic) Sunset Carson
- Caravan Trail ('46 PRC) Eddie Dean
- Stars Over Texas ('46 PRC) Eddie Dean
- Tumbleweed Trail ('46 PRC) Eddie Dean
- Law Of the Lash ('47 PRC) Lash LaRue
- Ride, Ryder, Ride ('49 Eagle Lion) Jim Bannon
- Roy Rogers: Treasure of Paradise Valley ('55) Roy Rogers

GREGG PALMER

A leading man career was in the works for Palmer Lee/Gregg Palmer at Universal-International in the early '50s until the studio system changed and U.I. dropped many of their contract players in the mid '50s.

Born Palmer Edwin Lee, January 25, 1927, in San Francisco, California, his father, Olaf Ludwig Lee, came to the U.S. from Norway in 1907 to join the American Army. The Norwegian spelling of the name is Lie, but it was changed to Lee in the U.S. Palmer's father, a carpenter who built houses, met his wife Emma Andrea Hammer in San Francisco.

Palmer graduated from Lowell High, a college prep school, in 1943 and signed up with the Army Air Corps who sent him to the University of Utah under their Army Specialized Training Reserve Program in 1944. This was followed by a cryptology (code) course. Most of Palmer's duty time was spent at Waller Field in Trinidad.

Discharged from the service in 1946, his plans to become a corporate attorney were altered when a friend invited him to go along on an audition for a radio staff announcer position at NBC. On a lark, Palmer auditioned himself. The friend wasn't hired but Palmer was.

Following a stint at NBC, he went to work at a new station, KEEN in San Jose, California. While there he was encouraged to entertain the possibility of becoming an actor by former '30s actress Noel Francis (who had been a leading lady to Tom Mix, Buck Jones and others).

Nothing came of it when Palmer auditioned in '49 at 20th Century Fox while still employed at KEEN. Then, while working as a floor officer (bouncer) at the Palladium in Los Angeles, he made the rounds of the studios. Without a studio contract, after a few bit roles, Palmer was nearly ready to return to San Francisco, when he

Gregg Palmer is machete-wielding John Goodfellow in John Wayne's "Big Jake" ('71 National General).

was offered a contract by Universal-International in late '51.

For some 15 films, including "Cimarron Kid" ('52), "Battle at Apache Pass" ('52), "Red Ball Express" ('52) and "The Raiders" ('52) he was billed as Palmer Lee. During the making of "Taza, Son of Cochise" ('54) U-I decided to build him into a top star as they had Tony Curtis, Rock Hudson and others. With the build-up came the name change to Gregg Palmer. Solid roles in "Playgirl" ('54), "Magnificent Obsession" ('54), "To Hell and Back" ('55) and others followed. Gregg mused on the name change, "Did it hurt me or help me? I dunno—as I look back now I would have liked to have kept my legal name. It didn't hurt Humphrey Bogart or Arnold Schwarzenegger. I think U-I was going for a heavy sound, like Tab…or Rock…"

Unfortunately, Gregg's timing was off, the studio system was changing and U-I released him and several others. Oddly, one of his first films freelancing was "The Creature Walks Among Us"—right back at U-I in 1956.

Gregg continued to freelance into the early '80s, including several films in Europe in the '70s, then six films with John Wayne, the most notable role being John Goodfellow, the vicious, wild-eyed, machete wielding member of Richard Boone's gang in "Big Jake".

Gregg married Ruth Stump Brooks, a nurse, in 1967. They had no children, but Gregg inherited a ready-made family of three children from Ruthie's prior marriage. She died of cancer in 1999.

Semi-retired today, Gregg Palmer, a consummate performer and comedian, is heavily involved attending various pro-celeb golf tourneys (long an avocation) and western film festivals.

Suggested Sampling of Palmer's Western Heavies:

- Cimarron Kid ('52 Universal-International) Audie Murphy
- Stories of the Century: Jack Slade ('55) Jim Davis
- Champion: A Bugle For Ricky ('55) Jim Bannon
- Tales of the Texas Rangers: Panhandle ('57) Willard Parker
- Restless Gun: The Hand Is Quicker ('58) John Payne
- Sky King: The Runaway ('58) Kirby Grant
- Frontier Doctor: Crooked Circle ('58) Rex Allen
- Jefferson Drum: Band of Iron ('58) Jeff Richards
- Death Valley Days: Perilous Cargo ('58)
- Cimarron City: Bitter Lesson ('59) John Smith
- State Trooper: Girl On Cloud Nine ('59) Rod Cameron
- Shotgun Slade: Freight Line ('59) Scott Brady
- Overland Trail: Vigilantes of Montana ('60) Doug McClure/William Bendix
- Deputy: Trail of Darkness ('60) Allen Case
- Lawman: Old Stefano ('60) John Russell
- Tall Man: A Gun Is For Killing ('61) Barry Sullivan/Clu Gulager
- Wyatt Earp: Doc Holliday Faces Death ('61) Hugh O'Brian
- Gun Fight ('61 United Artists) James Brown
- Five Guns to Tombstone ('61 United Artists) James Brown
- Cheyenne: Frightened Town ('61) Clint Walker
- Outlaws: Sam Bass ('61) Don Collier
- Wyatt Earp: Gunfight at the O.K. Corral ('61) Hugh O'Brian
- Tales of Wells Fargo: Death Raffle ('61) Dale Robertson
- Laramie: Long Road Back ('62) John Smith
- Gunsmoke: Phoebe Strunk ('62) James Arness
- Gunsmoke: Blind Man's Bluff ('63) James Arness
- Laramie: Badge of Glory ('63) Robert Fuller
- Gunsmoke: Odyssey of Jubal Tanner ('63) James Arness
- Quick Gun ('64 Columbia) Audie Murphy
- Laredo: Golden Trail ('65) Neville Brand/William Smith/Peter Brown
- Branded: $10,000 For Durango ('65) Chuck Connors
- Wild Wild West: Night of the Human Trigger ('65) Robert Conrad
- Legend of Jesse James: A Real Tough Town ('66) Christopher Jones
- Gunsmoke: Which Dr. ('66) James Arness
- Cimarron Strip: Journey To a Hanging ('67) Stuart Whitman
- Gunsmoke: Hide Cutters ('68) James Arness
- Rio Lobo ('70 20th Century Fox) John Wayne
- Chisum ('70 Warner Bros.) John Wayne
- Gunsmoke: Lynott ('71) James Arness
- Big Jake ('71 National General) John Wayne
- Sometimes Life Is Hard, Right, Providence? ('72) Tomás Milian

TEX PALMER

Tex "Squint" Palmer, with some 200 films in his saddlebags, was one of Hollywood's career cowpokes.

Commencing in 1930 with an uncredited role in Bob Steele's "Near the Rainbow's End" (Tiffany) and Ken Maynard's "Fighting Legion" (Universal), the squint-eyed badman worked regularly with virtually every B-western screen hero and at all studios. He was seldom given screen credit and, unlike most of his contemporaries, Tex *never* once ventured off the B-western/serial screen into A-productions, be they western or otherwise.

We last caught Tex in Johnny Mack Brown's "Man From the Black Hills" ('52 Monogram) as a member of the posse. He did hang around Gower Gulch through the mid '50s and was glimpsed in an "Adventures of Champion" episode as well as a "Gunsmoke", both in '55. A very healthy 25 year ride.

Only scant biographical material exists on Tex: born Luther William Palmer in Xenia, Ohio, July 31, 1904. He died in Mechanicsburg, Pennsylvania, March 22, 1982. He's apparently buried at San Fernando Mission Cemetery in California.

Suggested Sampling of Palmer's Western Heavies:

- Renegades of the West ('32 RKO) Tom Keene
- Dawn Rider ('35 Lone Star) John Wayne
- Rider of the Law ('35 Supreme) Bob Steele
- Law Rides ('36 Supreme) Bob Steele
- Boothill Brigade ('37 Republic) Johnny Mack Brown
- Trouble In Texas ('37 Grand National) Tex Ritter
- Sing, Cowboy, Sing ('37 Grand National) Tex Ritter
- Billy the Kid Returns ('38 Republic) Roy Rogers
- Rolling Caravans ('38 Columbia) Jack Luden
- Frontiers of '49 ('39 Columbia) Bill Elliott
- Where Trails End ('42 Monogram) Tom Keene
- Rock River Renegades ('42 Monogram) Range Busters
- Haunted Ranch ('43 Monogram) Range Busters

EDDIE PARKER

One of the best stuntmen in the business, Eddie Parker, hit the ground running in 1932 ("Hurricane Express" serial) and never showed down until his death in 1960.

Edwin (Eddie) Parker was born in Minnesota on December 12, 1900, and spent over a quarter century on the screen in well over 300 films either as a stuntman, actor or both. His mother's maiden name was Hazelden.

Parker tried four fields of endeavor before deciding to become an actor. At first he was handyman at a small newspaper, doing everything from selling ads to setting type. Dissatisfied, he took a job as a night attendant at a mortuary. Tiring of the dreary routine, the floral business attracted his attention and he prospered for a while but lost his savings in a bank crash in 1924. Acting interested him, so he began as a singer and dancer in a nightclub, graduating to vaudeville where he toured several circuits. With the downfall of vaudeville, he finally turned to motion pictures.

Some 60 serials attest to his action actor abilities. It would be hard in the '30s and '40s to avoid his serial derring-do at Republic ("Lone Ranger Rides Again", "Daredevils of the West", "Masked Marvel", "Crimson Ghost", "Ghost of Zorro" etc.), Universal ("Winners of the West", "Flash Gordon", "Ace Drummond", "Buck Rogers", "Red Barry" etc.), Columbia ("Mandrake the Magician", "The Phantom", "Black Arrow", "Chick Carter, Detective", "Jack Armstrong", "Tex Granger" etc.), Mascot ("Whispering Shadow", "Fighting Marines", "Adventures of Rex and Rinty"), even Stage and Screen ("Clutching Hand").

Aside from some good roles early on in several John Wayne 1934 Lone Star westerns, nearly all of Parker's acting assignments were bit roles in serials, westerns and action pictures until the mid to late '40s. Then about 1946 Parker began to play more dominant badman roles, particularly at Monogram and PRC opposite Johnny Mack Brown and Eddie Dean, all the while never slacking up on stuntwork in films and on TV ("Abbott and Costello Meet Frankenstein", "Bells of San Angelo", "Rear Window", "Mole People", "Tarantula", "Reprisal", "Around the World In 80 Days", "Colt .45" TVer and dozens more.)

Shortly after completing a role and some stuntwork in "Spartacus" ('60), Eddie Parker died in Sherman Oaks, California, following a heart attack suffered during the making of a "Jack Benny" TV episode on January 20, 1960.

Recalling his "Jack Armstrong" serial ('47 Columbia), John Hart chuckled about Parker's sense of humor. "Eddie Parker and Jack Ingram were buddy buddies. I would join them drinking after hours. I had a lot of fun with those guys. Eddie worked for a funeral home one time and every time the hearse would take a corpse to the cemetery, he'd jump in the back, ride along and try on the guy's shoes. (Laughs)"

Suggested Sampling of Parker's Western Heavies:

- Lucky Texan ('34 Lone Star) John Wayne
- Star Packer ('34 Lone Star) John Wayne
- Courageous Avenger ('35 Supreme) Johnny Mack Brown
- Lone Star Trail ('43 Universal) Johnny Mack Brown
- Black Arrow ('44 Columbia serial) Robert Scott
- Days of Buffalo Bill ('46 Republic) Sunset Carson
- Lost Trail ('45 Monogram) Johnny Mack Brown
- Trigger Fingers ('46 Monogram) Johnny Mack Brown
- Silver Range ('46 Monogram) Johnny Mack Brown
- Valley of Fear ('47 Monogram) Johnny Mack Brown
- Shadow Valley ('47 PRC) Eddie Dean
- Hawk of Powder River ('48 PRC) Eddie Dean
- Whirlwind Raiders ('48 Columbia) Charles Starrett
- Fighting Ranger ('48 Monogram) Johnny Mack Brown
- Range Justice ('49 Monogram) Johnny Mack Brown
- Law of the West ('49 Monogram) Johnny Mack Brown
- Cisco Kid: Trouble In Tonapah ('50) Duncan Renaldo
- Hawk of Wild River ('52 Columbia) Charles Starrett
- Hopalong Cassidy: Black Sheep ('52) William Boyd

Johnny Mack Brown has his "Trigger Fingers" full with outlaws Eddie Parker (L) and Riley Hill (R) ('46 Monogram).

MICHAEL PATE

Michael Pate is an Australian who conquered the screen Wild West by playing vicious killers and bloodthirsty Indians. As a matter of fact, at one time or another Pate portrayed every true life Indian chief there was—Crazy Horse, Sitting Bull, Victorio, Quanah Parker, Geronimo—as well as a lot of fictitious ones, Strongbow, Yellow Robe, Sleeping Dog, Blue Horse, Kotana, Sankeno, Toriano, Chato, Buffalo Calf, Running Horse, among others.

Pate was born February 26, 1920, in Drummoyne, a harborside suburb of Sydney, Australia. His father, Barney Pate, was a talented and well known horsebreaker, trainer and Royal Easter Show reinsman who later became a master pastry cook and baker. Schooled at home by his maternal Grandmother and his parents, Michael could read and write by the time he entered kindergarten.

A lover of western movies as a child, he thoroughly enjoyed dressing up for year end concerts as an Indian chief or a cowboy, never realizing as an adult he would continue to fulfill these childhood dreams.

Pate left school at 15 to get a job because it was not affordable for his family to send him on to University. Michael got a job as a junior cost accountant for several years. A few years later he quit a job as head accountant for an electrical firm when he met an influential young producer at the Australian Broadcasting Commission who, in 1938, mentored him into a career writing and broadcasting for radio. This led to radio acting, other parts on the stage and in films in '38 and '39. He became a young star of radio shows such as the "Colgate-Palmolive Youth Show" and "Lux Radio Theater", appeared at the Minerva Theater, the Theater Royal and various little theaters in many plays and was then cast in the epic film of the Australian Lighthorse in Mesapotamia during WWI—"40,000 Horsemen". Michael also wrote for several newspapers as a book and theater critic and had short stories published in Australian magazines and anthologies and in HARPER'S BAZAAR in the U.S.

WWII interrupted his burgeoning young career and he served in the S.W.P.A. of the Australian Army's entertainment unit in various combat areas until 1946.

From 1946-1950 Michael starred in various radio dramas, in the theatre, and in films in Australia. He also wrote theatrical plays.

In 1950 he came to the U.S. for the film version of his play "Bonaventure" which was released as "Thunder On the Hill" in 1951 by Universal.

Subsequently, he began to work steadily in Hollywood ("Strange Door" '51, "Ten Tall Men" '51, "Face to Face" '52, "Black Castle" '52, "Julius Caesar" '53, "The Maze" '53) until his first western, "Hondo" ('53 Warner Bros.), brought him into the cowboy and Indian mold he so dearly loved as a child. The role of Chief Vittorio instantly made Pate a recognizable western actor.

On November 19, 1951, Michael married actress Felippa ("Flip") Rock, daughter of noted Vitagraph comedian and later producer Joe Rock who, among other things, produced the first batch of silent Stan Laurel two-reelers. He also produced comedies with Chester Conklin, Slim Summerville and others. After winning an Academy Award in 1932 for "Krakatoa", a three-reel short, he relocated to England and began Rock Studios, producing many features there. His daughter, Felippa, was in "Moss Rose" ('47), "Kiss the Blood Off My Hands" ('48), "Bride of the Gorilla" ('51), "From the Terrace" ('60), among others.

While continuing to act in film and on TV, Michael began teaching acting and lectured on film acting as well as writing screenplays ("Escape from Fort Bravo", "Rawhide" TV episode, etc). In the theatre, he played two seasons of "Medea" in L.A. and Houston.

In 1968, after nearly 60 films and well over 200 TV episodes in the U.S., Michael elected to return home to write and co-produce "Age of Consent" ('69).

In Australia he acted in and produced shows in all areas, police dramas, musicals and variety series, one of which won four industry awards. He acted in over 250 TVers. For one, "Matlock Police", he did a stint of over 192 episodes over four years, being honored with Australia's coveted Penguin Award as Best Actor. He worked on some 15 films, also writing and directing.

Never idle, Michael wrote three books between 1970-1986, including THE FILM ACTOR textbook, an illustrated children's book and a book of his WWII experiences.

In 1977, he wrote and produced "The Mango Tree" which featured his son Christopher, who, by the way, was also in a "Gunsmoke" episode, "The Whispering Tree".

In 1978 he wrote, produced and directed "Tim", the film that launched Mel Gibson's career and garnered Michael a Best Screenplay Award from the Australian Writer's Guild. Son Chris was producer's assistant for the film.

In 1979 Michael was featured on Australia's "This Is Your Life" as he continued to do theatre in Melbourne and Sydney.

Michael and his son joined forces again from 1982-1984 to co-star and tour Australia on stage in "Mass Appeal".

Over the years since, Michael has done other legit plays, radio, voice-overs for TVmercials and narrations for various documentaries and corporate videos. He's also continued to write an Australian movie column and, since 1997, has contributed a bi-monthly column of his movie and TV remembrances for Boyd Magers' WESTERN CLIPPINGS.

In 1997 Michael was awarded, by his government, a medal of the Order of Australia (OAM) for services rendered to the arts and film industry.

Today, from his home in Wadalba, New South Wales, he continues to write books and scripts and remains active in various phases of the Australian film industry.

Suggested Sampling of Pate's Western Heavies:

- Hondo ('53 Warner Bros.) John Wayne
- A Lawless Street ('55 Columbia) Randolph Scott
- Reprisal! ('56 Columbia) Guy Madison
- Broken Arrow: Indian Agent ('56) John Lupton/Michael Ansara
- Zane Grey Theatre: Fearful Courage ('56)
- Cheyenne: Border Affair ('57) Clint Walker
- Gunsmoke: Big Girl Lost ('57) James Arness
- Wagon Train: A Man Called Horse ('58) Ward Bond/Robert Horton
- Zorro: Eagle's Brood/Zorro By Proxy/Quintana Makes a Choice/Zorro Lights a Fuse ('58) Guy Williams
- Rifleman: New Orleans Menace ('58) Chuck Connors
- Texan: No Tears For the Dead ('58) Rory Calhoun
- Westbound ('59 Warner Bros.) Randolph Scott
- Rin Tin Tin: The Devil Rides Point ('59) Lee Aaker
- Rifleman: Second Witness ('59) Chuck Connors
- Zane Grey Theatre: Trouble at Tres Cruces ('59) Brian Keith
- Wanted Dead or Alive: Bounty for a Bride ('59) Steve McQueen
- Gunsmoke: Renegade White ('59) James Arness
- Gunsmoke: Blue Horse ('59) James Arness
- Rifleman: The Visitors ('60) Chuck Connors
- Law of the Plainsman: Common Ground ('60) Michael Ansara
- Zane Grey Theatre: The Last Bugle ('60) Robert Cummings
- Rifleman: Mescalero Curse ('61) Chuck Connors
- Lawman: Cold One ('61) John Russell
- Tales of Wells Fargo: Kelly's Clover Girls ('61) Dale Robertson
- Laramie: Day of the Savage ('62) Robert Fuller/John Smith
- Rifleman: The Executioner ('62) Chuck Connors
- Cheyenne: Johnny Brassbuttons ('62) Clint Walker
- California ('63 American International) Jock Mahoney
- Virginian: Man of Violence ('63) Doug McClure
- Temple Houston: Gun that Swept the West ('64) Jeffrey Hunter
- Major Dundee ('65 Columbia) Charlton Heston
- Branded: Call to Glory (Pt. 1-3) ('66) Chuck Connors
- Hondo: Hondo and the Eagle Claw ('67) Ralph Taeger

LEONARD PENN

Leonard Penn's contributions to outlawry on the screen only lasted 10 years ('47-'56) in the latter days of the B-western as westerns made their transition into half hour shoot-'em-ups, but those contributions were significant.

The suave, mustached badman, almost always cast as the dress heavy, was born in Springfield, Massachusetts, November 13, 1907. Penn graduated from Columbia University with a BA degree, his major being drama. After working on Broadway in various character roles, Leonard Monson Pennario made his move to Hollywood in '37 with a stock contract at MGM, making four films at the major studio in his first year, the first being "Firefly" with Jeanette MacDonald.

Other than a role as Pedro in "Girl of the Golden West" ('38 MGM), he didn't make a western til 1947.

Obviously, Penn did a stint in the military, as there are no film credits from '40-'46.

His return found him freelancing and accepting work in B films and serials where we began to recognize him. "Chick Carter, Detective" ('46) was the first of eight serials he made for Columbia. He was also treacherous in "Brick Bradford" ('47), "Congo Bill" ('48), "Batman and Robin" ('49) and "King of the Congo" ('52).

Seventeen B-westerns from '47-'53 and nearly 50 western half-hour TVers also featured Penn.

Roles grew sparse in the mid '50s, so he accepted a recurring role as space villain Griff on the ultra lowbudget TVer "Rocky Jones, Space Ranger" ('56). His last part was as a garrison officer in "Spartacus" ('60).

Penn was once married to actress Gladys George (1900-1954) who was nominated for an Academy Award in 1936 for her work in "Valiant Is the Lady". The pair worked together in MGM's "Marie Antoinette" in '38. It's unknown when they were married but they were divorced in 1946. Penn then married Louise in 1947.

Penn died in Los Angeles of colon cancer May 20, 1975.

Please do not confuse him with actor/director Leo Penn, the father of actor Sean Penn.

Suggested Sampling of Penn's Western Heavies:

- Hoppy's Holiday ('47 United Artists) Hopalong Cassidy
- Courtin' Trouble ('48 Monogram) Jimmy Wakely
- Outlaw Brand ('48 Monogram) Jimmy Wakely
- Range Land ('49 Monogram) Whip Wilson
- Lone Ranger: War Horse ('49) Clayton Moore
- Silver Raiders ('50 Monogram) Whip Wilson
- Gene Autry: Black Rider ('50) Gene Autry
- Six Gun Mesa ('50 Monogram) Johnny Mack Brown
- Range Rider: Baron of Broken Bow ('51) Jock Mahoney
- Wanted Dead Or Alive ('51 Monogram) Whip Wilson
- Wild Bill Hickok: Mexican Rustlers Story ('51) Guy Madison
- Cisco Kid: Carrier Pigeon ('51) Duncan Renaldo
- Roy Rogers: The Knockout ('52) Roy Rogers
- Barbed Wire ('52 Columbia) Gene Autry
- Outlaw Women ('52 Howco/Lippert) Marie Windsor
- Fangs of the Arctic ('53 Monogram) Kirby Grant
- Buffalo Bill Jr.: Devil's Washbowl ('55) Dick Jones
- Champion: Deer Hunters ('55) Jim Bannon
- Annie Oakley: Outlaw Brand ('56) Gail Davis

HOUSE PETERS JR.

House Peters Jr.'s screen work began in 1936, but it was in the late '40s and early '50s that he hit his stride as a screen badman.

Robert House Peters Jr. was born in New Rochelle, New York, January 12, 1916. His father, silent screen matinee idol, Robert House Peters, was born March 12, 1880, in Bristol, England.

House Sr. left England and worked in a stock company in Durban, South Africa. Leaving there, he landed in Montreal and eventually New York about 1911. After working in New York theatre, he came to Hollywood in 1915 to do four films for Cecil B. DeMille, including "The Great Divide" and "Girl of the Golden West".

House grew up knowing many of the people associated with his father such as Tom Mix, Hoot Gibson and Art Acord. Although House used to go to the studio with his father, "He never allowed me to be in a picture. I was brought up under a fairly normal home life circumstance, both my parents led a very quiet and unassuming life style considering the position my father attained in the film industry. Drama classes in grammar and high school in Beverly Hills really provided me with the incentive to make it my life's work. Years later, I did find out there had been a few opportunities in some of Dad's films but he felt other less fortunate children should have such chances, probably wanting me to lead a more normal childhood."

His father's last film before leaving the business was "Rose Marie" with Joan Crawford in 1928. Many of his best scenes were cut, leaving Peters disgusted with the business. Fortunately, he had acquired enough wealth that he did not need to return to films.

However, in 1952, director George Archainbaud asked House Jr. if his father would play a role in the current Gene Autry western they were filming, "The Old West". Senior did the picture, the only one father and son made together.

House Jr. graduated high school in 1935 and was trying to get an agent when actor James Gleason arranged a bit part for him in "Hot Tip" ('36 RKO).

Next came the role of a heavy in Universal's "Adventures of Frank Merriwell" serial ('36) which featured a lot of other Juniors. Roles in two more serials, "Flash Gordon" and "Ace Drummond" (both '36), plus a heavy in Gene Autry's "Public Cowboy No. 1" ('37) followed, along with bits in a few other pictures.

1937-1941 were lean years for House in films, forcing him to find other employment…he mined for gold in Mexico, managed a Signal Gas Station and became assistant manager of the Hermosa Theatre in Manhattan Beach.

On the strength of a steady income in 1939, he and his first wife, Margaret, were married. Their daughter Linda was born in 1940. House was now working at North American Aviation Corporation.

When December 7, 1941, signaled WWII, House joined the Coast Guard Auxiliary.

When his marriage ended in divorce in 1942, House enlisted in the Signal Corps, eventually winding up in the Philippines which is where he met his new wife to be, Lucy Pickett, shortly after the end of the war. They were married February 22, 1946, at Fort McKinley.

Discharged in 1946, House joined Ben Bard Playhouse on his GI loan, appearing in several plays.

From there House began to find work, especially at Republic ("Old Los Angeles" with Bill Elliott was his first after the war) and built a solid career over the next 18 years in films and on TV.

Besides B-westerns, House had roles in major films such as "Lorna Doone" ('51), "Day the Earth Stood Still" ('51), "Strategic Air Command" ('55), "Rebel Without a Cause" ('55) and "Rio Conchos" ('64). He also worked in four more serials, the most noteworthy being "King of the Rocketmen" ('49), made many religious films for Family Films, industrial films and commercials, including his famous Mr. Clean advertisements.

House reminisced, "I liked making westerns, and most of the people who were associated with those productions. Roy Rogers was the easiest to work with. You became acquainted quickly with Roy. He was always at-

Johnny Mack Brown is "Gunning for Justice" with an arm lock on House Peters Jr. ('48 Monogram).

tentive to those who came in, even if it was just one day. Of course, I didn't get acquainted with all the cowboy stars. I guess I would say Allan Lane was the toughest, but then, I never got to know him well. Please bear in mind, of my 250 appearances (movies and television), only half were actually westerns. The balance of my work consisted of playing ministers, sheriffs, detectives, etc. and appearing in commercial and industrial films. I never reached the heights in the business that I wanted—never quite able to step out of my father's shadow. The closest I ever got to a big part was in the original 'Lassie' television series when I played the up-to-date sheriff for a number of years, alongside Jan Clayton and George Cleveland. But, I must say, I had a wonderful time and met lots of great people."

In 1965, after completing a role in "The Great Sioux Massacre" and a "Lassie" episode, at age 50, House Jr. retired from acting and went into real estate, eventually opening an office in Woodland Hills.

In 1976, he left that business behind and for the next 13 years he and Lucy began a snowbird existence in their motor home.

House was honored by the Motion Picture and TV Fund with a Golden Boot Award in August, 2000.

Today, he and Lucy reside comfortably in complete retirement at the Motion Picture and TV Home in Woodland Hills, California. House smiles, "It was very interesting—there were lean days—sometimes one year better than another—sometimes you had to do other work to keep going—raising a family with three children. I have a lovely wife, Lucy, daughter Kathy; Rob is the oldest boy and Jon is the youngest. Christmas trees—Christmas greens and a mistletoe company of 30 people kept us busy for 25 years during the holidays. There was never a day that I went to work on a picture that I didn't look forward to it. I thoroughly enjoyed my work—with the hope that I would advance in the business to the extent that better parts would be available. I wish I could do it all over again with what I now know—but no regrets. I'm looking forward to many more years, and I have lots of things to do."

In 2000, House self-published his memoirs, ANOTHER SIDE OF HOLLYWOOD, definitely recommended reading for the real story of a working actor.

Suggested Sampling of Peters' Western Heavies:

- Public Cowboy No. 1 ('37 Republic) Gene Autry
- Under California Stars ('48 Republic) Roy Rogers
- Gunning For Justice ('48 Monogram) Johnny Mack Brown
- Courtin' Trouble ('48 Monogram) Jimmy Wakely
- Outlaw Country ('49 Western Adventure) Lash LaRue
- Son of Billy the Kid ('49 Western Adventure) Lash LaRue
- Lone Ranger: Jim Tyler's Past ('50) Clayton Moore
- Gene Autry: Head For Texas ('50) Gene Autry
- Gene Autry: Star Toter ('50) Gene Autry
- Lone Ranger: Desert Adventure ('50) Clayton Moore
- Cow Town ('50 Columbia) Gene Autry
- Border Treasure ('50 RKO) Tim Holt
- Spoilers of the Plains ('51 Republic) Roy Rogers
- Range Rider: False Trail ('51) Jock Mahoney
- Range Rider: Shotgun Stage ('52) Jock Mahoney
- Old West ('52 Columbia) Gene Autry
- Kansas Territory ('52 Monogram) Bill Elliott
- Wyoming Roundup ('52 Monogram) Whip Wilson
- Sky King: Desperate Character ('52) Kirby Grant
- Cisco Kid: Pancho and the Pachyderm ('52) Duncan Renaldo
- Lone Ranger: Best Laid Plans ('52) John Hart
- Range Rider: West of Cheyenne ('53) Jock Mahoney
- Hopalong Cassidy: New Mexico Manhunt ('54) William Boyd
- Annie Oakley: Dude Stagecoach ('54) Gail Davis
- Lone Ranger: Gold Freight ('55) Clayton Moore
- Buffalo Bill Jr.: Little Mavericks ('55) Dick Jones
- Champion: Medicine Man Mystery ('55) Jim Bannon
- Wyatt Earp: The Gambler ('55) Hugh O'Brian
- Wyatt Earp: The Killer ('55) Hugh O'Brian
- Buffalo Bill Jr.: Golden Plant ('56) Dick Jones
- Annie Oakley: Outlaw Brand ('56) Gail Davis
- Roy Rogers: Toss Up ('56) Roy Rogers
- Lone Ranger: Breaking Point ('57) Clayton Moore
- Lone Ranger: Ghost Town Fury ('57) Clayton Moore
- Black Patch ('57 Warner Bros.) George Montgomery
- Jim Bowie: Intruder ('57) Scott Forbes
- Man From God's Country ('58 Allied Artists) George Montgomery
- Wagon Train: Charles Maury Story ('58) Ward Bond/Robert Horton
- Rough Riders: Counterfeiters ('58) Jan Merlin/Kent Taylor/Peter Whitney
- Terror at Black Falls ('62 Beckman) House Peters Jr.

BILL PHIPPS

William (Bill) Phipps' boyish blonde good looks often belied a vicious badman.

Born February 22, 1922, in St. Francisville, Illinois, Phipps knew from boyhood he was destined to become an actor. He appeared in grade school and high school plays and briefly at Eastern Illinois University.

Hitchhiking to Hollywood in 1941, he worked on the stage in "Families Are Like That".

WWII interrupted his career with three years in the Navy, sending Bill across the Pacific 16 times on six different ships.

Post WWII, Phipps entered the respected Actor's Lab on his G. I. Bill. Charles Laughton noticed him and cast him in "Galileo" at John Houseman's Coronet Theatre in Hollywood.

Bill's first film was RKO's controversial "Crossfire" in '47. RKO then used Bill as the juvenile in his first western, Tim Holt's "Arizona Ranger" ('48) as well as Dick Powell's "Station West" ('48).

In 1950 Bill auditioned for and received the voice role of Prince Charming in Walt Disney's "Cinderella" ('50). A year later he hid his boyish face beneath a stubble beard and starred in Arch Oboler's memorable end-of-the-world classic, "Five", a film he is always remembered for.

Appearing in over 80 films and some 200 TV episodes, as varied as "Julius Caesar" ('53), "Cat Women of the Moon" ('53), "Executive Suite" ('54) and "Lust For Life" ('56), Phipps became closely associated with westerns, especially on TV, again often sporting a two day beard and grungy clothes to hide his youthful good looks. Several westerns with "Rocky" Lane, Rex Allen and Monte Hale utilized Bill as a juvenile second-lead rather than as an outlaw.

Among his TV guest shots, Bill was a semi-regular as Curley Bill Brocius on "Wyatt Earp" from '58-'61.

Not a juvenile anymore, but not looking old enough to play fatherly roles, in late 1969 Phipps dropped out of acting for five years and moved to Maui, Hawaii. He returned to the mainland, and acting, in March 1975.

Phipps has continued to work, in films, TV, commercials and voiceover work. He provided the narration for a special 190 minute version of David Lynch's "Dune", was seen in "Homeward Bound: The Incredible Journey" for Disney in '93 and played a reverend in "Sordid Lives" in 2000, which he also co-produced.

Suggested Sampling of Phipps' Western Heavies:

- Belle Starr's Daughter ('47 20th Century Fox) George Montgomery
- Wild Bill Hickok: Yellow Haired Kid ('51) Guy Madison
- Rose of Cimarron ('52 20th Century Fox) Mala Powers
- Northern Patrol ('53 Allied Artists) Kirby Grant
- Cisco Kid: Double Deal ('54) Duncan Renaldo
- Jesse James Vs. the Daltons ('54 Columbia) Brett King
- Two Guns and a Badge ('54 Allied Artists) Wayne Morris
- Rin Tin Tin: Poor Little Rich Boy ('55) Lee Aaker
- Broken Arrow: The Raiders ('56) Michael Ansara/John Lupton
- Badlands of Montana ('57 20th Century Fox) Rex Reason
- Annie Oakley: Dude's Decision ('57) Gail Davis
- Broken Arrow: Black Moment ('57) Michael Ansara/John Lupton
- Colt .45: One Good Turn ('57) Wayde Preston
- Trackdown: Look For the Woman ('57) Robert Culp
- Tombstone Territory: Gun Fever ('58) Pat Conway
- Sugarfoot: Canary Kid ('58) Will Hutchins
- Wyatt Earp: Peacemaker ('58) Hugh O'Brian
- Texas John Slaughter: Ambush In Laredo ('58) Tom Tryon
- Cimarron City: McGowan's Debt ('58) George Montgomery
- Sugarfoot: Price on His Head ('58) Will Hutchins
- Wanted Dead or Alive: The Corner ('59) Steve McQueen
- Rifleman: Money Gun ('59) Chuck Connors
- Gunsmoke: Odd Man Out ('59) James Arness
- Tombstone Territory: The Capture ('60) Pat Conway
- Wanted Dead or Alive: Triple Vise ('60) Steve McQueen
- Rebel: The Guard ('61) Nick Adams
- Gunsmoke: Carter Caper ('63) James Arness

STANLEY PRICE

Spindly, lean, often the coward in the outlaw band, Stanley Price was at home in cowboy gear or suits in B-films from '32-'56.

A talented stage actor, Price was the original Abie in "Abie's Irish Rose" on Broadway, playing the part for 1,100 performances. He also portrayed Judas in "The Pilgrimage Play" for several seasons in California. Although he first tried films in 1922, "Your Best Friend" for director William Nigh, he returned to the legit stage.

By 1932 he'd returned to Hollywood, where his first film was as one of Edward Arnold's thugs in "Three On a Match" at Warner Bros. Until 1939, and over 30 films, his only western exposure was in Mascot's Tom Mix serial, "Miracle Rider" ('35).

With "Water Rustlers" in '39, opposite singing cowgirl Dorothy Page, his western roles became more frequent, especially at Monogram and PRC. By 1949 he was firmly entrenched in western roles at Lippert (all of the Jimmy Ellison/Russell Hayden series) and Monogram/Allied Artists.

Also by 1949, he supplemented his income by acting as dialogue coach or dialogue director on dozens of films, obviously relying back on his long stage experience.

Over his career, Price essayed roles in nearly 40 serials. He was a mindless Zombie-slave in "Buck Rogers" ('39 Universal), a terrified gangster in the Batcave in "Batman" ('43 Columbia), a subservient storekeeper-henchman in "The Tiger Woman" ('44 Republic), the native chief in "The Phantom" ('43 Columbia), ranch foreman Pancho assisting "The Son of Zorro" ('47 Republic) and a plastic surgeon "doc" in "G-Men Never Forget" ('48 Republic). But usually Price was a minor league, often whiney, minion, quickly disposed of. He reached his serial pinnacle as the egotistical Phantom Ruler for 12 chapters of "The Invisible Monster" in 1950 during Republic's waning days.

In major productions such as "Algiers" ('38), "Meet John Doe" ('41), "Road to Morocco" ('42), "Lost Weekend" ('45), "State of the Union" ('48) and "The Ten Commandments" ('56) (his last film), his roles were always brief and character driven.

Early television apparently held little appeal for Price as he can only be spotted in episodes of "Buffalo Bill Jr.", "Kit Carson" and sparse others.

Stanley L. Price was born in Kansas December 31, 1892, the son of Frank H. Price and Laura Elizabeth Pratt. He served with the armed forces in WWI and was married to minor actress Frances Severens. They were the parents of a son, Stanley, and a daughter, Frances. Price died of coronary thrombosis July 13, 1955, at 62. His remains were cremated and are at Rosedale Crematory in Los Angeles.

Perhaps Price's most unusual contribution to westerns was in Tom Keene's "Wanderers of the West" ('41 Monogram) in which rustler Price plans to steal a government buffalo herd, take 'em to Mexico, breed 'em with cattle and come up with cattleo. (!?!)

I. Stanford Jolley (L), Bill Elliott and Stanley Price (R) in Allied Artists' "Rebel City" ('53).

Suggested Sampling of Price's Western Heavies:

- Water Rustlers ('39 Grand National) Dorothy Page
- Golden Trail ('40 Monogram) Tex Ritter
- Wanderers of the West ('41 Monogram) Tom Keene
- Driftin' Kid ('41 Monogram) Tom Keene
- Dynamite Canyon ('41 Monogram) Tom Keene
- Lone Star Law Men ('41 Monogram) Tom Keene
- Arizona Stagecoach ('42 Monogram) Range Busters
- Texas Kid ('43 Monogram) Johnny Mack Brown
- Fighting Valley ('43 PRC) Dave O'Brien/James Newill
- Range Law ('44 Monogram) Johnny Mack Brown
- Sunset in El Dorado ('45 Republic) Roy Rogers
- Romance of the West ('46 PRC) Eddie Dean
- Dalton's Women ('51 Western Adventure) Lash LaRue
- Man From Sonora ('51 Monogram) Johnny Mack Brown
- Man From Black Hills ('52 Monogram) Johnny Mack Brown
- Rebel City ('53 Allied Artists) Bill Elliott

HUGH PROSSER

Tall, somewhat debonair bad guy Hugh Prosser, more often dressed in a coat and tie rather than boots and spurs, was usually found giving orders to his henchmen from the safe haven of his lawyer or back room saloon office.

Born Clarence Prosser, little is known of his background. Social Security records indicate his birth as March 2, 1907, although no state is recorded.

His earliest known film is "Millionaire Kid" ('36). Within one year Prosser was working steadily in westerns, serials and smaller parts in A-films such as "They Got Me Covered" ('43) with Bob Hope, "So Proudly We Hail" ('43) with Claudette Colbert and "Pardon My Past" ('45) with Fred MacMurray.

In westerns, Prosser primarily worked at Republic in the early '40s, with mid '40s roles tending to be with Universal and Monogram, then several Durango Kids at Columbia in the late '40s.

Serial producers and directors liked his work also as he can be spotted in some 16 serials, both in large and small roles, good guy and bad guy. He was sneaky in "Phantom Rider" ('46 Republic), then at Columbia in "Sea Hound" ('47) and "Bruce Gentry" ('49), but on the right side of the law in "Jack Armstrong" ('47) as scientist Vic Hardy, "The Vigilante" ('47) as Capt. Riley, and "Mysterious Island" ('51) as one of the lost balloon adventurers.

The polished Prosser had entered a productive period on TV ("Gene Autry", "Cisco Kid", "Lone Ranger") when he died from injuries received in an auto accident November 8, 1952, near Gallup, New Mexico, about which little is known.

Suggested Sampling of Prosser's Western Heavies:

- West of Cimarron ('41 Republic) 3 Mesquiteers
- Boss of Hangtown Mesa ('42 Universal) Johnny Mack Brown
- Riders of the Deadline ('43 U.A.) William Boyd
- Range Law ('44 Monogram) Johnny Mack Brown
- Code of the Lawless ('45 Universal) Kirby Grant
- Prairie Raiders ('47 Columbia) Charles Starrett
- Six Gun Law ('48 Columbia) Charles Starrett
- Trail to Laredo ('48 Columbia) Charles Starrett
- Lone Ranger: The Beeler Gang ('49) Clayton Moore
- Outlaw Gold ('50 Monogram) Johnny Mack Brown
- Cisco Kid: Sleeping Gas ('50) Duncan Renaldo
- Canyon Ambush ('52 Monogram) Johnny Mack Brown

DENVER PYLE

Denver Pyle started out as a western badman in the B's of "Rocky" Lane, Gene Autry, Tim Holt and others in the late '40s, then easily slipped into the rapidly expanding band of juvenile oriented TV westerns, appearing more than frequently on "Roy Rogers", "Gene Autry", "Range Rider", "Kit Carson", "Annie Oakley" and others. Prematurely gray (a family trait), he became a familiar player on "Gunsmoke", "Bonanza", "Have Gun Will Travel", "Zane Grey Theatre" and dozens more, still playing occasional badmen, but slowly slipping into more character oriented roles.

Pyle's more important movie and TV roles came late in his career. One of his most memorable film roles was in "Bonnie and Clyde" ('67) as Sheriff Frank Hamer, the handcuffed hostage of the outlaw duo who spits in Faye Dunaway's face after she coyly poses with him for the camera.

For TV he was Grandpa to "Tammy" ('65-'66), Doris Day's ranch owner father on "The Doris Day Show" ('68-'70), a regular on the brief run of "Karen" ('75), mountain man Mad Jack on "Grizzly Adams" ('77-'78), and finally, a role he will always be associated with, love it or not, Uncle Jesse Duke to the good-ol'-boy "Dukes of Hazzard" from '79-'85.

The crotchety hillbilly/mountain man with a full beard types he played on the latter two series fit him well, and he brought that presence to many other films ("Escape To Witch Mountain", "Winterhawk", "Adventures of Frontier Fremont", "Wind In the Wire" etc.) and TV series.

Named after the capital of the state where he was born, Denver Dell Pyle was born in the little Colorado town of Bethune on May 11, 1920. His parents, married in Smith Center, Kansas, struck out on horseback to stake out a homestead where his Dad built a sod house. He and his older brother Willie (later a noted Disney animator) and older sister Skippy grew up on that farm. Denver attended school through the eighth grade in Bethune at which time the three children moved to Boulder, Colorado, and found jobs there. His sister started in college, Willie in high school and Denver in junior high. Eventually their mother joined them and opened up a boarding house.

Denver later went to the University of Colorado for two years until wanderlust consumed him and he, in his words, "Went on the bum."

By now, his brother was working for Disney and his sister was at Benton and Bowles Advertising Agency in Hollywood. After working in the oil fields of Oklahoma and Texas for a couple of years, he decided to visit his siblings in California where he ended up getting a job as a page boy at NBC during the daytime while he worked at Lockheed as a riveter at night when WWII started.

Through the Merchant Marines he was able to enlist in the Navy. He was given a medical discharge in 1942 after receiving wounds at Guadalcanal.

After the war Denver was working in the defense system and was married to a lady named Marilee. (They divorced in 1966, but had two sons.)

Through a friend, actor Sidney Gordon, Denver was coaxed into auditioning for a play. He began to study acting and was overjoyed when noted actress and coach Maria Ouspenskaya requested him personally to study with her. To pay his tuition he built sets and helped around the American Rep Theatre.

Through a play, Michael Chekhov asked Denver to join a group he was coaching (Marc Lawrence, John Dehner, Akim Tamiroff, Bill Phipps, others). In six years of intensive study Denver overcame his wanderlust and found his calling. Over this time he did plays at the Glendale Center Theatre, The Actor's Lab and other little the-

atres while he earned his keep waiting on tables and selling hearing aids.

Six years of hard work paid off when he was cast for a bit role in "The Guilt of Janet Ames" in '47. Other roles quickly followed including a choice part as an informant in Glenn Ford's "Man From Colorado" ('48 Columbia). On this film Denver met Edgar Buchanan who became a life long friend and who, Denver admits, "I emulated and stole liberally from."

It took Denver til about 1955 when he was outlaw Ben Thompson on "Wyatt Earp" to get established as a full time actor.

Over the years Pyle received many honors...John Wayne (with whom he worked frequently) became impressed with his photography and designated Pyle as the official set photographer for "The Alamo". Cumberland College in the Appalachians honored him for his continuous contributions to their scholarship fund. He received a Golden Boot Award in '84 and a star on the Hollywood Walk of Fame just two weeks before his death at 77 in Burbank from lung cancer on December 25, 1997.

Denver's longtime friend and co-star on "Dukes of Hazzard", James Best, told us, "Denver was one of the building stones of the real old Hollywood. He was a superb talent. He made his living during the time when talent really meant something. He wasn't just a personality. Denver was certainly an icon among the character actors in Hollywood."

Character player Walter Reed said, "He was a dear old friend of mine. I knew him when he wasn't doing too well financially. He sold me a car one time for 50 bucks, and said, 'Give me $10 at a time'—cause he was that busted. (Laughs) He was one fine, fine actor...a hell of a good character man, and he could do Shakespeare too. When Gabby Hayes died, Denver said, 'Hell, I'm gonna grow a beard.' He reinvented himself about five times."

Veteran heavy Gregg Barton said at learning of

Wayne Morris disarms "Texas Badman" Denver Pyle ('53 Allied Artists).

Denver's death, "What a wonderful, thorough professional...*always* ready, always competent. Just *completely* cooperative in any way you wanted to work with the man. He'll be missed by a lot of us old timers."

Suggested Sampling of Pyle's Western Heavies:

- Where the North Begins ('47 Screen Guild) Russell Hayden
- Marshal of Amarillo ('48 Republic) Allan "Rocky" Lane
- Dynamite Pass ('50 RKO) Tim Holt
- Old Frontier ('50 Republic) Monte Hale
- Rough Riders of Durango ('51 Republic) Allan "Rocky" Lane
- Hills of Utah ('51 Columbia) Gene Autry
- Range Rider: Western Fugitive ('51) Jock Mahoney
- Range Rider: Gunslinger in Paradise ('51 Jock Mahoney
- Gene Autry: Frontier Guard ('51) Gene Autry
- Cisco Kid: Hypnotist Murder ('51) Duncan Renaldo
- Desert Passage ('52 RKO) Tim Holt
- The Maverick ('52 Allied Artists) Bill Elliott
- Range Rider: Secret of the Red Raven ('52) Jock Mahoney
- Roy Rogers: Treasure of Howling Dog Canyon ('52) Roy Rogers
- Cisco Kid: Ghost Town ('52) Duncan Renaldo
- Gene Autry: Bullets and Bows ('52) Gene Autry
- Roy Rogers: Doublecrosser ('52) Roy Rogers
- Hopalong Cassidy: Blind Encounter ('52) William Boyd
- Cowboy G-Men: Salted Mines ('52) Russell Hayden
- Rebel City ('53 Allied Artists) Bill Elliott
- Texas Bad Man ('53 Allied Artists) Wayne Morris
- Range Rider: Cherokee Round-Up ('53) Jock Mahoney
- Kit Carson: Renegade Wires ('53) Bill Williams
- Kit Carson: Counterfeit Country ('54) Bill Williams
- Hopalong Cassidy: Outlaw's Reward ('54) William Boyd
- Gene Autry: Outlaw of Blue Mesa ('54) Gene Autry
- Lone Ranger: The Fugitive ('54) Clayton Moore
- Buffalo Bill Jr.: Black Ghost ('55) Dick Jones
- I Killed Wild Bill Hickok ('56 Wheeler) Johnny Carpenter
- Yaqui Drums ('56 Allied Artists) Rod Cameron
- Lone Ranger: Cross of Santo Domingo ('56) Clayton Moore
- Wyatt Earp: Witness For the Defense ('57) Hugh O'Brian
- State Trooper: Trail of the Dead ('57) Rod Cameron
- Tales of Wells Fargo: Renegade Raiders ('57) Dale Robertson
- Casey Jones: Storm Warning ('57) Alan Hale Jr.
- Man Without a Gun: Shadow of a Gun ('58) Rex Reason
- Bat Masterson: Marked Deck ('59) Gene Barry
- Restless Gun: The Pawn ('59) John Payne
- Texan: Telegraph Story ('59) Rory Calhoun
- Lawman: The Conclave ('59) John Russell
- Rifleman: Bloodlines ('59) Chuck Connors
- Law of the Plainsman: The Matriarch ('60) Michael Ansara
- Wichita Town: Legend of Tom Horn ('60) Joel McCrea
- Man From Blackhawk: Man Who Wanted Everything ('60) Robert Rockwell
- Tall Man: Garrett and the Kid ('60) Barry Sullivan/Clu Gulager
- Wyatt Earp: Too Perfect Crime ('60) Hugh O'Brian
- Gunsmoke: The Wake ('60) James Arness
- Bat Masterson: End of the Line ('61) Gene Barry
- Deputy: The Example ('61) Henry Fonda/Allen Case
- Bronco: Guns of the Lawless ('61) Ty Hardin
- Gunsmoke: Us Haggens ('62) James Arness/Ken Curtis
- Laramie: Vengeance ('63) Robert Fuller
- Virginian: Vengeance Is the Spur ('63) Clu Gulager/James Drury
- Rawhide: Incident of the Rawhiders ('63) Clint Eastwood
- Gunsmoke: No Hands ('64) Milburn Stone/James Arness
- Gunsmoke: The Violators ('64) James Arness
- Gunsmoke: Deputy Festus ('65) Ken Curtis/James Arness
- Incident at Phantom Hill ('66 Universal-International) Robert Fuller
- Guns of Will Sonnett: The Warriors ('68) Walter Brennan
- Bonanza: The Wagon ('70) Dan Blocker

MARSHALL REED

Marshall Reed was to Monogram what Roy Barcroft was to Republic—their resident badman. He menaced the late '40s Monogram cowboys (Johnny Mack Brown, Whip Wilson, Jimmy Wakely) in as many films as he did the stars at all the other studios (Republic, PRC, Columbia, RKO) combined.

Coming to the business in an unbilled bit for Roy Rogers' "Silver Spurs" ('43 Republic), his tall handsome looks quickly advanced him to major roles such as in "Texas Kid" ('43 Monogram) with Johnny Mack Brown and "Haunted Harbor" ('44 Republic serial), almost as if the studios were eyeing him for a starring series. As a matter of fact, he almost made it a couple of times. He was one of many under consideration for the "Lone Ranger" TV series ('49-'57) which went to Clayton Moore and was nearly cast as Red Ryder at Republic.

Finally, in 1954, Columbia starred Reed in 15 chapters of "Riding With Buffalo Bill". But it was too late, the serials and westerns were all but over. Reed returned to playing heavies on all the early B-western-styled half hour TVers. Reed found a regular paycheck from '54-'59 as Lt. Fred Asher, a regular role on "The Lineup" for CBS (syndicated as "San Francisco Beat"). Roles were sparse in the '60s and his final films were sadly in ill-received lowbudget quickies ("They Saved Hitler's Brain" '68, "Hard Ride" '70 and "Til Death" made in '72 escaped in '78).

Thankfully, there were a few nice (but small) roles for TV during this period on "Adam-12", "Marcus Welby, M.D.", "Cannon" and "Apple's Way". He also produced and directed several TV documentaries for charitable organizations on behalf of crippled children and retarded adults.

Marshall Jewel Reed was born in Englewood, Colorado, May 28, 1917. His father, Walter George Reed, was a Colorado native and his mother, Ruth Dustin, was from New Mexico.

Marsh (as he was often called) began his acting career early, appearing in children's theatre at 10. During high school Reed managed two of his own theatre groups. After high school he supported himself with various odd jobs such as horse trainer, meter reader, bookkeeper and mail clerk. His professional career began with Elitch Gardens Summer Stock Theatre in Denver by building and painting scenery, making costumes. He eventually acted in some of the plays staged there, then began to write, produce and act for a variety of theatre groups in Denver. Following that, Reed toured throughout the U.S. with his repertory group and acted in summer stock in New York and Los Angeles.

Reed came to California in 1942 and worked nights at Lockheed while he started his career in pictures. Reed served with the Navy in the Pacific during the last portion of WWII (circa '44-'45), then returned to Hollywood to resume his film career.

Reed was active in the Masquers Club, a theatrical organization in Hollywood, where he was an officer on the board of directors as well as serving as chairman of the Theatre Committee from '65-'67. In this capacity, he designed and directed "Twelve Angry Men" and "The Royal Family" as well as designing sets and executing lighting for other Masquers productions. He was also the head of Marshall Reed Enterprises, his own film equipment rental company.

A few years before he died, Reed redesigned the Paramount Ranch in Agoura for "Shame, Shame On the Bixby Boys" ('78) which starred Monte Markham. Reed had a small role in the film.

The last of Reed's five wives was Carlyn Miller. They were living at 5111 Babcock Ave. in North Hollywood when Reed died of a massive hemorrhage at Tarzana Medical Center April 15, 1980, at only 62. He had suffered from an earlier brain tumor. He was cremated and placed at Harbor Lawn Memorial Park in Costa Mesa, California.

Reed once recalled, "Bill Elliott and I became very good friends. Did you know Bill was best man at my wedding? He had talked to Herb Yates, and I was supposed to do the Red Ryder series. It was all cut and dried. At the time this was happening, Allan Lane was working on the lot in a hockey picture ("Gay Blades" '46), and Herb Yates was looking at the dailies one day and, just like that, he decided Lane was going to be the new Red Ryder. I had talked to Yates, and everything was beautiful. But Yates was the kind of guy who would change his mind at the drop of a hat. So that was the end of my deal, and Allan Lane was the new Red Ryder. I had some tough breaks in the business. Then, I tried out for 'The Lone Ranger' role, and Clayton Moore got it. When Clayton went on strike, I tried out again, but this time, it went to John Hart."

"I'll never forget the time we were doing a Johnny Mack Brown western, up at Walker cabin, near Newhall. I was one of the heavies. The good guys were behind us and they were shooting at us and we were shooting back at them. Now, there were a couple of new boys on the job when we started the chase and were just about to go un-

"Night Raiders" Marshall Reed (L) and Terry Frost have the drop on Whip Wilson ('52 Monogram).

der a huge limb of a big oak tree when I heard 'zing!' It turned out it was the first time one of the new kids was involved in a picture, and he brought his own gun and ammunition. He was shooting real ammunition! The minute I heard the 'zing,' I knew something was for real. Suddenly, everybody scattered. Needless to say, somebody could have been killed. They took that young man right off the picture, and he was never heard from in pictures again."

Pierce Lyden told us, "Marshall was a great guy and deserved a break. We were very happy when we heard 'one of our own'—Marsh Reed got (the lead) in 'Riding with Buffalo Bill' serial. But Marsh, real or imagined, was always having woman trouble. We were always consoling him. His early death was a shock. Marsh always wanted to be a star. He always thought he would be."

Suggested Sampling of Reed's Western Heavies:

- Texas Kid ('43 Monogram) Johnny Mack Brown
- Mojave Firebrand ('44 Republic) Bill Elliott
- Gangsters of the Frontier ('44 PRC) Tex Ritter/Dave O'Brien
- Gentleman From Texas ('46 Monogram) Johnny Mack Brown
- On the Old Spanish Trail ('47 Republic) Roy Rogers
- Prairie Express ('47 Monogram) Johnny Mack Brown
- Song of the Wasteland ('47 Monogram) Jimmy Wakely
- West of Dodge City ('47 Columbia) Charles Starrett
- Back Trail ('48 Monogram) Johnny Mack Brown
- Fighting Ranger ('48 Monogram) Johnny Mack Brown
- Triggerman ('48 Monogram) Johnny Mack Brown
- Check Your Guns ('48 PRC) Eddie Dean
- Rangers Ride ('48 Monogram) Jimmy Wakely
- Courtin' Trouble ('48 Monogram) Jimmy Wakely
- Mark of the Lash ('48 Western Adventure) Lash LaRue
- Brand of Fear ('49 Monogram) Jimmy Wakely
- Law of the West ('49 Monogram) Johnny Mack Brown
- Cherokee Uprising ('50 Monogram) Whip Wilson
- Silver Raiders ('50 Monogram) Whip Wilson
- Outlaw Gold ('50 Monogram) Johnny Mack Brown
- Gene Autry: Hot Lead ('50) Gene Autry
- Cisco Kid: Lynching Story ('50) Duncan Renaldo
- Marshal of Gunsight Pass: Shotgun Messenger ('50) Eddie Dean
- Canyon Raiders ('51 Monogram) Whip Wilson
- Gunplay ('51 RKO) Tim Holt
- Lawless Cowboys ('51 Monogram) Whip Wilson
- Range Rider: Bad Medicine ('51) Jock Mahoney
- Cisco Kid: Pancho Hostage ('51) Duncan Renaldo
- Wild Bill Hickok: Dog Collar Story ('51) Guy Madison
- Gene Autry: Frame For Trouble ('51) Gene Autry
- Wild Bill Hickok: Trapper Story ('52) Guy Madison
- Roy Rogers: Ghost Town Gold ('52) Roy Rogers
- Cisco Kid: Laughing Badman ('52) Duncan Renaldo
- Kit Carson: Baron of Black Springs ('52) Bill Williams
- Cowboy G-Men: Pixilated ('52) Russell Hayden
- Night Raiders ('52 Monogram) Whip Wilson
- Range Rider: Blind Canyon ('52) Jock Mahoney
- Lone Ranger: The Map ('52) John Hart
- Hopalong Cassidy: Lawless Legacy ('52) William Boyd
- Texas City ('52 Monogram) Johnny Mack Brown
- Rough Tough West ('52 Columbia) Charles Starrett
- Fort Osage ('52 Monogram) Rod Cameron
- Range Rider: Western Edition ('53) Jock Mahoney
- Cisco Kid: Church In the Town ('53) Duncan Renaldo
- Cowboy G-Men: Rawhiders ('53) Russell Hayden
- Gene Autry: Narrow Escape ('53) Gene Autry
- Kit Carson: Renegade Wires ('53) Bill Williams
- Hopalong Cassidy: Frontier Law ('53) William Boyd
- Annie Oakley: Bull's Eye ('54) Gail Davis
- Gene Autry: Prize Winner ('54) Gene Autry
- Cisco Kid: Caution of Whitey Thompson ('54) Duncan Renaldo
- Bat Masterson: High Card Hangs ('60) Gene Barry
- Shotgun Slade: Marriage Circle ('60) Scott Brady

TOM REESE

The sullen, menacing, often chilling Tom Reese became a fixture on the TV westerns of the '60s, especially "Gunsmoke" on which he appeared 23 times.

Reese was born Thomas Allen in Chattanooga, Tennessee, in 1928 to Austin and Ethel Allen. Tom's father, and his uncle as well, were regional country-western singers with a fan base in the Nashville/Memphis/Chattanooga/Georgia area. Tom recalls traveling with his parents "in a trailer like a medicine show." His father made a few records but when his singing career petered out he went to New York as a steel worker during the war. "I kinda used to sing with him as a kid," Tom recalled, "sit on his knee, but I regret I never learned to play the guitar."

Tom started "singing in nightclubs, strip joints, amateur shows," he told us. "When I was 15 or so I got on the Major Bowes Amateur Hour radio show…then the Arthur Godfrey Show, Ted Mack. On the road, in clubs, I sang ballads, but finally realized I wasn't gonna make it as a singer, so I started doing impressions of singers. That was my ace in the hole…I did Frankie Laine, Tony Bennett, Johnny Mathis, Johnny Ray. That was my nightclub (act) but I worked mostly strip joints, traveled around the country quite a bit…Boston, Detroit, Pittsburgh…and a lot of stuff in Canada…Montreal, Toronto. At that time I was also studying at the American Theatre Wing in New York under the GI Bill when I got out of the Marines."

Tom served with the Marines from 1945-1951 in transportation and mess duty in Cherry Point and Camp Lejeune, North Carolina, then as an MP at Quantico, Virginia.

Discharged, Reese went on a "cattle call" and got

in a short-lived Broadway Show, "Out West of 8th Avenue", which was about the Madison Square Garden Rodeo. Dennis Weaver (with whom Tom later worked on "Gunsmoke") and Brian Keith were also in the play at the Ethel Barrymore Theatre, directed by Burgess Meredith.

Then it was back to studying, off Broadway, Equity Library Theatre and on the road again with nightclubs.

Luck reached out when Tom got involved with the John Cassavetes acting group, Variety Arts Studio of New York of which Cassavetes was the director. Armed with $40,000 and a 16mm camera, Cassavetes filmed "Shadows" in 1959, which was then blown up and printed on 35mm stock. Entered in the Cannes Film Festival, it won the Critics Award and was picked up for distribution by Lion International. Reese (under the name Tom Allen) was 6th billed. The film's success brought Cassavetes to Hollywood.

Starring in his TV series, "Johnny Staccato", Cassavetes arranged a part for Reese in "The Return" episode of the series (airing in December '59). "I had no agent," Tom smiles, "but an actor on the show, Garry Walberg, got me with his agent and I was with them for 20 years. I changed my last name to Reese as there was a kid actor called Tom Allen."

With Reese's tough demeanor, he was nearly always cast as a heavy, except for the role of Sgt. Velie on NBC's "Ellery Queen" ('75-'76).

As to the heavies Tom played, he says, "A lot of the anger that came out on the screen was the anger I was feeling because I had been working on the road in these strip joints. I hated it. I wanted to act, I wanted to be in the movies. I grew up going to the movies. Little southern boy in New York, they used to beat the hell out of me all the time, so I'd go hide out in the movies. So I grew up wanting to be an actor. So many years in clubs, I hated nightclubs, it was very hard work. Of course, the experience helped me with timing, delivery. A lot of that anger came out—I used that anger when I played the heavies. But acting was a dream come true for me. I loved all the dream factory MGM movies made in those days, but I loved Johnny Mack Brown, Charles Starrett, I loved all those B-westerns. Kinda wanted to get on a horse and ride, so I learned to ride in Central Park, but it's not the same (Laughs)."

Reese was married early—around '64 he recalls—to a girl singer named Carol whom he met in nightclubs. "She came out to Hollywood a few years later, we got married but it didn't work out," Tom explains. "I was working, she wasn't, that was a problem. We split up and I never remarried"—although he's had several liaisons over the years.

Reese's last "official" work was an episode of "Paradise" in '89, however there was an independent, never released picture with he and Don Stroud made in Silver City, New Mexico, "Legend of Doc Holliday" made about 1992.

Today, he is semi-retired, he'd work if he got a call, but doesn't want those 4am calls. He's recently done some theatre work in Los Angeles including the role of Oscar in "The Odd Couple" for dinner theatre.

Suggested Sampling of Reese's Western Heavies:

- Law of the Plainsman: Jeb's Daughter ('60) Michael Ansara
- Gunsmoke: Gentleman's Disagreement ('60) James Arness
- Have Gun Will Travel: Tender Gun ('60) Richard Boone
- Gunsmoke: Tall Trapper ('61) James Arness
- Lawman: The Son ('61) John Russell
- Gunsmoke: Harriett ('61) James Arness
- Virginian: Woman From White Wing ('62) Lee J. Cobb
- Gunsmoke: Friend ('64) James Arness
- Blood On the Arrow ('64 Allied Artists) Dale Robertson
- Taggart ('64 Universal-International) Tony Young
- Bonanza: Underdog ('64) Lorne Greene/Michael Landon
- Destry: Infernal Triangle ('64) John Gavin
- Gunsmoke: Pariah ('65) James Arness
- Laredo: Golden Trail ('65) Neville Brand/William Smith/Peter Brown
- Gunsmoke: Hostage ('65) James Arness
- Branded: McCord's Way ('66) Chuck Connors
- Iron Horse: Dynamite Drive ('66) Dale Robertson
- Gunsmoke: Nitro (Pt. 1-2) ('67) James Arness
- Stranger On the Run ('67 TVM) Henry Fonda
- Guns of Will Sonnett: Meeting at Devil's Fork ('67) Walter Brennan
- Hondo: Hondo and the Sudden Town ('67) Ralph Taeger
- Cimarron Strip: Last Wolf ('67) Stuart Whitman
- Gunsmoke: Waco ('68) James Arness
- Gunsmoke: The Squaw ('75) James Arness

RICHARD REEVES

Big, beefy, rough hewn, tough talking Richard Reeves made his mark playing no-nonsense heavies on '50s TV westerns.

Richard Jourdan Reeves was born in New York City August 10, 1912, and made his way into films at 31 in 1943's "This Is the Army" as a soldier/singer. His mother's maiden name was Titsink.

His next film was not until 1947, "The Long Night", so one suspects military service during WWII.

Unfortunately, there is no statistical data on Reeves who died March 17, 1967, in Northridge, California, of cirrhosis of the liver.

He was one of the many who made the TV westerns of the '50s and '60s fun to watch.

Suggested Sampling of Reeves' Western Heavies:

- The Maverick ('52 Allied Artists) Bill Elliott
- Kit Carson: Hawk Raiders ('53) Bill Williams
- Kit Carson: Secret Sheriff ('53) Bill Williams
- Hopalong Cassidy: Sole Survivor ('53) William Boyd
- Roy Rogers: Peddler From Pecos ('53) Roy Rogers
- Roy Rogers: Land Swindle ('54) Roy Rogers
- Annie Oakley: Annie and the Texas Sandman ('54) Gail Davis
- Lone Ranger: Bounty Hunter ('55) Clayton Moore
- Fury: Ghost Town ('55) Peter Graves
- Top Gun ('55 U.A.) Sterling Hayden
- Maverick: Long Hunt ('57) James Garner
- 26 Men: Big Rope ('57) Kelo Henderson/Tris Coffin
- Tales of Wells Fargo: Doc Bell ('58) Dale Robertson
- Tombstone Territory: Rebel's Last Charge ('58) Pat Conway
- Sugarfoot: Bullet Proof ('58) Will Hutchins
- Jim Bowie: Patron of the Arts ('58) Scott Forbes
- Jefferson Drum: Hanging of Joe Lavett ('58) Jeff Richards
- Maverick: Lonesome Reunion ('58) James Garner
- Bat Masterson: Double Trouble in Trinidad ('59) Gene Barry
- Deputy: Proof of Guilt ('59) Henry Fonda/Allen Case
- Sugarfoot: Return of the Canary Kid ('59) Will Hutchins
- 26 Men: Fighting Man ('59) Kelo Henderson/Tris Coffin
- Rough Riders: Highgraders ('59) Jan Merlin/Kent Taylor
- Two Faces West: Hot Water ('60) Charles Bateman
- Outlaws: Rape of Red Sky ('60) Don Collier
- Wyatt Earp: Terror In the Desert ('61) Hugh O'Brian
- Bronco: Stage to the Sky ('61) Ty Hardin
- Cheyenne: Storm Center ('61) Clint Walker
- Cheyenne: Sweet Sam ('62) Clint Walker
- Legend of Jesse James: Judas Boot ('65) Christopher Jones

ADDISON RICHARDS

In close to 300 movies and over 100 TV shows outstanding character player Addison Richards portrayed sincerity. His long, lean face with earnest eyes and reassuring voice held an undeniable charisma that spoke of understanding. Wise directors often used his kindly persona to great advantage, twisting it to belie an unscrupulous heavy. Another screen heavy, Bill Kennedy, termed Richards "a marvelous performer."

Addison Whitaker Richards Jr. was born October 20, 1902 (not 1887 as oft reported) in Zanesville, Ohio. Graduating with a B.A. from Washington State University, he did post-graduate work at Pomona College in California and launched his acting in the 1926 "Pilgrimage Play". In 1930 he became associate director of the fledgling Pasadena Community Playhouse and acted there as well.

Richards entered films in 1933 with "Riot Squad" and quickly became known as a reliable character actor.

He continued to work for 33 years with his last role coming in '64's "For Those Who Think Young". In that film he played a college dean, the type of authoritarian or dignified role (generals, bank presidents, community leaders, governors, judges, doctors) he'd turned to since the early '50s. He had a recurring role as Doc Landy on Henry Fonda's TV series, "The Deputy" ('59-'61).

His respected talent saw him cast in classic films such as "G-Men" ('35), "Petrified Forest" ('36), "My Little Chickadee" ('40), the Andy Hardy series at MGM, "They Died With Their Boots On" ('42), "Pride of the Yankees" ('42), "Flying Tigers" ('42), "Spellbound" ('45), "Dragonwyck" ('46), "Mighty Joe Young" ('49) and "Ensign Pulver" ('64) right alongside B-films with Charlie Chan, the Lone Wolf, the Crime Doctor, East Side Kids, Roy Rogers and Gene Autry.

For serials, Universal capitalized on his talents three times, he was honest in "Raiders of Ghost City" ('44) and "Royal Mounted Rides Again" ('45) but his sincerity proved him to be a traitorous Nazi in "The Master Key" ('45).

In his westerns, he was never better than in Gene Autry's "Back In the Saddle". It's really Richards' film all the way as a good/badman gambler. All his scenes are standouts, including the one where he smugly tells arrogant mine owner Arthur Loft, "Don't ever be alone with yourself, you wouldn't like it."

Richards died March 22, 1964, in Los Angeles of a heart attack. Survivors included a wife and daughter, Ann. He is buried at Forest Lawn Memorial Park in Glendale.

Suggested Sampling of Richards' Western Heavies:

- Home On the Range ('35 Paramount) Randolph Scott
- Eagle's Brood ('35 Paramount) William Boyd
- Trailin' West ('36 Warner Bros.) Dick Foran
- Pony Express Days ('40 Warner Bros.) George Reeves
- Back In the Saddle ('41 Republic) Gene Autry
- Sheriff of Tombstone ('41 Republic) Roy Rogers
- Texas ('41 Columbia) William Holden/Glenn Ford
- Cowboy Serenade ('42 Republic) Gene Autry
- Ridin' Down the Canyon ('42 Republic) Roy Rogers
- Bordertown Trail ('44 Republic) Sunset Carson
- Jim Bowie: A Horse for Old Hickory ('57) Scott Forbes

KEITH RICHARDS

1949 was a pivotal year for Keith Richards. Although he'd been in the business since 1940 he'd failed to make much of an impact. Then, in 1949, he starred as Jesse James in Republic's sanitized serial version of the James Boys' exploits, "The James Brothers of Missouri". Keith also began that year to appear on every western TV adventure that came along—most always as a heavy. "Lone Ranger", "Sky King", "Range Rider", "Cisco Kid", "Roy Rogers", "Wild Bill Hickok", "Annie Oakley", "Hopalong Cassidy", "Gene Autry"—he did them all and more.

Ted Huish was born July 18, 1914, in Pittsburgh, Pennsylvania, to Frank and Mary Emma Huish who both came to the U.S. from England. Frank had been a famous soccer player prior to immigrating to America. A brother, George, died young and when his father deserted the family, mother had to raise Ted and his sister, Edith.

Ted attended Osceola Grammar School in Pittsburgh, but by the 6th grade he was enrolled at prestigious Carson-Long Military Academy in New Bloomfield, Pennsylvania. Not only a standout in sports at the Academy, this is where he gained his early love of the stage in school plays and as captain of the debating team.

Graduating from Carson-Long in 1934, he attended the University of Pennsylvania for a year, then was known as Keith Huish with the George Sharpe Stock Company in Pittsburgh.

His love of Shakespearian plays led him to employment as assistant business manager with the company that constructed sets for the Laurence Olivier Broadway production of "Romeo and Juliet" in 1940. Learning of Keith's background, Olivier offered him a minor role in the show's road tour. Numerous talent scouts and other actors advised Keith to go to Hollywood, which he did. His initial role was in "Meet the Wildcat" ('40) as a gallery assistant. This is when he assumed the name Keith Richards.

Soon being groomed under contract at Paramount, his first western was "Secrets of the Wasteland" with William Boyd in '41. Keith was placed in many other large-scale Paramount pictures, "Reap the Wild Wind", "Forest Ranger", "Beyond the Blue Horizon", "Holiday Inn", "Wake Island", "Lucky Jordan" and "So Proudly We Hail".

WWII interrupted his blossoming career in late 1943. Due to his experience at the Military Academy, he was made Chief Petty Officer when he entered the Navy. Never seeing overseas duty, he was stationed at Bainbridge, Maryland, and Chicago.

Post WWII, 1946, Keith returned to Hollywood but his career never regained the foothold it once had. More and more he gravitated to the serials (his first was "Mysterious Mr. M", Universal's last in '46) and westerns for which we know Keith best. Besides "James Brothers of Missouri", Richards' only other major serial role was as the main heavy in Republic's final fling at chapterplays, "King of the Carnival" ('55).

Keith also worked in radio. For a long time in the mid to late '40s he was the announcer on "The Eddie Cantor Show".

Keith starred in a TV pilot for "Mandrake the Magician" but it went unsold.

When acting jobs for Keith became lean in 1962, he went to work at M&K Iron and Metal Company. In 1967 he left the movie business entirely and operated M&K, which he finally ended up owning.

Eventually selling the business, Keith retired and devoted his time to playing golf with buddies like Bob Wilke, James Garner and Peter Falk.

Throughout the years Keith was a member of the Hollywood Stars Baseball team, became an accomplished painter, and was quite adept at interior decorating.

Richards was 71 when cancer took his life on March 23, 1987, in Los Angeles.

Suggested Sampling of Richards' Western Heavies:

- Secrets of the Wasteland ('41 Paramount) William Boyd
- Where the North Begins ('47 Screen Guild) Russell Hayden
- Gay Ranchero ('48 Republic) Roy Rogers
- Shadows of the West ('49 Monogram) Whip Wilson
- Lone Ranger: Finders Keepers ('49) Clayton Moore
- Gene Autry: Kid Comes West ('51) Gene Autry
- Cisco Kid: Hidden Valley ('51) Duncan Renaldo
- Range Rider: Outlaw's Double ('52) Jock Mahoney
- Cisco Kid: Mad About Money ('52) Duncan Renaldo
- Sky King: Danger Point ('52) Kirby Grant
- Kit Carson: Wild Horses of Pala ('52) Bill Williams
- Hopalong Cassidy: Vanishing Herd ('52) William Boyd
- Lone Ranger: Godless Men ('53) John Hart
- Cisco Kid: Bodyguard ('53) Duncan Renaldo
- Wild Bill Hickok: Sheriff Was a Redhead ('53) Guy Madison
- Rebel City ('53 Allied Artists) Bill Elliott
- Cisco Kid: Steel Plow ('54) Duncan Renaldo
- Stories of the Century: Dalton Gang ('54) Jim Davis
- Annie Oakley: Annie Joins the Cavalry ('54) Gail Davis
- Lone Ranger: Trigger Finger ('55) Clayton Moore
- Cisco Kid: Kidnapped Cameraman ('55) Duncan Renaldo
- Wild Bill Hickok: Treasure Trail ('55) Guy Madison
- Gene Autry: Guns Below the Border ('55) Gene Autry
- Champion: Hangman's Noose ('55) Jim Bannon
- Judge Roy Bean: Judge's Dilemma ('56) Edgar Buckanan
- Roy Rogers: Morse Mix-up ('56) Roy Rogers
- Cisco Kid: Dangerous Shoemaker ('56) Duncan Renaldo
- Buffalo Bill Jr.: Secret of the Silverado ('56) Dick Jones
- Annie Oakley: Annie and the Lacemaker ('56) Gail Davis
- Lone Ranger: Breaking Point ('57) Clayton Moore
- Tombstone Territory: Revenge Town ('57) Pat Conway
- Casey Jones: Prison Train ('57) Alan Hale Jr.
- Wyatt Earp: Imitation Jesse James ('58) Hugh O'Brian
- Tales of Wells Fargo: The Prisoner ('58) Dale Robertson
- Tales of the Texas Rangers: Traitor's Gold ('58) Willard Parker
- Rough Riders: Strand of Wire ('58) Jan Merlin/Peter Whitney
- Rin Tin Tin: Stagecoach to Phoenix ('59) Lee Aaker
- Rebel: The Rattler ('60) Nick Adams
- Bronco: Beginner's Luck ('62) Ty Hardin

PAUL RICHARDS

With his expressive, brooding, troubled face, often exemplifying some sort of intense inner tragedy or misery, Paul Richards was the perfect candidate for the stream of adult TV westerns that proliferated in the '50s and '60s. At other times he could turn that inner turmoil into an icy-cold unforgiving killer. He always offered a commanding presence.

Paul Richards was born in Hollywood, California, November 23, 1924. Richards said he was only ten years old when he and some friends made some movies with an old 8mm camera then charged other kids a nickel admission to watch their "productions". He later commented, "Little did I think that one day the same people who paid five cents to see me in a movie would be paying two dollars to see me do almost the same thing…but, of course, the direction and scripting had improved. I feel most fortunate that I knew what I wanted when I was ten and now, two decades later, I have the same goal."

While he was working on a Masters degree in theatre arts at UCLA, Richards acted on radio, a medium well-suited to his distinctive deep, rich voice.

His first film was 1951's "Fixed Bayonets" at 20th Century Fox. He then began appearing in many TVers, including several "Dragnet" programs.

In '53 he made his first two westerns, a Hopalong Cassidy episode and as one of the troopers in "War Paint" (U.A.) with Robert Stack.

Richards starred as a dedicated psychiatrist in the short-lived ABC "Breaking Point" series in '63.

Richards was married in '53 to actress Monica Keating. He continued to work on TV episodes, TV commercials and films (his last was "I Escaped From Devil's Island" in '73) up until his death December 10, 1974, of cancer in Culver City, California. Richards was only 50.

Suggested Sampling of Richards' Western Heavies:

- Gunsmoke: Matt Gets It ('55) James Arness
- Brave Eagle: Code of the Chief ('55) Keith Larsen
- Tall Man Riding ('55 Warner Bros.) Randolph Scott
- Rin Tin Tin: Last Chance ('55) Lee Aaker
- Black Whip ('56 20th Century Fox) Hugh Marlowe
- Broken Arrow: Desperado ('57) John Lupton/Michael Ansara
- Gunsmoke: Joe Phy ('58) James Arness
- Blood Arrow ('58 Regal) Scott Brady
- Tombstone Territory: Thicker Than Water ('58) Pat Conway
- Rawhide: Incident at Barker Springs ('59) Eric Fleming/Clint Eastwood
- Black Saddle: Client: Martinez ('59) Peter Breck
- Rifleman: The Trade ('59) Chuck Connors
- Have Gun Will Travel: The Chase ('59) Richard Boone
- Johnny Ringo: The Hunters ('59) Don Durant
- Tombstone Territory: Noose That Broke ('59) Pat Conway
- U.S. Marshal: Kill or Be Killed ('60) John Bromfield
- Johnny Ringo: Vindicator ('60) Don Durant
- Tate: Voice of the Town ('60) David McLean
- Four Fast Guns ('60 Universal) James Craig
- Westerner: Mrs. Kennedy ('60) Brian Keith
- Bat Masterson: Death By Decree ('60) Gene Barry
- Bonanza: Lonely House ('61) Michael Landon
- Rawhide: Boss's Daughter ('62) Eric Fleming
- Guns of Will Sonnett: Of Lasting Summers and Jim Sonnett ('67) Walter Brennan
- Gunsmoke: The Jackals ('68) James Arness

WARNER RICHMOND

Throughout the '30s the snide, snarling presence of Warner Richmond elicited instantaneous boos from front row kids. Here was a no good lout if ever there was one. Tex Ritter, Jack Randall, Gene Autry, Bob Steele, Johnny Mack Brown, John Wayne and others were in for a rough ride against this scoundrel.

According to his death certificate, Werner Paul Raetzmann was born in Racine, Wisconsin (not Virginia as often reported), January 11, 1886. Racine is suspect, however, as, at the time, the family was living in Reedsburg, Wisconsin, half-a-state away. 1880, 1900 and 1910 census records all show the family, including Werner, living in Reedsburg. Other records indicate Werner's brothers and sisters as being born in Reedsburg.

Werner's father, William Raetzmann, was born in Hanover, Germany, and immigrated to the U.S. sometime prior to 1880 when he is found working as a printer in Reedsburg. His wife, Werner's mother, was Emilie (later spelled Amelia) Licht (later reported as Light) born in 1856 in Wisconsin. (She died in 1939.) Over the years Werner had seven brothers and sisters. Ewald was born in 1875 and remained a farmer in Illinois. Amandus was born in 1876. Meta was born in 1878. William was born in 1881. By 1930 he was superintendent on a horse farm in Kentucky and later moved to Monterey, California. Alfred, born in 1888, became a movie stuntman in 1919 for about seven years. He moved to Billings, Montana, in 1934 where he owned Al's Saddle Horse Service when he died in 1966. Paul was born in 1893. He became a policeman in Washington, D.C., and, some reports say, a member of the security force at the White House. He later moved to Clearwater, Florida. Pauline was born about 1890 and became a nurse in Chicago.

Some bios indicate Warner attended Virginia Military Institute in Lexington, Virginia. However, VMI alumni records prove this to be inaccurate, probably the result of an invented "studio bio". He also supposedly held an early job as a brakeman on the Baltimore and

Ohio railroad. This may be accurate or, again, it may be studio hype. According to 1910 census records, at age 24, Werner was dividing his time between stock company work in Chicago and as a traveling salesman of musical instruments in Wisconsin. Some reports indicate when stock work became slow, he operated a haberdashery shop in Chicago. Somewhere in these years he changed his name from Werner Raeztmann to Warner Richmond and invented the "fact' he was born in Virginia. Is it coincidence the city of "Richmond" is in Virginia? As is Virginia Military Institute and the University of Virginia.

Eventually, the 5' 11", 179 lb. Richmond came to New York and the old Vitagraph Studios which is where he met and married actress Felice Striker Rose. They had a son, Warner Jr. Felice gave up her career when they married but returned to acting after Warner died. Felice Richmond can be seen in "Fighting Vigilantes" ('47 PRC), "Rough Riders of Cheyenne" ('45 Republic), "Trail of the Mounties" ('47 Screen Guild), "Fighting Mustang" ('48 Yucca), "Loaded Pistols" ('49 Columbia), "Son of Billy the Kid" ('49 Western Adventure), "Cowtown" ('50 Columbia), "Westbound" ('49 Warner Bros.), among many others.

Richmond first appeared on screen in "The Godmother" (1912). His first western was as a doctor in House Peters Sr.'s "The Great Divide" (1915). In the developing years of silent films Richmond had romantic leads (or second leads) in dozens of films, with critics especially taking note of his work in "Tol'able David" in 1921, the year, incidentally, his son Warner P. Richmond Jr. was born.

Richmond's next western role wasn't until 1930, as gunman Bob Ballinger in Johnny Mack Brown's historically inaccurate "Billy the Kid". He was decent in George O'Brien's "Life In the Raw" ('33) but turned as vile as they make 'em in "Smokey Smith" ('35) as he shot off the finger of Bob Steele's father so he could steal a ring, then brutally threw lye in George Hayes' eyes, blinding him.

Richmond worked in six serials with his most prominent roles in "Lost Jungle" ('34 Mascot) and "Phantom Empire" ('35 Mascot). The die was forever cast. Richmond sneered, sneaked, snatched and snarled his way through over 20 more westerns until he suffered a serious head injury when he fell from his horse due to a loose cinch while filming a chase scene in Prescott, Arizona, for Tex Ritter's "Rainbow Over the Range" ('40). You'll

Tex Ritter protects pretty Eleanor Stewart from the evil Warner Richmond in "Headin' for the Rio Grande" ('36 Grand National).

note in the film how his character of Bart Griffin appears and disappears due to his inability to finish the picture.

Richmond was hospitalized in Arizona for eight months, then returned home with the left side of his face paralyzed. While sitting and reading, Richmond continually pinched and massaged his paralyzed face until he restored his reflexes after two and a half years, even though his eye still didn't work well.

Producer Bob Tansey helped him return to westerns, mean as ever in '44 ("Outlaw Trail" w/Trail Blazers), but Richmond made only two more with Eddie Dean before he retired to the Motion Picture Country Home. The life of one of the best of the badmen was cut short at 62 on June 19, 1948, by coronary thrombosis. He was cremated at the Chapel of the Pines.

Suggested Sampling of Richmond's Western Heavies:

- Phantom Empire ('35 Mascot serial) Gene Autry
- Smokey Smith ('35 Supreme) Bob Steele
- Rainbow's End ('35 First Division) Hoot Gibson
- New Frontier ('35 Republic) John Wayne
- Singing Vagabond ('35 Republic) Gene Autry
- Courageous Avenger ('35 Supreme) Johnny Mack Brown
- Song of the Gringo ('36 Grand National) Tex Ritter
- Headin' For the Rio Grande ('36 Grand National) Tex Ritter
- A Lawman Is Born ('37 Supreme) Johnny Mack Brown
- Riders of the Dawn ('37 Monogram) Jack Randall
- Trail of Vengeance ('37 Supreme) Johnny Mack Brown
- Where Trails Divide ('37 Monogram) Tom Keene
- Doomed at Sundown ('37 Republic) Bob Steele
- Six Shootin' Sheriff ('38 Grand National) Ken Maynard
- Wild Horse Canyon ('38 Monogram) Jack Randall
- Prairie Moon ('38 Republic) Gene Autry
- Water Rustlers ('39 Grand National) Dorothy Page
- Fighting Mad ('39 Monogram) James Newill
- Rhythm of the Rio Grande ('40 Monogram) Tex Ritter
- Rainbow Over the Range ('40 Monogram) Tex Ritter
- Colorado Serenade ('46 PRC) Eddie Dean
- Wild West ('46 PRC) Eddie Dean

LEE ROBERTS

"He was a good 'hand,'" badman Pierce Lyden wrote in his MOVIE BADMEN I RODE WITH book. "I always thought he would get a break and move up. Lee was quiet, steady and a real nice guy. When Katzman gave him a chance (to star) in the serial 'Blazing the Overland Trail' he looked great and it *could* have led to something big. It didn't."

Lee Roberts, real name Robert Allen, is one of the mystery men of westerns and a "lost player."

Roberts got his start under his real name in a couple of Trail Blazers Monograms in '43 (leading to the mistaken belief on some fronts that former Columbia star Bob Allen was in these films).

After apparent military service in '44-'45, Roberts returned to Hollywood finding western roles plentiful at PRC and Monogram where he did the bulk of his work.

Usually he was one of the gang out to rustle, steal or swindle, but on occasion he moved up to second lead with Whip Wilson ("Stage To Blue River" '51 Monogram, "Riders of the Dusk" '49 Monogram), Eddie Dean ("Stars Over Texas" '46 PRC), Johnny Mack Brown ("Canyon Ambush" '52 Monogram) and Sunset Carson ("Battling Marshal" '50 Yucca).

Lee's one chance at stardom came late in the game when Sam Katzman selected him as the lead for his "Blazing the Overland Trail" '56 Columbia serial, dressing Roberts to match stock footage of Buck Jones from earlier Columbia serials, "White Eagle" in particular. It was the last serial ever made.

Roberts was in 14 serials, with good roles also in "Pirates of the High Seas" ('50), "Great Adventures of Capt. Kidd" ('53), "Lost Planet" ('53) and "Adventures of Captain Africa" ('55). Roles in film and on TV were minimal after the serials and by 1960 Roberts had disap-

Doubtful, but it appears Lee Roberts (R) is on good terms with Whip Wilson as they prepare to take the "Stage to Blue River" ('51 Monogram).

peared. He was last seen on a few episodes of ZIV TV's syndicated "McKenzie's Raiders" and a "Laramie" in 1960—"Hour After Dawn".

Stuntlady/actress Evelyn Finley met Roberts while working (under the name Eve Anderson) in Katzman's "Perils of the Wilderness" Columbia serial in '56. They were soon married but it ended quickly when Finley discovered, as she told Boyd Magers, "Lee was a closet drinker. Literally. He hid his bottles in the closet. I never knew til a short while after we were married." Evelyn, a devout Christian Scientist, could not live with Roberts' drinking and they were divorced. Evelyn went on to say, "I have to say he had more talent and ability than anyone I ever knew. He could have gone far as an actor—if only someone would have 'pushed' him. He wouldn't 'push' himself, and I could only encourage him. I can't really put my finger on the real reason Lee wasn't successful in motion pictures—unless he just didn't care for acting. He was, without a doubt, the finest, most clean-minded man, a gentleman at all times. I still truly admired him—though we had our differences. One day he left! We have never heard from him since. He seems to have disappeared. I treasure the good times we had together, and I wish him the best of everything."

Shortly before Evelyn died in 1989, she tried to locate Roberts having heard rumors of his living on L.A.'s skid row or possibly having become an insurance salesman. Alas, her search ended in a cold trail. His whereabouts or demise still remains a mystery.

Suggested Sampling of Roberts' Western Heavies:

- Death Valley Rangers ('43 Monogram) Trail Blazers
- Caravan Trail ('46 PRC) Eddie Dean
- Tumbleweed Trail ('46 PRC) Eddie Dean
- Driftin' River ('46 PRC) Eddie Dean
- Law of the Lash ('47 PRC) Lash LaRue
- Deadline ('48 Yucca) Sunset Carson
- Mark of the Lash ('48 Western Adventure) Lash LaRue
- Haunted Trails ('49 Monogram) Whip Wilson
- Fighting Redhead ('49 Eagle Lion) Jim Bannon
- Dalton Gang ('49 Lippert) Don Barry
- Square Dance Jubilee ('49 Lippert) Don Barry
- Desperadoes of the West ('50 Republic serial) Richard (Tom Keene) Powers
- Law of the Panhandle ('50 Monogram) Johnny Mack Brown
- Abilene Trail ('51 Monogram) Whip Wilson
- Nevada Badmen ('51 Monogram) Whip Wilson
- Lawless Cowboys ('51 Monogram) Whip Wilson
- Texas Lawmen ('51 Monogram) Johnny Mack Brown
- Man From Sonora ('51 Monogram) Johnny Mack Brown
- Roy Rogers: Shoot To Kill ('51) Roy Rogers
- Desperadoes' Outpost ('52 Republic) Allan "Rocky" Lane
- Cowboy G-Men: Ozark Gold ('52) Russell Hayden
- Hopalong Cassidy: Vanishing Herd ('52) William Boyd
- Cisco Kid: Bandaged Badman ('53) Duncan Renaldo
- Stories of the Century: Jim Courtwright ('55) Jim Davis

JACK ROCKWELL

Jack Rockwell played a stolid, unsmiling Sheriff, Ranger Captain or U.S. Marshal more than he did a badman, but when he wasn't on the side of the law, he was an excellent villain.

Rockwell, whose true name was John Rockwell Trowbridge, was born in Vera Cruz, Mexico, October 6, 1890. His father was Charles Trowbridge from Decatur, Illinois, and his mother was Kate Stephens of Pachuca, Mexico. Jack's brother was actor Charles Trowbridge, also born in Vera Cruz on January 10, 1882. Eight years Jack's senior, Charles started in films around 1915 and it was no doubt he who got Jack into the business in the late '20s shortly after Jack had seen duty in WWI. His first credited film is "Prairie King" with Hoot Gibson in '27.

Unlike his brother, Charles Trowbridge did few westerns but was a prolific performer in both A and B films. Often seen as a lawyer, judge, military man, scientist, he had a commanding voice with a memorable enunciation of words. The handful of westerns he did do include a senator in "Cherokee Strip" ('40 WB), a Colonel in "Belle Starr" ('41 20th Century Fox) and the Governor in "The Paleface" ('48 Paramount). But he's also the Major in "Adventures of the Flying Cadets" ('43 Universal serial), the Commissioner in "Captain America" ('44 Republic serial), the Governor in "Mysterious Dr. Satan" ('40 Republic serial) and an official in "King of the Texas Rangers" ('41 Republic serial). He's in the cast of literally hundreds of non-westerns in the '30s, '40s and '50s. Charles died in 1967.

Jack's steely-eyed, tight-lipped, firm demeanor qualified him as a Sheriff or Ranger early on in Ken Maynard and Bob Steele B's, a role he was will suited for and pursued vigorously in nearly 100 B-westerns. Other times he was a rancher, father, townsman—or outlaw—for a total of over 250 films through 1947.

Jack was married to Helen B. Trowbridge. They lived at 461 W. Windsor Rd. in Glendale, California.

Jack died at 57 November 10, 1947, at Glendale (California) Sanitarium where he'd been a pneumonia patient for eleven days. His widow died in 1976, outliving Jack by over 30 years. Both are in vaultage at Grandview Memorial Park in Glendale.

Rick Vallin (R) watches closely as Wild Bill Elliott and Gabby Hayes put a hold on nefarious Jack Rockwell in Republic's "Wagon Tracks West" ('43 Republic).

Suggested Sampling of Rockwell's Western Heavies:

- When a Man Rides Alone ('33 Monarch) Tom Tyler
- Prescott Kid ('34 Columbia) Tim McCoy
- Outlaw Rule ('35 Kent) Reb Russell
- Justice of the Range ('35 Columbia) Tim McCoy
- Man From Guntown ('35 Puritan) Tim McCoy
- Lightning Triggers ('35 Kent) Reb Russell
- Lucky Terror ('36 Diversion) Hoot Gibson
- Reckless Ranger ('37 Columbia) Bob Allen
- Guilty Trails ('38 Universal) Bob Baker
- Prairie Justice ('38 Universal) Bob Baker
- Overland With Kit Carson ('39 Columbia serial) Bill Elliott
- Pony Post ('40 Universal) Johnny Mack Brown
- Bury Me Not On the Lone Prairie ('41 Universal) Johnny Mack Brown
- Riders of Death Valley ('41 Universal serial) Dick Foran
- Stick To Your Guns ('41 Paramount) William Boyd
- Tumbleweed Trail ('42 PRC) Lee Powell/Art Davis/Bill Boyd
- Overland Mail ('42 Universal serial) Lon Chaney Jr.
- Forty Thieves ('44 U.A.) William Boyd
- Beyond the Pecos ('45 Universal) Rod Cameron
- Scarlet Horseman ('46 Universal serial) Paul Guilfoyle

GENE ROTH

The large, imposing face and frame of Gene Roth is well remembered by western fans for a handful of B's in which he played the main heavy, dozens more films and TVers where he enacted various character parts, plus roles in 21 serials at Universal, Republic and Columbia.

The best of his serial roles are in "Sea Hound" ('47 Columbia), "Brick Bradford' ('47 Columbia), "Ghost of Zorro" ('49 Republic), "Mysterious Island" ('51 Columbia), "Captain Video" ('51 Columbia) and "Lost Planet" ('53 Columbia). Obviously, one of producer Sam Katzman's dependables at Columbia.

As for westerns, no one can forget the "break you in half" barroom battle between Roth and Allan Lane as Red Ryder in "Marshal of Cripple Creek".

Eugene Oliver Stutenroth was born in South Dakota January 8, 1903, to immigrant parents, his father from Germany and his mother from Sweden. After his parents moved, he became interested in dramatics during his junior year in Minneapolis West High School. From then on he often appeared for little theatres, later joining a Pantages troupe as a juvenile. In the summer he traveled with a carnival show.

Traveling to Hollywood he won a break at the Mack Sennett studios, appearing in several two-reel comedies. Deciding he wasn't progressing, Stutenroth turned to the boxing game as a promoter and then to building pipe organs. But acting was in his blood so he went to New York in 1930 resuming theatre roles and summer stock. By 1939 he was finding bit parts in films. "Mercy Plane" ('39) seems to be his first. His next credited role is as a Nazi agent (a role he was called on to repeat often in his long career) in "The Adventures of the Flying Cadets" 1943 Universal serial. From then until 1967, a period of 28 years, Roth was never unemployed on film or TV, amassing some 200 film credits and 60 plus TV shows.

When not appearing in films, Roth worked in a liquor store.

He had attended a huge film gathering in Los Angeles June 16-19, 1976, when, only a month later, on July 19, 1976, he was struck by a car while crossing the street mid-block of Oxford, south of Beverly, at 9:03 in the evening. He died at Queen of Angels Hospital in Los Angeles of multiple injuries. Divorced at the time, Roth was living at 1844 N. Bronson Avenue. Apparently, his daughter, Dorene Stutenroth, was the reporting party on Roth's death certificate.

Suggested Sampling of Roth's Western Heavies:

- Beyond the Pecos ('45 Universal) Rod Cameron
- Homesteaders of Paradise Valley ('47 Republic) Allan Lane
- Marshal of Cripple Creek ('47 Republic) Allan Lane
- Oklahoma Badlands ('48 Republic) Allan "Rocky" Lane
- Valiant Hombre ('48 U.A.) Duncan Renaldo
- Sheriff of Wichita ('49 Republic) Allan "Rocky" Lane
- Big Sombrero ('49 Columbia) Gene Autry
- Ghost of Zorro ('49 Republic serial) Clayton Moore
- Lone Ranger: The Renegades ('49) Clayton Moore
- Lone Ranger: Barnaby Boggs, Esquire ('50) Clayton Moore
- Lone Ranger: Trouble For Tonto ('50) Clayton Moore
- Lone Ranger: Behind the Law ('51) Clayton Moore
- Gold Fever ('52 Monogram) John Calvert
- Sky King: Deadly Cargo ('52) Kirby Grant
- The Maverick ('52 Monogram) Bill Elliott
- Lone Ranger: Deserter ('53) John Hart
- Roy Rogers: And Sudden Death ('55) Roy Rogers
- Sky King: Red Tentacles ('56) Kirby Grant
- 26 Men: Big Rope ('57) Kelo Henderson

Allan (Red Ryder) Lane (L) squares off with Gene Roth (center) and Mauritz Hugo to protect the "Homesteaders of Paradise Valley" ('47 Republic).

HENRY ROWLAND

Although born in Omaha, Nebraska, early in his career, due to his looks, Henry Rowland was typecast as a Nazi or saboteur ("International Squadron" '41, "A Yank in the R.A.F." '41, "Captains of the Clouds" '42, "Berlin Correspondent" '42, "Desperate Journey" '42, "Casablanca" '42, "Edge of Darkness" '43—and the 3 Mesquiteers' "Phantom Plainsmen" ('42 Republic).

Rowland was unable to break free of this type casting until the advent of TV when he began to play boss heavies as well as dog heavies on "The Lone Ranger", "Range Rider", "Wild Bill Hickok", "Roy Rogers", "Gene Autry", "Cisco Kid", "Wyatt Earp" and others. However, the Nazi and foreign agent roles continued to pursue him in movies. He's a foreign smuggler in Roy Rogers' "Bells of Coronado" ('50 Republic) and has other traitorous roles in "Operation Secret" ('52), "El Alamein" ('53), "Attack" ('56), "Imitation General" ('58), "Four Horsemen of the Apocalypse" ('62), among others.

Born December 28, 1913, in Omaha, his father conducted the Omaha Symphony and his mother was a concert singer.

Never even considering anything other than acting, he started out doing musical comedy and light opera at Pasadena Junior College, then attended Pasadena Playhouse from '34 to '37.

Possessed of an excellent voice, he found plenty of work at this time in dramatic radio.

Rowland's first film was "Thunder Afloat" in 1939 when he was cast as, you guessed it, a German officer.

After playing yet another German officer in "The Desert Song" ('43), Rowland was in the air corps during WWII and toured with "Winged Victory" (including the film version in '44).

After WWII it was back to the Gestapo with "Gallant Journey" ('46), "13 Rue Madeleine" ('47), "Battleground" ('49) and others.

By the time Rowland came to Republic serials, that Saturday matinee genre was on its last legs. He was a minor heavy in "Zombies of the Stratosphere" ('52), then moved up to lead heavy, representing another of those mysterious foreign powers, in "Jungle Drums of Africa" ('52).

At least the westerns gave him a break. In his MOVIE BADMEN I RODE WITH book, Pierce Lyden called Henry an "Unsung good actor. Henry just wasn't the rough and tumble kind and so had his problems. He was the mean heavy type that could really make you believe he must be the same off screen as on."

Rowland left films after 40 years with 1979's "Frisco Kid" playing an Amish farmer. At least he wasn't a Nazi.

Rowland died April 26, 1984, in Northridge, California.

Suggested Sampling of Rowland's Western Heavies:

- Phantom Plainsmen ('42 Republic) 3 Mesquiteers
- Range Rider: Peace Pipe ('51) Jock Mahoney
- Wild Bill Hickok: Professor's Daughter ('51) Guy Madison
- Hopalong Cassidy: Guns Across the Border ('51) William Boyd
- Cisco Kid: Lodestone ('52) Duncan Renaldo
- Wagon Team ('52 Columbia) Gene Autry
- Rebel City ('53 Allied Artists) Bill Elliott
- Gene Autry: Cold Decked ('53) Gene Autry
- Roy Rogers: M Stands For Murder ('53) Roy Rogers
- Cisco Kid: Gun Totin' Papa ('53) Duncan Renaldo
- Hopalong Cassidy: Valley Raiders ('53) William Boyd
- Kit Carson: Army Renegades ('53) Bill Williams
- Annie Oakley: Annie Joins the Cavalry ('54) Gail Davis
- Gene Autry: Santa Fe Raiders ('54) Gene Autry
- Gene Autry: Carnival Comes West ('54) Gene Autry
- Cisco Kid: Six Gun For No Pain ('54) Duncan Renaldo
- Wild Bill Hickok: Kid From Red Butte ('54) Guy Madison
- Roy Rogers: Strangers ('54) Roy Rogers
- Cisco Kid: Extradition Papers ('55) Duncan Renaldo
- Annie Oakley: Annie Breaks An Alibi ('55) Gail Davis
- Buffalo Bill Jr.: Trail of the Killer ('55) Dick Jones
- Wild Bill Hickok: Hideout ('55) Guy Madison
- Roy Rogers: Three Masked Men ('55) Roy Rogers
- Brave Eagle: Gold of Haunted Mountain ('55) Keith Larsen
- Roy Rogers: Ambush ('56) Roy Rogers
- Wyatt Earp: Killing at Cowskin Creek ('56) Hugh O'Brian
- Champion: Return of Red Cloud ('56) Jim Bannon
- Buffalo Bill Jr.: Secret of the Silverado ('56) Dick Jones
- Rin Tin Tin: Lost Treasure ('56) Lee Aaker
- Lone Ranger: Quicksand ('56) Clayton Moore
- Roy Rogers: Johnny Rover ('57) Roy Rogers
- Broken Arrow: Bounty Hunters ('57) Michael Ansara/John Lupton
- Sky King: Feathered Serpent ('58) Kirby Grant
- Wyatt Earp: Ballad and Truth ('58) Hugh O'Brian
- Zorro: Eagle's Flight ('58) Guy Williams
- Jefferson Drum: Stagecoach Episode ('58) Jeff Richards

- Jim Bowie: Ursula ('58) Scott Forbes
- Johnny Ringo: The Arrival ('59) Don Durant
- Texan: Dishonest Posse ('59) Rory Calhoun
- Rebel: The Unwanted ('59) Nick Adams
- Deputy: The World Against Me ('60) Allen Case/Henry Fonda

BING RUSSELL

Bing Russell was a baseball player before he became a television badman and, even then, he's probably best remembered as Clem Foster, the husky, dark-haired deputy of Virginia City on "Bonanza". He filled in when Sheriff Roy Coffee (Ray Teal) was otherwise occupied. When Teal/Coffee left the series, Bing/Clem became sheriff of Virginia City. But in scores of other TVers throughout the late '50s and the '60s, Bing played many a hard hombre.

Neil O. Russell was born May 5, 1926, in Maine. His father was a battler and bought his two year old son a punching bag. As the boy punched the bag He'd say "bing, bing, bing." Hence the nickname that stuck.

Bing's hotel owner father flew an airplane, so Bing learned to fly as a boy. Through his father's flying, they became acquainted with Lefty Gomez of the New York Yankees. When Bing was nine, Lefty took Bing traveling with the Yankees for six years.

With aspirations towards baseball, Bing belonged to the Yankees and Chicago Cubs until an injury sidelined that career.

Bartending in Rangely, Maine, he was offered a similar job in Florida which is where they happened to be filming "The Big Leaguer" ('53). Having played ball, Bing got a job as an umpire in that film, then decided to try his luck in Hollywood.

Obtaining an agent, it was a tough go for a while, but Bing began to connect solidly in the mid '50s. Bing once said during the years of '57-'59 there were only six weeks when he didn't appear before a camera.

In 1963, during the fourth season of "Bonanza", Bing was hired as Deputy Clem Foster. Bing told Tom and Jim Goldrup for their FEATURE PLAYERS Vol. II, "I really missed 'Bonanza' after 10 years (on it) when the show died. It was a fun place to be; wasn't like work at all. It was like an annuity. It fit my scheme perfectly. They'd call me at 10, I had the wardrobe at my house. I'd be in front of the camera at 11 and be through by 11:30. I was really fortunate to be part of 'Bonanza'. His other favorite roles were on "Horse Soldiers", "Cattle Empire" and "Ride a Violent Mile". "Except for Clem, I played one heavy after another and made one hell of a living."

With his son Kurt born in '51, Bing returned to his first love when he formed the Portland Mavericks baseball team in the Class A Northwest League in the early '70s. Helming the only independent team in the class A Northwest League, Russell was an innovator, keeping a 30 man roster because he believed that some of the players deserved to have one last season. He created a park that kept all corporate sponsorship outside the gates, hired the first female general manager in professional baseball, and the following year hired the first Asian-American general manager. That same season his team set a record for the highest attendance in minor league history, and went on to win the pennant. Ex-major leaguers and never-weres who couldn't stop playing the game flocked to his June tryouts, which were always open to anyone that showed up. From as far away as Capetown and France, players would head to Portland for a chance with Russell's Mavericks.

He basically quit acting in the mid '70s, although he essayed a film role every now and then, especially in a couple of son Kurt's movies ("Elvis" in '79, "Tango and Cash" in '89), with his last brief appearance as a club patron in "Dick Tracy" ('90).

At 76 Bing died of cancer April 8, 2003, in Thousand Oaks, California. He was survived by his wife Louise Crain.

Suggested Sampling of Russell's Western Heavies:

- Casey Jones: Prison Train ('57) Alan Hale Jr.
- Tombstone Territory: Guns of Silver ('57) Pat Conway
- Cattle Empire ('58 20th Century Fox) Joel McCrea
- Colt .45: Ghost Town ('58) Wayde Preston

- Maverick: Seed of Deception ('58) James Garner/Jack Kelly
- Sugarfoot: Guns For Big Bear ('58) Will Hutchins
- Wyatt Earp: General's Lady ('58) Hugh O'Brian
- Have Gun Will Travel: A Sense of Justice ('58) Richard Boone
- Gunsmoke: Lynching Man ('58) James Arness
- Colt .45: Dead Aim ('59) Wayde Preston
- Texan: Dishonest Posse ('59) Rory Calhoun
- Black Saddle: Long Rider ('59) Peter Breck
- Sugarfoot: Gitanos ('59) Will Hutchins
- Johnny Ringo: A Killing For Culley ('59) Don Durant
- Laramie: Company Man ('60) Robert Fuller/John Smith
- Wanted Dead or Alive: Triple Vise ('60) Steve McQueen
- Tate: The Reckoning ('60) David McLean
- Rifleman: Seven ('60) Chuck Connors
- Gunsmoke: Don Matteo ('60) James Arness
- Maverick: A Bullet For the Teacher ('60) Roger Moore
- Bronco: Stage to the Sky ('61) Ty Hardin
- Laramie: Lawless Seven ('61) Robert Fuller
- Bonanza: Long Night ('62) Pernell Roberts
- Laramie: Sometime Gambler ('63) Robert Fuller
- Iron Horse: Through Ticket to Gunsight ('66) Dale Robertson
- Monroes: The Hunter ('66) Michael Anderson Jr.
- Guns of Will Sonnett: Robber's Roost ('69) Walter Brennan
- Yuma ('71 TVM) Clint Walker

JOHN (JACK) RUTHERFORD

Lantern-jawed John Rutherford's background is a hard trail to follow, with some unanswered questions. Apparently Rutherford, who played loutish badmen in a host of '30s westerns, was apparently born in Germantown, Pennsylvania, April 12, 1893.

There is a silent 1920 anti-communism film, "The Great Shadow", starring Tyrone Power Sr. which features a John Rutherford. Since that film is among the array of lost silents, we cannot determine if this is "our" John Rutherford. Meanwhile, we know for certain "our" Rutherford was a noted stage actor on Broadway from September 1916 ("Paganini") til early 1929, appearing in at least 11 Broadway productions, including the smash hit "Whoopee!" (December 1928-1929).

The next film credits for a John Rutherford are two U.K. films in 1927 and 1929. This is most likely another performer of the same name born in England in 1893. Direct from the Broadway cast of "Whoopee!", Rutherford plays the Sheriff in the 1930 released Eddie Cantor film version of the musical comedy.

By 1932 the husky Rutherford found his way into B-westerns, his first being "Cowboy Counselor" with Hoot Gibson.

Some sources, including tradepaper obits, cite Rutherford as playing Buffalo Bill "in the film of the same name." This simply isn't accurate. Rutherford did play Buffalo Bill Cody in Universal's 1938 Johnny Mack Brown serial, "Flaming Frontiers". Oddly, sans Buffalo Bill goatee and mustache, Rutherford also plays Rand, one of the serial's heavies. Also, Rutherford played Buffalo Bill in the national company of Irving Berlin's "Annie Get Your Gun" starring Mary Martin which followed the musical hit's Broadway debut in May of '46.

For whatever reason, Rutherford's film roles after 1940 become sparse and often uncredited. He returned to Broadway for roles in "Soliloquy" in '38 and "Bigger Than Barnum" in '45-'46. These no doubt led to the role in "Annie Get Your Gun" which most likely began in '47 as there are no film credits at all for Rutherford from mid '47 until two TV roles in 1955 on "Sergeant Preston of the Yukon". A small uncredited role in "Mohawk" ('56) was his last film work.

Rutherford died August 21, 1982, at 89 in Patagonia (near Tucson), Arizona.

Hopalong Cassidy has a hold on outlaw Jack Rutherford in "North of the Rio Grande" ('37 Paramount).

Suggested Sampling of Rutherford's Western Heavies:

- Cowboy Counselor ('32 Allied) Hoot Gibson
- Justice of the Range ('35 Columbia) Tim McCoy
- Heart of the West ('36 Paramount) William Boyd
- North of the Rio Grande ('37 Paramount) William Boyd
- Raw Timber ('37 Crescent) Tom Keene
- Flaming Frontiers ('38 Universal serial) Johnny Mack Brown
- Riders of the Frontier ('39 Monogram) Tex Ritter
- Arizona Gangbusters ('40 PRC) Tim McCoy
- Trailing Double Trouble ('40 Monogram) Range Busters
- Riders of Black Mountain ('40 PRC) Tim McCoy
- Rollin' Home To Texas ('40 Monogram) Tex Ritter

WALTER SANDE

Serio-comical character player Walter Sande divided his 35 year screen and TV career ('37-'72) between the law and the lawless.

Sande essayed many sheriffs on "The Lone Ranger", "Wanted Dead or Alive", "Laramie" and in films such as "Last Train From Gun Hill" ('59) and "Noose For a Gunman" ('60). The versatile character player also worked as newspaper reporters, detectives, sailors, all types of military officers and various businessmen in B-films, A-productions and on TV.

As to serials, he was newspaper photog "Flash" Strong, Charles Quigley's buddy, in "The Iron Claw" ('41 Columbia), and in two Don Winslow serials at Universal he was Winslow's aide Lt. Red Pennington. In these three, his breezy, carefree manner offset the serious business at hand. He applied the same technique to his role as Detective Sergeant Matthews in the Boston Blackie Columbia B-mysteries of the '40s with Chester Morris. But—he could be crooked, as he was in serials like "Green Hornet Strikes Again" ('41 Universal) and "Sky Raiders" ('41 Universal).

Born in Denver, Colorado, July 9, 1906, he was studying music by age 6 and by 30 could play every musical instrument. He toured with a band and later became musical director for Fox West Coast Theatres before entering films with "Tenth Avenue Kid" in '37.

Sande never came near a western until some 82 films into his career with the lighthearted spoof on the genre, "Singing Sheriff" ('44 Universal) which starred Bob Crosby, brother of Bing.

Circa 1944-1946, Sande served in the Coast Guard while still appearing in several films. He had an excellent talent for building models of Japanese ships which were used in Coast Guard schools for study.

At 65, Sande died in Chicago, Illinois, November 22, 1971. He had just flown in from California. As he waited for an available cab, he suffered a fatal heart attack. Rushed to Resurrection Hospital, he was pronounced DOA. He was married to a sister of stone-faced actress Virginia O'Brien.

Suggested Sampling of Sande's Western Heavies:

- Singing Sheriff ('44 Universal) Bob Crosby
- Along Came Jones ('45 RKO) Gary Cooper
- Daltons Ride Again ('45 Universal) Alan Curtis
- Dakota Lil ('50 20th Century Fox) George Montgomery
- Red Mountain ('51 Paramount) Alan Ladd
- Canyon River ('56 Allied Artists) George Montgomery
- Gun Brothers ('56 United Artists) Buster Crabbe
- Black Saddle: Client Tagger ('59) Peter Breck
- The Rebel: The Crime ('60) Nick Adams
- Stagecoach West: By the Deep Six ('60) Robert Bray
- Redigo: The Hunters ('63) Richard Egan
- Quick Gun ('64 Columbia) Audie Murphy

HUGH SANDERS

Not only did the huge frame and commanding voice of Hugh Sanders delineate many sheriffs, military men and police officers, he also played his share of contemptible badmen, usually disguising his corruptibility behind the respectability of a business suit.

Sanders was born in Illinois on March 13, 1911.

He started out to be a radio actor but switched to film, first in 1949's "Undertow" at Universal, then permanently when producer Jerry Wald asked him to play a gangster in Joan Crawford's "The Damned Don't Cry" in 1950.

His first western was Randolph Scott's "Sugarfoot" in '51. He claims his most realistic bit of acting occurred during a knock-down-drag-out fight in Scott's "Thunder

Over the Plains" ('53).

Sanders was married to Janet Barrett, a former ballet dancer. They had at least one child, a girl, around 1953.

Sanders died in Los Angeles January 9, 1966.

Coming late to westerns as he did, his roles were few, but he impressed strongly in the ones he did.

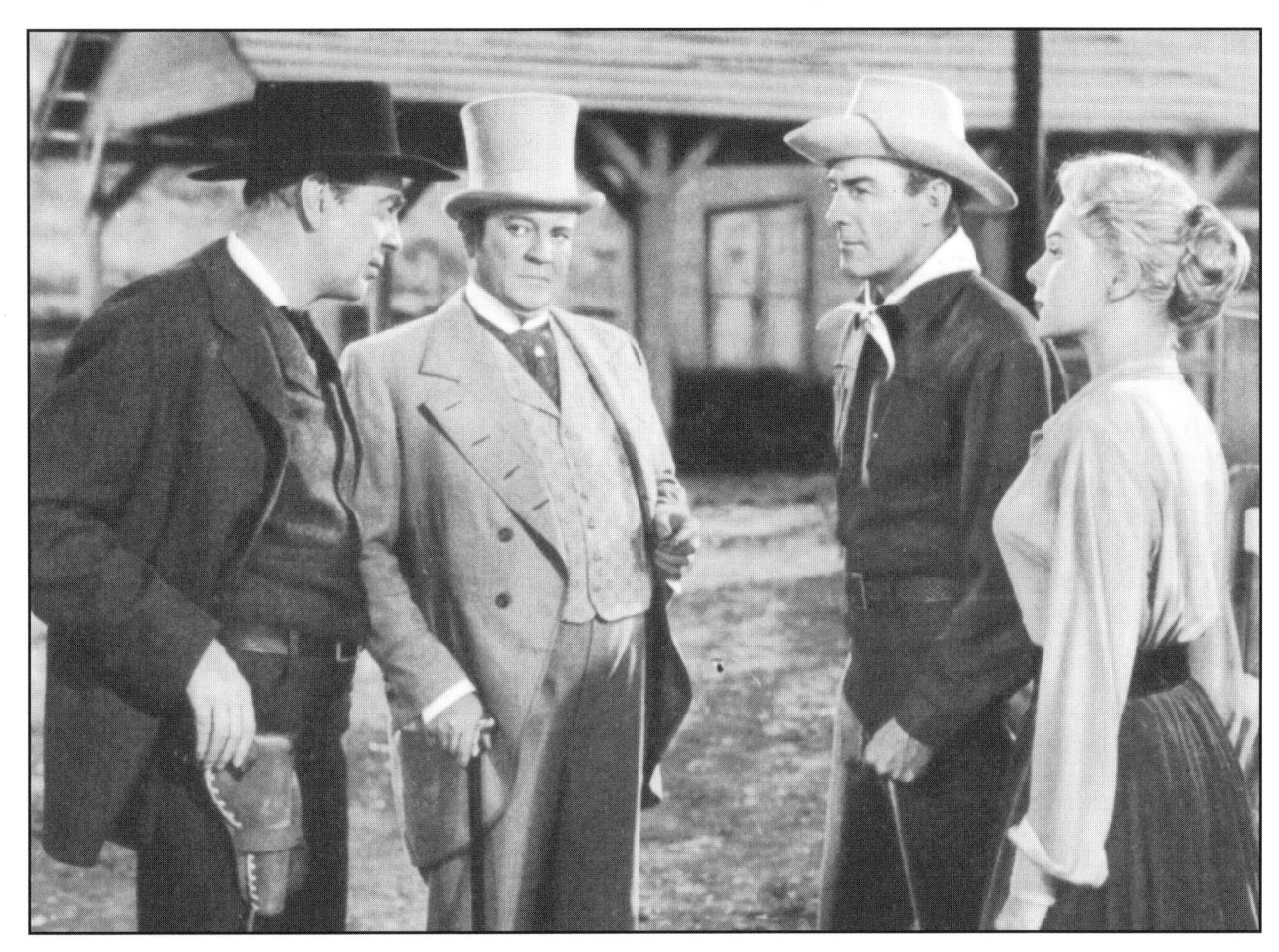

A tense moment from Warner Bros. "Sugarfoot" ('51) between Raymond Massey (L) and Hugh Sanders (top hat) as they confront Randolph Scott and Adele Jergens.

Suggested Sampling of Sanders' Western Heavies:

- Sugarfoot ('51 Warner Bros.) Randolph Scott
- Indian Uprising ('52 Columbia) George Montgomery
- Gun Belt ('53 United Artists) George Montgomery
- Lone Ranger: Godless Men ('53) Clayton Moore
- Thunder Over the Plains ('53 Warner Bros.) Randolph Scott
- Lone Ranger: Rendezvous at Whipsaw ('54) Clayton Moore
- Lone Ranger: Sheriff's Wife ('55) Clayton Moore
- Phantom Stagecoach ('57 Columbia) William Bishop
- Sugarfoot: Price on his Head ('58) Will Hutchins
- Man Without a Gun: Dream Weaver ('58) Rex Reason
- Tombstone Territory: Payroll to Tombstone ('59) Pat Conway
- Yancy Derringer: Duel at the Oaks ('59) Jock Mahoney
- Colt .45: Man Who Loved Lincoln ('59) Wayde Preston
- Bronco: Red Water North ('59) Ty Hardin
- Bat Masterson: Pigeon and the Hawk ('60) Gene Barry
- Deputy: Return of Simon Fry ('60) Henry Fonda

ALLAN SEARS

The depraved look of Allan Sears brought an extra dimension to his evilness because he truly possessed a ruthless, loathsome screen persona. Lamentably, his western screen appearances were few.

Born Alfred Daniel Sears (his mother's maiden name was Gould) in San Antonio, Texas, March 9, 1887, in his teens he was termed a big, handsome leading player when he began to appear in top supporting roles, usually listed third or fourth in the cast, in 1914. At this time, until 1918, he was being billed as A. D. Sears. From there on he adopted Allen Sears, Al Sears, Alan Sears and Allan Sears.

Prior to coming to films he was a candy salesman.

Census records indicate he was married to a lady from Missouri named Lucille in 1907 with a daughter, Ada, born in 1909. However by 1917 he was divorced. No record of any further marriages.

Only a few westerns grace his credits in the silent era, but he did play Davy Crockett in "Martyrs of the Alamo" in 1915.

Unexplainably, Sears is absent from the screen in 1921-1922 and seems to have made only one film per year from 1923-1925, none in '27, four in '28 and then is absent again until he returned in 1933 with Mary Pickford in "Secrets".

From 1935-1938 he played crazy killers and rat-like heavies in 13 westerns, mostly at Columbia and Universal. He's especially memorable as laughing badman Bill Slagg in "Two Fisted Sheriff" with Charles Starrett. No doubt he would have created many more nasty characterizations had he not suffered an early death at 55 in Los Angeles on August 18, 1942.

Suggested Sampling of Sears' Western Heavies:

- Law Beyond the Range ('35 Columbia) Tim McCoy
- Revenge Rider ('35 Columbia) Tim McCoy
- Justice of the Range ('35 Columbia) Tim McCoy
- Singing Vagabond ('35 Republic) Gene Autry
- Sunset of Power ('35 Universal) Buck Jones
- Boss Rider of Gun Creek ('36 Universal) Buck Jones
- Trapped ('37 Columbia) Charles Starrett
- Two Fisted Sheriff ('37 Columbia) Charles Starrett

FRED SEARS

Acting and directing, Fred Sears seldom strayed from his home base at Columbia.

Frederick Francis Sears was born in Boston, Massachusetts, July 7, 1912. His mother's name was Grusey.

Sears graduated from Boston College, then joined a regional theatre where he acted, produced and directed. He later moved to Memphis, Tennessee, where he founded the Little Theatre of Memphis. He then taught dramatic Arts at Southwestern University in Memphis before going to work at Columbia as a dialogue coach in late 1945.

By 1946 he was turning up in uncredited bit parts in Columbia's Blondie and Rusty series.

By 1947 he had his first non-villainous and villainous roles in Charles Starrett Durango Kid pictures—"Lone Hand Texan" and "West of Dodge City" respectively. From then until 1952 Sears acted in 19 Durango westerns and directed 13 of them.

He directed Columbia's "Blackhawk" serial in '52, then as the Durango pictures ended, Sears stopped acting altogether and concentrated on directing minor A-westerns for the studio—"Nebraskan" ('53), "Wyoming Renegades" ('54), "Massacre Canyon" ('54), "Apache Ambush" ('55) along with some memorable sci-fi films—"Earth Vs. the Flying Saucers" ('56) and "The Werewolf" ('56). Sears also worked with producer Sam Katzman cashing in on the Rock 'n' Roll craze ("Rock Around the Clock", "Don't Knock the Rock"), the calypso fad ("Calypso Heat Wave") and the juvenile delinquent trend in films ("Teenage Crime Wave").

Apparently, a boyhood injury caused a blood vessel in Sears' head to swell when he drank alcohol, especially to excess. He was alone in a bathroom at offices he had with Columbia at Lyman Place and Sunset on November 30, 1957. He'd been drinking and the blood vessel in question burst, causing his death.

Suggested Sampling of Sears' Western Heavies:

- West of Dodge City ('47 Columbia) Charles Starrett
- Law of the Canyon ('47 Columbia) Charles Starrett
- Whirlwind Raiders ('48 Columbia) Charles Starrett
- Blazing Trail ('49 Columbia) Charles Starrett
- South of Death Valley ('49 Columbia) Charles Starrett
- Bonanza Town ('51 Columbia) Charles Starrett
- Kid From Amarillo ('51 Columbia) Charles Starrett
- Laramie Mountains ('52 Columbia) Charles Starrett

CARL SEPULVEDA

Credited and uncredited, usually "one of the gang", Carl Sepulveda was born February 5, 1897, in Utah. His father, Alex Sepulveda, was from Spain and his mother, Louisa Teeples, was a native of Utah.

Nothing is known of Carl's background before he made his first silent westerns in 1927 ("Fangs of Destiny") and 1928 ("Four Footed Ranger") at Universal with Dynamite, the Dog and Edmund Cobb. He's also in Syndicate's "Chinatown Mystery" silent serial in 1928 starring legendary strongman and serial ace Joe Bonomo. There is an unexplained eleven year hiatus in his filmography until his next couple of serial roles at Republic in 1939 ("Lone Ranger Rides Again" and "Zorro's Fighting Legion") and several westerns that year at Republic and Columbia.

Carl worked steadily throughout the '30s and '40s at Columbia, Universal, Republic, PRC and Monogram. He supported most of the B-western heroes but was seen most frequently in the films of Charles Starrett, Johnny Mack Brown and Jimmy Wakely.

Usually bad, it's odd that perhaps his strongest role was as a Sheriff in the Range Busters' "Black Market Rustlers" ('43 Monogram).

As his quarter century of films came to an end, he worked on TV on the "Gene Autry" TV series and was seen in small roles in A-films such as "Annie Get Your Gun" ('50). "Callaway Went Thataway" ('51) and his last, "Lusty Men" ('52), a rodeo yarn with Robert Mitchum. Carl was widowed and residing in Carmichael, California, a small town north of Sacramento, where he'd been employed as a construction worker, when he died of a stroke August 24, 1974, at 77.

The rather quiet Sepulveda was "well thought of in the business" according to stuntman Whitey Hughes, except for one incident related in Universal-International production notes for Audie Murphy's "Kansas Raiders" ('50). It was necessary for assistant director Ronnie Rondell to call Sepulveda out of a riding scene at Idyllwild because he was making excessive noise and disrupting the morale of other riders. Sepulveda, asked to return to "base", was accompanied on his own by wrangler/extra Chet Bias. Later that evening, in the lobby of the hotel, Sepulveda spoke in a "belligerent and profane manner" to Rondell and second assistant director George Loper. Sepulveda publicly admitted he'd been drinking that day, then struck Rondell in the chest. Rondell did

Two bad men—Carl Sepulveda (L) and Hal Taliaferro in Johnny Mack Brown's "Little Joe the Wrangler" ('42 Universal).

not return the blow. Both Sepulveda and Bias were restrained at this time by stuntman/actor Roy Bucko (8/22/93-8/6/54) and other members of the crew and were returned to the studio the next day.

Carl is buried at Oak Hill Cemetery in Red Bluff, California, some 60-80 miles north of Sacramento.

Suggested Sampling of Sepulveda's Western Heavies:

- Code of the Cactus ('39 Victory)—Tim McCoy
- Riders of Black River ('39 Columbia)—Charles Starrett
- Little Joe, the Wrangler ('42 Universal)—Johnny Mack Brown
- Lone Rider and the Bandit ('42 PRC)—George Houston
- Black Market Rustlers ('43 Monogram)—Range Busters
- Raiders of San Joaquin ('43 Universal)—Johnny Mack Brown
- Plainsman and the Lady ('46 Republic)—William Elliott
- Partners of the Sunset ('48 Monogram)—Jimmy Wakely

MICKEY SIMPSON

Town bully. Troublemaker. Outlaw. At 6'5", overpowering, rugged Mickey Simpson was sent for when the screenplay called for an immense and imposing presence to challenge "The Lone Ranger", "The Range Rider", "Maverick", "Sky King", "The Cisco Kid", "The Rifleman", "Cheyenne", "Bronco" or a number of others.

Simpson got his start with minor roles in "Panama Lady" ('39), "Abbott and Costello In the Navy" ('40) and "Keep 'Em Flying" ('41), a couple of serials ("Sea Raiders" '41 and "Gang Busters" '42), John Wayne's "The Spoilers" ('42), "Arabian Nights" ('42) and then broke through when prominent director John Ford cast him as Sam Clanton in "My Darling Clementine" in '46. He became a Ford favorite over the years, appearing in "Fort Apache" ('48), "She Wore a Yellow Ribbon" ('49) and "Wagonmaster" ('50).

Charles Henry Simpson was born December 3, 1913, in Rochester, New York, the son of an ex-policeman.

At 18, he headed west intending to be a logger. After spending some time in the Marshfield, Oregon, logging camps, Mickey drifted south to Los Angeles, met a girl and they were married.

Joining the Navy, the formidable Simpson was placed in the Shore Patrol and assigned duty at the Hollywood Canteen. A chance meeting there with John Ford's wife, Mary, and others set Mickey on the path to filmdom. As a struggling young actor, Simpson made ends meet working as actress Claudette Colbert's chauffeur.

"Clementine" opened doors in Hollywood for Simpson who continued to work in major films ("Tarzan and the Huntress", "Wistful Widow of Wagon Gap", "Three Musketeers", "Wake of the Red Witch", "Fighting Kentuckian", "Ten Tall Men", "What Price Glory", "Lion In the Streets", "Prince Valiant", "Long Gray Line", "Donovan's Reef", "Greatest Story Ever Told" and dozens more, as well as all the major TV westerns of the '50s and '60s. Simpson was only in one serial, "Roar of the Iron Horse" ('51 Columbia).

He was a regular on two TV series, the seldom remembered "Captain David Grief" ('55) based on Jack London's sea stories and starring Maxwell Reed, as well as a recurring role on "Rocky Jones, Space Ranger" in '54.

But of all this work, Simpson is undoubtedly best remembered as Sarge, the prejudiced small restaurant owner who has a classic fight with Rock Hudson at the end of "Giant".

In the '60s Simpson had a roadshow called "The Badmen of Hollywood" in which they'd shoot up the town and put on action skits. Rand Brooks, Jay Silverheels and others went out on this show at times with Simpson.

Still in good health, but seeing the business changing, Simpson's last credit was "The Great Bank Robbery" in '69. With over 200 films and TV shows to his credit, he took early retirement at 62.

Simpson died of a heart attack at 71 in Northridge, California, on September 23, 1985.

Suggested Sampling of Simpson's Western Heavies:

- My Darling Clementine ('46 20th Century Fox) Henry Fonda
- Wagonmaster ('50 RKO) Ben Johnson
- Lone Ranger: Drink of Water ('50) Clayton Moore
- Range Rider: Fight Town ('51) Jock Mahoney
- Roar of the Iron Horse ('51 Columbia serial) Jock Mahoney
- Lone Ranger: The Outcast ('51) Clayton Moore
- Leadville Gunslinger ('52 Republic) Allan "Rocky" Lane
- Cisco Kid: Spanish Dagger ('52) Duncan Renaldo
- Sky King: Danger Point ('52) Kirby Grant
- Lone Ranger: Trial by Fire ('52) Clayton Moore
- Apache Country ('52 Columbia) Gene Autry
- Star of Texas ('53 Allied Artists) Wayne Morris
- Saginaw Trail ('53 Columbia) Gene Autry
- Range Rider: Outlaw Territory ('53) Jock Mahoney
- Lone Ranger: Midnight Rider ('53) John Hart
- Annie Oakley: Sharpshooting Annie ('54) Gail Davis
- Lone Ranger: Dan Reid's Fight For Life ('54) Clayton Moore
- Lone Ranger: Trigger Finger ('55) Clayton Moore
- Cisco Kid: Jumping Beans ('55) Duncan Renaldo
- The Lone Ranger ('56 Warner Bros.) Clayton Moore
- Giant ('56 Warner Bros.) Rock Hudson
- Cheyenne: Storm Riders ('56) Clint Walker
- Gunsmoke: No Indians ('56) James Arness
- Maverick: Hostage ('57) James Garner/Jack Kelly
- 26 Men: Valley of Fear ('57) Tris Coffin/Kelo Henderson
- Gunfight at the O.K. Corral ('57 Paramount) Burt Lancaster
- 26 Men: Hondo Man ('57) Tris Coffin/Kelo Henderson
- Rifleman: Sharpshooter ('57) Chuck Connors
- Maverick: Thirty Ninth Star ('57) Jack Kelly
- Bronco: Trail to Taos ('57) Ty Hardin
- Lawman: Intruders ('57) John Russell
- Rifleman: The Indian ('58) Cluck Connors
- Yancy Derringer: Wayward Warrior ('58) Jock Mahoney
- Lawman: The Huntress ('58) John Russell
- Rough Riders: The Rifle ('58) Jan Merlin/Kent Taylor
- Lawman: To Capture the West ('60) John Russell
- Maverick: Bundle From Britain ('60) Jack Kelly/Roger Moore
- Bat Masterson: The Hunter ('60) Gene Barry
- Sugarfoot: Man From Medora ('60) Will Hutchins
- Cheyenne: Cross Purpose ('61) Clint Walker
- Bronco: A Sure Thing ('62) Ty Hardin
- Cheyenne: Durango Brothers ('62) Clint Walker
- Dakotas: Reformation at Big Nose Butte ('63) Jack Elam

ARTHUR SPACE

Character actor Arthur Space lent a dignified, erudite presence to the occasional untrustworthy cads he played in westerns.

Primarily, Space was a character man who came from eastern stage work and landed in Hollywood for a role in "The Bugle Sounds" at MGM in 1941. For the next five years he essayed parts in over 50 pictures, many of them classics ("Rio Rita", "Random Harvest", "A Guy Named Joe", "A Wing and a Prayer", "Wilson", "30 Seconds Over Tokyo", "Gentle Annie", "Woman In the Window", "Our Vines Have Tender Grapes", "Black Beauty") before he made his first western as one of the heavies in "Home In Oklahoma" at Republic in 1946 with Roy Rogers.

The 6 ft. tall Space certainly never devoted full time to westerns, but continued along the character actor route, returning now and then to westerns to portray an evil doer.

Perhaps his heavies with a stately bearing are best viewed in Monte Hale's "Vanishing Westerner" ('50) and as cultivated stick-up man Black Bart on "Stories of the Century" ('54).

Many of his western roles on television are as physicians, bankers, lawyers or other professional men.

Space's aloofness worked well in two latter day Republic serials, as foreign agent Marlof in "Canadian Mounties Vs. Atomic Invaders" ('53) and as renegade research chemist Dr. Morgan in "Panther Girl of the Kongo" ('55). Space is also a suspect on the board of the Interstate Truck Owners Association in "Government Agents Vs. Phantom Legion", although the mysterious Voice actually turns out to be Pierce Lyden.

But perhaps Space is best remembered as kindly Doc Weaver on "Lassie" ('54-'64) and on the TV adaptation of "National Velvet" ('60-'62) as Herbert Brown, Velvet's father.

Space was born in New Brunswick, New Jersey, October 12, 1908, to Charles Augustus Space and Isabelle

Barrett. A rather rebellious youth, he connected with a wonderful drama coach in his senior year and was selected to play male leads at the New Jersey College for Women as they needed men for their shows.

After becoming an assistant professor there and appearing in their shows from 1927-1935, he joined the East Orange Stock Company, then a road company and was in various New York plays with Bide Dudley's Players Group.

It was Sylvan Simon, a former director with Bide Dudley, then a director at MGM, who summoned Space to Hollywood for a role in Wallace Beery's "The Bugle Sounds".

Space continued to work in film and TV until 1980. He died of cancer January 13, 1983. He was survived by a wife and two daughters.

Suggested Sampling of Space's Western Heavies:

- Home In Oklahoma ('46 Republic) Roy Rogers
- Rustlers of Devil's Canyon ('47 Republic) Allan Lane
- Vanishing Westerner ('50 Republic) Monte Hale
- Night Riders of Montana ('51 Republic) Allan "Rocky" Lane
- Utah Wagon Train ('51 Republic) Rex Allen
- Fargo ('52 Monogram) Bill Elliott
- Last of the Pony Riders ('52 Columbia) Gene Autry
- Canadian Mounties Vs. Atomic Invaders ('53 Republic) Bill Henry
- Stories of the Century: Black Bart ('54) Jim Davis
- Gene Autry: Holdup ('54) Gene Autry
- Gene Autry: Hoodoo Canyon ('54) Gene Autry
- Gene Autry: Feuding Friends ('55) Gene Autry
- 26 Men: Trail of Revenge ('59) Tris Coffin/Kelo Henderson

CHARLES STEVENS

Charles Stevens, Hollywood's greatest shifty-eyed, sneaky Indian, was either born in Arizona and was the grandson of the great Apache Chief Geronimo, or—that information is simply another motion picture publicity con-game.

According to his California death certificate, Charles G. Stevens was born March 3, 1893, in Solomonsville, Arizona, to James H. Stevens and Eloisa (maiden name unknown). Reportedly, he was half Apache and half Mexican. Eloisa is a common Mexican feminine first name. Puzzling is the fact no information has ever been presented as to whether James H. Stevens was a "son" of Geronimo or was Eloisa a daughter? So many questions, so few answers.

Whatever the reality of Stevens' link to Geronimo (1829-1909), he did play Mexicans and Indians or half-breeds (often named Injun Joe, Breed, Jose or Lopez) on screen in a career that spanned 47 years from "The Birth of a Nation" ('15) to "The Outsider" ('62).

Sources claim Stevens worked for two years with Miller Brothers 101 Ranch Wild West Show in a cowboy sketch before entering pictures. This *could* also be more Hollywood hype as no written records verify this.

Following "Birth of a Nation", Stevens worked in some 40 silent films including "Empty Hands" ('24) w/ Jack Holt, "Six Shooter Andy" ('18) w/Tom Mix and "Vanishing American ('25) w/Richard Dix. During this period, he was befriended by Douglas Fairbanks Sr. and appeared in most of Fairbanks' films such as "Mark of Zorro" ('20).

Beginning with Paramount's "The Virginian" in 1929 with Gary Cooper, the 5' 10", 150 lb. Stevens appeared in some 150 films, dominated by westerns and serials. Many of his myriad parts are uncredited. Some of his best (read most vicious) roles were in Universal serials— "Winners of the West" ('40), "Overland Mail" ('42), "Oregon Trail ('39), "Flaming Frontiers" ('38) and "Wild West Days" ('37).

His dialogue delivery was slow, calculated and precise. As he got older, Stevens' face became more weathered and wrinkled making it easy to spot the "crow's feet" by his eyes when he gave us a squint or quizzical look of concern.

Stevens worked plenty on western TVers as well— "Lone Ranger", "Kit Carson", "Range Rider", "Rin Tin Tin" (on which he once played Geronimo), "Wild Bill Hickok", "Wagon Train", "Zorro", "Jim Bowie" and others, with one of his last being an episode of "Rawhide" in early '62, "Incident of the Buffalo Soldiers".

Charles Stevens is roped and tied by Johnny Mack Brown in Universal's "Wild West Days" '37 serial.

Incidentally, the Charles Stevens listed as a property master in many '30s-'40s films is not "our" Charles Stevens according to research conducted by writer Les Adams.

Stevens served in the Armed Forces during WWI and was a noted authority on Indian history and folklore.

On August 22, 1964, Stevens died of heart disease at his home at 1926 N. Whitley Ave. in L.A. at age 71. Widowed at the time, he is buried at Valhalla Cemetery in North Hollywood.

Suggested Sampling of Stevens' Western Heavies:

- Heritage of the Desert ('32 Paramount) Randolph Scott
- Mystery Ranch ('32 Fox) George O'Brien
- Drum Taps ('33 World Wide) Ken Maynard
- Wild West Days ('37 Universal serial) Johnny Mack Brown
- Flaming Frontiers ('38 Universal serial) Johnny Mack Brown
- Oregon Trail ('39 Universal serial) Johnny Mack Brown
- Winners of the West ('40 Universal serial) Dick Foran
- Marked Trails ('44 Monogram) Bob Steele/Hoot Gibson
- Bandits of the Badlands ('45 Republic) Sunset Carson
- Border Bandits ('46 Monogram) Johnny Mack Brown
- Gunfighters of the Northwest ('54 Columbia serial) Jock Mahoney
- Vanishing American ('55 Republic) Scott Brady
- Adventures of Rin Tin Tin: Tomahawk Tubbs ('58) Lee Aaker
- Maverick: Arizona Black Maria ('60) Jack Kelly

HAROLD J. STONE

Harold J. Stone was a perfect name for the heavyset, strong, swarthy visage of the actor with an intense, domineering presence that dominated dozens of TV westerns in the '50s and '60s. Stone was equally adept at portraying underworld bosses and syndicate killers as well as having a flair for comedy on several sit-coms on which he was a regular—"The Hartmans" ('49), "The Goldbergs" ('52), "My World and Welcome To It" ('69) and "Bridget Loves Bernie" ('72).

Harold Hochstein was born March 3, 1913, in New York City, the son of Jacob Hochstein, an actor, owner and stage manager in Yiddish Theatre, and his wife Jennie Levison. His grandfather, Charles Hochstein, was also a well known New York actor. Harold, himself, began acting in a Yiddish production at age 6.

Stone was educated at New Utrecht High in Brooklyn and, wanting to study medicine, enrolled at NYU for a pre-med course, received his B.A., then followed with two years at the University of Buffalo Medical School. In school and college he was active in sports and played the double bass in the orchestra yet, despite his family's acting tradition, was never considered good enough for plays.

Upon his father's death in '31, to support the family, Stone left medical school, working at odd jobs in New York. At the same time he was studying nights at NYU.

In 1936 he made his radio debut, working at WTIC, Hartford, Connecticut. With this experience, he returned to New York in 1938 and obtained small roles, including

Audie Murphy and Harold J. Stone (R) have a "Showdown" while chained to the iron maypole prison ('63 Universal).

one with George Jessell's "Little Old New York" at the World's Fair in 1939.

Stone made his Broadway debut in "The World We Make" in '39 followed by excellent recognition in 1940 for "Morning Star". He did many other plays, including "A Bell For Adano" in '44-'45, all the while supplementing his income by driving a taxi. During his Broadway period is when he changed his last name to Stone. He also toured with Anita Louise in "Mr. and Mrs. North" in '41. Many more plays, including "Stalag 17" on Broadway, followed.

Stone has an uncredited role in Alan Ladd's "Blue Dahlia" ('46 Paramount), then came the two sit-com series in '49 and '52. From '53-'56 Stone was heard on CBS radio's "Twenty-First Precinct". He began to work on TV series such as "Man Behind the Badge" in '54, then was cast as Rocky Graziano's father in "Somebody Up There Likes Me" at MGM in '56. The Broadway actor, now in his mid '40s, had achieved success in Hollywood and began to work steadily in films and on TV.

In 1959 both he and Lyle Bettger, both best known as screen heavies, turned to the right side of the law as investigators on TV's "Grand Jury". Stone also had a recurring role on "I Spy" in '65.

Stone was married to nonprofessional Joan Blumenthal in 1946. They had two children, Jennifer (born in '49) and Robert James. When his wife passed away of rheumatoid arthritis in '61, Stone remarried in '62.

Stone's last acting job was a "Highway to Heaven" episode in '84. Now in his 90s, the acting pioneer lives in quiet retirement in the Villa at the Motion Picture Retirement Home in Woodland Hills, California.

Stone loved acting and making people happy. He told interviewers Tom and Jim Goldrup, "I think the greatest compliment I get from people is that you do me more good than doctors and I always say it is one of the reasons I went into acting. I would have loved to be a physician but it's got to be the way it's got to be."

Stone, 92, died November 18, 2005, at the Motion Picture Home in Woodland Hills, California.

Suggested Sampling of Stone's Western Heavies:

- Gunsmoke: Who Lives By the Sword ('57) James Arness
- Have Gun Will Travel: A Matter of Ethics ('57) Richard Boone
- Cheyenne: Last Comanchero ('58) Clint Walker
- Restless Gun: Sheriff Billy ('58) John Payne
- Tales of Wells Fargo: Sniper ('58) Dale Robertson
- Rifleman: Home Ranch ('58) Chuck Connors
- Trackdown: The School Teacher ('58) Robert Culp
- Sugarfoot: Yampa Crossing ('58) Will Hutchins
- Trackdown: Fear ('59) Robert Culp
- Gunsmoke: Buffalo Hunter ('59) James Arness
- Overland Trail: The Reckoning ('60) Doug McClure/William Bendix
- Rifleman: Trail of Hate ('60) Chuck Connors
- Tall Man: The Parson ('60) Barry Sullivan/Clu Gulager
- Stagecoach West: Red Sand ('60) Robert Bray
- Wyatt Earp: The Fanatic ('60) Hugh O'Brian
- Have Gun Will Travel: Last Judgement ('61) Richard Boone
- Cheyenne: Wedding Rings ('62) Clint Walker
- Showdown ('63 Universal) Audie Murphy
- Gunsmoke: Homecoming ('64) James Arness
- Bonanza: The Hostage ('64) Lorne Greene
- Big Valley: Teacher of Outlaws ('66) Barbara Stanwyck
- Virginian: Ride to Delphi ('66) James Drury
- Iron Horse: Steel Chain to a Music Box ('67) Dale Robertson
- Virginian: Death Wait ('69) David Hartman

GLENN STRANGE

The Frankenstein monster. Petro—the "Mad Monster". Sam the bartender on "Gunsmoke". Tested for the role of Tarzan. Dick Foran's sidekick "Pee Wee". Fiddle player and noted songwriter. Veteran of nine serials including "Flash Gordon". Butch Cavendish who ambushed Clayton Moore on TV's "Lone Ranger". But most of all, 6' 3" craggy-faced Glenn Strange was a B-western badman in over 200 features and 50 or so TV episodes.

Born August 16, 1899, in Weed, New Mexico, of Irish-Cherokee parentage, his father, William R. Strange, who some reports indicate was a Cherokee Indian—or at least had Cherokee blood, was a bartender and a rancher. (No wonder Glenn looked so natural as Sam the bartender on "Gunsmoke".) Glenn's mother, Sarah E. Byrd, was of Irish heritage. A little known fact is that Glenn was a first cousin to B-western sidekick Lee "Lasses" White.

Glenn quit school after the 8th grade to help his father in the cattle business, probably now living in Crosscut, Texas, but after learning to play the fiddle at about age 12, he started drifting around the country with various type shows.

Glenn did a brief stint as a heavyweight boxer (Eddie Dean says Glenn was a protégé of Jack Dempsey until he broke his hand) and worked briefly as a deputy sheriff in New Mexico.

Glenn started in radio in El Paso in 1928, he hooked up with the Arizona Wranglers, a group who at the time included Jack Kirk and, another cousin of Glenn's, Curtis

"Cactus Mack" McPeters. Working on tours in the southwest, the group eventually could be heard on KNX radio, Hollywood. Films were the next logical step and Glenn can be spotted playing fiddle with Kirk, Mack, Charles Baldra, Charley Sargent and other musicians in such '30s B-westerns as "Lawless Range", "Stormy", "Westward Ho", "New Frontier", "Sundown Rider" and "Cyclone of the Saddle". You'll even see him during his later "Gunsmoke" years playing the fiddle at some Dodge City social.

Glenn worked for a while as a rodeo rider which is where he picked up the nickname Pee Wee. "I did a lot of westerns with Dick Foran at Warner Bros.," Glenn explained. "At the opening (credits), they'd show a picture of Dick, then a picture of me, Glenn 'Pee Wee' Strange. (Laughs) I got that name way back during when Hugh Strickland was World Champion Cowboy. My brother and I was rodeoing then, and Bud was bigger than I am. We went to the Fort Worth Fat Stock Show. Hugh was announcing and he announced us as we'd come out, and why Hugh did it, I don't know…my Bud came out before I did and he called him Puny. (Laughs) He was as big as (James) Arness! Then when I got ready to come out—Pee Wee! (Laughs) Puny and Pee Wee—and we never lost those names, not ever. I was still rodeoing when Warners pulled me over there with Foran. (Director) Breezy Eason knew me real well, the producer knew me real well, so they said, 'Most people know you as Pee Wee, we'll just call you that.'"

Riding rodeo, Glenn spent time with Hoot Gibson's rodeo at Saugus, California. (Gibson bought the Baker Ranch and Rodeo in April '30.) Strange remembered Hoot helping him over the rough spots in his first films. Hooter's "Mounted Stranger" ('30) and "Wild Horse" ('31) were Glenn's first two features. Strange once told researcher John Brooker, "I came to Hollywood in 1929 with Hoot Gibson's rodeo. Hoot had a ranch out there. I broke my leg and stayed at the ranch until I recuperated. Hoot brought me into working in westerns. My favorite B-western star was Buck Jones…we were friends…I met him on the rodeo."

Glenn's roles were chiefly unbilled bits from '31-'35. Strange remembers Buck Jones insisting he stay in bed on the second day of shooting when Glenn awoke with the flu. Jones put on Glenn's wardrobe and did his riding for him. Besides playing outlaws, Glenn was Jack Randall's sidekick in "Land of the Six Guns" ('40 Monogram) and Dick Foran's buddy, Pee Wee, in several of Foran's Warner westerns and portrayed sheriffs in several films as well, such as Bob Baker's "Honor of the

Bob Baker makes his "Last Stand" against outlaw odds, Glenn Strange (L) and Jack Kirk (R) ('38 Universal).

West". And there were dangerous moments in making these fast-paced B-westerns. Glenn recalled in talking with interviewers Don Glut, Bart Andrews, Bob Burns and Larry Byrd, "One time, on a Foran picture up at Chatsworth, we were coming right down between two rocks, just about room for a horse and man to get through. I had a guy coming from the other way with what they call a falling horse—they cue 'em, you know, and they fall. He was to fall that horse here (indicating with a finger) and we'd go right by him. Well, the horse, they cued him a little late and he fell right across our trail. My horse's front feet hit him and turned over with me. It was on the side of a hill and I was afraid he'd roll over on me. I reached under the side of his head and grabbed the bit and jerked his head down against the ground so he wouldn't come on over. I was laying there seeing these other horses turning over me. There was seven of us and nobody got hurt! Every horse was down and every man was down."

Then on Bob Baker's "Last Stand" in 1938, Glenn told of another close call, "I was up at Sonora, California, out at a place called Phoenix Lake. It had been up but the water had receded. There were round driftwood sticks (or logs) laying around. I was chasin' a stagecoach. The pony I was ridin' was about a half quarter horse. He could really fly! Jumped this log with me, and when he lit on the other side, his feet hit on one of these driftwood sticks and the thing rolled out from under him. This is on film, he went right over and hit on his nose, in fact, broke his nose. I thought he was gonna bleed to death. Of course, he lost me on the first turnover. He lit on his hip and turned completely over again. I hit into some rocks and sticks and it knocked me goofy for a minute, which it didn't have to knock me too hard. (Chuckles) To show you how things work out, I got up and grabbed the gun, I'd lost my gun which I'd had out and was shooting, and my hat, and got on this horse as he was getting up and rode about 40-50 feet out of camera range and fell on my face. I was still out! It's on film with Bob Baker. I rode the rest of that picture with two broken ribs from that fall. What a hurt I had!"

In yet another incident Strange related to Glut, Andrews, Burns and Byrd, "We went to Arizona in early 1930, some independent company. I jumped this horse off of this cliff—and I tried to leave him, but it's a little hard if you've never tried this, when a horse is falling and you're falling with him, you try to get off him—but I did somehow and I never straightened up. I just lay up there like this (erect motion) and that's the way I hit the water and I don't think I ever went under. You talk about being blistered—I just bounced! They had a coupla boats together and had kind of a raft built across that with cameras on it. They had a camera on the shore shooting up this way and they had a camera for the take-off back here. I never stunted very much, I just stunted a little-while and then started trying to act... and I'm still trying. (Chuckles) It was the last day's shooting on this picture,

just after lunch. They had to go back and get a heavy and shoot all of my stuff over because I couldn't finish the picture. You can imagine what it cost to do that. That's why they double. Many stars can do stunts, but (the studio) can't afford to let 'em try; if anything happens, they're in Dutch."

Over the ensuing years Strange worked with nearly every western star but, for whatever reason, he was on screen more for Warner Bros., Monogram, Universal and PRC than he ever was for Republic where he only did about 20-21 with several of those being '50s A-westerns. One of his standouts is as the dim-witted killer, The Maverick ("That ain't friendly"), in the Range Busters' "Boot Hill Bandits" ('42).

While still appearing in scores of westerns, Strange won over the horror audience by becoming the Frankenstein monster in three Universals—"House of Dracula", "House of Frankenstein" and "Abbott and Costello Meet Frankenstein". He also appeared as the monster with Abbott and Costello on their "Colgate Comedy Hour".

In her book COWBOY PRINCESS, Cheryl Rogers-Barnett wrote, "Glenn was a gentleman who genuinely loved kids. By the time I saw him as the monster in 'Abbott and Costello Meet Frankenstein' ('48), I was eight years old. Even with the gruesome makeup, I knew it was Glenn—but I got hysterical anyway and had to be taken home early."

Glenn's early musical training allowed him to compose several songs for films, the most recognized being "On the Banks of the Sunny San Juan" which he wrote with Eddie Dean who performed it in "Wildfire" ('45) and "Harmony Trail" ('44). Smiley Burnette sings it in "El Dorado Pass" ('48). Other Strange songs were sung by Tex Ritter ("Renegade Song") in "Hittin' the Trail" ('37), Eddie Dean's title song to "Tumbleweed Trail" ('46) and Dean again ("Sands of the Old Rio Grande") in "Stars Over Texas" ('46). Earlier, Glenn contributed music to John Wayne's "Westward Ho" ('35) and "Winds of the Wasteland" ('36).

Sidekick Slim Andrews related the following story: "One day Glenn Strange and his band stopped by my house to spend the night. After supper, my wife started to clean off the table, Glenn said, 'Now wait a minute! After a good meal like this, we sure ain't gonna let this little lady wash the dishes.' So Glenn and one of his boys did the dishes. Now that was a sight—big old Glenn Strange in an apron washing dishes."

Somewhere around late '49 or in 1950, as best we can determine, Strange was injured badly. Badman Pierce Lyden said, "Once a stagecoach slid off the road and went down an embankment. Inside was Glenn Strange. He rolled around inside and was busted up pretty badly. After a year in the hospital, with many operations, he was up and around, but his stunting days were over."

Strange told it this way, "I got my leg broke. When you're sitting in a stagecoach and the horses are running just as fast as they possibly can run, and the door is wired—you can't get it open—and nobody up there to drive 'em, that'll give you kind of a rough feeling. I was doing a heavy. Ted Mapes had been doubling me that day. He'd made all these wild rides in this coach and they came to the place where they were shooting a closeup of me over Charles Starrett's shoulder…he was on a parallel on his horse. They're shooting over his shoulder into the coach on me. Horses bolted, took off with me in there. I wound up in Cedars of Lebanon Hospital with a leg smashed all to pieces including the knee joint. I'd come off every pinnacle in the country and horse falls—of course you're always leading the pack if you're the heavy—I've had horses fall and the whole pack run over me."

Still making feature films, Glenn entered the early days of TV in 1949 as he waylaid Clayton Moore and a group of Texas Rangers on the first three continued-storyline episodes of "The Lone Ranger". He returned as Butch Cavendish a year later in the "Never Say Die" episode. He was also seen on 75 or so other TV western episodes.

Glenn came to "Gunsmoke" when he met James Arness in '59. Jim asked when he was going to do an episode, explaining he liked to work with tall guys and Glenn fit the bill. Glenn's first "Gunsmoke" was "Old Faces" in March '61, but he didn't become a regular as mild mannered, craggy-faced Sam the barkeep for Miss Kitty until the next season's shows in Fall '61. He continued with the series until his death September 20, 1973, at 74.

Archivist/actor Bob Burns smiled, "Glenn was closer to me than my own Dad. He was one of the most loved guys in the business. At his funeral there must have been over 900 people. It overflowed the church. Every old-time western actor or stuntman still around was there. Some were in wheelchairs, walkers, etc. They all came to pay their respects to Pee Wee. Dick Foran, who had just lost his nose to cancer, said to me, 'He was one of the best human beings on the face of this good earth.' Eddie Dean was Glenn's best friend. He was supposed to sing at the funeral but was so distraught he couldn't do it. Luckily, he had prerecorded it just in case that happened and they played that. And what a wonderful guy Jim Arness is. At the funeral, he really helped me get through it. We were honorary Pallbearers and I was doing pretty well until we had to move with the coffin and I completely fell apart. He put his arm around my shoulder and said how much we would all miss Glenn. The way he said it and the look in his eyes was so comforting to me. I'll be forever grateful to him for that. Glenn so loved Jim. He kept Glenn working when he had his cancer until he just couldn't work any longer. I think that's really a measure of a man."

On the 1/21/74 episode of "Gunsmoke", Robert Brubaker as Floyd has replaced Sam. When Nehemiah Persoff asks the whereabouts of Sam, Floyd replies, "We lost him awhile back…everybody around here misses him a lot."

Strange was married to Min Thompson and they had a daughter. They lived at 926 East Valencia St. in Burbank.

Strange, a heavy smoker in his life, died of a carcinoma of the lung which he'd had for about a year prior to his death September 20, 1973, at St. Joseph Hospital in Burbank. He is buried at Forest Lawn Memorial Park in Hollywood Hills.

Suggested Sampling of Strange's Western Heavies:

- Single Handed Saunders ('32 Monogram) Tom Tyler
- Somewhere In Sonora ('33 Warner Bros.) John Wayne
- Lawless Range ('35 Republic) John Wayne
- Arizona Days ('37 Grand National) Tex Ritter
- Whirlwind Horseman ('38 Grand National) Ken Maynard
- Six Shootin' Sheriff ('38 Grand National) Ken Maynard
- Pride of the West ('38 Paramount) William Boyd
- California Frontier ('38 Columbia) Buck Jones
- Ghost Town Riders ('38 Universal) Bob Baker
- Blue Montana Skies ('39 Republic) Gene Autry
- Law of the Pampas ('39 Paramount) William Boyd
- Fighting Gringo ('39 RKO) George O'Brien
- Covered Wagon Trails ('40 Monogram) Jack Randall
- Pals of the Silver Sage ('40 Monogram) Tex Ritter
- Stage to Chino ('40 RKO) George O'Brien
- Three Men From Texas ('40 Paramount) William Boyd
- Kid's Last Ride ('41 Monogram) Range Busters
- Fugitive Valley ('41 Monogram) Range Busters
- Wide Open Town ('41 Paramount) William Boyd
- Billy the Kid Wanted ('41 PRC) Buster Crabbe
- Bandit Trail ('41 RKO) Tim Holt
- Forbidden Trails ('41 Monogram) Rough Riders
- Arizona Cyclone ('41 Universal) Johnny Mack Brown
- Lone Rider and the Bandit ('42 PRC) George Houston
- Stagecoach Buckaroo ('42 Universal) Johnny Mack Brown
- Raiders of the West ('42 PRC) Lee Powell/Art Davis/Bill Boyd
- Billy the Kid Trapped ('42 PRC) Buster Crabbe
- Boot Hill Bandits ('42 Monogram) Range Busters
- Romance On the Range ('42 Republic) Roy Rogers
- Come On Danger ('42 RKO) Tim Holt
- Overland Stagecoach ('42 PRC) Bob Livingston
- Kid Rides Again ('43 PRC) Buster Crabbe
- Haunted Ranch ('43 Monogram) Range Busters
- Wild Horse Stampede ('43 Monogram) Trail Blazers
- Western Cyclone ('43 PRC) Buster Crabbe
- Arizona Trail ('43 Universal) Tex Ritter
- Return of the Rangers ('43 PRC) James Newill/Dave O'Brien
- False Colors ('43 United Artists) William Boyd
- Forty Thieves (44 United Artists) William Boyd
- Silver City Kid ('44 Republic) Allan Lane
- San Antonio Kid ('44 Republic) Bill Elliott
- Trail to Gunsight ('44 Universal) Eddie Dew
- Renegades of the Rio Grande ('45 Universal) Rod Cameron
- Roll Thunder Roll ('49 Equity) Jim Bannon
- Lone Ranger: Enter the Lone Ranger ('49) Clayton Moore
- Lone Ranger: Never Say Die ('50) Clayton Moore
- Sky King: Stagecoach Robbers (52) Kirby Grant
- Hopalong Cassidy: Alien Range ('52) William Boyd

- Cisco Kid: Cisco and the Giant ('55) Duncan Renaldo
- Champion: Outlaw's Secret ('55) Jim Bannon
- Gene Autry: Dynamite ('55) Gene Autry
- Judge Roy Bean: Cross Draw Kid ('56) Edgar Buchanan
- Annie Oakley: Outlaw Brand ('56) Gail Davis
- Sky King: Dead Giveaway ('59) Kirby Grant

LYLE TALBOT

For a man who hated horses, Lyle Talbot sure rode a lot of them. Under contract to Warner Bros., Lyle was offered the singing cowboy role that made Dick Foran famous in 1935 but, because of his dislike and fear of horses, he begged off. Finally, in 1944, his starring career at WB over, Lyle made his first western, as a U.S. Marshal, supporting Eddie Dew in "Trail to Gunsight" at Universal.

Now in his early '40s, he began to accept a few western and serial heavy roles, but tried to stay off horses as much as possible. In the '50s Lyle became a staple on early TV westerns, sometimes representing judges or doctors, but often the outlaw boss.

Lysle Henderson was born February 8, 1902, in Pittsburgh, Pennsylvania, but calls Nebraska his home because he grew up there. Tracing his heritage is quite intriguing. Lyle's grandfather, Mr. Hollywood, immigrated to America with his family from Ireland. A coal miner, he settled near Pittsburgh later moving to Wyoming. One of his daughters married a Talbot and the Talbot's daughter living in Brainard, Nebraska, at 18, married a Scotchman named Henderson. They moved to Pittsburgh where Lysle was born. However, when his mother became quite ill, they moved back to Nebraska. Lysle's mother died four months later and his grandmother took charge of raising the boy. At odds with his father, his grandmother Talbot legally adopted Lysle, changing his name to Talbot.

Lysle never saw his father again until he was about 15. By this time his Dad had married Anna Nielsen and they'd gone into show business as actors who toured with traveling repertory companies throughout the Midwest.

Lyle started in 1919 as a teenager touring with a traveling hypnotist. He sang, did a little magic and performed in a couple of sketches. Graduating to a resident stock company, he worked in Sioux Falls, South Dakota, for two years and eventually opened his own stock company, The Talbot Players, in Memphis, Tennessee.

With the Depression of the '30s and the advent of talking pictures, repertory work and theatres that supported those actors began to close down. Many of the actors, like Lysle, migrated to Hollywood, however his first film was a 20 minute short with Pat O'Brien lensed in New York in 1930, "The Nightingale", released by Warner Bros. He then made a test at Warner Bros. and was signed to a seven year contract, which is when the 's' was dropped from his first name.

Over the next six years Lyle starred in dozens of

Charles Starrett warns Lyle Talbot not to be so "Quick on the Trigger" ('48 Columbia).

top flight Warner Bros. films—"Three On a Match", "20,000 Years in Sing Sing", "Life of Jimmy Dolan", "College Coach", "No More Orchids", "Fog Over Frisco", "Dragon Murder Case", "Oil for the Lamps of China", among others.

Lyle was frequently loaned to other studios during his Warners tenure, most notably for "The 13th Guest" at Monogram in '32 and "Trapped By Television" at Columbia in '36.

Released from his WB contract after 6 years, Lyle began to freelance in 1937. He was always fond of pointing out that in his over 60 years in show business he seldom went more than a week without working in a play, radio, a movie or a TV show. "I worked a lot because I liked working. I did some real dogs, but I believe I gave my best performances in the theatre."

Lyle made his first serial (of nine) in 1944 as an agent for a foreign power in the swamplands of Louisiana for Universal's "Mystery of the Riverboat". Then he was the star of "Chick Carter, Detective" at Columbia in 1946. He went from clean-cut detective hero to nightclub-owning crook the next year with "The Vigilante" ('47 Columbia). He was back helping "Batman and Robin" in 1949 at Columbia as Commissioner Gordon. Then came his tour-de-force as bald, mad professor Lex Luthor in "Atom Man Vs. Superman" ('50 Columbia).

Other lesser roles followed for Sam Katzman at Columbia as well as spy leader Borent in Republic's "Trader Tom of the China Seas" ('54).

Lyle continued appearing on stage in dinner theatres through the late '80s until his wife of nearly 42 years, Margaret Epple, died in 1989. They were married in 1948 and had four children, including, now journalist, David Talbot and child actor Stephen Talbot. Previously Lyle was married to Marjorie Kramer in 1937 until their divorce.

Lyle sold his house of many years in Studio City when Margaret died and moved to an apartment in the heart of San Francisco to be near his children. Lyle's best friend in show business was Walter Reed, who sadly told us, "He had an amazing career. He ran a stock company in Memphis when I was still a youngster. I first saw Lyle on stage at the El Capitan Theatre in Hollywood when I was 13. That's when I decided to become an actor. In pictures he played opposite the best—Mae West, Shirley Temple, Barbara Stanwyck, Carole Lombard. Later in life he took some lesser parts. Why not? He had four kids to support. Lyle always believed you weren't an actor unless you were acting…no small parts, only small actors. We worked together in Mexican Spitfire pictures, 'Lone Ranger', a commercial and more. Then Lyle did shows with Ozzie and Harriett as well as many plays. As young actors we were hell raisers. We partied hard and worked hard but never let the two get in the way of each other. Maybe that's why we liked each other so much. We respected each other's acting. He really didn't know how much I'd learned from him. Lyle never thought about quitting acting, even when he was using a walker in his 90s he would have considered a role. His body was falling apart but his mind was sharp right to the last. Lyle had a lot of love for his family, his two sons and two daughters. He talked about them constantly. They are all very successful and he was very proud of them. I'm still trying to figure out how he lived so long. Maybe it's his Irish blood, his family name way back was Hollywood. I loved him as a brother, Heaven is lucky to have him."

Lyle Talbot was a respected stage actor, a star at Warner Bros. in the '30s, a star and supporting actor in dozens of westerns and serials, featured in scores of TV shows including Bob Cummings' buddy Paul Fonda in "Love That Bob", neighbor Joe Randolph on "The Adventures of Ozzie and Harriett", he was in the acknowledged "worst film ever made"—"Plan Nine From Outer Space" and he was the last living actor of the 21 who founded the Screen Actor's Guild.

After several days illness, at 94, the legendary Lyle Talbot died March 3, 1996, at his San Francisco apartment.

Suggested Sampling of Talbot's Western Heavies:

- Song of Arizona ('46 Republic) Roy Rogers
- Gun Town ('46 Universal) Kirby Grant
- Quick On the Trigger ('48 Columbia) Charles Starrett
- Gold Raiders ('51 U.A.) George O'Brien
- Stage to Blue River ('51 Monogram) Whip Wilson
- Wild Bill Hickok: Boulder City Election ('51) Guy Madison
- Desperadoes Outpost ('52 Republic) Allan "Rocky" Lane
- Wyoming Roundup ('52 Monogram) Whip Wilson
- Cowboy G-Men: Center Fire ('52) Russell Hayden
- Crossroad Avenger: Adventures of the Tucson Kid ('53) Tom Keene
- Range Rider: West of Cheyenne ('53) Jock Mahoney
- Cowboy G-Men: General Delivery ('53) Russell Hayden
- Lone Ranger: Trouble in Town ('53) Clayton Moore
- Gene Autry: Gypsy Wagon ('53) Gene Autry
- Hopalong Cassidy: Valley Raiders ('53) William Boyd
- Lone Ranger: Code of the Pioneers ('55) Clayton Moore
- Rin Tin Tin: Legacy of Sean O'Hara ('55) Lee Aaker
- Buffalo Bill Jr.: Six Gun Symphony ('55) Dick Jones
- Rin Tin Tin: Witch of the Woods ('56) Lee Aaker
- Wild Bill Hickok: Wild Bill's Odyssey ('56) Guy Madison
- Restless Gun: The Englishman ('59) John Payne
- Lawman: By the Book ('61) John Russell

HAL TALIAFERRO (WALLY WALES)

From silents to talkies. From hero to heavy. From sidekick to character player. Features, shorts, serials. A films and B films. Call him Wally Wales or Hal Taliaferro, for over 30 years, 1921-1952, he gave viewers a world of western adventure.

Floyd Taliaferro Alderson was born in Sheridan, Wyoming, November 13, 1895, and raised on Hanging Woman Creek in Montana at his father's homestead. His father sold the ranch about 1900 and moved to Sheridan where he went into the café business. After his mother died in 1907, Floyd and his two brothers came to his uncle's ranch and were raised by him. In the spring of 1914 the 5' 11", 165 lb. handsome youth with brown hair and blue eyes left home and found work a year later driving a stage in Yellowstone Park. In the fall of 1915 he bummed his way to San Francisco to see the World's Fair, then headed for Hollywood.

His entrance into the movies as an extra in 1915

was cut short for WWI Army service from 1917-1919 while he served with the 91st Division and in the Spruce Division. Returning from the war, working bits in films and supplementing his income with odd jobs, finally by 1925 he was making $500 per picture starring in his own westerns as Wally Wales for Artclass. With several of those under his belt, in 1927 he switched to Pathé to star in 10 more.

As talkies came in, Wally was the hero of the first all sound serial, the 10 chapter "Voice From the Sky" (G.Y.B. Pictures '30).

Serials remained a strong part of Wales/Taliaferro's work throughout his career, appearing in 20 cliffhangers…with noteworthy appearances on the right side of the law also in "Painted Stallion" ('37 Republic), "Lone Ranger" ('38 Republic), "Adventures of Red Ryder" ('40 Republic) and "Phantom Rider" ('46 Republic). With the acting ability to switch back and forth from good to bad, he menaced the hero in "Zorro's Black Whip" ('44 Republic) and "Federal Operator 99" ('45 Republic).

With an excellent voice, great cowboying abilities, a handsome look and build and a four year string of starring silents to his credit, you'd think a major studio would have snapped Wally up to star in sound westerns. At least a mid-range outfit like Monogram, Tiffany or World Wide. But no, Wally wound up starring for lowly poverty row outfits like Big 4, Imperial and Superior.

He managed these starring nickel-and-dime B's through 1934, all the while honing his character acting abilities in other westerns and serials with Ken Maynard, Bob Steele, Tom Tyler, Tim McCoy, Rex Bell and Bill Cody.

By 1936 he changed his name to Hal Taliaferro, often sporting a scruffy beard, and settled in on character roles…whether it be sheriffs, girl's brother, rancher, townsman or outlaw.

He briefly had a fling playing the sidekick from '35-'38 in a handful of pictures with Ken Maynard ("Lawless Riders" '35 Columbia), Bob Allen ("Rio Grande Ranger" '36 Columbia, "Law of the Ranger" '37 Columbia) and Bob Baker ("Prairie Justice", "Black Bandit" both '38 Universal). If one has any doubts as to his comic abilities, take a look at him performing "Frankie's Flaming Fandango" in Bob Allen's "Unknown Ranger" ('36 Columbia). These gay cavaliers are a real hoot!

Perhaps a hint of the reason he turned from leading man to character roles is revealed in a portion of a letter he sent to a researcher late in his life after he'd returned to work in 1954 on the family Bones Brothers ranch in Montana. "I was never what one would call very social. The picture game calls for that, and much more, in order to be successful, but I'm a loner. Some, in order to stay on top, kill themselves by going the booze and dope route. There are many like this. I had three or four friends go over the big river (commit suicide) by the use of the .45 Colt. Many drank themselves to death. The glory trail is dangerous unless you know a Sampson, have guts, strength, will, wisdom, and character, and unless you know the game. Few stay on top for keeps. I'm a most fortunate man, I saw it coming (the ending of his career), the dark days, and the black cloud. I would like very much to contribute my long list of memories to the history of those early Hollywood days. I am interested in those who do historicals, and will try to cooperate. I do not mind looking backward, but I do not want to live looking backward. I'm not in show business; I'm in another world. And, my work here on the ranch keeps me pretty busy."

Taliaferro's last film was "Sea Hornet" ('51 Republic). Leaving Hollywood he lived in Alaska in 1952 working for a mill construction firm before moving back to being a real cowboy in Montana on his nephew's ranch. For the last 20 years of his life he devoted his spare time to his favorite hobby, portrait painting.

He was twice married, both briefly, first to Mary Bell Towers, then Gwendolyn Costello sometime in the '50s. He suffered a crippling stroke in 1976 and was confined for a while to a nursing home in Sheridan. One of the finest supporting players in westerns died of pneumonia on the family ranch on February 12, 1980, at 84.

Taliaferro's nephew, Irv Alderson (born 1930), still owns and manages the Bones Brothers Ranch near Birney, Montana.

Suggested Sampling of Taliaferro's Western Heavies:

- Law and Lawless ('32 Majestic) Jack Hoxie
- Rusty Rides Alone ('33 Columbia) Tim McCoy
- Trail Drive ('33 Universal) Ken Maynard
- Six Gun Justice ('35 Spectrum) Bill Cody
- Fighting Caballero ('35 Superior) Rex Lease
- Five Bad Men ('35 Sunset) Noah Beery Jr.
- Pecos Kid ('35 Commodore) Fred Kohler Jr.
- Silent Valley ('35 Reliable) Tom Tyler
- Vanishing Riders ('35 Spectrum) Bill Cody
- Danger Trails ('35 Beacon) Big Boy Williams
- Trigger Tom ('35 Reliable) Tom Tyler
- Lucky Terror ('36 Diversion) Hoot Gibson
- Law and Lead ('37 Colony) Rex Bell
- Rangers Step In ('37 Columbia) Bob Allen
- Trigger Trio ('37 Republic) 3 Mesquiteers
- Phantom Gold ('38 Columbia) Jack Luden
- Riders of the Frontier ('39 Monogram) Tex Ritter
- Saga of Death Valley ('39 Republic) Roy Rogers
- Young Bill Hickok ('40 Republic) Roy Rogers
- In Old Cheyenne ('41 Republic) Roy Rogers
- Sheriff of Tombstone ('41 Republic) Roy Rogers
- Bad Man of Deadwood ('41 Republic) Roy Rogers
- Jesse James at Bay ('41 Republic) Roy Rogers
- Border Vigilantes ('41 Paramount) William Boyd
- Hoppy Serves a Writ ('42 United Artists) William Boyd
- Leather Burners ('43 United Artists) William Boyd
- Silver Spurs ('43 Republic) Roy Rogers
- Man From Music Mountain ('43 Republic) Roy Rogers
- Lumberjack ('44 United Artists) William Boyd
- Forty Thieves ('44 United Artists) William Boyd
- Yellow Rose of Texas ('44 Republic) Roy Rogers
- Zorro's Black Whip ('44 Republic serial) Linda Stirling
- Utah ('45 Republic) Roy Rogers
- Springtime in Texas ('45 Monogram) Jimmy Wakely
- West of Sonora ('48 Columbia) Charles Starrett
- Gallant Legion ('48 Republic) Bill Elliott
- Red River ('48 United Artists) John Wayne
- Brimstone ('49 Republic) Rod Cameron

SHERRY TANSEY

Sherry Tansey, with over 140 films to his credit, usually as one of B-westerns' dirty rotten polecats, made his movie debut in the 1915 silent saga, "Destruction". He did not play one of the bad guys in the film as he was only 9 years old.

Beginning his Hollywood career in 1916, as a child actor (under the name Sheridan Tansey), there was nothing to indicate he would become one of the oater's busiest henchmen. His roles were limited to appearances in melodramas popular in those days with titles such as "The Foolish Virgin" ('17), "The Two Brides" ('19) and "Over the Hill To the Poorhouse" ('20).

Tansey's first western film was apparently as a 19 year only boy in Buddy Roosevelt's "Fast Fightin'" ('25 Artclass). This was followed by parts with some of the early silent western stars such as "Fighting Boobs" ('26) with Bob Custer, "Obligin' Buckaroo" ('27) with Buffalo Bill Jr., "Code of the Cow Country" ('27) with Buddy Roosevelt and "Riders of the Rio" ('30) with Lane Chandler.

For his early films, he used his birth name of Sheridan (James) Tansey, switching to Sherry Tansey by 1923. In the '30s and '40s he seemed to alternate between Sherry Tansey and James Sheridan.

Sheridan James Tansey was born July 29, 1904, in New York City. Although no information could be located on Tansey's father, Tansey's mother was actress Emma Tansey who was born in Louisville, Kentucky, September 12, 1870. It's possible Tansey may have even been Emma's maiden name and that she never married.

In any event, sometime near the end of the 1800s, Emma migrated from the Blue Grass of Kentucky to the streets of New York. One possible reason, not confirmed, may have been Emma seeking a career in the world of entertainment.

While in New York, Emma spawned three sons. Son number one was Robert Emmett Tansey, born June 28, 1897, in Brooklyn. Son number two was John Foster Tansey, born October 8, 1901, in New York. Son number three was henchman Sherry Tansey.

Early in the 1900s, following the births of the three Tansey sons, the family moved to the Los Angeles area where all, mother and three sons, carved out a career in Hollywood.

The first of the Tansey clan to latch onto the Hollywood bandwagon was son John, who proved to be the lesser light in the family's film lives. John made his first appearance at the age of seven in "The Red Man and the Child" ('08). He's credited with 15 films, the final being "Silent Sentinel" ('29).

There is a gap between 1918 and 1924 which may indicate service during World War I for the older brother. However, a 1920 census has them all living at 162 Anderson Ave. in Palisades Park, New Jersey.

John and Ruth Tansey co-wrote and directed one of the last silent westerns, "Romance of the West" starring Jack Perrin, released by Capital in '30. John and brother Robert produced and John directed "Riders of the Rio", an independent early 1931 talkie with Lane Chandler in which Sherry Tansey has a role. John's last fling at films seems to be "Taming of the Jungle" in 1933 which he co-directed with Bob. What he did after he left films is unknown. John died in North Hollywood on April 28, 1971.

The next of the Tansey's to have an acting career was Robert commencing with "Hazel Kirke" ('12) when he was about 15. Robert's acting career was brief, as he quickly found a home behind the cameras as a writer and director of lowbudget westerns throughout the '30s and '40s right on up until his death in Los Angeles of a heart attack on June 17, 1951, just before his 54th birthday.

Screenwriter Frances Kavanaugh worked often with Bob Tansey and recalled, "Bob's mother, Emma, had been an actress in silents. She had three sons and she took them all over the states. The troupe traveled by train for plays. She raised them as actors on the stage. Bob told me he was in a comedy billed as Robert Emmett Tansey, his real name. He did a comedy series as a young child."

Emma Tansey herself made her screen debut in "When You and I Were Young" ('17). Emma's 24-some credits consisted of roles in dramatic films, "Les Miserables" ('35), westerns including Bob Steele's "Gun Lords of Stirrup Basin" ('37) (which featured son Sherry as a heavy) and the W. C. Fields comedy "The Bank Dick" ('40). Earlier, in "Fast Fightin'" ('25) she also shared billing with son Sherry. Her final film was "Never Give a Sucker An Even Break" ('41). Emma Tansey, 71, passed away in Los Angeles, on March 23, 1942.

Whether billed as Sherry Tansey or James Sheridan, his lean, sharp-featured countenance was seen repeatedly in the B-westerns of Wally Wales, Bob Steele, Tim McCoy, John Wayne, Johnny Mack Brown, Tom Tyler, Tex Ritter, Tom Keene, Fred Scott, Jack Randall and others up until his final film, "Harmony Trail' ('44) with Ken Maynard.

Naturally, when brother Bob was directing, there was usually a role for Sherry. Frances Kavanaugh recalls, "Oh yeah, Sherry was a heavy a lot of times. He was the youngest. Sherry was a very slender, sensitive young man. He always loved to work in westerns. We didn't see much of him…he lived with his mother, Emma. When she passed on it nearly killed him." (You'll note Sherry's credits cease in 1942, the year of his mother's death with only his final film coming two years later in '44.) "Emma had a beautiful big, white cat, so he got the cat when she died and he loved that cat. But young men on their own, they don't know how to take care of a cat, so the cat got away. And do you know, Sherry moved away and we never, never heard from him. Bob never mentioned it and I didn't either, but I sure did miss Sherry. He was such a sweet person."

Sherry Tansey never served in the Armed Forces and never married. He spent the last years of his life living in Broderick, California, directly across the river from Sacramento. He was employed as a custodian at a labor union hall in Broderick.

Sherry died April 12, 1961, in Sacramento County Hospital at age 56 of heart disease. His body lies at rest at the Woodland Cemetery in Yolo County, California.

There's "Thunder in the Desert" as Lew Meehan (L) and Sherry Tansey (center) face off against Bob Steele ('38 Republic).

Suggested Sampling of Tansey's Western Heavies:

- Timber Terrors ('34 Stage and Screen) John Preston
- Arizona Cyclone ('34 Imperial) Wally Wales
- Between Men ('35 Supreme) Johnny Mack Brown
- Roamin' Wild ('36 Reliable) Tom Tyler
- Silver Trail ('37 Reliable) Rex Lease
- Gambling Terror ('37 Republic) Johnny Mack Brown
- Doomed at Sundown ('37 Republic) Bob Steele
- Lightning Carson Rides Again ('38 Victory) Tim McCoy
- Paroled to Die ('38 Republic) Bob Steele
- Songs and Bullets ('38 Spectrum) Fred Scott
- Sundown on the Prairie ('39 Monogram) Tex Ritter
- Trigger Smith ('39 Monogram) Jack Randall
- Silver On the Sage ('39 Paramount) William Boyd
- Billy the Kid Outlawed ('40 PRC) Bob Steele
- Phantom Rancher ('40 Colony) Ken Maynard
- Lone Star Law Men ('41 Monogram) Tom Keene
- Billy the Kid's Fighting Pals ('41 PRC) Bob Steele

FORREST TAYLOR

Veteran heavy—and sometimes father figure—Edwin Forrest Taylor began in films in 1915. Born December 29, 1883, in Bloomington, Illinois, his father (Christopher C. Taylor from New Jersey) was a prominent newspaperman. Taylor spent a few years in publishing before turning thespian with his first picture an Art

Acord western for American, "Man-Afraid-of-His-Wardrobe" ('15). Billed as E. Forrest Taylor, he starred in at least three more 2-reelers for American and at least 5 Mustang 2-reelers, all in 1915.

In 1917, he deserted movies for the legitimate stage, working as a leading man with Clara Kimball Young, enjoying success on Broadway in "The Fool" ('22), "In Love With Love" and "Nervous Wreck" (both '23) and even heading his own stock company for seven years. Although he's in "No Man's Gold" ('26) with Tom Mix at Fox, he returned to his screen career in earnest in 1933 ("Death Kiss" with Bela Lugosi, then "Riders of Destiny" with John Wayne) and worked opposite virtually every western star for the next 26 years, retiring in 1959.

His malevolence was at its best in the '30s when Taylor employed his gray-haired "fatherly figure" outwardly to disarm all around him while he plied his evil schemes with his henchies. In this type of role, viewers were never quite sure at first, because Taylor was often cast simply as a down-to-earth, honest father or uncle. As a matter of fact, by 1950, now in his late 60s, he'd pretty much shed his bad-guy image for strictly father-sheriff-doctor-townsman roles.

Some 350 films boast his name as well as dozens of TVers including a recurring role as Doc Brannon on "Man Without a Gun" ('57-'59) which starred Rex Reason. Taylor also starred as the family patriarch on the long running religious TV series "This Is the Life" ('52-'56). His last appearance was as a minister in "The FBI Story" ('59).

In serials, some 35, he was the most prolific chapterplay "pawn" or "suspect" in "Fighting Devil Dogs" ('38), "Iron Claw" ('41), "Manhunt of Mystery Island" ('45), "Crimson Ghost" ('46) and others. He arranged his own kidnapping and was revealed in the final chapter to be the mysterious Recorder in "Bruce Gentry" ('49). He's also in "Shadow of Chinatown" ('36), "Lone Ranger Rides Again" ('39), "Green Archer" ('40), "Terry and the Pirates" ('40), "Overland Mail" ('42) and others with his last being "Lost Planet" in '53 for Columbia.

Taylor never served in the military. He was married to Ann H. Taylor with at least one son, Jack F. Taylor. The Taylors resided at 8111 Stanford in Garden Grove, Orange County, California.

One of the kindliest appearing but most deadly screen heavies, Forrest Taylor died February 19, 1965, at 81, while a patient at Palm Harbor General Hospital in Garden Grove. Cause of death was pulmonary edema and congestive heart failure. He'd also suffered from emphysema. Taylor is laid to rest at Forest Lawn, Hollywood Hills Cemetery.

Forrest Taylor (center) and his gun-rannies (L-R) Ted Mapes, George Chesebro and Jack Kirk in "Texas Panhandle" with Charles Starrett ('45 Columbia).

Suggested Sampling of Taylor's Western Heavies:

- Riders of Destiny ('33 Lone Star) John Wayne
- Trail of Terror ('35 Supreme) Bob Steele
- Men of the Plains ('36 Colony) Rex Bell
- West of Nevada ('36 Colony) Rex Bell
- Phantom of the Range ('36 Victory) Tom Tyler
- Orphan of the Pecos ('37 Victory) Tom Tyler
- Lost Ranch ('37 Victory) Tom Tyler
- Roaming Cowboy ('37 Spectrum) Fred Scott
- Tex Rides With the Boy Scouts ('37 Grand National) Tex Ritter
- Arizona Days ('37 Grand National) Tex Ritter
- Ghost Town Riders ('38 Universal) Bob Baker
- Desert Patrol ('38 Supreme) Bob Steele
- Phantom Stage ('39 Universal) Bob Baker
- Code of the Cactus ('39 Victory) Tim McCoy
- Frontier Crusader ('40 PRC) Tim McCoy
- Ridin' the Cherokee Trail ('41 Monogram) Tex Ritter
- Mojave Firebrand ('44 Republic) Bill Elliott
- Texas Panhandle ('45 Columbia) Charles Starrett
- Lawless Empire ('45 Columbia) Charles Starrett
- Caravan Trail ('46 PRC) Eddie Dean
- Buckaroo From Powder River ('47 Columbia) Charles Starrett
- Stranger From Ponca City ('47 Columbia) Charles Starrett
- Stallion Canyon ('49 Astor) Ken Curtis

RAY TEAL

Ray Teal was best known as capable Sheriff Roy Coffee on TV's "Bonanza' for some ten years. But, in his over 300 movie and TV appearances in four decades (from '37-'74) he often played heavies as well as brave sheriffs, weak townsmen, bartenders, cavalry officers, doctors and other character roles.

Born in Grand Rapids, Michigan, January 12, 1902, Teal furthered his education at the Universities of Texas and California. A talented musician, he helped pay his way through college by playing the alto saxophone, even forming his own small band after graduation, Ray Teal and his Floridians. Teal spent some 15 years playing the sax in dance bands, eventually working in stock until making his way to Hollywood in '37. After study at the Actors Lab in Hollywood and work at the Pasadena Playhouse (under the name Raymond Steele), his screen debut was, appropriately enough, as an orchestra leader in "Sweethearts of the Navy".

The solidly built Teal, who always sported a thick mustache, quickly fell into B-westerns and serials at Republic ("Western Jamboree" '38 with Gene Autry, "Zorro Rides Again" '37 Republic serial), Columbia, Warner Bros. and others turning out program westerns and serials. During his formative years, Teal appeared in seven serials: "Zorro Rides Again" ('37 Republic), "Adventures of Red Ryder" ('40 Republic), "Green Hornet Strikes Again" ('41 Universal), "Don Winslow of the Navy" ('42 Universal), "Capt. Midnight" ('42 Columbia), "Raiders of Ghost City" ('44 Universal) and "Black Arrow" ('48).

By the '40s the always dependable Teal worked his way up into bigger pictures, essaying a variety of character parts in such classics as "Wing and a Prayer" ('44), "Thin Man Goes Home" ('45), "Sudan" ('45), "Captain Kidd" ('45), "Best Years of Our Lives" ('46), "Joan of Arc" ('48), "Great Gatsby" ('49), "Desperate Hours" ('55), "Judgement at Nuremberg" ('61) etc. Nevertheless, Teal always found time to return to his western roots in A's like "Gentle Annie" ('44), "Along Came Jones" ('45), "Don't Fence Me In" ('45), "Canyon Passage" ('46), "Pursued" ('47), "Cheyenne" ('47), "Fabulous Texan" ('47), "Black Bart" ('48), "Whispering Smith" ('48), "Ambush" ('49), "Oh! Susanna" ('51), "Distant Drums" ('51), "Cattle Town" ('52), "Man From Bitter Ridge" ('55) and many more.

"I never had a real yen to be an actor," Teal told an interviewer, "but it looked like a good way to make money. I enjoyed playing heavies if the parts were good and I could make it believable."

Teal entered television early on, specifically in 1950 for "The Lone Ranger". He also appeared on "Cheyenne", "Broken Arrow", "Tales of Wells Fargo", "Wagon Train", "Zorro", "Restless Gun", "Bronco", "Texan",

"Laramie", "Rawhide" and dozens more. He joined the cast of "Bonanza" in 1960 during the second season and remained until the '71-'72 (13th) season.

Teal continued to work—his last appearance was on the TV movie "The Hanged Man" in '74.

Following a long illness, the 74 year old actor died April 2, 1976, at St. John's Hospital in Santa Monica, California.

Suggested Sampling of Teal's Western Heavies:

- Western Jamboree ('38 Republic) Gene Autry
- Adventures of Red Ryder ('40 Republic serial) Don Barry
- Prairie Schooners ('40 Columbia) Bill Elliott
- Pony Post ('40 Universal) Johnny Mack Brown
- Along Came Jones ('45 RKO) Gary Cooper
- Whispering Smith ('48 Paramount) Alan Ladd
- Streets of Laredo ('49 Paramount) William Holden
- Lone Ranger: Never Say Die ('50) Clayton Moore
- Fort Worth ('51 WB) Randolph Scott
- Montana Belle ('52 Republic) Jane Russell
- Cattle Town ('52 Warner Bros.) Dennis Morgan
- Man From Bitter Ridge ('55 Universal) Lex Barker
- Rage at Dawn ('55 RKO) Randolph Scott
- Burning Hills ('56 Warner Bros.) Tab Hunter
- Guns of Fort Petticoat ('57 Columbia) Audie Murphy
- Utah Blaine ('57 Columbia) Rory Calhoun
- Maverick: Stage West ('57) James Garner
- Broken Arrow: Bounty Hunters ('57) John Lupton/Michael Ansara

TEX TERRY

Mild mannered in real life, the stocky, quiet Tex Terry, usually sporting a few days growth of whiskers, played uncredited henchmen, ranchers, bartenders and ranch hands throughout the '40s and '50s.

It's difficult to single out a western in which Terry had a really big role—but he can be spotted riding with the gang (or the posse) from Gene Autry's "Rovin' Tumbleweeds" ('39 Republic) on through Fred MacMurray's "Oregon Trail" ('59 20th Century Fox).

Virtually all of his roles in the '40s were at Repub-

Off screen, Tex Terry (R) was a good guy, seen here helping Roy Rogers and Dale Evans sell tickets for a Down's Syndrome fund-raiser. (Photo courtesy Whitey Hughes.)

lic with the Sunset Carson series making the best use of his character player abilities and dexterity with a bullwhip, which he later displayed at a Memphis Film Festival in the late '70s. (More than likely, Tex doubled Sunset using a whip in his westerns.)

Stuntman Whitey Hughes fondly recalls Tex as a "good buddy" of Roy Rogers and Dale Evans. "He loved Roy and Dale. Tex, Bill Coontz and I did a barroom brawl on stage at a little picture house in Newhall—then, we did it at the Shrine Auditorium in Los Angeles with Roy and Dale as a fund raiser for Down Syndrome. The Sons of the Pioneers, Doye O'Dell, Hoot Gibson, Andy Devine and others were there. He was a good whip man. Tex was a good man, a laid back kinda guy."

Edward Earl Terry was born August 22, 1902, in Coxville, Indiana. His first exposure to the world of entertainment was as part of a vaudeville team. Arriving in Hollywood circa 1922 as part of a troupe, he decided to stay, starting his career as a stuntman and bullwhip expert.

"When I first started working in moving pictures," Tex recalled, "I think my second western was with William S. Hart. It was near the end of his career. I did stunts for a long time. I'd get $2.50 a day for rides and falls or fights. If we'd get up to $7.50 a day we'd think we were great actors at work for a big future."

As Whitey Hughes noticed, "Tex left town early." Terry was 57 at the time of his last film in '59. At age 60, through a friend, he met Isabelle Draesemer, a motion picture agent. The couple married two years later in 1964. In '67 the couple moved back home to Indiana, finally settling down in Tex's hometown of Coxville in '78.

Terry's health declined. He had both kidneys removed and spent extended time in and out of hospitals. He had returned home on April 26, 1985, following his fourth hospital stay when he suffered a "gasping attack" while eating. He was rushed to Union Hospital in Terre Haute where he died at 82 on May 18, 1985. Terry is buried at the Coxville cemetery.

Suggested Sampling of Terry's Westerns:
- Covered Wagon Trails ('40 Monogram) Jack Randall
- Oregon Trail ('45 Republic) Sunset Carson
- Sunset In El Dorado ('45 Republic) Roy Rogers
- Alias Billy the Kid ('46 Republic) Sunset Carson
- El Paso Kid ('46 Republic) Sunset Carson
- Sioux City Sue ('46 Republic) Gene Autry
- Apache Rose ('47 Republic) Roy Rogers
- Gallant Legion ('48 Republic) William Elliott
- Gene Autry: Outlaw of Blue Mesa ('54) Gene Autry

GUY USHER

Dapperly deceitful Guy Usher's film career was brief (11 years) but prolific, crowding in roles in some 175 films from late '32 to early '43.

In 1935 alone Usher was featured in a staggering 28 films! 1935 saw him oppose Tim McCoy in Usher's first western at Columbia, "Law Beyond the Range" (made in late '34) when he was already 59.

Usher was born in Mason City, Iowa, May 9, 1875. Prior to his stage and screen career, Usher worked as a railroad engineer. Beginning his show business career in stock in Denver, Colorado, Usher came to the coast in mid '32 making his film debut uncredited in "Payment Deferred" ('32 MGM). A consummate actor, Usher played fathers, attorneys, detectives, doctors, editors, sheriffs, judges, senators—and heavies in nearly 30 westerns, primarily at RKO, Columbia and Republic stealing ranches and the like and being corralled by Gene Autry, George O'Brien, Charles Starrett, Roy Rogers and others. He did slip to poverty row once to make "Danger Ahead", a 1940 Renfrew of the Royal Mounted epic with James Newill. His serial work was minimal, a good role in "Buck Rogers" ('39 Universal) and minor roles in "Green Hornet" ('39 Universal) and "Junior G-Men of the Air" ('42 Universal).

Usher retired from screen work due to ill health and died at his ranch near San Diego June 16, 1944, at 69. He was survived by his wife.

Suggested Sampling of Usher's Western Heavies:
- Law of the Range ('35 Columbia) Tim McCoy
- Justice of the Range ('35 Columbia) Tim McCoy
- Old Wyoming Trail ('37 Columbia) Charles Starrett
- Timber Stampede ('39 RKO) George O'Brien
- King of Dodge City ('41 Columbia) Bill Elliott/Tex Ritter

RICK VALLIN

Rick (Richard) Vallin was born September 24, 1919, in Russia to a onetime prima ballerina of the Moscow Ballet. Following the Russian revolution, his mother and her young son escaped safely, arriving in New York in 1922. After five years in New York, he and his mother went to California where most of Rick's education was acquired.

While studying at the Pasadena Playhouse, Bliss-Hayden Theatre and the Masque Playhouse, Vallin supplemented his income by working as salesman, private detective, radio announcer, nightclub doorman, theatre usher, commercial fisherman, newsboy and dishwasher.

Rick appeared in a long succession of plays and made his screen debut among the students in MGM's "Dramatic School" in 1938.

Reportedly, but unconfirmed, Vallin enlisted in the Seabees where he did public relations and entertainment stints for the service. Timelines here seem a bit murky as by late 1941, he was making pictures for PRC, having reportedly been spotted while appearing in a Los Angeles stage play.

From the start, Rick had wanted to appear in westerns but never got the chance until he bought some cowboy garb and started wearing it into town. It worked. His first western was "King of the Stallions" in '42, followed by quite a few more opposite the 3 Mesquiteers, Bill Elliott, Wayne Morris, Tim Holt, Jon Hall and others—often playing Indians.

During the '40s and early '50s Rick appeared in all sorts of other films, especially at Monogram and Columbia.

Also during this time Rick made 17 serials (mostly for Sam Katzman): "Perils of the Royal Mounted" ('42 Columbia), " Desert Hawk" ('44 Columbia), "Brick Bradford" ('47 Columbia), "Sea Hound" ('47 Columbia), "Adventures of Sir Galahad" ('49 Columbia), "Batman and Robin" ('49 Columbia), "Cody of the Pony Express" ('50 Columbia), "Atom Man Vs. Superman" ('50 Columbia), "Roar of the Iron Horse" ('51 Columbia), "Captain Video" ('51 Columbia), "King of the Congo" ('52 Columbia), "Blackhawk" ('52 Columbia), "Son of Geronimo" ('52 Columbia), "Riding With Buffalo Bill" ('54 Columbia), "King of the Carnival" ('55 Republic), "Adventures of Captain Africa" ('55 Columbia), "Perils of the Wilderness" ('56 Columbia). Note that all of these were Columbia except one.

Actor John Hart told us, "He was one of my best friends for 15-20 years. His mother was a big wheel in the Russian community around Hollywood although Ricky didn't seem to take any part in it or care about it. I was doubling Jon Hall in a Sam Katzman feature ("Last of the Redmen" '47) when I met Rick. He was playing an Indian, he was dark-complexioned. He was a very competent actor. He started me fishing. We went fishing together for years…down to Mexico, out on boats, a lot of surf fishing at a cove up around Malibu that nobody went to much. I just had a lot of fun with Ricky. He lived with Victoria Faust, sort of an actress, very wealthy. She was married to a director and the three of them lived in the same house in Beverly Hills. The director, can't recall his name, was a nice guy and just put up with Rick moving in. We used to get together and do radio scripts and tape 'em just to keep our wits going. He never talked about his background. I lost track of him when I did the 'Lone Ranger' then went to Canada to do 'Hawkeye'. His life with Victoria fell apart when she remarried and moved to Mexico and he didn't have a home anymore."

Rick's career as a western heavy really blossomed with early TV. Throughout the '50s and '60s he worked in hundreds of TV shows, mostly westerns.

Rick also had lesser roles during the '50s in westerns like "Man From Bitter Ridge" ('55) with Lex Barker, "At Gunpoint" ('55) with Fred MacMurray, "Frontier Gambler" ('56) with Kent Taylor and "Raiders of Old California" ('57) with Jim Davis.

His last film was an unbilled part in Audie Murphy's "Quick Gun" in '64. What he did after leaving the screen is unknown but according to reports he drank quite heavily. Vallin was only 57 when he died August 31, 1977.

Suggested Sampling of Vallin's Western Heavies:

- Wagon Tracks West ('44 Republic) Bill Elliott
- Comanche Territory ('50 Universal-International) Macdonald Carey
- Cody of the Pony Express ('50 Columbia serial) Jock O'Mahoney
- Cowboy G-Men: Centerfire ('52) Russell Hayden
- Kit Carson: Range Master ('52) Bill Williams
- Kit Carson: Curse of the Albas ('52) Bill Williams
- Kit Carson: Badman's Escape ('53) Bill Williams
- Marksman ('53 Monogram) Wayne Morris
- Cowboy G-Men: High Heeled Boots ('53) Russell Hayden
- Topeka ('53 Monogram) Bill Elliott
- Homesteaders ('53 Monogram) Bill Elliott
- Gene Autry: Narrow Escape ('53) Gene Autry
- Riding With Buffalo Bill ('54 Columbia serial) Marshall Reed
- Annie Oakley: Annie and the Outlaw's Son ('54) Gail Davis
- Wild Bill Hickok: Boy and the Hound Dog ('54) Guy Madison
- Gene Autry: Prize Winner ('54) Gene Autry
- Gene Autry: Battle Axe ('54) Gene Autry
- Treasure of Ruby Hills ('55 Allied Artists) Zachary Scott
- Brave Eagle: The Challenge ('55) Keith Larsen
- Annie Oakley: Renegade's Return ('56) Gail Davis
- Buffalo Bill Jr.: Devil's Washbowl ('55) Dick Jones
- Annie Oakley: Front Trail ('56) Gail Davis
- Tales of Wells Fargo: Renegade Raiders ('57) Dale Robertson

LEE VAN CLEEF

They nicknamed him Angel Eyes. "Being born with a beady-eyed sneer was the best thing that ever happened to me," Lee Van Cleef smiled as only he could.

Tall and lean, pointed nose, high cheekbones, cruel mouth, balding head—and those cold-steel squinty eyes, these physical attributes served to make Van Cleef one of the major heavies of screen westerns.

Born Clarence Leroy Van Cleef Jr., January 9, 1925, in Somerville, New Jersey, his parents (Clarence Leroy Van Cleef and Marian L. Van Fleet) were both new Jersey natives of Dutch extraction. Lee's father, a WWI veteran who served two years in Europe, worked as an accountant and bank cashier. His mother, by some reports, was once a professional singer. His father, an outdoorsman, taught Lee to shoot by age 10.

In June '42, after his junior year in high school, Lee took a summer job on an area farm. He quit the farming job in September to begin his senior year, but in October '42 the 17 year old left high school to enlist in the Navy. During this era, many high school seniors were given condensed courses to complete high school before entering service. Navy documents attest Lee did receive a high school diploma. Following recruit training as a Sound Man and in Mine Craft, he was assigned to the USS Incredible.

On December 10, 1943, Lee married high school sweetheart Patsy Ruth Kahle before he was sent to sea, eventually serving in the Atlantic and Pacific. He was discharged from the Navy March 6, 1946. During the war Lee had seen service aboard a subchaser in the Caribbean and a mine-sweeper in the Mediterranean and the China Sea, earning him several medals.

After Van Cleef was discharged, he and his wife worked in a Maine hunting/fishing camp. Before '46 was over, he was a farmer on the estate of a prominent socialite.

With the birth of two children, Alan in '47, Deborah in '48, Lee found better paying work at a Somerville factory. Also from '46-'50 he maintained a private practice as an accountant for several local businesses.

Encouraged by a factory co-worker, Lee became involved with the Clinton (NJ) Music Hall Players, appearing in "Our Town" and "Heaven Can Wait".

Enamored with stage work, Lee went to New York and obtained a small role in "Mister Roberts", then toured for 15 months in '50-'51 with the hit play. It was his work as a policeman in this production that caught the eye of producer Stanley Kramer who was preparing "High Noon". Kramer initially offered Lee the role of the deputy (which eventually went to Lloyd Bridges) with the stipulation Van Cleef have his nose surgically altered to appear less menacing. Lee refused and Kramer cast him as one of the heavies at $500 a week.

Van Cleef quickly learned to ride and, as production on "High Noon" didn't start til September '51, Lee was able to find work as a heavy on two episodes of Jock Mahoney's "Range Rider": "Greed Rides the Range" and "Outlaw's Double". Dick Jones, Dick West on "The Range Rider", was unaware these were Van Cleef's first screen roles, "He came on as an old professional. I liked working with him. He was very handy…did a good fight scene. I sure didn't know it was his first job."

Van Cleef is the first character seen on screen in "High Noon" and, without a word of dialogue, made a lasting impression in the Academy Award winning film, forever establishing Lee as a heavy.

After appearing in dozens of film and TV westerns, Lee was driving home from Lone Pine, California, in the Fall of '58 (after completing location work on "Ride Lonesome") with his wife and three children (a third son David had been born by this time) when he was involved in a head on collision with another car. The wreck fractured his left arm in two places and shattered his left kneecap, hospitalizing him for a month. Lee was told he may never walk again without a limp or ride a horse. However, in a struggle Lee later termed "mind over matter," he disproved the doctor's theories.

Tragically, the accident and aftermath led to a drinking problem for Lee which ended his 15 year marriage.

In 1960, Lee remarried, to Joan Miller. They adopted a daughter, Denise.

With westerns on the decline by the mid '60s, Lee hit bad financial times. Joan was working as an IBM secretary and Lee was doing freelance house painting and living off residuals. Good fortune returned in the person of Italian director Sergio Leone who had struck gold with Clint Eastwood in "A Fistful of Dollars". For the follow-up, "For a Few Dollars More", Leone wanted Van Cleef for his bounty hunter protagonist. That film, like "High Noon", changed Van Cleef's life.

Lee went on to make over 20 more Spaghetti westerns through the late '70s, never returning to the TV screen again until he starred in his own short-lived series, "The Master" in 1984. More than any other actor, he brought prestige to the Italian western.

While making 1974's "The Stranger and the Gunfighter", Lee met Barbara Hevelone, a concert pianist working on the score for the film. By 1975, he divorced Joan and married Barbara on July 13, 1976.

Heart disease slowed his work in the late '70s. He had a pacemaker installed in the early '80s.

Besides the failed 13 episode run of his series "The Master", Lee's screen roles were on a definite downturn as he accepted parts in lesser budgeted films.

On December 16, 1989, a few weeks shy of his 65th birthday, heart disease caught up with "the man with gunsight eyes" as he collapsed at his home in Oxnard, California. He was taken to St. John's Hospital where he died. Throat cancer was listed as a secondary cause of death. Lee had taken up smoking a pipe while in the Navy and can be seen smoking in many of his films. He was buried at Forest Lawn Cemetery in Hollywood Hills, California. His friend from "Mr. Roberts", actor Rance Howard gave the eulogy. Rory Calhoun, Harry Carey Jr. and others were pallbearers.

"Bad guys have always been my bag," Lee once explained, "I look mean without even trying. Audiences just naturally hate me on screen. I could play a role in a tuxedo and people would think I was rotten. You can do much more with a villain part. Movies are full of leading men—most of whom aren't working. It's much harder to find a good villain."

Suggested Sampling of Van Cleef's Western Heavies:

- Range Rider: Outlaw's Double ('52) Jock Mahoney
- High Noon ('52 Columbia) Gary Cooper
- Untamed Frontier ('52 Universal) Joseph Cotton
- Lone Ranger: Brown Pony ('53) John Hart
- Lawless Breed ('53 Universal) Rock Hudson
- Nebraskan ('53 Columbia) Phil Carey
- Tumbleweed ('53 Universal) Audie Murphy
- Stories of the Century: Frank and Jesse James ('54) Jim Davis
- The Desperado ('54 Allied Artists) Wayne Morris
- Yellow Tomahawk ('54 United Artists) Rory Calhoun
- Gene Autry: Outlaw Warning ('54) Gene Autry
- Kit Carson: Missing Hacienda ('54) Bill Williams
- Rin Tin Tin: Rin Tin Tin and the Raging River ('54) Lee Aaker
- Rails Into Laramie ('54 Universal) John Payne
- Annie Oakley: Annie Breaks an Alibi ('55) Gail Davis
- Buffalo Bill Jr.: Boomer's Blunder ('55) Dick Jones
- Treasure of Ruby Hills ('55 Allied Artists) Zachary Scott
- A Man Alone ('55 Republic) Ray Milland
- Brave Eagle: Shield of Honor ('55) Keith Larsen
- Badge of Marshal Brennan ('57 Allied Artists) Jim Davis
- Last Stagecoach West ('57 Republic) Jim Davis
- Tales of Wells Fargo: Alder Gulch ('57) Dale Robertson
- Trackdown: The Town ('57) Robert Culp
- Joe Dakota: ('57 Universal) Jock Mahoney
- The Bravados ('58 TCR) Gregory Peck
- Lawman: The Deputy ('58) John Russell
- Frontier Doctor: Great Stagecoach Robbery ('58) Rex Allen
- Rifleman: Deadly Wait ('59) Chuck Connors
- Tombstone Territory: Gun Hostage ('59) Pat Conway
- Yancy Derringer: Outlaw at Liberty ('59) Jock Mahoney
- Wanted Dead or Alive: The Hostage ('59) Steve McQueen
- Law of the Plainsman: Clear Title ('59) Michael Ansara
- Ride Lonesome ('59 Columbia) Randolph Scott
- Cimarron City: Town Is a Prisoner ('59) George Montgomery
- Northwest Passage: Fourth Brother ('59) Keith Larsen
- Deputy: Palace of Chance ('60) Henry Fonda
- Gunsmoke: Old Flame ('60) James Arness
- Lawman: Return of Owny O'Reilly ('60) John Russell
- Laramie: .45 Calibre ('60) Robert Fuller

- Bonanza: Blood Line ('60) Lorne Greene
- Posse From Hell ('61 Universal-International) Audie Murphy
- Rifleman: Clarence Bibbs Story ('61) Chuck Connors
- Stagecoach West: Never Walk Alone ('61) Wayne Rogers
- Cheyenne: Trouble Street ('61) Clint Walker
- Man Who Shot Liberty Valance ('62 Paramount) John Wayne
- Rifleman: Death Never Rides Alone ('62) Chuck Connors
- Destry: Destry Had a Little Lamb ('64) John Gavin
- For a Few Dollars More ('65 United Artists) Clint Eastwood
- Laredo: Quarter Past Eleven ('66) Peter Brown
- Gunsmoke: My Father, My Son ('66) James Arness
- The Good, The Bad and the Ugly ('66 United Artists) Clint Eastwood
- Take a Hard Ride ('75 20th Century Fox) Jim Brown

GREGORY WALCOTT

Gregory Walcott grew up in North Carolina and wisely retained his southern accent which he often used to great advantage in creating laid-back, soft spoken characters that belied their evil intents. This malevolence was never better portrayed than as cold blooded killer Farmer Perkins on "Death at Dawn", a first season "Bonanza" episode.

Greg was born Bernard Mattox on January 13, 1928, in Wendell, North Carolina, and raised in nearby Wilson beginning when Greg was six. His parents were Robert and Mabel Mattox who lived in North Carolina all their lives. Greg's dad worked as a salesman in the furniture business.

For three months in the summer of '44, at 16, Greg worked in wartime Washington, D.C., as a messenger for the Civil Service Commission. Returning to Wilson, in his junior year, he played 2nd string on the 1944 North Carolina State Champion football team. His senior year of 1945 he was supposed to graduate but stayed behind another year to play football, hoping to win a college scholarship. He played on the '46 team which were state champs once again.

Greg left school in January of '47, joining the Army on an 18 month enlistment. Following basic training at Ft. Bragg, he served as an athletic instructor at Ft. Monmouth, New Jersey, and rose to the rank of corporal.

Discharged in July of '48, Greg attended Furman University for a couple of semesters but left in '49.

Enthralled with the movies from a young age, with $100 in his pocket, Greg decided in September of 1949 to hitchhike to Hollywood and become an actor. Six days and several YMCA nights later, Greg arrived in California.

Attending Ben Bard drama school on his G.I. bill, he kept himself alive by dong odd jobs. Soon he began to appear in plays.

Finding an agent through an actor friend, Greg obtained his first film role as a smoke jumper in "Red Skies of Montana" ('52 20th Century Fox).

Other roles followed, including a part on Republic's "Stories of the Century" in '54 as one of the Younger Brothers, but Greg's breakthrough came as a tough drill instructor in Warner Bros.' realistic "Battle Cry" ('55). As a result of that role, Warners placed Greg under contract and cast him in several other major films ("Mr. Roberts", "Court Martial of Billy Mitchell", etc.) as well as episodes of their TV westerns such as "Cheyenne" and "Sugarfoot".

In 1954 Greg married former Miss San Diego runner-up Barbara Watkins. The couple are parents to Jina, Pamela and Todd. Barbara and Greg met at a meeting of the Hollywood Christian Group in Encino under the auspices of Roy Rogers and Dale Evans.

Throughout the '50s and early '60s, Greg appeared on nearly every major TV western, but it was another drill sergeant role in "The Outsider" in '61 that led to another studio contract, this one with Universal who placed him on the TV series "87th Precinct" as one of the lead detectives.

Now better established, the '70s saw Greg in several major films with Clint Eastwood, a friend since guest starring on several "Rawhide" episodes. Greg was in Eastwood's "Joe Kidd", "Thunderbolt and Lightfoot",

"Eiger Sanction" and "Every Which Way But Loose".

But Greg always enjoyed the role of the heavy. "The villains always seemed to have a little more dimension, a little more color, a little more character. Roles that force me to stretch my range as an actor. I rather feel challenged by doing a role that is not me at all, it's kind of fun too." And anyone who has met Greg at one of the several film festivals he's attended can attest to the fact this "good guy" is no heavy.

In recent years Greg became a lay minister and a renowned speaker at colleges and civic clubs. In 1967 an honorary Doctor of Laws degree was conferred on him by Georgetown University in Kentucky. He's made numerous commencement addresses and received a number of civic honors.

In 2004 Greg published his memoirs of 40 years in the business in HOLLYWOOD ADVENTURES (Wilson Daily Times Press).

Suggested Sampling of Walcott's Western Heavies:

- Stories of the Century: Younger Brothers ('54) Jim Davis
- Cheyenne: The Travelers ('56) Clint Walker
- Sugarfoot: Bullet Proof ('58) Will Hutchins
- Rifleman: Angry Gun ('58) Chuck Connors
- Trackdown: The Vote ('59) Robert Culp
- Tales of Wells Fargo: Desert Showdown ('59) Dale Robertson
- Maverick: Full House ('59) James Garner
- Bat Masterson: Mr. Fourpaws ('60) Gene Barry
- Bonanza: Death at Dawn ('60) Lorne Greene
- Deputy: Ma Mack ('60) Henry Fonda/Allen Case
- Tall Man: The Shawl ('60) Barry Sullivan, Clu Gulager
- Wyatt Earp: The Doctor ('60) Hugh O'Brian
- Laramie: Drifter's Gold ('60) John Smith/Robert Fuller
- Rawhide: Incident at Poco Tiempo ('60) Clint Eastwood
- Tales of Wells Fargo: Escort to Santa Fe ('60) Dale Robertson
- Laramie: Trigger Point ('61) Robert Fuller
- Bat Masterson: Farmer With a Badge ('61) Gene Barry
- Bonanza: Song In the Dark ('63) Pernell Roberts
- Dakotas: Thunder In Pleasant Valley ('63) Larry Ward
- Rawhide: Incident of the Gallows Tree ('63) Eric Fleming
- A Man Called Shenandoah: The Accused ('66) Robert Horton
- Shane: Day of the Hawk ('66) David Carradine
- Big Valley: Man From Nowhere ('66) Richard Long
- Bonanza: Amigo ('67) Lorne Greene
- Daniel Boone: The Renegade ('67) Fess Parker
- Bonanza: A Darker Shadow ('69) Michael Landon
- Bonanza: Thornton's Account ('70) Michael Landon
- Bonanza: Riot ('72) Lorne Greene
- The Cowboys: The Avengers ('74) Jim Davis

FRANCIS WALKER

Francis (Frank) Walker, with over 100 screen credits as an actor and often stunt-double from '34-'45, is one of the western screen's mystery men. We could locate no biographical information on Walker.

Walker made his screen debut playing the uncredited role of a deputy in 1934's "Man Trailer" with Buck Jones.

Throughout the rest of the '30s Walker stunted in or played uncredited small roles in some 50 independent B-westerns opposite Harry Carey, Bill Cody, Tom Tyler, John Wayne, Big Boy Williams, Tim McCoy, Kermit Maynard and others. Also during this period, he can be spotted in several serials, "Spider's Web" ('38 Columbia), "Robinson Crusoe of Clipper Island" ('37 Republic) and "Great Adventures of Wild Bill Hickok" ('38 Columbia).

By 1939 Walker was most likely under contract to Columbia as all three of his films were Columbia B's opposite Bill Elliott, Charles Starrett, Bob Allen.

Walker's credits come to a halt in 1942 and it's quite likely he was involved in WWII. We find one appearance in 1945 ("Return of the Durango Kid"), leaving about a three year gap, which further indicates military service. Speculation is Walker at first tried to return to film work in 1945 after the War but then decided on another line of work as, at the time, he would only have been in his early 30s. Perhaps he surmised that, not having made a huge mark on the film industry, it was time to move on. A postcard from actor Pierce Lyden to Ralph Absher indicated that apparently sometime in the '60s Walker was employed as a truck driver in northern California.

But for western fans, he left us with a satisfying decade of villainous roles. He probably died not realizing how important he was to '30s front row kids.

Suggested Sampling of Walker's Western Heavies:

- Reckless Buckaroo ('36 Spectrum) Bill Cody
- Law of the Ranger ('37 Columbia) Bob Allen
- Galloping Dynamite ('37 Ambassador) Kermit Maynard
- Rolling Caravans ('38 Columbia) Jack Luden
- Return of Wild Bill ('40 Columbia) Bill Elliott
- Man From Tumbleweeds ('40 Columbia) Bill Elliott
- Roaring Frontiers ('41 Columbia) Bill Elliott/Tex Ritter
- King of Dodge City ('41 Columbia) Bill Elliott/Tex Ritter
- Lawless Plainsmen ('42 Columbia) Charles Starrett/Russell Hayden
- Prairie Gunsmoke ('42 Columbia) Bill Elliott/Tex Ritter

Russell Hayden to the rescue of pal Charles Starrett as he's held fast by Francis Walker in Columbia's "Overland to Deadwood" ('42).

ROBERT WALKER

Six foot tall, 160 lb. Robert Donald Walker entered films with the Edison Company in 1913 and is not to be confused with the much later actor (1918-1951) who was married to Jennifer Jones and is the father of Robert Walker Jr. Nor is he to be confused with screenwriter Robert G. Walker.

Our Robert Walker was born in Bethlehem, Pennsylvania, June 18, 1888. His mother's maiden name was Hilliard. Her brother, Walker's uncle, was noted Broadway stage actor Robert Cochran Hilliard (1857-1927), active on Broadway from 1887-1917. Walker was educated at the prestigious Horace Mann School in New York. He was not only a stage, musical and screen actor, but wrote a few screen stories.

For an actor who appeared in over 70 silent features from 1913-1929, he's received little attention in film history. He was a leading man in 13 features from 1915-1920 before he made his first westerns with Tom Mix ("The Texan") and House Peters Sr. ("Isobel or The Trail's End") in '20.

In the '20s he regularly appeared in westerns opposite William S. Hart, Tom Mix, J. P. McGowan, Franklyn Farnum, Dick Hatton, Ben Wilson, Buffalo Bill

Jr., Ken Maynard, Billy Sullivan, Yakima Canutt (Walker wrote the scenario for "Three Outcasts"), Buddy Roosevelt and others.

In the sound era, already 42, most of the pictures he worked in were of the poverty row level. He was a mainstay with anything Harry S. Webb was producing or directing from 1930-1940. In the '30s he added a mustache to his handsome face to enhance his villainous demeanor. Walker appeared in at least 16 sound serials with his most noteworthy roles in "Voice From the Sky" ('30 Universal), "Custer's Last Stand" ('36 Stage and Screen) and "Black Coin" ('36 Stage and Screen).

As he grew older, his parts became smaller and he was often uncredited in small roles from the late '30s until his last part as a townsman in Gene Autry's "Riders In the Sky" in '49.

Robert Walker died in Los Angeles, California, March 4, 1954, at 65.

Suggested Sampling of Walker's Western Heavies:

- Rip Snorter ('25 Arrow) Dick Hatton
- Upland Rider ('28 First National) Ken Maynard
- Canyon Hawks ('30 Big 4) Yakima Canutt
- Phantom of the Desert ('30 Syndicate) Jack Perrin
- Breed of the West ('30 Big 4) Wally Wales
- Sign of the Wolf ('31 Metropolitan serial) Rex Lease
- Kid From Arizona ('31 Cosmos) Jack Perrin
- Headin' For Trouble ('31 Big 4) Bob Custer
- Man From New Mexico ('32 Monogram) Tom Tyler
- Scarlet Brand ('32 Big 4) Bob Custer
- Strawberry Roan ('33 Universal) Ken Maynard
- Jaws of Justice ('33 Principal) Richard Terry (aka Jack Perrin)
- Potluck Pards ('34 Reliable) Bud 'n' Ben (Harry Myers, Ben Corbett)
- Rawhide Mail ('34 Reliable) Jack Perrin
- Loser's End ('35 Reliable) Jack Perrin
- Fighting Caballero ('35 Superior) Rex Lease
- Texas Jack ('35 Reliable) Jack Perrin
- Rough Riding Ranger ('35 Superior) Rex Lease
- Custer's Last Stand ('36 Stage and Screen serial) Rex Lease
- Caryl of the Mountains ('36 Reliable) Francis X. Bushman Jr.
- Mysterious Pilot ('37 Columbia serial) Frank Hawks
- El Diablo Rides ('39 Metropolitan) Bob Steele
- Pioneer Days ('40 Monogram) Jack Randall

ANTHONY WARDE

You automatically distrusted Anthony Warde on sight. Under a snap-brim hat, with thin lips, roughly dimpled, but firmly set chin and cold steely eyes, he was the perfect henchman, appearing in 23 serials at Republic, Universal and Columbia from 1937's "Tim Tyler's Luck" (as Spider Webb's henchman Garry Drake) to 1950's "Radar Patrol Vs. Sky King". 13 years of serial villainy! Plus several westerns.

Born November 4, 1908, in Philadelphia, Pennsylvania, he grew up in Danbury, Connecticut, where his father was a hatter. Tony's early interest was in music and he played for a while with his brother's dance band. Tony went to Los Angeles in 1930 during the Depression and enrolled in a drama class, supporting himself through odd jobs. He read for a part at the Beverly Hills Little Theatre and won the role. Later, in 1933, he was accepted at the Pasadena Playhouse. Although he preferred comedy and found it easier to do (unlike many actors), he did a play, "Blind Alley" where he portrayed a neurotic killer which led to film roles, forever cast as a heavy. Warde called it quits in 1956 (except for a small role in "The Carpetbaggers" in '64) and opened a successful clothing store in Hollywood.

In "Flash Gordon's Trip To Mars" in '38 Warde was the Mighty Toran of the Forest People. He's well remembered as Killer Kane, arch enemy of Buster Crabbe's "Buck Rogers" in '39. He was paid $100 a day for two days work, however, he completed the part, 113 camera set-ups, in one day and was paid the full $200.

Other important serial roles were in "Dick Tracy Vs. Crime Inc." ('41), "Masked Marvel" ('43), "Monster and the Ape" ('45), "King of the Forest Rangers" ('46), "Hop Harrigan" ('46), "Black Widow" ('47) and "Dangers of the Canadian Mounted" ('48). Tony told interviewer Greg Jackson in 1974 that he preferred working at Universal because, "…generally speaking, Universal spent more money on their serials. Columbia was the cheapest. But it was a matter of the personalities you worked with at the time. We had fun in those days wherever we were."

Having been likened to a new Paul Muni in stage productions, Warde said he only did serials "as a livelihood. I wasn't given the opportunity…the time…to do anything of a serious nature. I always felt self conscious playing a heavy. I'm really a nice guy. (Laughs)" Warde recalls "Masked Marvel" as a horrible experience because the four leading men, hired because of their similar appearance, could not act or remember their lines. Warde also offered up great praise for the stuntmen… "Duke Green was really the mentor. Dale Van Sickel would double for me for obvious reasons, if he was available."

Anthony Warde died in Hollywood, January 8, 1975, of cancer. He was survived by his wife, Frances.

Suggested Sampling of Warde's Western Heavies:

- Chip of the Flying U ('39 Universal) Johnny Mack Brown
- Ridin' On a Rainbow ('41 Republic) Gene Autry
- Riders of the Deadline ('43 United Artists) William Boyd
- Cisco Kid Returns ('45 Monogram) Duncan Renaldo
- North of the Border ('46 Screen Guild) Russell Hayden
- King of the Bandits ('47 Monogram) Gilbert Roland
- King of the Forest Rangers ('46 Republic serial) Larry Thompson
- Where the North Begins ('47 Screen Guild) Russell Hayden
- Dangers of the Canadian Mounted ('48 Republic serial) Jim Bannon
- Trail of the Yukon ('49 Monogram) Kirby Grant
- Sky King: Threatening Bomb ('52) Kirby Grant
- Jim Bowie: Jim Bowie and His Slave ('56) Scott Forbes
- Wyatt Earp: The Judge ('60) Hugh O'Brian

WALLY WEST

Wally West was usually uncredited and seldom said much of anything on screen although he was one of western films' busiest support players and stuntmen.

West, whose true name was Theo A. Wynn, was born in Gough, Texas, October 11, 1903. His father was a Texan with his mother (maiden name Adams) coming from Georgia. He honed his skills as a rider during his younger years as a working cowboy on a Texas ranch.

Although he may have gotten into the film business as early as 1926 as a rider and stuntman, this is unconfirmed as 1930 census records place him in Dallas, Texas, living with his wife, Mary E. (to whom he was married when he was 20), his 7 year old stepdaughter, his mother-in-law and five roomers. At that time he was working as a muligraph operator for an insurance company.

His first noticed, uncredited role is as a detective in "Her Forgotten Past" ('33 Mayfair) with Henry B. Walthall. By 1935 though he was doubling Gene Autry in Mascot's "Phantom Empire" serial as well as essaying the part of a Muranian soldier, being a bartender in Lane Chandler's "Lone Bandit", seen as a poker player in John Wayne's "Desert Trail", riding as a cowhand in Tim McCoy's "Riding Wild", portraying a sheriff's deputy in Bob Steele's "Alias John Law"—and much more.

Possessed with a Texas twang but firmly established as a stuntman and bit player he was working in virtually everyone's B-westerns in one capacity or the other (or both) from then on through 1956.

West doubled Bob Livingston at Republic, Tim McCoy at PRC, George Houston at PRC, Ken Maynard at Colony, Buster Crabbe at PRC and badmen of every stripe at all the studios. Even in the early television years director Earl Bellamy remembers West, who was not a particularly large man, doubling Lee Aaker on "The Adventures of Rin Tin Tin" from time to time. (West was also a regular on that TV series as one of the Cavalrymen.) He was also seen on such TVers as "Brave Eagle", "Roy Rogers", "Kit Carson", "Buffalo Bill Jr." and "Lone Ranger". West can also be glimpsed doing bits and stunts in over 13 serials, including "Vigilantes Are Coming" ('36 Republic), "Mysterious Dr. Satan" ('40 Republic), "Son Of Geronimo" ('52 Columbia), "The Vigilante" ('47 Columbia) and "Atom Man Vs. Superman" ('50 Columbia).

When he first really got rolling in 1935, West even got to star once, under the name Tom Wynn, in Victor Adamson's independently produced Security Pictures cheapie, "Desert Mesa", unfortunately a lost title.

Stuntman Whitey Hughes recalled Wally with a smile, "Wally was just a good down-to-earth guy. He was just a guy to like, a real nice, nice man. As far as I'm concerned, he was a qualified stunt guy…he was a good hand."

His last big screen appearance was in Allan "Rocky" Lane's "El Paso Stampede" ('53 Republic) (also Lane's last starrer) although West continued to work on TV til '56.

West was 79 when he died in Los Angeles, May 16, 1984.

Suggested Sampling of West's Western Heavies:

- Roamin' Wild ('36 Reliable) Tom Tyler
- Vengeance of Rannah ('36 Reliable) Bob Custer
- Billy the Kid's Fighting Pals ('41 PRC) Bob Steele
- Billy the Kid Trapped ('42 PRC) Bob Steele
- Pioneer Justice ('47 PRC) Lash LaRue

CHARLES "SLIM" WHITAKER

Charles "Slim" Whitaker came off the real west range to become one of the B-western's earliest and principal no-good, dirty, rotten polecats. Through the years the pounds began to pile up on him so that he was not only a "heavy" on screen, but heavy in real life.

Charles Orby (not Orbie as often reported, according to family members) Whitaker was born July 29, 1893, in Kansas City, Missouri. His parents were Sherman Whitaker, a Missouri native, and Bell Shepered, place of birth unknown. Slim's background is supplied by Tom Bahn, who is married to Slim's great granddaughter, and was fortunate enough to glean information on the family from Leota Whitaker Gandrau, Slim's daughter and Rose Banks, Slim's granddaughter.

Slim married Ethel Maze in 1910 and shortly thereafter left Missouri, heading for California. Over the years the couple had three children—Leota born 1915, June born 1917 and Charles in 1920.

After a brief career on the rodeo circuit, Slim joined several cattle drives, eventually ending up as a cowboy at the Chowchilla Ranch in California's San Joaquin Valley where hands earned about a dollar a day and the days were 18 hours long. During this period Slim became friends with other cowboys who would all find their way into the burgeoning motion picture business—Bill Gillis, Hank Bell, Jack Montgomery, Ed Hendershot.

In 1912, the Chowchilla Ranch owner announced he had sold the ranch. Somehow the cowhands got the mistaken idea the new owner was a British concern and, pledging they'd never work for a foreigner, the five friends "up and quit," riding north looking for ranch work. After traveling 120 miles on horseback, they stumbled upon Broncho Billy filming a western in Niles Canyon where they were hired as riding extras and stuntmen. Unfortunately, the work wasn't steady and they were only paid for the days they worked.

In late 1913, Slim headed south hoping to find jobs in Southern California. Thanks to his short stint with Broncho Billy, the film studios were quick to hire him as a riding extra in westerns where he earned five times the wages he'd been drawing as a ranch hand. Although his first film was "Tested By Fire" in '14, his first credited western is the one-reeler "When Thieves Fall Out" ('14 Selig) with Harold Lockwood. Plenty more opposite William Farnum, Wally Wales, Buffalo Bill Jr., Bob Custer, Buddy Roosevelt, Yakima Canutt, Pete Morrison and Ken Maynard followed.

Leota says whenever the kids were around show business folks, Slim protected his children from studio riff-raff. He was a big, easy-going man, Leota declared, "You didn't want to get him mad."

In April of 1920, Jack Montgomery and Hank Bell had migrated to Southern California and met Slim at his favorite Hollywood bar. Unable to find work as ranch hands, Slim introduced them to film production in Edendale where both men became well known and had long careers in westerns.

According to Leota, the actors were required to supply their own clothes, saddle, guns and spurs. Players were to be on the job at five in the morning if they were shooting at the studio. If they were working on location they could catch a ride at the studio or, as Slim usually did, wait by the curb in front of his North Hollywood house. Leota remembers Wally Wales, Charlie King and Al Bridge were like her uncles, spending so much time at her house that it was if they lived there. Charlie and Al were regular drinking buddies of Slim's with the poker games always at Slim's place.

After 34 years of marriage, Ethel became tired of rowdy cowboys playing poker, getting drunk and passing out at her house. She divorced Slim in '44, remarried and bought a restaurant on San Fernando Rd. in Sunland, California. She and Slim remained friends and he was often seen having a meal or coffee at the restaurant—which is probably the basis for the erroneous oft-printed info that Slim was a restaurant short-order cook in his later years. Actually, after leaving films in 1949, Slim worked as a bartender at a cowboy bar in Sunland and later as a fireman for a couple of years, then retired.

Slim had five grandchildren and lived to see the first of 13 great-grandchildren. He died at 66 June 27, 1960, at Cedars of Lebanon Hospital from a heart attack and was buried at Valhalla Cemetery in North Hollywood.

During the post silent era, Slim was among the busiest of support players. English film historian Nick Nichols once calculated Slim appeared in over 584 films over 35 years, most of which were westerns. It would be hard to find a B-western star to whom Slim had not been a nemesis. His last westerns were a pair with Eddie Dean ("Westward Trail" and "Black Hills", both '48 PRC) and a bit in Universal's "Gal Who Took the West" ('49).

Whitaker maintained a frequent presence in some 22 serials with his best parts in "Law of the Wild" ('34 Mascot), "Roaring West" ('35 Universal) and "Lost Jungle" ('34 Mascot).

Montie Montana once said, "Slim was a hard drinking cowboy that enjoyed kidding and telling jokes. He should have been a comedian." As a matter of fact, RKO, after letting Ray Whitley and Chill Wills be George O'Brien's saddlepals, gave ol' Slim a crack at it in "Fighting Gringo" ("39), "Bullet Code" ('40) and as Silent in the best of the bunch (with good billing too), "Prairie Law" ('40). And he was downright good at it! But there were to be no more.

No matter, he was soon right back at his nasty, underhanded villainy, right where we expected him to be. Undoubtedly, one of the Top 10 western screen badmen.

Wild Bill Elliott brings law to the "Frontiers of '49" as he manhandles hefty Slim Whitaker ('39 Columbia).

Suggested Sampling of Whitaker's Western Heavies:

- Shadow Ranch ('30 Columbia) Buck Jones
- Under Montana Skies ('30 Tiffany) Kenneth Harlan
- Oklahoma Cyclone ('30 Tiffany) Bob Steele
- In Old Cheyenne ('31 SonoArt-World Wide) Rex Lease
- One Way Trail ('31 Columbia) Tim McCoy
- Freighters of Destiny ('31 RKO) Tom Keene
- Rider of the Plains ('31 Syndicate) Tom Tyler
- Texas Tornado ('32 Kent) Lane Chandler
- Law and Lawless ('32 Majestic) Jack Hoxie
- Somewhere In Sonora ('33 Warner Bros.) John Wayne
- Trouble Busters ('33 Majestic) Jack Hoxie
- Deadwood Pass ('33 Monarch) Tom Tyler
- Drum Taps ('33 World Wide) Ken Maynard
- Cactus Kid ('34 Reliable) Jack Perrin
- Terror of the Plains ('34 Reliable) Tom Tyler
- Silent Valley ('35 Reliable) Tom Tyler
- Arizona Bad Man ('35 Kent) Reb Russell
- Lone Bandit ('35 Empire) Lane Chandler
- Rio Rattler ('35 Reliable) Tom Tyler
- Coyote Trails ('35 Reliable) Tom Tyler
- Outlaw Tamer ('35 Empire) Lane Chandler
- Range Warfare ('35 Kent) Reb Russell
- Lawless Range ('35 Republic) John Wayne
- Last of the Clintons ('35 Ajax) Harry Carey
- Santa Fe Bound ('36 Reliable) Bob Custer
- Ridin' On ('36 Reliable) Tom Tyler
- Ghost Patrol ('36 Puritan) Tim McCoy
- Fast Bullets ('36 Reliable) Tom Tyler
- Rio Grande Ranger ('36 Columbia) Bob Allen
- Melody of the Plains ('37 Spectrum) Fred Scott
- Silver Trail ('37 Reliable) Rex Lease
- Stagecoach Days ('38 Columbia) Jack Luden
- In Early Arizona ('38 Columbia) Bill Elliott
- Pioneer Trail ('38 Columbia) Jack Luden
- Phantom Gold ('38 Columbia) Jack Luden
- Lightning Carson Rides Again ('38 Victory) Tim McCoy
- Frontiers of '49 ('39 Columbia) Bill Elliott
- Law Comes to Texas ('39 Columbia) Bill Elliott
- Arizona Bound ('41 RKO) Rough Riders
- Along the Rio Grande ('41 RKO) Tim Holt
- Arizona Stagecoach ('42 Monogram) Range Busters
- Mysterious Rider ('42 PRC) Buster Crabbe
- Silver Bullet ('42 Universal) Johnny Mack Brown
- Raiders of Red Gap ('43 PRC) Bob Livingston
- Marshal of Gunsmoke ('44 Universal) Tex Ritter
- Law of the Lash ('47 PRC) Lash LaRue
- Return of the Lash ('47 PRC) Lash LaRue

DAN WHITE

Dan White's leathery high-cheekboned face with its tight-drawn expressionless mouth and snake eyes were perfect casting for western badmen in the '40s and '50s.

Dan White was born March 25, 1908, to George and Orpha White about a mile from the Suwannee River in the sleepy little town of Falmouth, Florida. Dan was one of 12 siblings who were moved to Lakeland, Florida, sometime around WWI.

In 1922, at the age of 14, Dan ran away from home joining tent, minstrel, vaudeville and theatre shows that played throughout the South. He hearkened back to that life in 1943 for a role as a minstrel performer with Guy Wilkerson in PRC's "Boss of Rawhide".

Dan performed on stage with his brother Willard for nine years with a stock company in Tampa's old Rialto Theatre.

During this period Dan met Mathilda Mae Spivey on the stage and married her in February of 1933. Tilda had a child by a previous marriage. Times were tough, so Dan found work in 1934 with the Conservation Corps in Homestead, Florida, where he could make a better wage.

Still longing to "make it" in the movies, Dan decided to move his family to California in 1935. They had to stop frequently in various cities across the country in order to make extra money to continue their journey. Dan was a very good auto mechanic so he never had a problem finding that type of work. They lived in Panama City, Florida, Shreveport, Louisiana, and Texarkana, Arkansas, for short periods.

According to Dan's grandson, John F. White, a daughter, June Larue White, was born to them in Texarkana February 14, 1937. On April 1 they continued their journey to California arriving in mid April.

Finding work hard to come by in films, Dan took a job for six months working on the Pan American Highway in Panama.

When he returned in 1938, he found work in several Gene Autry and Roy Rogers B's including "Prairie Moon" (as a henchman). Dan always related he made $55 a week working in that production.

In the late '30s and early '40s White was just as likely to be cast as a townsman, settler or rancher as he was a bit part henchie. During this period he popped up in B-westerns with Bill Elliott, Tim McCoy, Bob Steele, Ken Maynard, 3 Mesquiteers and George Houston, but also elevated his status in the business being selected for small roles in several prestigious pictures including "Gone With the Wind" ('39), "Grapes of Wrath" ('40), "Our Town" ('40) and "Back Street" ('41).

A third child, Donald Curtis White, was born November 9, 1941.

His parts in B-westerns became better in the '40s as he enacted baddies opposite the Rough Riders, Buster Crabbe, the Trail Blazers, Kirby Grant, Dave O'Brien and James Newill, Tex Ritter, Charles Starrett, Lash LaRue and others. He otherwise worked in six serials in the '40s, with his best parts noticeable in "The Phantom" ('43 Columbia) and "Black Arrow" ('44 Columbia).

As his status in the business grew, by the mid '40s he began to turn to character driven roles in A-westerns ("San Antonio" '45; "Duel In the Sun" '46; "Albuquerque" '48; "Station West" '48; "Red River" '48; "Four Faces West" '48; "The Gunfighter" '50; "Rawhide" '51; "Distant Drums" '51; "Taza, Son of Cochise" '54; "Giant" '56; "Sheepman" '58; among others).

By the same token, White played good character roles in non-westerns as well— "Sudan" ('45), "Unknown Island" ('48), "David and Bathsheba" ('51), "Inferno" ('53), "Suddenly" ('54), "Country Girl" ('54), "The Rainmaker" ('56), "Touch of Evil" ('58), "Attack of the Giant Leeches" ('59) and as the mob leader in "To Kill A Mockingbird" ('62).

Dan's last roles in the '60s were in several of producer A. C. Lyles' "final-roundup" westerns—"Apache Uprising" ('66), "Waco" ('66) and "Red Tomahawk" ('67). Lyles told us, "Dan was a very interesting man. Western parts, the west was part of his life. If you had a part you thought he could do well, he *could* do it well."

White worked only sporadically in the '70s, but producer-brothers Whitey and Billy Hughes cast him as an old Colonel in their 1975 independently produced "Smoke In the Wind". Whitey remembers Dan as "…a real down to earth old character, honest. He really lived his part in 'Smoke' and I think he did a pretty good job in the film. He'd been around a *long* time. He was very likeable, you couldn't help but liking Dan because he was an outgoing, honest man."

White also worked extensively in TV beginning in 1951 on through 1973. After playing heavies in several of the juvenile oriented TVers of the '50s, he began to essay sheriffs, shop keepers and townspeople on "Sugarfoot", "Rawhide", "Bonanza", "Gunsmoke", "The Deputy", "Wagon Train", "Laramie", "Rifleman", "Virginian" and others.

Upon retirement in the mid '70s, the Whites returned to Tampa, Florida, where it all started. He died there on July 7, 1980.

For a 1974 interview Dan said, "Western pictures are Americana…this stuff really happened. The James Gang, the Hole in the Wall Gang, they were all real. What you saw in a western picture, we actually had to do. In those days you had to do all your own stunts. I had four men killed right beside me once! And in those days you went behind a rock to change…a far cry from the portable dressing rooms of today."

Suggested Sampling of White's Western Heavies:
✪ Trail of Terror ('43 PRC) Dave O'Brien/James Newill
✪ Blazing Guns ('43 Monogram) Trail Blazers
✪ Westward Bound ('44 Monogram) Trail Blazers
✪ Utah Kid ('44 Monogram) Bob Steele/Hoot Gibson
✪ Harmony Trail ('44 Mattox) Ken Maynard
✪ Rough Ridin' Justice ('45 Columbia) Charles Starrett
✪ Trail to Vengeance ('45 Universal) Kirby Grant
✪ Gun Town ('46 Universal) Kirby Grant
✪ Station West ('48 RKO) Dick Powell
✪ Red River ('48 United Artists) John Wayne
✪ Outlaw Country ('49 Western Adventure) Lash LaRue
✪ Wild Bill Hickok: Outlaw's Son ('52) Guy Madison
✪ Cisco Kid: Iron Mask ('54) Duncan Renaldo
✪ Cisco Kid: Cisco Plays the Ghost ('54) Duncan Renaldo
✪ Stories of the Century: Jim Courtwright ('55) Jim Davis

BLACKIE WHITEFORD

Unshaven, untidy, his left eye in a perennial droop, Blackie Whiteford always appeared to have just come off a three day drunk.

Whiteford was one of the few-lines-but-always-there henchmen all through the '30s, '40s and '50s. His biggest roles in westerns came during his time spent with the Gower Gulch independents of the '30s. By 1936 he'd hooked up with Columbia where he worked constantly (but not exclusively) in the B's of Charles Starrett, Bill Elliott and Russell Hayden but the roles were seldom labeled more than henchman, rustler, holdup man or barfly. The latter seemed to fit him well.

Whiteford once told Lee Koonce of Colorado, "I've been a cowboy ever since there were cows."

Not unsurprisingly, his repellant polecat appearance also served him well in comic roles opposite Laurel and Hardy ("Hoose Gow" '29—apparently his first film, "Pardon Us" '31), W. C. Fields ("My Little Chickadee" '40), 3 Stooges ("Phony Express" '43; "Out West" '47), Wheeler and Woolsey ("Silly Billies" '48), Andy Clyde ("Peppery Salt" '36) and many other two-reelers.

Although they weren't big parts, A-films also made use of Blackie's tough countenance—for "King Kong" ('33) he was a sailor, for "Captain Blood" ('35) he was a pirate, for "Gilda' ('46) as a crap game spectator and "Knock On Any Door" ('49) as the suspect without a shirt. His last film appearance was in John Ford's classic "Man Who Shot Liberty Valance" ('62) although not much had been seen of him since the mid '50s.

Serials? Certainly. At least 10 including "Black Coin" ('36 Stage and Screen), "Secret of Treasure Island" ('38 Columbia) and "Great Adventures of Wild Bill Hickok" ('38 Columbia).

John P. "Blackie" Whiteford was born in New York City, April 27, 1889. Names of his parents are unknown. Whiteford never served in the Armed Forces. We speculate this could be due to his bad left eye.

He'd been living at 5230 Clinton St. in Los Angeles but he died at the Motion Picture Country Hospital March 21, 1962, at 72 of post operative evisceration following surgery for a gastric ulcer about a week before.

Whiteford was buried at Valhalla Memorial Park in North Hollywood.

Suggested Sampling of Whiteford's Western Heavies:

- Cyclone Kid ('31 Big 4) Buzz Barton
- Mark of the Spur ('32 Big 4) Bob Custer
- Man From New Mexico ('32 Monogram) Tom Tyler
- Man From Hell's Edges ('32 SonoArt–World Wide) Bob Steele
- Deadwood Pass ('33 Monarch) Tom Tyler
- When Lightning Strikes ('34 Regal) Lightning, the Wonder Dog
- West of the Divide ('34 Lone Star) John Wayne
- Ghost Rider ('35 Superior) Rex Lease
- Last of the Warrens ('36 Supreme) Bob Steele
- Law Rides ('36 Supreme) Bob Steele
- Valley of the Lawless ('36 Supreme) Johnny Mack Brown
- Old Wyoming Trail ('37 Columbia) Charles Starrett
- Sundown Valley ('44 Columbia) Charles Starrett
- Last Horseman ('44 Columbia) Russell Hayden

PETER WHITNEY

Jan Merlin, often a vicious heavy in his own right, remembers his "Rough Riders" TV series ('58-'59) co-star Peter Whitney as, "a wonderful guy, a raconteur with stories that just didn't stop. He was so massive, enormous, about 6' 4". A huge, huge man. I remember the first time Pete came over to the house. I had ordinary furniture and he sat on a chair which just *shattered* under him! We laughed and I said, 'Why don't you sit on the couch?'—and even that groaned. But we kidded about it."

Peter Whitney was born Peter Engle in Long Branch, New Jersey, May 24, 1916. He migrated west with his father after the family fortune was wiped out in the Depression.

Pete first enrolled at an art institute in California, changing to the Pasadena Playhouse a year later. He appeared in stock and Shakespearean companies around the country before Warner Bros. signed him to a four year contract with his first film being "Underground" in '41.

Whitney worked steadily in major films ("Whistling In Dixie" '42 with Red Skelton, "Rio Rita" '42, "Valley of the Sun" '42, "Notorious Lone Wolf" '46, "Destination Tokyo" '43, etc.) until 1948 at which time there is an unexplained four year gap in Pete's career until 1952 when he returned to film John Wayne's "Big Jim McLain".

Pete turned almost exclusively to westerns, especially on TV, in 1955 and never let up until 1971, appearing in over 100 TV westerns but only 10 western movies. He was especially good at playing religious fanatics.

Jan Merlin recalls, "When 'The Rough Riders' was over, Pete and his wife (Barbara) went to Hawaii and opened a little boutique. He'd spend six months in Hawaii growing a beard and a lot of hair, then come to Hollywood and spend three months doing shows with his beard and all his hair. Then he'd get a haircut, shave off the beard and spend the other three months doing shows without all that hair. Then he'd go back to Hawaii again for six months."

Whitney, who had several mild heart attacks during his career but had not been seriously ill, died at 55 March 30, 1972, from a heart attack at a Santa Barbara, California, home. He was survived by Barbara, an artist, and six children.

Suggested Sampling of Whitney's Western Heavies:

- Lone Ranger: Heritage of Treason ('55) Clayton Moore
- Man From Del Rio ('56 United Artists) Anthony Quinn
- Tombstone Territory: Apache Vendetta ('57) Pat Conway
- Gunsmoke: Sins of the Father ('57) James Arness
- Domino Kid ('57 Columbia) Rory Calhoun
- Buchanan Rides Alone ('58 Columbia) Randolph Scott
- Texan: Dishonest Posse ('59) Rory Calhoun
- Gunsmoke: Kangaroo ('59) James Arness
- Law of the Plainsman: The Hostiles ('59) Michael Ansara
- Cheyenne: Imposter ('59) Clint Walker
- Rifleman: Eddie's Daughter ('59) Chuck Connors
- Johnny Ringo: Dead Wait ('59) Don Durant
- Alaskans: Seal-Skin Game ('60) Roger Moore
- Lawman: Surface of Truth ('60) John Russell
- Rawhide: Incident of the Music Maker ('60) Eric Fleming
- Tate: Before Sunup ('60) David McLean
- Maverick: Dodge City or Bust ('60) Jack Kelly
- Rifleman: The Queue ('61) Chuck Connors
- Gunsmoke: Harper's Blood ('61) James Arness
- Rebel: The Promise ('61) Nick Adams
- Gunsmoke: Run, Sheep, Run ('65) James Arness
- Legend of Jesse James: The Raiders ('65) Christopher Jones
- Virginian: Nobody Said Hello ('66) James Drury
- Iron Horse: T Is For Traitor ('66) Dale Robertson
- Bonanza: Commitment at Angelus ('68) Michael Landon

FRANK WILCOX

While western roles were in a minority to his film and TV total of over 300 roles, Frank Wilcox's very first film was an oater, supporting Dennis Morgan in the Warner Bros. two-reeler "Ride, Cowboy, Ride" in '39. It was a genre he returned to often.

Frank Reppy Wilcox, certainly among the more versatile of character actors with roles ranging from Abraham Lincoln in "Old Hickory" ('40) to a crooked land agent in Tim Holt's "Mysterious Desperado" ('40), was born March 13, 1907, in DeSoto, Missouri. His father, Roger V. Wilcox was a physician from Kansas. His mother, Mabel Irene Reppy, was a native of Arkansas.

Wilcox graduated from the University of Kansas and was torn between becoming a physician or entering the business world in the field of oil exploration. Unable to decide between the two careers, he auditioned for the Kansas City Civic Theatre. The audition was a success and he both acted and directed at that locale until 1934 when he moved to California intending to pursue a career in sales, but again the acting bug bit and he studied at the famed Pasadena Playhouse and helped found the Pomona Theatre Guild. In 1939 Hollywood beckoned, and other than serving in the Navy during WWII, the world of entertainment remained his forté.

Wilcox played in an enormous number of films over the next three decades, often in small supporting roles. His 6' 3" refined appearance served him well as businessmen, doctors, attorneys and historical figures. Perhaps he's best known in the TV role of oil company president John Brewster on "The Beverly Hillbillies" ('62-'66).

His A-film credits are varied—"They Drive By Night" ('40), "Fighting 69th" ('40), "Sergeant York" ('41), "They Died With Their Boots On" ('42), "Across the Pacific" ('42), "The Sullivans" ('44), "Cass Timberlane" ('47), "Samson and Delilah" ('49), "Show Boat" ('51), among others.

Wilcox certainly appeared in A-westerns throughout the '40s ("Virginia City", "Santa Fe Trail", "Wild Bill Hickok Rides", "Bad Men of Missouri") but never entered the field of B-westerns until he was cast as the dress heavy in a pair of 1949 Tim Holts at RKO, "Mysterious Desperado" and "Masked Raiders". He repeated his villainy with Holt in "Trail Guide" ('52).

Mixed in with his continuing character roles, more A-westerns followed—"Half Breed" ('52), "Pony Express" ('53), "Black Dakotas" ('54), "Man From God's Country" ('58).

Wilcox also moved heavily into TV in 1949, staying busy on through 1972. His westerns included "Lone Ranger", "Sugarfoot", "Jim Bowie", "Cisco Kid", "Restless Gun", "Zorro", "Rifleman", "Bat Masterson", "Wagon Train", "Bronco", "Texan", "Rawhide", "Wild Wild West", "Laramie", "Broken Arrow" and others.

Married to M. Joy Langston, the couple resided on Vanalden Avenue in Northridge, California.

In addition to his acting, Wilcox was co-owner for 13 years of The Oak Room, a restaurant on Ventura Blvd. in Encino, California. Wilcox also served as a greeter according to actor Gary Gray who often dined there.

On March 3, 1974, in Granada Hills Community Hospital, at age 66, Frank Wilcox died from cardio-vascular disease. He is buried at San Fernando Mission in Mission Hills, California.

Suggested Sampling of Wilcox's Western Heavies:

- Masked Raiders ('49 RKO) Tim Holt
- Mysterious Desperado ('49 RKO) Tim Holt
- Kid From Texas ('50 Universal-International) Audie Murphy
- Lone Ranger: The Map ('52) John Hart
- Trail Guide ('52 RKO) Tim Holt
- Lone Ranger: Prisoner in Jeopardy ('53) John Hart
- Cisco Kid: Freedom of the Press ('53) Duncan Renaldo
- Man From God's Country ('58 Allied Artists) George Montgomery

ROBERT J. (BOB) WILKE

"Here was a guy that could be described as a human dynamo, a veritable windmill with an inexhaustible supply of energy," so wrote B-badman Pierce Lyden of his friend and cohort in screen crime, Bob Wilke.

Another shifty-eyed co-worker, Zon Murray, used to refer to Wilke as "old ugly." They were "good friends" though and could "party" all night, according to Lyden, then "play a round of golf in the morning and still do a great job of whatever was required that day on a western."

The 6' 2", 200 lb. Wilke was said to be an excellent golfer. Actor Claude Akins remarked Wilke earned more money on the golf course than he ever did in movies. Lyden said, "Bob was an avid golfer and very good, playing in some big Pro-Am meets with the best. When you were playing Pebble Beach in the Crosby, you had to be good."

Robert Joseph Wilke was born in Cincinnati, Ohio, May 18, 1914. His father, name unknown, was born in Germany. His mother's name and origin are not known. Wilke attended Parochial school in Cincinnati, one year of high school, Elder High in Cincinnati and the Miller Business School also in Cincinnati.

Wilke left Cincinnati as a youth to work at a series of odd jobs that found him in '33-'34 performing a high dive at the Chicago World's Fair.

Wilke was working as a lifeguard at a Miami, Florida, hotel where he made show business contacts which led him to Hollywood, finding work as a stuntman in 1935 with his first film being the blockbuster "San Francisco" ('36) starring Clark Gable.

Bob knocked around in serials and B-westerns, particularly at Republic, in over 40 films as a stage guard, deputy, background badman and other stuntmen/bit parts until obtaining more meaningful henchman roles in Sunset Carson and Allan Lane films at Republic in '45.

Lyden recalled, "Wilke was a good stuntman. Maybe too good. It paid more money than acting jobs and that was hard to turn down. You can get 'typed' or locked into a groove."

As to serials, most people do not realize Bob worked in 21 Republic serials, principally because he never had more than a bit role in any of them. Republic really missed the boat on Wilke, not utilizing his talents as a badman by putting him under contract and elevating him to lead heavy parts as they did with Roy Barcroft, Kenne Duncan, Bud Geary and LeRoy Mason. Even when Wilke began to obtain bigger roles at Columbia with Charles Starrett B's in '46-'48, Republic still cast Bob in bit roles.

By the early '50s Bob was a lead heavy in RKO Tim Holts where he was often better than the material. Regarding his B-western work Bob remembered, "Those were rough days, calls at four o'clock in the morning, be ready to start at five-thirty, drive to locations, eat a terrible box lunch, and work 14 hours a day. But we had fun, that was the important thing. We used to start as soon as the sun came up, then, we would just keep getting higher and higher, by the end of the evening, we're on top of the mountain getting the last of the sun."

Then, in 1952, director Fred Zinnemann cast Bob as one of the four badmen (along with Ian MacDonald, Lee Van Cleef, Sheb Wooley, out to kill Marshal Will Kane (Gary Cooper) in "High Noon". Zinnemann had considered Wilke for the main heavy role of Frank Miller but eventually selected Ian MacDonald, relegating Wilke to the lesser, but still star-making, breakthrough role of Pierce. In later years Bob said, "I think 'High Noon' was the greatest western ever made. I am proud I was a part of it. Without a doubt, it is the best thing I've ever done."

The "High Noon" role greatly elevated Wilke's salary and visibility at a very opportune time, just as the B-western era he'd been so associated with was coming to a close. Although he did work in a few more medium budget westerns, the weathered visage of Wilke was now considered for, and cast in, more major westerns ("Powder River" '53, "Arrowhead" '53, "Far Country" '55, "Night Passage" '57, "Man of the West" '58, "Magnificent Seven" '60, "Cheyenne Social Club" '70).

Good roles in important non-western films were also now being offered him—"From Here to Eternity" '53, "20,000 Leagues Under the Sea" '54, "Written On the Wind" '56, "Spartacus" '60, "Tony Rome" '67.

Television provided Wilke a great deal of work in the '50s and '60s, with again, "High Noon" elevating his roles from the juvenile TV westerns of Cisco, Roy, Annie and Gene to meatier roles on "Have Gun Will Travel", "Gunsmoke", "Lawman", "Wanted Dead or Alive", "Laramie", "Bat Masterson", "Maverick" etc. Over 140 TVers, nearly all westerns. He turned to the right side of the law as Marshal Sam Corbett in his only TV series "The Legend of Jesse James" in '65-'66, unfortunately the series never took off and is not well remembered today.

Bob tapered off his work load drastically in the late '70s and early '80s, preferring to spend more time at his Makato Inn on Riverside Dr. spinning yarns, telling gags and doing gimmicky magic tricks. Pierce Lyden tells us Bob also owned a bar years earlier on Ventura Blvd. in Studio City. "When Bob wasn't working, he was back of the bar. You couldn't go in the place that he didn't have everyone in 'stitches,'" Lyden smiled.

Upon his death, Boyd Magers gathered several remembrances of Bob for his column then in THE BIG REEL. Director William Witney: "He was a most pleasant person…he was always there…a good actor and a hell of a good golfer. He'd classify as one of the good guys." Harry Lauter: "He was a very dear friend of mine. We must have worked off and on together for 15-20 years. He was a very versatile actor, and he was a big man—probably 6' 2"—looked like a bear but had a heart as big as he was. A great golfer…and he was a hustler…had a handicap of 4 or 5. Good sense of humor. A very amusing thing, he sold a watch to a director of ours without any works in it. I always looked forward to working with Robert…he was excellent." Sheb Wooley, one of the Miller Brothers in "High Noon": "We were a mean team…raisin' hell and goin' after it. He was a fine golfer too." Lois Hall, co-star in Charles Starrett's "Frontier Outpost": "He was a very nice person—a real gentleman—extremely helpful. He'd talk with the extras and stagehands and that's always nice."

Bob's last part was that of a train engineer in the TV movie "The Texas Rangers" with Jeff Osterhage in '81.

Bob was married to Patricia Kesinger at the time of his death. They had one son, Bob. They lived at 12550 Ostetgo St. in North Hollywood.

Without a doubt, one of the finest, most menacing western heavies died March 28, 1989, from lung cancer at St. Joseph's Medical Center in Burbank, California. He was 74.

Suggested Sampling of Wilke's Western Heavies:

- Sheriff of Sundown ('44 Republic) Allan Lane
- Bandits of the Badlands ('45 Republic) Sunset Carson
- Sunset In El Dorado ('45 Republic) Roy Rogers
- Roaring Rangers ('46 Columbia) Charles Starrett
- West of Dodge City ('47 Columbia) Charles Starrett
- Law of the Canyon ('47 Columbia) Charles Starrett
- Six Gun Law ('48 Columbia) Charles Starrett
- West of Sonora ('48 Columbia) Charles Starrett
- Laramie ('49 Columbia) Charles Starrett
- Across the Badlands ('50 Columbia) Charles Starrett
- Gene Autry: The Posse ('50) Gene Autry
- Saddle Legion ('51 RKO) Tim Holt
- Gunplay ('51 RKO) Tim Holt
- Bonanza Town ('51 Columbia) Charles Starrett
- Pistol Harvest ('51 RKO) Tim Holt
- Hot Lead ('51 RKO) Tim Holt
- Laramie Mountains ('52 Columbia) Charles Starrett
- High Noon ('52 Columbia) Gary Cooper
- Cattle Town ('52 Warner Bros.) Dennis Morgan
- Fargo ('52 Monogram) Bill Elliott
- Wyoming Roundup ('52 Monogram) Whip Wilson
- Maverick ('52 Allied Artists) Bill Elliott
- Range Rider: Border Trouble ('52) Jock Mahoney
- Roy Rogers: Train Robbery ('52) Roy Rogers
- Cisco Kid: Mad About Money ('52) Duncan Renaldo
- Lone Ranger: Trial By Fire ('52) Clayton Moore
- Cowboy G-Men: Frontier Smugglers ('52) Russell Hayden
- Road Agent ('53 RKO) Tim Holt
- Cow Country ('53 Allied Artists) Edmond O'Brien
- Powder River ('53 20th Century Fox) Rory Calhoun
- Roy Rogers: M Stands for Murder ('53) Roy Rogers
- Lone Gun ('54 United Artists) George Montgomery
- Two Guns and a Badge ('54 Allied Artists) Wayne Morris
- Far Country ('54 Universal) James Stewart
- Shotgun ('55 Allied Artists) Sterling Hayden
- Wichita ('55 Allied Artists) Joel McCrea
- The Lone Ranger ('56 Warner Bros.) Clayton Moore
- Raw Edge ('56 Universal) Rory Calhoun
- Canyon River ('56 Allied Artists) George Montgomery
- Gun the Man Down ('56 United Artists) James Arness
- Cheyenne: Long Winter ('56) Clint Walker
- Jim Bowie: Bound Girl ('57) Scott Forbes
- Cheyenne: Mutton Puncher ('57) Clint Walker
- Return to Warbow ('58 Columbia) Phil Carey
- Man of the West ('58 United Artists) Gary Cooper
- Rifleman: The Marshal ('58) Chuck Connors
- Bat Masterson: The Fighter ('58) Gene Barry
- Lawman: Wanted ('58) John Russell
- Man Without a Gun: Buried Treasure ('58) Rex Reason
- Have Gun Will Travel: Man Who Lost ('59) Richard Boone
- Zorro: Man From Spain ('59) Guy Williams
- Tombstone Territory: Grave Near Tombstone ('59) Pat Conway
- Deputy: The Deputy ('59) Henry Fonda/Allen Case
- Wichita Town: Bullet for a Friend ('59) Joel McCrea
- Gunsmoke: Saludos ('59) James Arness
- Law of the Plainsman: Desperate Decision ('59) Michael Ansara
- Wanted Dead Or Alive: No Trail Back ('59) Steve McQueen
- Lawman: The Press ('59) John Russell
- Texan: Cowards Don't Die ('59) Rory Calhoun
- Have Gun Will Travel: Naked Gun ('59) Richard Boone
- Overland Trail: Perilous Passage ('60) William Bendix/Doug McClure
- Cheyenne: Outcast of Cripple Creek ('60) Clint Walker
- Westerner: The Old Man ('60) Brian Keith
- Tales of Wells Fargo: The Wade Place ('60) Dale Robertson
- Tall Man: Last Resource ('61) Barry Sullivan
- Rawhide: Incident of the Running Man ('61) Clint Eastwood
- Outlaws: Night Riders ('61) Don Collier/Slim Pickens
- Maverick: Epitaph For a Gambler ('62) Jack Kelly

- Gun Hawk ('63 Allied Artists) Rory Calhoun
- Have Gun Will Travel: American Primitive ('63) Richard Boone
- Laramie: The Marshals ('63) Robert Fuller
- Gunsmoke: The Bassops ('64) James Arness
- Death Valley Days: Brute Angel ('66)
- Gunsmoke: Cattle Barons ('67) James Arness
- Wild Wild West: Night of the Arrow ('67) Robert Conrad
- Bonanza: Trouble Town ('68) Lorne Greene/Michael Landon
- Guns of Will Sonnett: Meeting In a Small Town ('68) Walter Brennan
- Bonanza: Old Friends ('69) Lorne Greene

ROGER WILLIAMS

In spite of a Hollywood career of over 100 films from 1933-1939, almost all westerns and serials, there is scant biographical information to be located on this extremely popular western badman.

Finally, after following many cold trails, we obtained a verified Social Security number on a Roger Williams from a 1937 Republic Studio contract. However, coincidentally, *that* Roger Williams (born 1898 in Colorado) turned out to be a production man who had worked with Republic prexy Herbert J. Yates for several years.

Then, members of the Slim Whitaker family located an obituary in the LOS ANGELES TIMES archives proving *our* Roger Williams died "suddenly" of angina pectoris July 6, 1939, at Wildyrie Camp, Mammoth Lakes, California, in the San Bernardino Mountains while apparently filming two back-to-back Harry S. Webb epics, "Law of the Wolf" and "Fangs of the Wild". The casts of these two adventures are virtually the same (Dennis Moore, Luana Walters, George Chesebro, Martin Spellman, Rin Tin Tin Jr.) with a couple of exceptions, one being Roger Williams who is in "Law of the Wolf" but not "Fangs of the Wild". Even the production crews are identical. Supposition is, Williams died on location while working on these two pictures. Williams' widow never remarried and lived until 1984, nearly 96 years of age.

Born in 1890 in Ohio, according to 1930 census records (but July 13, 1889 according to the death certificate), Williams was married (at 35) to Ethel Moore and living at 214 N. Oakhurst Dr. in Beverly Hills. He was then employed as a public accountant.

Somehow, he arrived on screen for the first time (as a sheriff) in "Trouble Busters" ('33 Majestic) with Jack Hoxie. Throughout the rest of the '30s Williams worked in as many as 25-30 films per year.

Over the years in trying to find "our" Roger Williams, a common name, much misinformation and supposition has been put forth on Williams' life in his early years, all of which can now be discarded.
- His father was *not* Charles H. Williams, an actor in the 1866 hit Broadway play "The Black Crook".
- Roger was not educated at the Colorado School of Mines earning two degrees.
- He obviously was not in films as early as 1915 in "White Feather".
- He apparently never served in the Army field artillery during WWI.
- He is not a purported Roger N. Williams of Denver who became an architectural draftsman in Indiana.
- "Our" Roger is often confused with a Roger Williams born in Germany.

Suggested Sampling of Williams' Western Heavies:

- Gun Play ('35 Beacon) Big Boy Williams
- Range Warfare ('35 Kent) Reb Russell
- Lawless Border ('35 Spectrum) Bill Cody
- Men of the Plains ('36 Colony) Rex Bell
- Reckless Buckaroo ('36 Spectrum) Bill Cody
- Ridin' On ('36 Reliable) Tom Tyler
- Gun Grit ('36 Atlantic) Jack Perrin
- Desert Justice ('36 Atlantic) Jack Perrin
- Aces Wild ('36 Astor) Harry Carey
- Wagon Trail ('36 Ajax) Harry Carey
- Wildcat Trooper ('36 Ambassador) Kermit Maynard
- Brothers of the West ('37 Victory) Tom Tyler
- Singing Buckaroo ('37 Spectrum) Fred Scott
- Roaming Cowboy ('37 Spectrum) Fred Scott
- Santa Fe Rides ('37 Reliable) Bob Custer
- Silver Trail ('37 Reliable) Rex Lease

- Mystery Range ('37 Victory) Tom Tyler
- Riders of the Whistling Skull ('37 Republic) 3 Mesquiteers
- Six Shootin' Sheriff ('38 Grand National) Ken Maynard
- Feud Maker ('38 Republic) Bob Steele

NORMAN WILLIS

Norman Willis truly entered the Hall of Infamy when he cut two fingers off of young Charles Starrett's right hand in "Outlaws of the Prairie" and with his role as "Spider" Webb in Universal's "Tim Tyler's Luck" serial, both in '37. In the serial, leading lady Frances Robinson described Spider Webb as "everything a man shouldn't be, a brutal, killing crook." That he was. For a serial, the nastier the villain, the better the hero fares, and Norman Willis made Frankie (Tim Tyler) Thomas look terrific!

Born Willis Ira Norman May 27, 1903, in Chicago, Illinois, his parents, Laurence and Anna Pelton, were both Illinois natives. As a young boy he attended Hyde Park High in Chicago and later became a radio announcer on Chicago stations WGN and WBBM. Interested in acting, he joined a stock company and was also an announcer for the Chicago World's Fair in 1933.

Rearranging his name to Norman Willis and trying his luck in Hollywood, he finally won a small role as a gangster in "Mary Burns, Fugitive" in '35 which led to a short contract at Warner Bros. After that he began to freelance. Dozens of westerns with Richard Arlen, Charles Starrett, George O'Brien, Johnny Mack Brown, Bill Elliott, 3 Mesquiteers, Tim Holt and others as well as meaty parts in A-films such as "They Drive By Night", "Trail of the Lonesome Pine", "Roaring Twenties", "Adventures of Mark Twain", etc. plus roles in early TV ("Cheyenne", "Lone Ranger", "Deputy", etc.) kept Willis busy for over 25 years. Producer Alex Gordon gave him his last job in "Bounty Killer" ('65).

Other serial roles were in "Iron Claw" as one of the "brother suspects", "Desert Hawk" as Andor with minor roles in "King of the Royal Mounted", "G-Men Vs. the Black Dragon" and "Zombies of the Stratosphere".

For whatever reason, for two or three years in the late '40s, he made a few films under the name Jack Norman.

Married for many years to a Margaret Huckin, Willis was retired when he died at 84 on January 27, 1988, at Kaiser Foundation Hospital in Los Angeles of an instantaneous heart attack. He had suffered from heart disease for many years.

Looking back at "Tim Tyler's Luck", Tim Tyler himself, Frankie Thomas said, "He filled that old saying, the nicest people are the villains, 'cause he was absolutely charming. Wonderful to work with, although we had only a few scenes together as he was always off in the Jungle Cruiser. He had this terribly menacing voice but he was the nicest guy."

Willis was cremated with his ashes at rest in the Chapel of the Pines in Los Angeles.

Charles Starrett is gunning for revenge on Norman Willis and the "Outlaws of the Panhandle" ('41 Columbia).

Suggested Sampling of Willis' Western Heavies:

- Outlaws of the Prairie ('37 Columbia) Charles Starrett
- Badman From Red Butte ('40 Universal) Johnny Mack Brown
- Legion of the Lawless ('40 RKO) George O'Brien
- Beyond the Sacramento ('40 Columbia) Bill Elliott
- Twilight On the Trail ('41 Paramount) William Boyd
- Gauchos of El Dorado ('41 Republic) 3 Mesquiteers
- Down Rio Grande Way ('42 Columbia) Charles Starrett, Russell Hayden
- Avenging Rider ('43 RKO) Tim Holt
- In Old New Mexico ('45 Monogram) Duncan Renaldo
- Heading West ('46 Columbia) Charles Starrett
- Lone Ranger: Six Gun Artist ('55) Clayton Moore

GRANT WITHERS

Grant Withers loved women and wine in real life. On screen we loved to see him ply his evil trade.

Granville Gustavus Withers was born January 17, 1905, in Pueblo, Colorado. His parents, Ernst E. Withers and Noma D. Newton were both from Colorado.

Educated at Kemper Military School in Boonville, Missouri, and the University of Colorado where he majored in journalism, he later moved to California where he worked as a salesman for an oil company and as a police beat reporter for the LOS ANGELES RECORD for three years before taking a shot at the movies in the final heyday of silents (circa 1926).

By the mid '30s the 6' 3", 230 lb. actor was a leading man in lower budget B-films such as "Valley of Wanted Men" ('35), "The Test" ('35), "Fighting Marines" serial ('35), "Jungle Jim" serial ('36), "Radio Patrol" serial ('37) and "Navy Secrets" ('39). In the early '40s he was usually seen playing second lead, such as his recurring role as Police Captain Bill Street in Monogram's Mr. Wong (Boris Karloff) series.

Withers drifted into smaller character roles, often uncredited, until Republic began to utilize him as a western heavy in 1944. He also landed plum roles in director John Ford's "My Darling Clementine" ('46) and "Fort Apache" ('48). During this period Withers was renown as one of John Wayne's drinking buddies. Republic kept Withers busy until their demise in the late '50s at which time he made an easy transition to TV, finding character work on "Have Gun Will Travel", "Elfego Baca", "Circus Boy", "Zane Grey Theatre", "Wyatt Earp" and others.

Although credited with service in WWII, Withers managed to work in films steadily as did many others who somehow "served".

Withers was married five times. Of those, the most publicized was his elopement to Yuma, Arizona, in 1930 with Loretta Young when she was only 17. That marriage was annulled in 1931. Two other wives were Gladys Joyce Walsh and Republic regular Estelita Rodriguez (his fifth, '53-'58).

In spite of his taste for marriage, he was divorced at the time he took his own life by barbiturate poisoning at his home at 4817 Ben Ave. in Los Angeles on March 27, 1959. There was a suicide note by his side.

A quite sad end to the 6' 3" leading man and western heavy who cut a memorable screen swath over three decades.

Suggested Sampling of Withers' Western Heavies:

- Red Rider ('34 Universal serial) Buck Jones
- Arizona Raiders ('36 Paramount) Buster Crabbe
- Hollywood Round-Up ('37 Columbia) Buck Jones
- Masked Rider ('41 Universal) Johnny Mack Brown
- Yellow Rose of Texas ('44 Republic) Roy Rogers
- Bells of Rosarita ('45 Republic) Roy Rogers
- Utah ('45 Republic) Roy Rogers
- Dakota ('45 Republic) John Wayne
- My Darling Clementine ('46 20th Century Fox) Henry Fonda
- Gallant Legion ('48 Republic) William Elliott
- Night Time In Nevada ('48 Republic) Roy Rogers
- Last Bandit ('49 Republic) William Elliott
- Savage Horde ('50 Republic) William Elliott
- Trigger Jr. ('50 Republic) Roy Rogers
- Spoilers of the Plains ('51 Republic) Roy Rogers
- Captive of Billy the Kid ('52 Republic) Allan "Rocky" Lane
- Leadville Gunslinger ('52 Republic) Allan "Rocky" Lane
- Iron Mountain Trail ('53) Rex Allen
- 26 Men: Fighting Man ('59) Kelo Henderson/Tris Coffin

HARRY WOODS

Roy Barcroft, favorite badman of many people, always acknowledged Harry Woods as his role model.

Born Harry Lewis Woods May 5, 1889, in Cleveland, OH, at maturity his 6' 2" frame carried about 210 lbs. He had brown hair and greenish-hazel eyes. Harry married Helen Hokenberry on October 28, 1911, with three children (Maril Lee, Richard, Harrison) being born in 1913, 1916 and 1918 respectively.

Although earning a living as a millinery salesman, friends urged Woods toward trying his luck on the stage, which he did with a stock company out of Lakewood (Cleveland), OH. He alternated stage work with a job as sales manager for a large rubber company before he finally decided to try his luck in Hollywood, eventually landing work around 1921 first as a grip then as a actor reportedly in some of the Ruth Roland serials. Harry may have worked uncredited in some of them but there is no documented evidence to this effect.

He did appear, credited, in William Duncan's 1923 15 chapter Universal serial, "Steel Trail". The same year he was a knight in Jack Hoxie's "Don Quickshot of the Rio Grande".

From then on Harry began to work steadily in silent serials ("Fast Express", "Ten Scars Make a Man", "Wolves of the North") and in features opposite Fred Thomson, Tom Tyler, Tim McCoy and others.

With the advent of sound, his suave demeanor, cobra-like eyes and deep resonate voice made him a truly convincing badman—whether it be dress heavy or dog heavy—he played both to the hilt. All the major studios making westerns employed him. So much in demand was Woods, he never had to seek employment at the lower ranks of PRC.

He was reportedly a one-time skating champion and golf addict. His hobby was remodeling houses and, when not employed in film, he made a lot of money in the remodeling business.

In the '50s, B-westerns gone, Harry worked more infrequently with his last role being in "Bat Masterson: Run For Your Money" in '61…a good solid western on which to end a 37 year screen career.

Harry Woods, who in the early days ranked up there as a badman's badman with Fred Kohler, Noah Beery, Walter Miller, Bob Kortman, and in the later days was a role model for Roy Barcroft, Stan Jolley and others, died December 28, 1968, in L. A. of uremia while confined at King Manor Convalescent Hospital in Santa Ana, California. He was 79. He is buried at Valhalla Memorial Park in North Hollywood.

With over 230 films to his credit (over 190 talkies)—and mainly westerns, he is considered the dean of western heavies.

Tim Holt brings gun law to top screen badman Harry Woods in RKO's "Western Heritage" ('48).

Suggested Sampling of Woods' Western Heavies:

- Bandit's Baby ('25 FBO) Fred Thomson
- Tyrant of Red Gulch ('28 FBO) Tom Tyler
- Lone Rider ('30 Columbia) Buck Jones
- Men Without Law ('30 Columbia) Buck Jones
- West of Cheyenne ('31 Syndicate) Tom Tyler
- Texas Ranger ('31 Columbia) Buck Jones
- In Old Cheyenne ('31 SonoArt–World Wide) Rex Lease
- Texas Gunfighter ('32 Tiffany) Ken Maynard
- Haunted Gold ('32 Warner Bros.) John Wayne
- Law and Order ('32 Universal) Walter Huston
- Rustlers of Red Dog ('35 Universal serial) Johnny Mack Brown
- When a Man's a Man ('35 Fox) George O'Brien
- Adventures of Rex and Rinty ('35 Mascot serial) Kane Richmond
- Gallant Defender ('35 Columbia) Charles Starrett
- Lawless Riders ('35 Columbia) Ken Maynard
- Phantom Rider ('36 Universal serial) Buck Jones
- Lawless Nineties ('36 Republic) John Wayne
- Land Beyond the Law ('37 Warner Bros.) Dick Foran
- Reckless Ranger ('37 Columbia) Bob Allen
- Range Defenders ('37 Republic) 3 Mesquiteers
- Courage of the West ('37 Universal) Bob Baker
- Rolling Caravans ('38 Columbia) Jack Luden

- Panamints Bad Man ('38 20th Century Fox) Smith Ballew
- In Early Arizona ('38 Columbia) Bill Elliott
- Blue Montana Skies ('39 Republic) Gene Autry
- Days of Jesse James ('39 Republic) Roy Rogers
- West of Carson City ('40 Universal) Johnny Mack Brown
- Boss of Bullion City ('40 Universal) Johnny Mack Brown
- Bullet Code ('40 RKO) George O'Brien
- Winners of the West ('40 Universal serial) Dick Foran
- Ranger and the Lady ('40 Republic) Roy Rogers
- Sheriff of Tombstone ('41 Republic) Roy Rogers
- Riders of the West ('42 Monogram) Rough Riders
- West of the Law ('42 Monogram) Rough Riders
- Deep In the Heart of Texas ('42 Universal) Johnny Mack Brown/Tex Ritter
- Cheyenne Roundup ('43 Universal) Johnny Mack Brown/Tex Ritter
- Outlaws of Stampede Pass ('43 Monogram) Johnny Mack Brown
- Nevada ('44 RKO) Robert Mitchum
- Westward Bound ('44 Monogram) Trail Blazers
- Marshal of Gunsmoke ('44 Universal) Tex Ritter
- Call of the Rockies ('44 Republic) Sunset Carson
- Silver City Kid ('44 Republic) Allan Lane
- West of the Pecos ('45 RKO) Robert Mitchum
- South of Monterey ('46 Monogram) Gilbert Roland
- Sunset Pass ('46 RKO) James Warren
- Wild Horse Mesa ('47 RKO) Tim Holt
- Thunder Mountain ('47 RKO) Tim Holt
- Western Heritage ('47 RKO) Tim Holt
- Indian Agent ('48 RKO) Tim Holt
- Masked Raiders ('49 RKO) Tim Holt
- Kit Carson: Savage Outpost ('53) Bill Williams
- Lone Ranger: Midnight Rider ('53) Clayton Moore

BOB WOODWARD

I'll never understand why Bob Woodward didn't get the recognition he deserved for his very prolific and enduring stunt career. He is as visible and active as any of the so-called well known stuntmen.

Born Robert D. Woodward March 5, 1909, in Oklahoma, Bob first appeared on the Hollywood scene in '31's Tom Tyler film, "Rider of the Plains". He spent the next 30 years as a stuntman, actor and double for such stalwarts as Gene Autry, Lash LaRue, Jimmy Wakely, Dick Foran (although a little short for Foran) and Buck Jones. Woodward appeared in hundreds more at every studio.

Bob Woodward (L) and Tris Coffin in Charles Starrett's final western, "Kid from Broken Gun" ('52 Columbia).

Bob worked heavily at PRC in '47, then seemed to find a home at Monogram in the late '40s, appearing in over 22 of their titles in '48 alone.

Joining with Gene Autry in 1950, the singing cowboy used Woodward quite heavily. Bob is visible in virtually every one of the "Gene Autry" TV shows, as well as other series produced by Autry, "Champion", "Range Rider", "Annie Oakley", "Buffalo Bill Jr.". Bob and Sandy Sanders are the two doubles for Gene that are easily discerned in the numerous brawls in each episode. Woodward can easily be spotted as he always ducked his head close to his chest.

Besides being a good fight man, Woodward was adept at horsemanship as well as team and buggy driving, even showing up as the stagecoach driver of a four-up team on occasion.

Woodward worked A-westerns too—"Cattle Queen of Montana", "Wyoming Renegades", "Apache Territory", etc.

By the time most of the westerns being done in Hollywood were for the television audience, Bob easily made the transition to the small screen, appearing in and performing stunts on over 100 episodic westerns including "Lone Ranger", "Annie Oakley", "Kit Carson", "Buffalo Bill Jr.", "Cisco Kid", "Range Rider", "Wild Bill Hickok", "Tales of Wells Fargo", "Sgt. Preston", "Gray Ghost" and "Laramie".

House Peters Jr. told us, "I worked with a lot of great stuntmen: Yakima Canutt, Dave Sharpe, Bob Woodward, etc. I probably owe my life to Bob—he stopped a two-up team before I was run down after I had been given a 'falling horse' to ride who did his trick fall in front of Bob's team coming along at full speed."

When age and infirmity began to creep up on Bob, he kept his hand in doing bit parts and extra work on "Gunsmoke", "Wagon Train" and "Have Gun Will

Travel". His last film seems to be "Gun Fight" ('61 United Artists) with James Brown.

After a four decade career in front of the camera, Robert D. Woodward, 62, succumbed to a massive heart attack February 7, 1972, in Hollywood, CA. He was survived by his wife and two daughters as well as a fabulous, productive career in stunt work and playing heavies that anyone can be proud of.

Suggested Sampling of Woodward's Western Heavies:

- Fighting Texan ('37 Ambassador) Kermit Maynard
- Santa Fe Stampede ('38 Republic) 3 Mesquiteers
- California Mail ('39 Warner Bros.) Dick Foran
- Taming of the West ('39 Columbia) Bill Elliott
- Gauchos of El Dorado ('41 Republic) 3 Mesquiteers
- Shadow Valley ('47 PRC) Eddie Dean
- Courtin' Trouble ('48 Monogram) Jimmy Wakely
- Fighting Ranger ('48 Monogram) Johnny Mack Brown
- Overland Trails ('48 Monogram) Johnny Mack Brown
- Rangers Ride ('48 Monogram) Jimmy Wakely
- Sheriff of Medicine Bow ('48 Monogram) Johnny Mack Brown
- Range Justice ('49 Monogram) Johnny Mack Brown
- Shadows of the West ('49 Monogram) Whip Wilson
- Gene Autry TV series ('50-'55) Stunts and parts in most episodes

MORGAN WOODWARD

Stern, no nonsense, craggy-faced 6' 3" Morgan Woodward's persona is exemplified by his chilling performance of the mirrored-sunglasses-wearing "man with no eyes" in "Cool Hand Luke" ('67). But for over 10 years prior to that hit film Woodward had been building on that persona with astonishingly realistic and gritty performances on dozens of TV westerns…and he would continue to do so for many years afterward. Morgan logged in nearly 160 TV guest star roles (20 on "Gunsmoke" alone—the most for any guest actor) and some 50 films.

Thomas Morgan Woodward was born September 16, 1925, in Fort Worth, Texas, the son of Dr. Valin R. and Frances (McKinley) Woodward. His father was one of seven brothers, all of whom were doctors. Morgan's uncle, Dr. S. A. Woodward, living in the San Angelo, Texas, area, was one day called to deliver a baby. In honor of the doctor's service, the parents named the child Woodward Maurice Ritter. Later, he was better known as Tex Ritter.

Morgan has four brothers, one who is a doctor. Another brother, Lee, was a widely known TV weatherman in Tulsa, Oklahoma.

Morgan grew up in Arlington, Texas, where the town has honored him with a street, Morgan Woodward Way. Morgan graduated from Arlington High School where he played football.

Upon graduation, Morgan entered the Army Air Corps during WWII. Discharged in December 1945, he enrolled in junior college at Arlington State in January '46. Introduced there to theatre, his aspiration was in musical theatre where he sang light opera. He had hopes of joining the Metropolitan Opera, but decided instead to change his major from music and drama. Studying at the University of Texas, he graduated in 1951 with a BBA degree in Corporation Finance. He then attended law school there. All the while, Morgan hosted a variety show on KTMX radio, fronted a dance band and a barbershop quartet.

With the outbreak of the Korean War, he was recalled into the Air Force with the Military Air Transport Command, spending two years overseas.

Returning home, a job with Lone Star Steel Co. in Dallas as a junior exec was not to Morgan's liking, so he decided to pursue his ambition of acting and singing. Leaving Texas in '55 for Hollywood, an old fraternity brother, Fess Parker, had become a star on Disney's "Davy Crockett" and opened a few doors for Morgan who soon did three pictures for Disney in rapid succession—"The Great Locomotive Chase", "Along the Oregon Trail" and "Westward Ho the Wagons", all in '56.

It was a lean period for awhile after that, and even though he found some roles on "Zane Grey Theatre", "Sugarfoot", "Broken Arrow" and others, Woodward still had to support himself with odd jobs.

He clicked in 1958 on "The Life and Legend of Wyatt Earp" (as the fourth season of the popular series began) playing frontiersman Shotgun Gibbs, a role that took him through 1961. Then it was back to guest-starring on "Wagon Train", "Tales of Wells Fargo", "Rawhide", "Big Valley" and others until the turning-point role in his career came along in "Cool Hand Luke".

Over the ensuing years Morgan was nominated for three Emmys, two from "Gunsmoke"—"Lobo" (one of his personal favorites), "Vengeance" and "Star Trek: Daggers of the Mind".

In the '80s Woodward's career spiked again as he essayed the role of "Punk" Anderson on "Dallas" and had a 10 month run on the daytime soap "Days of Our Lives" as Phillip Colville.

Following an excellent "Millennium" episode in early '97, Woodward retired.

Long interested in aviation, Morgan's chief hobby is restoring and rebuilding antique airplanes and he's regarded as an authority on early American aircraft. Additionally, Morgan is among the very active members on the Golden Boot Awards committee.

In his 2001 autobiography James Arness referred to Morgan as "a superb character actor," "a wonderful person" and a "a real pro."

Suggested Sampling of Woodward's Western Heavies:

- Tales of Wells Fargo: Renegade Raiders ('57) Dale Robertson
- Gunsight Ridge ('57 United Artists) Joel McCrea
- Restless Gun: Manhunters ('58) John Payne
- Ride A Crooked Trail ('58 Universal) Audie Murphy
- Frontier Doctor: Strange Cargo ('59) Rex Allen
- Restless Gun: The Way Back ('59) John Payne
- Wagon Train: Alexander Portlass Story ('60) Robert Horton
- Bat Masterson: Big Gamble ('60) Gene Barry
- Tales of Wells Fargo: Trackback ('61) Dale Robertson
- Wagon Train: Martin Onyx Story ('62) Robert Horton
- Wagon Train: Charlie Wooster, Outlaw ('63) Frank McGrath
- Gun Hawk ('63 Allied Artists) Rory Calhoun
- Wagon Train: Hide Hunters ('64) Robert Fuller
- Branded: The Wolfers ('66) Chuck Connors
- Gunpoint ('66 Universal) Audie Murphy
- Gunsmoke: The Good People ('66) James Arness
- Bonanza: Four Sisters From Boston ('66) Lorne Greene
- Gunsmoke: Vengeance (Pt. 1-2) James Arness
- Hondo: Hanging Town ('67) Ralph Taeger
- Cimarron Strip: The Last Wolf ('67) Stuart Whitman
- Bonanza: Pride of a Man ('68) Michael Landon
- Gunsmoke: Lyle's Kid ('68) James Arness
- High Chaparral: Buffalo Soldiers ('68) Leif Erickson
- Fire Creek ('68 Warner Bros.) James Stewart
- Gunsmoke: Lobo ('68) James Arness
- Guns of Will Sonnett: Trail's End ('69) Walter Brennan
- Gunsmoke: Stryker ('69) James Arness
- Bonanza: Old Friends ('69) Lorne Greene/Dan Blocker
- High Chaparral: Journal of Death ('70) Leif Erickson
- Gunsmoke: Hackett ('70) James Arness
- Gunsmoke: Luke ('70) James Arness
- Yuma ('71 TVM) Clint Walker
- Gunsmoke: The Wedding ('72) James Arness
- Gunsmoke: Sodbusters ('72) James Arness
- Kung Fu: Sun and Cloud Shadow ('73) David Carradine
- Gunsmoke: A Game of Death…An Act of Love (Pt. 1-2) ('73) James Arness
- Kung Fu: Nature of Evil ('74) David Carradine
- Gunsmoke: Matt Dillon Must Die ('74) James Arness

HARRY WORTH

Harry Worth created some of the most unforgettable villains in western film. He often brought distinct, quirky character aspects to his heavies not normally seen in B-westerns.

In "Bar 20 Rides Again" he is a calculatingly cold, meticulously dressed, snuff-savoring Eastern snob-rustler obsessed by Napoleon. His love for chess is a metaphor for the "real" chess game he and Hoppy play.

In "Lightnin' Bill Carson" he is a timid-killer bookkeeper.

In "Phantom Patrol" he essays a dual role of a dapper-Dan badman and a novelist.

In "Hopalong Rides Again" he's a slightly limp-wristed paleontologist.

Born February 6, 1903, in England, all his films from 1919 to 1929 are British made ("Bleak House", "Becket", "Third Eye", several in the series of Sherlock Holmes two-reelers, etc.). Coming to the U.S. in 1929 at 26, Harry J. Worth's English film experience gave him the background to find his way to the Broadway stage where he appeared in various productions until coming to Hollywood in 1935.

His first role for American films was in Universal's "Tailspin Tommy In the Great Air Mystery" serial. Although he was an ally of Tommy in that serial, Worth returned to chapterplays twice more at Republic—as crooked banker Calvin Drake in "Adventures of Red Ryder" ('40) and as the archaeologist who turns out to be the masked Scorpion in "Adventures of Captain Marvel" ('41).

Late producer Alex Gordon once told me, "I met Harry Worth when he turned out to be the cousin of a woman who worked for the gas company in New York and a temp agency where I had a job part-time in between Gene Autry tours after being at Walter Reade Theatres as assistant booker for a couple of years, '48-'50. When she arranged a meeting with Worth, I was thrilled and he gave me an autographed photo of himself as 'The Scorpion'."

I'm sure Worth considered himself an "actor" rather than a western film player, as only 11 of his 53 films are B-western features. For whatever reason, he worked under the name Michael Worth in a few films, such as when he played Frank James in "Days of Jesse James" ('39 Republic) with Roy Rogers.

Worth also had roles in such major films as "Sea Spoilers" ('36), "Life of Emile Zola ('37), Beau Geste" ('39), "Mark of Zorro" ('40), "Honky Tonk" ('41) and "Desert Song" ('43).

Worth left films after playing a gambler in "Adventures of Mark Twain" in '44. At only age 41, he may have returned to the stage. Social Security records have him in California until 1951. At any rate, his whereabouts are unaccounted for until 1965 when he retired in Albuquerque, New Mexico, where he lived with an older sister, Beatrice Gregg, a former actress, until his death on November 3, 1975, at an Albuquerque hospital. Private cremation services took place at Fairview Park Crematory. Worth was survived by one sister, Beatrice Greig of Albuquerque and a cousin in Los Angeles.

Suggested Sampling of Worth's Western Heavies:

- Bar 20 Rides Again ('35 Paramount) William Boyd
- Lightnin' Bill Carson ('36 Puritan) Tim McCoy
- Cowboy and the Kid ('36 Universal) Buck Jones
- Phantom Patrol ('36 Ambassador) Kermit Maynard
- Big Show ('36 Republic) Gene Autry
- Hopalong Rides Again ('37 Paramount) William Boyd
- Adventures of Red Ryder ('40 Republic serial) Don Barry
- Cyclone On Horseback ('41 RKO) Tim Holt
- Kansas Cyclone ('41 Republic) Don Barry
- Riders of the Rio Grande ('43 Republic) 3 Mesquiteers

H. M. WYNANT

Born February 12, 1927, in Detroit, Michigan, handsome, roguish H. M. Wynant's many faceted acting career began at the tender age of 19 when he left Detroit after having attended Wayne University for just two years. He arrived in New York with only $125 in his pocket and a lot of ambition.

Choreographer/producer Jerry Robbins hired him on the spot when Wynant went to his first audition; an open call for the Broadway musical, "High Button Shoes" ('47) starring Eddie Foy. Wynant was working as a draftsman and told Robbins he had to go to work the next day. Robbins said, "Then quit." Thus began a career in theatre which included productions such as "As You Like It" ('50) with Katharine Hepburn, "Love Of Four Colonels" ('53) starring Rex Harrison and Lilli Palmer, "Venus Observed" ('52) directed by Laurence Olivier, "The Sound of Music" ('59) with Shirley Jones, and "Teahouse of the August Moon" ('53) starring David Wayne. These performances garnered him many outstanding reviews and led to a prolific motion picture and TV career.

In 1956 RKO cast Wynant based on his theatrical

reputation, sight unseen, in the co-starring role of Crazy Wolf in the western, "Run of the Arrow". In those days he was known as Haim Weiner which was his given name. Producer Samuel Fuller changed this to H. M. Wynant as he was known from then on.

A budding film career ensued with Wynant cast in varying film roles including many westerns and TV episodes, either as Indians, smooth scamps or treacherous renegades. Wynant became part of television history by appearing in many live, dramatic television shows such as "Chrysler Video Theatre", "Lux Video Theatre", "Playhouse 90", "Matinee Theatre" and "Studio One". Television credits also include more than 500 episodic and soap opera shows in guest-starring roles and many appearances in Movies-Of-the-Week. As David Ellington, Wynant kept the devil at bay in one of the most bizarre episodes of the classic "Twilight Zone: The Howling Man". Soap fans recognize him from recurring roles on "Days of Our Lives" and "General Hospital".

In recent years Wynant's Los Angeles stage performances have included playing the lead role in "Karalaboy", a suspense ghost story. Jules Aaron directed him in his last two performances as Mervyn in "The Sisters Rosensweig", and as Seth Lord in "Philadelphia Story" starring Alison Eastwood as his daughter. Coming back to the stage has brought H. M. full circle to his beginnings. He's also continued to appear on TV shows such as "West Wing" and "Sea Quest DSV".

Wynant's first wife was Ethel ?? ('51-'71) with three children. He married his present wife Paula in '93 and they have a daughter, Paula.

Suggested Sampling of Wynant's Western Heavies:

- Playhouse 90: Massacre at Sand Creek ('56) John Derek
- Run of the Arrow ('57 RKO) Rod Steiger
- Decision at Sundown ('57 Columbia) Randolph Scott
- Oregon Passage ('57 Allied Artists) John Ericson
- Tonka ('58 Buena Vista) Sal Mineo
- Restless Gun: Woman From Sacramento ('57) John Payne
- Cheyenne: Standoff ('58) Clint Walker
- Sugarfoot: Devil to Pay ('58) Will Hutchins
- Mackenzie's Raiders: Long Day ('58) Richard Carlson
- Bat Masterson: One Bullet From Broken Bow ('59) Gene Barry
- Rawhide: Incident of a Burst of Evil ('59) Clint Eastwood/Eric Fleming
- Maverick: Goose Downder ('59) Jack Kelly
- Shotgun Slade: Ring of Death ('60) Scott Brady
- Deputy: The Higher Law ('60) Henry Fonda/Allen Case
- Bat Masterson: Wanted Alive Please ('60) Gene Barry
- Frontier Circus: Lippizan ('61) John Derek
- Gunsmoke: The Do-Badder ('62) James Arness
- Cheyenne: Indian Gold ('62) Clint Walker
- Gunsmoke: Old York ('63) James Arness
- Gunsmoke: Trip West ('64) James Arness
- Gunsmoke: Winner Take All ('65) James Arness
- Wild Wild West: Night of the Sudden Plague ('66) Robert Conrad
- Gunsmoke: A Hat ('67) James Arness
- Virginian: The Fortress ('67) James Drury
- Outcasts: How Tall Is Blood ('69) Don Murray/Otis Young

CARLETON YOUNG

There were two actors who used the name Carleton Young. Carleton Scott Young (1905-1994) appeared in some 190 sound films from '36-'71 and dozens of TV shows in the '50s and '60s. Well over 50 of his movies were westerns battling Gene Autry, Bob Baker, Bob Steele and Tex Ritter.

The "other" actor was Carleton G. Young (1907-1971), a noted radio actor ("Count of Monte Cristo", "Ellery Queen", etc.). He is the father of Tony Young, noted for his TV series "Gunslinger" and two B-westerns at Universal, "Taggart" and "He Rides Tall". Carleton G.'s film career was brief, less than a dozen movies and TV roles. The two Youngs were unrelated.

Our Carleton Young was able to reinvent his career several times over—from character player to heavy to second lead and back to character player again.

Young was born October 21, 1905, in New York City. His parents were Joseph Young of Massachusetts and Minna Adler, a native of Germany. Young made his Broadway debut in the early '30s appearing in such plays as "Page Pygmalion", "Man Who Reclaimed His Head", "Late Wisdom" and "Yesterday's Orchids".

Moving to Hollywood in 1936, he was under a Republic term players contract from October 5, 1936, to October 4, 1937. This is where he scored a hit as Dick Tracy's brother, Gordon, who gets surgically transformed into a vicious criminal in Republic's first Tracy serial. During this time he had bit parts on several Gene Autry and 3 Mesquiteers westerns and a couple more serials.

Freelancing from '38 on, he was able to mix character roles in non-westerns with heavies at Universal, Paramount, Metropolitan and others, second lead roles as Bob Steele and Buster Crabbe's pal Jeff at PRC, and even more serial appearances at Republic ("Red Ryder", "Captain Marvel") and Universal ("Gang Busters", "Overland Mail").

In a couple Metropolitan quickies, for some unknown reason, he was billed as Gordon Roberts.

Young is credited with serving in the armed forces during WWII from '41-'46, although he amassed over

25 film credits during those years. It should be noted that during the war many Hollywood players are credited with service, yet continued their acting chores. Many avoided duty by joining a National Guard Reserve Unit and were never called for actual service.

By the '50s Young worked primarily as a character man in A-productions ("American Guerilla In the Philippines", "Operation Pacific", "Deadline U.S.A.", "Niagara", "From Here to Eternity") reverting now and then to B-westerns ("Bitter Creek", "Gene Autry and the Mounties".)

In the late '50s and early '60s Young became a favored member of John Ford's stock company, appearing in "Last Hurrah", "Cheyenne Autumn", "How the West Was Won", "Sergeant Rutledge", "Horse Soldiers" and the excellent part of a physician in despair on the "Wagon Train" episode directed by Ford, "The Colter Craven Story". In "Man Who Shot Liberty Valance" it is Young who delivers the oft quoted line, "This is the west, sir. When the legend becomes fact, print the legend." This line has become synonymous with Ford.

During this time Young also worked as a public relations representative for either a real estate company or mortgage firm.

At 65, Young retired in 1970 and lived quietly until his death November 7, 1994, at 89. He was a patient at the West L.A. Veteran's Administration Medical Center with death attributed to blockage of the bronchial tree and advanced pulmonary emphysema.

Carleton Young (L) and Ted Adams are making plans in Bob Steele's "Pal from Texas" ('39 Metropolitan).

Young was married to Noel Toy. His remains were cremated and scattered at sea off the coast of California near Santa Monica.

Suggested Sampling of Young's Western Heavies:

- Old Barn Dance ('38 Republic) Gene Autry
- Billy the Kid in Texas ('40 PRC) Bob Steele
- Cassidy of Bar 20 ('38 Paramount) Hopalong Cassidy
- Black Bandit ('38 Universal) Bob Baker
- Prairie Justice ('38 Universal) Bob Baker
- Honor of the West ('39 Universal) Bob Baker
- Pal From Texas ('39 Metropolitan) Bob Steele
- Smoky Trails ('39 Metropolitan) Bob Steele
- Trigger Fingers ('39 Victory) Tim McCoy
- Riders of the Sage ('39 Metropolitan) Bob Steele
- Zorro's Fighting Legion ('39 Republic serial) Reed Hadley
- One Man's Law ('40 Republic) Don Barry
- Pals of the Silver Sage ('40 Monogram) Tex Ritter
- Gun Code ('40 PRC) Tim McCoy
- Gene Autry and the Mounties ('51 Columbia) Gene Autry
- Goldtown Ghost Riders ('53 Columbia) Gene Autry
- Bitter Creek ('54 Allied Artists) Bill Elliott
- Buffalo Bill Jr.: Legacy of Jesse James ('55) Dick Jones
- Frontier Doctor: Confidence Gang ('59) Rex Allen

THE REST OF THE GANG

RODOLFO (RUDY) ACOSTA

Rodolfo Acosta was a character actor with grim and swarthy Mexican/Indian features, dark eyes, a burly frame and lightning quick changes of expression that usually condemned him to playing bandidos and Indians in westerns.

Acosta was born July 29, 1920, near El Paso, Texas, in the then U.S. community of Chamizac, midway between El Paso and Juarez, Mexico, an area later ceded back to Mexico. At age three, the family moved to California where a fascination with acting led him to later attend Los Angeles City College and UCLA where he studied drama. Still later he moved on to the famed Pasadena Playhouse for additional training. At age 19 his success in dramatics resulted in his receiving a scholarship at Palacio de Bellas Artes in Mexico City where he remained for three years.

Returning to the United States, he served in the intelligence branch of the U.S. Navy during WWII.

Following the war, while he was performing in a stage play, his performance was viewed by John Ford, who offered him a role in "The Fugitive" ('47). Based on this successful role, Mexican director Emilio Fernandez wrote for him the role of Paco, a gigolo, in the Mexican classic film "Salon Mexico" ('48), a performance that won him Mexico's highest acting award, an Ariel.

More than 20 other Mexican films ensued through '52, as well as a role in director Budd Boetticher's "Bullfighter and the Lady" ('51). By 1952, Acosta began to focus on American films, occasionally returning to Mexico to appear in a movie there. During the '50s and '60s he was seen in such A-westerns as "San Antone" ('53) with Rod Cameron, "Hondo" ('53) with John Wayne, "Trooper Hook" ('57) with Joel McCrea, "Flaming Star" ('60) with Elvis Presley and "Rio Conchos" ('64) with Richard Boone. Acosta continued to perform in films and on TV (including a running part as "High Chaparral" ranch hand Vaquero, '68-'71).

Acosta died of cancer November 7, 1974, at the Motion Picture Hospital in Woodland Hills, California. Buried at Forest Lawn, Hollywood Hills, his survivors included five children.

RICHARD ANDERSON

Tall (6' 4") and handsome, Richard Anderson (born August 8, 1926) left hometown Long Branch, New Jersey, for stage and radio in New York after appearing in high school plays. After a hitch in the Army he began doing summer stock, radio work and bit parts in films. Cary Grant heard him on a radio show and brought him to MGM in the very late '40s.

Playing a vicious Dave Rudabaugh in Joel McCrea's "Gunfight at Dodge City" ('59 United Artists) showed how nasty he could be, which he continued to do on TV's "Rifleman", "Zorro", "Law of the Plainsman", "Stagecoach West", "Wanted Dead or Alive", "Virginian", "Gunsmoke", "Big Valley" and others.

Anderson's first wife ('55-'56) was the daughter of Alan Ladd, Carol Lee Ladd. His second wife in 1961 was Katharine Thalberg, daughter of actress Norma Shearer and producer Irving Thalberg. They had three daughters but divorced after 12 years in 1973.

ROBERT G. (BOB) ANDERSON

Robert G. (Bob) Anderson (June 14, 1923-January 4, 1996) began in the late '30s as an RKO contract player and eventually became a staple on TV westerns. He was last known living in San Gabriel, California.

His first western was "West of the Pecos" at RKO with Robert Mitchum in 1945. Of his 75 plus films and well over 100 TV shows, most of his heavies were on TVers such as "Frontier", "Zane Grey Theatre", "Colt .45", "Wyatt Earp", "Jefferson Drum", "Tales of Wells Fargo", "Wagon Train", "Have Gun Will Travel", "Pony Express", "Shotgun Slade", "Daniel Boone", "High Chaparral", "Broken Arrow", etc. Last seen as a gambler in "Young Billy Young" ('69).

STANLEY ANDREWS

Character actor Stanley Andrews is best remembered as the Old Ranger, host of TV's original "Death Valley Days", and for playing tough, stubborn ranchers (such as in Johnny Mack Brown's "West of Wyoming" '50 Monogram) and old coots on various TV westerns. Although the bulk of his 250 or so movie roles in the '30s and '40s were not westerns, one cannot overlook his exemplary work as carpet-bagging renegade Confederate Army Captain Mark Smith in "The Lone Ranger" Republic serial of 1938 as he schemed to become dictator of Texas. He was also excellent the same year as vicious outlaw Jackson in Roy Rogers' "Shine On Harvest Moon". Other early badmen roles came in "Nevada" ('35 Paramount) with Buster Crabbe, "Drift Fence" ('36 Paramount) with Tom Keene, "Wild Brian Kent" ('36 RKO) with Ralph Bellamy, "Mysterious Rider" ('38 Paramount) with Douglass Dumbrille, "Prairie Moon" ('38 Republic) with Gene Autry and "Tucson Raiders" ('44) with Bill Elliott.

By the mid '40s Andrews was essaying sheriffs, marshals, judges and governors in more and more westerns and as television entered the picture in '49, he was playing old coots, fathers, sheriffs and homesteaders on "Lone Ranger", "Gene Autry", "Range Rider", "Cisco Kid", "Kit Carson", "Roy Rogers", "Buffalo Bill Jr.", "Annie Oakley" and others. However, an occasional badman role would still come along as with Rory Calhoun's excellent "Dawn at Socorro" ('54 Universal-International)

Andrews was born August 28, 1891, in Chicago, Illinois, of parents who emigrated from Cornwall, England. He became a successful radio actor in the '30s, notably as capitalist Daddy Warbucks on "Little Orphan Annie", and started in films with bit roles in 1933. Respected by his peers, the kindly Andrews died in Los Angeles on June 23, 1969.

JACQUES AUBUCHON

Jacques Aubuchon (born October 30, 1924), a heavyweight character actor in the Victor Buono/Dan Seymour mold, began on Broadway in 1949. Perhaps best remembered as Robert Mitchum's nemesis in "Thunder Road" ('58), he's also in "Gun Glory" ('57) with Stewart Granger, but the bulk of his screen villainy is on TV: "Sugarfoot", "Cheyenne", "Laredo", "Johnny Ringo", "Trackdown", "Wanted Dead Or Alive", "Restless Gun", "Have Gun Will Travel", "Gunsmoke", "Law of the Plainsman", "Man From Blackhawk", "Northwest Passage" etc.

Will ("Sugarfoot") Hutchins remembers him as "…an imposing fellow…Laird Cregar type. I recall how good his acting was—he stole the show. He was a typical Eastern actor with a horse though—having a little trouble. I was impressed by him."

Aubuchon died December 28, 1991, of heart failure in Woodland Hills. He was 67.

TOL AVERY

Heavyset, smug, arrogant, haughty Tol Avery was a dress heavy who usually portrayed crooked politicos or businessmen on TV. Avery was especially effective in a number of '60s Warner Bros. TV westerns—"Maverick", "Bronco", "Sugarfoot", "Lawman", "Colt .45", "Cheyenne".

Born Taliaferro Avery in Ft. Worth, Texas, August 28, 1915, to Harve J. Avery and Elizabeth Boyce, his family included four brothers. His father was a commissioner of livestock in the Amarillo area for many years.

Tol came to the West Coast at 18. During WWII he became a second lieutenant with Armed Forces Radio. Following the war, he resumed an acting career which included radio and the stage as well as film and TV beginning in 1950 with "Where Danger Lives".

In 1958 Avery was one of the corrupt Agry brothers who troubled Randolph Scott in "Buchanan Rides Alone". For TV he was also seen on "Kit Carson", "Gray Ghost", "Bonanza", "Death Valley Days", "Iron Horse", "F-Troop", "Wild Wild West", among others.

Besides acting, Avery was at one time president of the Overweight Research Center for Hypno/Science Inc. on Wilshire Blvd. in Los Angeles. He was also president of the California Professional Hypnotists.

When he died one day short of 58, August 27, 1973, in Encino, California, he was survived by a son Michael Tol Avery and Yvonne Michelle Avery.

ROBERT BARRON

Second string western/serial badman Robert Barron just couldn't seem to get "established" as one of the top heavies, although he worked steadily throughout the '40s in about 55 movies and at least 19 serials. His serial work was first at Universal and Republic in lower echelon henchmen type roles, becoming better established as a member of producer Sam Katzman's stock players in '47-'48 with his best roles as Dr. Albour in "Jack Armstrong", Prince Amil in "The Vigilante", Zuntar in "Brick Bradford" and especially as the swarthy, ruthless pirate leader known as The Admiral in "Sea Hound" with Buster Crabbe.

"Stories" have him born in Cody, Wyoming, in 1923 with his father partnering in a mercantile business with Buffalo Bill Cody who reportedly bounced Barron on his knee when he was six. No doubt studio hype as Robert H. Barron was actually born March 13, 1896, in Alabama. His background is hazy, but he entered films in 1939. He's seen to best advantage as a heavy in "King of the Texas Rangers" serial ('41 Republic), "Boss of Hangtown Mesa" ('42 Universal), "Cheyenne Roundup" ('43 Universal) both with Johnny Mack Brown, "Overland Mail" ('42 Universal serial), "West of Texas" and "Return of the Rangers" (both '43 PRC), "Gunsmoke Mesa" ('44 PRC) all with Dave O'Brien/James Newill, "Boss of Boomtown" ('44 Universal) with Rod Cameron, "Both Barrels Blazing" ('45 Columbia) with Charles Starrett, "Springtime in Texas" ('45 Monogram) with Jimmy Wakely, "Song of Old Wyoming" ('45 PRC) and "Caravan Trail" ('46 PRC) both with Eddie Dean.

Barron left Hollywood in 1949, his further life a mystery. He died June 21, 1971, in Los Angeles, California, at 75.

MATTHEW BETZ

Matthew Betz was already 49 by the time talking films came along, leaving him little room to establish himself. Born Matthew L. Von Betz in St. Louis, Missouri, September 13, 1881, the cruel, iron-faced actor came to silent films in 1914 with a background in stock companies, burlesque and vaudeville. His first sound western was "Fighting Marshal" ('31 Columbia) starring Tim McCoy, with whom he also made "Silent Men" and "Whirlwind", both '33. His mobster-like skulduggery also shows up in "Gold" ('32) and "Via Pony Express" ('33) both with Jack Hoxie at Majestic, "Trails of the Wild" ('35 Ambassador) with Kermit Maynard and finally "Law Commands" ('37 Crescent) opposite Tom Keene. Of his six sound serials, he's most prominent in "Hurricane Express" ('32 Mascot) and "Tarzan the Fearless" ('33 Principal).

Betz died January 26, 1938, in Los Angeles, California.

LYNTON BRENT

Lynton Brent spent 24 years before the camera, from 1930-1954, but seldom rose above an unbilled henchman.

Born August 2, 1897, in Chicago, Illinois, he was a captain of the Cavalry in WWI. Acting wasn't his only interest, he was author of a score of magazine stories, earning a considerable reputation. He was a painter as well. His father, a pioneer resident of Los Angeles, bought 600 acres of wilderness land in 1903, selling the property at 100% profit five years after purchasing it. It still bears the family name—Brentwood Park.

Although Brent appeared in at least 17 serials, his only decent role is as Dr. Edwards, suspected of being The Rattler, in Ken Maynard's "Mystery Mountain" ('34 Mascot).

Of Brent's over 60 B-western roles, he's seen to best advantage in "Frontier Town", "Rollin' Plains" and "Utah Trail" (all '38 Grand National), "The Pioneers" ('41 Monogram) all with Tex Ritter, "South of Santa Fe" ('42 Republic) with Roy Rogers, "Lone Rider In Cheyenne" ('42 PRC) with George Houston, "Rangers Take Over" ('42 PRC) with Dave O'Brien/James Newill, "Stranger From Pecos" and "Texas Kid" (both '43 Monogram) and "Partners of the Trail" ('44 Monogram) all with Johnny Mack Brown and "Valley of Vengeance" ('44 PRC) with Buster Crabbe.

Brent died July 12, 1981, in Los Angeles, California.

DAVID BRIAN

David Brian's suave, sardonic smile and distinctive voice quickly typed him as a heavy in both westerns and crime movies, especially the melodramas of Joan Crawford.

Brian was a dancer before Warner Bros. signed him to a contract in '49. Leaving Warners after four years, he never seemed as effective outside their environment.

Brian was married to Republic leading lady Adrian Booth from 1949 til his death.

Best western heavies were in "Fort Worth" ('51 WB) with Randolph Scott, "Springfield Rifle" ('52 WB) with Gary Cooper, "Ambush at Tomahawk Gap" ('53 Columbia) with John Hodiak, "Dawn at Socorro" ('54 Universal) with Rory Calhoun, "Fury at Gunsight Pass" ('56 Columbia) with Richard Long, "White Squaw" ('56 Columbia) with William Bishop, as well as TV episodes of "Laramie", "Dakotas", "Branded", "Hondo", "Gunsmoke" and others.

Born August 5, 1914, Brian died July 15, 1993, in Sherman Oaks, California, of cancer and heart failure.

WILLIAM BRYANT

Handsome western character actor William Bryant was born William Robert Klein in Detroit, Michigan, January 31, 1924; growing up with his mother in many towns and cities throughout the South then spending WWII as a gunner on a B-17 over Germany.

In 1947, attending the Celeste Rush Radio School of Drama with aspirations to be a radio actor, he instead wound up in films when an agent spotted him. Bryant told Tom and Jim Goldrup for their FEATURE PLAYERS: STORIES BEHIND THE FACES Vol. 3, "I went though 40 years in this business unconcerned about billing. I never pushed the issue. I didn't care. All I wanted to do was work. I loved it."

After hundreds of film and TV roles, Bryant did six months on "General Hospital" that gained him more recognition than he'd ever had. He then broke into the voice-over business which became a full time endeavor. He felt lucky to have been part of the Golden Age, but as he looked back he told the Goldrups, "I have gone from nothing to poverty in 40 years and loved every minute of it."

Some of Bryant's best western roles were as President Grant on "The Rebel" and a 3-part "Branded". Many viewers remember him as Gen. Crook on the "Hondo" TV series ('67).

Many other cavalry roles are among his credits, as well as a fair share of heavies on "Wyatt Earp", "Tales of the Texas Rangers", "Rifleman", "Sugarfoot", "Hotel de Paree", "Man From Blackhawk", "Rebel", "Outlaws", "Laramie", "Guns of Will Sonnett", "Monroes", among others.

At 77, Bryant died of a brain tumor June 26, 2001, in Woodland Hills, California.

BRUCE CABOT

Bruce Cabot may be best known for his heroic role in "King Kong" ('33), but he enacted his share of screen badmen.

Born Jacques Etienne de Bujac April 20, 1904, in Carlsbad, New Mexico, he was the grandson of a French Ambassador to the U.S. Educated at the University of the South in Sewanee, Tennessee, Cabot knocked around in a variety of jobs before taking a screen test in the early '30s. He plied his skull-duggery in "Bad Man of Brimstone" ('38 MGM) with Wallace Beery, "Dodge City" ('39 WB) with Errol Flynn, "Angel and the Badman" ('47 Republic) with John Wayne, "Gunfighters" ('47 Columbia) with Randolph Scott, "Gallant Legion" ('48 Republic) with Bill Elliott, "Rock Island Trail" ('50 Republic) with Forrest Tucker, "Best of the Badmen" ('51 RKO) With Robert Ryan, "Town Tamer" ('65 Paramount) with Dana Andrews and "War Wagon" ('67 Universal) with John Wayne.

Cabot was first married to '30s actress Adrienne Ames in 1933. Divorced in '37, he married Francesca DeScaffa, but they were divorced in 1951.

Cabot died of lung and throat cancer May 4, 1972, at the Motion Picture Hospital in Woodland Hills, California, and is buried in Carlsbad, New Mexico.

JOHN DAVIS CHANDLER

John Davis Chandler is the scroungy bounty hunter to whom Clint Eastwood remarks, "Dyin' ain't much of a livin' boy", before he unceremoniously guns down the arrogant little rat.

Born in Hinton, West Virginia, on January 28, 1937, the heavy-lidded, sleepy-eyed look of Chandler was first evident on screen as Columbia's "Mad Dog Coll" in 1961.

As a member of director Sam Peckinpah's stock company, Chandler appeared in three of the director's westerns. He is the youngest of the five uncivilized and dangerous Hammond brothers in "Ride The High Country" ('62 MGM), one of the motley misfit participants of the unusual expedition of "Major Dundee" ('65 Columbia) into Mexico and is also in Sam Peckinpah's "Pat Garrett and Billy the Kid" ('73 MGM).

Chandler has continually carved out a career playing no-goods and still works today, with his most recent appearance being on TV's "Star Trek: Deep Space Nine" in '98.

Also evil in "Return of the Gunfighter" ('67 MGM), "Good Guys and the Bad Guys" ('69 WB), "Barquero" ('70 United Artists) and TV episodes of "Travels of Jamie McPheeters", "A Man Called Shenandoah" and "High Chaparral".

JEFF COREY

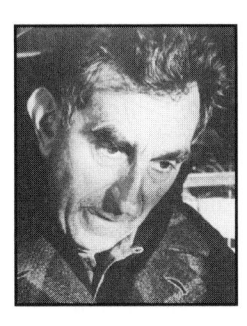

Gifted Jeff Corey (August 10, 1914-August 16, 2002) became an actor because "I just didn't want to relinquish the fun of being young and imaginative and making believe."

Following dramatic school and several plays in New York, where he was born, Corey moved to Los Angeles in '40 where he found work in film. He was a Navy combat photographer during WWII then returned to films in '46. His career came to a halt in late '51 when he refused to name names before the House Committee on Un-American Activities. He didn't work again until 1963. During this time, through word of mouth, he became one of the most respected acting coaches in Hollywood.

Actress Jean Rouverol ("Bar 20 Rides Again", "Law West of Tombstone", etc.) told us, "He knew more about theatre all over the world than anybody. If I had taken classes from Jeff, I'd have been a far better screen actress. If I'd have done it earlier, I'd have been a far better screenwriter because his classes were also invaluable even for writers. I learned from Jeff the most important thing in a scene is not what's said but what isn't said. He was private, his whole family was private. The primary thing (to him) was his family."

Corey's westerns aren't plentiful, but his strong characterizations make him notable in "The Nevadan" ('50 Columbia) with Randolph Scott, "Singing Guns" ('50 Republic) with Vaughn Monroe, "The Outriders" ('50 MGM) with Joel McCrea and "True Grit" ('69 Paramount) with John Wayne. Also played heavies on "Rawhide", "Wild Wild West" and "Bonanza".

JOHN CRAWFORD

John Crawford, born March 26, 1926, in Los Angeles, California, made his mark in B-westerns and serials beginning after WWII in 1945. He worked in a succession of nine Republic and three Columbia serials between 1948 and 1954. His best roles were as a thug in "Invisible Monster" ('50), "Blackhawk" ('52) as Chuck, one of the Blackhawks, and "Great Adventures of Captain Kidd" ('53) as the title pirate. For B-westerns he's a heavy in "Northwest Territory" ('51 Monogram) with Kirby Grant, "Old Oklahoma Plains" ('52 Republic) with Rex Allen, "Son of Geronimo" ('52 Columbia serial) with Jock Mahoney, "Marshal of Cedar Rock" ('53 Republic) with Allan "Rocky" Lane, "Rebel City" ('53 Allied Artists) with Bill Elliott and "Battle of Rogue River" ('54 Columbia) with George Montgomery. Crawford also enacted cut-throats on "Lone Ranger", "Wild Bill Hickok", "Gunsmoke" and "Daniel Boone" before beginning to do solid character parts on TV and in prestigious films such as "Solomon and Sheba" ('59), "Exodus" ('60), "Longest Day" ('62), "Greatest Story Ever Told" ('65), "Towering Inferno" ('74). He's also recalled as Sheriff Bridger on TV's "The Waltons".

Crawford is legendary stuntman Yakima Canutt's nephew.

Today, Crawford is completely retired.

ROYAL DANO

Gangly and weather-beaten with a hang-dog, sad-faced appearance, Royal Dano was cast in a variety of western roles in the '50s and '60s, sometimes as a heavy, but more often as a sympathetic, downtrodden character. Often weak and helpless, sometimes half-loony, Dano was a consummate actor who could evoke sympathy or contempt. Perhaps Dano's gentler side was defined early on with his first major role in John Huston's "Red Badge of Courage" ('51) as the Tattered Soldier. Hard to believe this New York born man could play such roughhewn, often backwoods bumpkins—he even turned up as Lambert Haggen, Ken Curtis as Festus' backwoods cousin on episodes of "Gunsmoke".

"A supporting actor has to work harder," Dano stated, "carefully planning his performance to enhance the entire storyline and star players."

For a sympathetic view of Dano, watch "Gunsmoke: Obie Tater", "Restless Gun: Cheyenne Express", "Wanted Dead Or Alive: The Matchmaker" or Audie Murphy's "Posse From Hell" ('61 Universal). But for the vicious side of Dano see "Tribute To a Bad Man" ('56 MGM), "Man of the West" ('58 U.A.), "Gunpoint" ('66 Universal) as well as "Tales of Wells Fargo" as "Cole Younger", "Have Gun Will Travel", "The Rebel", "Iron Horse", "Big Valley", "Guns of Will Sonnett", among others.

Dano was born November 16, 1922, in New York City. When he was 12 he ran away from home and bummed his way all over the country, a not uncommon occurrence during the Depression '30s. Eventually returning home, he graduated high school in 1942. Working for the NEW YORK DAILY NEWS (where his father was employed) in a menial job and taking a course at NYU, he decided to enlist in the Army. He was placed in a truck regiment and sent to India.

Finding he had a talent for acting, he began to work in shows for the troops. When Dano returned to New York after the war he obtained his Equity Card and began to work small parts on Broadway starting with "Finian's Rainbow" in '47 and '48. Continuing to work on Broadway though '52, he also found sporadic film work. While in New York, Dano worked on numerous live TV shows but his future was set when he did his first westerns, "Bend of the River" ('54 Universal-International) and "Johnny Guitar" ('54 Republic).

Dano, 71, died of pulmonary fibrosis at his Santa Monica, California, home May 15, 1994.

RAY DANTON

Ray Danton (born Raymond Kaplan September 19, 1931) started as a child performer on radio in "Let's Pretend". After the Korean war he began appearing on live TV shows, eventually moving to Hollywood. His most acclaimed screen role is in director Budd Boetticher's "The Rise and Fall of Legs Diamond" ('60). After several off-the-record stories attesting to Danton's brashness, Budd Boetticher told us, "Out of respect to Ray, I think together we were responsible for the best performance of his life. I understand he turned into a good TV director."

Danton was once married to lovely actress Julie Adams.

In the late '50s and '60s Danton played many cocky, self-assured heavies on "Sugarfoot", "Trackdown", "Wagon Train", "Bronco", "Yancy Derringer", "Bat Masterson", "Lawman", "Colt .45", "Cheyenne", "Maverick", "Temple Houston' and "Big Valley".

He died February 12, 1992, at a Los Angeles, California, hospital after a life long bout with kidney disease.

ALBERT DEKKER

Always up to no good, smirking beneath his mustache, whether in costume dramas ("Marie Antoinette"), horror films ("Dr. Cyclops"), gangster classics ("The Killers") or westerns, Albert Dekker was a consummate villain.

Born December 20, 1905, in Brooklyn, New York, he made his Broadway debut in the '20s after graduation from Bowdoin College in Brunswick, Maine. He entered films in 1937.

From '45-'46 he served a term in the California legislature representing the Hollywood district. As he got older, he turned more to the stage and achieved much success on the college lecture circuit.

Dekker's last role was memorable, as the tough railroad detective tracking down an outlaw gang in "The Wild Bunch" ('69).

Western heavies include "Honky Tonk" ('41 MGM) with Clark Gable, "In Old California" ('42 Republic) and "In Old Oklahoma" ('43 Republic) both with John Wayne, "Salome, Where She Danced" ('45 Universal) with Rod Cameron, "California" ('47 Paramount) with Ray Milland, "Wyoming" and "Fabulous Texan" (both '47 Republic) with William Elliott and "Fury at Furnace Creek" ('48 20th Century Fox) with Victor Mature.

His death on May 5, 1968, by strangulation was ruled accidental but speculation revolved around suicide.

JIM DIEHL

Jim Diehl made westerns and serials exclusively for a brief seven years, 1946-1952, then disappeared. Born James F. Diehl in Indiana, December 20, 1916, his work in films was pretty much limited to Sam Katzman Columbia serials (at least 6) and Durango Kid Columbia B-westerns (at least 7). Not much of an actor, nevertheless he *was* a presence in the waning days of B-westerns and serials.

Look for Diehl in "South of the Chisholm Trail"

('47), "Stranger From Ponca City" ('47) and "Laramie" ('49), all with Charles Starrett, "Over the Santa Fe Trail" ('47) with Ken Curtis, and serials like "Tex Granger" ('48) and "Cody of the Pony Express" ('50). Also on TV's "Cisco Kid", "Wild Bill Hickok", "Hopalong Cassidy", "Roy Rogers", "Annie Oakley", "Kit Carson" and "Lone Ranger".

Diehl died at 56 in Los Angeles, California, on January 9, 1973.

CHARLES "ART" DILLARD

In a 23 year period from 1932 to 1955, Texas born stuntman/actor Charles "Art" Dillard (February 20, 1907-March 30, 1960) appeared as a background henchman in a couple of hundred B-westerns. He was regularly featured on Gene Autry's TV series and other Flying-A productions in the '50s. After working with virtually every B-western star imaginable, he died of a heart attack in "Black" Jack O'Shea's Trading Post in Chatsworth, California.

EARL DOUGLAS

Earl Douglas was the younger brother of Frank Yaconelli who played Mexican sidekicks to Ken Maynard, Gilbert Roland's Cisco Kid and others. His real name was Lou Yaconelli.

Although there's quite a bit of information available on Frank, who was born in Italy in 1898 and died of lung cancer in 1965, very little is known of brother Lou, but he seems to have been born April 16, 1906, in Boston, Massachusetts.

Apparently, the 5' 8", 155 lb. Earl spent some time on the stage before entering silent films in the late teens, making quite a few with silent comic Larry Semon. He was also with Al Christie and Educational Comedies.

Earl was seen in at least 11 serials beginning with "The Whirlwind" ('19 All Good) with Charles Hutchinson.

His first sound film was the serial "King of the Wild" ('31 Mascot). He was next seen as Rex Lease's Mexican sidekick (a role his brother really specialized in) for "Fighting Caballero" ('35 Superior). Serials and westerns kept him going for the next six years, but he vanishes in 1941. One wonders if he entered the service and was killed, or if he just got into another line of work. Brother Frank's final days were spent operating a small Italian restaurant on Western Ave. in Hollywood where he used to play and sing for customers.

It's known Frank Yaconelli's nephew, Steve (Lou's son?), is now a director of photography with a close relationship to James Garner.

Lou's primary badman roles in his active six year period were mostly for Monogram, including "Trigger Pals" ('39 Grand National) with Art Jarrett, "Down the Wyoming Trail" ('39 Monogram) and "Rhythm of the Rio Grande" ('40 Monogram) both with Tex Ritter, "Riders of the Sage" ('39 Metropolitan) with Bob Steele, "Danger Ahead" ('40 Monogram) with James Newill, "Driftin' Kid" and "Riding the Sunset Trail" (both '41 Monogram) with Tom Keene.

VICTOR FRENCH

Like the Barrymores, the Fondas, the Carradines, the Beerys, the Holts and the Fairbanks, the Frenchs were also a "family" of actors beginning with Charles K. French and continuing through his "son" Ted and "grandson" Victor. Actually, as Victor once related, "Charles was my *adopted* grandfather," explaining that his father, Ted, and Charles were extremely close friends. Since they shared the same last name, and because Victor's real grandfather was deceased, "he became my adopted grandfather."

Charles E. Krauss was born January 17, 1860, in Columbus, Ohio, the son of Elizabeth Bond and Christian Krauss. Educated at Columbus High School, he later went to New York and got into stage work. As Charles French he began his career touring with minstrel shows, making a series of banjo recordings on cylinders for the old Edison Phonograph.

His screen career started around 1907 at the Biograph Studios in New York where he was one of the early East Coast western leads in films like "Davy Crockett–In Hearts United" ('09), "A True Indian's Heart" ('09) and "Prisoner of the Mohicans" ('11). During this period he also did writing and directorial work. The versatile French went on to character roles as fathers, sheriffs and badmen in silent westerns.

As sound came in, he was featured in the first all-talking B-western, "Overland Bound" ('29) with Leo Maloney, Jack Perrin and Wally Wales. His sound work found him playing sheriffs, fathers (especially to Bob Steele) and other roles up until he was 85 years old.

Charles was married three times, first to a stage actress with the first name Helen from 1912 til her death on March 12, 1917, then to Isabelle Gurton from 1919 til her death in 1928 and finally to Doris Herbert from 1938 til her death in 1948.

French died of a heart attack in Hollywood at 92 on August 2, 1952.

Victor Trenwith "Ted" French was born April 21, 1899 (not 1903 as often reported). Ted was a wrangler at 16 on the San Marcus Ranch in Santa Barbara. When the film studios moved in to do westerns, Ted became a stuntman in 1916, finally accepting acting parts circa 1944. Working as a stuntman and bit-player badman, his last films were in the early '60s. He was often spotted in bit parts on "Gunsmoke" in the '60s, a series his son Victor often guested on. Ted was a known alcoholic, so it's likely Victor obtained these small roles for his father. Ted died in Northridge, California, July 3, 1978, at 79.

Ted's son, Victor French, was born December 4, 1934, in Santa Barbara, California. His mother's maiden name was Cowles. He made his screen debut on an episode of "Lassie" and by the '60s was appearing as heavies on "Gunsmoke" (17 episodes, also directing 5), "Bonanza" (5 episodes), "Two Faces West", "Virginian", "Dakotas", "Wild Wild West", "Iron Horse", "Daniel Boone", "Lancer" and others. His unkempt beard and scowling countenance made him an ideal badman.

Playing badmen changed when his good friend Michael Landon cast him in 1974 as Isaiah Edwards for "Little House On the Prairie". French left in 1977 to star in his own sitcom, "Carter Country". Landon hired him again in 1984 for his "Highway to Heaven" TV series.

French directed in Los Angeles theatres, winning the Critic's Circle Award for "12 Angry Men". He was inducted into the Hall of Great Western Performers of the National Cowboy and Western Heritage Museum in 1998 as a cast member of "Little House On the Prairie".

Married from 1966-1968 to noted TV actress Julie Cobb. They were divorced.

French died of lung cancer at 54 in Sherman Oaks, California, on June 15, 1989, shortly after finishing the last episode of "Highway to Heaven".

BARNEY FUREY

J. Barney Furey, who made his name as a heavy in silent westerns from 1912-1929, was born September 7, 1888, in Boise, Idaho.

Of Furey's over 70 silent features, two-reelers and serials, the bulk were westerns. Furey played opposite Tom Tyler at least 15 times and also worked with Franklyn Farnum, William Farnum, Tom Mix, Pete Morrison, Dick Hatton, Leo Maloney, Bob Steele and others.

Usually seen with a well trimmed mustache, the rather smallish appearing Furey was 44 when sound came in and was relegated to decent badman roles in poverty row features or bit parts in bigger westerns such as "Cimarron" ('31), "Powdersmoke Range" ('35) and "Wells Fargo" ('37)—his last role before his death at only 51 on January 18, 1938, of liver disease in Los Angeles.

Of his talkies, his best heavies are in "Kid Courageous" ('35 Supreme) with Bob Steele, "Thunderbolt" ('35 Regal) with Kane Richmond, "Silent Code" ('35 Stage and Screen) with Kane Richmond and "The Law Rides" ('36 Supreme) with Steele. Furey can also be seen in three serials: "Mystery Squadron" ('33 Mascot), "Queen of the Jungle" ('35 Screen Attractions) and "Custer's Last Stand" ('36 Stage and Screen)—but not as heavies.

Had he lived, there is no doubt Furey would have been seen in numerous more talkies.

WILLIAM GOULD

Heavy set, often pompous, William N. Gould had a long and varied career in films, beginning in 1922 and lasting some 30 years til the early '50s, but virtually all of his scoundrelous western roles were in a three year period from '33 to '36. After that he began to portray fathers, cattle inspectors, ranchers, lots of lawyers, and various other official types.

Gould played heavies opposite Ken Maynard ("Phantom Thunderbolt", "Trail Drive", "Smoking Guns"), Tom Tyler ("Terror of the Plains", "Unconquered Bandit", "Rio Rattler", "Trigger Tom"), Big Boy Williams ("Big Boy Rides Again"), Jack Perrin ("Loser's End", "Wolf Riders"), Conway Tearle ("Desert Guns", "Judgment Book") and Hoot Gibson ("Swifty") all in that three year period. He was last seen as a heavy in RKO's "Fighting Frontier" with Tim Holt in '43.

Gould lived through the San Francisco earthquake of 1906. He spent 20 years on the legitimate and musical comedy stage and five years in radio before coming to silent films in 1922.

Born in 1886 (not circa 1915 as several sources indicate), he died tragically in a fire in Long Beach, California, on March 29, 1960.

CHICK HANNON

Nondescript, plain looking B-western henchman Chick Hannon appeared in over 160 films beginning with Kermit Maynard's "Valley of Terror" in 1937, yet he received screen credit in but a scant handful.

Chester William Hannan was born in Iron River, Michigan, May 24, 1901, and died in Los Angeles, California, August 14, 1980. Beyond that, nothing is known about this western screen rider who played not only henchmen, but members of the posse, ranchers, townsmen, stage guards, saloon patrons, card players—whatever sort of utility no-line job was called for. Tex Ritter's wife and actress, Dorothy Fay, even stated Hannon doubled her. Seldom referred to in westerns by any character name, but when he was, it was nearly always Pete.

He worked in films with everybody at all studios, but seemed to find his most camera time with Tex Ritter, such as in "Rhythm of the Rio Grande" ('40 Monogram). He hung around the business 18 years, with his last film being an extra in "Around the World In Eighty Days" in 1956.

JOE HAWORTH

Joe Haworth (October 21, 1914-July 2, 2000) came from a theatrical family out of Cleveland, Ohio. His father, William Haworth, was a famous playwright; his uncle, Joe Haworth, was a noted American stage actor working with such greats as Edwin Booth. His brother-in-law was Wallace Ford and his brother is Academy Award winning art director Ted Haworth.

After appearing on the New York stage, Joe operated his own theatre in Nyack, New York, then came to Hollywood making his film debut in "Gung Ho" ('43). When actor Jack Randall was killed on location filming for Universal's serial "Royal Mounted Rides Again" ('45), it was Joe who replaced him as a gold raider. Later in life he became a respected Hollywood publicity photographer.

Also in "Frontier Gal" ('45 Universal) with Rod Cameron, "Singing On the Trail" ('46 Columbia) with Ken Curtis, "Outcasts of Poker Flat" ('52 20th Century Fox) with Dale Robertson, "Five Guns to Tombstone" ('61 U.A.) with James Brown and TV episodes of "Lone Ranger", "Annie Oakley", "Kit Carson", "Tombstone Territory", "Rifleman", "Laredo", others.

RON HAYES

Ron Hayes, born February 26, 1929, in San Francisco, California, was a heavy of one kind or another on virtually every TV western made from 1958-1970. Ron's father, Sam Hayes, was a newscaster and his mother, Marian Brune, was a director of children's theatre, so Ron had acted since childhood. A battle with polio when he was a toddler left him with a permanently weakened right arm. Prior to his TV and movie work, Hayes was a mountain climber, airplane pilot, and served a stint as a platoon leader with the Marines in Korea. Always an outdoors type, he supplemented his income during his acting days as owner of a tree pruning service.

During his tenure in Hollywood he was on "Bronco", "Maverick", "26 Men", "Tombstone Territory", "Texan", "Destry", "Rawhide", "Bat Masterson", "Gunsmoke", "Wichita Town", "Tales of Wells Fargo", "Bonanza", "Wagon Train", "Laramie", "A Man Called Shenandoah" and several others. He starred for one season on "Everglades", syndicated in 1961.

Jan Shepard worked with Hayes on "Everglades". "Ron reminded me a lot of Eric Fleming, in that he seemed like a loner, a quiet man. He was just a doll, a wonderful man. He was very kind and a real professional. He laughed very easily."

Hayes' last notable screen work was a 45 episode stint on "General Hospital" soap opera in 1986 playing a honky Southern sheriff.

Hayes died in Malibu, California, at 75, on October 1, 2004.

"SKIP" (GEORGE) HOMEIER

"Skip" (George) Homeier, born October 5, 1930, in Chicago, Illinois, a child actor of the early '40s, found early stage and screen success as a young Nazi in "Tomorrow the World" ('44). Thereafter, his sullen, arrogant nature propelled him into roles as a variety of vicious or vindictive villains in such westerns as "The Gunfighter" ('50 20th Century Fox) with Gregory Peck, "Dawn at Socorro" ('54 Universal) with Rory Calhoun, "At Gunpoint" ('55 Allied Artists) with Fred MacMurray, "Road to Denver" ('55 Republic) with John Payne, "Dakota Incident" ('56 Republic) with Dale Robertson, "The Tall T" ('57 Columbia) with Randolph Scott, "Comanche Station" ('60 Columbia) with Randolph Scott, "Showdown" ('63 Columbia) with Audie Murphy, along with good work on TV in "Rawhide", "Wanted Dead Or Alive", "Lawman", "Rifleman", "Outlaws", "Elfego Baca", "Virginian", "Iron Horse" and others. Homeier, slightly bitter about his career, left films completely in 1978 and remains reclusive as far as public appearances or interviews.

CHARLES HORVATH

Born October 27, 1920, in Pennsylvania, Charles Horvath began a remarkable career as a stuntman and actor in 1946 after serving in WWII with the Marines. His hulking, sullen, menacing appearance created castings on most TV westerns, often portraying vicious Indian chiefs or renegades. He died July 23, 1978.

Seen on "Lone Ranger", "Cheyenne", "Black Saddle", "Texan", "Bonanza", "Lawman", "Outlaws", "Wild Wild West", "Jim Bowie", "Laredo", "Big Valley", "Iron Horse", "High Chaparral", "Northwest Passage" and films such as "Roar of the Iron Horse" ('51 Columbia serial) with Jock Mahoney, "Snake River Desperadoes" and "Bonanza Town" (both '51 Columbia) with Charles Starrett, "Border River" ('54 Universal) with Joel McCrea, "Rails Into Laramie" ('54 Universal) with John Payne, "Vera Cruz" ('54 U.A.) with Gary Cooper, "Pawnee" ('57 Republic) with George Montgomery, "Gunmen From Laredo" ('59 Columbia) with Robert Knapp, "Posse From Hell" ('61 Universal) and "Showdown" ('63 Universal) both with Audie Murphy.

Horvath was twice married, first from 1953-1961, then to a dancer named Margot.

EDWARD M. HOWARD

Lanky, long-faced Edward M. Howard may have had the shortest badman career in westerns, only a scant three years, but in that time he managed to be a menace in 16 B-westerns and three Universal serials. His first film, however, came in 1942…a bit as a "citizen" in "The Magnificent Ambersons". A few more bits followed until he turned to westerns as a gunman with Bud Geary against Bill "Red Ryder" Elliott in "Tucson Raiders" ('44 Republic).

Always with hat cocked a little askew, Howard's best parts came in "Three In the Saddle ('45 PRC) with Tex Ritter/Dave O'Brien, "Rustlers of the Badlands" and "Texas Panhandle" (both '45 Columbia) with Charles Starrett, "Code of the Lawless" ('45 Universal) and "Bad Men of the Border" ('46 Universal) both with Kirby Grant, "Navajo Kid" ('45 PRC) and "Thunder Town" ('46 PRC) both with Bob Steele and as the notorious Zero Quick in Universal's "Scarlet Horseman" serial ('46).

Edward M. Howard was born September 12, 1909 (or possibly 1913) in Illinois. He died of a cerebral hemorrhage May 23, 1963, in Palm Desert, California.

JOHN IRELAND

Slim, heavy browed, tough looking John Ireland was born January 30, 1914, in Vancouver, B.C., Canada, and rose nicely from supporting roles, mostly as heavies, to star parts, but failed to maintain his head of the cast position, slipping back into supporting parts and foreign-made Bs.

Ireland died of leukemia March 21, 1992, in Santa Barbara, California. He was married (second of three) to Joanne Dru from 1949-1956.

Seen to best advantage in "My Darling Clementine" ('46 20th Century Fox) with Henry Fonda, "Red River" ('48 United Artists) with John Wayne, "Doolins of Oklahoma" ('49 Columbia) with Randolph Scott, "I Shot Jesse James" ('49 Lippert), "The Return of Jesse James" ('50 Lippert), "Little Big Horn" ('51 Lippert) with Lloyd Bridges, "Red Mountain" ('51 Paramount) with Alan Ladd, "Vengeance Valley" ('51 MGM) with Burt Lancaster and "Gunfight at the OK Corral" ('57 Paramount) with Burt Lancaster.

Macdonald Carey once told Boyd Magers, "John was a naturalistic actor—not a method actor—played it right off his chest. His personality transferred into many characters, mostly heavies because of his features. John's facial features were, shall we say, oversize. He physically adapted more to the mind's eye of heavies."

FRANK JAQUET

When Republic and Universal needed a short, fat, often pompous windbag of a badman, they frequently called on Frank Jaquet (sometimes spelled Jacquet) who was born Frant Garnier Jaquet March 16, 1885, in Wisconsin.

The role of crooked politician, medical doctor, banker or judge fit Jaquet to a "T" and he played the type perfectly in "Shine On Harvest Moon" ('38 Republic) with Roy Rogers, "Raiders of the Range" ('42 Republic) with the Three Mesquiteers, "Beneath Western Skies" ('44 Republic) with Bob Livingston, "Call of the Rockies" ('44 Republic) with Sunset Carson, "Silver City Kid" and "Topeka Terror" ('44 and '45 Republic) both with Allan Lane, "Beyond the Pecos" ('45 Universal) with Rod Cameron, "Trail to Vengeance" ('45 Universal) with Kirby Grant, "Colorado Pioneers" ('45 Republic) with Bill Elliott, "Mule Train" ('50 Columbia) with Gene Autry and on the "Lone Ranger" episode "Bullets For Ballots" ('50).

Jaquet died at 73 May 11, 1958, of a heart attack in Los Angeles, California.

NOBLE JOHNSON

Although African-American by birth, the statuesque 6'2" Noble Johnson portrayed Indians of all types on screen from 1915 til 1950, a marvelous 35 year career. Born in Marshall, Missouri, on April 18, 1881, his family moved to Colorado Springs, Colorado, when he was quite young.

In 1916 he and his business partner, George P. Johnson, became pioneers in the production of black films for black audiences with their Lincoln Motion Picture Company. They produced some 10 features before closing down in the early '20s. Meantime, he began to find work playing Indians and badmen on the silent screen opposite Fred Church, Buck Jones, Bill Patton, Hoot Gibson, William Desmond, Don Coleman and Richard Dix (the classic "Redskin" in '29). Johnson also worked on serials with Marie Walcamp ("Red Ace" '17), Eddie Polo ("Bull's Eye" '17), Jack Hoxie ("Lightning Bryce" '19) and others.

By the time he terrified us as Mudo, the mute killer, in George O'Brien's "Mystery Ranch" ('32 RKO) he was already 51. The next year he made the film everyone remembers him for—"King Kong" as the savage native chief. (He's also in "Son of Kong".) He impressed B-western audiences in two Roy Rogers films, "Frontier Pony Express" ('39 Republic) and "Ranger and the Lady" ('40 Republic), then played Indians in many other classic films ("The Plainsman", "Union Pacific", "Allegheny Uprising", "Northwest Mounted Police", "Shut My Big Mouth", "She Wore A Yellow Ribbon") and closed out his career at 69 (looking far younger) as Nagura, the Oseka chief, in Roy Rogers' "North of the Great Divide" ('50 Republic).

He was married early on in 1912 to a Ruth Thornton and later to Gladys Mae Blackwell.

Always in great physical shape, the somewhat "mysterious" Noble Johnson died January 9, 1978, at 96, in Yucaipa, California. He is buried at Eternal Valley Memorial Park in Newhall, California, under the name Mark Noble.

DONALD KIRKE

Who was Donald Kirke? Why didn't he make more than 40 films and a quartet of TV shows from 1930-1960? Certainly he didn't earn a living appearing in this scant number of films. Odd that he didn't work more or with consistency as he always turned in a creditable performance. Virtually nothing is known about his life other than he was born May 17, 1901, in Jersey City, New Jersey, came to films in 1930, and died May 18, 1971, at 70.

Seen to good advantage with Tom Mix in "Fourth Horseman" and "Hidden Gold" (both '32 Universal), opposite Buck Jones in "Sunset of Power" ('35 Universal), "Ride 'Em Cowboy" ('36 Universal) and "Smoketree Range" ('37 Universal), trying to outwit Gene Autry in "Oh, Susanna" ('36 Republic), and threatening Don Barry in "Outlaws of Pine Ridge" ('42 Republic). Wish that we would have seen more of the sleazy Kirke.

JOHN LARCH

The cynical look of tall, rugged looking John Larch made him a perfect heavy for the adult TV westerns of the '50s and '60s, as well as several big screen A-westerns. His powerful voice and commanding presence made him ideal for authoritarian roles.

Born October 4, 1922, in Salem, Massachusetts, but raised in Brooklyn, New York, the fine character actor began acting on television in 1953. His first western was also his first movie, "Bitter Creek" ('54 Allied Artists) starring Bill Elliott.

During the same period (June '53-May '54), Larch starred as Captain Rocky Starr of the Nova Space Station on ABC Radio's short-lived and long-forgotten "Starr of Space".

After a solid role in 1955's "Phenix City Story", Larch's acting credibility was assured. He went on to work in some 50 movies and over 300 TV episodes through 1981.

Larch was married to actress Vivi Janiss until her death in 1988. He later remarried, to actress Claudia Bryar. At last report, Larch was living in retirement in Sherman Oaks, California.

Ruthless roles in westerns include "Seven Men From Now" ('56 WB) with Randolph Scott, "Quantez" ('57 Universal) with Fred MacMurray, "Saga of Hemp Brown" ('58 Universal) with Rory Calhoun and TV episodes of "Gunsmoke", "Broken Arrow", "Restless Gun", "Wagon Train", "Jefferson Drum", "Texan", "Wanted Dead Or Alive", "Rough Riders", "Bat Masterson", "Bonanza", "Wichita Town", "Laramie", "Johnny Ringo", "Deputy", "Yancy Derringer", "Rebel", and scads of others.

Larch died at 91 October 16, 2005, in Woodland Hills, California.

KEN LYNCH

Ken Lynch (July 15, 1910-February 13, 1990) of Cleveland, Ohio, began his career doing three to four shows a day on radio, including a long running role as Tank on "Hop Harrigan", before entering films in 1956. His snarling attitude and distinctive growly voice was utilized in a couple of Audie Murphy westerns, "Seven Ways From Sundown" ('60 Universal-International) and "Apache Rifles" ('64 20th Century Fox) but was far more evident on TVers like "Gunsmoke", "Californians", "Have Gun Will Travel", "Maverick", "Lawman", "Rifleman", "Tales of Wells Fargo", "Bronco", "Rawhide", "Virginian", "Wagon Train", "Destry" and others.

GEORGE LLOYD

George Harrington Lloyd had a solid 22 year career in over 200 movies as a character actor. But his end was a sad one. Born November 5, 1892, in Edinburgh, Illinois, he served in the 'Great War' in 1918 as a staff sergeant but was mustered out due to an injury.

After stage work he came to films in 1933, usually playing hoods, mugs, truck drivers, guards or detective assistants, often with comic overtones. Columbia saw his potential and memorably featured him as a western heavy in "Return of Wild Bill" and "Wildcat of Tucson" (both '40) with Bill Elliott. During the '40s he can be spotted in four serials. Dozens more character roles came his way until Republic utilized him often in the late '40s not only as a character player but as scoundrelous heavy "Pop" Jordan in "Under California Stars" ('48) with Roy Rogers, as well as "Denver Kid" ('48) and "Bandit King of Texas" ('49) both with Allan "Rocky" Lane.

Lloyd retired in '55 and settled down, but in '62 he and his wife divorced. Lloyd lost his home to his wife and was reduced to living in a run-down section of Los Angeles on Hoover St. His last surviving daughter, Georgene Lloyd Kelly, stood by in the hard times til he died of heart problems August 15, 1967, at the Veterans Hospital in West Los Angeles.

Sadly, Lloyd died in obscurity, but having served his country, was afforded free burial in a veteran's cemetery.

CACTUS MACK

Cactus Mack, whose true name was Taylor Curtis McPeters, often rode in the outlaw band, but just as often he was a rancher, posse member or townsman. He was one of Jack Luden's sidekicks in "Rolling Caravans" ('38 Columbia) and a pal of George O'Brien's in "Fighting Gringo" ('39 RKO). But mainly he was a talented musician, featured with Ray Whitley's Six Bar Cowboys (see "Molly Cures a Cowboy" '40 RKO), Fred Scott's Cimarron Cowboys, Johnny Luther's Cowboy Band ("Rough Riding Ranger" '35 Superior), The Arizona Wranglers ("Stormy" '35 Universal) and quite often with Jack Kirk's ad-hoc group of musicians ("Westward Ho" '35 Republic; "New Frontier" '35 Republic). His work is mostly uncredited in over 130 westerns from '30-'56 and many TV episodes. Pierce Lyden referred to him as, "A barrel of laughs, always with some new gag. But make no mistake, Cactus was all cowboy."

The tall, lanky, mustached Mack, a cousin of Glenn Strange and Rex Allen, was born in Weed, New Mexico, August 8, 1899. His parents were John McPeters and Leona Byrd. He died of a massive heart attack April 17, 1962, as he was walking to a studio car about to take him on location for a role in Marlon Brando's "The Ugly American".

PETER MAMAKOS

Peter Mamakos' parents came to America from the Island of Lesbos, Greece. Peter was born in Somerville, Massachusetts, December 14, 1918. His father owned three restaurants with several of Peter's uncles. Always a movie buff, Peter began acting in high school plays, receiving a scholarship to Bishop-Lee School of Drama in Boston. After three years there he joined a stock company out of Berkshire, Massachusetts, for two years, then on to another company in Florida. As WWII approached, Peter applied and was accepted for O.C.S., graduating as a Lieutenant. Leaving the service a major, he used his G.I. Bill to attend Pasadena Playhouse.

With his first films in 1949 (one of them Kirby Grant's "Trail of the Yukon"), Peter's course in acting was set for the next 40 years. He played many villains of many nationalities in "Silver Canyon" ('51 Columbia) with Gene Autry, "The Marauders" ('55 MGM) with Jeff Richards, "Quincannon–Frontier Scout" ('56 United Artists) with Tony Martin, "Terror at Black Falls" ('62 Beckman) with House Peters Jr. and TVers such as "Lone Ranger", "Zorro", "Jim Bowie", "Kit Carson", "Brave Eagle", "Cisco Kid", "Broken Arrow", "Gunsmoke", "Wyatt Earp", "Rin Tin Tin", "Deputy", "Rawhide" and "Virginian".

Peter has occasionally turned his hand to writing, scripting episodes of "Zane Grey Theatre", "Rifleman", "Checkmate" and others. Most of Peter's time in recent years has been devoted to work for the Greek Orthodox Church.

JAMES (JIM) MASON

Pierce Lyden called James (Jim) Mason "a suave gentleman heavy," but Mason (no relation to the English dramatic actor) could just as easily be one of the dog heavies. Lean and lanky, Mason was actually French, born in Paris February 3, 1889. Educated in private schools and at Cornell University, he started in films as early as 1914. Under several variances of his given name (James Mason, Jim Mason, J. M. Mason, etc.) he worked in some 70 silents. His greatest glory came as a badman in the silent westerns of William S. Hart, Ken Maynard, Hoot Gibson, Pete Morrison, Buck Jones, Jack Holt, Harry Carey and Tom Mix.

With the advent of sound, he found a few plum outlaw roles in "Last of the Duanes" ('30 Fox) with George O'Brien, "Concentratin' Kid" ('30 Universal) with Hoot Gibson, "Caught" ('31 Paramount) with Richard Arlen, "Border Law" ('31 Columbia) with Buck Jones, "Texas Gunfighter" ('32 Tiffany) with Ken Maynard, "Renegades of the West" ('32 RKO) with Tom Keene, "Dude Ranger" ('34 RKO) with George O'Brien, "Fighting Shadows" ('35 Columbia) with Tim McCoy and "The Phantom Rider" serial ('36 Universal) with Buck Jones. By the mid '30s, now nearing 50, producers and directors usually cast Mason as 4th or 5th henchman through the door; he was seldom credited in the westerns of George O'Brien, Hopalong Cassidy, Tex Ritter, Charles Starrett, Buck Jones, Tom Keene, Bill Elliott or Gene Autry. By the '40s his roles had fallen to bit parts with his last appearance in "Kansas Territory" ('52) with Bill Elliott relegated to simply a card player in the saloon.

Mason was 70 when he died of a heart attack in Hollywood on November 7, 1959.

GEORGE MEEKER

Tall, thinly mustached, gray-blond, cultured-looking, born in Brooklyn, New York, George Meeker (March 5, 1904-August 19, 1984) had a long and usually menacing career in films (23 years) from 1928 to 1951.

As a character actor, Germanic or society playboy roles were often his lot and many classic A-films are among his nearly 200 screen credits—"Tess of Storm Country" ('32), "Life of Jimmy Dolan" ('33), "Stella Dallas" ('37), "Marie Antoinette" ('38), "Roaring Twenties" ('39), "Gone With the Wind" ('39), "High Sierra' ('41), "Captains of the Clouds" ('42) and "Casablanca" ('42).

Most of his slippery western contemptibles came opposite Roy Rogers at Republic. Watch for his underhanded dirty dealings in "Rough Riders' Round-Up" ('39), "Song of Nevada" ('44), "Home in Oklahoma" ('46), "Apache Rose" ('47), "Gay Ranchero" ('48) and "Twilight In the Sierras" ('50). Meeker's also in "Singing Hill" ('41) with Gene Autry, "Northwest Trail" ('45) with Bob Steele, "Silver Trails" ('48) with Jimmy Wakely, "Ranger of Cherokee Strip" ('49) with Monte Hale and "Wells Fargo Gunmaster" ('51) with Allan "Rocky" Lane. Meeker had roles in six serials towards the end of his term in Hollywood, with his best roles coming in "Brenda Starr, Reporter" ('45 Columbia) and as loan shark Nick Pollo in "Chick Carter, Detective" ('46 Columbia).

Meeker succumbed to Alzheimer's disease in Carpenteria, California.

JOHN MILJAN

From matinee idol of virtually every tank town in the U.S. to playing unsympathetic roles on screen is the road traveled by John Miljan. Born November 8, 1893, in Lead City, South Dakota, the suave deceiver was on the stage in roadshows, stock companies and repertoire for 14 years prior to making his first film in 1922. He played handsome, debonair romantics in silents but turned into a smooth talking, oily villain in scores of sound pictures after realizing his aristocratic good looks had a certain cold, shady quality.

Miljan was married to Victoria Lowe, a former wife of actor Creighton Hale. They had three sons.

His crafty dealings were evident in "Arizona Mahoney" ('36 Paramount) with Buster Crabbe, "Border G-Man" ('38 RKO) with George O'Brien, "Young Bill Hickok" ('40 Republic) with Roy Rogers, "North of the Rockies" ('42 Columbia) with Bill Elliott and Tex Ritter, "Wildfire" ('45 Action) with Bob Steele and a few others. In his 60s he turned to playing old Indian chiefs in "The Savage" ('52), "Wild Dakotas" ('56), "Apache Warrior" ('57) and his last, "Lone Ranger and the Lost City of Gold" ('58).

Miljan, 66, died of cancer in Hollywood on January 24, 1960.

IVAN MILLER

When Republic needed an unscrupulous businessman-type badman, they often called on Ivan Miller (November 13, 1888-September 27, 1967). Busy on the screen from 1935-1944, he was often seen as a G-Man, detective, policeman, attorney, or other official. It was to Republic's credit that they played him "against type", and it worked quite well in "The Old Barn Dance" ('38), "Man From Music Mountain" ('38), "Under Fiesta Stars" ('41) all with Gene Autry; "Wall Street Cowboy" ('39) and "Jesse James at Bay" ('41) with Roy Rogers, "Cowboys From Texas" ('39) with 3 Mesquiteers, and "Frontier Vengeance" ('40) with Don Barry. Also seen as the crooked Turk Mortenson in Universal's "Scouts to the Rescue" serial ('39).

BOYD "RED" MORGAN

Boyd "Red" Morgan was literally born in the saddle October 24, 1915, at Waurika, Oklahoma, and lived his first 12 years on a combination farm/cattle ranch. Red (so nicknamed for his bright red hair) stated he was hard pressed to remember when he didn't ride. His first taste of show business came when he was living for 15 months with an uncle who was a rancher and rodeo performer.

Red started high school in Hobbs, New Mexico, but finished after moving to Holtville, California. He was outstanding in athletics and received a football scholarship from U.S.C. in 1935. Arriving at the university in July for football practice, Red was recruited for his first professional job…playing halfback in a football picture. He joined the Screen Actors Guild in 1936, but after graduating from U.S.C. was recruited by the Washington Redskins. He joined the Pacific Coast League in 1940 and played a little with the Hollywood Bears and later with the Birmingham Generals.

WWII was going full bore in 1942. Graduating from U. S. Naval Academy as an ensign, he was sent to St. Mary's Pre-flight Training Center for 16 months. Upon leaving the service he coached football at Polytechnic High School in Long Beach until 1948 when he gave up the backfield for the backlot. One of the greatest stunt and heavy careers was about to begin.

Big, burly Red found himself in high demand due to his prowess with horses and soon became one of Hollywood's top stuntmen. Just some of the badguy roles to Red's credit: "Snake River Desperadoes" ('51), "Smoky Canyon" ('52), "Rough, Tough West" ('52) all with Charles Starrett, "Desert of Lost Men" ('51) and "Thundering Caravans" ('52) with Allan "Rocky" Lane, "Waco" ('52) with Bill Elliott, "Last Musketeer" ('52) with Rex Allen, "Winning of the West" ('53) with Gene Autry, "Gun Belt" ('53), "Robber's Roost" ('55) and "Gun Duel In Durango" ('57) all with George Montgomery, "Ten Wanted Men" ('55) with Randolph Scott, plus numerous episodes of "Range Rider", "Roy Rogers", "Cisco Kid", "Gene Autry", "Annie Oakley" and others throughout the '50s.

Morgan died January 8, 1988, in Tarzana, California, of a heart attack, leaving behind wife Lucille and two children.

PERRY MURDOCK

Perry Murdock was one of the lesser acclaimed but more talented of the western support players. Of Murdock's relatively few (less than 50) film credits, over 30 of them were in support of Bob Steele. The reason was a friendship issue, as Steele's younger brother Jim Bradbury says Bob and Perry were close friends.

Murdock was first seen in Steele's two 1928 FBO silents "Lightning Speed" and "Captain Careless", both non-westerns. From there a bond was formed and Murdock played various roles up through 1937, seldom venturing off Bob's range.

Mostly we recognize him for his vile henchmen, as when he contemplated selling pretty heroine Harley Wood to a Chinese-brides-for-sale ring in "Border Phantom" and the hideously ugly assayer/killer in "Big Calibre".

The multi-talented Murdock's musical talent can be viewed when he's part of a vaudeville song and dance team with Steele in "Headin' North" ('30), when he sings (with Steele) "Ragtime Cowboy Joe" and another ditty in "Near the Rainbow's End" ('30), as a guitar player in "Kid Courageous" ('35), as a tramp/singer in "Tombstone Terror" ('35) and as Ike of the duo Mike and Ike singing in John Wayne's "Paradise Canyon" ('35).

Murdock was active on the other side of the camera too, writing the original stories for "Captain Careless" (Steele served as co-writer); "Pals of the Prairie" ('33), a low rent Ben Corbett/Buck Owens (not the later country singer) vest pocket oater; and Steele's "Big Calibre" ('35) (writing in a good role for himself as noted above) and "Tombstone Terror" ('35).

Murdock had a go at being an assistant director under Steele's father, Robert North Bradbury, on "Danger Valley" ('37), one of Jack Randall's best Monograms.

Assuredly, Murdock worked in films in one capacity or another (second or first assistant director, writing, set decoration, etc.) from '38-'43 although none of his work was credited, but that's not unusual in B-films with sparse on-screen credits.

In 1944 he began to receive on-screen credit as a set decorator at Republic on such titles as "Silver City Kid" ('44), "Bordertown Trail" ('44) and "Haunted Harbor" serial ('44). He continued to labor in this field, eventually moving over to TV with series like "Stories of the Century", "Leave It To Beaver", "Coronado 9", "Thriller", "Overland Trail" and "Night Gallery", taking him into the early '70s. For years he was employed as a set decorator at Universal.

The talented Perry Harrison Murdock was born November 18, 1901, in Oklahoma. His father's name is unknown but his mother's maiden name was Jessie Lou Davis. Murdock never served in the Armed Forces.

At the time of his death, Murdock was married to Erma Gertrude Purviance. In an effort to learn more of Murdock's background, Bob Nareau spoke to Bob Steele's younger brother, Jim Bradbury, who confirmed Bob and Perry were close friends, that Perry spent a lot of time at the Bradbury ranch in the San Fernando Valley but at that time neither Bob nor Perry were married and "when the two of them were together, they really tore up the place."

Murdock died at 86 April 19, 1988, at the Beverly Manor Convalescent Hospital in Van Nuys, California, of respiratory arrest. He'd suffered from Alzheimer's disease for eight years prior to his demise. His remains were cremated.

BRADLEY PAGE

Born in Seattle, Washington, September 8, 1901, Bradley Page later became one of the original founders of the Screen Actors Guild. His parents were Mr. and Mrs. Sherman Page Brown. For generations the family was influential in the early life of the American Colonies. Bradley's father was a member of President Lincoln's Intelligence Department and later became an executive with the Union Pacific railroad in Chicago and Northern Pacific in Seattle. Bradley was christened Sherman Page Brown II.

After attending the University of Washington for two years, his life long interest in acting had him joining a Seattle musical stock company as an assistant electrician, followed by a stint with an English company in Victoria, British Columbia, circa 1920. Back in Washington, he joined a touring vaudeville act using the name Sherold Page up through 1927. From vaudeville, Bradley went into stock in various cities, including New York, alternating between Broadway and road shows.

Closing the hit play "House of Fear", Bradley came west to Hollywood in 1931, immediately finding work. By '32 he was the dress heavy in Buck Jones' "Sundown Rider". Also in Jones' "Fighting Ranger" ('34); "Beyond the Sacramento" ('40) with Bill Elliott; "Roaring Frontiers" ('41) with Elliott and Tex Ritter; "Outcasts of Poker Flat" ('37); "Sons of the Pioneers" ('42) with Roy Rogers and Republic's "King of the Mounties" Allan Lane serial ('42).

Page freelanced all of his 12 years in Hollywood in over 110 films. He continually supplemented his income by working on radio and stage.

Page left Hollywood in May 1943 and ranched along the lower Rogue River in Oregon til 1947 at which time he went into real estate in Brookings. Later approached to manage the Chamber of Commerce in Crescent City, Oregon, he was employed there for nine and a half years. He left to manage the Lake Tahoe South Shore for three and a half years.

Page died December 8, 1985, in Brookings.

JACK PALANCE

It was in director George Stevens' classic western "Shane" starring Alan Ladd where the cadaverous features and quiet, breathless way of talking made such an impact for ruthless, Jack Palance as hired killer Wilson. Also villainous in "Arrowhead" ('53 Paramount), "The Professionals" ('66 Columbia) and several Euro-westerns in the '70s.

Born Vladimir Palanuik February 18, 1919, in Lattimer Mines, Pennsylvania, he is the son of a Ukrainian coal miner. After being badly burned in an air crash in WWII, Palance underwent plastic surgery, the results of which are still visible in his taut, angular features. Palance came to Hollywood from the New York stage.

DENNIS PATRICK

Distinguished looking character actor Dennis Patrick, who usually played heavies, then crooked executives as his hair turned to silver, was born Dennis Patrick Harrison March 14, 1918, in Philadelphia, Pennsylvania. His father's family came from Ireland.

Patrick made his acting debut at eight in a children's show. Besides acting, he often directed. Some of his best known work is non-western. He was Jason McGuire (in '67) and Paul Stoddard (in '69) on "Dark Shadows" and Vaughn Leland from '79-'84 on "Dallas". He delightfully played western heavies on "Sugarfoot", "The Deputy", "U. S. Marshal", "Laramie", "Wanted Dead or Alive", "Tales of Wells Fargo", "Outlaws", "Stagecoach West", "Tall Man", "Dakotas", "Big Valley" and others.

While Patrick suffered from cancer and needed kidney dialysis, he died October 13, 2002, from smoke inhalation when his Studio City, California, condo caught fire. He was found on the third floor.

He was once married to actress Barbara Cason (1933-1990).

GAYLORD "STEVE" PENDLETON

Gaylord "Steve" Pendleton had a checkered, up-and-down acting career, never quite grabbing the gold ring, but to his credit he kept at it for over 50 years from 1923 to 1976.

Born September 16, 1908, in New York state, he entered films with the questionable name of Gaylord Pendleton, certainly not "western", although by 1933 he was appearing in his first westerns opposite Buck Jones ("Unknown Valley") and George O'Brien ("Life In the Raw"). He often played the youth—or juvenile lead—in westerns such as "Circle of Death" ('35) with Montie Montana, "Young Buffalo Bill" ('40) with Roy Rogers, even two later Jim Bannon Red Ryders—"Ride, Ryder, Ride" and "Roll, Thunder, Roll" along with "Buckaroo Sheriff of Texas" ('51) with the Rough Ridin' Kids. Many of his roles in bigger non-western pictures such as "Sergeant York" ('41), "Wild Harvest" ('47), "He Walked by Night" ('48) and "Battleground" ('49) are uncredited so we're not sure exactly when Pendleton dropped the Gaylord moniker and became Steve, but by 1951, now in his 40s, he was employing Steve as he played scores of badmen on TV's "Wild Bill Hickok", "Roy Rogers", "Gene Autry", "Hopalong Cassidy", "Annie Oakley", "Buffalo Bill Jr.", "Wyatt Earp", "Tales of the Texas Rangers", "26 Men", and other such fare. He's also a heavy in two 1935 Conway Tearle Beaumont offerings, "Gunfire" ('50) with Don Barry, "Sunset In the West" ('50) with Roy Rogers and "The Great Missouri Raid" ('51) with Wendell Corey and Macdonald Carey. Pendleton kept working in small roles on TV up through a "Cannon" episode in 1976.

He died October 3, 1984, in Pasadena, California.

JOHN PICKARD

Versatile John Pickard played both heavies and good guys. He was often cast as a tough cavalry Sergeant.

Born on a farm outside of Nashville, Tennessee, June 25, 1913, his entrance into showbiz came by singing in a Major Bowe's Amateur talent contest. Singing on the radio in Tennessee and male modeling jobs followed before John joined the Navy in 1942 for three and a half years. After the war John was in the cast of the "Diamond Jubilee Show" that toured the country, a few plays in Hollywood, and finally came to pictures with a bit in "Wake of the Red Witch" ('49).

Working on all the western TV series, John eventually co-starred on TV's "Gunslinger" in 1961 and starred as Cavalry Captain Shank Adams on "Boots and Saddles" ('57-'58).

Pickard was on over 200 TV episodes, including heavy roles on "Lone Ranger", "Cisco Kid", "Hopalong Cassidy", "Rin Tin Tin", "Kit Carson", "Wyatt Earp", "Death Valley Days", "Rawhide", "Lawman", "Laramie", "Johnny Ringo", "Gunsmoke", etc. Big screen badmen roles came with "Twilight In the Sierras" ('50 Republic) with Roy Rogers, "The Gunfighter" ('50 20th Century Fox) with Gregory Peck, "Snake River Desperadoes" ('51 Columbia) with Charles Starrett, "Trail Guide" ('52 RKO) with Tim Holt, "Bitter Creek" ('54 Allied Artists) with Bill Elliott, "Badlands of Montana" ('57 20th Century Fox) with Rex Reason and "Outlaw's Son" ('57 United Artists) with Dane Clark, among others.

John's good friend Gene Evans told us, "He was a straight up guy. John was well liked—and the best way to be that way is to always say what you mean and mean what you say and that's what he did. He wasn't a pushy guy. He made a living in that business for a long while and that's a hard thing to do. He could play anything—good guys, bad guys. He was really a good actor…much better than he ever got the chance to show. If you had a big scene to do and he was in it, you never worried that he was gonna let you down. He'd always bring a little more than was there."

Tony Young, star of "Gunslinger", on which John co-starred, stated, "I never saw him angry. He seemed to be at ease with life…he was like John Ireland that way. A very genuine, warm guy. He was very helpful to me, 'cause I was pretty green. He was always there for me. We were under tremendous pressure…12-14 hour days were not unusual. It took the cooperation of everybody and John was just terrific."

John died in an accident August 4, 1993, on the farm near Murfreesboro, Tennessee, that had sustained his family since 1829. Pickard was killed as he fell and broke his neck when a 1,300 lb. bull apparently knocked him down. Sheriff's authorities concluded Pickard was walking across a field to open a gate so the animals would have access to a spring.

WALTER REED

Walter Reed was a Golden Boot Award winner in 2000 and at times a "member" of both John Ford and Budd Boetticher's acting "families". To western and serial aficionados and film festival attendees over the years he'd become a well respected man, always full of life and ready with a wallet full of new jokes.

Born Reed Smith on Bainbridge Island, Washington, February 10, 1916, the son of a Coast Artillery Major, the family moved to Los Angeles when his father retired and became VP of a bond and stock company. Both Walter and his brother (Jack Smith, a popular singer and radio star of the '40s) were interested in showbiz when they were teens causing Walter to go on a mass interview in 1929 where he was chosen to play one of the Indian children in Richard Dix's "Redskin", filmed in Gallup, New Mexico.

However, Walter didn't join the Screen Actors Guild until 1936 when he appeared in several comedy shorts in New York with Tom Patricola and Buster West. Walter honed his craft appearing in stock companies in Rhode Island, Chattanooga, and New York. Joel McCrea saw Walter in a play and McCrea's agent worked out a contract for him at RKO in 1941.

After appearing in "Bombardier" and several other hit films, his career was interrupted by WWII. During the service he toured with dozens of other actors in the Army play, "Winged Victory".

Returning to RKO in 1946 he became a respected character actor, including three westerns with Tim Holt, "Western Heritage" ('48), "Target" ('52) and "Desert Passage" ('52). He's Bob Dalton in Randolph Scott's "Return of the Badmen" ('48) and was a heavy in dozens of juvenile-type TV westerns throughout the '50s ("Lone Ranger", "Hopalong Cassidy", "Annie Oakley", "Buffalo Bill Jr.", "Champion", "Wyatt Earp", "State Trooper", etc.)

As a lead, he starred in two Republic serials, "Flying Disc Man from Mars" ('51) and "Government Agents Vs. Phantom Legion" ('51).

After a major heart attack in the '60s (at age 49), Walter slowed down and became successful in real estate (partnering at times with old friend and stuntman Chuck Roberson).

At 85, Walter died of natural causes August 20, 2001, at his retirement home in Santa Cruz, California.

At the time, his friends and co-workers remembered him in Boyd Magers' WESTERN CLIPPINGS.

Myrna Dell (longtime friend from RKO years): "I loved him and I think he knew it. He was one of the best actors I've ever worked with. He was one of the nicest people I've ever known. I will always love him."

Myron Healey: "He determined his way to go. He was a hell of a man! If you can be happy for somebody's passing, I'm proud of him for wanting to go at a certain time and saying this is it, I'm going. He's fantastic. He made his exit at the Golden Boot with dignity which was wonderful. Everybody was proud of him."

Richard Simmons: "We were friends for over 50 years. Knowing Walter was really a privilege. He was a wonderful guy, very special, an exceptional guy."

Bruce Gordon: "We go back to 1937. We did melodramas at the American Music Hall. We did 'Girl of the Golden West', 'Fireman's Flame'…we were dancing and singing and jumping around and twitching, all for $21 a week. (Laughs) But we had a lot of fun!"

Russell Wade (RKO colleague): "He was one of the nicest people, a great actor and a credit to the industry. We were very good close friends. He was always a funny guy. He'd say, 'I'm Walter Reed, the actor, not the hospital!' He was funny."

Elaine Riley (RKO leading lady): "Heaven will never be the same after Walter gets there! (Laughs) He and Betty (his wife) and Dick (Elaine's husband Richard Martin) and I were longtime friends—we all lived in the Valley and we used to get together about once a week—the backyard in the summertime or the fireplace in the winter—we had such fun with them."

Dick Jones (worked with Walter on "Buffalo Bill Jr." and other Gene Autry produced shows): "He made my job in the motion picture and television industry a pleasure. He was fun to work with and to be around. He made one comment—said, 'You guys have cowboyed a lot…you get on those horses and you're gone! I'm still puttin' the saddlebags on.' I told him, 'You're not expected to, you're an ac–tor.' He puffed up and he says, 'You're right, I'm not a cowboy!' (Laughs) I could sit and talk with him for the longest time about anything and everything and nothin' at all. I enjoyed his company."

Harry Carey Jr.: "What can I say except he was one of the nicest guys I've ever known. Walter Reed could make a cloudy day sunny."

Rand Brooks: "His acting potential was really never realized. The field of acting has some wonderful people in it, but there have been a few times when I've been a little embarrassed to be an actor because of some of them. But Walter was the kind that made you proud to be an actor. He had class, humor and warmth."

DICK RICH

Dick Rich (February 27, 1909-March 29, 1967) played hoods, loudmouths, ruffians and bullies in dozens of films and TV shows from 1937 to 1958.

Without ever reaching any degree of stardom, his rugged mug was seen fleshing out character roles in B-films ("Racket Busters" '38, "Smashing the Money Ring" '39, "Phantom Raiders" '40, "Mob Town" '41, "In Old Oklahoma" '43, "Radar Men From the Moon" serial '52, etc.) as well as A-classics ("Angels With Dirty Faces" '38, "Each Dawn I Die" '39, "Grapes of Wrath" '40, "Brigham Young—Frontiersman" '40, "Ox Bow Incident" '43, "Story of G. I. Joe" '45, "Sea of Grass" '47, "Jailhouse Rock" '57, etc.).

Although more often cast in gangster films, it's fitting his first western heavy was in Buck Jones' "Headin' East" ('37 Columbia), followed by "Danger Ahead" ('40 Monogram), a James Newill Renfrew entry. Also in "Devil's Canyon" ('53) with Dale Robertson, "Fighting Lawman" ('53) with Wayne Morris and his last, "The Sheepman" ('58) with Glenn Ford—as well as dozens of TV heavies on "Lone Ranger", "Cisco Kid", "Wild Bill Hickok", "Kit Carson", "Hopalong Cassidy", "Gene Autry", "Roy Rogers", "Gunsmoke", "Colt .45", "Tales of Wells Fargo", among others.

Rich died in Palmdale, California.

FRANK RICHARDS

Burly, gorilla-faced Frank Richards, born September 15, 1909, in New York City, grew up in Fall River, Massachusetts. Although he had one bad eye, a lifelong habit of going to the gym led to a young career in the boxing ring in 1930-1931.

Richards operated a wholesale fruit and vegetable business for years while he tried to break into an acting stock company on Cape Cod. Soon, he began to get a few breaks, including a small role on Broadway in "The Brown Danube" ('39).

Eventually, Frank broke into films with Boris Karloff's "Before I Hang" ('40) followed by a henchman role in Universal's "Sky Raiders" serial ('41).

WWII interrupted his fledgling career while he served 18 months with the Army.

Following the war he resumed his career. Equally at home as a gangster or western heavy, some of his better westerns were "South of Caliente" ('51 Republic) with Roy Rogers, "Cowboy and the Indians" ('49 Columbia) with Gene Autry, "Wyoming Mail" ('50 Universal-International) with Stephen McNally, "Destry" ('54 Universal-International) with Audie Murphy, "Storm Rider" ('57 20th Century Fox) with Scott Brady, "Hard Man" ('57 Columbia) with Guy Madison and TVers such as "Lone Ranger", "Sky King", "Stories of the Century" (as Ike Clanton), "Cisco Kid", "Fury", "Annie Oakley", "Restless Gun", "26 Men", "Pony Express" and "Shotgun Slade".

Phasing out of the acting business, Frank entered real estate in 1960 and did terrific in his new field through 1984.

About 1989, Frank and his wife moved from the San Fernando Valley and settled in Las Vegas, Nevada, where he died on April 15, 1992.

ROY ROBERTS

"The Perils of Pauline" thrilled Roy Roberts so much at 18 that he decided to become an actor. Born Roy Barnes Jones March 19, 1906, in Tampa, Florida, he was the youngest of six children. He started as a musical (ukulele) song and dance man in Tampa, continued on to Baltimore where he was seen and encouraged. He dropped his southern accent by reading Shakespeare aloud. By the early '30s he was on the Broadway stage.

Roy's screen career didn't begin until after WWII where he was a rifle instructor with the Army Signal Corps. His film debut came in 1943 with "Guadalcanal Diary".

Writer Gary Brumbaugh described Roberts as "The prototype of the gruff, steely executive, the no-nonsense mayor, the assured banker, the stentorian leader. Roberts looked out of place without his patented dark suit and power tie. He was a solid, memorable presence who added stature wherever he was, no matter how far down the credits list."

A memorable TV appearance that grants him 'Best of the Badmen' status is his filibustering crooked Washington senator opposing Clint Walker in "Cheyenne: Vanishing Breed". Roberts totally embodies the thoroughly detestable Senator Matson.

Roberts also left his wicked mark on "Zane Grey Theatre", "Restless Gun", "Gunsmoke", "Lawman", "Bonanza", "Rawhide" and "Laredo" as well as a group of '50s B-plus westerns: "Wyoming Mail" ('50 Universal-International) with Stephen McNally, "Stage to Tucson" ('50 Columbia) with Rod Cameron, "Santa Fe" ('51 Warner Bros.) with Randolph Scott, "Cripple Creek" ('52 Columbia) with George Montgomery, "Man Behind the Gun" ('53 Warner Bros.) with Randolph Scott and "Yaqui Drums" ('56 Allied Artists) with Rod Cameron, among others.

The stocky Roberts died of a heart attack May 28, 1975, in Los Angeles and was buried in Ft. Worth, Texas. He was survived by his wife, actress Lillian Moore.

JACK ROPER

Stone-faced Jack Roper didn't make many westerns, but when he did, his rigid, stone-cold appearance was abjectly noticeable such as in, perhaps his best, "North From the Lone Star" ('41 Columbia) opposing Bill Elliott.

Actually a prizefighter from 1924 to 1940, the aging Roper finally managed to arrange a title bout with Joe Louis for the World Heavyweight boxing championship in February 1939. Roper's vision of the heavyweight title was stopped when Louis knocked him out 2 minutes and 20 seconds into the first round. Roper continued on for another year, but quit the ring when he lost an Oriental Heavyweight title fight to Luis Logan. Roper's final record: 53 wins (26 KO's), 42 losses, 10 draws for 105 bouts. He sometimes boxed under the alias Clifford Byron Hammond, which *may* have been his real name, but we have no information to substantiate that.

Roper was born in Pontchoula, Louisiana (not Mississippi or Michigan, as often reported), on March 25, 1904. He died at 62, November 28, 1966, of throat cancer at the Motion Picture Country House in Woodland Hills, California, where he'd been a resident for some time.

Certainly, many of his films were fight pictures— "Tough Kid" ('39), "Leather Pushers" ('40), "Pittsburgh Kid" ('41), "Kid From Brooklyn" ('46), and six of the Joe Palooka Monograms.

Roper's other western heavies were in "Flaming Frontiers" ('38 Universal serial) with Johnny Mack Brown, "Wall Street Cowboy" ('39 Republic) with Roy Rogers, "Heroes of the Saddle" ('40 Republic) with 3 Mesquiteers, "West of Carson City" ('40 Universal) with Johnny Mack Brown, "My Little Chickadee" ('40 Universal) with W. C. Fields and "Ridin' the Cherokee Trail" ('41 Monogram) with Tex Ritter.

Roper's final screen appearance was in John Wayne's "The Quiet Man" in '52—once again as a boxer, Tony Godello.

WILLIAM ROYLE

Swindler, crooked saloon owner, political boss, counterfeiter, dignified looking William Royle was a businessman-badman in some 20 westerns and serials during his brief four year career in Hollywood.

Born March 22, 1887, in Rochester, New York, the erudite Royle was obviously stage trained when he arrived in Hollywood in 1936 at age 49.

Perhaps his most important role was that of Raschid Ali Kahn in Darryl F. Zanuck's "The Rains Came" at Fox in 1939. However, to serial watchers he will always be remembered as Sir Dennis Nayland Smith in Republic's classic "Drums of Fu Manchu" serial ('40). But he was up to no good in two 1938 serials, "Flaming Frontiers" (Universal) with Johnny Mack Brown and "Hawk of the Wilderness" (Republic) with Bruce Bennett, and in "Wild West Days" ('37 Universal) with Brown. Royle was also one sort of cad or another in "Rebellion" ('36 Crescent) with Tom Keene, "Renfrew of the Royal Mounted" ('37 Grand National) and "Murder on the Yukon" ('40 Monogram) both with James Newill, "Renegade Ranger" ('38 RKO), "Arizona Legion" ('39 RKO) and "Fighting Gringo" ('39 RKO) all with George O'Brien, "Mexicali Rose" ('39 Republic) with Gene Autry and "Heroes of the Saddle" ('40 Republic) with the Three Mesquiteers.

Royle was only 53 when he died August 9, 1940, in Los Angeles, California.

WILLIAM H. RUHL

William H. (for Harris) Ruhl is probably not better known as a western badman because, in his character actor career of nearly 20 years, he didn't concentrate solely on western films. But among his 120 films are some 26 westerns, the bulk of them as heavies at Republic in the early '40s and Monogram in the late '40s. Also in his varied career are five serials with his best two roles in "Red Barry" ('38 Universal) as gangster Mannix and in "Scouts to the Rescue" ('39 Universal) as G-Man Hal Marvin.

His primary B-western back-stabbers were seen in "Gaucho Serenade" ('40 Republic) with Gene Autry; "Oklahoma Renegades" ('40 Republic) and "Gauchos of El dorado" ('41 Republic) both with the Three Mesquiteers; "Texas Terrors" ('40 Republic) and "Days of Old Cheyenne" ('43 Republic) with Don Barry; "Law Comes to Gunsight" ('47 Monogram), "Prairie Express" ('47 Monogram) and "Western Renegades" ('49 Monogram) all with Johnny Mack Brown; "Song of the Drifter" ('48 Monogram), "Cowboy Cavalier" ('48 Monogram) and "Brand of Fear" ('49 Monogram) all with Jimmy Wakely; "Shadows of the West" ('49 Monogram) and "Haunted Trails" ('49 Monogram) both with Whip Wilson. Ruhl played a few sheriffs on TV before retiring in 1951.

He was born October 25, 1901, in Oregon and died March 12, 1956, in Hollywood due to shock, secondary to a perforated ulcer.

LEE SHUMWAY

Lee Shumway had a marvelous 44 year screen career as a character actor and western heavy.

Born Leonard C. Shumway in Salt Lake City, Utah, March 4, 1884, he was educated in Salt Lake public schools and the University of Salt Lake, then taught dramatics and worked in various stock companies before entering films practically at the beginning in 1909.

The 6 foot, 180 lb. actor, often billed early on as L. C. Shumway, appeared in a variety of films, including westerns opposite such silent heroes as Harry Carey, Tom Mix, William Farnum, Buck Jones and Bob Custer.

Already 46 by the time sound came in, Shumway found lead heavy roles increasingly harder to come by. One of his most brutish is framing Tom Keene for murder in "Partners" ('32 RKO). He was also a notable gun-buzzard of one sort or another in "Lone Star Ranger" ('30 Fox) with George O'Brien; "Santa Fe Trail" ('30 Paramount) with Richard Arlen; the notorious Cactus Kid in Mascot's "Lone Defender" serial ('30); "Ivory Handled Gun" ('35 Universal) and "Outlawed Guns" ('35 Universal) both with Buck Jones; "Ghost Town" ('36 Commodore) with Harry Carey; "Song of the Trail" ('36 Ambassador) with Kermit Maynard; Universal's "Phantom Rider" serial ('36) with Buck Jones; "Painted Desert" ('38 RKO) with George O'Brien, and his last real hurrah as a lead heavy in two early Bill Elliott Columbias—"Lone Star Pioneers" and "Law Comes to Texas" (both '39).

In his mid '50s, Shumway turned to playing ranchers, fathers, sheriffs, businessmen, police officers, etc., winding up his career in a couple of Republic B's with Allan "Rocky" Lane ("Savage Frontier" as a doctor) and Rex Allen ("Old Overland Trail" as an elderly uncle).

At 74, Shumway's distinguished career ended when he died January 4, 1959, in Los Angeles, California.

K. L. (KENNETH L.) SMITH

Virtually nothing is known about K. L. (Kenneth L.) Smith, a rather smallish heavy with a stern, worried look on his pockmarked face who was prolific on one TV western after another in the '50s and '60s. Seen on "Gunsmoke", "Broken Arrow", "Sugarfoot", "Bat Masterson", "Lawman", "Bronco", "Maverick", "Rough Riders", "Colt .45", "Have Gun Will Travel",

"Cheyenne", "Rebel", "Laramie", "Rawhide", "Laredo" and others. The Oklahoma-born Smith, born October 22, 1922, worked from 1955 to 1971 in Hollywood, then was forgotten. He died August 24, 1981, in San Diego, California, at only 58.

WILLIAM SMITH

William Smith is perhaps best known for his portrayal of Falconetti on TV's "Rich Man, Poor Man" mini-series in 1976, or possibly as Texas Ranger Joe Riley on "Laredo" ('65-'67). But as a heavy, he will never be forgotten as psychotic, savage Jude Bonner who beats, rapes and nearly kills Miss Kitty (Amanda Blake) on the classic "Gunsmoke" episode, "Hostage!" ('72).

The 6' 2" Smith was born March 24, 1934, on Rolling Acres, a Hereford cattle ranch near Columbia, Missouri. Losing everything to the dust bowl, the family moved west to California, where, from 1942 when he was eight, until 1947, Bill appeared in many movies beginning with the part of a village boy in Universal's "Ghost of Frankenstein" ('42).

After high school, Bill joined the Air Force and served during the Korean War, receiving a Purple Heart. Bill studied at the University of Munich, Syracuse University and graduated cum laude at UCLA.

His list of life-achievements are stunning: He received a Lifetime Achievement Award from the Academy of Bodybuilding and Fitness; is two-time Arm Wrestling World Champion in the 200 lb. class; was a TV Marlboro Man; is fluent in Russian, German, French and Serbo-Croatian; has a 31-1 record as an amateur boxer; held the light-heavyweight weightlifting championship; played semi-pro football for the Wiesbaden Flyers in Germany; taught Russian at UCLA; was the training partner of Mr. Olympia, Larry Scott; fought California wildfires in the '50s; worked as a trainer at Bert Goodrich's Hollywood Gym; received a Golden Boot Award for his westerns; and has become a noted cowboy poet.

Returning to films in 1951, Smith was especially active on screen during the biker-flick craze in the late '60s and early '70s. Throughout the '70s, '80s, '90s and into the new century, Smith has continued to work, hop-scotching from A-films to B-films and even pure straight-to-video schlock. Nevertheless, he's always maintained a distinctive presence to this day; frequently appearing at western film festivals with his wife Joanne.

Other notable western scoundrels Bill played were on "Virginian", "Wagon Train", "Guns of Will Sonnett", "Custer", "Daniel Boone", "Yellow Rose" and in the big screen western comedy with Gene Wilder, "Frisco Kid" ('79).

RON SOBLE

Veteran heavy Ron Soble, 74, died in Los Angeles May 2, 2002, of lung and brain cancer. He was awarded the Golden Boot at his home only weeks before his death.

Born in Chicago, Illinois, March 28, 1932, Soble was a Golden Gloves boxing champ in 1944 and played football for the University of Michigan. After entering films, he was a longtime Screen Actors Guild activist, being twice elected third VP.

Soble enacted vicious heavies in "Walk Tall" ('60 20th Century Fox) with Willard Parker; "Gun Fight" ('61 United Artists) with James Brown; "True Grit" ('69 Paramount) and "Chisum" ('70 Warner Bros.) both with John Wayne and "Joe Kidd" ('72 Universal) with Clint Eastwood as well as TV episodes of "Virginian", "Lawman", "Texan", "Rawhide", "Bonanza", "Deputy", "Tall Man", "Two Faces West", "Gunslinger", "Laramie", "Cimarron Strip", "Daniel Boone", and others.

He played the part of Dirty Jim on the '66-'67 TV series "The Monroes".

KELLY THORSDEN

Another of the familiar faces that came into being with the advent of the TV western was gruff, brawny Kelly Thorsden, always projecting a strong, authoritative image whether playing heavies, which he did a lot, or cops.

Born January 19, 1917, in Deadwood, South Dakota, what he did for 40 years before coming to Hollywood in 1957 is unknown. He was employed from then on, usually as a hulking brutal or savage menace, on such shows as "Cheyenne", "Gunsmoke", "Californians", "Sugarfoot", "Tales of the Texas Rangers", "Lawman", "Texan", "Bronco", "Wyatt Earp", "Maverick" (as Sam Bass), "Overland Trail", "Laramie", "Rifleman", "Tales of Wells Fargo", "Bonanza", "Rawhide" and others. Also in "Gunpoint" ('66 Universal) with Audie Murphy. Thorsden was a semi-regular as Colorado Charlie, Yancy Derringer's compadre on that 1959 series.

He left the business in 1976 and died at 61 on January 23, 1978, in Sun Valley, California, of cancer.

MICHAEL VALLON

Shortish, pudgy, slightly balding…with an "everyman" appearance, Michael Vallon might be termed a character-actor badman.

Born July 21, 1897, in Dover, Minnesota, he came to films after some touring stage work as Rollo Dix in a few films in 1935. Quickly switching to Michael Vallon, he had small parts in some seven serials through 1944 (including "Valley of Vanishing Men" '42 Columbia and "Batman" '43 Columbia). He essayed heavies of various types in "Lightning Strikes West" ('40 Colony) with Ken Maynard, "Silver Bullet" ('42 Universal), "Boss of Hangtown Mesa" ('42 Universal), "Raiders of San Joaquin" ('43 Universal), "Lone Star Trail" ('43 Universal) all with Johnny Mack Brown, "Bad Men of Thunder Gap" ('43 PRC) and "Border Buckaroos" ('43 PRC) both with Dave O'Brien/James Newill, "Frontier Law" ('43 Universal) with Russell Hayden and "Trigger Trail" ('44 Universal) with Rod Cameron. He played a Mexican bandit on TV's "Rin Tin Tin: Border Incident" and a crooked bootmaker in "Cisco Kid: Robber Crow".

Working on through 1960, Vallon died November 13, 1973, at 76, in Los Angeles, California.

NILES WELCH

Niles Welch was a second string leading man, or "other" man, in dozens of silent era drawing room dramas who eventually came to playing several heavies in the early '30s. However, his life after the movies was far more interesting and productive.

Born July 29, 1888, in Hartford, Connecticut, the handsome, wavy-haired Welch began his film career for Vitagraph in 1913 and remained active til 1938.

Married to actress Elaine Baker, and possessed of a rich, deep voice, Welch turned to radio in 1939 and was the announcer for "The American School of the Air" and "Campbell Playhouse", both on CBS. During WWII he did foreign language broadcasts for Voice of America.

While working for the State Department, Welch was blinded and, as a resident of the Industrial Home for the Blind in Brooklyn, New York, he helped develop the program for the blind.

At 88, he died November 21, 1976, in Laguna Niguel, California.

Welch is prominent as a heavy in "Rainbow Trail" ('32 Fox) with George O'Brien, "McKenna of the Mounted" ('32 Columbia) and "Sundown Rider" ('33 Columbia) both starring Buck Jones, "Come On, Tarzan" ('32 World Wide) and "Lone Avenger" ('33 World Wide) both opposite Ken Maynard, "Riding Wild" ('35 Columbia) with Tim McCoy, and "Singing Vagabond" ('35 Republic) with Gene Autry.

Welch also played the "other" man in several westerns with an especially effective role as a Reverend in Buck Jones' "Stone of Silver Creek" ('35 Universal).

Welch also helped imperil both Frankie Darro and Tom Mix in two Mascot serials, "Wolf Dog" ('33) and "Miracle Rider" ('35).

ALAN WELLS

Alan Wells is another of that later group of heavies who primarily made their mark in TV westerns. In Wells' case he played juvenile leads on "Lone Ranger", "Cisco Kid", "Roy Rogers", "Hopalong Cassidy" and others, but slowly gravitated to heavies.

He's possibly at his best as hate-filled, vengeance-seeking, sneering Sheriff Mark Rote on "The Avenger", a 1957 color "Lone Ranger".

George Alan Wells was born March 23, 1926, in Greenville, Illinois, to George and Marie Wells. His father later became head of security at Disney Studios.

Alan was doing plays in Los Angeles when an agent spotted him doing the lead in "Mr. and Mrs. North" and sent him out to 20th Century Fox where he was cast as Cesar Romero's bodyguard in the gangster-comedy "Love That Brute" ('50). Directly after, he won the role of Lame Bull in Russell Hayden's "Apache Chief" at Lippert ('49) which was actually released before "Love That Brute".

Wells often played Indians—on "The Lone Ranger", "Wild Bill Hickok", "Champion" and in Republic's "Man With the Steel Whip" serial ('54).

Wells and actress Claudia Barrett met while doing a play and were married for seven years. They also appeared on seven TV shows together. The couple ran a poultry store when they weren't acting. Although divorced, Claudia and Alan remain good friends to this day.

Wells was later married several other times, including actress Barbara Lang.

As "parts were getting thinner, this opportunity came along," Wells told us in describing how he purchased the failing Jerry Lewis Restaurant on Sunset Blvd. circa 1966 and turned it into a prosperous nightclub, The Classic Cat. Wells had a ten year lease and ran out the whole "very successful" ten years.

Closing the club in 1976, he retired and traveled to Europe for several years, then settled in Lake Tahoe, Nevada. He found he liked Reno better and has been there for the last 15 years or so.

At 78, Wells keeps fit with a daily morning workout and swim.

Look for Wells as a heavy in "Last of the Desperadoes" ('55 Associated) as well as TV episodes of "Stories of the Century", "Annie Oakley", "Roy Rogers", "Tales of the Texas Rangers", "Tales of Wells Fargo", "26 Men", "Wanted Dead or Alive", "Mackenzie's Raiders" and "Wyatt Earp".

NORMAN (RUSTY) WESCOATT

Born in Hawaii, Norman (Rusty) Wescoatt (August 2, 1911-September 3, 1987) held three world records as a swimmer and was a professional football player and wrestler before coming to films in 1947 as a member of Columbia serial producer Sam Katzman's group of stock players.

The big, burly Wescoatt regularly got roughed up by smaller adversaries in 16 Columbia serials beginning with "The Vigilante" in 1947. Rusty's also in "Sea Hound" ('47), "Superman" ('48), "Tex Granger" ('48), "Congo Bill" ('48), "Batman and Robin" ('49), "Adventures of Sir Galahad" ('49), "Cody of the Pony Express" ('50), "Pirates of the High Seas" ('50), "Atom Man Vs. Superman" ('50), "Roar of the Iron Horse" ('51), "Mysterious Island" ('51), "Captain Video" ('51) "King of the Congo" ('52), "Riding With Buffalo Bill" ('54) and "Perils of the Wilderness" ('56). Wescoatt also worked for Katzman in several Jungle Jim thrillers; "When the Redskins Rode" ('51) and "Brave Warrior" ('52).

Branching out a bit in the '50s, Rusty was a heavy in Gene Autry's "Pack Train" ('53 Columbia), "Snowfire" ('58 Allied Artists) and TVers "Kit Carson", "Gene Autry", "Wild Bill Hickok", "Hopalong Cassidy", "Roy Rogers", "Sky King", "Tales of the Texas Rangers", "Casey Jones", and others.

Towards the end of his time in Hollywood, Rusty snagged two semi-regular roles…as the bartender on Robert Culp's "Trackdown" ('57-'59) and as the slightly crafty, but somewhat dim-witted Sgt. Holcomb on "Perry Mason". Rusty left the business in '65.

ADAM WILLIAMS

A familiar, always effective, supporting player on TV, Adam Williams also occasionally wrote screenplays. Williams, born in New York City, was usually cast as a heavy in westerns with two of his most vicious roles coming in "The Westerner: Dos Pinos" ('60) and "Bonanza: Vengeance" ('61) seeking to kill Hoss for the "murder" of his brother, for which Hoss was not responsible.

Williams can otherwise be seen in "Gunfight at Comanche Creek" ('63 Allied Artists) with Audie Murphy and TV segments of "Have Gun Will Travel", "Rifleman", "Black Saddle", "Rawhide", "Texan", "Zane Grey Theatre", "Outlaws", "Lawman", "Gunsmoke", "Maverick", "Cheyenne", "Northwest Passage" and "A Man Called Shenandoah".

Williams, 84, died December 4, 2006, of lymphoma.

MASTON P. "MACK" WILLIAMS

Mustachioed, scroungy looking screen badman Maston P. "Mack" Williams is a real enigma. Born April 23, 1879, in Mississippi, best information indicates Williams moved at a young age to Corsicana, Texas. He was married and operated a small grocery store until the marriage broke up. Supposition is, this is when he headed west for California where he entered films at 52 in 1931. He only worked eight years in the industry, appearing in nearly 40 movies, of which 21 were westerns and serials.

Finishing a role in Charles Starrett's "Riders of Black River" in 1939, Williams returned to Corsicana where he continued to operate the grocery. He died in Corsicana on July 15, 1978, at 99.

The busy bandit can be seen in "Cavalier of the West" ('31 Artclass) with Harry Carey; "Fighting With Kit Carson" ('33 Mascot serial) with Johnny Mack Brown; "To the Last Man" ('33 Paramount) with Randolph Scott; "Outlaw Tamer" ('35 Empire) with Lane Chandler; "Whistling Bullets" ('37 Ambassador) with Kermit Maynard; "Painted Stallion" ('37 Republic serial) with Ray Corrigan, "One Man Justice" ('37 Columbia) with Charles Starrett, "Public Cowboy No. 1" ('37 Republic) with Gene Autry; "Heart of the Rockies" ('37 Republic) and "Call the Mesquiteers" ('38 Republic) both with the Three Mesquiteers and "Overland Express" ('38 Columbia) starring with Buck Jones.

CLIFTON YOUNG

Born Robert Young September 15, 1917, Clifton Young was 31 and had already been in the movies for 23 years when, in 1948, he made "Blood On the Moon" as one of Robert Preston's hired guns.

Young arrived in showbiz early in life appearing in vaudeville with his parents. By age eight in 1926 he was the "juvenile villain" Bonedust in at least 16 of the late silent and early talkie "Our Gang" comedies at MGM, often using the name Bobby Young. Clifton was actually his mother's maiden name.

After a bit in John Wayne's "Lonely Trail" in 1936, Young left the screen for 10 years during which time he worked in radio and served in WWII.

Re-entering movies in 1946 he appeared as Joe McDoakes' loudmouth pal in several Warner Bros. shorts and had bit roles in several major films—he was the flophouse bum in "Treasure of the Sierra Madre" ('48).

After "Blood On the Moon" he seemed to find a "calling" as a western heavy in "Calamity Jane and Sam Bass" ('49 Universal-International); "Salt Lake Raiders" ('50 Republic) with Allan "Rocky" Lane; "Return of Jesse James" ('50)…very effective as Bob Ford; and in Roy Rogers' "Bells of Coronado" ('50) and, especially, "Trail of Robin Hood" ('50).

Just before his 34th birthday, on September 10, 1951, a promising career as a western heavy was cut short when Young apparently fell asleep while smoking and died of asphyxiation.

BIBLIOGRAPHY

Books
Aaker, Everett. TELEVISION WESTERN PLAYERS OF THE FIFTIES. McFarland, 1997.
Adams, Les and Rainey, Buck. SHOOT 'EM UPS. Arlington House, 1978.
AFI CATALOG: FEATURE FILMS 1931-1940; 1941-1950. University of California Press, 1982; 1999.
Barabas, SuzAnne and Barabas, Gabor. GUNSMOKE: A COMPLETE HISTORY. McFarland, 1990.
Bartelt, Chuck and Bergeron, Barbara. VARIETY OBITUARIES. Garland, 1988.
Blum, Daniel. AMERICAN THEATRE 100 YEARS. Chilton, 1960.
Canutt, Yakima. STUNT MAN. Walker and Co., 1979.
Carey Jr., Harry. COMPANY OF HEROES. Scarecrow, 1994.
Carman, Bob and Scapperotti, Dan. ADVENTURES OF THE DURANGO KID. Self-published, 1983.
Cary, Diana Serra. HOLLYWOOD POSSE. Houghton Mifflin, 1975.
Cline, William. IN THE NICK OF TIME. McFarland, 1984.
Copeland, Bobby. B-WESTERN BOOT HILL. Empire, 1999.
Copeland, Bobby. CHARLIE KING, WE CALLED HIM BLACKIE. Empire, 2003.
Copeland, Bobby. ROY BARCROFT, KING OF THE BADMEN. Empire, 2000.
Copeland, Bobby. TRAIL TALK. Empire, 1996.
Drake, Oliver. WRITTEN, PRODUCED AND DIRECTED BY OLIVER DRAKE. Hale-Ken, 1990.
Eyles, Allen. THE WESTERN. A. S. Barnes, 1975.
Goldrup, Tom and Jim. FEATURE PLAYERS VOL. 1, 2, 3, Self-published, 1986; 1992; 1997.
Hoffman, Henryk. "A" WESTERN FILMMAKERS. McFarland, 2000.
Holland, Ted. B-WESTERN ACTOR'S ENCYCLOPEDIA. McFarland, 1989.
Horner, William. BAD AT THE BIJOU. McFarland, 1982.
Jones, Ken and McClure, Arthur. HEROES, HEAVIES AND SAGEBRUSH. A. S. Barnes, 1972.
Jones, Ken and McClure, Arthur. INTERNATIONAL FILM NECROLOGY. Garland, 1981.
Katchmer, George. A BIOGRAPHICAL DICTIONARY OF SILENT FILM WESTERN ACTORS AND ACTRESSES. McFarland, 2002.
Kinnard, Roy. FIFTY YEARS OF SERIAL THRILLS. Scarecrow, 1983.
Landesman, Fred. THE JOHN WAYNE FILMOGRAPHY. McFarland, 2004.
Langman, Larry. A GUIDE TO SILENT WESTERNS. Greenwood Press, 1992.
Lentz, Harris. TELEVISION WESTERNS EPISODE GUIDE. McFarland, 1997.
Lentz, Harris. WESTERN AND FRONTIER FILM AND TV CREDITS. McFarland, 1996.
Lloyd, Ann and Fuller, Graham. ILLUSTRATED WHO'S WHO OF CINEMA. Macmillan, 1983.
Lyden, Pierce. CAMERA! ROLL 'EM! ACTION. Self-published, 1986.
Lyden, Pierce. FROM THE B'S TO TV'S. Self-published, 1987.
Lyden, Pierce. THE MOVIE BADMAN. Self-published, 1985.
Lyden, Pierce. THE MOVIE BADMEN I RODE WITH. Self-published, 1988.
Lyden, Pierce. THOSE SATURDAY SERIALS. Self-published, 1991.
Magers, Boyd and Fitzgerald, Michael. LADIES OF THE WESTERN. McFarland, 2002.
Magers, Boyd and Fitzgerald, Michael. WESTERNS WOMEN. McFarland, 1999.
Malloy, Mike. LEE VAN CLEEF. McFarland, 1998.
McClure, Arthur, Twomey, Alfred and Jones, Ken. MORE CHARACTER PEOPLE. Citadel, 1984.
McCord, Merrill. BROTHERS OF THE WEST. Self-published, 2003.
Miller, Don. HOLLYWOOD CORRAL. Riverwood, 1993.

Moyer, Donn. COWPOKES 'N' COWBELLES. Wild West, 2003.
Nareau, Bob. BITS AND SPURS. Self-published, 2001.
Nareau, Bob. BOB STEELE, STARS AND SUPPORT PLAYERS. Self-published, 1998.
Nareau, Bob. THE FILMS OF BOB STEELE. Self-published, 1997.
Nareau, Bob. THE REAL BOB STEELE AND A MAN CALLED BRAD. Da' Kine, 1991.
Nareau, Bob. THOSE B WESTERN COWBOY HEROES WHO RODE THE HOLLYWOOD RANGE WITH BOB STEELE. Self-published, 1999.
Nevins, Francis. FILMS OF HOPALONG CASSIDY. World of Yesterday, 1988.
Nevins, Francis. FILMS OF THE CISCO KID. World of Yesterday, 1998.
Peters Jr., House. ANOTHER SIDE OF HOLLYWOOD. Empire, 2000.
Pitts, Michael. POVERTY ROW STUDIOS. McFarland, 1997.
Quinlan, David. ILLUSTRATED DIRECTORY OF FILM STARS. Hippocrene, 1981.
Quinlan, David. ILLUSTRATED ENCYCLOPEDIA OF MOVIE CHARACTER ACTORS. Harmony Books, 1986.
Ragan, David. WHO'S WHO IN HOLLYWOOD. Facts on File, 1992.
Rainey, Buck. SERIALS AND SERIES. McFarland, 1999.
Rainey, Buck. THE STRONG, SILENT TYPE. McFarland, 2004.
Reyes, Luis and Rubie, Peter. HISPANICS IN HOLLYWOOD. Lone Eagle, 2000.
Schutz, Wayne. MOTION PICTURE SERIAL. Scarecrow, 1992.
Truitt, Evelyn Mack. WHO WAS WHO ON SCREEN. R. R. Bowker, 1983.
Vazzana, Eugene Michael. SILENT FILM NECROLOGY. McFarland, 2001.
Wakely, Linda Lee. SEE 'YA UP THERE, BABY: THE JIMMY WAKELY STORY. Shasta, 1992.
Ward, Jack. SUPPORTING PLAYERS OF TELEVISION. Lakeshore West, 1996.
Ward, Jack. TELEVISION GUEST STARS. McFarland, 1993.
Wise, James E. and Wildersen III, Paul. STARS IN KHAKI. Naval Institute Press, 2000.
Witney, William. IN A DOOR, INTO A FIGHT, OUT A DOOR, INTO A CHASE. McFarland, 1996.

PERIODICALS
CLASSIC IMAGES, various issues (1979-2004).
CLIFFHANGER, various issues (1983-2000).
FAVORITE WESTERNS, various issues (1981-1987).
Magers, Boyd. WESTERN CLIPPINGS, various issues (1994-2004).
UNDER WESTERN SKIES, various issues (1978-2000).
WESTERN FILM COLLECTOR VOL. 1 #2 (May 1973).
WRANGLER'S ROOST, various issues (#74-119).

WEBSITES
Chuck Anderson's Old Corral
IBDB (Internet Broadway Database)
IMDb (Internet Movie Database)

ABOUT THE AUTHOR

Boyd Magers has always felt he grew up in the right time and place for a full appreciation of all westerns…the late '40s–early '60s. Born in Kansas City, Kansas, in 1940, he grew up with a western influence in Independence, Kansas (near where the Dalton and James Gangs rode) and Ponca City, Oklahoma (the site of the famed 101 Ranch). Beginning in late 1946 he attended the Beldorf in Independence and the Center in Ponca City, riding the range with the current crop of B-western heroes—Roy Rogers, Gene Autry, Rex Allen, Monte Hale, Tim Holt, Eddie Dean, Jimmy Wakely, Durango Kid, Johnny Mack Brown and others. By 1953 the new medium of television offered him a steady hour upon hour appreciation of the early screen cowboys—Buck Jones, Bob Steele, Hoot Gibson, Ken Maynard, George O'Brien, Rex Bell, Tim McCoy and the rest. The early '50s was also the time for the dawning of the TV western—"Hopalong Cassidy", "Kit Carson", "Cisco Kid", "Stories of the Century" and the others which slowly matured into the so-called adult TV western of the late '50s early '60s, "Gunsmoke", "Cheyenne", "Sugarfoot", "Restless Gun" and dozens more. Therefore, he came to appreciate all eras of westerns.

Following Armed Forces Radio Network military service in Korea from '60-'61, and during a fifteen year career in radio ('62-'77), Boyd began to contribute articles on westerns to publications such as COUNTRY STYLE and others.

In 1977 he established VideoWest which soon became the most respected source for western movies and TV episodes on video for over 25 years. From 1987 to 1994 he contributed a regular column on westerns to THE BIG REEL. Over the ensuing years he wrote regular columns or contributed articles to COUNTRY AND WESTERN VARIETY, UNDER WESTERN SKIES, CLASSIC IMAGES, FILM COLLECTOR'S REGISTRY, among several others. Over the years he's also provided research data and material to over 40 books and several TV/video documentaries. He wrote hundreds of B-western film reviews still being used annually in VIDEO MOVIE GUIDE. In 2005 he wrote all the Roy Rogers and Gene Autry film reviews for Leonard Maltin's CLASSIC MOVIE GUIDE.

In 1994 he began self-publishing WESTERN CLIPPINGS which has become *the* primary source and authority for thousands of western readers. He also self-publishes SERIAL REPORT.

Knowledgeable about all phases of western films, over the last thirteen years Boyd has moderated over 120 western celebrity guest star discussion panels at western film festivals all over the country. In addition, Boyd currently has over 1,750 reviews and observations ("The Best and Worst of the West") of western films online at Chuck Anderson's Old Corral <www.surfnetinc.com/chuck/magers.htm>

Boyd's first book, WESTERNS WOMEN, was published by McFarland in 1999 and was followed in 2002 by LADIES OF THE WESTERN. SO YOU WANT TO SEE COWBOY STUFF was his third book in 2003, followed by THE FILMS OF AUDIE MURPHY in 2004. THE FILMS OF GENE AUTRY is scheduled for 2007.

Boyd is dedicated to preserving the rich heritage and enduring memories of small and big screen westerns and the people who populated them.

ABOUT THE AUTHOR

Bob Nareau was born in Keene, New Hampshire. Early in life, his main interests were sports and movie cowboys. That interest never left him.

Following the attack on Pearl Harbor, Bob enlisted in the U.S. Navy. Following the war, he attended Columbia University in New York City, where he graduated with the degrees Bachelor of Science, Master of Arts, and completed work on an Education Doctorate. It was at Columbia that Bob had his first contact with the magic of the world of films. Contacted by Boris Kaplan, a talent scout for Paramount Pictures, he was offered a chance at Hollywood. Still not too smart, he declined.

Nareau's first job after college was coaching at a school in the Sacramento, California, area. Following two successful years, a new elementary school was opened in the district, and he was appointed principal. Five years of writing articles for various educational journals on programs he instigated, and coping with the woes of 22 women teachers convinced him to move on. For his efforts, Bob was awarded a California Congress of Parents and Teacher Award as Man of the Year.

He then opened his own swimming and tennis club in Carmichael, California, acting as the teaching professional, while attending evening classes at University of Pacific School of Law. Graduating from law school with both a Bachelor and Doctorate of Law, he opened a law practice in San Diego County where for several years he had the largest criminal law defense practice in the county. During this tenure, Nareau managed to change the laws a dozen times in the appellate and supreme courts. He was admitted to practice and argued in the Supreme Court of the United States.

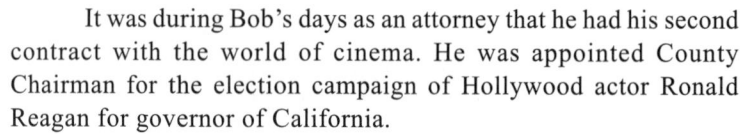

It was during Bob's days as an attorney that he had his second contract with the world of cinema. He was appointed County Chairman for the election campaign of Hollywood actor Ronald Reagan for governor of California.

The urge to write continued during Bob's practice of law and resulted in articles in various law journals. After many years as a criminal defense attorney, he realized his work was resulting in putting back on the streets many whom he knew in his heart belonged locked up. He sold his practice and moved with his wife, Greta, to the beautiful Island of Kauai in the state of Hawaii where, along with ample beach time, he taught law in the University of Hawaii system.

Today retired, he, Greta, and granddaughter "Punky" spend their days between attending film festivals, "existing" in Arizona, and "living" on Kauai.

Bob Nareau's other books include THE REAL BOB STEELE AND A MAN CALLED "BRAD", THE FILMS OF BOB STEELE, BOB STEELE: STARS AND SUPPORT PLAYERS, BOB STEELE: HIS "REEL" WOMEN, THOSE "B" WESTERN COWBOY HEROES WHO RODE THE HOLLYWOOD RANGE WITH BOB STEELE, BITS AND SPURS: "B" WESTERN TRIVIA and KID KOWBOYS.

ABOUT THE AUTHOR

Bobby Copeland was reared in Oak Ridge, Tennessee, and began going to the Saturday matinee B-Western movies at nearby theaters. He was immediately impressed by the moral code of these films, and has tried to pattern his life after the example set by the cowboy heroes. After graduating from high school and attending Carson-Newman College and the University of Tennessee, he set out to raise a family and start a career at the Oak Ridge National Laboratory. His love for the old Western films was put on the shelf and lay dormant for some 35 years. One Saturday, in the mid-eighties, he happened to turn on his television and the station was showing a Lash LaRue movie. This rekindled his interest. He contacted the TV program's host ("Marshal" Andy Smalls), and was invited to appear on the program. Since that time, Bobby has had some 100 articles published, written nine books, contributed to twelve books, made several speeches, appeared on television over 30 times, and has been interviewed by several newspapers and four independent radio stations as well as the Public Radio Broadcasting System to provide commentary and promote interest in B-Western films. In 1985 he was a co-founder of the Knoxville, Tennessee-based "Riders of the Silver Screen Club," serving five times as president. He initiated and edited the club's newsletter for several years.

In 1996, his first book TRAIL TALK was published by Empire Publishing, Inc. (one of the world's largest publishers of books on Western films and performers) It was followed by B-WESTERN BOOT HILL, BILL ELLIOTT: THE PEACEABLE MAN, ROY BARCROFT—KING OF THE BADMEN, CHARLIE KING—WE CALLED HIM BLACKIE, and JOHNNY MACK BROWN—UP CLOSE AND PERSONAL. In addition to these popular books, Bobby also self-published THE BOB BAKER STORY, THE WHIP WILSON STORY, and FIVE HEROES. He has attended some 60 Western film festivals, and met many of the Western movie performers. He continues to contribute articles to the various Western magazines, and he is a regular columnist for *Western Clippings*. In 1988, Bobby received the "Buck Jones Rangers Trophy," presented annually to individuals demonstrating consistent dedication to keeping the spirit of the B-Western alive. In 1994, Don Key (Empire Publishing) and Boyd Magers (Video West, Inc. & *Western Clippings*) awarded Bobby the "Buck Rainey Shoot-em-Ups Pioneer Award," which yearly honors a fan who has made significant contributions towards the preservation of interest in the B-Westerns. He will soon be featured on a four-hour DVD about the history of B-Western films.

Bobby is an active member at Oak Ridge's Central Baptist Church. He retired in 1996 after 40 years at the same workplace. Bobby plans to continue his church work, write more B-Western articles, and enjoy his retirement with his faithful sidekick, Joan.

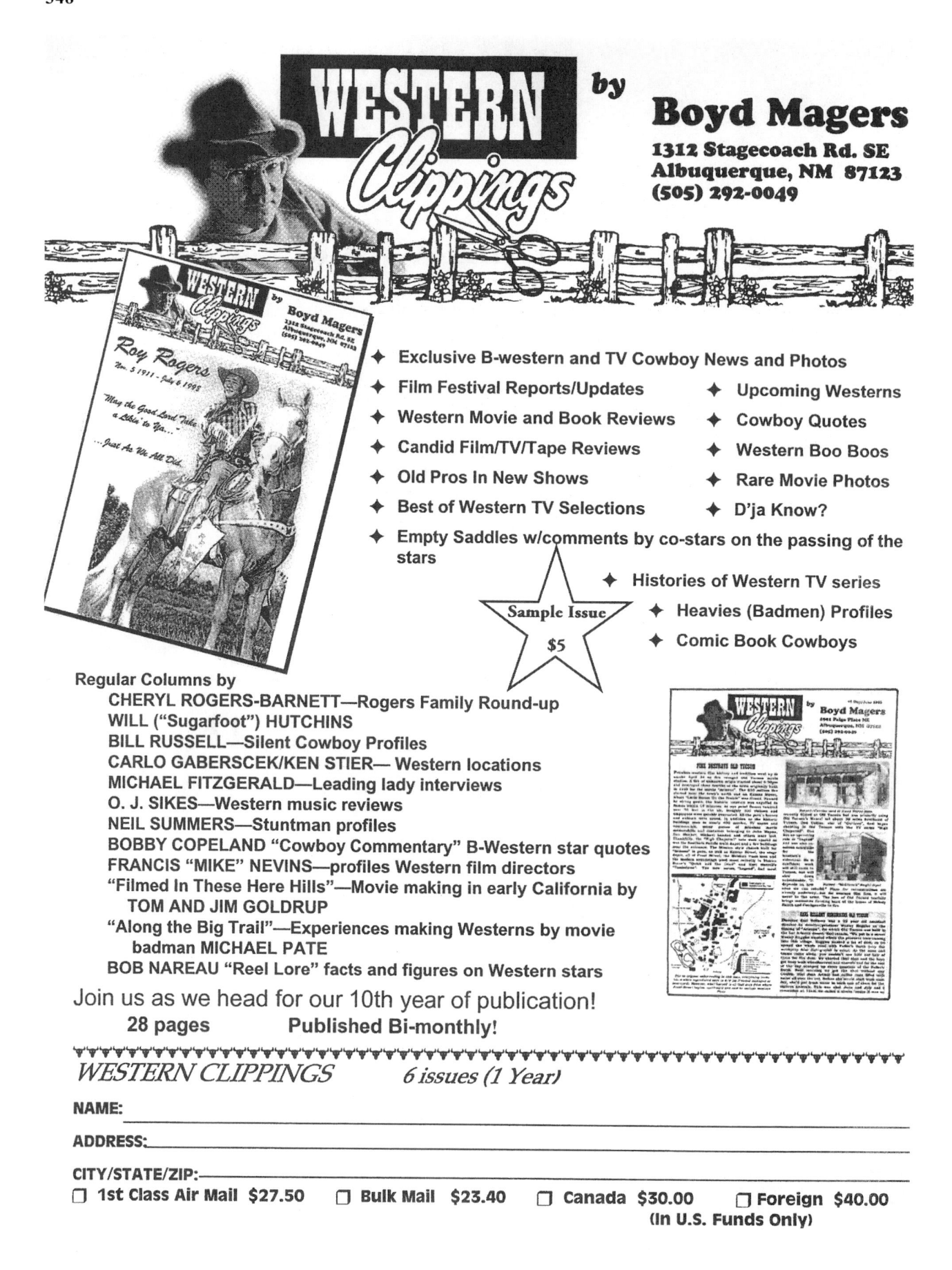

WESTERN Clippings by Boyd Magers

1312 Stagecoach Rd. SE
Albuquerque, NM 87123
(505) 292-0049

- Exclusive B-western and TV Cowboy News and Photos
- Film Festival Reports/Updates
- Upcoming Westerns
- Western Movie and Book Reviews
- Cowboy Quotes
- Candid Film/TV/Tape Reviews
- Western Boo Boos
- Old Pros In New Shows
- Rare Movie Photos
- Best of Western TV Selections
- D'ja Know?
- Empty Saddles w/comments by co-stars on the passing of the stars
- Histories of Western TV series
- Heavies (Badmen) Profiles
- Comic Book Cowboys

Sample Issue $5

Regular Columns by
CHERYL ROGERS-BARNETT—Rogers Family Round-up
WILL ("Sugarfoot") HUTCHINS
BILL RUSSELL—Silent Cowboy Profiles
CARLO GABERSCEK/KEN STIER— Western locations
MICHAEL FITZGERALD—Leading lady interviews
O. J. SIKES—Western music reviews
NEIL SUMMERS—Stuntman profiles
BOBBY COPELAND "Cowboy Commentary" B-Western star quotes
FRANCIS "MIKE" NEVINS—profiles Western film directors
"Filmed In These Here Hills"—Movie making in early California by TOM AND JIM GOLDRUP
"Along the Big Trail"—Experiences making Westerns by movie badman MICHAEL PATE
BOB NAREAU "Reel Lore" facts and figures on Western stars

Join us as we head for our 10th year of publication!
28 pages   Published Bi-monthly!

WESTERN CLIPPINGS   6 issues (1 Year)

NAME: _____

ADDRESS: _____

CITY/STATE/ZIP: _____

☐ 1st Class Air Mail $27.50   ☐ Bulk Mail $23.40   ☐ Canada $30.00   ☐ Foreign $40.00
(In U.S. Funds Only)

SO YOU WANNA SEE COWBOY STUFF?

The Western Movie/TV Tour Guide

by Boyd Magers

Here's the only complete tour guide ever assembled leading you directly to all the western movie and TV memorabilia as well as filming locations in the entire United States!

From California to Maine you will find:

- Exact filming locations where Roy Rogers, Gene Autry, Hopalong Cassidy, Bill Elliott, John Wayne, "Bonanza", The Durango Kid and all the rest shot their western films. Iverson's Corriganville, Old Tucson, Lone Pine, Sedona, Melody Ranch, Jauregui Ranch, Kernville, Moab, Walker Ranch, Bronson Cave, Monument Valley, Vasquez Rocks, Pioneertown, Big Bear, Kanab.
- Murals, Birthplaces, Monuments, Statues, Parks, Exhibits, Rodeos, Road Markers, Hotels, Bronzes and more!
- The Top Western Museums in the Country—Gene Autry, Roy Rogers, Rex Allen, Will Rogers, John Wayne, Andy Devine, Warner Bros., George Montgomery, Red Ryder, Buddy Roosevelt, Ken Maynard, Tom Mix, James Stewart, Audie Murphy, Tex Ritter, Yakima Canutt.
- Detailed Studio Guides to Republic, Warner Bros., Universal, Monogram.
- Birthplaces, Childhood Homes and Former Residences of Roy Rogers, Hopalong Cassidy, Gail Davis, Tom Mix, William S. Hart, Joel McCrea, Ken Maynard, John Wayne, Dale Evans, Gene Autry, Audie Murphy.
- Detailed Guide to Western Stars on the Hollywood Walk of Fame, Newhall Walk of Stars, Palm Springs Walk of Fame and others.
- How to Find, Visit and See Gower Gulch, Ray "Crash" Corrigan's Grill, Fess Parker's Winery, John Wayne's Wild Goose yacht, Clint Eastwood's Mission Ranch, the Pro Rodeo Hall of Fame, the Lone Ranger's Mask, Hoot Gibson's Rodeo, the John Ford Memorial, Roy Rogers Restaurants, Sky King's Songbird, The Ponderosa "Bonanza" Ranch, Rex Bell's Ranch, the bar used on "Gunsmoke", Buck Jones' Circus Wagon, Railroads and Locomotives used in dozens of westerns.
- Gravesites of John Wayne, Roy Rogers, Gene Autry, Audie Murphy, Hoppy's Topper and others.
- Complete Listing of All the Annual Western Film Festivals!

$35.00 + $3.00 s/h

Written and Extensively Researched Over a Three Year Period by Boyd Magers, Author of WESTERN CLIPPINGS Magazine, WESTERNS WOMEN and LADIES OF THE WESTERN among others. Special Movie Locations Contributions in Association with Noted Authority Tinsley Yarbrough.

- Hardcover; 8-1/2 x 11"
- Glossy Stock throughout
- 264 pages
- Hundreds of photographs

EMPIRE PUBLISHING, INC. • PO BOX 717 • MADISON, NC 27025-0717 • PH: 336-427-5850 • FAX 336-427-7372

B-WESTERN BOOT HILL
A Final Tribute to the Cowboys and Cowgirls Who Rode the Saturday Matinee Movie Range
by Bobby J. Copeland

$15.00 (+ $2.00 s/h)

NEWLY REVISED AND UPDATED! Now includes the obituaries of Rex Allen, Dale Evans, Walter Reed, Clayton Moore, and others. *You asked for it—now here it is . . . an extensively updated version of B-WESTERN BOOT HILL. (The first printing sold out!) An easy reference guide with hundreds of new entries, updates, and revisions. If you've worn out your original BOOT HILL, or are looking for a more complete B-Western reference book, this is the book for you!*

* 1000+ ENTRIES *
The Most Complete List Ever Assembled of Birth Dates, Death Dates, and Real Names of Those Beloved B-Western Performers.

* IT'S A LITERARY MILESTONE *
Bobby Copeland has produced a literary milestone which surely will rank at the top among those important Western film history books printed within the past 30 years. *Richard B. Smith, III*

* OBITUARIES AND BURIAL LOCATIONS *
Through the years, Bobby Copeland has collected actual obituaries of hundreds of B-Western heroes, heavies, helpers, heroines and sidekicks. Also included is a listing of actual burial locations of many of the stars.

* MANY PHOTOS THROUGHOUT *

ROY BARCROFT: King of the Badmen
by Bobby J. Copeland

A WONDERFUL BOOK ABOUT A GREAT CHARACTER ACTOR

In this book, you will find:
- A detailed biography
- Foreword by Monte Hale
- How he selected the name "Roy Barcroft"
- Letters and comments by Roy
- Roy's views about his co-workers
- Co-workers' comments about Roy
- Roy's fans speak out
- Other writers' opinions of Roy Barcraft
- Filmography

$15.00 (+ $2.00 s/h)

CHARLIE KING
We called him "Blackie"
by Bobby J. Copeland

Who was the "baddest" of the badmen?
Many will say it was Charlie King.

This book is a salute to Charles "Blackie" King— one of the premiere B-Western badmen.

Includes:
- The most comprehensive information ever printed on "Blackie"
- The truth about Charlie's death... including his death certificate
- Comments by noted Western film historians
- Remarks by co-workers
- Writers' opinions of Charlie's acting and his career
- Cowboys with whom he worked
- Studios that employed him
- Filmography
- Many photos
- Much, much more

ONLY $15.00 (+ $2.00 s/h)

EMPIRE PUBLISHING, INC. • PO BOX 717 • MADISON, NC 27025 • PH 336-427-5850 • FAX 336-427-7372

The ROUND-UP

A Pictorial History of WESTERN Movie & Television STARS Through the Years!

by Donald Key

"This book brings back memories for me... makes me think back to those days at Republic."
—Monte Hale

Relive those treasured Saturday afternoons of your youth when you cheered on your favorite B-Western cowboy heroes: Tom Mix, Hoot Gibson, Ken Maynard, Tim McCoy, Gene Autry, Dale Evans, Roy Rogers, Lash LaRue, the Durango Kid, Buck Jones, Hopalong Cassidy, Wild Bill Elliott, Sunset Carson. And bring back memories of the Classic TV-Western cowboys and the more recent A-Western stars.

They're all here in what may be the mot comprehensive (and attractive) Western star picture book ever produced. You get 298 heroes, heroines, stuntmen, sidekicks, villains, and cattlepunchers, plus 2 musical groups (the Cass County Boys and the Sons of the Pioneers). From old-time stuntman Art Acord to Tony Young (who played Cord in TV's *Gunslinger),* from Harry Carey to Clint Eastwood, this handsome volume includes all your favorites from the turn of the century through the 1990s, arranged in alphabetical order for easy reference. But this is more than just a pictorial. Each full-page entry includes a discretely placed one-paragraph background summary of the actor of group, with dates of birth and death. PLUS you get all these EXTRAS:

- Revised 2005
- Foreword by Monte Hale
- Afterword by Neil Summers
- Bibliography
- Quality hardcover to withstand repeated use.

$27.00 + $3.00 s/h

"As time marches on, and so many of our screen and personal friends leave us, books like The Round-Up become even more important to us and to the history of Westerns."
—Neil Summers

Those Great COWBOY SIDEKICKS

by David Rothel

- 8-1/2 x 11
- BEAUTIFUL COLOR COVER
- 300+ PAGES
- OVER 200 PHOTOS

$25.00 + $3.00 s/h

This book features in-depth profiles of such fondly-remembered character actors as George "Gabby" Hayes, Smiley Burnette, Andy Devine, Al "Fuzzy" St. John, Pat Buttram, Max Terhune, Fuzzy Knight, and many other sidekicks of the B-Westerns—thirty-nine in all! Much of *Those Great Cowboy Sidekicks* is told through the reminiscences of the sidekicks themselves and the cowboy stars who enjoyed the company of these often bewhiskered, tobacco-chewing saddle pals. Mr. Rothel provides the reader with the rare opportunity to go behind the scenes to discover the manner in which Western screen comedy was created.

Author David Rothel is a Western film historian who has also written AN AMBUSH OF GHOSTS, RIM HOLT, RICHARD BOONE: A KNIGHT WITHOUT ARMOR IN A SAVAGE LAND, THE ROY ROGERS BOOK, THE GENE AUTRY BOOK, and several other titles.

EMPIRE PUBLISHING, INC. · PO BOX 717 · MADISON, NC 27025 · PH 336-427-5850 · FAX 336-427-7372

Other Fine Western Books Available from Empire Publishing, Inc:

ABC's of Movie Cowboys by Edgar M. Wyatt. $5.00.
Art Acord and the Movies by Grange B. McKinney. $15.00.
Audie Murphy: Now Showing by Sue Gossett. $30.00.
Back in the Saddle: Essays on Western Film and Television Actors edited by Garry Yoggy. $24.95.
Bill Elliott, The Peaceable Man by Bobby Copeland. $15.00.
B-Western Actors Encyclopedia by Ted Holland. $30.00.
Buster Crabbe, A Self-Portrait as told to Karl Whitezel. $24.95.
B-Western Boot Hill: A Final Tribute to the Cowboys and Cowgirls Who Rode the Saturday Matinee Movie Range by Bobby Copeland. $15.00.
The Cowboy and the Kid by Jefferson Brim Crow, III. $5.90.
Crusaders of the Sagebrush by Hank Williams. $29.95.
Duke, The Life and Image of John Wayne by Ronald L. Davis. $12.95.
The Films and Career of Audie Murphy by Sue Gossett. $18.00.
The Golden Corral, A Roundup of Magnificent Western Films by Ed Andreychuk. $29.95.
The Hollywood Posse, The Story of a Gallant Band of Horsemen Who Made Movie History by Diana Serra Cary. $16.95.
Hoppy by Hank Williams. $29.95.
In a Door, Into a Fight, Out a Door, Into a Chase, Movie-Making Remembered by the Guy at the Door by William Witney. $32.50.
John Ford, Hollywood's Old Master by Ronald L. Davis. $14.95.
John Wayne—Actor, Artist, Hero by Richard D. McGhee. $25.00.
John Wayne, An American Legend by Roger M. Crowley. $29.95.
Johnny Mack Brown—Up Close and Personal by Bobby Copeland. $20.00.
Kid Kowboys: Juveniles in Western Films by Bob Nareau. $20.00.
Lash LaRue, King of the Bullwhip by Chuck Thornton and David Rothel. $25.00.
Last of the Cowboy Heroes by Budd Boetticher. $32.50.
More Cowboy Shooting Stars by John A. Rutherford and Richard B. Smith, III. $18.00.
The Official TV Western Roundup Book by Neil Summers and Roger M. Crowley. $34.95.
Randolph Scott, A Film Biography by Jefferson Brim Crow, III. $25.00.
Richard Boone: A Knight Without Armor in a Savage Land by David Rothel. $30.00.
Riding the (Silver Screen) Range, The Ultimate Western Movie Trivia Book by Ann Snuggs. $15.00.
Riding the Video Range, The Rise and Fall of the Western on Television by Garry A. Yoggy. $75.00.
The Round-Up, A Pictorial History of Western Movie and Television Stars Through the Years by Donald R. Key. $27.00.
Roy Rogers, A Biography, Radio History, Television Career Chronicle, Discography, Filmography, etc. by Robert W. Phillips. $65.00.
The Roy Rogers Reference-Trivia-Scrapbook by David Rothel. $25.00.
Saddle Gals, A Filmography of Female Players in B-Westerns of the Sound Era by Edgar M. Wyatt and Steve Turner. $10.00.
Silent Hoofbeats: A Salute to the Horses and Riders of the Bygone B-Western Era by Bobby Copeland. $20.00.
Singing in the Saddle by Douglas B. Green. $34.95.
Sixty Great Cowboy Movie Posters by Bruce Hershenson. $14.99.
The Sons of the Pioneers by Bill O'Neal and Fred Goodwin. $26.95.
So You Wanna See Cowboy Stuff? by Boyd Magers.
Television Westerns Episode Guide by Harris M. Lentz, III. $95.00.
Tex Ritter: America's Most Beloved Cowboy by Bill O'Neal. $21.95.
Those Great Cowboy Sidekicks by David Rothel. $25.00.
Trail Talk, Candid Comments and Quotes by Performers and Participants of The Saturday Matinee Western Films by Bobby Copeland. $12.50.
The Western Films of Sunset Carson by Bob Carman and Dan Scapperotti. $20.00.
Western Movies: A TV and Video Guide to 4200 Genre Films **compiled by Michael R. Pitts. $25.00.**
Westerns Women by Boyd Magers and Michael G. Fitzgerald. $36.50.
Whatever Happened to Randolph Scott? by C. H. Scott. $12.95.
White Hats and Silver Spurs, Interviews with 24 Stars of Film and Television Westerns of the 1930s-1960s. $38.50.
Written, Produced, and Directed by Oliver Drake. $30.00.

Ask for our complete listing of 300+ MOVIE BOOKS!

Add $3.00 shipping/handling for first book + $1.00 for each additional book ordered.
Empire Publishing, Inc. • PO Box 717 • Madison, NC 27025-0717 • Ph 336-427-5850 • Fax 336-427-7372